The Monfort Plan

The Monfort Plan

*The New Architecture
of Capitalism*

JAIME POZUELO-MONFORT

WILEY
John Wiley & Sons, Inc.

To the Extreme Poor

Published by John Wiley & Sons, Inc., Hoboken, New Jersey.
Published simultaneously in Canada.

For general information on our other products and services or for technical support, please contact our Customer Care Department within the United States at (800) 762-2974, outside the United States at (317) 572-3993 or fax (317) 572-4002.

Wiley also publishes its books in a variety of electronic formats. Some content that appears in print may not be available in electronic books. For more information about Wiley products, visit our web site at www.wiley.com.

Library of Congress Cataloging-in-Publication Data:

Pozuelo-Monfort, Jaime.
    The Monfort plan : The new architecture of capitalism / Jaime Pozuelo-Monfort.
        p. cm. — (Wiley finance series)
    Includes bibliographical references and index.
    ISBN 978-0-470-29363-8 (cloth)
        1. Economic development—Social aspects.   2. Capitalism—Social aspects.
3. Sustainable development—Social aspects.   I. Title.
    HD75.P69 2010
    330.12′2—dc22   2009041479

Printed in the United States of America.

10 9 8 7 6 5 4 3 2 1

Contents

Foreword

In an article published in *This Is Africa*, the quarterly magazine of the *Financial Times*, Columbia University professor Jeffrey Sachs wonders whether world leaders would be courageous enough to invent and design new programs and institutions with the legitimacy and the engagement to pull the world out of and away from the current crisis and target a more fair and sustainable future. A new architecture is the only path toward a better world that we dream of, a utopia (universal welfare state).

So far, world leaders have not been courageous (although there have always been exceptions—leaders who have had to pay a high price, sometimes compromising their own lives), and the peoples have not been motivated to stand up and rebel. In fact, we have been spectators, impassive eyewitnesses. Aid funds were substituted for loans; international cooperation for exploitation; and democratic multilateralism for plutocratic groups from the most prosperous and developed countries. Worst of all was (before a total absence of reaction capability) the substitution of the values for which we had fought hard so many years, for the laws of the market. These plutocratic groups squeezed the United Nations, and the globalizers declared and started an unbelievable race to increase weaponry stocks (for past wars, by the way). The result is an economy of war ($3 billion is spent every day on arms whereas 60,000 to 70,000 individuals starve to death), a virtual economy based on an unbridled speculation with no regulation. In 1991, I wrote, "with the Berlin Wall a system has sunk in which equality had forgotten freedom. Now, if the system does not change radically, the alternative system based on freedom that has forgotten equality will also fall." And both systems had forgotten justice.

As could be expected, capitalism has now also sunk . . . but it has been rescued. We must be on alert, because we could forsake a great opportunity and accept one more time that the rescued do not rescue those who suffer from hunger and thirst. It is time for the rebellion of the masses, peacefully, quietly, with tenacity, to transition from a saturation economy that includes 20 percent of humanity (the prosperous district of the global village) to a global economy of sustainable development, which in addition to improving the livability of the planet increases its number of customers.

"Extreme poverty originates and perpetuates," writes Jaime Pozuelo-Monfort, "because developed countries have failed to reform the six components of the Axis of Feeble, an Axis that must be defeated in an intellectual war that uses the Weapons of Mass Persuasion. The six components of the Axis of Feeble are: agriculture, trade and labor rights, small arms trade" (what about the big ones?) "extractive industries, financial architecture, and brain drain."

Numerous wars of the past defeated the Axis powers and the East Powers, and current wars—based on lies and simulation—try to defeat the so-called Axis of Evil. The Axis of Feeble is maintained thanks to the hard work of the Pirates of Heartless Capitalism and the Bretton Woods Elites, who have been serving the plutocrats and who, if things do not change, will use their propaganda instruments to oppose a paradigm shift.

In the first part of his autobiography, the American diplomat George F. Kennan noted, "We of this generation did not create the civilization of which we are part and, only too obviously, it is not we who are destined to complete it. We are not the owners of the planet we inhabit; we are only its custodians." We will not defeat the Axis of Feeble if all custodians do not become active passengers and not mere spectators.

The Monfort Plan is of particular interest because now that the peoples can have an active virtual participation, each and every one of us can begin and take off on the journey of a lifetime. The Monfort Plan is designed, with astonishing imagination, to attract many readers and individuals to key issues for the future of the planet and humankind. It is through education that the average citizen can increase her or his level of consciousness. Only if, as a society, we widen our cognitive space will we be able to compare and be motivated to work without pause for the benefit and sake of future generations.

It is urgent that we accomplish decisions when dealing with questions and processes that, because of their very own nature, are potentially irreversible. Years ago, I stressed the importance of this "ethics of time," because we can reach levels of no return in social issues (migratory flows, radicalization of those who have time and again seen unfulfilled promises that were previously formulated), as well as in environmental issues.

We are approaching a tipping point as a global society. We must become women and men capable of inventing a new tomorrow. The creative capacity, this mystery, is our hope. Jaime Pozuelo-Monfort has identified 100 Expert Dreamers, disciples of Roosevelt and Marshall, of Clayton and Kennan, of Monnet and Schuman, who can serve the global public interest. The Expert Dreamers will defeat the Axis of Feeble and the Pirates of Heartless Capitalism with their wisdom and intellectual strength.

The inhabitants of the blue planet, its custodians, must recover the courage of the visionaries of the 1940s and 1950s, who created an architecture that changed the world for good. Today's dominant oligarchies have been incapable of embracing change and have been driven by inertia, the great enemy of progress. Certain financiers and entrepreneurs—"because of their greed and irresponsibility," in the words of President Barack Obama—have led us all to this multifaceted crisis (financial, geopolitical, food-related, ethical, and democratic) and to a geopolitical situation absolutely paradoxical and overwhelming: China is the world's most capitalist country and Pakistan is a nuclear power! While the guidelines of Reagan and Thatcher were inexorably implemented, the world remained silent. Now, with a perplexed and irritated world, it is very likely that the scientific, academic, and intellectual communities will lead this transition from the force to the word.

We must start living a life with a different look, in full color. We must, one more time, dream and love. The Sleeping Beauty must wake up and rescue the Forgotten Continent. The American Giant will fall in love, one more time, with the Sleeping Beauty.

As it is so beautifully advocated by the Earth charter, it is necessary, in this beginning of the century and the millennium, to initiate a new order, "a new beginning."

FEDERICO MAYOR ZARAGOZA
Former Director General of UNESCO (1987–1999)
January 2010

Today's world is a world of increasing inequality, poverty, and despair, a world in which the current players are incapable of coping with a reality that is too rough to acknowledge, too uncomfortable to deal with, and too disproportionately harsh to face. Thirty plus years of development aid have proven ineffective. The major international players in the financial arena are incapable of providing solutions. The Bretton Woods era is gone and the so-called Washington Consensus is a mere reflection of what it once was. We are living in a new world, a new reality where the Cold War and Reagonomics no longer exist, and where globalization and unilateralism have gained relevance as drivers of the first years in the twenty-first century.

The private equity shops and hedge funds of the world acquire major relevance in a financial landscape that is more and more sophisticated and hard to understand and cope with. This is especially true for a majority of individuals in the developed and developing worlds, who no longer control their financial stability, as it is subject to international traders, hedgers, brokers, and speculators. Microfinance is claimed to be the most important tool devised to fight against poverty in the last 30 years, but it only reaches a fraction of the extreme poor. New financial services for the poor do not arise because the poor have no collateral, and because the poor lack the ability to earn, save, and repay. Western financial institutions are timidly entering emerging markets to offer financial services, and are more often investing and de-investing to speculate on the short-term and earn positive returns above the benchmark that beat the market. In the meantime, the price of basic food skyrockets because of the turmoil in the oil markets, and because the West needs to satisfy its hunger for energy with alterative energy sources, namely biofuel.

A world based on the maximization of economic profit, in an extreme derivative of capitalism led by the wealthiest, is leaving equity and global justice behind. By failing to incorporate redistribution to the global agenda, this economic basis forsakes the poor, leaving those with no safety nets to the mercy of the better-off and the corporations—both of whom claim to have become sustainable and responsible with their philanthropic activity, reaching a point of equilibrium where they will stand for years to come.

It is, however, time to change the course of this journey and admit that capitalism is not heading in the right direction. We need more regulation. We need Institutions to be above Markets, we need to protect the more vulnerable with Global Redistribution schemes and welfare systems that enable the incorporation of the poor to the benefits of the lifestyle enjoyed in the West (underlined terms will appear throughout this book and are included in the two-page figure located between Chapter 15 and Chapter 16, which summarizes the New Architecture of Capitalism. Readers are encouraged to identify the terms in the two-page figure as they are found in the text, so as to understand step-by-step the New Architecture of Capitalism).

We need to provide the basic infrastructure to those who lack it, so that the poor get on the ladder of development and become economically self-reliant once and for all. Investors have to start looking at the social return of their investments. Investors have to start computing the collateral damage of some of their investment decisions, which are sound economically speaking in the short term, but bring about calamity and turmoil in the long run. Consumers have to start discriminating among products, and penalizing those manufacturers who are not ethical and sustainable, thereby rewarding those who strictly comply with a set of internationally established standards. These standards must define an ambitious agenda to ensure the respectful treatment of the environment and humankind.

There is a trend that needs to be accelerated. Muhammad Yunus won the Nobel Peace Prize in 2006 for his contributions to fighting poverty through microfinance. Albert Gore won the Nobel Peace Prize in 2007 for his activism against Global Warming. Society acknowledges the efforts of key individuals who have decided to fight the world's most serious threats. But the trend has to be accelerated. We need our politicians, corporate leaders, and investors to become aware of the challenges of an unequal world. We need our politicians, corporate leaders, and investors to make every effort toward sustainability.

A NEW GENERATION

I believe I belong to a generation that has to step forward and lead the change of approach to politics, corporate strategy, and finance. It is a new approach that has to come from the very roots of the society and from the society's own citizens. These citizens must stand up for sustainability; they must stand up and denounce unethical behavior among politicians, corporate leaders, financiers, and money managers. The pressure of those who vote, the pressure of those who buy and invest is a Trojan horse with the potential to boost and accelerate a trend some have timidly started to adopt.

I become multidisciplinary to better understand a complex world in which solutions to problems are no longer easy. I become multidisciplinary to consensuate approaches to the crises we face, to hear experts from different disciplines, and to reach agreement with the leaders of society. I become multidisciplinary to communicate and expose the problems—*our* problems—and to propose and engineer solutions to social problems. In doing so, I hope to contribute to making of this world a place where our children and grandchildren can live comfortably regardless of where they are born or where they choose to settle.

I am a hunter of impossible dreams, an explorer of the twenty-first century, a consultant of the twenty-second century, and a representative of a forward-looking mentality that is not anchored in the ideas of the past. I am an inhabitant of Decemland, the land of 10 percent. I am a dreamer who loves and a lover who dreams. This mentality is one that asks *why not* instead of *why*, prefers alternative to continuous, and prefers to start from scratch rather than persist in pursuing the wrong path.

The academic and professional trajectory I have decided to pursue is as unusual as my ideas, but it is not less appropriate for that reason. The unusual and nonstandard has the ability to innovate and make a difference. Innovation sets the new forward-looking trend to be followed by the standard approach, by those who argue the default logic should become little more than an input assumption to understand the rationale of why we move in a certain direction.

I look around and realize I am obligated to be a social entrepreneur, because those around me lack the ability or the energy to react. It is my responsibility to continue deepening my knowledge, because my energy and enthusiasm are a gift that I have been given for the purpose of awakening in others the necessary realizations. We must abandon the de-facto thinking process and shift our focus to more important issues, to another dimension concentrating on the welfare of all and not only of a fraction of the global population. My desire to change is a reflection of all of us, many of whom do not dare to move. I am not afraid to lead. I am not afraid to suggest change. I dare, therefore I am.

Changing today's reality of finance for development requires creativity, the ability to propose unheard-of mechanisms within the developed world and to implement them via public policy. The public administrations of the developed economies have been so far incapable of taking the current level of development aid to the next level. It is no longer a matter of devoting the 0.7 percent of a country's gross domestic product (GDP) to development aid, which most developed economies do not even fulfill to date. It is, rather, about setting mechanisms in place able to considerably raise the amount of funds available for development. This must be executed in a consistent and sustainable way, so as to make a significant impact on our ability to radically change the basic infrastructure in extreme poor countries.

In this context, my aim is to offer an alternative to today's economic architecture: an alternative with a different color and flavor, an alternative able to suggest—from a profound understanding of today's complex economic and financial reality—public policies exclusively centered in coping with the increasing gap in income and inequality between rich and poor nations, a niche player in the fields of economic development and finance for development.

The political class in Europe is static and anchored in past issues, which although once important in essence and nature, will not take Europe a step further and make it the leading power of the first half of the twenty-first century. Europe needs a new generation of public administrators, consisting of those who are truly European, understanding of Europe's multicultural reality, but also of Europe's set of values. These values are rooted in the conception of universal rights of <u>Health Care</u> and <u>Education</u>, in a society centered around the idea of a welfare nation-state.

I belong to a generation that has not undergone war. I belong to a generation that has seen Europe grow larger and more stable, and continue to expand and integrate. I belong to a generation that has for the first time lived in different parts of Europe, made international friendships, and learned not only the language, but also the culture of each country of residence. I am, first and foremost, European.

I believe a new set of revolutionary ideas will depart from the young, enthusiastic individuals of my generation. I am ready to step forward and become part of that generation of leading contributors to a changing world, and I have a plan for change.

IT IS TIME

For years, the neoliberal economic principles based on Milton Friedmann's work and the Chicago school tradition have emphasized that the results of Adam Smith's theory of the invisible hand maximize the aggregate welfare of society based on an individual's pursuit of happiness. This approach reinforces the greed and the unsustainable quest for economic profit that lack regard for basic human dignity and the environment. This greed is behind the 2007 to 2008 financial crisis of Wall Street bankers. Regulation is only a first response to a deeper problem dwelling in the very roots of capitalism.

Robert Bates, a professor of government at Harvard University, emphasizes that economic reform is strongly attached to democratic reform, inferring that the former is only possible if the latter occurs (Bates 2004).

In their book *For the Common Good*, H.E. Daly and J.B. Cobb (1989) point out, "The axiom of greed must be rejected because real people, unlike Homo Economicus, are not insatiable." They add, "The view of Homo Economicus derived from anthropology and still underlying the existing discipline is radically individualistic," concluding, "Society as a whole is viewed as an aggregate of such individuals" (Daly and Cobb 1989).

Economic growth has been emphasized by the political, economic, and corporate elites. This economic growth failed to incorporate the sustainability clause. Natural resources are finite. The depletion of natural resources harms the environment and the viability of capitalism in the long run. Sustainability comes into play in a new economic paradigm. Marcel Jeucken (2004) describes sustainable development as a triple bottom line that includes the three Ps: people, profit, and planet.

Once upon a time in 1944, in a small town in New Hampshire called Bretton Woods, the economic elite of 44 nations met to determine the skeleton of the subsequent economic and financial architecture. Such economic architecture would aim at avoiding the pitfalls of the interwar period, which led to the emergence of Nazi Germany and the eruption of World War II. Those times are no longer representative of the current climate. Today's challenges are of a different nature. They include extreme poverty, inequality, widespread disease, conflicts that are exacerbated by the availability of weaponry, corruption, money laundering, and tax evasion, all of which contribute to the persistence of unethical behavior in today's capitalist economies.

It is time to look beyond the present tense to imagine the kind of world we intend to devise for 2050. The Bretton Woods Elites represent an older generation of retiring baby boomers who have proven ineffective in dealing with the problems of our time: extreme poverty, environmental sustainability, human dignity, and climate change.

It is time to transition from the old paradigms and consensuses to new approaches. The transition has to ensure the whole of society and its operating mechanism turns sustainable, thus being respectful of basic human dignity and the environment. In order to accomplish this, the transition must also propose international standards fulfilled by nation-states and design new institutions with the ability to provide Global Public Goods, which work based on the principle of Global Redistribution.

We lived a fairy tale that is over. We were part of a Western society that slept a beautiful dream. I decided to wake up to the reality of an unequal world and realized that our current economic institutions are ineffective. The European Union as Sleeping Beauty must wake up and assume a historic responsibility it owes to the African continent and the United States and lead the path toward a New Paradigm, financing the change, and proposing and executing reform.

On the quest to find the <u>Expert Dreamers</u> of today who will help build a new capitalism, I interacted with thousands of individuals throughout Europe, the United States, and the developing world.

I met **Rodrigo de Rato Figaredo** (FMN) in June 2008 at the Lazard branch office in Madrid (Spain) (names in bold throughout the book belong in the category of Expert Dreamers, and three letter initials correspond to organizational areas). In March 2006, I sent Rodrigo a letter with some of my thoughts for a redefined capitalism. Rodrigo was Spain's finance minister from 1996 to 2004, and managing director of the International Monetary Fund from 2004 to 2007. The letter was part of a group of 10 letters that I sent to the following individuals besides Rodrigo: Joaquín Almunia, Raymond Baker, Josep Borrell, Jimmy Carter, Bill Clinton, Hernando De Soto, Susan George, William Greider, and Jeffrey Sachs.

At the end of our meeting, I gave Rodrigo a paper I had finished a few days before in the class "The European Union and the Challenges of the Twenty-first Century," which I took at Columbia University in 2008. I finished the paper in May 2008. Subsequently, I mailed a copy of the paper and a letter to the European Union's 27 Commissioners and to President José Manuel Durão Barroso in an attempt to tell these important leaders that it is time. It is time to move ahead. It is time to never give up and to fight the great evils of our time. It is time to start materializing utopia, to start dreaming of the <u>History of Tomorrow</u>.

We need to become, one more time, men and women of stature and embrace the vision of the great men of the twentieth century. We need to become disciples of Marshall and Truman to defeat, once and for all, the great evils of our time. There is a <u>Window of Opportunity</u>. There is no other exit out of the crisis. Let the <u>Glorious Forty</u> begin.

For updated information about The Monfort Plan, please visit www.The MonfortPlan.com.

JAIME POZUELO-MONFORT
January 2010

A note about the artwork in *The Monfort Plan*: Artwork is credited as follows: Richard Cole illustrated Chapters 1 to 5, Claudio Muñoz illustrated Chapters 6 to 11, Andrzej Krauze illustrated Chapters 12 to 15, Bill Butcher illustrated Chapters 16 to 20, David Bromley illustrated Chapters 21 to 25, Mike Luckovich illustrated Chapters 26 to 30, Nigel Holmes designed the Summary Figure featured in the central pages, Peral designed the African map featured in Chapter 19, and finally, Joe Cummings illustrated the Who is Who in The Monfort Plan featured in Chapter 29.

One

A New Paradigm

The time of international crisis in the financial markets; the ongoing food shortage triggering riots among the extreme poor; the failure of the Doha Round and the inability of the World Trade Organization to sell a framework of multilateral agreements in which the European Union and the United States are not willing to give up their agricultural subsidies; the questioned role of the International Monetary Fund; the politicization of the World Bank in the post-Wolfensohn era; and the increase of inequality and extreme poverty numbers on a global scale put us in a scenario in which a new economic paradigm is necessary—a new consensus able to substitute the old-fashioned and virtually dead Washington Consensus.

It is time to embrace the problems of today, of our generation, and to remind our politicians that extreme poverty and hunger are behind many of the relevant issues they have to deal with today in their foreign policy agendas. Chapters 1 to 5 propose a new consensus and explain what a paradigm shift should involve. They also explain, in detail, the impact of globalization on poverty, the reality of aid, and recent trends in income inequality and income distribution, as well as introduce Global Redistribution as a first step prior to the creation of Global Public Goods and a Universal Welfare.

After reading Part I, the reader should understand why a New Economic Architecture is necessary in today's environment. A New Economic Architecture involves reforming six key areas that originate and perpetuate poverty. Without reform, the North and the South will never be on the same page. Before we start writing the History of Tomorrow, it is essential to depart from a <u>Page One</u> that is representative of everyone on the globe.

A NEW SAPLING IN BRETTON WOODS

Artwork by Richard Cole.

CHAPTER 1

Bretton Woods and the Washington Consensus

To have one's name not known at all is to confront a barrier that can be broken through only with much effort and luck. To become known, on the other hand, too widely—to become known, in particular, as having something to offer that a great many people want—is to step out onto the slippery path that leads to fragmentation of effort, hyperactivity and— eventually—sterility.

—George F. Kennan, *Memoirs 1950–1963*

Seven hundred and fifty delegates from 44 nations met in Bretton Woods, New Hampshire (United States), in July 1944. The meeting designed a new international financial architecture that could help reconstruct a devastated Europe and foster world trade after the protectionism that emerged in the interwar period 1918 to 1939, and more precisely in the Great Depression that followed Black Monday of 1929.

The Bretton Woods summit was the successful beginning of a phenomenal creation process that designed from scratch the International Bank for Reconstruction and Development, which would later become the World Bank, and the International Monetary Fund (IMF); resurrected the League of Nations to create the United Nations (San Francisco, 1946); and started the General Agreement on Tariffs and Trade (GATT 1947) that would later become the World Trade Organization. The Bretton Woods summit also fostered an environment in the United States in which the Economic Recovery Program for European Reconstruction (Marshall Plan) could be widely agreed upon by the political elite and explained to the American electorate.

The World Bank and the International Monetary Fund awarded a majority vote to the economic powers of the time. The voting power has not shifted ever since. Today, Belgium has more representative power than India in the World Bank. The United States has veto power in the International Monetary Fund. Both institutions are based in Washington, DC, and subject to political bias and interference of the U.S. administration.

The president of the World Bank has traditionally been an American. The managing director of the International Monetary Fund has traditionally been a European. The United States and Europe have monopolized the institutions since their creation. The presidents and managing directors of both institutions have exerted their personal operating approaches to development aid from the institutions they represent. Well-known World Bank presidents Robert McNamara (1968 to 1981) and James Wolfehnson (1995 to 2005) fought poverty in different, relatively successful ways. World Bank presidents in the 1980s and early 1990s applied lending policies that were biased by the ongoing Cold War between the United States and the Soviet Union. They fostered economic regime changes from socialism to capitalism in many developing countries triggering episodes of negative growth and exacerbating conflicts between Marxist and right-wing guerrillas.

The term Washington Consensus was coined by the economist John Williamson. Williamson is now promoting a revised version of his consensus, hoping to leave behind "the stale ideological rhetoric of the 1990s" (Clift 2004). In a 2002 speech entitled "Did the Washington Consensus Fail?" Williamson, an economist at the Peterson Institute for International Economics, enumerated "the ten reforms that I originally presented as a summary of what most people in Washington believed Latin America ought to be undertaking as of 1989": fiscal discipline, reordering public expenditure priorities, tax reform, liberalizing interest rates, a competitive exchange rate, trade liberalization, liberalization of inward foreign direct investment, privatization, deregulation, and property rights (Williamson 2002).

In an op-ed published on the International Monetary Fund's *Review of Finance and Development*, Jeremy Clift (2004) summarized his vision beyond the Washington Consensus. Clift reckons that the term Washington Consensus "became a lightning rod for those disenchanted with globalization and neoliberalism or with the perceived diktats of the U.S. Treasury." Clift adds, "Around the world 10 middle-income developing countries experienced major financial crises between 1994 and 1999 that damaged living standards and, in some cases, toppled governments and left millions worse off." The bailout packages of the IMF proved unsuccessful in repeated instances. The macroeconomic conditionality attached to many bailout packages of the IMF and certain loans of the World Bank only deepened the poverty trap of many developing countries.

In 1996, Michael Camdessus, who then headed the IMF as managing director, pointed out, "Even though the monetary system had changed since 1944 the goals of Bretton Woods were as valid today as they had been in the past" (Dammasch 2000). The fellow French native Dominique Strauss-Kahn was appointed managing director of the IMF in 2007 with the support of French President Nicolas Sarkozy. Unlike the French visionaries of the 1950s, Robert Schuman and Jean Monnet, Camdessus and Strauss-Kahn seem to be determined to perpetuate the current status quo.

According to J. Barkley Rosser and Marina Vcherashnaya Rosser of James Madison University, the Washington Consensus took for granted that inequality would be fundamentally positive for economic growth and prosperity. Inequality was to be promoted in the post-Soviet world that followed the fall of the Berlin Wall in 1989 as an expected yet desired outcome. The James Madison scholars conclude, "We also now see that income inequality itself may well play a role in increasing the size of the underground economy through social alienation and general dislocation, especially in conjunction with macroeconomic instability" (Rosser and Rosser 2001).

The Bretton Woods institutions are in serious need of reform. The Washington Consensus is virtually nonexistent. Out of Williamson's 10 requirements, fiscal discipline and property rights are the only two that would hold sway in today's environment, although fiscal discipline has been undermined by Western democracies that have run exorbitant deficits in the aftermath of the 2008 economic crisis during the Great Recession. Since 2000, a handful of goals, rounds, and consensuses have proliferated in the international arena, but none have become the new de facto approach to be embraced by both the developing and the developed world. The variety of consensuses is presented hereafter.

THE MILLENNIUM DEVELOPMENT GOALS

In 2000, the 189 members of the United Nations unanimously approved the Millennium Development Goals (MDGs), a set of eight goals primarily related to education and health. The men behind the definition and successful approval of the eight development goals were Kofi Annan, a native of Ghana and former secretary general of the United Nations, and Jeffrey Sachs, an American professor of economics at the Earth Institute of Columbia University.

The eight goals are ambitious and set a 2015 deadline for fulfillment. Generally speaking the goals were on their road to completion in most areas of the world prior to the 2008–2009 economic crisis, with the exception of sub-Saharan Africa, where not only were many countries not approaching fulfillment of the goals, but they were actually worsening it. The economic crisis slowed down the progress. The goals are financed by an increase in the allocation of foreign aid through innovative financial instruments such as debt relief to the Heavily Indebted Poor Countries (HIPC) or investment vehicles such as the Global Fund for AIDS, Malaria, and Tuberculosis.

According to the report *Millennium Development Goals at Midpoint*, global progress has been outstanding on income poverty thanks to the high performance of mostly Asian countries. The global income poverty target should, thus, be reached. Other regions in the world are either less concerned by the MDGs, possibly because they are made up of mostly middle-income countries, or performed poorly, most notably sub-Saharan Africa (Bourguignon, Benassy-Quere, et al., 2008).

The MDGs are arguably a result of the development conferences in the 1990s. For Karen A. Mingst and Margaret P. Karns, "Those conferences stimulated research, introduced new ideas and approaches, and energized Civil Society on human development issues." The authors conclude, "Consensus on the need for new forms of cooperation and partnerships does not guarantee success of the effort" (Karns and Mingst 2007).

There are two question marks regarding the MDGs. First, they demand an increase in aid without increasing the monitoring of its spending, nor the accountability on behalf of both the donors and recipients. Second, they do not seek to eliminate the roots of extreme poverty, which often require reform in the industrialized countries. The roots of extreme poverty are explained in Part II of this book (The Axis of Feeble). However, the MDGs are only a first step in the right direction. They represent a noteworthy accomplishment that puts developed and developing countries on the same page and acknowledge the urgency of tackling the shortage of education and health-care coverage in a majority of extreme poor countries.

It is unlikely that the MDGs will be accomplished by 2015 in the current state of affairs. The development community is in need of new ideas that may contribute to the fulfillment of the goals and reach further faster.

THE MONTERREY CONSENSUS

On March 21 to 22, 2002, the heads of state met in Monterrey (Mexico) to move forward in the financing for development agenda. The original purpose of the summit is summarized by the second paragraph of the summit memorandum (United Nations 2002):

> *We the heads of State and Government, gathered in Monterrey, Mexico, on 21 and 22 March 2002, have resolved to address the challenges of financing for development around the world, particularly in developing countries. Our goal is to eradicate poverty, achieve sustained economic growth and promote sustainable development as we advance to a fully inclusive and equitable global economic system.*

In a subsequent joint summary paper, the World Bank and the IMF concluded, "Overall the results of the conference are quite positive, creating a powerful momentum to put development at the center of the global agenda and arguably reinvigorated an international partnership for development" (IMF 2002).

The Monterrey summit proposed leading actions that included the following (United Nations 2002): (a) mobilizing domestic financial resources for development; (b) mobilizing international resources for development (foreign direct investment and other private flows); (c) enhancing international trade as an engine for development; (d) increasing international financial and technical cooperation for development; and (e) reducing external debt.

A 2005 report by the World Economic Forum entitled "Building on the Monterrey Consensus" (WEF 2005) examines "how public-private partnerships can best be harnessed to extend the reach and effectiveness of aid to address international and national development challenges," exploring the cooperation between the public and the private initiatives in the provision of basic services such as Water or Sanitation. A majority of poor countries are still largely underserved in the areas of water and sanitation, a gap that public-private partnerships have been incapable of filling effectively.

In October 2007, the United Nations Economic Commission for Africa released a report entitled *Perspectives of African Countries on the Monterrey Consensus* (UNECA 2007). The survey sent 106 questionnaires to African policy-makers, out of which 57 were returned from 32 countries in Africa's five sub regions. According to the survey: "Respondents identified the mobilization of international resources and domestic resource mobilization as areas where progress has been very limited" (UNECA 2007).

Six years later, the participants in the Monterrey summit met in Doha (Qatar) between November 29 and December 2, 2008. The *Doha Declaration on Funding for Development* aimed at following up on the progress built up by the Monterrey Consensus (United Nations 2008a). The Doha summit took place only three weeks after G20 countries met in Washington, DC, on November 15, 2008, to discuss financial reform. The conclusions of the Doha summit reaffirm the Monterrey Consensus "in its entirety, in its integrity and holistic approach, and recognize that mobilizing financial resources for development and the effective use of all those resources are central to the global partnership for sustainable development, including the support of the achievement of the internationally agreed development goals, including the Millennium Development Goals" (United Nations 2008a).

Susanne Soederberg, an associate professor of global political economy at Queens University, points out, "The basic assumption of the Monterrey consensus, substantial poverty reduction, is more about disciplining the poor to accept the dictates of neoliberal domination than creating a more just world" (Soederberg 2004). Failed agendas, lack of economic reform, and inability to engage the Civil Society, are all symptoms of a backward-looking perspective, which does not foster an environment that facilitates the adoption of new economic principles. The recent history of the development community is a concatenation of summits and conferences that issue the same diagnosis, emphasizing the same economic indicators, and that use the same economic jargon. All are indicative of a lack of willingness on behalf of the Lobbies and Elites, the better off. All are further indicative of a lack of imagination on behalf of the policy-makers of our time.

THE FAILED DOHA ROUND

The *General Agreement on Tariffs and Trade* (GATT) was signed in 1947 in the constructive environment that was started at the Bretton Woods conference. GATT's main purpose was to foster international trade after the protectionism that emerged in the 1930s. In 1995, GATT became the World Trade Organization (WTO).

Subsequent trade rounds have embraced an agenda that pushes for the elimination of barriers to trade or tariffs. Trade theory shows that producers and consumers maximize their economic benefit if tariffs are eliminated. But tariffs are also used as a political and economic weapon in the developed and developing worlds with a variety of goals such as protecting national agriculture, farming, or the manufacturing industries.

Trade agreements can be bilateral or multilateral. The WTO has stressed the importance of negotiating multilateral trade agreements, in which all WTO members are subject to the same conditions. Bilateral trade agreements include the well-known notion of most favored nation, in which an importer country, for instance the United States, decides to lower tariffs on the products or services imported from an exporting country, such as Colombia.

Since the formation of GATT, the world has undergone nine trade negotiation rounds. In each trade round, WTO members meet to reach agreement on the elimination of tariffs aiming at increasing international trade. The first negotiation round took place in Geneva in 1947. The longest negotiation round, the Uruguay Round, lasted from 1986 to 1994. The last negotiation round, known as the Doha Round, collapsed in 2008.

The Doha Round failed to reach consensus in key areas related to the elimination of tariffs in agricultural and farming produce. Developing countries refused to continue discussing the reduction and elimination of tariffs on agricultural and farming produce if the European Union and the United States maintained their subsidies. Subsidies are a de facto trade barrier, acting as a deterrent to the produce originated in the developing world, whose price, in spite of being more competitive, cannot compete with the subsidized European or U.S.-based food staples.

Within the European Union, the ongoing battle to defend or attack agricultural subsidies has involved the French president Nicolas Sarkozy and the European Union's former trade commissioner Peter Mandelson. Sarkozy is an advocate of subsidies, which he justifies based on the protection of the French countryside that, some argue, would literally disappear if subsidies were eliminated. Some policy-makers in Brussels talk about food security, increasing the priority of raising crops locally to avoid food shortages that could endanger the provision of food staples within the European Union's borders. Peter Mandelson, along with the French WTO director general, Pascal Lamy, has strongly argued for trade liberalization based on the advantages claimed by trade economists.

The European Union spends 40 percent of its budget (about 1 percent of Europe's gross domestic product) in subsidizing agriculture and farming. This amount is a multiple of the overall funding available for development in the developing world. In the meantime, the reality of international trade is turning sour. Developed and developing nations are more and more protecting their own markets, forsaking David Ricardo's theories that discovered the wonders of specialization.

We forgot to grant an opportunity to the products that are competitive in many low-income countries. Eliminating agricultural subsidies would carry a huge political cost, which French politicians are not ready to assume. The rice lobbies in the United States are powerful and well connected and would put tremendous pressure on the Obama Administration and its trade representative if subsidies were reduced or eliminated.

Trade theory works on paper, but does not work in reality. The United States bailed out its auto sector to protect its uncompetitive car industry. For years, U.S. automakers forgot to focus on fuel efficiency and continued to manufacture popular SUVs that could continue to run on cheap oil. In 2009, thousands of workers in Michigan risked losing their jobs. Based on trade theory, the United States should focus on sectors in which it is more competitive, including biotechnology, communications, and education. But it will not because forsaking its autoworkers carries a collateral damage of incalculable cost, which economists forgot to incorporate with their models.

This book is about incorporating the collateral damage of Western policies and determining their impact. This book is about reforming in key areas that carry much collateral damage, originating and perpetuating an avoidable poverty trap.

International trade is important. But human dignity and the respect of the environment are more important. David Ricardo and Adam Smith were right three hundred years ago. Their constrained views[1] ought to be left behind or complemented, in a globalized world that facilitates financial and trade flows, but forsakes migration flows of unskilled labor, which would flood Europe and the United States with millions of individuals, and harm the social fabric of many developed countries.

THE COPENHAGEN CONSENSUS

In March 2004, the British Magazine *The Economist* published an article that raised the following question: "*What would be the best ways to spend additional resources on helping the developing countries?*" (*Economist*, 2004a). The article reviewed the effort led by Danish economist Bjorn Lomborg, author of two best-selling books that include *The Skeptical Environmentalist* (2001) and *Solutions for the World's Biggest Problems* (2007).

Lomborg's argumentation is known as Copenhagen Consensus. Williamson's Washington Consensus focused on 10 key areas back in 1989. Lomborg's key areas include air pollution, conflicts, diseases, education, global warming, malnutrition and hunger, sanitation and water, subsidies and trade barriers, terrorism, and women and development.

Every additional consensus departs from where the previous one left off. Lomborg's Copenhagen Consensus includes déjà-vu areas such as education and health care. Jeffrey Sachs' Millennium Development Goals already incorporate disease prevention and treatment, education, malnutrition and hunger, water and sanitation, and women and development. The diagnosis of the problem is more often shared by experts, who continue to fail to propose policies that can then translate into action and be implemented. The value chain of the idea is broken halfway because of a lack of innovation, a lack of persuasion, or the unwillingness of our political elites to embrace new and creative policy-making.

The punch line of *The Economist*'s article stresses the importance of smart spending. "How should a limited amount of new money for development initiatives, say an extra $50 billion, be spent?" the article asks (*Economist* 2004a). The Copenhagen Consensus' panel of experts proposes new ideas in the aforementioned key areas that are then evaluated by a team of referees.

Pablo Rodríguez-Suanzes summarizes the conclusions of the second edition of the Copenhagen Consensus. Rodríguez-Suanzes interviews one of the referees of the ideas put forth by Lomborg's panel of experts. Nobel Prize winner Thomas Schelling argues, "It would be a mistake that each of these challenges and its solution be considered separately." Schelling adds, "A good nutrition does not only avoid deaths, but brings about a good health thanks to which children can attend school and avoid a fatal fate" (Rodríguez-Suanzes 2008).

According to Rodríguez-Suanzes, the Copenhagen Consensus proposes market-based policies in nutrition, health, and education. On the topic of nutrition, the panel of experts proposes to concentrate on the quality and not the quantity of food, emphasizing the use of iron or iodum micronutrients. In health, the panel of experts suggests that low-cost treatment in malaria and tuberculosis could help save millions of lives. The treatment should incorporate the use of inexpensive drugs that have proven effective and are widely available. In education, the panel of experts proposed to reward with an economic incentive the parents who decide to send their children to school.

REINVENTING BRETTON WOODS

In February 2008, I traveled to Berkeley, California, where three years earlier I had graduated with a master's in financial engineering from the University of California.[2] During my visit I met with Barry Eichengreen, one of the world's best economic historians. The 45-minute conversation with the Berkeley economist included a discussion on the Bretton Woods Institutions. Eichengreen suggested that I contact Marc Uzan, the executive director of Paris-based think-tank, The Reinventing Bretton Woods Committee.

In June 2008, I spent three days in Paris, where I had lived for two years in 1997 to 1998 and 2000 to 2001. In the morning of a beautiful June day, I met with Uzan. I waited at a French café for 45 minutes while putting my ideas together and drinking a French café au lait. The two-hour meeting with Uzan was productive. He is a forward-looking thinker whose late proposal is a change of governance of the international financial system. Uzan co-authored a book in 2007 entitled *The International Monetary System, the IMF and the G20*, along with Richard Samans and Augusto Lopez-Claros of the World Economic Forum.

The idea that the very institutions that have failed to anticipate the financial crisis and have actively participated in the economic fiasco are invited to the reform process along the G20 is absurd. It is similar to inviting Robert Mugabe and Mobuto Sese Seko to a round on how to improve public governance in Africa. Or to asking former Illinois Governor Rod Blagojevich to maintain his position and participate in a wave of reform to decrease the incidence of corruption in Chicago-politics.

The Wall Street investment banks Bear Stearns and Lehman Brothers defaulted and were not bailed out. When will the World Bank and the International Monetary Fund default? Are they too big to fail? Do the shareholders have veto power that continues and perpetuates the maintenance of a majority vote that grants an insignificant share of representative power to the BRIC countries (Brazil, Russia, India, and China)? According to the *Financial Times*, "Capitalism's worst crisis in 70 years has not prompted a serious alternative vision of society. It has, however, laid bare that our current national framework for financial regulation is incapable of governing a global financial system" (*Financial Times* 2009).

Being provocative is only a first step to gaining the appeal and attention needed to shake the average citizen's conscience in Western Europe and the United States and raise his or her awareness. I see a Window of Opportunity that will not last long. I sense times of change that could be forsaken if the visionaries of our time do not react. It is our generation's duty and obligation to move forward with an agenda that embraces the poor and the environment, for we all are created equal, and human dignity should be valued above economic profit.

IN TRANSITION

Historians are well aware of the challenges of the first half of the twentieth century. Humankind underwent the most violent stage of modern times, with two almost consecutive World Wars that devastated Europe between 1914 to 1918 and 1939 to 1945.

The period in which we live today is a time of economic recession and potential depression, increasing protectionism and barriers to trade. In many respects, it resembles that of the 1930s and the Great Depression, which started in the United States. Ben Bernanke, chairman of the Federal Reserve Bank of the United States, is a reputed economist and one of the best experts on the Great Depression. His designation in 2005 to succeed former Chairman Alan Greenspan had to do with the then foreseeable crisis that some pessimistic economists such as Nouriel Roubini anticipated.

Nouriel Roubini is a professor of economics at New York University. I explained what the New Architecture of capitalism was all about to Roubini on May 14, 2009, at the RGEmonitor headquarters in New York City. Roubini mentioned several times that the ideas presented in this book were overly ambitious. He may be right. But if we are not the dreamers of today, we will never reach <u>Decemland</u>, the land of 10 percent, which will be presented in its fullness in Part VI of this book.

I look back at the years that followed the carnage of World War II. I see forward-looking policy-makers who were able to set the basis of the economic principles that enabled thirty years of phenomenal economic growth and stability in Western Europe. I see forward-looking policy-makers who had the obligation to dare, who created the structures that enabled the emergence of the European Union and secured once and for all Europe's peace.

Subsequent events accelerated the European recovery and construction. Quincy Wright (1961) comments that "the success of Mao Tse-tung in adding China to the Communist camp in 1949, followed by the Korean war, stimulated the integration of Western European states in the Steel and Coal Community, later developed by the Common Market and Euratom." But the success of today's Europe could not and would not have happened in the absence of a plan of action.

In his book *Global Covenant*, David Held presents "the Social Democratic Alternative to the Washington Consensus." Held focuses on "the relation between globalization and social integration" and "seeks to unfold a programme which might help weave together the processes of globalization, the bonds of social integration, and the priorities of social solidarity and justice." The author's progressive economic agenda "needs to calibrate the freeing of markets with poverty reduction programmes and the immediate protection of the vulnerable." Held's concluding remarks point in the direction of a new development agenda that emphasizes the protection of the vulnerable (Held 2004).

We decided to forsake and forget the devastation many extreme poor countries suffer today. We decided, as a society, to ignore the underlying roots of poverty. We neglected to demand of our political elite the accountability needed to move forward with the reform agenda. It is time to raise our voices as citizens of a globalized world, to demand the kind of change and reform our ancestors once dared to put on the table.

It is the poor's mandate. They demand change but have no representative power because many live in undemocratic societies. They demand change but cannot effect it because the World Bank, the International Monetary Fund, and the United Nations were designed to grant a majority vote to the economic powers of the time (World Bank and IMF), or to the victors of World War II (Security Council at the United Nations). The change must come from below and from within. The approach has to be bottom up. The Western world has to displace the political elite who are not ready to reform. On February 4, 2009, Martin Wolf of the *Financial Times* wrote the following statement (2009b):

> *Decisions taken in the next few months will shape the world for a generation. If we get through this crisis without collapse, we will have the time and the chance to construct a better and more stable global order. If we do not, that opportunity may not recur for decades.*

I replied to Wolf raising the following questions: What about reforming key policies in trade, agriculture, and financial architecture? What about cleaning the dirt out of the system including tax havens, and fighting tax evasion and money laundering? What about dismantling agricultural subsidies and giving more representative power to the emerging economies in the international institutions? What about a currency for the poor? What is the role of microfinance in enhancing the lives of the poor?

The *Financial Times* published a report in May 2009 entitled "The Future of Capitalism," which included the 50 leaders who would shape the debate. Surprisingly enough, Koffi Annan, Hernando De Soto, and Muhammad Yunus were not among the aforementioned leaders, the majority of whom are from developed nations.

The world economic and corporate elites meet in Davos, the land of the Pirates of Heartless Capitalism. These elites hang out with the pirates who hide in tax havens behind banking secrecy. The world economic and corporate elites are not pirates but they allow pirates to continue operating. Switzerland is a totalitarian monetary regime that ought to be embargoed.

It is time to look beyond the formulae anybody can find on academic papers from reputed journals. It is time to look at the details of our lack of ethics and our double standards in many key areas. The opportunity may arise if reform is followed by innovative policy-making that proposes alternative thinking, which the orthodox, mainstream thinkers of our time refused to believe in, pressured by lobbies, by the financial and economic elites, by the shareholders of multinationals, by the arms industry, and by the banking sector.

We are in transition from the old-fashioned economic principles of free-market economics. It must be a dynamic transition. I wish to contribute with a forward-looking rationale that aims at building up an alternative success story to today's unhopeful dynamics.

Artwork by Richard Cole.

CHAPTER 2

Redefining Capitalism

The age of nations is past. It remains for us now, if we do not wish to perish,
to set aside the ancient prejudices and build the Earth.
—Pierre Theilhard de Chardin, S.J.

Today's world is a world of increasing differences. Anti-globalists like Susan George are pessimistic about the system as a whole. She criticizes the Washington Consensus and the Bretton Woods Institutions that Keynes suggested as a way to take off after World War II (George 2004). Economist and Nobel Prize winner Joseph E. Stiglitz, who during the Clinton administration headed as chief economist both the Council for Economic Advisors at the White House and the World Bank, argues that the IMF and its policies have not helped developing economies in the past 20 years (Stiglitz 2003).

The income gap between the rich and the poor is latent, whether or not one may argue that it is actually widening. Many would support the argument that there exists a gap, a gap that stops many emerging economies from departing in the appropriate direction once and for all. There is overconfidence and a lack of realism in the first world regarding how to tackle a situation that worsens day after day. Many individuals in the rich world who are not familiar with the difficulties that emerging economies face, do not realize the depth and severity of the problems they encounter, and how much the latter affect the daily lives of millions of people.

No easy solution seems feasible. There have been, and there are interesting initiatives including microfinance and Hernando De Soto's work, which, provided their success, could bring rich and poor closer together in terms of income, growth opportunities, and share of the pie. As it has happened in the past, capitalism may need to be revisited. The trend of present capitalism will be that of increasing differences. Inequality tends to increase not only worldwide, but also within developed nations. The system is heading in the wrong direction.

TOWARD A NEW ECONOMIC PARADIGM

Capitalism has always been revisited after major crises or crashes. The Great Depression in the 1930s, the crash of the Stock Market in 1987, the major macroeconomic crisis in Asia and Latin America of the 1990s, or the collapse and subsequent bankruptcy of giants like Enron or Worldcom in 2001 are all examples of situations in which the major players of the game have redefined their roles. Many in the first world may be optimistic, true believers in a process we label globalization, which brings about good for everyone.

As has happened in the past, capitalism may need to be revisited. The current trend does not serve the goals set by the United Nations, which given the current state of the world, are unlikely to be accomplished by the year 2015. This is, of course, contrary to Jeffrey Sachs' remarks that "we can realistically envision a world without extreme poverty by the year 2025 because technological progress enables us to meet basic human needs on a global scale and to achieve a margin above basic needs unprecedented in history" (Sachs 2006).

Global poverty has a huge cost, because the potential contribution of the extreme poor is undermined and severely reduced. In his best-selling book *Obamanomics*, John Talbott, an economist at the University of California at Los Angeles (UCLA), estimates the total loss associated with extreme poverty at $100 trillion (Talbott 2008). When I asked Talbott how he determined this number he mentioned that the "two billion living on next to nothing, they have the human potential to contribute $50,000 per year to the world economy. That is $100 trillion just in the first year."

Jeremy Rifkin has been writing about the future of capitalism since 2005. In his essay "Europe and the Future of Capitalism," Rifkin stresses the importance of the European social model that relies on the welfare state as a cohesive instrument. Rifkin raises the question *Can capitalism be saved?* For Rifkin, capitalism is superior to any other economic system in areas such as technological innovation, entrepreneurship, productivity increases, and the assumption of individual risks. But capitalism does not distribute fairly the dividends of economic progress. Redistribution comes into play at this point (Rifkin 2005).

Kurt Eichenwald of New York University raises the question *Will capitalists ruin capitalism?* For Eichenwald, capitalists only measure their return in economic terms. Eichenwald points out that capitalism is able to correct itself when the abuses go far enough (Eichenwald 2002).

Can capitalists redefine capitalism?

ALTERNATIVE THINKING IN FINANCIAL MARKETS

There is already regulation in the financial markets that, through taxation, raises public funds for public spending. If corporations were asked whether to pay corporate or dividend tax, they would definitely choose not to do so, based on the maximization of the present value of their future cash flows, which equals the company's equity value. Or equivalently, they would adopt the strategy that most benefits their shareholders. Similarly, corporations in today's world tend to respect the current regulation, but are able to skip ethical codes of conduct, always aiming at maximizing their profits, since there is no such regulation set in place.

The concept of financial rating is crucial to a public corporation, because it determines the cost of capital it will incur on whatever funds are borrowed from investors or the markets. The rating agencies impose strong constraints to assign certain ratings that are indicative of a firm's financial strength. In addition, financial auditors make sure a public corporation's financial statements fulfill international standards and are trustworthy.

Consequently, there is a system in place with which the modern corporation has to comply. A corporation's unique approach is to adapt to the regulation and the set of operating rules established by regulators and rating agencies. Top executives at large corporations work hard to be transparent, to not use confidential information in their own advantage. There is a growing trend in the corporate world to adopt a code of ethical conduct and develop sustainable policies accordingly. However a firm's financial rating will not change whether or not the company is ethically responsible. Today's financial markets only reward the financial manners of a corporation, with no repercussion on the ethical space.

We cannot live in a world governed by multinational corporations that do not have strong codes of conduct, that invest and divest as they wish, and that outsource a share of their operations to developing countries under deplorable working conditions. The rich world has succeeded at building up a system that works in the industrialized nations, but does not work globally.

Along with the financial rating, a company should have an ethical rating of a similar nature. The ethical rating would affect a company's success in the consumer market, as much as its financial rating does in the financial markets. Rating agencies will determine the ethical actions of a corporation, whether or not it outsources, how it invests its money, the working conditions of its employees, whether its operating policies respect the environment, what part of their corporate tax is devoted to social action, and so on. There will be ethical auditors that confirm whether the corporation complies with the set of ethical criteria established. A globalized economy characterized by the immediate diffusion of information should not tolerate a firm's unethical policies that oftentimes remain undisclosed.

Every potential investor looks at a corporation's financial rating prior to purchasing stock or corporate debt. The financial rating has become a guarantee for an investor because it is a proxy for the firm's probability of default. The ethical rating will play the same role for the consumer.

Products and services will be labeled with a company's ethical rating. Consumers will at all times know whether a company is ethically responsible, and in the end, reward or penalize a firm for not complying with the rules of the system. Consumers will likely purchase products or services that align with their values, ethically speaking. In order to be successful in the marketplace, a firm will have to be ethically responsible. The better ethical rating, the better the consumer's opinion on the corporation, and the more likely the consumer will be to purchase a certain product or service.

Multinational corporations will not determine a consumer's choice through advertising techniques and marketing. Rather, consumers will determine a corporation's set of operating policies. It is about reversing the rules of the game. It is about giving the individual consumer the power to believe that his or her actions have a direct impact on a firm's well-being. It is about consumers pushing out of the market those corporations that are not ethically responsible.

RAISING FUNDS THROUGH REGULATION

Within a century, society will look back in anger and will not understand the extreme inequality of personal wealth and income that currently exists in the world. The wealthiest fortunes in our planet represent the net income of millions of people in poor countries. This extreme asymmetry only proves that the current system has produced enormous disparities. We are eyewitnesses of this phenomenon, yet convinced nothing can be done. The situation is taken as is; inequality has always existed, as it is an intrinsical attribute of the human race.

Personal wealth over a certain amount should be subject to taxation. The current regulation taxes income and gains on assets, but does not tax personal wealth. Somehow the more a person owns, the greater his or her social compromise is in the current state of the world. Nobody should be eligible to have above a certain amount of money and not contribute through taxation to redistribution. From a global sense of justice, it is simply not sustainable. And this can and should be accomplished through regulation with changes in the tax code.

Corporations will be entitled to invest 10 percent of their net earnings in a development fund over a certain time horizon. This contribution would not be lost, but woud be an asset on the asset side of a firm's balance sheet. Should the firm go bankrupt, the firm's senior debt holders would also recover the part of a firm's income invested in the development fund over the years. The fund will keep the profits linked to the investment strategies and allocate them to sustainable development strategies.

Rich economies will issue as much as the equivalent of 10 percent of their gross domestic product in public debt and devote this money to the investment fund. Again, only the profits from the investment strategies will be used as development aid. Surpluses of the rich economies of the world will also feed the development fund.

The money accumulated in the development fund will be managed by an independent entity, which will only invest in companies that are ethically responsible. Companies that are ethically sound, besides being financially driven, will see their financing opportunities increased. It is not unlikely to picture a world with strong multinational corporations that are ethically responsible. It is not utopic to imagine a development fund that only invests in companies with strong ethical codes of conduct, one that devotes the rates of return of its investment strategies to development aid, and in so doing, encourages ethical operating policies within corporations.

The fund will become a redistribution instrument, from the rich to the poor. With an annual budget equal to the profits of its investment strategies, the fund will contribute to funding the provision of Global Public Goods (as described in Chapter 5), which includes a free, basic, and Universal Welfare. The development fund will be able to influence, with its equity investment criteria, the corporate strategy of numerous multinational corporations, aiming at investing only in those that defend and effectively apply ethical management principles.

A development fund, conceived in the manner presented above, will substantially increase the amount of funding available for development in developing countries and therefore have a direct influence on the causes of poverty. A development fund, conceived in the manner presented above, will become the heart of a redefined capitalism. The world will then observe the rise of a redefined, stronger capitalism, which after all, as F.A. Hayek properly said, "is the only mechanism that has ever been discovered for achieving participatory democracy" (Hayek 1944).

A PARADIGM SHIFT

We live in times of uncertainty and volatility,[1] not only in the financial markets, but also in the thought processes, in the ideologies, and in the structures that have determined capitalism's operating principles since the aftermath of World War II. There is no leadership because the complexity of the concatenation of crises reaches a level approaching the absolute unkown. There is no leadership because today's powers, elites, and lobbies are shortsighted and work to defend their own interests. They continue to support an old-fashioned paradigm that should have been left behind in the 1990s.

We ought to propose new standards in times of crisis, a sentiment echoed by many international and institutional leaders. We ought to define new frames of understanding, and new architectures able to transition a globalized world, the world of the twenty-first century, into reform—into the convergence of income, human rights, respect of the environment, wealth, and equality.

In my travels, I meet with representatives from international institutions. They are representatives of an old paradigm that made sense in the second half of the twentieth century, of an old paradigm that today can only perpetuate the problems of our time. The handful of international institutions is unable to solve the severe challenges of today, mainly because of the intromission of the foreign policy agendas of the United States and the European Union.

I hear that donor countries impose operating conditions to the international institutions, and that the former dictate how the latter should allocate humanitarian aid. I read how for decades the World Bank and the International Monetary Fund have applied lending policies in a context of macroeconomic conditionality that forced the neediest countries to tighten their belts and shrink the budget devoted to health care and education. These countries will never leave the poverty trap behind without health care and education.

Looking for the ultimate causes of extreme poverty, I find the urgency of reform in the developed and developing worlds. I am surprised by the banking secrecy and the existence of tax havens that facilitate tax evasion and money laundering. I am startled by the maintenance of agricultural subsidies and the lowering of tariffs on products and services that are primarily manufactured in the industrialized world. I am fascinated by the lack of representation of the developing world in the voting bodies of the international institutions.

The current economic paradigm benefits the rich. I criticize constructively the complacency that shields our stealing of the most valuable resource of the developing world, a phenomenon we call brain drain. I am concerned by the migratory policies that import unskilled labor when it is convenient and gets rid of it when the economic slowdown knocks on the door. Extreme poverty feeds derived problems such as illegal immigration, international terrorism, and mafias. Global warming increases the impact of natural crises and smashes those who lack access to a social protection network.

A new consensus is necessary. A new economic paradigm is feasible. Perhaps we need more regulation in the international financial markets. Perhaps we need new standards that reassure the provision of food staples to the malnourished before they are available to trade in the international markets. Perhaps trade should be fair before it is free.

Buying the surplus of subsidized food staples in the United States to lessen the burden of the food crisis in sub-Saharan Africa is not a permanent solution. It is a shortsighted solution that benefits the producers of the developed nations. Let's once and for all move food production to poor countries, enabling them to produce locally and sell their surplus. Let's incentivize the farmer in Europe and the United States to become competitive, specializing in niche markets characterized by more quality produce. Let's incentivize the uncompetitive European and North American farmers to learn other skills that would allow them to work in more competitive sectors.

Let's take advantage of the times of crisis. Let's suggest a New Paradigm able to contribute to the change in the structures that represent the skeleton of our institutions, a New Paradigm able to create the ideological and operational basis of a reformed capitalism. The new economic paradigm will materialize a new international consensus that dignifies the human being, maximizes social welfare along with global justice and equity, and embracing dialogue and diplomacy by utilizing the Weapons of Mass Persuasion.

Change must come. Progressive instead of radical change is appropriate. When I attended the London School of Economics (LSE) in 2006 to 2007, I had the privilege of listening to Michael Storper, a professor of economic geography at LSE and the University of California at Los Angeles (UCLA). In his paper "The Poverty of Radical Theory Today: from the false promises of Marxism to the mirage of the cultural turn," Storper argues against the radical Marxist approaches in vogue in the United States and the United Kingdom twenty years earlier. Storper concludes, "A critical pragmatism, combined with a firm rejection of relativism, is necessary, as well as not shying away from openly embracing certain elements of philosophical liberalism and normative ethics" (Storper 2001).

Change has to be brought on board in today's society through persuasion, and never through imposition. The severity of today's global reality is so acute that policy-makers have plenty of evidence to construct a message of urgency able to impregnate the electorate of Western countries.

REDEFINED CAPITALISM

Major global threats endanger the existence of the human being and the planet we inhabit. The lack of leadership of our current political class coupled with the status quo of the current economic paradigm puts the world at an inflection point that faces the risk of free fall. The 2007 to 2008 crisis in the financial markets was a triple crisis (liquidity, credit, and real estate) that triggered a severe economic slowdown on both sides of the Atlantic. And it was all largely because of the greediness and moral hazard of financiers in the credit risk chain, and the determination of the Federal Reserve and the Bank of England to bail out banks that should have gone bankrupt under the principles of free markets, endorsed by Milton Friedman and his successors.

Keynes and The New Deal came back when many had forsaken public spending and government intervention for the sake of the welfare and well-being of a country's citizens. A new economic paradigm has to put the extreme poor at the very center of reform, securing transnational consensus and agreements that protect those who lack a social protection network from the ups and downs of the economy—cycles that are magnified by the activity of financial speculators. Today's institutions must be reinvented and redesigned. In an environment where the unwillingness to reinvent and redesign today's institutions is manifest, new institutions may emerge as a strategy that represents the shortest path to Cornucopia and Eutopia.

Exciting times of convergence lie ahead of us. The bottom billion have to become the core of any new strategies that aim at reducing the widening income gap between the high incomes and the low incomes of our time. Convergence must prioritize the adoption of a world's minimum wage in purchasing power parity (PPP) terms that guarantees a decent standard of living. Convergence must incorporate Global Redistribution from the better off to the worse off that enables the provision of a basic welfare state to the most vulnerable. It is our generation's obligation. It is the poor's mandate.

The lack of political leadership is supine. Our political leaders in Europe and the United States lack the ability and the vision, or are invaded by the fear and inundated by the dominance of the economic and corporate elites. I read the history of the 1930s. I read the history of the 1940s. I found individuals of extreme political caliber, policy-makers to whom we owe the peace and stability we enjoy in today's Europe and the United States. Where are the Claytons, Monnets, Schumans, and Kennans of our time? Who is in charge of shouting the urgency of the moment?

Our sole priority is to fight extreme poverty. Our only goal is to depoliticize the policy-making of foreign aid. We left the World Wars behind. We left the Cold War behind. We started to leave nuclear proliferation behind. We flirted with preventive war and decided to forego the international consensus of the United Nations. We were no Knights of the Middle Ages; we were coward instruments of foreign policy, which perpetuates a world order that imposes our own rules of the game, defined by our elites without incorporating the Southern Hemisphere. Where are the Robin Hoods of our time? Who are the Robin Hoods of our time?

I dreamt of a better world. I dreamt of a society that brings more equity into the plethora of negotiation rounds, a society that grants more representative power to the worse off. I dreamt of consumers who are sensitive to human rights and do not tolerate the operation of multinational corporations that do not respect human beings or the environment. A new society will emerge from the vestiges of this old-fashioned capitalism that is unable to survive, and is unable to sustain its very own rules.

"Capitalist Crumbs"

Artwork by Richard Cole.

CHAPTER 3

Globalization and Poverty

The critics of globalization accuse Western countries of hypocrisy, and the critics are right. The Western countries have pushed poor countries to eliminate trade barriers, but kept up their own barriers, preventing developing countries from exporting their agricultural products and so depriving them of desperately needed export income.
— Joseph E. Stiglitz, *Globalization and Its Discontents*

Globalization and poverty do not have to be interrelated, but they are. Globalization is a process whereby barriers to trade and to financial flows are reduced or eliminated, bringing about, on paper, an increase in economic activity conducive to economic growth and prosperity.

On September 26, 2008, I talked with Don Sillers. Sillers is an economist, who at the time worked for the Office of Poverty Reduction at the United States Agency for International Development (USAID). After our phone conversation, I sent Sillers a one-page summary of this chapter, which included the statement, "Globalization empowers the rich and undermines the poor," without providing further evidence. The sentence was, after all, part of a one-page summary. On January 2, 2009, Sillers replied with comments to my one-page summary. He mentioned that the aforementioned statement was naïve and even laughable. Sillers was right. Without further commentary, a simple statement such as this, which draws such a generalization, could be inaccurate, misleading, and potentially wrong. I am now writing this chapter to provide Sillers and the readers of this book with further commentary.

I could have argued, "Globalization empowers the poor and undermines the rich," or perhaps, "Globalization is a win-win situation for both rich and poor." But the fact of the matter is that from the very core of my brain and bottom of my heart, I fundamentally disagree with these two sentences.

Generally speaking, economists can be classified according to the emphasis they give to the power of free-markets or to the need of regulation and intervention to arrive at the optimum outcome in the economy. For example, neoclassical or new classical economists believe in free markets more than Keynessian or new Keynessian economists. Milton Friedman and other Chicago school economists like Robert Lucas or Gary Becker are examples of market economists who have strong affinity with the power of the market mechanism. In development economics, William Easterly from New York University would have a more pro-market view while

Jeffrey Sachs from Columbia University would not. Depending on whether you are on one or the other side, your judgment will put the free-markets and the forces of supply and demand above state intervention and regulation, or vice versa.[1]

Unlike Easterly or Sachs, I am not an economist. I never earned a doctorate and will not be an academic. Unlike Easterly or Sachs, I am an architect who designs solutions to lessen the burden of poverty. I use the theory of the social sciences developed by academia to engineer forward-looking solutions for a challenging, unequal world. Contrary to what orthodox thinkers believe, there is much to learn from both Easterly and Sachs. The future of policy-making is neither conservative nor progressive, and it is neither neoclassical nor Keynesian; it is a hybrid that combines the best of each approach to delineate instruments of social return. It is perhaps time to leave ideology behind and embrace pragmatism.

When assessing the statement, "Globalization empowers the rich and undermines the poor," the direction of the causality tends to be: (1) What kind of economist am I? (2) Based on whether I am neoclassical or Keynesian, would I then find that globalization is good for the rich and bad for the poor, or vice versa?

Your answers to the above questions depend on whether you see the glass half empty or half full. Wealthy countries can only see the glass half full. I see the glass half empty and subsequently find reasons to support my view. This is the case in most arguments in today's challenging environment. Most issues have reached such a level of complexity that depending on how you frame the evidence and argumentation, you can persuade policy-makers to be for or against it.

Many economists debate about whether the number of people living under the poverty line has decreased or increased. Depending on what methodology you believe or what school of thought you support, you can find optimistic or pessimistic scenarios. The academic debate feeds the brains of some of the world's most talented academics, but does little to lessen the burden of poverty. Raymond Baker, a fellow at the Brookings Institution, concludes on globalization (Baker 2005):

> *The potentially beneficial forces of globalization and its corollaries, free trade and financial liberalization, work well in the presence of the rule of law, political integration, institutional stability and domestic accord. Absent these, the process can instead have a negative impact on growth and cohesion. What globalization must not be is a license to plunder, disrupt, and further weaken already fragile states.*

As a European who frequently sees double standards everywhere in our policy-making, in this analysis I have decided to examine the issues from a developing country's perspective. This is a difficult undertaking, many in the developing world would argue, if not impossible. But at least I have made the commitment to try.

Globalization works in Europe and the United States because we have strong currencies whose exchange rates can be defended if attacked by financial speculators. It works in Europe and the United States because we have independent Central Banks and Governors of Central Banks who are able to run appropriate monetary policy and control inflation. We have strong institutions and rule of law.

Globalization works in Europe and the United States because we maintain agricultural subsidies that protect our uncompetitive agriculture and farming sectors from being overtaken by the cheaper produce coming from the developing world. It works because we have social protection networks and public goods that are universally provided and financed through redistribution.

Globalization works in Europe and the United States because we have strong multinational corporations that are able to outsource the unfair working and environmental conditions to developing countries. Multinationals have muscle. Developing countries do not. Multinationals can negotiate their conditions under the threat that they will relocate to a more permissive environment. Poor countries cannot compete with each other and are subject to the free-rider problem in which corporations seek the location with cheaper labor costs and lesser environmental standards.

The European Union (EU) created the European Globalisation Adjustment Fund (EGF) in 2005. According to the European Commission,[2] the EGF "aims to help workers made redundant as a result of changing global trade patterns to find another job as quickly as possible." The fund was launched in 2007 with a yearly contribution of 500 million euros. On March 1, 2006, the *International Herald Tribune* published an article entitled "EU Fund to Ease Globalization Pain" (Kanter 2006). According to Kanter, "The Global Adjustment Fund would help retrain and relocate 35,000 to 50,000 workers a year when jobs are lost to the dynamics of global trade, rather than by mismanagement or loss of production to another EU member state." Kanter concludes, "Governments would be able to use the EU money in cases where a company, its suppliers and its associated producers laid off at least 1,000 people in a region with a population of up to 800,000, and where the unemployment already is higher than the European or the national average." As a result, the European Union has the financial muscle to hedge against the collateral damage of globalization. A majority of developing countries simply do not.

The fact of the matter is that today's world should not be taken at face value. Poor countries may be to blame for their mismanagement, corruption, and lack of governance. However, Europe and the United States may also be to blame for other reasons. Europe's colonization of Africa proved detrimental. Many mistakes were committed in the past, yet we are still working to exonerate ourselves of blame today. Blame is useless if it is not coupled with action. But sometimes blame is a necessary departure to acknowledge the necessity of moving forward.

What justice has been done regarding our pitfalls in the colonization period? It is time to move forward and understand our obligation to undertake a Second Marshall Plan for sub-Saharan Africa and the remainder of the extreme poor countries. It was the conviction of the United States after World War II that Europe's reconstruction was vital for its economic recovery and the maintenance of democratic capitalism in the fight against the expansion of Soviet communism and influence in Eastern Europe.

I understand the corollary of our time. Globalization does not alleviate or reduce poverty in low-income countries because of the lack of international standards to guarantee minimum working conditions for the poor. Furthermore, globalization is ineffective at reducing poverty in low-income countries because their governments do not have the means to finance a social protection network that provides a Universal Welfare state including universal health care and education, financed through redistribution.

The market will not solve Africa's tragedy, as it will not solve the French farmers' survival, or the Detroit automakers' revival. The market is not always the answer. Markets work under a set of assumptions that are not always fulfilled. Extreme poor countries may be ready to adopt the rules of our game called democratic capitalism in the future, but they are not ready to do so today so long as they remain poor.

Paul Krugman argues, "The influence of ideas that have not been expressed as models disappears soon" (Krugman 1995). In modern economic theory, Krugman, who won the Nobel Prize of Economics in 2008, may be right. That is why John Kenneth Galbraith, one of the most influential economists of the twentieth century, did not have the relevance of Keynes or Friedman. There are ideas that simply cannot be expressed as models, such as the myriad of plans that emerged in the late 1940s (Marshall, Schuman, and Monnet's plans).

PROS AND CONS OF GLOBALIZATION

This section reviews reasons for and against globalization from eight different authors, which includes *Financial Times*' Martin Wolf and Columbia University's Joseph E. Stiglitz. The reader should bear in mind that the glass is never full or empty, but rather half full or half empty. The side you choose determines to a large extent the orientation of your arguments. I chose the thinkers, experts, and scholars who inspired me. As an architect of solutions, I choose the bricks of the building I design to construct a message able to impregnate the societies of Europe and North America.

Why Globalization Works

Martin Wolf runs a weekly column in the *Financial Times*. His book *Why Globalization Works* was written in 2004 at the top of the economic bonanza of that time. His arguments touch upon agricultural subsidies and low labor standards in developing countries. Wolf recalls, "Total assistance to rich country farmers was $311 billion in 2001, six times as much as all development assistance, indeed more than the GDP of Subsaharan Africans." He then adds, "The United States and the European Union account for around half of all world wheat exports, with prices 46 and 34 percent respectively below costs of production" (Wolf 2004b).

Regarding labor standards, Wolf notes, "For a western visitor such jobs may seem unimaginably bad, but some of the alternatives—total dependency as housewife or despised daughter, prostitution, agricultural labor or begging—are worse." Wolf may be right; it is better to have a 12-hours-a-day, low-paying job at a crowded and dirty textile factory in Bangladesh with no vacation days than it is to beg or to become a prostitute. But it is even better to have an 8-hours-a-day, well-paying job at a clean, un-crowded textile factory in Bangladesh with a fair allocation of vacation days. We seem to compare the worse with the second to worse, without realizing the second to worse could be much better if standards were agreed upon. The 64-hour workweek was banned by the European Parliament in December 2008 because Europeans felt they have fought too long the 40-hour workweek to let those benefits evaporate. We now have to fight for global working standards that improve the working conditions for the worse off.

Wolf comments, "International economic integration is undermining the capacity of sovereign states to choose their tax and regulatory structures. In particular it is destroying the high-tax, high-regulation European economic model. More specifically, it has made the redistributive policies of the welfare state impossible." (Wolf 2004b). What if Europe were to export its welfare state model? What if instead of threatening to disappear, the welfare state model expanded to low-income countries? Then, the welfare state would no longer be in danger of extinction.

When I moved to Paris (France) in September 1997 to study for one academic year at Télécom Paris, the French Grande École for Telecommunications Engineering, I did not need to sign up for private medical insurance. When I moved to Berkeley, California in March 2004, to study at the Haas School of Business, not only did I have to pay a high tuition, but also a private medical insurance fee. Countries that offer social protection networks establish agreements with countries that offer equivalent protection levels, for the very benefit of their own citizens. As a Spaniard in Canada, I am covered by the Canadian public health-care system, but I am not covered in the United States. In terms of health care, it is more cost-effective for a European to spend one year in Canada than it is to spend one year in the United States.

If certain developing countries embraced the welfare-state paradigm, Europeans and Canadians would be able to travel to certain developing countries and be entitled to access their public health-care systems, and vice versa. Cooperation fosters the enlargement of protection networks. Globalization could bring about extended geographical coverage, instead of the opposite. A new welfare-state paradigm could be embraced. The Euro-Consensus would then become the substitute for the Washington Consensus. The old paradigm privatized education and health care and shrank the welfare state of developing countries. The New Paradigm exports Europe's welfare-state to the extreme-poor, helping them finance it and run efficient organizations that hire local doctors and teachers and take advantage of economies of scale to minimize the cost of delivery and eliminate the middleman.

Wolf concludes, "Why, people quite reasonably ask, should innocent people have to repay debt incurred by the tyrants who persecuted them when in office?" (Wolf 2004b).

George Soros on Globalization

The Hungary-born philanthropist and billionaire[3] George Soros, who studied at the London School of Economics, wrote an interesting piece on globalization in 2002. Soros defines globalization as "the free movement of capital and the increasing domination of national economies by global financial markets and multinational corporations" (Soros 2002). Soros' goal is "to reform and strengthen our international institutions and create new ones where necessary to address the social concerns that have fueled the current discontent."

For Soros, globalization has a negative side, particularly in less-developed countries, where "many people have been hurt without being supported by a social safety net." Soros notes, "The Monterrey Conference on Financing for Development ought to focus on the provision of public goods on a global scale," later adding, "We ought to provide the resources for universal primary education" (Soros 2002).

Soros further asserts, "To mobilize public opinion in favor of increased international assistance, the proposal must show not only how the money will be raised but also how it will be spent." He concludes (Soros 2002):

> *The fight against terrorism cannot succeed unless we can also project the vision of a better world. The United States must lead the fight against poverty, ignorance, and repression with the same urgency, determination, and commitment of resources as the war against terrorism.*

Making Globalization Work for the Least Developed Countries

The United Nations Ministerial Conference of the Least Developed Countries[4] (LDCs) met in Istanbul in July 2007, to issue the *Istanbul Declaration on Least Developed Countries*. The conference focused on four themes: trade and investment, transfer of technology, agricultural productivity and food security, and finally, socially acceptable forms of energy. The conference report acknowledges that "while many posit that globalization has led to substantial gains in the well-being of millions of people around the globe, a darker side to globalization coexists, manifested in increasing, unprecedented inequalities both between and within the vast majority of countries." The report adds, "LDCs as a group receive proportionately fewer benefits of globalization, but are exposed to proportionately more of the costs and risks" (United Nations 2008b).

Out of the policy responses suggested, the following are noteworthy. At the national level, "promoting greater transparency and measures for managing natural resource rents, including through the Extractive Industries Transparency Initiative" and "further investigating migration and development issues, including their impact on local capacities, and identifying the incentives necessary to attract return migrants." At the international level, "reforming the governance of existing multilateral cooperation institutions so as not only to reflect the increasing power of southern emerging economies, but also the perspectives of least developed countries and low-income country aid recipients" and "ensuring that there is institutionalized asymmetry in trade agreements involving the least developed countries members, in their favour" (United Nations 2008b).

A New Paradigm needs a leading voice able to persuade the leaders of the Least Developed Countries (LDCs) that the New Architecture of capitalism proposed in this book prioritizes their interests. **CHEICK DIARRA** (CEO) is the United Nations under-secretary general and high representative for the Least Developed Countries, Landlocked Developing Countries, and Small Island Developing States. I met Cheick at his office on the seventh floor of the United Nations Headquarters in New York City on September 8, 2008, and again on May 15, 2009. For Cheick, the ideas put forth in this book are controversial and will wake up the attention of a sleeping establishment unable to look beyond the orthodoxy of our time.

Debating Globalization

David Held is a professor of political science at the London School of Economics. In his book *Debating Globalization* (2005), Held exposes his views on globalization. Held argues, "Over the coming few years between now and 2010 choices will be made that will determine the fate of the globe for decades to come." He concludes, "Understanding that effective, transparent and accountable global governance requires reliable income streams, from aid to new financial facilities and, in due course, new tax revenues" (Held 2005).

Globalization and Its Discontents

Globalization under its current version emphasizes international trade and privatization. Columbia economist Joseph E. Stiglitz adds, "The United States supports free trade, but all too often, when a poor country does manage to find a commodity it can export to the United States, domestic protectionist interests are galvanized." Stiglitz concludes, "U.S. unfair trade laws are not written on the basis of economic principles, they exist solely to protect American industries adversely affected by imports" (Stiglitz 2003).

Has Globalization Gone Too Far?

Harvard economist Dani Rodrik argues, "In Western Europe, where unions have remained stronger and the policy environment more supportive, the wages of the less skilled have not collapsed, but the price has been an increase in unemployment." Rodrik believes, "The identity of the gainers and losers matters," and "Rawlsian conceptions of justice, for example, imply that redistributions that enhance the well-being of the most disadvantaged groups should receive priority" (Rodrik 1997).

Regarding labor standards Rodrik points out, "In 1993, the European Commission took the view that competition within the Community on the basis of unacceptably low social standards, rather than the productivity of enterprises, will undermine the economic objectives of the Union." Rodrik concludes, "Globalization reduces the ability of governments to spend resources on social programs, it makes it more difficult to tax capital, and labor now carries a growing share of the tax burden" (Rodrik 1997).

Another World is Possible If

Susan George is a leading thinker of the anti-globalization movement. George defines globalization as "the freedom for my group of companies to invest where it wants when it wants; to produce what it wants, to buy and sell where it wants and to support the fewest restrictions possible coming from labour laws or social conventions" (George 2004).

George's *The Lugano Report* (2001) became the reference reading among anti-globalists. In the more recent *Another World is Possible If* (2004), she claims an evil view of capitalism represented by the myriad of multinational companies. She points out, "Achieving any improvement at all is difficult enough without telling people they must bring down, preferably tomorrow, the most powerful and pervasive economic system the world has ever known" (George 2004).

The Silent Takeover

Noorena Hertz is one of the leading thinkers of her generation. In her 2002 masterpiece *The Silent Takeover* she claims that multinational corporations are taking over democratic societies. She explains it as follows: "We stand today at a critical juncture. If we do nothing, if we do not challenge the Silent Takeover, do not question our belief system, do not admit our own culpability in the creation of this 'new world order,' all is lost" (Hertz 2002).

In a world dominated by the private actors, the role of the state and of the society is diminishing. Hertz adds, "In the world of the Silent Takeover, in which the social contract between government and the people is increasingly meaningless, popular pressure is doing something that governments can't or won't: demanding that corporations be judged by non-economic criteria, holding them accountable in a way that we cannot hold our elected representatives" (Hertz 2002). In an environment where the political elite lack the reaction capacity to compensate for the imbalances of global capitalism, it is through pressure from Civil Society that the pitfalls of globalization may be overcome.

In the developing world where the absence of public provision of education and health care is noteworthy, corporations are stepping in to undo the market failure. Hertz argues, "In parts of the Third World, in countries in which the state is so moribund that it cannot deliver even the most fundamental of public goods such as education, basic health, roads and infrastructure, corporations are deciding to meet the shortfall themselves" (Hertz 2002). This is not how we decided to design the delivery of public services in the industrialized world. Consequently this is not the right approach for the developing world.

AFRICA'S TRAGEDY

In 1997, William Easterly and Ross Levine published *Africa's Growth Tragedy*. Easterly and Levine note, "The borders of African nations were determined through a tragicomic series of negotiations between European powers in the nineteenth century that split up ethnic groups and exacerbated preexisting high levels of ethnic and linguistic diversity" (Easterly and Levine 1997). Africa's growth tragedy can be explained by a variety of factors including short civil wars and failed policies based on ethnic division.

The white man's burden in Africa has been detrimental since the beginning of times. First through colonization and then through failed foreign aid, Western countries have not found the magic recipe to pull sub-Saharan Africa out of poverty. Perhaps there is no magic recipe, but only incremental improvement. Perhaps foreign aid should be discontinued. But, most likely, we need smarter aid. Barack Obama argued during the 2008 presidential campaign that the debate was not whether the United States needed more or less government. The United States needed smarter government. The analogy can be extrapolated to foreign aid.

Civil War and Ethnic Division

According to Oxford economist Paul Collier, countries experience higher growth rates after long civil wars than after short civil wars. Because civil wars are used with much lower technology than international wars, they cause less damage. In particular, Collier concludes, "If a country immiserises itself through civil war it will have an enhanced post-war growth rate by virtue of its poverty. This effect would predict that the post-war growth rate would be faster the longer the duration of the previous war" (Collier 1999). Wars in general and civil wars in particular ruin the structural features that make an economy work, deteriorating infrastructure and undermining the enforcement of property rights. GDP growth does not only increase after the war the longer the war lasts, but it also shrinks by an average 2.2 percent per year during the years of war.

William Easterly and Ross Levine study the relation between a country's ethnic diversity and how it indirectly impacts economic growth. They use the variable ETHNIC as a proxy for a country's ethnic diversity. ETHNIC is an abbreviation for *Ethnolinguistic Fractionalization Index*, which represents a proxy of the number of competing groups in a society, and as a result its potential degree of conflict. Easterly and Levine examine "the direct effect of ethnic diversity on economic growth and evaluate the indirect effect of ethnic diversity on public-policy choices that in turn influence long-run growth rates.". They determine that ethnic diversity and division may create polarization and favor the ruling group in expense of other ethnic groups. The authors conclude, "The data indicate that high levels of ethnic diversity are strongly linked to high black market premiums, poor financial development, low provision of infrastructure, and low levels of education" (Easterly and Levine 1997).

The combination of Collier's and Easterly and Levine's conclusions is counterproductive for Africa. A combination of short civil wars and a high ethnic diversity is likely to sink a country in a poverty trap that will be difficult to overcome. This combination is common across Africa and undermines the ability of many sub-Saharan African countries to leave the poverty trap behind.

Africans are not only to blame for their repetitive episodes of civil war. So are Americans and Russians for having financed right-wing and Marxist guerrillas during the Cold War. So are Europeans for having conducted a disastrous decolonization process that ignored Africa's rich ethnic heritage. So are Western governments that supported dictatorial regimes that guaranteed and unfortunately still guarantee the operations of Western oil and mining companies on African soil. So are Western governments for allowing the operations of arms manufacturers that export weaponry and ammunition to extreme poor countries without enforcing disclosure and transparency clauses. We need to reform the small arms industry and determine in what direction reform should be undertaken, which will be discussed further in Chapter 9.

Colonization

David Welsh writes in *Ethnicity in Subsaharan Africa* (1996), "Colonial Africa's boundaries had been the product of an imperial carve-up that cut through territories inhabited by indigenous societies and arbitrarily jumbled together a diversity of ethnic communities inside unitary administrative structures." The arbitrary division of Africa's borders in the Berlin Conference of 1884 anticipated the abundance of armed conflicts that has devastated Africa since the time of independence. Thomas H. Johnson (1984) writes in this direction:

African independence was achieved in two waves, the first from 1956 (Sudan) through 1968 (Equaterial Guinea, Mauritius, and Swaziland) when 36 states became independent, and a second wave from 1974 (Guinea-Bissau) through 1980 (Zimbabwe), when nine more states were decolonized.

From 1960 through 1982, of the 45 majority-ruled states of Sub-Saharan Africa 25 (55 percent) have experienced 52 successful military coups d'etat. There were also 56 attempted coups and 102 reported coup plots. In sum, 38 of the 45 countries (84 percent) saw some form of military intervention between the beginning of 1960 and the end of 1982.

Throughout centuries, European colonization was a sign of exploitation of human labor to secure natural resources. The pride that today characterizes Europeans, who advocate human rights, good governance, and transparency abroad, was not a common feature in the societies of prior decades and centuries that colonized and imposed their views on the local populations. Apartheid in South Africa and segregation in the United States were the last piece of evidence of an exploitation that lasted centuries for which we do not feel accountable, as a society, today. In 1957, the highest-paid African at the mines earned less than a third of the lowest paid Europeans, whereas the average white-black wage ratio was almost 20 to 1. Europeans were given educational preference to monopolize the small number of elite jobs (Franck 1961). In broader terms, colonization benefited the wealth and welfare of the rulers at the expense of the colonized.

The Cold War

The Cold War between the United States and the Soviet Union along with nuclear proliferation exacerbated the politicization of foreign aid that oftentimes supported Marxist or right-wing guerrillas with the goal of winning the battle that would perpetuate one economic system over its rival (capitalism versus socialism). Sam C. Nolutshungu, a former professor of political science and African politics at the University of Rochester, writes, "The USSR remained in Guinea under Sekou Toure despite provocative policies on its host's part, and it persevered in Somalia long after perceiving that progress could not be achieved in any direction." He then concludes: "The Soviet Union encouraged the creation of vanguard parties based on Marxism-Leninism, but it clearly did not favor a break in economic relations with the West or even a sudden change in economic specializations during the long preliminary phase before socialism could be constructed" (Nolutshungu 1985).

In 2005, Janice Love, dean of the School of Theology at Emory University, published *Southern Africa in World Politics* (Love 2005). Love raises the following questions: *Why did regional and global powers take such an interest in these countries and their internal disputes? Would these wars have lasted so long and caused such devastation if they had remained local?* In addition, the Emory scholar points out (Love, 2005):

On the day of Angola's formal independence, November 11, 1975, the impact of fairly extensive and intensive military globalization was clearly evident. The three guerrilla groups vying for power fought one another on many fronts across the country, each backed by potent allies from outside. Although the South African military had provided supplies to UNITA for some time, troops from the South African Defense Forces (SADF) launched a massive invasion from bases in Namibia (then South-West Africa) in mid-October. Previously, in August, the U.S. Central Intelligence Agency (CIA)

*had shipped large quantities of arms to the ENLA. Cuban troops arrived
in early October, and Soviet military supplies continued to flow into the
country to bolster the MLPA.*

We should perhaps ask ourselves why we make explicit the credit that our past
ruling elites may deserve while we minimize their pitfalls. Only if we acknowledge
their wrongdoing will we be able to trigger a new era of understanding that puts
North and South on the same page, Page One of the History of Tomorrow.

Solutions for an Abandoned Continent

The Africa Progress Panel (APP) concluded in the aftermath of the 2008 economic
crisis that two of the priorities for Africa going forward would be the immediate
assistance and access to resources, that the main responsibility to act rests with
African leaders, and that Africa needs a stronger voice in the international institutional architecture (APP, 2009). APP noted that "we call on the IMF, World Bank,
and the African Development Bank to ease access to credit and provide urgently-
needed funds, preferably grants rather than loans, to compensate for the loss of
domestic revenues, remittances and foreign direct investment and to address urgent
social needs" (APP, 2009). APP concluded, "we call on Africa's leaders to press
for substantial reforms on the world's governance structures to make them more
representative, supportive and ultimately effective" (APP, 2009).

For Tidjane Tall, author of *Fixing Africa Once and for All* (2009), "Africa
needs leaders who'll work collaboratively to combat its widespread instabilities."
Tall concludes that International Organizations (IOs) "have stopped believing that
real change is possible in Africa," and that as IO employees move forward in their
careers, "their mortgages and university fees for their children gain in prominence,
and they have less appetite for rocking the boat" (Tall 2009).

SUCCESS STORIES

For years the four Asian tigers (Hong Kong, Singapore, South Korea, and Taiwan)
have been mentioned as success stories in development and economic growth. China
did not enter the WTO until 2001 and has ruled its capitalism from a centrally
driven communist regime. Korea's economic growth was based on the chaebols, or
industrial conglomerates owned by the state and later divided and privatized such as
Daewoo or Samsung. According to Stiglitz (2003):

*For three decades Korea enjoyed remarkable economic growth without sig-
nificant international investment. Growth had come based on the nation's
own savings and on its own firms managed by its own people. It did not
need Western funds and had demonstrated an alternative route for the im-
portation of modern technology and market access.*

India is a good example of a democracy that has entered the path of economic
growth and prosperity embracing the principles of the free markets. But a comparison
with its Northern neighbor China leads to the conclusion that China's thriving,

infrastructure-abundant economy has been better directed from Beijing by its ruling elite, than India by its widespread and buoyant entrepreneurial class spread out throughout the country.

Dani Rodrik, a Harvard professor of development economics, argues, "The Chinese experience represents not the exception, but the rule: transitions to high growth are typically sparked by a relatively narrow range of reforms that mix orthodoxy with domestic institutional innovations, and not by comprehensive transformations that mimic best practice institutions from the West" (Rodrik 2002).

Three success stories have emerged in Africa over the course of the last fifty years, since the independence from the former colonial powers started to occur in the 1960s. Tunisia in Northern Africa, and Botswana and Mauritius in sub-Saharan Africa are countries that in spite of facing most of the problems of their neighbors, managed to reach steady growth leading to prosperity. Botswana is further reviewed in Chapter 28; Mauritius and Tunisia are reviewed in the remaining sections of this chapter.

Mauritius

James Meade, a former Nobel Prize winner in economics, wrote in two seminal papers in the 1960s that Mauritius would suffer a demographic explosion and predicted population growth from roughly one million in the early 1960s to three million in 2000, which would lead to Malthusian, widespread starvation episodes. The small, remote island of the Indian Ocean, with an area of just above 2,000 square kilometers, has controlled its population growth, a population that stands at 1.3 million. The small island-state topped the ranking on good governance in Africa in 2005 and also earns outstanding marks in transparency and economic freedom. In 2005, it ranked 65 in the Human Development Index of the United Nations out of a total of 177 countries.

Mauritius is composed of four ethnic groups that profess different religions. It is a well-balanced environment with a well-educated workforce that has allowed the country to diversify from an export-based mono-crop agricultural economy, which mostly produced and exported sugar cane to the European Union in the 1960s and 1970s, to a multi-sector economy that has become a technological, financial, and tourism center.

Paul Collier writes about Mauritius, "When Mauritius escaped the traps in the 1980s it rocketed to middle-income levels; when neighboring Madagascar finally escaped the traps two decades later, there was no rocket" (Collier 2007). In a paper entitled "Ethnicity in Subsaharan Africa," David Welsh (1996) reviews why Mauritius, in spite of its ethnic diversity, has been able to become one of the few success stories in the area. Welsh comments, "Out of the few African states that have coped with ethnicity in ways that have proved compatible with democracy, Botswana and Mauritius have had the enormous advantage of high economic growth rates for sustained periods of time" (Welsh 1996).

Tunisia

Tunisia's success story in Northern Africa has catapulted the country to having the area's second highest per capita income and the second highest Human Development

Index behind Libya. Tunisian President Ben Ali devised the National Solidarity Fund (NSF) in 1992 as a redistribution instrument able to improve the living of inhabitants of poor areas and to help them establish microenterprises through the provision of funding. The philosophy of the NSF is based on the provision of basic rights to the individual, which include the right to health, education, and culture, and the right to economic integration. The number of donors has increased from 180,000 in 1994 to more than two million in 2002.[5]

During the Millennium Summit in September of 2007, Tunisia's president Zine El Abidine Ben Ali suggested the creation of a World Solidarity Fund (WSF). In 2002, the then United Nations Secretary General Kofi Annan submitted to the General Assembly specific proposals regarding the implementation of a WSF. Later in 2004, president Ben Ali announced that Tunisia's NSF would allocate 10 percent of the donations to the WSF.[6] The WSF becomes the <u>Decemfund</u>, which is presented in more detail in Chapter 24.

Artwork by Richard Cole.

CHAPTER 4

The Reality of Aid

The only way to avoid deceiving yourself like this is to work to the limits. If your reports never get an outraged reaction, you are lying. If they are never rejected, you are lying. If you are never fired from a contract, you are lying. You are lying to your clients and you are lying to yourself. You are killing people.

—Peter Griffiths, *The Econonomist's Tale*

Is 0.7 percent of a country's GDP the right amount of aid? How was this number assessed and what is its significance today? In their paper *Ghost of 0.7 percent: Origins and Relevance of the International Aid Target*, Michael A. Clemens and Todd J. Moss of the Center for Global Development review the rationale behind the determination of the percentage and its significance in today's environment. Clemens and Moss provide evidence that "no government ever agreed in a UN forum to actually reach 0.7 percent." They also point out, "The eventual 0.7 percent target was mostly arbitrary, based on a series of assumptions that are no longer true, and justified by a model that is no longer considered credible" (Clemens and Moss 2007).

WHAT IS THE RIGHT NUMBER?

The Pearson Commission is credited with having set the 0.7 percent target. Lester B. Pearson was the Canadian prime minister when the then president of the World Bank Robert McNamara asked him to form a Commission on International Development. It is in the Commission's report where the 0.7 percentage first appears. McNamara was president of the World Bank between 1968 and 1981. The final report entitled "Partners in Development" concluded that "we therefore recommend that each aid-giver increase commitments of official development assistance for net disbursements to reach 0.70 percent of its gross national product by 1975 or shortly thereafter, but in no case later than 1980" (Oxfam 2005). How did the Pearson Commission come up with the 0.7 percent number? According to Clemens and Moss (2007), former Pearson Commission staffer Sartaj Aziz recalls:

> *By the time the Pearson Commission met, there was a virtual consensus on the 1 percent target. From there, the rationale for reaching the 0.70 percent*

*target for Overseas Development Aid (ODA) was straightforward. ODA
had already reached 0.54 percent in 1961. An increase to 0.60 percent
would have been considered too modest since countries like France had
reached 0.72 percent by 1968. I remember one staff discussion in which we
debated whether the ODA target should be 0.70 percent or 0.75 percent.
Consensus reached was in favor of 0.70 percent, as a 'simple, attainable and
adequate' target.*

The 1-percent consensus was built up during the 1950s and the 1960s and was
confirmed by a group of influential economists in the 1960s. According to Clemens
and Moss (2007), Paul Rosenstein-Rodan and Hollis Chenery, both of who were
chief economist of the World Bank at different times, conducted separate calculations
on "how much foreign capital would be needed by low income-countries in the early
1960s."

Is more aid necessary? Does the amount of additional funding make the commitment to reach the 0.7 percent a priority? A variety of reports have pointed out
the necessity of increasing foreign aid. Reaching the 0.7 percent threshold is only an
intermediate step. The 0.7 percent has lost its significance in today's environment,
very different from that of the 1960s. More emphasis has to be put on how additional
funding is spent. We need more aid, but above all we need smarter aid. As a result,
it is important that countries increase their contribution. It is yet more important
that any additional contribution be spent in new schemes that show the recipient
country's explicit desire to receive the funding based on an improvement on the
country's social and economic fabric. In other words, donors and recipients have to
be accountable for the aid dispensed. Aid must have a social return. Its impact must
be tracked down and appropriate changes should be incorporated to its allocation
in the absence of any social improvement. Aid's time horizon must be a compromise
between the short and the long runs.

Aid Commitments

Today only a handful of countries have reached the magic number. Percentage-wise,
the United States is the country in the OECD that devotes the least amount of public
money to development aid. As Robert Calderisi points out, "The United States has
never spent more than one quarter of one percent of its national income on foreign
aid, and two thirds of that has been devoted to just two countries: Israel and Egypt"
(Calderisi 2006).

Some would argue that the contribution from corporate donors in the United
States well exceeds that of other European countries. As a result, the aggregate
contribution, both public and private, could approach the 0.7 percent. The reality is
different. According to the Committee Encouraging Corporate Philanthropy (CECP),
the 155 companies (including 69 of Fortune Magazine's Top 100) that participated in
the 2007 *Corporate Giving Standard* (CGS) *Survey of Philanthropy* donated a total
of $11.6 billion in both cash and non-cash contributions to communities around the
globe, which represents a median contribution of 0.92 percent of pre-tax profit for all
companies and of 0.83 percent for the 69 Fortune 100 Companies that participated
in the survey (CECP 2008), down from a median of 1.3 percent of pre-tax profit
in 2004. Out of this percentage, Fortune 100 companies provide an average of
14 percent of their aid to international end-recipients, whereas all other companies

give an average of 10 percent to international end-recipients. Consequently, these companies give 0.12 percent of their pre-tax profit to international end-recipients, whereas all other companies give 0.09 percent of their pre-tax profit to international end-recipients.

According to *Fortune Magazine*, the top 1,000 companies in terms of revenue in the United States had an aggregate profit of $724 billion in 2007. If we assume that each of them devoted on average 0.12 percent of their pre-tax profit to international end-recipients, the total dollar amount devoted to international end-recipients was $869 million, or roughly 0.0063 percent of the United States' GDP.[1] This is a miniscule amount compared to the target 0.7 percent and its contribution is quasi-negligible. The United States is far from reaching the 0.7 percent target.

Forbes ranks the top 200 charities in the United States. According to the U.S. magazine the total volume of private contributions for the 200 largest charities for 2008 amounted to $40.75 billion, up 5 percent from a year before (Barrett 2008). Of this amount, $9.44 billion or 23 percent of the total was spent in international needs.

The Foundation Center features the endowments and the annual giving of the top 100 U.S. Foundations.[2] The aggregate endowment of the top 100 U.S. Foundations amounted to $263.4 billion in 2008. Total giving for the 2007 to 2008 fiscal year amounted to $15.6 billion, of which $2.0 billion corresponded to the Bill and Melinda Gates Foundation and $526 million corresponded to the Ford Foundation. The Foundation Center does not disclose what share of the total giving ($15.6 billion in 2007 to 2008) was spent in the United States and what share was spent internationally. According to *The Economist*, in 2008 American Foundations spent $5.4 billion internationally (*Economist* 2009a). Joel L. Fleishman, author of *The Foundation*, summarizes the foundation sector in the United States as follows (2007):

> *In 2005, about 68,000 foundations of all kinds existed in the United States, controlling estimated assets of half a trillion dollars and making annual grants totaling $33.6 billion. As of December 31, 2003, forty-six foundations had assets of over one billion dollars, while another sixty-four had assets between five hundred million and one billion dollars. Fully 70 percent of all foundation assets were controlled by just 2 percent of foundations.*

According to Oxfam, "Meeting the UN target of allocating just 0.7 percent of national income to aid would generate $120 billion, enough to meet the MDGs and other vital poverty-reduction goals". Oxfam adds, "By 2003, spending on aid and debt relief to all developing countries, measured per person in rich countries, was just $80 per year, or $1.53 from each person per week" (Oxfam 2005). As a percentage of Gross National Income (GNI), governments spend less today than ever before on aid. As pointed out by Figure 4.1, the percentage has decreased from 0.5 percent in 1961 to just above 0.2 percent in 2002. In aggregate total, development assistance of the 22 OECD member countries of the OECD Development Assistance Committee (the world's major donors) went down from $104 billion or (0.31 percent of GNI) in 2006 (0.31 percent) to $103 billion in 2007 (0.28 percent of GNI) (OECD 2008).

As of 2007, only five OECD countries reached the 0.7 percent target (Norway, Sweden, Luxembourg, the Netherlands, and Denmark), with the United States and Greece in the last position at 0.14 percent. In 2007 the United States' ODA amounted to $21.75 billion or 0.16 percent of the country's GDP. If corporate giving in the amount of $869 million, charities expenditure in the amount of $9.44 billion, and

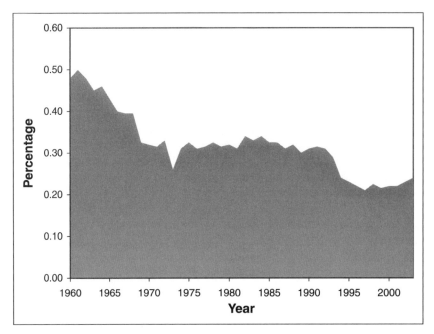

FIGURE 4.1   Net ODA as a Percentage of GNI, OECD countries
Source: Fraser and Emmett, 2005. Reproduced with the permission of Oxfam
GB, www.oxfam.org.uk

foundations expenditure in the amount of $5.4 billion were added to the United
States ODA, the sum of public and private development assistance would amount to
0.25 percent, which would put the United States ahead of Portugal, Italy, and Japan
but still behind many other European countries and Canada.

Oxfam also illustrates how a large percentage of aid from G7 countries is still
tied to serving their own domestic interests. In the case of Italy and the United
States, their percentages of tied aid, as of 2002, were 92 percent and 70 percent,
respectively (Oxfam 2005). Many of Oxfam's concluding recommendations have not
been satisfied since they were proposed in 2005, including "providing at least $50
billion in aid immediately," and "providing long-term, predictable aid for investment
in the provision of universal, free, and high-quality public services" (Oxfam 2005).

Blair's Commission

The Blair Commission for Africa was established by former British Premier Tony
Blair in February 2004. The purpose of the Commission was to delve into Africa's
complexity and determine what major undertakings should be accomplished to help
the continent combat poverty. The Commission consisted of 17 renowned experts,
nine of which were African. The Commission identified the following five goals
(GRIPS 2005):

1. Generate new ideas and action.
2. Support the best of existing African initiated effort.

3. Encourage the realization of existing international commitments.
4. Present a fresh and positive view of Africa.
5. Learn from Africans what their aspirations are and help them in satisfying them.

The Commission's 450-page concluding report points out that a big push is necessary to help the continent join the global community and become competitive. According to the Tokyo-based National Graduate Institute for Policy Studies (GRIPS), "the big push would aim to generate an annual growth rate of 7 percent by the end of the decade, compared with 3.8 percent in 2004" (GRIPS 2005). This big push would be translated into additional foreign aid of $75 billion per year that would effectively double 2004's foreign aid standing at $78.5 billion. The proposed $75 billion increase in foreign aid would be allocated as follows (GRIPS 2005): governance (4 percent), peace and security (2 percent), HIV/AIDS (13 percent), education (10 percent), health (26 percent), social inclusion (5 percent), growth, infrastructure and trade (27 percent), mitigation of shocks (5 percent), and contingencies (7 percent).

Tidjane Thiam (FMN) is the chief executive officer of Prudential, an insurance company, and the former minister of planning and development of Cote d'Ivoire. I talked to Tidjane on November 13, 2008. Tidjane was one of the nine African members of The Blair Commission for Africa, which also included Trevor Manuel (former South African Finance Minister), Graça Machel (Nelson Mandela's wife), Benjamin W. Mkapa (former president of Tanzania), and Meles Zenawi (prime minister of Ethiopia). According to Tidjane, the Commission for Africa culminated with the Gleneagles Summit of 2005.

In *The False Promise of Gleneagles*, Marian L. Tupy (2008) of the CATO Institute analyzes the mid-term results of the summit that in 2005 gathered representatives from the world's seven most industrialized nations and Russia (G8) in Gleneagles (Scotland) to tackle extreme poverty in Africa. For the CATO scholar, "The Gleneagles Summit, for all its good intentions, gave rise to unrealistic expectations. The heavy emphasis on aid and debt relief made Western actions appear to be chiefly responsible for poverty alleviation in Africa" (Tuly 2009).

Arnab Banerji was appointed Tony Blair's financial advisor in 2002. Banerji is the man Blair chose to patch up Downing Street's failing relations with the markets (Morgan 2002). I met Banerji at Brooks's gentlemen's club in London on July 6, 2009. Banerji acknowledges the need to invest in agriculture to transition from a world of food scarcity to a world of food abundance, otherwise called Cornucopia.

AID EFFECTIVENESS

In the context of the role played by development institutes and international economic institutions, New York University economist William Easterly argues in favor of adopting a market-driven approach to foreign aid or development aid, where supply naturally meets demand. The current approach to foreign-aid, Easterly argues, is more of an oligopoly based on a central planning system that puts together a variety of development institutions, which are not pressured to accomplish a good job based on the demand of their clients, in this case the extreme poor. Easterly calls the international development aid structure a cartel, whose purpose is to "thrive when customers have little opportunity to complain or find alternative suppliers."

Easterly concludes by saying if foreign aid is to make an impact and be efficient, it has to adopt the structure of a private enterprise that fulfills their customers' needs through means that maximize their economic return (Easterly 2002). In his book *The Elusive Quest for Growth*, Easterly adds a conclusion that captures well his thoughts on foreign aid allocation (2001):

> *We can envision a world in which governments do not devote themselves to theft, but one in which governments do provide national infrastructure— health clinics, primary schools, well maintained-schools, widespread phone and electricity services—and they do provide assistance to the poor within each society. The act of making loans will be rewarded rather than the act of helping the poor in each country. The solution is to have public visible "aid contests" in which each government vies for loans from a common pool on the basis of its track record and its credibly and publicly stated intentions.*

Easterly's aid allocation paradigm is exemplified by GlobalGiving, a nonprofit organization based in Washington DC. I first read about GlobalGiving in Easterly's book *The White Man's Burden* (2006). I then decided to contact the Washington-based group. GlobalGiving is one of the leading innovators in the field of development aid. The organization has collected over $14 million since 2002 and has invested in over 1,300 projects throughout the world.

MARI KURAISHI (CON) is the president of GlobalGiving. I phoned Mari on February 17, 2009. Mari points out that "GlobalGiving was founded on a key premise about innovation in international development, that in the first 50 years of development there was far less innovation than there might have been because the field was limited to larger scale (and fewer) top-down projects." Mari concludes, "the ultimate goal of GlobalGiving is to create an environment where many more experiments can be undertaken so that the rate of innovation can pick up."

How does GlobalGiving measure investment success? For GlobalGiving's president, "The more ultimate measure of course is whether 50 years from now we might have played a role in getting future Muhammad Yunuses off the ground."

Aid has been an instrument of foreign policy that has or has not proven effective at different times and locations. The history of aid in Africa is well summarized by the Zambian economist Dambisa Moyo (2009):

> *Post-war aid can be broken down into seven broad categories: its birth at Bretton Woods in the 1940s; the era of the Marshall Plan in the 1950s; the decade of industrialization of the 1960s; the shift towards aid as an answer to poverty in the 1970s; aid as the tool for stabilization and structural adjust-ment in the 1980s; aid as a buttress of democracy in the 1990s; culminating in the present-day obsession with aid as the only solution to Africa's myriad of problems.*

World Bank economist Charles Kenny points out that "the assumption has been that effective aid is that which increases recipient country GDP per capita growth rates." He concludes, "Given reconstruction has a better record than development efforts in general," and then suggests that the Marshall Plan should be compared to aid to Africa (Kenny 2006). The problem of aid delivery is exemplified by Easterly (2003):

> *Aid agencies face a peculiar incentive problem: they spend one group of people's money on a different group of people. The intended beneficiaries have almost no voice in how the money is spent. There has been surprisingly little research thinking about how to design proper incentives for aid agencies to achieve results in this situation, as well as how the aid agencies can design contracts to create good incentives for recipients.*

Santayanan Devarajan, William Easterly, and Howard Pack (2002) point out, "Low investment is not the constraint on African Development... one of the most famous predictions in development economics is that increases in investment ratios lead to growth accelerations, which fails to hold in Africa" (Devarajan, Easterly, et al., 2002).

In his paper "Why did the poorest countries fail to catch up?" Branko Milanovic explains some of the reasons why the poorest countries did not manage to reach sustainable growth (2005). The World Bank economist argues, "The poorest countries have lost, on average, some 40 percent of their output through much greater frequency of war compared with the rest of the world." The second reason involves the delay in reforms among Least Developed Countries (LDCs). The Serbian economist concludes, "While the middle-income countries' reformed from the mid-1980s onwards, comprehensive reforms among the poorest countries started only some ten years later" (Milanovic 2005).

Smart Aid

James A. Yunker is a professor of economics at Western Illinois University. In his 2005 book *Rethinking World Government* (Yunker 2005), the American scholar proposes a World Economic Equalization Program (WEEP). Yunker's WEEP is a Global Redistribution program that would shift income from high-income to low-income countries. This income would be spent in what he calls generalized capital, a category that includes, in addition to business physical capital (plant and equipment), social overhead capital (roads) and human capital (education). Yunker makes the explicit distinction between generalized capital and capital spent in consumption goods and services. His plan would shift from the rich to the poor percentages that go well beyond the 0.7 percent of a country's GDP.

A New Paradigm needs a chief executive officer. The Millennium Challenge Corporation (MCC) is a United States Agency created in 2005 by President George W. Bush. Between 2005 and 2009, the MCC was headed by Ambassador **JOHN DANILOVICH** (CEO), a businessman, diplomat, and former ambassador of the United States to Costa Rica and Brazil. I had the opportunity to meet the charming ambassador at his beautiful corner office in Washington, DC, on September 18, 2008, and on December 3, 2008, and again at his residence in London on March 8, 2009.

In its first fours years of operation since 2005, the MCC allocated $6.1 billion to 18 countries (10 of which are in sub-Saharan Africa) on a basis of conditionality. Participant countries have to show their explicit interest in obtaining aid from the MCC and demonstrate their improving performance across a number of indicators that emphasize economic growth. Easterly (2003) points out that "the White House said on its website that the new aid was motivated by the idea that 'economic development assistance can be successful only if it is linked to sound policies in developing countries.'"

The MCC has been praised as an innovative instrument of foreign aid. Easterly mentions that "the Millennium Challenge Account of the Bush administration is one interesting experiment in trying to keep money out of the hands of gangsters" (Easterly 2006). **Roy Cullen** (FIN) is a former member of parliament in Canada and the head of anti-money laundering at the Group of Parliamentarians Against Corruption (GOPAC). I talked to Roy on September 19, 2008. The Canadian comments, "I believe the Millennium Challenge Corporation is a good idea, we need more of them" (Cullen 2008). Paul Collier notes, "President Bush launched his new Millennium Challenge Account, wisely choosing not to allocate the additional American aid money through the established American aid agency" (Collier 2007).

The difference between conventional and conditional aid does not have to be significant if the conditionality is well designed and satisfies both ends of the aid spectrum, namely the donor and the recipient. Aid with conditionality can prove the right approach, if the conditionality is defined and agreed upon by both ends. New forms of development assistance should be considered going forward. Any new designs should find inspiration in structures that worked in the past (Marshall Plan) and seem to be working today (MCC and Tunisia's National Solidarity Fund).

Allocation Redefined

Two remarks draw from the history of foreign aid and its allocation—from both its successes and failures throughout the last 60 years. The first deals with who demands what. During the Marshall Plan years, it was crucial that Europe requested the aid and made the demand explicit (The Marshall Plan is described in detail in Chapter 16). A second conclusion deals with the purpose of the development aid and the topic of macroeconomic conditionality. Western countries should not pursue their own political agendas in a world where a Cold War no longer exists, in which once upon a time two rival superpowers spread out propaganda on their respective economic systems.

The new approach must remove intermediaries and involve a final delivery based on infrastructure building along with the provision of basic health care, education, clean water supply, and sanitation. The provision of basic infrastructure should guarantee a minimum level of welfare that dignifies the human being. A basic welfare state may bring about stability with the potential of helping the extreme poor to build up assets through savings in order to become economically self-reliant.

Market-Driven vs. Centrally Planned Allocation   Foreign aid allocated to finance the provision of basic services that should not be privatized can be compared to the public funding of the welfare state in developed nations. In a majority of Western countries, public goods such as the postal service, the army, the police, health care, and education are not market-driven and are publicly managed to make certain the social returns are maximized.

The allocation of foreign aid must not seek the economic efficiency of profit-maximizing businesses. It has to look at the maximization of social return, of the level of comfort and welfare of the needy and extreme poor. Foreign aid must concentrate in the construction of basic infrastructure, thereby allowing the poor to become economically self-reliant.

Formal vs. Informal Sectors   Informal sectors represent a larger part of a developing country's economy and might jeopardize a development institution's efforts to bring part of the economic activity to the formal sector. A policy that favors the formal over the informal sector might prove wrong because it leaves a majority of the poor beyond the reach of aid.

Microfinance is a perfect example of the effectiveness of foreign aid policies that favor the consolidation of the informal sector, granting the poor financial tools that bring them to the mainstream sector of the economy, where they can contribute to a country's revenues through appropriate taxation schemes. Supporting the consolidation of the informal sector through the establishment of Microfinance Institutions, which will on the mid-term become financially sustainable, could prove the right strategy.

NEW INSTRUMENTS OF FOREIGN AID

New instruments of foreign aid are suggested in this section. The premise that developed countries will continue increasing their development aid until it reaches 0.7 percent of their GDP is plausible. The incremental aid should be channeled through new schemes that explore ideas that have not been tried before.

Literature Review

In his best-selling book *The Bottom Billion* (2007), Oxford economist Paul Collier writes about the spillover effects that countries experience if a neighboring country is successful and undergoes strong economic growth:

> *In Africa, if the neighbors grow an extra 1 percent, how much does this spill over into the growth of a landlocked country? [...] The world average for all countries, landlocked or not, is 0.4 percent; for the non-African landlocked it is 0.7 percent, and for the African landlocked it is 0.2 percent.*

The lesson from Collier's argument is that if a low-income country were to become successful and concatenate a series of periods of strong economic growth, the neighboring countries could benefit by an extra increase in their GDP growth of between 0.2 and 0.7 percent. Collier identifies the failing states that are most likely to undergo a sustained turnaround. He points out that "starting from being a failing state, a country was more likely to achieve a sustained turnaround the larger its population, the greater the proportion of its population that had secondary education, and—perhaps more surprisingly—if it had recently emerged from civil war". One of Collier's new proposals is what he calls Independent Service Authorities (2007):

> *The idea is that in countries where basic public services such as primary education and health clinics are utterly failing, the government, civil society, and donors combined could try to build an alternative system for spending*

*public money. It would finance not just the building of schools and clinics
but also their day-to-day operation. As it demonstrated that it was spending money well, donors would increase the flow of money. If performance
deteriorated, the donor money would dry up.*

According to Collier, Independent Service Authorities have a downside. "It is
that you start afresh rather than trying to reform the government ministries step by
step from within the system, and so it is appropriate means" he writes. Collier adds,
"global public goods are grossly undersupplied because nobody has much interest
in providing them" (Collier 2007).

Robert Calderisi's *The Trouble with Africa: Why Foreign Aid isn't Working* is
another major piece of literature worth exploring. Calderisi proposes to cut development aid to all countries by half and reward the performance of countries that
have reformed in the direction of prosperity. Calderisi points out that he would
focus at first on five countries whose governments "deserve much more than they are
receiving at the moment" (Calderisi 2006). The five countries are Uganda, Tanzania,
Mozambique, Ghana, and Mali. Calderisi's last section summarizes *Ten Ways of
Changing Africa*, and concludes as follows (2006):

*Is it reasonable to insist on international supervision of primary school
and HIV/AIDS services? Would this not be even more humiliating than
traditional aid? Perhaps, but no government that is unwilling to look after
the basic needs of its citizens should want to hold its head very high.*

The international supervision of primary school and HIV/AIDS services that
Calderisi points out is very similar to Collier's Independent Service Authorities.
Calderisi would, however, focus on a handful of five successful countries, contrary
to Collier's preference for failed states.

In the book *Beyond Humanitarianism* (Lyman and Dorff 2007), a handful of
experts write about foreign aid to Africa on a historical basis, along the successes and
failures experienced over time. The authors remark, "Many on the African continent
have come to see foreign aid as nothing more than a cow to be milked." The authors
propose a new approach to foreign aid as follows (Lyman and Dorff 2007):

*The West should adopt a new, enlightened form of self-interest and be open
to engaging in new sorts of involvement in Africa. Sick states there cannot be
restored with the medicines and surgical techniques of a bygone era. What is
required instead are international joint ventures. These arrangements would
avoid the evils of colonialism and the errors of more recent peace-keeping
and state-building efforts.*

The aforementioned joint ventures resemble again Collier's Independent Service
Authorities or Calderisi's international supervision of primary school and HIV/AIDS
services. The authors include a quote by former President Bill Clinton that reinforces
the arguments (Lyman and Dorff 2007):

*If you first develop the health infrastructure throughout the whole country,
particularly in Africa, to deal with AIDS, you will increase the infrastructure
of dealing with maternal and child health, malaria, and tuberculosis. Then I*

think you have to look at nutrition, water, and sanitation. All these things, when you build it up, you'll be helping to promote economic development and alleviate poverty.

Improving health care and education is only a first step to changing the reality of aid. Inhabitants of poor countries deserve a better outcome. Inhabitants of rich countries deserve more accountability of their tax dollars. New approaches to foreign aid ought to be considered. "What lessons can we draw from the experience of the past twenty years that would help Least Developed Countries' future growth?" asks Branko Milanovic (2005). He mentions the following three lessons:

1. Less war and less civil strife are key.
2. The reliance on multilateral lenders is unlikely to help the poorest countries.
3. Democratization and better education in poor countries are worthy goals, but neither seems to be an instrument for economic development, particularly so if other enabling conditions, like peace, are not present.

In her best-selling and controversial book *Dead Aid*, the Zambian economist Dambisa Moyo proposes to discontinue the flow of foreign aid within five years (2009):

> *What if, one by one, African countries each received a phone call (agreed upon by all their major aid donors—the World Bank, Western countries, etc.), telling them that in exactly five years the aid taps would be shut off— permanently? Although exceptions would be made for isolated emergency relief such as famine and natural disasters, aid would no longer attempt to address Africa's generic economic plight.*

What if Moyo's suggestion was reformulated? We could propose to shut off the current approach to foreign aid and embrace a new approach to development that would channel funds through new schemes able to secure the provision of Global Public Goods through Collier's independent service authorities in Calderisi's best-performing countries subject to an ex-ante conditionality inspired in the Millennium Challenge Corporation.

EXPLORING NEW TERRITORY

The provision of basic infrastructure is at the very core of any new approach of foreign aid. Education and health care are crucial in securing the extreme poor's turnaround. No society will move forward unless their youth is healthy and educated. This is the reality of poverty. The vicious cycle that many developing countries are trapped in limits their ability to take off. Countries lack the ability to generate growth opportunities because their population is sick and uneducated. Many countries have had to reimburse the external debt awarded to a plethora of corrupt leaders. Many countries have had to reimburse the loans of the World Bank and the International Monetary Fund that were oftentimes awarded to bail out Western investors.

I remain convinced that incremental improvement will never close the gap between the top and the bottom billions. I am confident that the traditional approach to poverty eradication based on project-based lending and macroeconomic conditionality will never trigger significant improvement among a majority of the extreme poor. The poor need what we need to move forward. They need publicly managed health care and education, subsidized water, and sanitation.

There is a Window of Opportunity. Academics are turning to new ideas that point in the direction of providing a Universal Welfare for the extreme poor. I am not sure the reality of aid could have accomplished a task of this caliber in the past, but it is our obligation today. I remain convinced a global effort can be designed and implemented. I hear Sachs' hope. I am determined to apply Collier and Easterly's conservative approaches that demand accountability for each dollar of foreign aid spent, independent from the source.

It is time. It is time to move one step forward. The provision of Global Public Goods must start. Welcome to the era of Global Redistribution. Global inequality must be monitored. We cannot continue to maintain the course on the wrong path. Let's slow the pace and redefine the structures under which democratic capitalism operates. It is time. It is time to reform our policies in the West. You can do it. I can help. It is time to define international standards that are enforced on nations and multinational corporations.

I dreamt of a New International Territory that could host the New Institutions of a redefined capitalism. I dreamt of a New International Territory that would be established away from the political and financial centers of our time, from Washington, DC, and New York City, from Brussels and Geneva. I dreamt of a New Consensus, the Euro-Consensus that would export the welfare state to the neediest countries. I dreamt of depoliticized institutions whose sole goal would be to fight extreme poverty. It is our generation's challenge. My heart breathes the hopeful wind that comes from ahead. I feel a harmony coming from the society of 2050. Let's start building the society of tomorrow. We need world institutions once and for all. A globalized world cannot only benefit the better off; a globalized world must benefit all.

This book describes a path towards the establishment of a New International Territory that could host the New Organizations of a redefined capitalism, including The New Institution. The New Institution will provide the extreme poor with a Universal Welfare consisting of universal, free, and basic education and health care, and a subsidized clean water supply and sanitation. The delivery will be based on the ideas shared by Collier and Calderisi, and will start in a group of six willing sub-Saharan countries that have expressed a common, explicit desire to move ahead and leave the poverty trap behind.

This book presents how to raise the financing needed to fund the provision of the Universal Welfare. It presents the individuals that will be part of the team in charge of implementing a New Paradigm, a New Consensus. Read carefully, and you will encounter the Hundred Individuals that in the years ahead will bring excitement to the policy-making process, a process that is forward-looking and shall never stop. A World Solidarity Fund will be established. The Fund will become the Poor's Endowment, able to finance a Universal Welfare State for the next 40 years and beyond. The next 40 years become the Glorious Forty.

Read the histories of the Marshall Plan and the formation of the European Union, including the European Coal and Steel Community and its six founding members. Substitute Coal and Steel with Health Care and Education. Substitute the core of Europe with the core of sub-Saharan Africa. Imagine an African Community of Healthcare and Education. Imagine the elimination of intermediaries, and the hiring of local teachers and doctors. Imagine an environment in which NGOs no longer need to operate. Imagine similar structures arising in Asia and Latin America.

I believe those that first embrace the New Paradigm will become the pioneers of a New Capitalism. The current proposal is sophisticated and involves intuition, thinking, creativity, persuasion, and a necessary degree of strategy and luck. This is The Monfort Plan. It is Collier's rocket, an accelerator of trends, a well-needed catalyst, the big push of the Blair's Commission for Africa.

William Greider writes in his book *One World Ready or Not*, "Perhaps, in the next age of capitalism, an original thinker will arise somewhere in the world with a new theory that reconciles the market's imperatives with unfilled human needs, without having to destroy the marketplace to do so" (Greider 2003). We are in desperate need of new ideas that fulfill Greider's premise.

"THE SEEDS OF GLOBAL REDISTRIBUTION"

Artwork by Richard Cole.

CHAPTER 5

The World's Income Distribution

Does economic inequality breed political conflict? In other words, are nations with a more unequal distribution of income and wealth more subject to phenomena like revolution, rebellion, terrorism, demonstrations, and coups than those with a more equal distribution? Most students of conflict would answer yes. All major theorists of conflict believe that economic inequality is, at least, a potentially important cause of dissent.

—Mark I. Lichbach, *An Evaluation of "Does Economic Inequality Breed Political Conflict?" Studies*

The world's income distribution has continued to widen over the last one hundred years. According to Angus Maddison (1995), the ratio between the income of the richest countries and the income of the poorest countries has gone up from 3:1 in 1820 to 72:1 in 1992. The richest countries have continued to grow while the poorest countries have sunk in their poverty trap.

Many have attempted to explain this paradox with relative success. Macroeconomists have elaborated growth models that explain what inputs (savings, technology, education) matter so that a country can reach a stage of sustainable economic growth. Political scientists have focused on the importance of institutions and the rule of law when assessing the conditions that foster economic growth. Development economists look at geography and ethnicity as indicators that can anticipate economic stagnation. Historians take into account the pitfalls of slavery and colonization to explain some of today's differences in income.

A New Architecture whose goal is to boost the incomes of the extreme poor and reduce inequality needs a leading expert in inequality. **BRANKO MILANOVIC** (INI) is a lead economist at the development research department of the World Bank. I met Branko at the London School of Economics on January 17, 2007. Branko, an authority on inequality, explains the plethora of academic interpretations to the prevalence of poverty in his outstanding book *Worlds Apart* (Milanovic 2005):

These empirical facts that are difficult to square with economic theory have led to two reactions. First was endogenous growth theory, which holds that in addition to the "usual suspects" (improved education, increasing labor force, and capital accumulation) there are many other important factors that affect growth. They are either political (democracy, rule of law, social stability) or economic (inflation, fiscal deficit, openness). Allowing for these variables permits a number of authors to claim that conditional convergence holds—namely that after controlling for these variables, poor countries still grow faster than the rich. But while "controlling" for other factors may make sense in a regression, it can hardly make sense in real life.

The last fifty years have only widened the difference between the richest and the poorest. A majority of the African countries that obtained independence failed to catch up. As Branko points out "the most extraordinary thing, therefore, is that out of the twenty-two countries that, in 1960, were within the striking distance of joining the club of the rich, only two—Singapore and Hong Kong—succeeded, while all the others not merely failed but slipped into the lower categories" (Milanovic 2005). For Branko, the years 1979 to 1980 were crucial in explaining some of the disparities we see today. He points out, "the changes that occurred around 1978-1980, namely the increase in world interest rates, the increased debt burden of developing countries, the growth slowdown in the industrial world, and the skill-biased technological change may have contributed to the developing countries' stagnation and to the bifurcation of the developing world" (Milanovic 2005).

In his paper "Where in the World Are You?" Branko stresses how "the richest people in India (as a group—admittedly a large one since it contains more than 50 million people) have lower per capita income than the poorest people (as a group) in Germany" (Milanovic 2007). There is, as a result, no overlap in income between India and Germany. An individual would, on average, be better off in the poorest 5 percent in Germany and in the richest 5 percent in India.

A 2004 article published in *The Economist* raised the question "Is the familiar claim that capitalism makes global inequality worse actually true?" The magazine remarks, "it so happens that average incomes in India and China are going up extremely rapidly. Without knowing anything else, one should therefore be sceptical [*sic*] about all the claims that are so confidently made about rising global inequality" (*Economist*, 2004b). China and India are typically presented as the success stories of global capitalism and globalization.

Xavier Sala-i-Martin is a Columbia University economist well-known for his research on income inequality and income distribution. The aforementioned article says "work by Surjit Bhalla and Xavier Sala-i-Martin shows rapid—indeed historically unprecedented—falls in poverty during the 1980s and 1990s, the new golden age of global capitalism." Branko refers to Sala-i-Martin's research and points out, "this is due to the very strong assumptions made by both authors" (Milanovic 2005). Sala-i-Martin's research outcome diverges from that of the World Bank.

Is worldwide inequality increasing or decreasing? Professor Francisco Rivera-Batiz, a well-known economist who teaches at Columbia University, offers one of the best answers to this question. He argues that in actuality Sala-i-Martin's and the World Bank's methodologies yield the same results. Sala-i-Martin uses national account data from each of the countries for which he measures income inequality to come up with his income distribution curves. The World Bank uses household data. If a country's gross domestic product is divided by its population, the result is the average per-capita-income for the country, which is total income.

Household data is based on individual household surveys conducted on a case-by-case basis. Household data is reflective of a person's disposable income. Total income is, generally speaking, greater than disposable income. Disposable income is total income minus tax payments and interest payments on any outstanding debt such as microcredits or consumption loans. The rule of thumb is that disposable income is about half of total income. As a result according to Sala-i-Martin's methodology an individual's income is twice as large as the income in the World Bank's methodology.

The above results are then used to determine the number of people in the world who live in extreme poverty. Extreme poverty is defined[1] by the World Bank as having less than $1 per day or less than $2 per day (in purchasing power parity of 1993 U.S. dollars). Because Sala-i-Martin's incomes are about twice those of the World Bank's, the former is more optimistic than the latter in the evolution of extreme poverty. For the World Bank, the number of extreme poor living under $1 or $2 a day is twice as large as for Sala-i-Martin.

The case of China and India deserves further commentary. Sala-i-Martin's methodology is based on national account data that relies on a country's self-reported GDP. In January 2008, the World Bank revised China and India's GDP downwards by 40 percent, "highlighting the need for better data" (Birdsall 2008). The impact on total income is severe. Average total income (a country's gross domestic product divided by its population) should be revised downwards by 40 percent in the case of China and India. This means that the number of people originally estimated to live under the extreme poverty line in China and India would go up significantly. *The Economist*'s statement that "it so happens that average incomes in India and China are going up extremely rapidly" should be revised downwards. As a result, the second part of statement, "without knowing anything else, one should therefore be sceptical [*sic*] about all the claims that are so confidently made about rising global inequality," no longer holds.

SANJAY REDDY (INI) is an economist at Barnard College in New York City. I had a productive conversation with Sanjay at his office of Barnard College on September 8, 2008. Sanjay works very closely with Yale philosopher Thomas Pogge. The tandem has criticized the World Bank's methodology on measuring poverty. In their paper "How not to count the poor," they challenge the World Bank's poverty line as arbitrary, remarking, "the international poverty line is not adequately anchored in any specification of the real requirements of human beings." They add, "the World Bank extrapolates incorrectly from limited data and thereby creates an appearance of precision that masks the high probable error of its estimates." As a result, they propose "a new methodology of global poverty assessment, focused directly on what is needed to achieve elementary human requirements." What do they propose exactly? In the concluding section of their paper, an alternative is provided (Pogge and Reddy 2005):

> *This alternative procedure would construct poverty lines in each country that possess a common achievement interpretation. Each poverty line would refer to the local cost requirements of achieving a specific set of ends. [...] The proposed procedure focuses not on whether the incomes of poor people are sufficient in relation to an abstract International Poverty Line (IPL)*

but rather on whether they are sufficient to achieve a set of elementary requirements. In effect, it does away with the need for an IPL, by focusing instead on a common poverty concept to be applied in all countries.

Their methodology has not been implemented and for the time being remains only on paper. It could prove challenging to adopt different standards for different countries and ethnic groups based on the local needs to achieve the basic requirements they talk about. In a way the Grameen Bank of Bangladesh proposes a measure of poverty that is similar to that of Sanjay's. Muhammad Yunus, founder of Grameen Bank and Nobel Peace Prize winner in 2006, explains how Grameen measures poverty as follows: "We developed a ten-point system that describes specific living conditions. Once a family has succeeded in clearing all ten of these hurdles, then we at Grameen Bank consider them to have escaped from poverty" (Yunus 2007).

POVERTY AND INEQUALITY

When I was 16 years old, I decided to spend a year abroad as an exchange student. I contacted Intercultura, the Spanish Chapter of American Field Service (AFS), and signed up for the year-abroad program. In early August 1992, I landed in San Antonio, Texas.[2] I now return every year to spend two weeks in San Antonio with my Texan host parents Bill and Barbara Sano. Every year I talk with Bill while he drives to the City Police Department in downtown San Antonio. Bill agrees with me that it is important to fight poverty globally. But he is more concerned about the poverty he sees, the poverty that surrounds him, which is the homeless in the San Antonio area.

Bill and Barbara flew to California to attend my graduation from the master's in financial engineering program at the University of California at Berkeley in March 2005. They were impressed by the number of homeless in San Francisco compared to San Antonio. It is a natural reaction to blame those who have not worked hard. But most often, it can only help to have a network of social protection that offers support to those in the bottom of the income distribution. This provides the worse off with a means to climb up and have a decent living.

It is also natural to try to take care of one's problems before taking care of a neighbor's problem. The neighborhood is also a relative concept. For those who do not travel, the neighborhood may be their city or their country. For international travelers their neighborhood may be the world. Consequently, poverty is a relative concept with geographical bounds. In the European Union poverty is defined as earning 60 percent or less of the average income. Poverty is again a relative concept. Extreme poverty is a different beast. Inequality is also a relative concept. In a capitalist democracy, there will always be inequality if there is difference in income. Extreme inequality is a different beast.

I am concerned with poverty and inequality in Europe and the United States, which I often travel between. Therefore I am a supporter of redistribution within Europe and the United States. The European Union has implemented continental redistribution through its Structural Funds, which "allow the European Union to grant financial assistance to resolve structural economic and social problems".[3] Spain surpassed Italy in per capita income in 2008, which would have seemed unthinkable when Spain joined the European Union in 1986. Since 1986, Spain has been receiving Structural Funds from the European Union in an amount close to 1 percent of its GDP. Many economists acknowledge that between 1994 and 2007, the Structural Funds helped Spain concatenate fourteen years of average economic growth above the 3 percent mark.

The next stop is Global Redistribution. It is knocking on our door, finally. But this time Global Redistribution is coming to stay. The world cannot continue to base its international cooperation on the charity of the better off. Contributions must turn systematic and foreseeable. Charity must turn long-tern investment.

Pedro Pablo Kuczynski (FMN) was Peru's Finance Minister from 2001 to 2002 and 2004 to 2005, and Peru's Prime Minister from 2005 to 2006. I met the Peruvian politician at his office in the District of Miraflores on June 22, 2009, in Lima (Peru). For Pedro Pablo redistribution is a key element of a country's economic agenda, and there must be cross-subsidies that help finance basic public goods to the most vulnerable.

Jeremy Rifkin wrote his book *The European Dream* in 2004. Rifkin's punch line is "how Europe's vision is quietly eclipsing the American Dream." Rifkin points out that "the fledging European Dream represents humanity's best aspirations for a better tomorrow." I have lived two years in France, one in Germany, one in the United Kingdom, and five in the United States. I know the realities on both sides of the Atlantic very well. I have identified the strengths and weaknesses of both societies. I hear Rifkin's words. I believe it is time for Europe to step forward and universalize its welfare-state paradigm. I am confident Americans will follow with the Obama Administration and the Health Care Bill. Rifkin writes (Rifkin 2004):

> *There are more people living in poverty in America than in the sixteen European nations for which data is available. Seventeen percent of all Americans are in poverty, or one out of every six people. By contrast 5.1 percent of the people in Finland are in poverty, 6.6 percent in Sweden, 7.5 percent in Germany, 8 percent in France, 8.1 percent in the Netherlands, 8.2 percent in Belgium, 10.1 percent in Spain, 11.1 percent in Ireland, and 14.2 percent in Italy.*

Rifkin concludes, "According to the OECD, while the U.S. devotes only 11 percent of its GDP to redistributing income by way of transfers and other social benefits, the EU countries contribute more than 26 percent of their GDP to social benefits."

THE KUZNETS CURVE

Simon Kuznets was an American economist who won the Nobel Prize in Economics in 1971. Kuznets was born in Russia, where he began his university studies that he would later complete at Columbia University. In the lecture[4] to the memory of Alfred Nobel that Kuznets gave upon receiving the Nobel Prize, he observed, "Modern economic growth, with the rapid succession of innovations and shortening period of their mass diffusion, must be accompanied by a relatively high incidence of negative effects." This is precisely what the Kuznets Curve is all about. A developing country, as it grows, will increase the incidence of negative effects. As a result, its income inequality will tend to rise.

James A. Robinson and Daron Acemoglu, economists of Harvard and the Massachusetts Institute of Technology (MIT) respectively, developed "The Political Economy of the Kuznets Curve" (Acemoglu and Robinson 2002). They conclude that when development occurs and income inequality increases, social unrest may lead to political democratization. Democratization embraces redistribution, which leads to a reduction of income inequality. This is the logical sequence of steps that should naturally develop. However, this pattern does not always take place. Robinson and Acemoglu state, "Development does not necessarily induce a Kuznets curve, and it is shown that development may be associated with two types of nondemocratic paths: an authocratic disaster, and an East Asian Miracle" (Acemoglu and Robinson 2002). An example of the former would be North Korea. An example of the latter would be any of the four Asian tigers (Hong Kong, Singapore, South Korea, and Taiwan).

What levels of inequality are bearable? Branko Milanovic points out that there should be an explicit difference between developed and developing countries. According to the Kuznets curve, countries that are more developed will tend to have a lower level of inequality in the long run. It is based on this premise that when establishing operating bounds, there has to be an explicit distinction between developed and developing countries.

Branko proposes two operating bands for inequality purposes. The goal is to avoid situations in which extreme inequality occurs within a specific country. The bands would monitor the main indicator for income inequality, the Gini coefficient.[5] Gini coefficients should, therefore, stay within the band of 0.25 to 0.35 for developed countries and 0.30 to 0.45 for developing countries. What are the priorities for the next 40 years in the development arena regarding income levels and inequality? First, we must make sure average incomes shift upwards for low-income countries. Second, we must make sure Gini coefficients stay within the proposed bands.

Why does the second condition listed above need to hold? Consider the case of Namibia, the world's most unequal country. Namibia's per capita income stands at $7,586 (PPP U.S. $ as of 2007), the fourth highest in sub-Saharan Africa after that of Mauritius ($12,715), Botswana ($12,387), and South Africa ($11,110). However, wealth is extremely badly allocated in Namibia. 35 percent of Namibia's population lives under $1 a day and 56 percent lives under $2 a day. These numbers compare with Botswana's 28 percent and 55 percent, or South Africa's 10 percent and 34 percent respectively (World Bank 2007c).

What do we do if the Gini coefficient for a specific country goes beyond the upper threshold? Consider the case of Great Britain. As of year-end 2007, Britain's Gini coefficient was 0.36 (World Bank 2007c) when it should be between 0.25 and 0.35 according to Branko, our authority on inequality. Two straightforward policies can be implemented: either raise income taxes and make them more progressive, or increase minimum wage levels so that those in the bottom of the income distribution earn more.

One of the conclusions for policy-makers would be to establish a worldwide minimum wage in PPP terms. This would help reduce national inequality. Global Redistribution schemes able to sustain a basic welfare state would help reduce international inequality. Average worldwide income has to continue increasing. Economic growth is important. But global inequality has to drop. It follows that worldwide minimum wage standards and Global Redistribution are simply the next step in the development agenda.

GLOBAL PUBLIC GOODS

Public goods are generally defined in terms of their excludability and rivalry. In an article published on *Le Monde Diplomatique* Inge Kaul explains "What is a public good?". Kaul describes private goods as follows (2000):

> *Private goods are typically traded in markets. Buyers and sellers meet through the price mechanism. If they agree on a price, the ownership or use of the good (or service) can be transferred. Thus private goods tend to be excludable. They have clearly identified owners; and they tend to be rival. For example, others cannot enjoy a piece of cake, once consumed.*

A public good is non-tradable and non-excludable. The result is that consumers cannot buy or sell a public good, and cannot stop other consumers from utilizing it. Public goods are also non-rival: others can enjoy their use, in spite of one individual's consumption. Global Public Goods are public goods that can be enjoyed on a global scale, and therefore on a worldwide scale. If we associate the concept of national public goods with universal access to health care and education, we are implicitly referring to a national welfare. Global Public Goods that incorporate health care and education are implicitly referring to a global welfare or world welfare, otherwise called Universal Welfare.

Global Public Goods have been part of the Bretton Woods architecture even if their delivery has not yet been accomplished. For instance, the United Nations (UN) was established "to solve problems of international coordination and to enhance regional and international cooperation." The 81 organizations of the UN system are "core providers of regional and international public goods" (Kaul, Grunberg, et al., 1999).

For Nancy Birdsall and Devesh Kapur of the Center for Global Development, the presidency of the World Bank is *The Hardest Job in the World*. Birdsall and Kapur give five recommendations to the then appointed President Paul Wolfowitz, one of which is to "obtain an explicit mandate, an adequate grant instrument, and a special governance structure for the Bank's work on Global Public Goods." For the authors, "past investments in global public goods have had impressive rates of return: as high as 40 percent for agricultural research" (Birdsall and Kapur 2005).

Branko notes, regarding a world welfare, that "as Gunnar Myrdal observed more than thirty years ago, the very idea that rich countries should help the poor countries is both novel—since it dates from the end of World War II—and implies the conception of World welfare" (Milanovic 2005). The transition from national public goods to Global Public Goods is well described by David Held (2004):

> *The provision of public goods can no longer be equated with state-provided goods alone. Some core public goods have to be provided regionally and globally if they are to be provided at all. From the establishment of fair trade*

rules and financial stability to the fight against hunger and environmental degradation, the emphasis is on finding durable modes of international and transnational cooperation and collaboration.

Although a majority of OECD countries have publicly managed and run health care and education systems, many at the World Bank and the International Monetary Fund have for decades advocated for a privatized delivery in low-income countries.

In 2008 Lawrence D. Brown and Lawrence R. Jacobs wrote a book entitled *The Private Abuse of the Public Interest*. Brown and Jacobs cannot be more explicit about the beginning of new times for the interaction between the market and the public interest. The authors note, "conservative aspirations to expand markets and shrink government have often disappointed citizens and resulted in more extensive government rules and routines" (Brown and Jacobs 2008). Perhaps we need smarter regulation and smarter government, as opposed to entering the debate or more vs. less regulation, or more vs. less government.

According to the authors, Nixon's victory in 1968 and not Reagan's, was a clear indication that market doctrine had to be embraced. Nixon campaigned against Lyndon B. Johnson's Great Society and War on Poverty. Are we back to Johnson's policies along Roosevelt's New Deal? The authors conclude, "When faced with concrete, most Americans expect government to intervene even if they remain uneasy in the abstract about the effectiveness and trustworthiness of government" (Brown and Jacobs 2008). I cannot help thinking that this was the case in the financial collapse, in the mortgage crisis, or in the automobile bailout. When the market is not able to correct its own excesses, regulators need to enforce regulation and governments have to step in to guarantee that the public interest is above the market.

For decades our emphasis on privately run health care and education providers for the extreme poor was misleading. The macroeconomic conditionality imposed by the Bretton Woods institutions in the 1980s and early 1990s targeted the minimal state, forcing developing countries to run fiscal austerity, thereby shrinking budget allocations to health care and education. There is perhaps a new opportunity to insist on what has yielded positive outcomes in Western Europe and other developed countries. The provision of Global Public Goods is now only possible if a welfare state is designed for the extreme poor.

GLOBAL REDISTRIBUTION OF WEALTH

Global Redistribution implies a worldwide shift of income from high-income countries to low-income countries. Redistribution has been part of democratic capitalism in the Bretton Woods era and incorporates progressivity into the tax system. As a result, those who earn more pay a larger share of their income in taxes. Redistribution is executed through the delivery of public services in developed countries. Public services represent the skeleton of the welfare state, are universally provided, and typically consist of education and health care.

A different type of redistribution is advocated by the supporters of the basic income, a theoretical concept that has not been implemented in Western countries with the exception of the state of Alaska in the United States. Daniel Raventós is the president of the Spain-based Basic Income Network and a professor of economics at

Universitat de Barcelona. I met Raventós at Plaza Catalunya in Barcelona (Spain) on March 26, 2009.

In his piece *Beyond the Welfare State: the Proposal of the Basic Income*, Raventós explains the benefits of the basic income as an improved version of the traditional welfare state (Raventós 2006). He argues that the basic income would add flexibility to the labor market and protection to the worker. It grants the individual more freedom to undertake whatever occupation to which he or she is more eager to devote his or her time, including those that are nonprofit or household-based. Raventós notes that the state of Alaska implemented the basic income in 1982. This basic income is the dividend from Alaska's oil fund. Similarly, a basic income could be appropriate in any resource-rich nation-state that is able to accumulate wealth in a fund. Norway is a good example. For Raventós, "criticising basic income because it will not put an end to the injustices of the capitalist system is a bit like sneering at a malaria vaccine because it does not put an end to infant mortality" (Raventós 2007).

Paul Segal is an Oxford economist who has written extensively on the basic income for the extreme poor. I met Segal on July 31, 2008, at Oxford University. Segal proposes that each resource-rich country "distribute its resource rents directly to citizens as a universal and unconditional cash transfer," which he calls resource dividend (Segal 2009). For the Oxford economist, this policy would halve the World Bank's $1 global poverty line. Resource-rich countries are oftentimes trapped in the resource curse, which is studied in detail in Chapter 9.

Dambisa Moyo suggests that "instead of writing out a single $250 million check to a country's government, why not distribute the money equally among its population?" (Moyo 2009).

There is a dilemma around the idea of Global Redistribution and global transfers from high-income to low-income countries. Should Global Redistribution be provided through public services universally available to the extreme poor, or through a basic income? If the poor had a basic income to spare, they would decide how and when to spend it, eventually choosing private providers of education and health care.

I think that any Global Redistribution proposal has to be based on the provision of the welfare state that has worked in a majority of developed countries. A basic income inspired in the Alaskan example could complement the provision of a basic welfare state for the extreme poor in those countries that are resource-rich and have accumulated wealth by piling up the revenues from the exploitation of natural resources such as oil, gas, or minerals.

Branko warns against the likelihood that global transfers are regressive. He points out that in order to design transfers that can reduce world poverty "we may want to avoid the likelihood of a regressive transfer, that is, the possibility that the transfer is generated by taxing somebody in a rich country who may turn out to be poorer than the recipient in a poor country" (Milanovic 2005). Branko further remarks:

> *That some systemic redistribution, in contrast to the current system of bi-lateral and voluntary contributions from rich countries, will eventually take place is a view that is now being shared by the World Bank. Its chief economist François Bourguignon noted that there was convergence with the alter-globalists on a certain topics including the creation of international*

taxes—whether it be a Tobin tax on financial flows, or a tax on plane tickets, on CO_2 emission, or on weapon exports. This convergence, if indeed real, represents a major step forward.

François Bourguignon is the former chief economist of the World Bank and director of the Paris School of Economics. I talked to Bourguignon on August 27, 2008. In 2006 the French economist co-authored a paper entitled "Global Redistribution of Income" (Bourguignon, Levin, et al., 2006), in which notes that global inequality is extremely high with a Gini coefficient estimated at between 0.64 and 0.66. The former chief economist concludes, "If this level of inequality were to exist within a single country, that country would probably experience substantial social strife." The world has been suffering from substantial social strife and Western countries have barely noticed.

Global Taxes

In 2009 Ecuador's President Rafael Correa suggested the taxation on oil production to establish a global tax aimed at the compensation for environmental damage. Correa holds a Ph.D. in economics from the University of Illinois at Urbana Champaign. This taxation would represent a tool to fight poverty and inequality in the developing world. The fact of the matter is that this proposal, along with many others, such as the historically demanded Tobin-tax or the Chirac-led air transportation levy, are either rejected by the financial or corporate elites or not subscribed to by the international community.

In a world of increasing differences, the words *global justice* and *equity* become inevitable in the daily conversation of wannabe technocrats. Redistribution schemes were established in Europe and the United States after World War II as a way to provide safety nets for a population severely impacted by 31 years of destruction, instability, and economic depression. Intra-nation redistribution schemes are schemes of the past, whose implementation was deemed appropriate 60 years ago. Inter-nation redistribution schemes are a must-have in today's unequal world. The lack of an international authority that implements Global Redistribution stops supporters from claiming that such a measure would be feasible and enforceable.

Global taxes will become common and widespread in the society of the twenty-second century. In the meantime, we have to consensuate international taxation schemes that will become precursors of future global taxes. The international community needs to set common ground for the establishment of an agenda leading to the adoption of international standards towards Global Redistribution, in which the better off in developed and developing nations are required to contribute to a global welfare state with the potential to guarantee the extreme poor with universal access to basic health care, education, water, and sanitation.

Western countries believe in the welfare state because healthy and educated citizens are in better shape to cope with the challenges of globalization, because a healthy and educated population can better contribute to a country's aggregate output and can become economically self-reliant. The industrialized world has secured the provision of public goods. A part of the developing world has begun to acknowledge access to these public goods as a right. The new constitution in Bolivia, approved in

2009, included an explicit mention to the consideration as a human right of access to water, energy, and telecommunications.

I hear many arguing that we should not raise the amount of funding available for development in the developing world. I hear many stating we should better allocate the existing resources, so that the errors of the past are no longer repeated. I believe our generation has to work on two fronts: accomplishing a considerable increase in current funding for development and maximizing its output by designing better allocation schemes. Moreover, I cannot think of a better way to allocate resources than by establishing a basic global welfare scheme that delivers the provision of health care, education, water, and sanitation to the extreme poor.

Fernando Villalonga (CON) was Spain's Deputy Minister for International Cooperation from 1996 to 2000. I met Fernando at his office of the Spanish Consulate in New York City on June 26, 2009. Fernando welcomes new venues of innovation and creativity in the development space. It is time we realize our scope goes beyond our borders. It is time we become aware that human beings deserve dignity independent from their nationality. It is possible in today's world to grant minimum standards of dignity to make sure that no matter where one is born, the hope to live a better life will be attainable. The extreme levels of income and despair we observe today should not coexist in a world where globalization is utilized at our own convenience and for our own benefit. We cannot ignore the crude reality of a large percentage of a population in desperate need of basic infrastructure, without which no one can move forward.

TWO

The Axis of Feeble

Throughout history the word *axis* has been commonly used in the West to denote the enemy that must be defeated. During World War II the enemy represented by Germany, Italy, and Japan was denoted the Axis Powers. In the aftermath of September 11, 2001, former U.S. president George W. Bush embraced the expression *Axis of evil* to denote the threat of international terrorism. Today we must acknowledge the existence of an axis that has remained ignored. It is a lethal axis that originates and perpetuates poverty. It is an axis that feeds and fosters mafias, corruption, crime, and terrorism. The Axis of Feeble is our new enemy if we are to redefine capitalism and build a new economic architecture that works for benefit of the extreme poor.

In his best-selling book *Capitalism's Achilles Heel*, Raymond Baker, director of the think-tank Global Financial Integrity, identifies one of the components of the Axis of Feeble: the international financial architecture with its loopholes, its tax havens, and its banking secrecy (Baker 2005). The remaining five components of the Axis of Feeble are: agriculture, trade and labor rights, small arms trade, mining and extractive industries, and brain drain.

The G20 summits of Washington, DC, and London that took place in 2008 and 2009 only addressed one of the components of the Axis of Feeble. The G20 technocrats who met in the United States and the United Kingdom did not speak about agriculture, fair trade, or brain drain. The G20 technocrats who met in the United States and the United Kingdom did not speak about small arms trade and labor rights. Trying to defeat the Axis of Feeble focusing only on financial reform is like trying to defeat the Axis powers fighting only Italy and Japan and forgetting Hitler's Nazi Germany, or like trying to defeat the Axis of evil focusing solely on Afghanistan and forgeting Pakistan.

Western society continues to defend national priorities and forgets that the global priorities will sooner or later have to be addressed if we are to prevail. Never before have we as a society been closer to starting the Journey of our Lifetime. Never have we as a society been closer to taking off to explore new territory that has remained in the imagination of the Expert Dreamers. We are at a tipping point in history where we might enter the Era of Sustainability. But first, we must defeat the Axis of Feeble.

Artwork by Claudio Muñoz.

CHAPTER 6

Agriculture

Few people in Europe, America, and Japan know anything about the relationship between food, feed, and hunger in the world. But if they did, would they feel morally compelled to eat lower on the global food chain with a more vegetable-oriented diet so that more agricultural land could be freed up to raise food grain rather than feed grain?
                                                        —Jeremy Rifkin, *The European Dream*

Agriculture and population growth have long been debated among economists. Thomas Robert Malthus was an English economist born south of London in the late eighteenth century. Malthus is frequently cited for his prediction that the human population would experience severe famines going forward if population growth outpaced increases in food production. According to the New School for Social Research's biography on Malthus,[1] "Malthus' hypothesis implied that actual population always has a tendency to push above the food supply." Malthus inspired Charles Darwin who would later write in his autobiography[2]:

In October 1838, that is, fifteen months after I had begun my systematic inquiry, I happened to read for amusement Malthus on Population, *and being well prepared to appreciate the struggle for existence which everywhere goes on from long-continued observation of the habits of animals and plants, it at once struck me that under these circumstances favorable variations would tend to be preserved, and unfavorable ones to be destroyed. The results of this would be the formation of a new species. Here, then I had at last got a theory by which to work.*

MALTHUS, MEADE, AND MAURITIUS ON POPULATION GROWTH

Malthus' *Essay on the Principle of Population* was written in 1798 and includes the following statement: "It is an obvious truth, which has been taken notice of by many writers that population must always be kept down to the level of the means of subsistence."

James Meade won the Nobel Prize in Economics in 1977 for his contributions to international trade. Two of his papers written in the 1960s, while he was chair of political economy at Cambridge, involved a Malthusian prediction on the small island-state of Mauritius. I first heard about Malthus' Mauritian predictions during a phone conversation with the former World Bank country representative for Madagascar, James Bond. Bond, who later became chief operating officer at the World Bank's Multilateral Investment Guarantee Agency (MIGA), referred to Meade's predictions that failed because of Mauritius' serious work on diversification and control of demographics.

Meade predicted in 1961, based on the demographic growth of the time, that the population of Mauritius would grow from one million to three million by the year 2000. Consequently, the island-state would not be able to increase food production at the same rate, and the inhabitants of the small country would either die or migrate. With an area of 2,000 square kilometers, Mauritius has a very limited availability of arable land.

Malthus and Meade were wrong on Mauritius. There is much to learn from the successful island-state. The hope is that Malthus and Meade will be wrong again on the world's ability to resolve once and for all the repetitive episodes of famine and starvation. The world has to do serious work on demographics and agriculture. We need to transition from a world of food scarcity to a world of food abundance. The objective of this chapter is to discover the challenges to overcome, the drivers of food prices, and what can be accomplished going forward to materialize a Second Green Revolution.

THE FOOD CRISIS

The World Bank reported in 2008 that "for many countries and regions where progress has been slow, the negative poverty impact of rising food prices risks undermining the poverty gains of the last five to ten years, at least in the short term," thereby concluding that prices would not return to the levels of 2000 until 2015 (Bryant and Blas 2008a). Jacques Diouf, director general of the Food and Agriculture Organization, notes, "there is a risk that this unrest will spread in countries where 50–60 percent of income goes to food" (Bryant and Blas 2008a).

Highlights from 30 Years of Research

A Grand Agricultural Design conducive to a Second Green Revolution requires the intellectual power of a leading agricultural thinker. **JOACHIM VON BRAUN** (AGR) is one of the world's leading authorities in agriculture. He is the director general of the International Food Policy Research Institute (IFPRI), an independent think-tank based in Washington, DC. I met Joachim on August 19, 2008, at his office of the IFPRI headquarters in DC. Later, on October 14, 2008, I phoned **Rajul Pandya-Lorch** (AGR). Rajul is the chief of staff of the Director General's Office and head of IFPRI's 2020 Vision Initiative.

In their joint piece "Food Policy for the Poor: Expanding the Research Frontiers," Joachim and Rajul review the "highlights from 30 years of IFPRI research" (Von Braun and Pandya-Lorch 2005). The following commentary refers to pieces included in the compendium edited by Joachim and Rajul:

In *2020 Global Food Outlook: Trends, Alternatives, and Choices*, Mark W. Rosegrant, Michael S. Paisner, Siet Meijer, and Julie Witcover (2001) try to answer the following question: *How would the world be different in 2020 as a result of a concentrated effort to improve the global food situation?* They picture the following two scenarios (Von Braun and Pandya-Lorch 2005):

> *Compare two alternative futures, an optimistic scenario characterized by increased attention to key drivers of food security and a pessimistic scenario characterized by relative neglect of these key drivers. In the first, economic growth accelerates by 25 percent, compared with the baseline projection, and population growth rates decline. The number of people with access to clean water and the number of women with access to secondary education both increase by 10 percent. Depending on the region, agricultural yields increase between 10 and 20 percent faster than anticipated by the baseline scenario. The area of irrigated land increases substantially.*

The authors conclude, "In the first scenario, food becomes much cheaper and rice, for instance, falls in price by 44 percent compared with the 2020 baseline projection," and point out, "Under the optimistic scenario, the number of malnourished children in developing nations would decline from 166 million in 1997 to 94 million in 2020, well below the 132 million of the baseline scenario" (Von Braun and Pandya-Lorch 2005).

C. Ford Runge, Benjamin Senauer, Philip G. Pardey, and Mark W. Rosegrant (2003) look at the major changes to be accomplished going forward to end hunger in our lifetime. For example, we must "increase investments in poor people, pursue new innovations in agricultural science and environmental sustainability, and create new institutional remedies to global dilemmas." According to the authors, "more research should focus on the needs of farmers in tropical areas, especially small peasant farmers," and "water resources will need to be more carefully and efficiently used." (Von Braun and Pandya-Lorch 2005) For Samyuktha Varma of the International Water Management Institute, "most information on the food crisis ignores that improving water management is the only way to produce food in the first place".

In "Accelerating Food Production in sub-Saharan Africa," John W. Mellor, Cristopher L. Delgado, and Malcom J. Blackie (1987) review the weaknesses and strengths of African agriculture (Von Braun and Pandya-Lorch 2005). They note:

> *African agriculture has numerous bright spots other than the perennial export crops such as smallholder cocoa, coffee, oil palm, and tea. Annual crops such as cotton and groundnuts have had periods of rapid growth when they were properly supported by public services and policies. Hybrid maize varieties have had a sweeping impact in wide areas of East Africa, where key institutional and policy complements were available.*

Joachim Von Braun, Tesfaye Teklu, and Patrick Webb (1999) look at the causes and reactions behind starvation episodes in Africa. The authors point out, "The development of rural financial markets and agricultural technology and the dissemination of assets and information remain fundamental for overcoming famine risks." The authors conclude, "A different legal code, including the rethinking of states' rights vs. citizens' rights may be required" (Von Braun and Pandya-Lorch 2005).

The Crisis According to IFPRI

In a Food Policy Report entitled "The World Food Situation," Joachim (2007) summarizes the "new driving forces and required actions" in the recent environment of food shortage and increasing prices. Joachim smartly points out, "Another major force altering the food equation is shifting rural-urban populations and the resulting impact on spending and consumer preferences." As of 2006, 61 percent of the world's population was expected to live in urban areas, although "three quarters of the poor remain in rural areas" (Von Braun 2007).

Stocks and production of cereal decreased in recent years. As Joachim explains, "world cereal production in 2006 was about 2 million ton, 2.4 percent less than in 2005," adding that "between 2004 and 2006, wheat and maize production in the European Union and the United States decreased by 12 to 16 percent." Global stocks for cereal were at their lowest level since the 1980s, and China's stocks have only decreased in recent years. Climate change will negatively impact the world's agricultural production, predicted to shrink 16 percent by 2020. Changes in the corporate food system have also impacted the overall reality of food production, as Joachim details (Von Braun 2007):

> *Transactions along the corporate food chain have increased in the past two years. Between 2004 and 2006, total global food spending grew by 16 percent, from $5.5 trillion to 6.4 trillion. In the same period, the sales of food retailers increased by a disproportionately large amount compared to the sales of food processors and of companies in the food input industry. The sales of the top food processors and traders grew by 13 percent, and the sales of the top 10 companies producing agricultural inputs (agrochemicals, seeds, and traits) increased by 8 percent.*

Following up on Joachim's observations about the corporate food chain, the *Financial Times* published an article on April 14, 2008, in which it reported, "Cargill, one of the world's largest privately held companies, said profits increased 86 percent from the same period last year, from $553 million to $1.03 billion in the third quarter ending on February 29" (Weitzman 2008). Joachim's intuitive piece concludes: (1) "Developed countries should facilitate flexible responses to drastic price changes by eliminating trade barriers and programs that set aside agriculture resources"; and (2) "The acute risks facing the poor require expanded social-protection measures" (Von Braun 2007).

Recent views on the food crisis contrast starkly from the situation in the late 1990s. In October 1999, IFPRI released a piece entitled "World Food Prospects: Critical Issues for the Early Twenty-First Century," co-authored by Per Pinstrup-Andersen, Rajul Pandya-Lorch, and Mark W. Rosegrant (Pinstrup-Andersen, Pandya-Lorch, et al., 1999). The reality of the food markets was radically different from that of 2008.

Prices for basic food commodities increased significantly in 1995 and dropped to very low levels. Food prices experienced severe fluctuations in subsequent years. According to IFPRI, a number of factors "coincided in 1995 to raise prices: adverse weather conditions in Canada and the United States, drought and civil conflict in sub-Saharan Africa, stagnating grain yields in Asia, set-aside programs and reduced subsidies in the European Union, and decreased food production in the former

Soviet Union and China." Prices subsequently fell because "the production increases exceeded demand at existing prices." With low prices the stock of grain in the world continued to increase and reached 18 percent of annual consumption by 1999 (Pinstrup-Andersen, Pandya-Lorch, et al., 1999). Some of the reasons why prices experienced severe volatility in 1995 and thereafter are also present today. But contrary to 1995, the emergence of biofuel and the deregulation of financial markets have altered the variables of the equation. The equation is now much more complex.

Many countries in Western Africa are net importers of food. The Food and Agriculture Organization (FAO) points out that "in the western part of the subregion including Cape Verde, Guinea-Bissau, Mauritania and Senegal, food prices are driven mainly by international market trends due to the high dependence of these countries on wheat and rice imports from the international market." Therefore, these countries are most vulnerable to price fluctuations. FAO concludes that "Senegal's domestic production, for instance, covers only about half of the country's cereal utilization requirements, so its rice and wheat imports amount to an average of about 900,000 tonnes per annum, from the international market" (FAO 2008).

I dreamt of a world of Cornucopia. I dreamt of a world of food abundance in which the provision of food is prioritized over its trading by profit-maximizing corporations, over its speculation by money managers. I dreamt of a world in which Africa becomes the breadbasket of the world. I dreamt of the World of 2050, the World of Decemland.

The Rice Crisis

The implementation of a Second Green Revolution needs to be directed by a chief scientist. **Robert Zeigler** (AGR) is the Director General of the International Rice Research Institute (IRRI) based in the Philippines. IRRI is the leading research center for rice in the world. I talked to Robert on May 7, 2008. Speaking with Robert helped me better understand the phenomena driving up food prices worldwide.

In the piece "The rice crisis: What needs to be done?" IRRI elaborates on some of the factors behind the increase in food prices, and particularly those behind the increase in the price of rice, experienced in the three-year period ending in 2008. Rice is the main food staple for almost two-thirds of the world's poor, or around 700 million who live in countries that rely on their domestic rice production to feed their population. The Green Revolution that started in the 1960s helped increase rice production and decrease prices, a trend that abruptly ended in 2001. Between December 2007 and April 2008, the world price of Thai rice (a popular export grade according to IRRI) almost tripled from $362 per ton to $1,000 per ton (IRRI 2008).

The International Institute for Geo-Information Science and Earth Observation (ITC) in the Netherlands is one of the world's leading academic institutions in the study of agriculture. **Eric Smaling** (AGR) is a professor at ITC whom I met at Dupont Circle in Washington, DC, on September 25, 2008. Eric sent me a short message at 3:31 A.M. the day before we met saying: "Dear Jaime: I am in Washington DC right now. I know it is short notice, but if you have time we could meet somewhere tomorrow." In addition Eric is a senator for Holland. I asked Eric how he had heard from me. When Eric mentioned he was a Dutch senator, I figured out he should have received one of the messages I regularly sent to 13,627 senators and members of Parliament from 80 different countries. By sampling the planet's political elite, I find talented visionaries that are willing to get on the journey of optimism that will lead us to the society of 2050. I am now confident Eric will help write the History of Tomorrow.

Eric's inaugural address as chair of sustainable agriculture at ITC took place on November 2, 2005. Eric presented an address entitled "Harvest the World" (Smaling 2005). In his address Eric remarked that "several studies have shown that the world as a whole is able to supply enough food for over 10 billion people," adding that "a harvest for the world is technically possible" (Smaling 2005). Eric also points out that Millennium Development Goal 1 will not be fulfilled in Africa "with projections for 2030 showing more hungry people than in the early 1990s" (Smaling 2005). Eric raises the question of whether or not it would make sense for Africa "to focus on its own and growing regional markets, and be allowed to protect itself to a certain extent from more or less artificially cheap imports" (Smaling 2005).

What would policy-makers do to protect their domestic consumers? Rice exporters should restrict exports to shift a majority of the local production to local consumption, minimizing the risk of malnutrition among their fellow citizens. The result of this increasing protectionism was a shrinking supply of rice in the international markets that is behind the skyrocketing trend of prices. According to Eric, countries should be allowed and even stimulated to aim at food sovereignty, without necessarily becoming fully self-sufficient. Eric adds, "there is basically no point in transporting huge amounts of food stuffs over the globe as long as it can just as well be obtained from within the country and region."

Many factors have contributed to the rice crisis, including an increasing demand that has surpassed production (IRRI 2008). The consequence is that rice stocks "are being rapidly depleted, with current stocks at their lowest since 1988" (IRRI 2008). Figure 6.1 shows how the stock of global grains has declined in recent years.

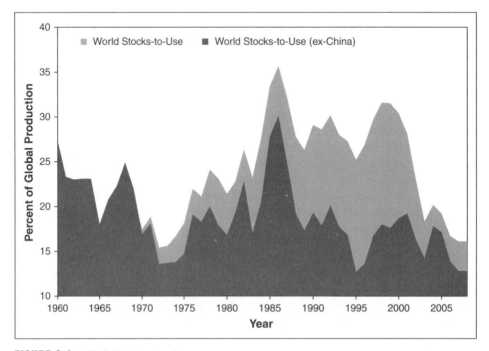

FIGURE 6.1 Global Grain Stocks
Source: World Bank (2009).

One of the reasons why demand has surpassed production is the decreasing trend of yield growth. In densely populated Asia the number of hectares available for rice production is limited. In order to increase rice production it is most often feasible to increase the yield (agricultural output per hectare), as opposed to increasing the number of hectares available. Productivity growth would measure the increase in rice production per hectare over a predetermined time horizon of, for instance, one year. The Green Revolution of the 1960s increased productivity growth significantly.

Are we in need of a Second Green Revolution? For Eric, we certainly are in need of a Second Green Revolution if we do not wish to strip the globe of all its natural vegetation. Eric notes that "higher production can only be achieved by better technologies and management." What would be required for a Second Green Revolution to take off? Eric suggests major investments in agrotechnology development for a broad global research group, including universities and to-be-developed centers of excellence in the tropics, with an emphasis in sub-Saharan Africa.

Demand for rice is increasing in Africa but also in Asia. According to IRRI, "it is projected that in 2015 Asia will need to produce 38 million more tons of rough (unmilled) rice than it produced in 2005" (IRRI 2008). Land competition is fierce in densely populated areas. Land devoted to rice production has to compete with real estate developments, crops for animal feeding, or biofuel. The picture is not pretty. IRRI points out that "the best strategy for keeping the price of rice low is to ensure that production increases faster than demand" and concludes (IRRI 2008):

> *Rice production can be increased by expanding the area planted to rice, by increasing the yield per unit area, or by a combination of both. The opportunity for further increase the rice area in Asia is now quite limited. The total rice area in Asia is unlikely to increase much beyond the current estimate of 136 million hectares. Although some increase in cropping intensity is still possible, rice land is being lost to industrialization, urbanization, or conversion to other crops.*

Agriculture comes first among the priorities we face as a global society. The importance of agricultural research in increasing output per hectare motivated my trip to IRRI[3] in the Philippines from February 21 to 27, 2009. At IRRI, I interacted with some of the world's most knowledgeable rice scientists. Some of the conclusions are included hereafter.

Hunger and Health

HENK-JAN BRINKMAN (AGR) is the senior advisor for economic policy at the World Food Programme. I met Henk-Jan on July 22, 2008, at the Headquarters of the World Food Programme[4] (WFP) in Rome (Italy). At the WFP premises I also met with Alan Jury, WFP's director of external relations. Henk-Jan is now based in New York and Jury is based in Washington, DC. Neither could wait to return to Obama's United States any longer. I met Henk-Jan a second time in New York City on September 8, 2008. Henk-Jan's New York office rocks and is much nicer than the one he had in Rome. His window overlooks Manhattan's midtown, with the Chrysler and the Empire State Buildings included in the view.

The World Food Programme released a piece in 2007 under the name "World Hunger Series 2007: Hunger and Health." In it, the Rome-based institution explains the relationship between hunger and health among the extreme poor as follows (WFP 2007):

1. Hunger and poor health are strongly related to political and economic choices, which in turn reflect the priorities attached to budget allocations, quality of social services, and community values.
2. Undernutrition leads to a state of poor health that puts the individual at risk of infectious and chronic disease.
3. It is imperative that national frameworks and programs are designed to consider the relationship between hunger and poor health.
4. Well-fed and healthy populations contribute to economic growth more effectively.
5. There is increasing evidence that nutrition and food support accompanying treatment for tuberculosis, human immunodeficiency virus (HIV), and other infectious diseases increases adherence and improves outcomes, particularly for the poor.

Hunger and health are intrinsically related. Hunger feeds malnutrition, which causes death. D. John Shaw points out that "hunger and malnutrition kill more people every year than AIDS, malaria and tuberculosis combined, and more people die from hunger than in wars" (Shaw 2009).

WHAT DRIVES AGRICULTURAL PRICES?

Two major variables have joined the complex equation of agricultural prices in recent times. The incidence of biofuels and of agricultural subsidies has impacted the supply and demand of agricultural produce, altering the price trends of previous years.

Biofuels

According to the *Financial Times*, "the World Bank, the Food and Agriculture Organization and the International Monetary Fund were unanimous in concluding that the rising appetite for biofuel was part of the reason for the increase in food prices" (Bryant and Blas 2008a). Only in the space of a few years, as much as one-fifth of the U.S. harvested grain has been diverted to produce ethanol, which is a direct consequence of subsidies (Shaw 2009).

Joachim Von Braun looks at the changes in world prices for five food staples by 2020 under two scenarios. Scenario 1 involves a mild expansion in biofuel production, whereas Scenario 2 involves a drastic increase in biofuel expansion. The forecast is disconcerting. The price increases compared with baseline levels are as follows: Cassava (Scenario 1: 11.2 percent of price increase; Scenario 2: 26.7 percent of price increase), Maize (26.3 percent, 71.8 percent), Oilseeds (18.1 percent, 44.4 percent), Sugar (11.5 percent, 26.6 percent), and Wheat (8.3 percent, 20.0 percent). Joachim concludes, "Biofuel production has contributed to the changing world food equation and currently adversely affects the poor through price-level and price-volatility effects" (Von Braun 2007).

Biofuel became popular as an alternative to high oil prices in 2007 and 2008. The barrel of oil crossed the $140 line in June 2008. On the verge of worldwide recession, the barrel of oil was trading under $50 at the end of 2008. Above certain thresholds, alternative energy sources start to make sense. Biofuel is one more energy source in the myriad of energy alternatives that include nuclear, solar, wind, and hydropower.

For decades, Brazil has been a pioneer in the use of biofuel. Brazil obtains biofuel from sugar cane, one of the major crops in the giant emerging economy from Latin America. Petrobras is one of the world's largest energy companies and it is state-owned. In 2008, Petrobras announced its intent to become Brazil's largest producer of biofuel. According to the *International Herald Tribune*, "the new subsidiary will coordinate biofuel investments that currently are run by various units of the company" (IHT 2008). Lula da Silva, Brazil's president, is a strong advocate of poverty eradication. He is also a strong supporter of biofuel. After all, much of Brazil's tax revenue originates from Petrobras' activity that includes the exploitation of biofuel. Biofuel dollars help Brazil mitigate poverty.

Countries are sovereign over their territory. Brazil can decide to shift agricultural production to biofuel or completely avoid it. But in an increasingly interconnected and globalized world, arable land devoted to food crops should be given priority over biofuel, particularly in developing countries that suffer from food shortages and are net food importers. Nation-states dictate national priorities. Nobody dictates global priorities.

The world's second largest producer of biofuel is the United States (Reuters 2005). In June 2008, *The Guardian* published an article entitled "U.S. Biofuel Subsidies Under Attack at Food Summit." The article describes Jacques Diouf's opening statement at a UN food summit in Rome. Diouf is director general of the Food and Agriculture Organization (FAO). Diouf said regarding U.S. subsidies to biofuel that "nobody understands why $11–12 billion of subsidies in 2006 and protective tariff policies should be used to divert 100 million tonnes of cereals from human consumption, mostly to satisfy a thirst for fuel for vehicles" (Borger 2008). Diouf was fundamentally right. It is morally wrong to divert agricultural consumption to satisfy the energy demand of the industrialized nations. It is contemporaneous nonsense to subsidize and perpetuate the absurdity.

The article also points out, "the International Monetary Fund has estimated that 20 to 30 percent of the food price increases in the past two years are accounted for by biofuels, and that last year they accounted for about half the increase in demand for principle food crops" (Berger 2008). Our generation's *war* is different than wars in generations past. This is a war on hunger, on poverty, and on disease. This is war on the Axis of Feeble. This is war on the preservation of our environment, and of our planet. It is a war that must be won with Weapons of Mass Persuasion, with rhetoric and the use of the mass media.

In May 2007, my parents visited me while I was completing a master's degree in local economic development at the London School of Economics. Mr. Pozuelo and Madame Monfort[5] are used to long-lasting discussions on poverty and sustainability. I frequently ask them if they have turned sustainable. "What does it mean?" they once asked.

Turning sustainable involves being fully aware of the collateral damage of our actions and reacting in order to minimize it. Did you turn sustainable today? The consumer market must incorporate a third dimension to the traditional quality vs. price dilemma. We need to incorporate sustainability. Is the company that manufactures this product or service sustainable?

I presented Mr. Pozuelo and Madame Monfort the following analogy while walking around the beautiful gardens of Hyde Park and Green Park in central London. Imagine a kidnapper who earns a living and maintains a family through an activity he deems appropriate within the bounds established by his own code of morality. Perhaps he believes kidnapping is okay but murdering is not okay. What would he do if he did not kidnap? After all at the end of the day, when he gets home and kisses his children good night, he realizes he has a family to feed, which encourages him to wake up the next day and be ready to continue with his outrageous kidnapping activity. The same principle applies to drug dealing, human trafficking, or prostitution.

There is a similar trend in industrialized nations. We think that agricultural subsidies, banking secrecy, or tax havens are okay within the bounds established by our own code of morality. Have we double-checked the lack of transparency of our arms manufacturers and the collateral damage they cause in many developing countries? Have we reviewed the lending policies of our financial institutions and the environmental damage some of the projects to which they lend money cause?

Agricultural Subsidies

In 2007 the OECD published a report entitled "Agricultural Policies in OECD Countries". The report remarks, "greater progress has been made in changing the way in which support is provided to producers" (OECD 2007). For developing countries, support continues to be support, independent from the way in which it is provided to producers. At the end of the day, it does not matter as much with what weapon you kill if the final outcome is death. The tremendous backwardness of today's agricultural policies, particularly in the European Union, raises a big question mark about our willingness, as Westerners, to continue supporting the political elites that sustain the European construction from Brussels and Strasbourg.

The Doha Round collapsed because of Europeans. We have to be brutally honest. This is the outcome of years of imposition of our interest in the trade negotiation rounds, nothing else. Developing countries reached the best decision when they turned their backs to Doha (the Doha Round is described in Chapter 7). They were free riders. They played the prisoner's dilemma. Yes, the same game Europeans have been playing for a long time now. For the OECD, the good news is that "declines in producer support were seen in most countries in 2006" (OECD 2007). Thanks for delaying the final outcome of death.

The European Union (EU) spends 40 percent of its yearly budget, which amounts to 1 percent of its GDP, in its Common Agriculture Policy (CAP). France is CAP's largest recipient, followed by Spain and Germany. Subsidies keep 3.3 percent of the French in their beloved *campagne*, whereas the more efficient British agriculture only employs 1.2 of the population in farming (Clark 2007). The strongest defender of subsidies in Europe is Nicolas Sarkozy. The dynamic and hyperactive French président de la République has not been honest to himself or his constituents. Generally two reasons are given to justify the maintenance of subsidies. The first is food security. The second is the preservation of rural Europe. We must be kidding.

Are we aware of the collateral damage of our decision making, of our rhetoric? Welcome to the unequal world of the Bretton Woods Elites. This is the downside of our inheritance. It is our obligation to start incorporating to the decision-making process the collateral damage of our decisions.

I am all for food security and rural preservation, if it does not obstruct our ability, as a global community, to eradicate once and for all extreme poverty and hunger. It is a world of priorities, and I know very well what comes first. The dignity of the human being and respect for the environment come first. I discover our blame and from the bottom of the hole I dig, I will present a plan of action that incorporates and embraces the developing world, once and for all.

I dreamt of a World of no hunger. I dreamt of a World of no disease. I see changing times. It is time to move ahead, to think forward. I discover a New Paradigm. I discover the World of 2050, the World of Decemland, the land of 10 percent.

A Multilayered Priority World   At a time when the world faces challenges that will determine the fate of Humankind, countries have set different layers of priority that are incompatible with each other. Unfortunately, nation-states have long played the game of non-cooperation. France's Sarkozy defends agricultural subsidies because of the preservation of rural France. In reality banning agricultural subsidies would carry a huge political cost in France, and Sarkozy would risk losing an election. Brazil's Da Silva defends biofuels because they are a clean alternative to oil. But the reality is that he is defending the biofuel industry in Brazil because of the tax dollars the state-owned Petrobras contributes to the country's budget.

THE EFFECT OF CLIMATE CHANGE ON FOOD CONSUMPTION

This section explains how an increasing incidence of rising temperatures has implications in food consumption that should be embraced by the developed and the emerging countries.

Food Safety

The Food and Agriculture Organization (FAO) released a report entitled "Climate Change: Implications for Food Safety" (Clark, Jaykus, et al., 2008), in which a pool of experts from the Rome-based institution reviews the connection between climate change and food safety. The authors analyze the likely impact of climate change on the agricultural sector.

According to the report, climate change "affects the microbial population of the macro-environment and the population of other vectors," all of which affect plant health and productivity. Climate change also has implications on animal production and fisheries. In particular the report notes that climate change could affect the *zoonoses* (diseases naturally transmitted between vertebrate animals and humans), "increasing the transmission cycle of many vectors and the range and prevalence of vectors and animal reservoirs." Regarding fisheries the report points out, "global fisheries should remain the same; however, the spatial distribution of fish stocks may change due to the migration of fish from one region to another in search of suitable conditions" (Clark, Jaykus, et al., 2008).

Meat Consumption

Climate change is contributing to increasing temperatures. According to IRRI, "some evidence suggests that rising temperatures may have already contributed to lower rice yields in recent years" (IRRI 2008).

Rajendra Pachauri is the chairman of the Intergovernmental Panel on Climate Change (IPCC). In 2006, the IPCC and Al Gore shared the Nobel Peace Prize. Pachauri also heads TERI, the TATA Environmental Research Institute based in Delhi, India. I phoned Pachauri on October 28, 2008. Our conversation focused on an article published in the English newspaper *The Observer*, in which Pachauri called for a reduction in meat consumption (Jowit 2008).

What does meat consumption have to do with food shortage and climate change? According to FAO, "meat production accounts for nearly a fifth of global greenhouse gas emissions" (Jowit 2008). Surprisingly, cows are methane-emitting animals. Methane is "23 times more effective as a global warming agent than carbon dioxide." Pachauri acknowledges IPCC's own discovery as follows (Jowit 2008):

In terms of immediacy of action and the feasibility of bringing about reductions in a short period of time, it clearly is the most attractive opportunity. Give up meat for one day a week initially and decrease it from there.

A second reason to diminish meat consumption is related to land competition. It takes about seven kilograms of cereals to produce one kilogram of beef. It takes 1,000 liters of water to grow one kilogram of wheat, but 15,000 liters of water to produce one kilogram of meat (*Economist*, 2009c). These ratios are lower for pork and poultry. Cereal production to feed cattle is undermining the world's ability to feed the hungry. The good news is that projected mean consumption annual growth is expected to drop (World Bank 2007b). It is perhaps a good idea to accelerate this trend.

The World Wildlife Fund (WWF) is one of the leading nonprofit organizations fighting climate change globally. Hans Verolme, director of WWF's Global Climate Change Programme, comments, "The planet is running a fever and people are working with WWF to cool it—global warming is costing us dearly already but by acting now we can avoid future calamities" (ENS 2007). Owen Cylke is WWF's director for African Development Institutions and is based in Washington, DC. I met the experienced American on December 16, 2008. Cylke's first impression was to be speaking with a lunatic: *A New International Territory? New Institutions? A New Consensus?* I reckon his impression radically changed in the 90 minutes we spent together.

I encourage and challenge the elites of our time to read the book and listen to the ideas put forth. There may be a before and an after in their systematic belief that the orthodox savoir-faire is the de facto approach to solving today's challenges. Cylke's phenomenal experience with the United States Agency for International Development (USAID) in India and Africa was not enough to tear down an infinite desire to move ahead with creativity, optimism, and persuasion. Everything is possible. The only requirement is a good explanation.

In conclusion, an excess of consumption can or cannot be justified depending on the framework and the reach. I would agree with the statement that consumption is a matter of income if society was fair globally, with Global Redistribution schemes that guarantee a minimum welfare state, with global institutions that guarantee the rule of law, and without the major powers interfering with their foreign policy agendas in the work of the international organizations. These international organizations grant a representative majority to countries that no longer represent a majority of the world's population.

We need international regulation that protects the extreme poor and guarantees the provision of a minimum amount of food, so that the poor avoid malnutrition and hunger. If there is no excess production at this point, it is wrong to feed a cow before we feed a person. Global priorities have to be defined and implemented: people first, then cows, then cars.

Going vegetarian is a short-term solution to the challenges of food scarcity and climate change. If meat consumption is reduced, less methane will be released into the atmosphere. If meat consumption is reduced, less cereal will have to be produced to feed cattle, more cereal will be available for human consumption, and more arable land will become available to grow other food staples.

A SECOND GREEN REVOLUTION

The first Green Revolution took off in South Asia when the development community realized the importance of increasing agricultural production in the mid 1960s, "in the aftermath of two consecutive droughts in the populous countries of South Asia" (Shaw 2009). According to IRRI, "a Second Green Revolution is needed now as much as the first Green Revolution was needed to avoid famine and mass starvation" (IRRI 2008). In order to succeed, IRRI suggests, "increased research investment together with policy reforms that make rice markets more efficient will help bring rice prices down to a level affordable to the poor" (IRRI 2008). What actions could lead to a Second Green Revolution?

Increase Yields

In their joint piece "Down to Earth: Agriculture and Poverty Reduction in Africa," Luc Christiaensen and Lionel Demery look at the growth potential of agriculture. The World Bank economists point out that "a review of the overall sectoral growth rates since 1960 indicated that agricultural GDP growth has on average lagged behind nonagricultural GDP growth" (Christiaensen and Demery 2007).

The authors focus on "enhancing agricultural productivity" (Christiaensen and Demery 2007). They claim that substantial improvement in productivity is feasible in Africa if cereal yields per hectare are compared. For instance, yields per hectare contrast starkly between countries like Madagascar (2,380 kilograms per hectare) and the average in East Asia and the Pacific (4,518 kilograms per hectare in 2005). They mention the work of Randrianarisoa and Minten, who "present supporting evidence of the potential efficacy" of revised agronomic practices in Madagascar (Christiaensen and Demery 2007). Only 6 percent of Madagascar's farmers use fertilizer. Phenomenal improvement is within the farmer's reach if more fertilizer is used.

In their third policy message, the authors state that "better water management and strengthened ex-post coping strategies will be critical in raising agricultural

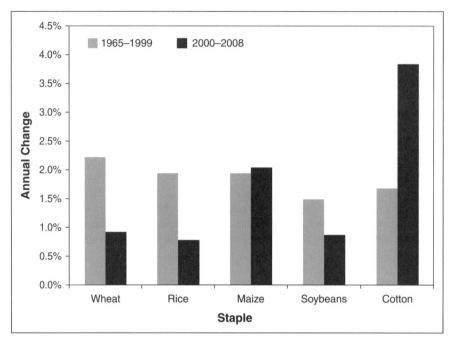

FIGURE 6.2   Annual Percentage Change in Yields
Source: World Bank (2009).

productivity." Their fourth policy message proposes an increased "adoption and use of modern inputs," which include credit access and connectivity. Their fifth policy recommendation suggests that "payoffs to improved rural road infrastructure are substantial and so are the costs, underscoring the need for careful and comprehensive cost-benefit analyses" (Christiaensen and Demery 2007).

Figure 6.2 shows that yields have decreased in the period 2000 to 2008, compared with the previous period 1965 to 1999, particularly for wheat and rice. Figure 6.3 shows that in the period 1960 to 2007, increases in agricultural production were more related to yield growth rather than area growth.

Genetically Modified Crops

In my efforts to reach out to experts in the field, I contacted Monsanto's Chief Executive Officer Hugh Grant and Bread's David Beckman. My repeated attempts were unsuccessful. However, over the course of the preparation of the book I had the opportunity to meet with three other celebrities: James Bond, Enrique Iglesias, and Michael Jackson. James Bond is chief operating officer of the World Bank's Multilateral Investment Guarantee Agency and was introduced earlier in this chapter. Enrique Iglesias is the former president of the Inter American Development Bank. Enrique is introduced in Chapter 22.

Michael Jackson is IRRI's director for program planning and communications. I met Jackson on February 26, 2009, in Los Baños (The Philippines). From 1991 to 2001, Jackson was director of IRRI's Gene Bank, the world's largest repository

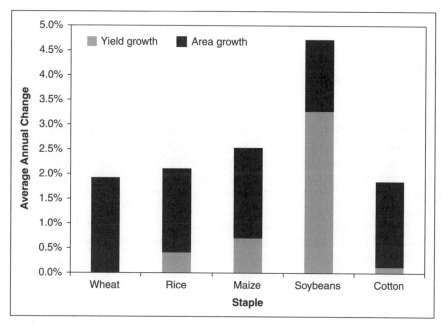

FIGURE 6.3 Average Annual Percentage Change in Area and Yields, 1960–2007
Source: World Bank (2009).

of rice samples that are publicly available, contrary to genetically modified crops. Jackson points out, "We are constantly collecting rice samples. The idea is to conserve whatever is out there" (Gluckman 1992).

Per Pinstrup-Andersen and Ebbe Schioler (2001) review some of the advantages of Genetically Modified (GM) crops (Von Braun and Pandya-Lorch 2005). The authors comment, "We find it extremely worrying that a minority that has more than enough to eat should make life so difficult for those who do not," adding that "developing countries, with the possible exception of China, will have no chance to benefit from GM food research unless they can draw on knowledge and contacts in the wealthy part of the world" (Von Braun and Pandya-Lorch 2005).

Kym Anderson, Lee Ann Jackson, and Chantal Pohl Nielsen look at the implications of the use of GM rice for welfare and poverty alleviation (Anderson, Jackson, et al., 2005). What is the impact of GM rice on producers and poor households? The authors' geographic focus is Asia. A GM variety of rice is golden rice. Golden rice "has the potential to improve health in regions where rice is or could be a dietary staple for poor people." In addition, golden rice is "the most important imminent GM crop" (Anderson, Jackson, et al., 2005).

To what extent can golden rice help boost rice productivity in Asia? Are there any tradeoffs? The authors focus on the health impact of using golden rice over a standard non-GM variety of rice. They comment, "A recent study found that introducing golden rice in the Philippines could decrease the number of disability-adjusted life years due to Vitamin A Deficiency by between 6 and 47 percent, or between 23,000 and 137,000." Overall, the authors conclude, "The first-generation, farm-productivity enhancing GM varieties alone will boost welfare in the adopting countries, and more so if adoption extends beyond rice to maize and oilseeds" (Anderson, Jackson, et al., 2005).

GM technology is typically owned by private corporations. As a result, these corporations that are generally for profit commercialize the GM varieties for the purpose of maximizing economic profit and reward their shareholders. There is nothing wrong with maximizing profit in developed markets and rewarding share-holders accordingly. There is, however, a great deal of wrongdoing when corpora-tions enter extreme-poor markets aiming at making a profit. The trade-off for the extreme poor is risky. GM varieties may be advantageous, but carry patent-filing and copyright material. Compare GM's research with that of IRRI. IRRI's research is internationally and publicly available. It is a Global Public Good. This is the kind of research we need going forward. Kofi Annan is in agreement, as he ruled out the use of GM crops in AGRA's programs (Mahajan 2008). AGRA is the Alliance for Green Revolution in Africa, and Kofi Annan will lead, along with IFPRI's Joachim Von Braun and IRRI's Robert Zeigler, the Second Green Revolution in sub-Saharan Africa. The Annan Plan is presented in Chapter 17.

Investment in Research and Development

Africa continues to be well below its potential in agriculture. In 2008, the World Bank announced it would double its agricultural loans to sub-Saharan Africa from $450 million to $800 million in the next year (Bellemare 2008). Marc F. Bellemare points out that "what Subsaharan Africa needs most are new roads, better trained and better remunerated police forces, improved means of transportation, and access to better food storage technologies" (Bellemare 2008). Productivity growth has been slow in sub-Saharan Africa since the time of independence. Experts think that some of the drivers of the slow productivity growth are the use of inappropriate technology and the mismanagement of agricultural systems (Ogodo 2008). With millions in sub-Saharan Africa going hungry every month, it is important to prioritize policies that allow rural farmers throughout the continent to increase the output through increases in productivity growth. Former UN secretary general Kofi Annan is leading the Alliance for an African Green Revolution (AGRA) with the support of a $150 million grant from the Rockefeller Foundation. Annan commented at the inauguration of the Nairobi-based AGRA that he hoped Africa could double its agricultural productivity in 10 to 20 years (Kanina 2007). Mafa Chipeta, sub-regional coordinator for the United Nations Food and Agricultural Organization (FAO) in East Africa thinks output could be boosted by as much as three or four times (Reuters 2008a). According to the U.K. Overseas Development Institute, 17 of the 30 fastest-growing agricultural economies are in sub-Saharan Africa (Perkins 2008).

In its 2007 Annual Report, the Rockefeller Foundation devotes an entire section to the Green Revolution in Africa. AGRA's purpose is to support 30 organizations in eight different countries in Africa and train African agricultural scientists at African Universities (Rockefeller Foundation 2007). The sponsored scientists are expected to continue working in Africa. For Simeon Ehui of the World Bank and Marinos E. Tsigas of the United States International Trade Commission, "Subsaharan Africa research and development in crops would generate higher welfare benefits than sharing research and development between crops and livestock" (Ehui and Tsigas 2006). The fact of the matter is that African governments only spend 4 percent of their national budgets in agriculture, with pre-colonial land rights only making investment tougher (Dowden 2008). Spending on agriculture averaged 7 percent of total government spending between 1975 and 1990 (Khan and Khan 1995).

In "The 10 Percent that Could Change Africa," Abigail Somma of IFPRI reports the pledge that African leaders made in 2003 to invest 10 percent of their national budgets in agriculture by 2010 (Somma 2008). The pledge was made in Maputo (Mozambique) and is known as the *Maputo Declaration*. What progress has been made since the *Maputo Declaration* of 2003? In 2008 out of Africa's 53 nations, only six reached the ten percent target: Burkina Faso, Cape Verde, Chad, Ethiopia, Mali, Malawi, and Niger. Thirteen spent between 5 and 10 percent of their government budget in agriculture, fifteen invested less than 5 percent, and eighteen countries did not report any data. Why was the target set at 10 percent? The 10 percent target was designed to fulfill the first Millennium Development Goal of cutting, by half, poverty and hunger by the deadline of 2015.

Only 4 percent of current development aid targets agriculture and USAID has cut its agricultural budget by 75 percent in the last twenty years (Hanson 2008). There are mixed signals. Japan announced in 2008 that it would provide enough agricultural assistance to African countries with the goal of doubling rice production in ten years (Asia-Pacific News 2008).

Leaders of the world's richest nations gathered in L'Aquila (Italy) during the G8 summit of July 2009. They decided to pledge $15 billion to boost food supply (Reuters 2009). According to *The Times*, L'Aquila Food Security Initiative would be "one of the biggest aid shifts in decades and could be controversial in America, whose farmers are the largest exporters of some crops" (Webster 2009).

Nienke M. Beintema and Gert-Jan Stads of the Agricultural Science & Technology Indicators look at worldwide investment in agriculture (Beintema and Stads 2008). They remark that global spending in research and development in agriculture has been decreasing. They also note that developed countries still spend more on public research in agriculture than do developing countries (Beintema and Stads 2008). Table 6.1 compares agricultural spending in different geographic areas between 1981 and 2000.

Sushil Pandey and Humnath Bhandari of IRRI and Mark W. Rosegrant and Timothy Sulser of IFPRI look at the impact of investing in agriculture. The four agricultural economists devise three different scenarios they compare to the baseline scenario. The three scenarios are described as follows (Pandey, Bhandari, et al., 2009):

1. Low scenario: presents declining rates of investment in agricultural research and development.
2. High scenario: has governments and other agencies prioritizing agricultural investments to improve productivity, particularly in the developing world.
3. Very high scenario: augments the improved high situation with increased investment in yield improvements, intensification of existing agricultural systems, increased investment in irrigation infrastructure, as well as higher investment in other poverty and malnutrition-reducing strategies.

The optimistic scenarios (high and very high) are promising. By 2050, rice prices would decline relative to the starting year 2000 (Pandey, Bhandari, et al., 2009), adjusted for inflation.

TABLE 6.1   Agricultural Research Expenditures, 1981 and 2000

Country Category	Public Agricultural R&D Spending		Regional Share of Global Total	
	1981	2000	1981	2000
	(Million 2005 PPP U.S. Dollars)		Percent	
Country Grouping by Income Class				
Low income (46)	1,410	2,564	9	11
Middle income (62)	4,639	7,555	29	32
High income (32)	9,774	13,313	62	57
Total (140)	*15,823*	*23,432*	*100*	*100*
Low- and Middle-Income Countries by Region				
sub-Saharan Africa (45)	1,084	1,239	7	5
China	713	1,891	5	8
India	400	1,301	3	6
Asia-Pacific (26)	1,971	4,758	12	20
Brazil	1,005	1,209	6	5
Latin America and the Caribbean (25)	2,274	2,710	14	12
West Asia and North Africa (12)	720	1,412	5	6
Subtotal (108)	*6,049*	*10,119*	*38*	*43*

Source: Beintema et al. (2008).

Green Revolution in Africa

In 1995 the United Nations released its *World Economic and Social Survey* with a special article devoted to the Green Revolution in Africa. The article, "It is time for a Green Revolution in Africa," noted that food production had been declining in Africa since the early 1970s contrary to the evolution in Asia and Latin America (United Nations 1995). The need for further research was already clear at the time. The report indicates, "in the light of Africa's food situation, research should focus on the development of drought-resistant, low-risk and low-cost seed varieties for rain-fed agriculture that do not need many external inputs." The report remarks, "The Green Revolution of the 1960s and 1970s was almost completely a product of international public research, in particular of the International Rice Research Institute and the Centro Internacional de Mejoramiento de Maíz y Trigo" (United Nations 1995). It is a fair assessment that more funding in international agricultural public research is needed to trigger a Second Green Revolution.

Out of the 20 countries in the world where a majority of the population suffers from hunger, 17 are in sub-Saharan Africa. Figure 6.4 shows the twenty countries that score highest in IFPRI's Global Hunger Index. Only three of the countries (Tajikistan, Yemen and Bangladesh) in the top twenty are not in sub-Saharan Africa.

Kei Kajisa is an agricultural economist in IRRI's Social Sciences Division. I met Kajisa on February 24, 2008, at IRRI in Los Baños (the Philippines). Kajisa is active researching the potential of Mozambique and Tanzania to become major rice producers. A Second Green Revolution could be triggered in these two countries

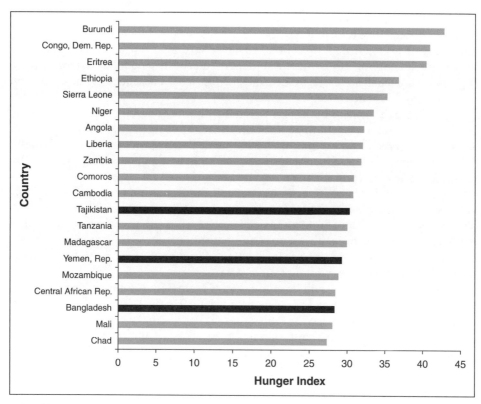

FIGURE 6.4 Global Hunger Index, 2003
Source: IFPRI (2006).

and later on in Madagascar if appropriate investments are undertaken in research, fertilizer, irrigation systems, and infrastructure. IRRI recently opened its African branch in Mozambique.

Joseph Rickman (AGR) is the regional coordinator for East and Southern Africa at the International Rice Research Institute. I met Joseph on July 10, 2009, at the Pestana Rovuma Hotel in Maputo (Mozambique). For Joseph, Mozambique and Tanzania have the right conditions to trigger a Second Green Revolution: some of the best soil that in addition is water-abundant and unlimited land of very high quality.

Maria Zimmermann (AGR) is the FAO representative for Mozambique and Swaziland. FAO is the Food and Agriculture Organization, a UN Agency. I met Maria at the FAO Representative Office in Maputo (Mozambique) on July 8, 2009. Maria is well aware of the potential of a Second Green Revolution on sub-Saharan African soil and more in particular in Mozambique. Yearly output increases in Mozambique are reaching 10 percent, but for Maria, without appropriate investments in infrastructure (roads and storage facilities) and education, the surplus is either spoiled in bad storage facilities or does not reach potential buyers because of a lack of infrastructure. Appropriate investments in infrastructure, and education are a precondition if a Second Green Revolution is to take off.

Zakaria L. Kanyeka is the regional plant breeder for East and Southern Africa at the International Rice Research Institute. I met Kanyeka on July 15, 2009, at the West Africa Rice Development Association in Dar es Salaam[6] (Tanzania). For Kanyeka, major investments in infrastructure and particularly in irrigation systems would trigger phenomenal increases in rice production and, consequently, a significant return on the initial investment.

What were the benefits of the first Green Revolution? For Kajisa, the Asian Green Revolution "has contributed to poverty alleviation by reducing the real rice price on the world market by more than half without depleting producers' profit." Additional benefits include a reduction in childhood malnutrition and an improvement in children's education (Kajisa 2008).

Figure 6.5 and Figure 6.6 show the per capita consumption of rice by geographic area and the total consumption of rice, for the years 2005 and 2015. Major increases in rice consumption by Southeast Asia, South Asia, and sub-Saharan Africa are expected. In the case of Southeast Asia and South Asia, there is actually a decrease in per capita consumption. However, population growth is expected to be the main driver of increases in rice consumption in Asia.

World rice production will have to increase from 352,466 thousands of metric tons in 2005 to 388,508 thousands of metric tons in 2015. In Asia, population growth is likely to outpace rice production. Sub-Saharan Africa remains underdeveloped and could boost its productivity if appropriate investments are undertaken. Contrary to

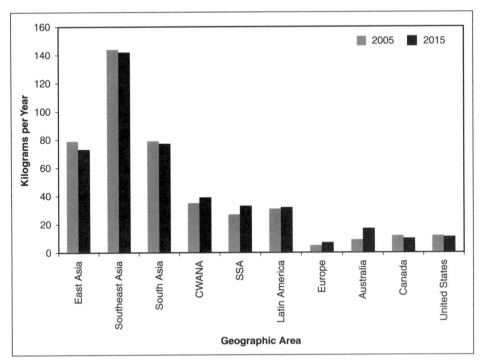

FIGURE 6.5 Rice Consumption per Capita, 2005 vs. 2015
Data Source: IRRI (2005).

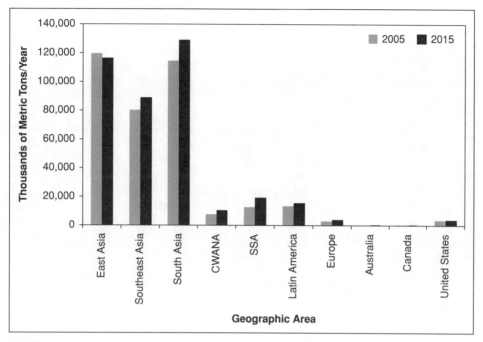

FIGURE 6.6 Total Rice Consumption, 2005 vs. 2015
Data Source: IRRI (2005).

Asia, sub-Saharan Africa is much more unpopulated, its farmers have barely used fertilizer, and appropriate rice varieties are only starting to be experimented on its soil. Land is abundant and weather conditions appropriate in countries such as Tanzania, Mozambique, and Madagascar.

Why does sub-Saharan agriculture remain underdeveloped at this point? There are many issues that have to be resolved in this region. On the technical side, average output per hectare remains under 1.5 metric tons, with a potential of up to 3 metric tons per hectare in Mozambique and Tanzania, well below the average output of 4.5 metric tons per hectare obtained in Asia. Among the reasons for the agricultural underdevelopment, V. Balasumbramanian and co-authors mention the following (2007):

- The cost of irrigated rice production is high in many sub-Saharan African countries, mainly because of the high initial investment in irrigation infrastructure and the poor operation of many irrigated rice schemes;
- Irrigated rice farmers have not realized the full potential of improved irrigated rice varieties.

Among the policies suggested to improve agricultural output in sub-Saharan Africa is the improvement of research and development capacity. In Mozambique, only two scientists are available to half a million farmers who cultivate 200,000 hectares of land, whereas in Tanzania only 23 researchers are available for a total of 322,000 hectares of land (Balasumbramanian, Sie, et al., 2007).

As of 2004, sub-Saharan Africa produced about 12,000 metric tons of rice and imported 7,000 metric tons of rice. The region could become self-sufficient or even a net exporter if only yields per hectare increased from the current 1.5 tons per hectare to a more reasonable 3 tons per hectare. In sub-Saharan Africa only Mauritania (4.53 metric tons/hectare) and Kenya (4.55) reach average rice yields that are more typical in Asia (Balasumbramanian, Sie, et al., 2007), with other countries such as Mozambique (1.12), Zambia (1.20), and Tanzania (1.96) falling behind.

The InterAcademy Council (IAC) acknowledges that Africa is fundamentally different from Asia and stresses the following disparities (IAC 2004): predominance of rain-fed agriculture as opposed to irrigated agriculture, lack of functioning competitive markets, under-investment in agricultural research and development and infrastructure, low and stagnant labor productivity and minimal mechanization, and predominance of customary land tenure. These fundamental differences make a Second Green Revolution on African soil more unlikely than the first Green Revolution that took place on Asian soil. In order to overcome these difficulties, IAC proposes the following drivers to boost African productivity (IAC 2004):

- Reduce land degradation and replenish soil fertility
- Recognize the potential of rain-fed agriculture
- Enhance the use of mechanical power
- Embrace information and communication technology at all levels

BOOSTING AGRICULTURAL OUTPUT

Game changers that could contribute to boosting agricultural yields include components of the agricultural product chain whose basic, widespread provision could make a difference in many underdeveloped areas. Fertilizer, access to credit, infrastructure and transportation, storage facilities, and appropriate land allocation through land reform are the most important components of a farmer's environment that could help boost productivity yields in underperforming regions.

Fertilizer

According to IRRI, "the world price of fertilizers—which are essential for rice production—has increased sharply, with the price of urea almost doubling over the past four years" (IRRI 2008).

In a paper prepared for the African Fertilizer Summit that took place in Abuja, Nigeria, between June 9 and 13, 2005, Eric Smaling, Moctar Toure, Nico de Ridder, Nteranya Sanginga, and Henk Breman (2005) review the use of fertilizer in Africa and its impact on the environment. According to the authors, "overuse of fertilizers causes other eco-system services to be jeopardized and under use of fertilizers contributes to depletion of soil carbon and soil fertility and too high rates of area expansion for crop and animal production" (Smaling, Toure, et al., 2005). The authors also conclude that because of under use in sub-Saharan Africa, "nutrient depletion is a reality at the macro-level." The overall conclusions remark that a more extended use of fertilizers is necessary in Africa. Among their international policy recommendations, they stress a "call for a revision of fertilizer subsidy systems at the International Level" (Smaling, Toure, et al., 2005).

Infrastructure and Transporation

Jerry Lebo and Dieter Schelling of the World Bank look at the gains in investing in basic rural infrastructure and transportation. Improvements in basic transportation and infrastructure in developing countries bring about spillover effects into nutrition or scholarization rates. For instance in Bangladesh, rickshaws are used as the major form of rural transportation to carry people and merchandise around. One driver in a rickshaw can carry up to 400 kilograms of weight per trip (Lebo and Schelling 2001). More time and an additional intake of food are necessary to ride a rickshaw on rough roads. Improved roads would bring down the cost of carrying one ton per kilometer from $0.50 for a rough road to $0.20 for a smooth road.

In Pakistan, Nepal, and Bhutan, mules are used as a common means of transportation. The actual cost is about three to four dollars per ton-kilometer, "including the cost of the mules and the persons walking with them." This rate should be compared to a cost of only $0.20 per ton-kilometer for trucking operations on improved roads (Lebo and Schelling 2001).

In Madagascar, a 50 percent reduction in travel time per kilometer on roads would increase rice productivity by 1 percent. In Ethiopia, access to all-weather roads reduced poverty by as much as 6.7 percent (World Bank 2007b).

Last distance to the nearest road can have a huge impact on scholarization rates. This is the case in Bhutan (Lebo and Schelling 2001). When roads are accessible (0 to 0.5 days walk to nearest road) the average income of a farm household is $176, which compares to $71 when roads are not accessible (one to three days walk to nearest road). Enrollment of boys and girls at schools also improves with accessible roads (73 percent boys, 64 percent girls) compared with not accessible roads (42 percent boys, 22 percent girls).

Agrarian Reform

Martin Ravallion and Dominique van de Walle of the World Bank look at the impact of land reform in China and Vietnam in poverty reduction. China's poverty rate decreased from 50 percent in 1981 to only 5 percent in 2005. Vietnam's poverty rate decreased from 60 percent in 1993 to 20 percent in 2004 (Ravallion and van de Walle 2008b). In both countries, land reform transformed cooperatives and collectives into individual landowners. Individual landowners would have to provide part of the production to the government, but could retain the rest for self-consumption or sale. The individual incentive to produce more output increases and yields are boosted upwards.

For Ravallion and van de Walle "compared with a market allocation, Vietnam's reforms to privatize land-use rights favored the poor" (Ravallion and van de Walle 2008b). For the World Bank economists, "as many developing countries strive to raise farm output in the wake of the dramatic increase in food prices, they should pay close attention to the reforms that may be needed to ensure that individual farmers can respond to market incentives" (Ravallion and van de Walle 2008a).

Improving Irrigation Systems

According to the *World Bank Development Report 2008* substantial potential for expanding irrigation in sub-Saharan Africa is the right way (World Bank 2007b). Only 4 percent of the cultivated land in sub-Saharan Africa is irrigated. For the World Bank, "With the new generation of better-designed irrigation projects, costs in Subsaharan Africa are now comparable to those in other regions, thanks to improvements in institutions, technology, and market opportunities for high-value products" (World Bank 2007b).

Financing and Storage

Other areas that would help boost agricultural productivity are related to financing and storage. Agriculture is the first component of the Axis of Feeble. Reform is needed in the developed markets, which perpetuate subsidies that undermine the ability of developing countries to export agricultural and farming produce. Biofuels and the trading of food staples also contribute to food scarcity and skyrocketing prices. The right investments in agriculture could trigger a Second Green Revolution in sub-Saharan Africa that would benefit the world as a whole. Major reform is also needed in the remaining five components of the Axis of Feeble, which are presented in further detail in Chapters 7 through 11.

Artwork by Claudio Muñoz.

CHAPTER 7

Trade Liberalization and Labor Rights

Certainly, I think that everyone should play by the rules of the game. But when it comes to supply, capacity, capital and technology, Africa will certainly find itself at a disadvantage. It is like saying that the rules of the game of rugby are the same for everybody. Then you bring in a team of professional rugby players to compete against a bunch of twelve-year-old kids. The rules are the same, but who is going to win?
—Kamran Kousari, *There is no level playing field for Africa*

Any introduction on trade must start with the English economist David Ricardo. Ricardo, born in 1772, was the pioneer of trade theory. The New School for Social Research's biography of Ricardo emphasizes his work when he was only fourteen at the London Stock Exchange.[1] In 1814, when he turned 41, he found himself "sufficiently rich to satisfy all my desires and the reasonable desires of all those about me." Ricardo's basic example is often used by economics faculty to teach trade theory. Ricardo proposes a simple world with two nations (Portugal and England) and two commodities (wine and cloth). Initially both countries manufacture both commodities. Ricardo proposes that each country specializes in the commodity in which it has a comparative advantage, a Ricardian comparative advantage. Later on, nations would trade with each other in the commodity that they have not manufactured.

David Held, professor of political science at the London School of Economics comments, "It is a misunderstanding to say that trade liberalization per se has fuelled China and India's economic growth; rather, it is the case that these countries developed relatively quickly behind protective barriers, before they liberalized their trade" (Held 2004). He adds, "Nearly all of today's developed countries initiated their growth behind tariff barriers, and only lowered these once their economies were relatively robust."

What is the impact of full trade liberalization? Is trade liberalization a precondition for sustained economic growth, or only a result of it? In "The Expected Benefits of Trade Liberalization for World Income and Development," Antoine Bouet reviews, in spite of the environment at the time, the long-term advantages of embracing trade liberalization (Bouet 2008). Bouet categorizes the impact at the world level and at the country level.

At the world level, Bouet (2008) notes that full trade liberalization, compared with the baseline estimate, would increase real income by 0.33 percent or

$99.6 billion. In his projection, world trade increases by 5.25 percent and agricultural trade increases 6.5 times more or by 33.67 percent. At the country level, the distribution of welfare gains mostly benefits rich countries, which get 73.8 percent of the total welfare gain. Middle-income countries get 24.1 percent, and least-developed countries get only 2.2 percent. Agrifood production increases significantly in Australia/New Zealand (+18.3 percent), Brazil (+12.2 percent), and Argentina (+7.5 percent); decreases significantly in the European Union (−10.8 percent), the Middle East and North Africa (−6.1 percent), and Mexico (−4.9 percent); and remains unchanged in the United States (+0.5 percent). Non-agrifood production does not undergo significant changes in any country.

Are there any winners and losers under full trade liberalization? Real incomes would generally go up, but no country would enjoy a significant improvement in real income compared to the average performer. Trade liberalization would leave the poor poor and the rich rich, but everybody would be slightly better off. Agricultural production would shift from the European Union to Australia/New Zealand and Brazil/Argentina. In terms of inequality distribution, full trade liberalization would not affect the world's inequality distribution, and 63 percent of the world population would still receive 8 percent of the world income (Bouet 2008).

Will Martin is one of the leading trade experts at the World Bank. I met Martin on December 15, 2008, at the World Bank in Washington, DC. Martin is acting research manager of the Development Research Group at the World Bank, and specializes in trade. Martin, along with World Bank economist Aaditya Mattoo, looks at what's on the table in "The Doha Development Agenda." For the World Bank trade experts, Doha offered three key benefits: "reduced uncertainty of market access in goods and services; improved market access in agriculture and manufacturing; and the mobilization of resources to deal with the trade problems of least developed countries" (Martin and Mattoo 2008). The comments of the Australian-born were released prior to the collapse of the Doha Round. What happened with the key benefits? Were they benefits fundamentally targeted to the developed nations? The authors include a section entitled "Aid for Trade." Doha negotiators emphasized this category of agreement based on the following three grounds (Martin and Mattoo 2008):

1. Overcome supply side constraints that would otherwise impede many from taking advantage of new Doha-associated market access.
2. Implement any Doha commitments by providing technical assistance and finance.
3. Provide assistance for domestic adjustment.

As a category of aid, Aid for Trade reached $24 billion in 2006. This is conditional aid based on the adoption of a set of rules that embrace trade liberalization. Trade liberalization is part of the Washington Consensus paradigm that collapsed well before Doha.

We decided to outsource the intellectual skills of the World Bank and the International Monetary Fund bureaucracies to the Bretton Woods Elites whose goal is to perpetuate the asymmetry defined in the 1940s that predominantly benefits the better off. It is time to use the brain power of the Washington technocrats to materialize the dream of a better world, the utopia of fair then free trade.

There is no momentum to reform the Bretton Woods Institutions. There is no push to move them out of Washington, DC, and New York City. Ask the Chambers of Commerce of both cities to comment on the negative impact the move would carry for the cities' economies. Ask the White House and the U.S. Department of State to reflect upon the reduction of political influence the removal would mean for their foreign policy agendas. Ask the employees of the World Bank, the International Monetary Fund or the United Nations the standard of living they would give up if they were required to move to a developing country.

It is not about lack of ideological momentum or inertia. It is about tangible losses, about a collateral damage that would affect the lives of thousands of World Bank employees, of thousands of UN employees, of thousands of IMF employees. We refuse to move forward in spite of hundreds of millions of people who today are demanding change with no voice, with no representation. I hear them. I hear the extreme poor. It is their mandate. We are only perpetuating a shortsighted approach that benefits a few thousand at the expense of hundreds of millions.

PROTECTIONISM

The collapse of the Doha Round presented in Chapter 1 is only the beginning of a trend leading countries to embrace protectionism, a word that was once forgotten and forsaken by trade economists. Protectionism will be here to stay if we do not react promptly. For Nigel Lawson, former U.K.'s chancellor of the exchequer from 1983 to 1989, "although capitalism survives it is capable of retreating behind a protectionist shell, at great cost to global prosperity" (Lawson 2009).

What can we do to avoid the pitfalls of protectionism? The question is answered by a group of leading economists from the European think-tank Centre for Economic Policy Research. In an electronic book entitled *What world leaders must do to halt the spread of protectionism* (Baldwin and Evenett 2008), the group of economists whose essays appear in the compilation present policy-makers with a framework leading to the rescue of years of trade negotiations.

In "The crisis and protectionism: History doesn't repeat itself, but sometimes it rhymes," Richard Baldwin of MIT compares the increasing protectionism that arose after the collapse of Doha with the Asian financial crisis of the late 1990s. Observing a similar trend, Baldwin points out that "the latest data from the International Trade Centre shows that many nations raised tariffs in 2008." The author also sees a stark contrast between the two crises: in 1997 the multilateral trade system was running smoothly, whereas in 2008 the Doha Round had literally collapsed (Baldwin and Evenett 2008). Baldwin concludes that whereas the 1997 Asian crisis was geographically bound to Southeast Asia, today's crisis is global.Simon J. Evenett of the University of St. Gallen presents his recommendations under the title "No turning back: Lock-in 20 years of reforms at the WTO." Evenett suggests, "Senior officials could agree to limit—for the duration of the global recession—antidumping investigations to accusations that sales abroad are taking place at prices lower than in home markets" (Baldwin and Evenett 2008).

In "Trade and the global crisis: What it means for Africa and the response of African leaders," Peter Draper of the South African Institute of International Affairs notes, "African leaders must overcome protectionist instincts and contribute to completion of the Doha Round." According to Draper, some of the effects of the increasing protectionism for African economies are a direct financial contagion, as well as reduced remittances from Africans abroad and reduced prices and volumes of commodity exports. Among his policy advice for African leaders, Draper includes "avoiding liberalisation of domestic services markets ostensibly because we do not have services to export" (Baldwin and Evenett 2008).

ROBERT WADE (TLR) is a professor of development studies at the London School of Economics (LSE) and is one of the world's leading authorities on international economics. I met Robert in the Senior Common Room at the London School of Economics on July 30, 2008. On December 2, 2008, the *Financial Times* published an article authored by Robert, entitled "Some forms of protection have to be deployed" (Wade 2008).

In his article, Robert argues that protection or protectionism is not an end, but a means to other ends, and "like any powerful instrument can be used well or badly." He calls for the deployment of some forms of protection "to achieve a sustained reduction of the huge global payments imbalances that are an underlying cause of the elevated level of global financial instability over the past 25 years." The English scholar does not hesitate to undermine the liberal trading system that emphasizes trade liberalization, which has turned the world economy into "an extremely unbalanced pattern of global production," in which the exports of China's low-cost industrial products "prevented regions such as Subsaharan Africa from beginning to create industrial sectors" (Wade 2008).

Three years prior, Robert wrote another piece in the *Financial Times* entitled "Why free trade has costs for developing nations." Among the reasons the LSE professor mentions is the minimal increase in GDP growth provided by full removal of trade barriers, a mere 0.6 percent (Wade 2005).

THE WORLD TRADE ORGANIZATION

The World Trade Organization (WTO) is an international institution based in Geneva that promotes free trade and trade liberalization. The organization has 153 members[2] and was created in 1995. Its predecessor was GATT, the General Agreement on Tariffs and Trade. John Maynard Keynes originally proposed the creation of an International Trade Organization (ITO), very different from what the WTO has become (Shaw 2009).

In July 2007, Susan George wrote on *Le Monde Diplomatique* about "Keynes' revolutionary ideas for an international trade organisation." For George, although the ITO never materialized, "it tells us that, in a rational world, it would be possible to construct a trading system serving the needs of people in both North and South." Under Keynes' system, which included the world currency bancor (the bancor is introduced in Chapter 22), "crushing third world debt and the devastating structural adjustment policies applied by the World Bank and the IMF would have been unthinkable" (George 2007).

In June 2008, the International Food Policy Research Institute (IFPRI) released a piece, entitled "WTO Negotiations on Agriculture and Developing Country." In the report Anwarul Hoda and Ashok Gulati look at the ups and downs of the latest trade round, known as the Doha Round. As an introduction, the authors walk us through the history of agricultural trade liberalization. The authors explain that "trade liberalization began in 1947, when the representatives of 23 major trading nations met in Geneva and entered into a trade compact that was to provide the foundation of the multilateral trading system in the postwar world" (Hoda and Gulati 2008).

Why did the leaders of 23 major trading nations meet in Geneva? What precipitated the encounter? What urgency drove the policy-makers of the 1940s to agree on a common trade agenda? The context of the time is crucial to understanding why the leading nations of the world joined efforts to avoid the pitfalls of the interwar period, and the increasing protectionism seen in the years that followed the Great Depression in the United States in the 1930s, and to hedge against the emergence of radical political forces that embraced nationalism. The Great Depression also led to xenophobia and authoritarianism (Wolf 2009a).

In what circumstances did Nazi Germany emerge? In 1919 John Maynard Keynes wrote *The Economic Consequences of the Peace*. The British economist predicted that the debt burden Germany had to sustain would raise confrontation. Keynes wrote that "compensation will be made by Germany for all damage done to the civilian population of the Allies and to their property by the aggression of Germany by land, by sea, and from the air" (Keynes 1919). In 1930 the Nazis won 18 percent of the German vote. Two years later they secured as much as 37 percent (Wolf 2009a).

The book *Unhappy China* was published in 2009. According to Austin Ramzy's review in *TIME Magazine*, the book, to put it simply, reveals why China is unhappy (Ramzy 2009). As Ramzy details, the book authors "point to the protests along the route of the Olympic flame, complaints about pollution from China by Western nations that consume far more resources per capita, and the West's unwillingness to share key technology with China as examples of continuing foreign disdain for the Middle Kingdom." The *TIME Magazine* author adds that nationalism in China, "fueled by a century and a half of foreign occupation and an education system that emphasizes that era of national weakness, patriotic sentiment can flash at times when citizens feel that the nation's interests or dignity have been violated, as when the protests during the Olympic torch's global run spurred Chinese anger" (Ramzy 2009).

George W. Bush doubled the U.S. debt during his two terms at the White House. If the successive bailout packages of President Barack Obama are unsuccessful, U.S. debt may spike up along the worsening of its sovereign rating. The United States may find it increasingly difficult to pay back interest on its outstanding debt, including two trillion dollars owed that the Chinese have piled up in foreign reserves. The debt burden the United States will have to sustain may raise confrontation in worsening economic climates.

In the aftermath of World War II, trade fostered understanding between nations and was one of the legs of a new international architecture that relied on more economic cooperation and dialogue between the nations of the capitalist bloc. What is the consensus of our day? Where is the reaction of our political elites in the current environment? Wake up, Sleeping Beauty. Wake up to the reality of an unequal world. Breathe the freedom and stability that emerged thanks to the Marshall Plan dollars, thanks to the French visionaries of the time.

The Doha Round collapsed because of our lack of reaction. I encourage Western society to look around and acknowledge the urgency of our time. It is time to open our hearts and minds to new approaches, to a redefined capitalism, to new institutions that are designed to cope with the challenges of our time, to new institutions that are designed to tackle the great evils of our time: hunger, malnutrition, the disease of billions. Wake up Sleeping Beauty. Wake up to the crude reality around us. It is never too late.

Let's reform, let's design new institutions, let's start a creation process that only stops when we see the great evils of our time disappear. Let's consign extreme poverty to history. Let's make extreme poverty something that can be seen only by visitors to a museum of human history.[3]

The WTO sits on three legs: GATT, GATS, and TRIPS. The plethora of acronyms should not scare the reader. They are simply an abbreviation of the three general agreements with which all WTO members have to comply. If a nation-state is a member of a club it should abide by its rules. These are the rules all WTO members have to fulfill. If a nation-state cannot fulfill them, it should not be part of WTO.

GATT is the General Agreement on Tariffs and Trade, first established in 1947. GATS is the General Agreement on Trade in Services. Finally, TRIPS is the most recent and controversial piece of WTO legislation and stands for Agreement on Trade-Related Aspects of Intellectual Property Rights. Each of the agreements is reviewed more in depth in the next three subsections.

General Agreement on Tariffs and Trade

The General Agreement on Tariffs and Trade (GATT) was established in 1947 by 23 nations that negotiated a multilateral trade agreement. Since its establishment, GATT members have pursued an agenda of trade liberalization in the context of successive negotiation rounds whose main goal was tariff reduction. Nine rounds followed the creation of GATT in 1947: Geneva (1947), Annecy (1949), Torquay (1951), Geneva (1956), Geneva-Dillon (1960–1961), Geneva-Kennedy (1964–1967), Geneva-Tokyo (1973–1979), and Geneva-Uruguay (1986–1994). The Doha negotiation round that collapsed at the end of 2008 is the latest attempt to bring together developing and developed countries around the idea of trade liberalization.

General Agreement on Trade and Services

The General Agreement on Trade and Services (GATS) was established in 1995 and covers international trade in services (WTO 2001). Services are defined in four different categories: (1) services supplied from one country to another; (2) consumers from one country making use of a service in another country; (3) a company from one country setting up subsidiaries or branches to provide services in another country; and (4) individuals travelling from their own country to supply services in another (WTO 2001).

GATS has become a controversial piece of legislation confronting the WTO and the activist community. The WTO argues that the following statements are false (WTO 2001): The new round of services negotiations will force WTO member countries to open all their services sectors to foreign competition; the services negotiations mean that all public services will have to be open to foreign competition; liberalization under GATS means deregulation of services; GATS commitments are irreversible; and GATS negotiations are secretive and anti-democratic.

Vicente Paolo B. Yu of Friends of the Earth International provides further commentary on why GATS liberalization may be detrimental for developing countries.[4] Yu observes, "Countries that, in the past 50 years managed to become industrialized did so through protectionist economic regimes that nurtured domestic industries, and only started liberalizing once domestic industries became strong enough to penetrate foreign markets and compete effectively against new foreign entrants in the domestic market."

To a certain extent it is true that GATS followed up two decades of structural lending by the World Bank and the International Monetary Fund that squeezed the provision of public services in developing countries and fostered the privatization of health care, education, water supply, and sanitation. It may only be coincidental but it does seem causal. It is unfortunate that GATS immediately followed the fall of the Washington Consensus and in fact contributed to its collapse. Structural lending is reviewed in Chapter 13 and Chapter 19.

Trade Related Intellectual Property Rights

The WTO defines intellectual property rights[5] as "the rights given to persons over the creations of their minds" and adds that intellectual property rights "usually give the creator an exclusive right over the use of his/her creation for a certain period of time." Trade Related Intellectual Property Rights (TRIPS) have become a topic of hot debate in law schools across the world.

TRIPS' Article 31 allows WTO member countries to use "the subject matter of a patent without the authorization of the right holder." The same article specifies that the use may only be permitted if "prior to such use the proposed user has made efforts to obtain authorization from the right holder on reasonable commercial terms and conditions and that such efforts have not been successful within a reasonable period of time," a requirement that "may be waived by a member in the case of a national emergency or other circumstances of extreme urgency."[6] Is the AIDS pandemic a matter of national emergency? Brazil and Thailand called on Article 31 of TRIPS to be able to manufacture two patent-protected drugs to combat the AIDS pandemic. More precisely, Brazil manufactured Merck's Efavirenz and Thailand manufactured Abbot Lab's Kaletra.

The *Financial Times* published the article "AIDS drugs: Are property rights and human rights in conflict?" in May 2007 (Epstein 2007). In the article Richard A. Epstein, a professor of law at the University of Chicago, defends the rights of pharmaceutical companies to defend their patents. The author notes that "in the United States, the war cry is that American consumers must unfairly subsidise the rest of the world by paying far higher drug prices than anywhere else in the developed and developing world" (Epstein 2007). The Chicago-based professor also claims that "price reductions in Thailand and Brazil will not lead to price increases elsewhere, since presumably Merck and Abbott already charge whatever price they think maximises the uneasy mixture between profits and good will" (Epstein 2007). LSE Professor Robert Wade comments on TRIPS (2005):

> *The agreement requires the WTO's developing country members to adopt U.S.-style patent and copyright laws. Although clothed in the language of liberal economics, it is a massive protective device in favour of western companies. Developing countries have to pay far more for drugs, software, videos and many other items than otherwise. The costs to developing countries probably outweigh the gains from trade liberalization.*

In "What might globalization's critics believe?" Alan V. Deardorff criticizes the intellectual property agreements within the WTO negotiation rounds. Deardorff (2002) concludes:

> The TRIPs agreement was sought by a subset of corporate interests who perceived that they were losing profits from unauthorized use of their intellectual property (IP). They lobbied aggressively, first to include IP in the Uruguay Round negotiations under the heading of Trade Related Intellectual Property Rights (TRIPS), but then expanding the coverage of these negotiations well beyond what could plausibly be called trade related to include the entire domestic IP regimes of all member countries. The result was to require that all WTO members implement and enforce IP regimes comparable to those in the developed countries.

Jacylyn Shi of the World Trade Institute looks at the intersection of trade law and social development concerns (2004). The author points out that the "TRIPS agreement has to take social development concerns into account, not because of its benevolence, but to correct the damaging effect that it causes to social development from the South." In order to justify her views, she mentions the following three points (Shi 2004):

1. TRIPS' adverse impact overweighs its positive effect to development.
2. TRIPS were manipulated to protect the commercial interests of corporations.
3. TRIPS have to take up its social responsibility if they cannot be removed from WTO.

Regarding access to health care, Shi comments, "The need to avoid paying high prices for drugs has been a central concern of health strategies in many developing countries." She gives the following legal advice (Shi 2004):

> Drug products are vital to public health and they should be treated differently from other goods by WTO rules especially TRIPS. The suggested legal actions will be either the effect of patent protection on pharmaceutical prices should be qualified or exclude pharmaceuticals from patentable subject matter completely from TRIPS.

TERMS OF TRADE

Discussions on trade require the basic understanding of a variety of terms, which the reader should be able to grasp in the following paragraphs.

The Stolper-Samuelson Theorem

Wolfgang Stolper was an Austrian-born economist who moved to the United States in 1933 and studied economics at Harvard. Paul Samuelson is, for many, the best American economist of the twentieth century. Samuelson won the Nobel Prize in

Economics in 1970. In 1941 Stolper and Samuelson enunciated the theorem that carries their name. Harvard economist Dani Rodrik explains the theorem as follows:[7]

> *The Stolper-Samuelson theorem is a remarkable theorem: it says that in a world with two goods and two factors of production, where specialization remains incomplete, one of the two factors—the one that is scarce—must end up worse off as a result of opening up to international trade. Not in relative terms, but in absolute terms. But the theorem is also quite limited in its applicability. It applies only to a case with two goods and two factors, and so its real world relevance is always in question.*

The *Encyclopedia of World Trade Since 1450* comments, "The Stolper-Samuelson Theorem has been applied to a range of empirical issues, including the effects of increased globalization on income distribution in developed countries, and the long-run political allegiances of classes and interest groups" (Neary 2004). One of the conclusions of subsequent applications of the theorem deals with the relation between trade and inequality. The theorem predicts a reduction of inequality as developing nations liberalize and open to trade.

Joseph E. Stiglitz and Andrew Charlton point out that the Stolper-Samuelson Theorem does not apply to the trade liberalization of Argentina, Chile, Colombia, Costa Rica, and Uruguay, whose income inequality increased after they liberalized trade in different years (Stiglitz and Charlton 2005). This is the economist's dilemma. Models do not always reflect the complex reality of the real economy. Normally the number of goods is greater than two. Usually the number of factors of production is greater than two. Often human beings are not purely rational, and not purely Homo Economicus.

Fair vs. Free Trade

For Susan Aaronson, an associate professor of international affairs and business at George Washington University, President Barack Obama "had to reconcile his internationalist and co-operative world view with his promises to Democratic special interests" adding that "he has relied on jargon such as fair trade, without defining such terms in a global context" (Aaronson 2008).

Clive Crook (2008) notes that the harder the Obama administration pushes for fair trade with poor countries, the more likely the United States will turn its back on trade. When would a politician use the term *fair trade*? Is it a fashionable term? Are Democratic voters in the United States and Socialist voters in Europe more likely to endorse a politician if he or she proves to know the jargon? While fair trade may have begun as a left-wing term, I am confident that it no longer is exclusively a left-wing term. It is a term of our time, a concept that must be incorporated into our economic reality and allowed to help set global priorities.

Fairtrade Labelling Organizations International (FLO) is a nonprofit association that involves 23 organizations operating in the Fairtrade certification of products worldwide. According to FLO, a product would be a fair trade product if it fulfills the Fairtrade Standards. The German company FLO-CERT GmbH is responsible for the inspection of products that presumably comply with the Fairtrade Standards. FLO-CERT is based in Bonn, in the German federal state of Nordrhein-Westfalen.

As of year-end 2008, FLO-CERT monitored 800,000 producers, workers, and their dependants in more than 45 countries. FLO is the predecessor of a World Fair Trade Organization, to which the WTO should evolute. The Fairtrade label concept has a recent history. It was launched in 1988 by a Dutch development agency. The first product to carry the Fairtrade label was Mexican coffee, which was sold in the Netherlands. The first Fairtrade label carried the name Max Havelaar.

When asked about the collapsed Doha Round, FLO chief executive officer Rob Cameron said, "The breakdown of the Doha talks is a significant blow for marginalized, smallholder farmers." Cameron adds, "Fairtrade provides an alternative and sustainable model for trade that strengthens the position of smallholder farmers and workers in developing countries" (Fairtrade 2008). The World Bank opened its first Fair Trade Store in May 2006 (Teruel-Soria 2006). Overall the fair trade movement benefits approximately 1.5 million producers and workers in 58 developing countries, with sales amounting to $3.6 billion in 2007 (Kohonen 2009).

Fair trade has also been explored by academia. In *Fair Trade: a Third Generation Welfare Mechanism to Make Globalisation Sustainable*, Fabrizio Adriani and Leonardo Becchetti implement a model of North-South trade (2004). They conclude, "Ethical concerns of consumers in the North might end up with reducing the welfare of workers in the South unless ethical concerned producers enter the market." The authors define fair trade as "a particular trade channel through which food and textile products from developing countries are exported in the industrialized countries." They note, "Fair trade products are required to respect a series of social and environmental criteria, defined by the Fair Trade Federation." The eight point criteria are enumerated as follows (Becchetti and Adriani 2004):

1. Paying for a fair wage in the local context.
2. Offering employees opportunities for advancement.
3. Providing equal employment opportunities for all people, particularly the most disadvantaged.
4. Engaging in environmentally sustainable practices.
5. Being open to public accountability.
6. Building long-term trade relationships.
7. Providing healthy and safe working conditions within the local context.
8. Providing financial and technical assistance to producers whenever possible.

The authors further conclude, "In a simple model where consumers care about the fairness of their consumption, we have shown that the entry of a Fair Trader may increase the welfare of both consumers in the North and workers in the South" (Becchetti and Adriani 2004).

In *Fair Trade*, Martin Richardson and Frank Stahler look at the vertical integration of a fair trade organization. The authors comment that a fair trade organization must be vertically integrated. This is an additional constraint that brings about an additional cost to consumers. The authors confirm, "This vertical integration limits the size of the fair trade organization compared to its rivals in international markets" (Richardson and Stahler 2007).

Leonardo Becchetti and Furio Rosati examine "Global Social Preferences and the Demand for Socially Responsible Products" (2007). In the paper, the authors conclude that a future development of fair trade depends on two issues: "the capacity of the fair trade movement of extending its outreach when investing in promotion and the solution of the problem of distributional bottlenecks of fair trade products aimed at reducing the negative effect of distance on consumption of fair trade products" (Becchetti and Rosati 2007).

Preferential Trade

According to the World Trade Organization (WTO), no country should grant privilege to another country or discriminate against it (Gibb 2000). The Lome Convention is a preferential trade agreement signed in 1975 between the former European Community (now European Union) and 71 African, Caribbean, and Pacific (ACP) states that were former European colonies. The Lome Convention seeks economic cooperation with ACP countries. The convention favors Europe's former colonies to the detriment of other developing nations. Lome's key feature is non-reciprocity, whereby ACP countries (but not the European Union) can export duty-free to the European Union and can raise tariffs on imports (Gibb 2000).

The Lome Convention violates the principles of tree trade and has been subject to strong criticism by the WTO, the Big Brother of free trade. In this context, the Lome Convention is being dismantled and the non-reciprocity principle should no longer hold between the European Union and its former colonies. The Lome Convention follows from the logic of supporting the development of Europe's former colonies through preferential trade, which would potentially allow the latter to develop the agriculture of certain products that can then be exported to the European Union. This special treatment has proven effective in explaining the economic success of a handful of economies, but has not represented a major factor in the development of a majority of countries.

The preferential trade agreements of the Lome Convention are contrary to the multilateral trade philosophy embraced by the World Trade Organization (WTO). In 1994 a WTO Panel examined the favorable treatment of the Lome Convention to banana exporters from the ACP countries. The WTO forced the then European Community to undertake "a long-term examination as to how a future trade regime with the ACP could be envisaged which would be ultimately WTO-compatible, without the necessity of requesting a waiver for an indefinite period of time" (Huber 2000). In this context, the EU and the ACP countries signed the Partnership Agreement (PA) in February of 2000.

How is the PA different from the previous Lome Convention? Does it fulfill the WTO's philosophy? According to Jurgen Huber (2000), "the PA provides for a preparatory period for all ACP states during which the non-reciprocal preferences of Lome will be maintained." The Partnership Agreement of 2000 would translate into Economic Partnership Agreements (EPAs) in 2008. EPAs are free trade areas among the signatory members. Huber remarks that "EPAs that will enter into force in 2008 will have to provide for the reciprocal elimination of trade obstacles in respect of substantially all the trade by the end of a transitional period of 10 years, or maybe 12 years in exceptional cases where it can be justified, which means that all ACP states that are parties to such EPAs will have to grant full reciprocity in trade preferences to the EC by 2018 or 2020 as the case may be" (Huber 2000).

MULTILATERAL VERSUS BILATERAL TRADE

Jagdish Bhagwati is one of the leading scholars on international trade. Bhagwati is a professor of international economics at Columbia University. His most recent book on international trade entitled *Termites in the Trading System* is a must-read to understand why the Indian scholar is a strong advocate of free trade (Bhagwati 2008). Bhagwati's working assumption is that Preferential Trade Agreements (PTAs) undermine trade. The most popular bilateral trade agreement is the Lome Convention signed between the European Union and 71 African, Caribbean, and Pacific States (ACP). The convention favors Europe's former colonies to the detriment of other developing nations.

Bhagwati argues against this framework of bilateral trade, which he deems discriminatory. The Indian economist argues that partial preferential reduction of trade barriers "directly contradicts the principle of nondiscrimination in trade that many economists and policy makers have traditionally valued as the sine qua non of sound trade policy and an essential cornerstone of the architecture of an efficient, even a fair, world trading system." According to Bhagwati, PTAs act like termites. The Indian scholar points out, "The analysis of PTAs has attracted nearly all of the best economists working in the theory of international trade in the past half-century." In the preface of his book Bhagwati raises the question, "How shall we return to the multilateralism that our trade policy makers have been extolling while their actions have been to undercut it?" (Bhagwati 2008).

Bhagwati argues that, starting in the early 1990s, he was the first economist to warn against the proliferation of PTAs, which he does not hesitate to call pandemic. On the other side of the hard-fought debate were renowned economists Paul Krugman and Lawrence Summers. Krugman is a 2008 Nobel Prize Laureate in Economics, professor of economics at Princeton University, and a disciple of Bhagwati. Lawrence Summers is director of the National Economic Council in the Obama Administration.

Bhagwati argues, "The effective emasculation of Article 24 for developing nations has thus been a contributory factor in the proliferation of Preferential Trade Agreements" (Bhagwati 2008). Oxford economist Paul Collier comments, "The WTO has an escape clause for least-developed countries, and in this context that should mean those low-income countries that have not yet established significant manufactured exports" (Collier 2007). Both Bhagwati and Collier are referring to WTO's Article 24 and the Enabling Clause. What are they? Why are they so controversial?

The Enabling Clause is an exception to GATT's Most Favourable Nation (MFN) Principle included in its Article 1. The MFN Principle is one of the pillars of the WTO trading system, whereby WTO member countries that grant tariff preferences to any country are required "to grant tariff preferences to all other WTO members immediately and unconditionally" (Ukpe 2007).

The 1971 Waiver Decision allows WTO member countries to grant preferential tariff treatment to imports from one specific developing country, without having to extend the benefit to other WTO member countries. As a result, the 1971 Waiver Decision overrides the WTO MFN Principle. The 1971 Waiver Decision was granted with a moratorium of 10 years. GATT members met in Tokyo in 1979, two years before the moratorium regarding the 1971 Waiver Decision expired. GATT members decided to introduce the Enabling Clause, whereby the 1971 Waiver Decision was extended indefinitely. As a result of the Enabling Clause, WTO member countries can pursue preferential trade agreements. Should the Enabling Clause be revised? And if so, in what way?

What does the leading international scholar on trade think about Obama and his change agenda? Bhagwati points out, "The freeing of trade is nearly impossible to achieve in times of macroeconomic crisis." According to the Columbia economist, Obama, who earned a bachelor's degree in political science at Columbia University, missed a golden opportunity to endorse the collapsed Doha Round. Bhagwati considers, "His pronouncements on the car bail-out disregard the lessons of the early 1930s when the Smoot-Hawley tariff was signed into law and a competitive raising of tariff barriers ensued" (Bhagwati 2009).

In the still world of Bretton Woods, any bailout has to be WTO-consistent, according to the influential Indian scholar, who concludes, "Mr. Obama, who has properly denounced unilateralism, should also not be the President who undermines respect for the rule of law that the WTO embodies at the multilateral level" (Bhagwati 2009). While Detroit's bailout may not be WTO-consistent, the WTO itself has lost much of the legitimacy it had a decade ago. We now live in a world in transition where WTO-consistency has lost much of the meaning it once had.

Bhagwati makes one more distinction, namely that Free Trade Areas (FTAs) such as NAFTA, are actually PTAs (2008). The European Union, ASEAN, Mercosur, or SADC would also be PTAs. Bhagwati is not only a leading economist, but also a historian. He knows very well how to explain why PTAs have proliferated. It is not a different reason why the Doha Round has collapsed. The tricycle theory, argues Bhagwati, helps explain why PTAs have proliferated among developing countries: ASEAN, Mercosur, or SADC. Bhagwati comments (2008):

> *The reluctant liberalizers who feared competition from the developed countries felt that they should learn to compete with countries their own size, then go on to general free trade on a Most Favourable Nation basis. This might be called the "tricycle" theory: you need to learn how to ride a tricycle before you move on to a bicycle.*

As far as I am concerned, I learned to ride a tricycle before I was able to ride a bike. I am not sure about the talented Indian scholar, who concludes, "If Doha does not settle in the next few years, there is no reason to think that protectionism will break out" (Bhagwati 2008). What do we do to transition from a world where PTAs proliferate to a truly multilaterist world in which multilateral free trade is the rule instead of the exception? The answer to Bhagwati's concern is only a footstep away.

Next door to Bhagwati's Columbia University office sits Professor Joseph E. Stiglitz, Nobel Prize Laureate in Economics in 2001. In 2005 Stiglitz co-authored the book *Free Trade for All* with Andrew Charlton (2005). Stiglitz and Charlton present a roadmap to free trade that incorporates the fairness clause to the agenda. While the final destination is where Bhagwati would like to arrive, the path and the means of motion may be different from what Bhagwati initially intended. In the authors' words, "The book attempts to support progress in the current round by asking what a true Development Round of trade negotiations would look like, one that reflects the interests and concerns of the developing countries and is designed to promote their development" (Stiglitz and Charlton 2005).

The authors claim that for many developing countries, "only through protection could their industries compete with the well-established firms of Europe and the United States." They also point out, "Concern that trade liberalization will lead to increased unemployment is perhaps the most important source of opposition to liberalization." The concern is particularly acute in countries lacking a social protection network. The authors acknowledge, "There is a middle ground between the extreme positions of the free-traders and the anti-globalizers," concluding, "This middle ground recognizes that even if one accepts the ultimate desirability of free trade, rushed liberalization may be harmful" (Stiglitz and Charlton 2005).

What do Stiglitz and Charlton propose as an intermediate solution between absolute liberalization and absolute protectionism? To start with, they suggest that developing countries should receive a special treatment from developed countries. This special treatment would translate into asymmetric preferential trade agreements, in which one country would have free access to the markets of a second country if either the aggregate GDP or the GDP per capita of the second is larger than that of the first. The authors explain this as follows (Stiglitz and Charlton 2005):

> *The proposal distributes new market access progressively, ensuring that the largest gains accrue to the smallest and poorest countries, and it distributes liberalization obligations progressively, requiring that the largest and richest countries liberalize most.*

TRADE WITH AFRICAN COUNTRIES

Two major initiatives have been proposed by the European Union and the United States in recent years to foster and increase trade with Africa. The two initiatives are reviewed in this section.

European Union's Everything But Arms (EBA)

The European Union enacted Everything But Arms (EBA) in 2001 to grant preferential access to imports from the 50 Least Developed Countries (LDCs). According to the OECD,[8] the EBA Initiative "eliminates EU import tariffs and restrictions for numerous goods, including agricultural products, from the least developed countries." EBA grants duty free access to imports from all LDCs, except arms and ammunitions. The list of LDCs contains 50 countries, a majority of which is in sub-Saharan Africa.

Three exceptions were incorporated to the full trade liberalization regime: bananas, rice, and sugar. As of 2001, these three products represented 40 percent of total exports from the LDCs to Europe. Between 2001 and July 1, 2009, quotas on sugar were applied to EU imports. Sugar quotas started at 74,000 tons in 2001 and increased by 15 percent per year to reach 197,335 tons in 2008 (Bruntrup 2006). Quotas were introduced due to pressure from U.K.'s National Farmers' Union and from parts of the multinational sugar industry, which felt that EBA with sugar would be a threat to U.K. sugar growers (Oxfam 2000).

United States' African Growth Opportunity Act (AGOA)

The African Growth Opportunity Act (AGOA) was signed between the United States and many African nations. Its goal appears similar to that of Europe's EBA. But in the long run, AGOA seeks to create full free trade agreements between the United States and every African nation and to eliminate tariffs among African nations so as to foster an environment of free trade. AGOA grants preferential treatment to sub-Saharan African exports, which can enter the United States duty-free until September 30, 2015 (Schaefer and Markheim 2006). Not every country is eligible to participate in AGOA. As of 2008, 40 of the 48 sub-Saharan African countries were eligible to participate. The two latest additions were Mauritania (June 2007) and Togo (April 2008). The selection is based on the following criteria (Schaefer and Markheim 2006):

> *The U.S. president must designate eligible countries based on their progress toward establishing market-based economies, representative government, strengthening the rule of law, combating corruption, eliminating barriers to U.S. trade and investment, protecting intellectual property, reducing poverty, expanding healthcare and educational opportunities, and adopting labor standards.*

Since its inception in 2000, AGOA has fostered trade between the United States and sub-Saharan Africa. Between 2000 and 2007 exports from sub-Saharan Africa to the United States more than tripled to $67.4 billion, 98 percent of which entered the United States duty-free (USTR 2008b). AGOA seeks to reduce tariffs among sub-Saharan African nations. It also seeks a reduction in tariffs imposed by these nations on U.S. imports by 2015.

In May 2008 Susan Schwab, the U.S. trade representative under President George W. Bush stated, "The improved business environment in Africa under AGOA has also helped to create new opportunities for U.S. exports to the region" (USTR 2008b). One of the problems of AGOA is that it allows the compliant country to define what is and what is not legally permissible regarding human and labor rights. In the case of Liberia, for instance, the Office of the United States Trade Representative comments, "Child labor remains widespread in almost every economic sector" (USTR 2008a).

In spite of this assessment, Liberia is AGOA-compliant. Considering a whole country compliant is a macro-approach that undermines local efforts to improve working conditions and grants government officials the opportunity of free-riding, which can be considered an exception. Fair trade labeling is a simpler and more easily monitored solution, which guarantees that the products imported by the United States or the European Union have indeed been manufactured according to a set of ethical standards, overcoming any exceptions outstanding in the current AGOA-environment.

LABOR RIGHTS

Christian Barry and Sanjay Reddy look at labor standards in their book *International Trade and Labor Standards* (2008). The authors argue that international trade should be conditional on improving basic labor standards that they define as "specified levels of attainment of wages and working conditions that are deemed minimally adequate in each country" (Barry and Reddy 2008). Here is their Proposition L:

> *Proposition L: it is desirable to bring about an institutional arrangement in which rights to trade are made conditional upon the promotion of labor standards, and there is reason to believe that such an arrangement can be brought about and sustained.*

Let's open the door to conditionality, but here in the North. I welcome this kind of conditionality because it raises our ethical standards, which we already deemed adequate. It is time to import the conditionality we exported for decades from the political power centers in Washington and Brussels. Are we embracing an agenda of Human Rights? Perhaps we should first double-check with some of our multinational corporations.

I am more likely to sign a contract with an employer who will pay the minimum wage and maintains healthy working conditions in a clean environment. I am more willing and likely to enter a contract that has exit clauses if the agreed conditions are broken. Otherwise we are embracing a contractual concept that approaches slavery. We have eliminated slavery from the developed world. But we decided to ignore its prevalence in many developing countries that today manufacture cheap products and services for us. This helps keep inflation down and allows us to continue to live in a multiple-choice capitalist regime.

International labor standards are needed to enforce minimum working conditions between employers and employees. The rule of law must be implemented in order to guarantee that those employers who break the code of conduct are penalized. I want to live in the world of Proposition L. What is necessary to enforce it? The authors conclude, "Should linkage of the kind we have described turn out to be infeasible because certain influential agents remain implacably opposed to it (perhaps for no other reason than that it would somewhat erode the privileges they enjoy at present), this would show not that linkage is undesirable but that reforms that would make international institutions more just are being resisted by those who do not prioritize the goal of justice" (Barry and Reddy 2008). More simply stated, in the above conclusion, linkage refers to Proposition L, and those who do not prioritize the goal of justice are the Pirates of Heartless Capitalism.

The International Labour Office

The International Labour Office (ILO) is based in Geneva, Switzerland. The ILO is one of the handful institutions that were not created in the 1940s. The ILO was founded in 1919, in the aftermath of World War I. It is a sister institution of the deceased League of Nations, the predecessor of the United Nations. The ILO became the United Nations' first specialized agency in 1946.

How does the ILO interpret the term decent work? For the ILO, "Decent work sums up the aspirations of people in their working lives." Decent work is subsequently defined according to four strategic objectives:[9] fundamental principles and rights at work and international labor standards; rights, voice, and recognition; family stability and personal development; and social dialogue and tripartism.

Going forward, labor standards are the most important of the four strategic objectives. The standards must be defined initially and subsequently respected and enforced. A piggyback mechanism is needed to penalize those that trespass the new standards. What kind of progress has the ILO made in this regard? Progress is always a relative concept. As a UN Agency the ILO has adopted more than 180 Conventions and 190 Recommendations covering every aspect of labor practices imaginable. However, the problem with UN Agencies is that they have limited enforcement capabilities. Multinational corporations abide by the rights and obligations of their countries of origin and of the countries where they operate. Multinational corporations are subject to global scrutiny, but unfortunately global scrutiny is not legally binding.

Multinational corporations are also hedged against abusive behavior with regard to the human being or the environment. Welcome back to the world of noncooperation, where nation-states pursue their interest while forsaking global priorities. This is not different from the ruling of a dictator that benefits his or her minority and mistreats the majority. This is not different from a feudal regime in the Middle Ages where only the nobility are protected from the abuse of the Lord.

KARL-JOHAN LONNROTH (TLR) was the ILO's director of employment from 1991 to 1996, where he was responsible for the ILO's World Employment Program. I spoke with Karl-Johan on September 19, 2008. At the time, Karl-Johan was the director general of translation at the European Commission. What international agency can define and enforce global labor standards that are legally binding? Do we need a new agency? Karl-Johan remains convinced that the ILO continues to hold the responsibility of enforcing global labor standards, while its structures should be adapted to the challenges of the twenty-first century. He concludes that the "ILO did in fact a magnificent job to develop the basic foundations of the international labour standards in the postwar period to enhance the dignity of working women and men." We now need to enforce the standards, and enforce them worldwide.

Artwork by Claudio Muñoz.

CHAPTER 8

Small Arms Trade

A thousand people die every day by gunshots, and three times as many are severy injured. Spinal cords severed, bones shattered, families destroyed, hearts broken. If the death, injury and disability resulting from small arms were categorised as a disease, we would view it as an epidemic. As a man-made vector of injury, guns are manifestly bad for human health.
—IANSA, *Gun Violence: The Global Crisis*

In the blame game, Spain is one of the relevant players in this chapter. Spain is the world's leading ammunition exporter to sub-Saharan Africa (*El Mundo* 2006). According to Oxfam, Spain is the world's eighth exporter of light weapons (small arms) and the main exporter to sub-Saharan Africa. Every year the world manufactures 38 million small arms. The final destination of 83 percent of this amount is unknown. Spaniards are perhaps not fully aware of the collateral damage of Spain's arms industry. The purpose of this chapter is precisely to raise their awareness along that of the rest of the truly learned readers. Welcome back to the World of the Bretton Woods Elites, where emphasis is put on the issues that do not harm our current status quo.

The total number of firearms outstanding in the world is estimated at between 875 million and one billion, of which between 2.5 percent and 3.5 percent corresponds to arms used for law enforcement. The military owns about 20 to 25 percent of the global stock, and the rest (between 650 million and 730 million) is owned by civilians. Country-wise, only Switzerland and Yemen approach the United States in per-capita rates of gun ownership. Germany, Finland, France, Iraq, and Serbia follow (Small Arms Survey 2007).

Oxfam released its research piece on arms trade, "Africa's Missing Billions," in 2007. Armed conflict costs Africa $18 billion per year. More precisely, $300 billion has been lost since 1990, an amount "equivalent to the international aid from major donors in the same period" (Oxfam 2007). This is equivalent to 15 percent of GDP for the whole of sub-Saharan Africa.

SMALL ARMS AND LIGHT WEAPONS

What are small arms? What are light weapons? Small arms are weapons designed for personal use, whereas light weapons are designed for a group of individuals organized as a crew. Examples of small arms are rifles and pistols. Examples of light weapons are machine guns and mounted grenades (Efrat 2006). The three main sources of small arms and light weapons (SALW) are illicit stocks, licit stocks that have become illicit, newly manufactured weapons that are built locally, or weapons imported from outside the region.

Seventy-four percent of the 875 million guns in circulation in the world as of 2008 were owned by non-state actors or civilians. Consequently, the number of weapons in the hands of private individuals triples the number of weapons owned by the government's police and armies. Developing countries top the list of countries with the highest gun homicide rate (International Action Network on Small Arms 2008).

Who manufactures them? The Russian assault weapon, the Kalashnikov AK-47, is the most popular light weapon. About 95 percent of all small arms are legal or illegal copies of the AK-47 and its derivatives. Legal AK-47s are manufactured by the Russian arms manufacturer Mashinostroitelnei Zavod, based in a remote town in the core of Russia called Izhevsk, in the Republic of Udmurtia, about 500 kilometers east of Moscow.

In April 2006, the English newpaper *The Independent* published an article entitled "Global Arms Trade: Africa and the Curse of the AK-47." The English newspaper refers to the AK-47 as "ageing cold weapons that represent the ultimate trickle-down of the global small arms industry." The article points out, "Until the mass killings in Darfur provoked an international arms embargo in 2003, the U.K. was a significant arms exporter to Sudan" (*Independent* 2006).

From a death toll point of view, small arms and light weapons kill more individuals in more places than weapons of mass destruction. Small arms and light weapons are somehow weapons of mass destruction, killing thousands, one person at a time. We label weapons of mass destruction the way it is convenient for our arms manufacturers. We decide to maintain our military and industrial complexes because otherwise our unemployment rates and our economies would sink even deeper. It is part of the Western hypocrisy to which we have grown so accustomed; we live in a world of double standards.

The mandatory ammunition to load the AK-47s and make them lethal weapons is manufactured outside Africa. According to Oxfam, "Of imports of ammunition to African countries worth $109.2 million, 98 percent came from outside Africa" (Oxfam 2007).

According to Matt Schroeder and Guy Lamb of the Federation of American Scientists, between 10 percent and 20 percent of the global trade on small arms is illicit (2006). Much of this illegal arms trade is related to illicit arms manufacturers. The authors conclude, "Unlicensed gunsmiths have the collective capacity to produce up to 200,000 firearms a year, some of quality comparable with industrially produced guns" (Schroeder and Lamb 2006).

Oxfam reports that in sub-Saharan Africa, at least 22 of the 34 countries that are least likely to reach the Millennium Development Goals by 2015 are undergoing armed conflict or have recently left armed conflict behind (Oxfam 2008). Arms trade exacerbates the incidence of armed conflict in many poor countries.

Oxford economist Philip Killicoat published a paper in April 2007 entitled "Weaponomics: The Global Market for Assault Rifles." Killicoat's work is a reference in the space of small arms trade. In his research, he examines the determinants of assault rifle prices. Among his conclusions, Killicoat mentions that regulation and supply costs are key determinants of the price of assault weapons. He emphasizes that the "historic focus on the supply side is justified" (Killicoat 2007).

In a report entitled "Who Takes the Bullet?" Church Aid outlines the impact of small arms violence (Jackson, Marsh, et al., 2005). The authors present a holistic approach on the issue of small arms trade. Their comments on children as a vulnerable group and on the global supply chain of small arms trade deserve our attention. The authors remark, "2 million children have been killed, 6 million seriously injured and traumatised, and 22 million displaced in conflicts in the 1990s." Gangs in developing countries have access to small arms and assault weapons. Only for Honduras, the Overseas Development Institute features a total of 340 gangs with nearly 15,000 youngsters enlisted. In El Salvador gangs can access major military weapons (Jackson, Marsh, et al., 2005).

Regarding the global supply chain of arms, the authors remark, "The overwhelming majority of small arms used to commit acts of violence have been legally produced, exported, bought, and stored" (Jackson, Marsh, et al., 2005). According to a 2003 survey conducted by the Omega Foundation, out of a total of 1,249 companies involved in small arms production, 42 percent are found in Europe and the former Soviet republics and 37 percent in North America. But most significantly, small arms are manufactured in Austria, Belgium, Brazil, China, France, Germany, Israel, Italy, Russia, Spain, Switzerland, the U.K., and the United States (Jackson, Marsh, et al., 2005). However, sub-Saharan Africa only represents 1 percent of the total sales from Western European countries.

Who supplies small arms to sub-Saharan Africa? According to the authors, "All arms currently in illegal circulation started off in the legal trade and under legal control. They were produced in government-licensed factories, stored under a variety of regulations, and often exported with a valid licence" (Jackson, Marsh, et al., 2005). But sooner or later many of the legal small arms are diverted into the illicit trade. The five methods of arms diversion are as described follows (Jackson, Marsh, et al., 2005):

1. Deliberate transfers of arms by governments to non-state parties involved in civil war.
2. Violations of the export licensing system through the use of forged documentation.
3. Theft or corrupt purchase from government stockpiles.
4. Battlefield recoveries of firearms after combat.
5. Purchases from gun shops by civilians that are then illegally passed on.

CHRISTIANE AGBOTON-JOHNSON (SAT) is the deputy director of the United Nations Institute for Disarmament Research (UNIDIR), headquartered in Geneva (Switzerland). Christiane was previously president of the Movement Against Small Arms in West Africa, based in Senegal. I talked to Christiane on August 6, 2009. I visited UNIDIR on July 16, 2008. The visit helped me to understand the key role played by the United Nations in the fight against the trade of illicit small arms— primarily, that the United Nations continues to lack the capability of enforcement.

According to Reverend Eugene Goussikindey, a Jesuit priest from Kenya, "the threat caused by the proliferation of light weapons on the African continent is of unprecedented magnitude and gravity, far greater than HIV/AIDS and malaria" (Goussikindey 2006). The Kenyan Jesuit believes that the proliferation of small arms and light weapons on African soil is destroying the fabric of society, a destruction from which it will take decades to recover. Goussikindey concludes, "Besides the death toll of actual combatants, one has to account for deaths directly related to the conflict as the consequence of displacement, and of dangerous and exhausting journeys on roads, through forests, across rivers and lakes" (Goussikindey 2006).

The link between arms trade and terrorism is stressed by Matt Schroeder, manager of the Federation of American Scientists' Arms Sales Monitoring Project in the United States. I phoned Schroeder on December 5, 2008. According to the American researcher,[1] "illicit arms trafficking feeds the arsenals of the world's worst terrorists." He then adds, "Of the roughly 175 terrorist attacks identified in 2003's *U.S. State Department Report on Patterns of Global Terrorism*, approximately half were committed with small arms or light weapons." The conclusion is straightforward: If the priority is to fight global terrorism, the priority must be to fight the illicit trade of small arms.

WEAPONS PRICING

The Kalashnikov assault rifle is the world's most popular light weapon. The key members of the Kalashnikov family are the AK-47, the AKM, the AK-74, and the AK-101. In the last five decades, the Kalashnikov has dominated the segment of assault rifles (Small Arms Survey 2007). Of the approximately 875 million small arms worldwide, between 50 million and 100 million are Kalashnikovs.

The price of the Kalashnikov is linked to the enforcement of a country's arms regulation. The more effective a country is in enforcing its regulation, the higher the price will be and vice versa. Porous borders enable the supply of weapons to meet the demand more easily (Small Arms Survey 2007).

Between 1986 and 2005, Africa was able to provide Kalashnikovs for under $200 a piece, well below the $600 needed in the Americas or Asia or the $800 needed in the Middle East (Small Arms Survey 2007). If the price of a Kalashnikov in Africa was higher, the supply would meet a lower demand and the total number of Kalashnikovs would decrease. In other words, "if the average world price of weapons were to rise by 10 percent, the risk of civil conflict would fall by approximately 0.5 percent" (Small Arms Survey 2007).

LICENSED VERSUS UNLICENSED PRODUCTION

Between 60 and 80 percent of all military and assault rifles were manufactured by producers who licensed the technology from the original manufacturer. There is, therefore, a key difference between licensed and unlicensed production. Licensed production involves two parties. A license agreement is "a partnership between an intellectual property owner and another who is authorized to use such rights under certain conditions" (Small Arms Survey 2007). The two parties that enter a partnership are called licensor and licensee.

The distribution of production of small arms and light weapons is as follows: licensed (57 percent), unlicensed (24 percent), and unclear (19 percent). The Russian Federation and Belgium provide the two most notorious examples of licensors exporting their arms production technology. Total annual production of small arms and light weapons for 2006 was estimated at between 530,000 and 580,000, of which 320,000 to 350,000 were assault rifles, 182,000 to 200,000 were rifles, and 28,000 to 30,000 were carbines. The geographic production of small arms and light weapons is concentrated as follows: Asia-Pacific (33 percent of the total), Europe (32 percent), Middle East and North Africa (18 percent), Americas (15 percent), and sub-Saharan Africa (2 percent).

For the time being there is no international regulation regarding licensed production. The enforcement of licensed production rests within the nation-state. "Improved transparency would help in particular to curb the irresponsible transfer of small arms and light weapons produced under licence," concludes the Small Arms Survey (2007). For Maria Haug, Martin Langvandslien, Lora Lumpe, and Nicholas Marsh, "a truly transparent export licensing system would require not only full and accurate reports on past arms export licenses and weapons shipments, but also prior parliamentary scrutiny of license approvals and open licensing procedure by governments" (Haug, Langvandslien, et al., 2002). We need more international standards for reporting arms transfers so that it is possible to understand and compare who exports what.

TRANSPARENCY

The Stockholm International Peace Research Institute (SIPRI) is the leading independent provider of research in the space of arms control and disarmament. SIPRI was established in 1966 and has published its Yearbook since 1969. Pieter Wezeman is a senior researcher at SIPRI. I phoned Wezeman on May 23, 2008. Is an international registry of small arms and light weapons necessary? For Wezeman, "international transparency by governments in arms trade and arms holdings, whether small or major arms or weapons of mass destruction, contributes to confidence building between states and helps to understand how arms may play a role in provoking, sustaining and aggravating conflict." Transparency by itself does not suffice. Wezeman concludes, "The information made available by governments needs to be incorporated in meaningful discussions between governments and within Civil Society aimed at understanding how arms may do damage and to inform adequate arms procurement and arms trade policies."

TRADE PREVENTION

Trade prevention is defined as the adoption of conventions that reduce the trade of small arms and light weapons (ex-ante policy). This section also examines arms embargoes and buy-back programs as policies able to reduce the burden of the trade of small arms once it has taken place (ex-post policy).

Asif Efrat is a visiting professor of law at Cornell University. In his research piece "Regulating Rifles: International Control of the Small Arms Trade" (2006), Efrat notes, "Given the enourmous death toll of small arms and the destruction they inflict, especially in Africa, one would expect international small arms regulation to be very tight" (2006). However we continue to live in a world of political declarations that are not legally binding, and that are not enforced. The current reality of international law is that a majority of its codes of conduct cannot be enforced. It is law for an autarchic world in which every nation-state behaves as it wishes, ignoring the collateral damage, externalities or repercussions of its actions. It is the world of Bretton Woods. Efrat adds, "I find that governments backing state-owned arms exporters favor weak international regulation of small arms, and so do non-democratic governments concerned about interference with their gun supply. By contrast, governments facing high rates of gun violence and governments with humanitarian foreign policy concerns support strong regulation" (Efrat 2006).

What happened to the spirit of the League of Nations? It was demolished by World War II. What happened to the spirit of the United Nations? It is being demolished by our own inability to design and implement international standards of behavior that benefit everyone. Our lack of compromise is latent with our own inability to sign international agreements.

Efrat's provocative essay draws a comparison between the WTO TRIPS agreement reviewed in Chapter 7 and the lack of consensus around the trade of small arms. Efrat talks about the externalities that were perceived in the West because of the continuous breach of patent laws that could not be internationally enforced. Through WTO TRIPS, patent laws are now internationally binding and breaches of the law can be prosecuted now through the WTO in any of the 153 members of the Geneva-based organization. We perceived the damage caused by the breach of patent laws and reacted accordingly. Our multinationals perceived the loss associated with the illegal copies of their products and reacted accordingly. The shareholders of our multinationals perceived the loss associated with lower earnings and reacted on time. Efrat expects two influences on behalf of governments that suffer the pain of arms and their trade (2006):

1. First, support for international regulation will increase with the magnitude of the negative externalities. For example, the higher the rate of gun violence or drug addiction, the greater should be the government's support for international restraints on the trade in small arms and drugs.
2. Second, support for international regulation will decrease as the government's ability to curb the trade on its own increases.

We are not able to react on time to the collateral damage, to the externalities that the trade of small arms causes beyond our own borders. We put the interest of our own arms manufacturers above the interests of the human beings who are born and live within borders where evil reigns, where violence perpetuates because of a lack of compromise that will bounce back to the developed world in the long run through an increase in riots, violence, terrorism, mafias, human trafficking, and the proliferation of organized crime.

This section reviews the number of declarations, treaties, and meetings that have emerged since 1997 to fight the exposure to the violence generated by armed conflicts.

This violence is exacerbated by a trade that remains beyond the control of national authorities in the absence of an international regulator able to enforce standards of mandatory fulfillment.

What lessons can we learn regarding the myriad of treaties and conventions ratified in the last 10 years? Welcome to the world of Bretton Woods, where our elites perpetuate the interest of a handful in expense of the welfare of millions. Welcome to the world of Bretton Woods, where the nation-states play the game of non-cooperation and continue to avoid reaching international understanding, which hedges their own citizens against crimes against humanity.

Yes, it is time to acknowledge it. The proliferation of small arms is a crime against humanity. It kills our neighbors south of the Mediterranean. It kills our neighbors south of the Mexican border. Let's face the reality of this unequal world that was designed by the Bretton Woods Elites sixty years ago. The blame game does not stop here. The blame game is only the beginning of a new approach. If we do not identify the problems of the current version of capitalism, we will not be able to fix it. That is why the current concatenation of international meetings is unable to reach the very root of the problem. That is why the European Troika (Sarkozy, Brown, and Merkel) is unable to lead Europe's emergence. No, we did not accomplish the mission to bring equity, justice, and sustainability to the very own system we praised for decades. We did not.

Convention on the Prohibition of the Use of Anti-Personnel Mines (1997)

Landmines are worth mentioning because there has been a recent accomplishment that may inspire optimism in the years to come. Landmines are dangerous weapons that mainly cause casualties. According to UNICEF,[2] over 110 million landmines remain hidden around the globe, particularly in Afghanistan, Angola, and Cambodia, where 85 percent of the related casualties have occurred.

The *Convention on the Prohibition of the Use, Stockpiling, Production and Transfer of Anti-Personnel Mines and on their Destruction* was ratified in 1997 by 122 governments in Ottawa (Canada). The International Campaign to Ban Landmines (ICBL) is a network of more than 1,400 non-governmental organizations in 90 countries that work on a global ban on landmines. In 2007, ICBL celebrated the tenth anniversary of the mine ban treaty. ICBL also won the Nobel Peace Prize in 1997 for its accomplishment on the global ban of landmines.

Kenneth Anderson, an associate professor of law at American University in Washington, DC, points out, "The most significant legal events of the entire 1990s were the signing of the Landmines Treaty and the signing of the International Criminal Court statute." He adds, "The Ottawa Convention represents the first time in over a century in which a major, traditional weapon system has been banned outright and not simply regulated in its use by a treaty that has a broad participation by states" (Anderson 2000). For the American scholar the Ottawa Convention signaled a romance between NGOs and International Organizations (Anderson 2000), as ICBL was a major effort leading to the global ban of landmines and the Nobel Peace Prize. The author talks about a partnership between Civil Society, sympathetic states, and international organizations.

What states are sympathetic? As of year-end 2008, the United States had not ratified the treaty. It was under the presidency of Bill Clinton that the United Sates did not attend the Ottawa summit in 1997. When and under what circumstances will the United States ratify a convention on small arms? The outcome is yet to be seen during the Obama Administration and beyond.

UN Convention to Control the Proliferation of Small Arms (2001)

The United Nations held a conference in 2001 that adopted the *Program of Action to Prevent, Combat, and Eradicate the Illicit Trade in Small Arms and Light Weapons in All Its Aspect.* Natalie J. Goldring, a senior fellow at the Edmund A. Walsh School of Foreign Service at Georgetown University, comments, "Unfortunately the world community is still far away from this goal." Goldring adds, "Governments can either continue with business as usual, which costs an estimated 1,000 deaths each day due to gun violence, or in the alternative, reach legally binding agreements to restrain illicit trade" (Deen 2008).

Judy Isacoff of the Africa Centre for Strategic Studies in Washington, DC points out that "not only do these weapons prolong violent conflicts, but their uncontrolled spread also poses a grave danger to long-term stability and development both domestically and within the region as a whole" (Deen, 2008).

Nairobi Protocol for the Prevention, Control, and Reduction of Small Arms and Light Weapons (2004)

The Nairobi Protocol brought together, on April 21, 2004, mandataries from eleven sub-Saharan African nations to acknowledge "the problem of the proliferation of illicit small arms and light weapons in the Great Lakes region and the Horn of Africa and the devastating consequences they have had in sustaining armed conflict and armed crime, degrading the environment, fuelling the illegal exploitation of natural resources and abetting terrorism and other serious crimes in the region" (Nairobi Protocol 2004).

The Protocol aims at: (1) preventing, combating and eradicating the illicit manufacturing of, trafficking in, possession of, and use of small arms and light weapons in the sub-region; and (2) preventing the excessive and destabilizing accumulation of small arms and light weapons in the sub-region (Nairobi Protocol 2004).

ECOWAS Convention on Small Arms and Light Weapons (2006)

The Economic Community of West African States (ECOWAS) is an association of 15 West African countries founded in 1975, whose mission is to promote economic integration in all fields of economic activity. The *ECOWAS Convention on Small Arms and Light Weapons, their Ammunition and other Related Materials* is a convention proposed by ECOWAS.

The president of the ECOWAS Commission, Mohammed Ibn Chambas, commented in October 2008, "The ECOWAS Convention on Small Arms is at the threshold of history, with only one country remaining to allow for the eventual entry into force of the legally binding instrument," adding, "it is our expectation that before the end of the year, the Convention will come into force" (AFRIK 2008).

Ilhan Berkol is a researcher at the Brussels-based Group for Research and Information on Peace and Security (GRIP). I phoned Berkol on January 9, 2008. In his analysis of the ECOWAS Convention, Berkol remarks, "The Small Arms Unit charged with overseeing the implementation of the Convention is a new entity that must have at its disposal the means necessary to carry out the tasks conferred on it by the Convention" (Berkol 2007).

The Oslo Convention on Cluster Ammunition (2008)

Cluster ammunition is defined as "a conventional ammunition that is designed to disperse or release explosive submunitions each weighing less than 20 kilograms, and includes those explosive submunitions" (CCM 2008).

The first significant use of cluster weapons took place during World War II when German planes threw butterfly bombs on English soil. The attack caused 1,000 casualties immediately and another 1,000 subsequently because of the weapons that did not detonate and were later activated by human contact. During the Vietnam War, more than nine million bomblets were left behind unexploded. These bomblets still cause casualties today. There are still significant stockpiles of cluster munitions, including 730 million cluster submunitions in the United States and a comparable amount in China and Russia (ICRC 2007).

Cluster munitions do not only cause civil casualties and lifelong mutilations. They also have an associated cost. It is estimated that only in Lebanon, 3,897 hectares of land were contaminated by cluster munitions, following the July to August 2006 war with Israel, of which 2,596 hectares were agricultural land. The loss for landowners is estimated at around $8,000 per year per landowner, for a total of 3,105 landowners (Crowther 2008).

107 countries adopted the convention on cluster ammunition in Dublin on May 30, 2008. The United States did not ratify the convention. Why did the United States remain outside the Oslo Convention? For years it was acknowledged that cluster munitions brought about a collateral damage in certain war-torn countries. The reality was finally addressed with the signature of the convention in 2008. The convention, which does not apply to mines, requires that each signatory member country agrees to never: (1) use cluster munitions; (2) develop, produce, otherwise acquire, stockpile, retain or transfer, directly or indirectly, cluster munitions; and (3) assist, encourage, or induce anyone to engage in any activity prohibited to a State Party under this Convention (CCM 2008).

The Geneva Declaration (2008)

The Geneva Declaration was signed by more than 90 states in September 2008 with a handful of exceptions, including George W. Bush's United States and Robert Mugabe's Zimbabwe. The declaration acknowledges the necessity to face the reality of the damage caused by small arms. The Geneva Declaration "calls on all signatories to strengthen efforts to integrate strategies for armed violence reduction and conflict prevention into national, regional, and multilateral development plans and programmes" (Geneva Declaration 2008). The declaration carries a 2015 deadline.

The declaration's report points out that of the 740,000 people who die each year because of armed conflict violence, as many as 490,000 take place outside war zones. Moreover, armed violence is the world's fourth cause of death for individuals aged between 15 and 44 (Geneva Declaration 2008).

Why did the United States remain outside the Geneva Declaration? The answer is connected to the United States Constitution's Second Amendment and the role of a strong lobby, the National Rifle Association. Lobbies are further analyzed in Chapter 12.

Arms Embargoes

In the joint report "United Nations Arms Embargoes: Their Impact on Arms Flows and Target Behaviour," SIPRI and Uppsala Universitet provide an analysis of the 27 arms embargoes the United Nations has imposed since 1990 (Fruchart, Holtom, et al., 2007). How effective are arms embargoes? To what extent do they limit the flow of arms? Is the United Nations able to enforce the embargoes?

The report classifies the 27 different embargoes along three categories: global security, government authority and conflict management. Global security refers to cases of Weapons of Mass Destruction and terrorism. Government authority includes cases in which illegitimate governments have taken power. Conflict management is related to armed conflicts where non-governmental armed forces may be acquiring arms through illicit means (Fruchart, Holtom, et al., 2007). As shown in Figure 8.1, the number of arms embargoes outstanding at the end of each year between 1990 and 2006 has continued to grow since 1990.[3]

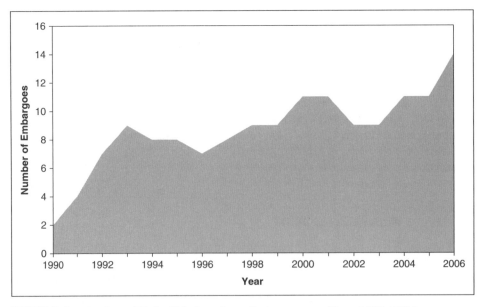

FIGURE 8.1   Number of United Nations Arms Embargoes per Year, 1990–2006
Source: Fruchart et al (2007). Reprinted with permission of the Stockholm International Peace Research Institute.

The report notes that in only six of the 27 embargoes the threat on behalf of the United Nations to the embargoed country was credible. The six cases were the former Yugoslavia (1991), Sierra Leone (1997), Taliban-controlled Afghanistan (2000), Liberia (2001), the Democratic Republic of the Congo (2005), and Eritrea and Ethiopia (2005).

Why is the United Nations not credible in 21 out of the 27 embargoes? There is a variety of factors described in the report. The first has to do with the timeframe between the threat and the imposition: "It is highly likely that there will not be any discernible increase in arms flows in these cases." The second has to do with the duration of the crisis: "The longer a crisis has been present, the more intractable the situation and the less likely it is that the threat will change target behaviour." The report provides two more interesting insights. Regarding the impact on arms flows to targets, in 9 out of 21 cases, "at least one state provided conventional arms to a target after a threat had been made." Regarding the impact on target behavior, in 7 of the 21 cases reviewed "at least one state publicly expressed its opposition to the actual imposition of an embargo" (Fruchart, Holtom, et al., 2007).

Post-Conflict Environment

ROBERT MUGGAH (SAT) is the research director at the Small Arms Trade of the Universit of Geneva, a Geneva-based think-tank in the small arms trade space. I paid a visit to the Small Arms Survey on July 16, 2008. Subsequently, I phoned Robert on October 31, 2008. Robert's paper "Emerging from the Shadow of War" reviews two effective methods to lessen the burden of small arms trade in post-conflict environments, methods that he calls interventions. The Canadian researcher notes, "Post-conflict environments can present as many risks to civilians as before or even during the armed conflict itself," pointing out the importance of assisting nation-states that have recently emerged from armed conflict (Muggah 2006).

The first intervention to assist in a post-conflict recovery is disarmament, demobilization, and reintegration (DDR). Robert observes, "By 1998, a report of the UN Secretary-General claimed that the reintegration of ex-combatants and others into productive society was one of the priorities of post-conflict peace building." The second intervention is the more obvious weapons reduction. Robert argues that in more recent times the connection between underdevelopment and terrorism has become more eloquent. As a result, bilateral donors and governments are paying more attention to arms reduction as an effective intervention that contributes to poverty reduction in failing states (Muggah 2006).

Buyback Programs

Buyback programs encompass an ex-post policy that aims at reducing the stock of small arms and light weapons by buying them back from their original owners. The program has proven effective in diminishing violence in Rio de Janeiro (Brazil). A study by Pablo Dreyfus, Luis Eduardo Guedes, Marcelo de Sousa Nascimiento, and others proves that "in Rio de Janeiro, small arms voluntary collection campaigns do indeed reduce armed violence," a conclusion that may help reduce the one hundred people who die each day in Brazil as a result of small arms (Dreyfus, Guedes, et al., 2008).

Of the 928,621 arms that circulate in Rio de Janeiro, 159,723 are regularly used in crime related activities. 29.6 percent of returned guns were registered, whereas 25.5 percent were unregistered. 31.7 percent of the individuals handing over guns had accomplished a high-school level of education, whereas 47.0 percent had stayed in school beyond high school. Overall the buyback program was successful in Rio de Janeiro, with a significant drop of 11 percent in the rate of firearms-related deaths in the city. The successful program was based on an 18-month awareness campaign and a broader small arms control strategy (Dreyfus, Guedes, et al., 2008).

Artwork by Claudio Muñoz.

CHAPTER 9

The Extractive Industries

If a state is to avoid the greatest plague of all—I mean civil war, though civil disintegration would be a better term—extreme poverty and wealth must not be allowed to arise in any section of the citizenbody, because both lead to both these disasters.

—Plato

Resource-rich countries are rich in oil, gas, and minerals. A handful of them have accomplished a successful management of their own natural resource wealth. Countries that have been successful are case studies from which unsuccessful countries can learn. Generally speaking, some of the more successful resource-rich countries serve as role models from which conclusions can be drawn—conclusions that can later be applied to developing countries that have, thus far, been unable to figure out an appropriate way to manage the revenue coming from the oil and extractive industries.

THE RESOURCE CURSE

The academic literature proposes different answers that explain why resource-rich countries tend to lag behind resource-poor countries. This chapter reviews a handful of countries that have been successful and draws conclusions on what resource-rich developing countries can learn from these strong performers. In the same manner, this chapter looks at countries that have become examples of bad revenue management. The literature review focuses on: (1) internal factors that explain the resource curse; (2) external factors; and (3) contract design between governments and multinationals.

Internal Factors

Countries with a good record of public governance are more likely to own their own mining companies and exploit their natural resources. This is the most appropriate scheme and maximizes the revenue states earn from the mining and extractive activity. Examples are Norway, Malaysia, and Chile. The advantage of this strategy is that "it avoids the agency problem of privatization itself, in the process of which the government may lose a substantial fraction of the value of the asset" (Humphreys, Sachs, et al., 2007).

Countries with a poor record of public governance are more likely to enter exploitation and exploration agreements with private companies whose goal is profit maximization. This coexistence of public and private interests generates an agency problem[1] between the state and the corporation. One additional difficulty faced by states that pursue this sort of agreement is the phenomenal bargaining power multinationals have over states. Multinationals will typically have access to a large pool of resources including consulting services, which countries oftentimes cannot access or afford. The ability of negotiating favorable terms in the exploration and exploitation agreements stems from a corporation's immense size compared to some developing economies. To counter this, smaller developing countries could pool their resources and profit from economies of scale.

Other secondary problems identified in academia are the onset of civil war, which is more likely to occur in oil-rich states (Humphreys, Sachs, et al., 2007), and the increase of inequality and widening of income differential between low-income and high-income households. These inequality and income disparities occur when the revenues collected by the government are not allocated appropriately across income levels and there are no redistributive policies in place. The exploitation of natural resources can also trigger regional confrontations and internal fights to secure revenue sharing. Regional confrontation sometimes leads to seccessionist movements that can drive an internal conflict to a regional war.[2]

The *Dutch disease* is a phenomenon associated with the appreciation of the local currency because of oil or mining exports. The Dutch disease makes the local agricultural and manufacturing goods less competitive in international markets. As a result, the proportion of the workforce employed in primary and secondary sectors (agriculture and manufacturing) tends to shrink as oil and minerals are exported. Due to the abundance of unskilled and inexpensive labor and the lack of industrial fabric, developing nations are better placed to be competitive in the primary (agriculture and farming) sector of the economy. The Dutch disease artificially alters the composition of the workforce and obliges some of the rural workforce to give up its once competitive agricultural activity to move to the city, seeking jobs in the manufacturing or services sector, which is not always feasible.

External Factors

External factors that contribute to the resource curse can be identified from what happens to resource-rich developing countries that have suffered economic decline in spite of their natural endowment. A strong argument is provided by Daniel Lederman and William F. Maloney in *Natural Resources: Neither Course nor Destiny* (2007). The authors argue, "The resource curse is not about resources per se, but about imperfect credit markets." Moreover, they conclude (Lederman and Maloney 2007):

> *In the 1970s commodity prices were high, which led developing countries to use them as collateral for debt. The 1980s saw a significant fall in those prices, leaving developing countries with a considerable amount of debt and a low flow of foreign resources to pay them. The low-growth curse appears to be a debt-overhang problem.*

The last of the statements above is conclusive and denotes that, among poor countries with a high endowment of natural resources, the least indebted are the least exposed to the resource curse. This is an important conclusion about the potential of resource-rich developing countries to prosper.

The price of natural resources is impacted by the increasing variability of commodity markets, driven by (1) the increasing sophistication of the financial instruments used to trade oil, gas, and minerals, and (2) the larger swings in supply and demand experienced with the participation of China and India along with other emerging powers in global trade. According to Graham A. Davis, a professor in the division of economics and business at the Colorado School of Mines, "price fluctuations of 30 percent or more within a year are common," as a result of which, "mineral-exporting countries suffer sharp swings in government revenues and foreign exchange earnings during the global business cycle" (Davis and Tilton 2007).

The ability of a state to borrow today against future revenues coming from the extractive industries is a matter of: (1) its repayment record; and (2) the present value of its future revenues. The first variable is measured by a country's sovereign rating, as determined by the international rating agencies Moody's, Standard and Poor's, and Fitch Ratings. The sovereign rating will be explained and studied later in this chapter. The second variable is a function of the future price of commodities. Commodities have suffered from increasing price volatility that makes it harder to forecast what the price of oil, gas, or minerals will be in the future. If a country borrows too much and commodity prices drop, the country could accumulate significant debt that it would then be unable to repay. This debt would carry a higher interest payment that the country would then have to pay to its creditors, thereby shrinking the budget allocated to the provision of public goods such as education and health care. The consequences could be detrimental to a country's ability to prosper.

Mansur Muhtar (FMN) is Nigeria's minister of finance and the former executive director representing Nigeria and Sao Tome and Prince at the African Development Bank. I spoke with Mansur on August 20, 2008. In March 2009, Nigeria announced it would issue $500 million in 10-year bonds that the country would pay with future proceeds from the sale of oil. But the economic slowdown and the descending oil prices made Mansur step back, pointing out that "we are hopeful, if not optimistic that by midyear, based on forecasts, oil prices will recover, at least we will be able to cover our benchmark" (Ghana Business News 2009). Consequently, borrowing against a country's future revenues is not always a good idea. A better approach is to build up a sovereign wealth fund that would then allow a country to smooth its revenues and cover the gap of running a deficit.

Contract Design

A third variable that can impact a country's success or failure is determined by the negotiation stage leading to the signature of an agreement between a country and a corporation. This dimension is neither internal nor external, but an area that can and should be carefully monitored by the local authorities in order to maximize the return on the resource they have decided to exploit in this way.

A country should first decide whether it runs a state-owned company or invites private corporations to exploit its natural resources. The former applies to countries like Norway, Malaysia, Venezuela, or Mexico. The latter is a more common arrangement in low-income countries with poor levels of public governance.

Once a country decides not to run a state-owned company, the next stage involves the negotiation of the contract terms between a foreign company and the local government. This negotiation includes choosing the type of contract and the nature of the revenues that the local government will receive.

Daniel Johnston is the founder and chief executive of Daniel Johnston & Co., Inc, consultants to the Petroleum Industry Worldwide. I phoned Johnston on December 16, 2008. According to Johnston (2003), there are two major types of contract between a multinational and a national government, namely concessionary systems and production-sharing contracts:

1. Under a concessionary system, the oil company has title to the crude oil produced, against which it typically pays royalties and taxes.
2. Under a production-sharing contract, the contractor carries out exploration and/or development work on behalf of the host country for a fee. All ordinary exploration risk is borne by the state. This kind of arrangement is more characteristic of the Middle Eastern region, where the state often has substantial capital but seeks only expertise. Under pure service contracts, the government retains title to the mineral resources.

In production-sharing contracts (PSC), the national government is still guaranteed a share of the revenues. Johnston comments, "With any PSC that has a cost recovery limit, the government will be guaranteed a share of production in each accounting period by virtue of the combination of the limit and the subsequent profit oil split" (Johnston 2003). Currently, the average royalty amounts to 7 percent.

There is no ideal contract to be signed between a government and a multinational. Governments that decide to invite private companies to exploit their natural resources should have the ability to change the terms of a contract in the case of a commodity boom.

How frequently should contracts be revised to update them to the conditions of the market and the global economy? The optimum contract typically changes depending on the value of commodities (low-medium-high price scenario). For model contracts, Johnston thinks that two to three years is not unreasonable, although a good design should be able to withstand a longer test period. For existing contracts, Johnston notes that the revision should be a contractual matter (Johnston 2003).

A CONTRIBUTOR TO PUBLIC BUDGETING

Revenues from oil and mining activity should feed a government's budget and help finance education, health care, and infrastructure. When revenues are not spent directly, they should be accumulated in a wealth fund that becomes an endowment to be spent by future generations.

Revenue management is successful if the revenue allocation process fulfills the citizen's basic needs via the provision of public goods such as education or health care. In order to succeed, revenue management should be administered by an administration that shows high levels of transparency and public governance. Transparency is necessary to make sure that each dollar of revenue is monitored and is not lost on its way from the mine to the government via corruption or bribery either at the governmental or the corporate level. Public governance guarantees the appropriate use of the available revenues.

More Transparency for Corporations

A meeting between campaigners and investors that took place in London in 2008, with representatives of some of the largest mining and oil companies and the International Accounting Standards Board, is likely to persuade the latter to introduce country-by-country reporting that would be adopted as soon as 2010 and help diminish the culture of secrecy and corruption present in some of the mining corporations (Mathiason 2008).

A piece published by the Tax Justice Network under the name "How to Make Multinational Companies More Transparent" (Murphy 2008) proposes country-by-country reporting as a way to enforce more accountability of corporations. There is concern that national governments do not profit from skyrocketing commodity prices, and that the upside is mostly allocated to corporations' shareholders through earnings and dividends. The report emphasizes that although all countries suffer from tax avoidance, poor countries are most vulnerable: "They rarely have the necessary resources and capability to challenge corporations trading in their countries. Poorer countries' public finances also often depend to a larger degree on corporate taxes than wealthier countries do, so tax avoidance by multinational corporations has proportionately greater impact on them" (Murphy 2008). Corporations will use three mechanisms to avoid or reduce taxes without breaking the law. These three mechanisms are described by Murphy (2008):

1. Finding and exploiting loopholes in domestic tax laws.
2. Adjusting a company's accounting to reduce its tax bill.
3. Shifting profits out of a country with a higher tax rate and into a country with a lower tax rate.

The most common way of shifting profits out of a country is by a transfer pricing arrangement, which can apply to the sale of raw materials, including commodities. In a transfer pricing arrangement, two national subsidiaries of a corporation can buy and sell from each other products and raw materials at prices that can be artificially set and do not relate to any market forces of supply and demand.

According to Murphy (2008), the International Accounting Standards Board has the ability to enforce country-by-country reporting that would end the malpractices of tax avoidance. More than 60 percent of world trade takes place within subsidiaries that belong in the same corporation.

In 2008 Transparency International released its *Bribe Payers Index*. According to the report, "companies based in emerging economic giants, such as China, India, and Russia, are perceived to routinely engage in bribery when doing business abroad" (Transparency 2008). The report ranks the top 25 exporters according to the likelihood that their corporations are getting involved in bribery while doing business abroad. The bottom five countries are from best to worst: Brazil, India, Mexico, China, and Russia. By regions, China, South Africa, and India are the worst performers in Africa and the Middle East; Taiwan, South Korea, and India are the worst performers in the Asia Pacific region; Spain, Italy, and China are the worst performers in Europe and the United States; and Italy, Spain, and China are the worst performers in Latin America.

Bribery is organized into three different categories, namely: (1) bribery to high-ranking politicians or political parties; (2) bribery to low-level public officials to speed things up; and (3) use of personal and family relationships in public contracting. The report also classifies bribery by 19 sectors. In the "bribery of public officials," Oil & Gas and Mining are in the top five of the sectors where bribes occur most often, and are more likely to be paid (Transparency 2008).

Reports of this nature are exemplary and essential to understanding the scope and repercussion of corruption. Oil, gas, and mining are among the sectors where the incidence of bribery is more widespread. Multinationals from China, India, and Russia, three emerging economies with a large representation in the oil and mining industries, are most likely to bribe public officials. This raises an additional concern, because China, India, and Russia have a large share of the market of multinationals operating in oil, gas, and mining.

Transparency of Governments

Developing countries have historically been less able to raise taxes than developed countries. A state finances the delivery of its public services through public expenditure. Public expenditure is a function of a government's ability to raise revenue through taxation. In developing countries, much of the economy is informal and immune to the taxation efforts of the relevant taxation authority. As a result, the government has little room for maneuvering and has to rely on two sources of revenue: (1) tariffs; and (2) corporate taxes on oil and mining companies. In many resource-rich countries, the latter is where a majority of taxation revenue comes from. Therefore, the ability to raise taxation revenue from the oil and mining industries, and utilize the revenue appropriately is crucial to securing the successful provision of public goods.

GAME CHANGERS

Based on what we know about why a majority of resource-rich developing countries have entered a trap they have rarely been able to leave, there is a series of structural features that, if applied systematically and if taken seriously, could help developing countries, which today are starting to explore and exploit their natural resources, thereby avoiding the resource curse.

Wotan Swiegers is the chairman of the Atomic Energy Board of Namibia and the principal officer of the Chamber of Mines of Namibia. I met Swiegers on April 14, 2009, at Kupferpfanne Restaurant in Swakopmund (Namibia). For Swiegers, drafting standards and the regulation that new mining companies would have to comply with are necessary prerequisites in countries that, like Namibia, are starting to tap their natural resources.

Monitoring of Revenue Management

Monitoring and reporting of each dollar earned from oil and mining activities should be carried out by both corporations and national governments. This monitoring and reporting is done today on a voluntary basis and there is no compulsion to subscribe to any rules or international standards.

Accountability

National governments and multinationals have to be accountable for their actions vis-à-vis their citizens and shareholders. Accountability must be enforced and acts of misconduct, bribery, and corruption should be publicized and penalized accordingly.

Improving Credit Ratings

Sovereign ratings play an indirect role in the likelihood of the occurrence of the resource curse. Resource-rich countries increased their external debt significantly in the 1970s, using their future revenues from the mining industry as collateral to be used for future repayments (Lederman and Maloney 2007). Only a handful of countries, mostly industrialized, had a sovereign rating in the 1970s. Thus, the interest rate attached to any outstanding loans granted to developing countries by Western banks was determined on an ad hoc basis between the relevant commercial bank and the resource-rich country.

Credit ratings are used to determine the appeal of a country as an investment destination. A credit rating also determines the cost of borrowing a country's government, and corporations have to assume when requesting a loan from the international markets. It is a better idea to improve a country's sovereign rating prior to increasing a country's external debt by borrowing from the international markets. Increasing a country's external debt under a mediocre sovereign rating implies assuming high interest payments throughout the life of the loan. Any significant borrowing should be postponed until the country has built up an investment-grade rating and is ready to demonstrate a repayment capability. In the meantime the revenues coming from the mining activity should be either spent in the provision of public goods, or accumulated via a sovereign wealth fund. A developing country should wait to improve its sovereign rating from below investment-grade to investment-grade before it starts issuing national debt.

Dutch Disease

A country that exports commodities such as oil and minerals will typically see its exchange rate appreciate. With a stronger local currency, the country's agricultural goods become less competitive in world markets. Accordingly, the share of agriculture in the labor force could shrink and lose workforce to the services sector. Resource-rich countries can thus become food importers instead of exporters.

Economic policies and financial instruments that maintain a competitive exchange rate and avoid or hedge against the appreciation of the local currency will help local farmers maintain their competitiveness in international markets.

Provision of Basic Welfare

Resource-rich countries may increase their inequality if the revenues coming from the oil and mining activity are not redistributed appropriately. Recent examples of extreme inequality are seen in resource-rich Equatorial Guinea or Namibia. The Gini coefficient (defined in Chapter 5) of Namibia is 0.74 (World Bank 2007c). Per capita income in Namibia has almost doubled since 2001, yet the country continues to be highly unequal. Per capita income in Equatorial Guinea has more than quadrupled since 2003, yet the oil revenues remain in the hands of the political elite.

A commitment on behalf of the local authorities to provide a minimum welfare state to the extreme poor, or a minimum basic income (see Chapter 5 for a discussion on basic income) could facilitate a reduction of inequality at the same time that it helps educate a healthier workforce. Equatorial Guinea is part of the Extractive Industries Transparency Initiative (EITI), whereas Namibia is not. EITI is presented in the next section.

WHAT IS BEING DONE

This section reviews what is being done to date in areas such as transparency and sustainability by international institutions, governments, and nonprofit and Civil Society organizations.

Transparency

In the area of transparency, three nonprofit organizations are making significant headway. They are the Extractive Industries Transparency Initiative (EITI), Publish What You Pay (PWYP), and the Revenue Watch Institute (RWI).

> The **Extractive Industries Transparency Initiative (EITI)** is a coalition that includes governments, corporations and Civil Society organizations that advise resource-rich developing countries on what is the appropriate roadmap to success in the management of their natural resource wealth. **EDDIE RICH** (MIN) is the deputy head and regional director for Anglophone/Lusophone Africa and the Middle East of EITI. I phoned Eddie on May 14, 2008. In his opinion, "There is strong evidence showing that transparency of the management of the revenues from natural resources is a necessary step in avoiding the resource curse."

> **Publish What You Pay (PWYP)** is a global Civil Society coalition that campaigns for greater transparency and accountability in the payment, receipt, and management of revenues from the oil, gas, and mining sectors. **Radhika Sarin** (MIN) is the international coordinator of the PWYP campaign. I phoned Radhika on June 23, 2008. How does PWYP work with EITI to make sure its intent is included in EITI's agenda? For Radhika, "PWYP members are the local watchdogs of EITI, often the first to capture the realities of EITI on the ground and the challenges and obstacles to successful implementation."

> The **Revenue Watch Institute (RWI)** encourages the responsible management of natural resources for the public good. RWI argues that an effective revenue management and an increased transparency can help drive development and national growth.

Sustainability

The Dow Jones Sustainability Index ranks the most sustainable companies in the world according to a total of 19 categories. Rio Tinto and Anglo American are the two most sustainable mining companies in the world. The Dow Jones assessment is an indicator that allows responsible investors to determine what companies are doing a better job at incorporating environmental and labor standards to their operations.

A new mining strategy requires a leading mining authority. **PRESTON CHIARO** (MIN) is the former global head of energy and minerals at Rio Tinto and the chairman of the World Coal Institute. I met Preston at the New Yorker Hotel on Eighth Avenue in New York City on May 27, 2008 and again at the Rio Tinto headquarters in London on March 8, 2009. Preston suggested that I visit Rio Tinto's subsidiary in Namibia, Rossing Uranium Limited, which is introduced in Chapter 19.

Mark Moody-Stuart is the chairman of Anglo American. Anglo American is one of the largest mining groups in the world. The company operates in 45 countries and has 190,000 employees, with earnings in 2008 amounting to $5.2 billion. I phoned Moody-Stuart on November 28, 2008.

What does Anglo American do to persuade its shareholders about the importance of sustainability? For Moody-Stuart, "Much of the value of a resource company lies in the expectation of its future development, so shareholders are interested in matters which can affect that future positively or negatively." Every year Anglo American publishes a *Report to Society*, which covers economic, social, and environmental aspects of the company's operations. The report is then reviewed by shareholders who can raise questions or point to issues on which they would like more information. Moody-Stuart concludes, "The shareholders can use the report to judge our performance against our competitors and to assess what risks we run."

WHAT CAN BE DONE

Innovative policy-making could help developing countries better manage their natural resources. This section presents several ideas for the improvement of revenue supervision, helping developing countries reach fair deals when they negotiate contract terms with corporations, and linking new foreign aid to the allocation of natural resource wealth.

Tracking the Use of Revenue

Promising initiatives such as EITI foster an environment of cooperation that aims at increasing the transparency and accountability of both governments and corporations. However, there is no supranational body with a supervisory role that denounces malpractices of oil and mining companies with regard to the environment or labor standards, and the mismanagement and misallocation of a country's natural resource wealth by its political elite. Any initiative that increases the level of supervision of the activities of both corporations and governments will act as a deterrent of bad conduct and the illicit/illegitimate appropriation of funds.

Fairness of a Contract

The bargaining power of corporations compared to that of governments of low-income countries puts the latter at a serious disadvantage when negotiating the terms of a contract. Developing countries suffer from the competition that takes place among poor countries that are sometimes desperate to attract foreign direct investment to their soil. Countries, states, and regions compete, lowering corporate taxes, labor standards, and environmental requirements. It is a practice that largely benefits the corporation seeking to minimize its operating costs and maximize its profit margins. Public corporations whose priority is profit maximization will naturally seek and find the lowest common denominator in countries that end up surrendering to the demands of corporate managers.

Many Latin American countries, including Bolivia and Ecuador, have either nationalized their natural resources or renegotiated contracts signed when commodities were not experiencing the boom in prices that came to an end in late 2008. Developing nations need to be able to access the expertise and know-how oftentimes only available to corporations. They also need to make sure the entities providing them with these services are ready to defend their interests and not that of the corporations. An independent body whose main goal is to help low-income, resource-rich countries reach better agreements could boost their ability to maximize the terms of an exploration and exploitation contract.

New Standards of Contract Design

To what extent would multinationals be willing to embrace new standards of contract design? Conditionality also has to apply to corporations if they are not undergoing a transition into more environmentally friendly operating models. Self-regulation on behalf of oil and mining companies may unfortunately be working in only a handful of instances, for example, in companies ranked and considered most sustainable in their category.

New standards of contract design could allocate a fair share of the revenue stream to developing countries, but would also require that corporations embrace sustainable operating methods that aim at developing the rural communities where they settle and respecting the environment.

John Tilton is a professor of economics at the Colorado School of Mines. I phoned Tilton on December 5, 2008. How important is asymmetric information when closing a mining contract? Are governments at a disadvantage compared with multinationals because the latter can tap into more brain power? Tilton points out, "In some countries there is no negotiation between the firm and the government; the firm simply has to comply with the requirements of the country's legal system to develop a mine." Tilton further notes, "The problem arises because the firm is likely to know much more about the specific deposit in question than the developing country."

Artwork by Claudio Muñoz.

CHAPTER 10

Financial Architecture

Enormous disparity, both economic and political, characterizes our shared world, and disparity, however caused or perceived, promotes among some powerful feelings of alienation and fatality. Capitalism can do a much better job of giving everyone a stake in prosperity, ameliorating part of the tendencies toward dissociation. Capitalism maintains the structure of tax havens, secrecy jurisdictions, dummy corporations, mispricings, fake transactions, and more, which terrorists utilize in the same way as criminal syndicates.
—Raymond Baker, *Capitalism's Achilles Heel*

ANew Architecture of capitalism requires a leading financial reformer. **RAYMOND BAKER** (FIN) is one of the leading authorities in financial integrity. I met Raymond on January 17, 2008, at the Brookings Institution in Washington, DC. Raymond is the director of Global Financial Integrity (GFI) and the author of *Capitalism's Achilles Heel*. I would fall short if I said that Raymond's book is a masterpiece.

Raymond begins his outstanding book by reminding readers, "I am all for the free-market system—free trade, free movement of capital, free convertibility of currencies. I do, however, add a proviso to this: provided it's legal" (Baker 2005). I could not agree more with Raymond, who continues his passionate discourse and points out that "because the business of falsified pricing underlies so much of global capitalism and has brought more money into Western coffers than it has taken out, Western nations are reticent to attack the goose that lays the golden egg" (Baker 2005). What is then so wrong with the current version of capitalism? What are the numbers? Why is it causing harm and what does this harm translate into? In an article published in the English newspaper *The Guardian*, entitled "A Chance to Crack Down on Africa's Loot-Seeking Elites," Oxford economist Paul Collier comments, "The loot-seeking elites that control parts of Africa illicitly send capital out of the region to the tune of $20 to $28 billion per year" (Collier 2008). Approximately $500 to $800 billion cross-border flow of proceeds related to corruption and tax-evasion leave the developing world and transitional economies every year (Baker and Joly 2008a), $30 billion of which leaves Africa (Kar and Cartwright-Smith 2009).

Raymond coauthored a piece in the September-October 2008 issue of *The American Interest* entitled "Catching Up With Corruption." Along with fellow writers John Christensen of Tax Justice Network and Nicholas Shaxson of the Chatam

House, Raymond calls for an expansion of the concept of corruption, and a refining of our perceptions of corruption. The extension of the concept should incorporate that "tax evasion is identified as a form of corruption, even if it does not involve the abuse of public office or entrusted power" (Baker, Christensen, et al., 2008b). Currently Transparency International, the independent civil society organization focusing on corruption, fails to incorporate tax evasion as a form of corruption. If it did, Singapore and Switzerland would fall in the international rankings of transparency.

Miguel Schloss (INI) was executive director of Transparency International from 1998 to 2002. I phoned Miguel on July 3, 2009. For the Chilean economist, "any definition, at the end of the day, is a convention on where one sets the boundaries on a concept. The wider the definition, and the more disparate the activities covered by it, the greater the prospect that effective action is bound to be constrained or diffused." It is time for Transparency International to expand the definition of corruption and adapt it to the reality of an unequal world where the North perpetuates a user's manual that benefits the better off in both Hemispheres.

For Raymond the explanation behind illicit money flows is linked either to portfolio diversification or to "fears of political or economic instability or fears of taxation, inflation or confiscation." GFI's best estimate is that "illicit financial flows out of developing countries are some $850 billion to $1 trillion a year," an estimate Raymond considers conservative (Kar and Cartwright-Smith 2009).

Today's capitalism is in desperate need of a new soul. Why does capitalism need a new soul? Raymond provides the answer: "A capitalist system with as much or more dirty money moving offshore illegally to the rich as the total amount of money available domestically to the poor is in deep trouble" (Baker 2005).

Thank you Raymond for being a giant on whose shoulders I can look ahead and contemplate a fairer capitalism. Thank you for concluding your masterpiece with the words "justice has the ability to be self-correcting, and it is in the direction of greater justice that capitalism must move" (Baker 2005). The new soul of capitalism is discussed in more depth in Chapter 17, where the writings of William Greider and John C. Bogle will shed light on what kind of soul is actually needed.

I hear the voice of the giants of today. I hear them shouting in desperate urgency that reform is necessary. Let's move ahead. Let's create a team of giants able to persuade our political elites that reform is needed, and that we need to bring more justice to the current version of capitalism.

REDEFINED CAPITALISM VERSUS MARXISM

In November 2005, I wrote the essay "Redefining Capitalism," which would become one of the finalist papers in the competition for the Robin Cosgrove Prize for Ethics in Finance. I finished writing the paper the very same day that I started reading Karl Marx's *Communist Manifesto*, the Manifesto of the Communist Party. I decided to read Marx's *Communist Manifesto* because some of the colleagues with whom I worked at an insurance company[1] in New York City would call me a communist. But while my colleagues may have thought I was a communist, I may have thought they were extreme capitalists. (Note that I said my colleagues and not my comrades.)

What does Marx's Manifesto argue? According to Martin Malia, an economist and former faculty member at the University of California at Berkeley, "the Manifesto's aim was to promote a Second Coming of the French Revolution in socialist guise" (Malia 1998). Malia concludes, "Marxism was born, not as a critique of mature capitalism, as is usually supposed, but as a theory of revolution to overcome German backwardness" (Malia 1998).

In the preface to the Manifesto's German edition of 1883, Marx comments, "All history has been a history of class struggles, of struggles between exploited and exploiting, between dominated and dominating clases at various stages of social evolution" (Marx 1848). For Marx, "The modern bourgeois society has but established new conditions of oppression, new forms of struggle in place of the old ones" (Marx 1848). He further remarks, "The theory of the Communists may be summed up in the single sentence: abolition of private property," and concludes, "It has been objected, that upon the abolition of private property all work will cease, and universal laziness will overtake us" (Marx 1848).

For Marx, Utopian Socialists are those who "reject all political, and especially all revolutionary action, they wish to attain their ends by peaceful means and endeavour, by small experiments, necessarily doomed to failure, and by the force of example, to pave the way for the new social gospel" (Marx 1848).

I would be what Marx understands as a Utopian Socialist. And many of those who advocate and demand more justice would also be Utopian Socialists. I reject all revolutionary action through violent means. I embrace peaceful means and endeavors and the use of Weapons of Mass Persuasion to deliver a message of urgency. Communism is a failed experiment of the twentieth century. The reference for capitalism is not on the other side of the political spectrum, it is above, in the sky. Capitalism has to mature and become fair and ethical.

Erik Ringmar may be a Social Utopian of the twenty-first century. In his book *Surviving Capitalism*, the former professor of political science at the London School of Economics illustrates the fight between extreme capitalism and democratic society (2005). For Ringmar, "The question is not how capitalism can be replaced with something else, the question is rather how its negative consequences can be avoided." The English scholar also points out (Ringmar 2005):

> *Instead of talking about the actual world, what economists typically do is to talk about the version of the world they have created in their theoretical models. Whereas the actual world is messy and full of awkward facts, the world of the model is neatly organized in accordance with a few basic principles.*

It is for this particular reason that economists are the mathematicians and physicists of capitalism, not its architects or engineers. It is urgent that we use their theory to build a New Architecture, a redefined version of today's old-fashioned capitalism, a capitalist system on the verge of collapse. Ringmar concludes, "While capitalism provided the welfare state with sufficient resources to discharge its functions, the welfare state provided the social infrastructure that made capitalism acceptable" (Ringmar 2005).

TAX HAVENS

Tax havens are also known as fiscal havens or offshore financial centers. In 1998 the OECD determined the four factors that define a tax haven: (1) no or nominal tax on the relevant income; (2) lack of effective exchange of information; (3) lack of transparency; and (4) no substantial activities (Owens and Saint-Amans 2009).

Daniel J. Mitchell, a senior fellow at the CATO Institute, thinks that *Tax Havens Are a Blessing* (2008). Mitchell forgot to add that tax havens are a blessing, but exclusively for the Pirates of Heartless Capitalism and their friends the Lobbies and the Elites. Mitchell argues that today's taxes in OECD countries are much lower than in 1980 thanks to tax havens. The reality is that starting in 1980, taxes started to lower because of the free-market economics praised and promoted by Ronald Reagan and Margaret Thatcher. You do not need tax havens to sell a logic that argues that the smaller size of a government, the better it will fare in terms of taxes. Mitchell also argues that the United States could be considered the world's largest tax haven. I welcome the suggestion. If this is the case, President Barack Obama and his successors have a lot of homework to do.

It is perhaps time to crackdown Delaware and Nevada, as it is time to crackdown Luxembourg and Ireland. Mitchell argues that thanks to the advantageous fiscal incentives of Delaware and Nevada, the United States has been able to attract $12 trillion in foreign investment (Mitchell 2008). I am confident that the Chinese have not bought over one trillion dollars in treasuries because of Delaware and Nevada, but because the United States has a triple-A sovereign rating and the dollar is the world's de facto reserve currency. Actually the idea that foreign direct investment flows into the United States because the United States is a tax haven undermines many more important factors that trigger foreign direct investment, such as property rights, the rule of law, or a low political risk. These are the factors that have determined the success of the United States. We have to compete to become better, not to become worse. Foreign direct investment is more closely reviewed in Chapter 25.

What are tax havens and how are they classified? According to the OECD there are currently 38 tax havens, categorized into cooperative and noncooperative. Prior to the second G20 summit that took place in London in April 2009, three tax havens were noncooperative, namely: Andorra, Liechenstein, and Monaco, three small nations located in the core of the European Union. The three small nations benefited from the regulator's oversight that allowed them to operate with substantial advantage in expense of the average investor and saver in the EU-27. According to the OECD, "Andorra, Liechtenstein and Monaco have endorsed the OECD standards and indicated their willingness to change their domestic legislation and to enter into agreements for the exchange of information." As of July 2009 all 38 tax havens had committed "to improving transparency and establishing effective exchange of information in tax matters" (Owens and Saint-Amans 2009). The ongoing impact of this effective exchange remains to be seen.

Out of the 38 tax havens, 39 percent are territory of a sovereign country, whereas 61 percent are a country itself. 79 percent of tax havens are located in islands with an aggregate population of barely five and a half million, the same number of inhabitants as the metropolitan area of Madrid (Spain). Subtracting the population of Malta and Cyprus, tax havens and members of the European Union, the aggregate population of the remainder of these paradise-islands adds up to slightly over four million.

Precisely a total of 22 out of 38 tax havens are either an overseas territory of the United Kingdom or one of its former colonies. The United Kingdom exploits its financial privilege to secure the maintenance of the world's most leveraged financial industry. This is a doubtful accomplishment if the collateral damage caused is greater than the aggregate gain that only benefits a few, a minority of lucky ones who intend to convince the rest of the world's population that the maximization of economic profit dictated by Adam Smith's invisible hand is the way to operate according to a set of orthodox market principles.[2]

Why are tax havens detrimental for economic growth and development? Tax havens hold a total of $13 trillion in untaxed wealth that represents $255 billion of additional revenue that governments would have at their disposal every year (Mathiason 2009).

Offshore Banking

The Offshore Group of Banking Supervisors (OGBS) is the association of international offshore banking centers. It is the equivalent of the Guild of Pirates of Heartless Capitalism. The association is chaired by Colin Powell, not to be mistaken with former Secretary of State Colin Powell.

In the twenty-fifth annual meeting of the OGBS that took place in the Cayman Islands on July 5, 2005, Chairman Powell pointed out, "For our part we are delighted that our high standards of compliance are increasingly being recognized internationally."[3] The OGBS has two levels of membership. On the one hand, pirates can be members. Among the members we find the following: Aruba, Bahamas, Barbados, Bermuda, British Virgin Islands, Guernsey, Isle of Man, Jersey, Labuan, Macau (China), Mauritius, Netherlands, Antilles, Panama, Samoa, and Vanuatu. Pirates can also be observers. Among the observers we find the following: Eastern Caribbean Central Bank, Antigua-Barbuda, and the Cook Islands.

Welcome to the World of the Bretton Woods Elites, where pirates can organize themselves in a guild and choose between two levels of membership. You can be a member pirate or an observer pirate. Pirates are pirates, independent from how they market themselves. I would like to make this clear. Offshore bankers are masters of the public campaign, and magicians in the use of the words. A bad-smelling individual is a bad-smelling individual, independent from the amount of perfume he or she wears. A bold individual is bold, independent from how good and expensive the wig he or she wears is.

Remember the quote from Abraham Lincoln: "You can fool all the people some of the time, and some of the people all the time, but you cannot fool all the people all the time." The Pirates of Heartless Capitalism have fooled a majority of us all of the time. But this has got to stop. Abraham Lincoln's words are inspiring at this time and President Barack Obama is a big fan of Abraham Lincoln. What are the requirements to become a member pirate? The conditions of membership are clearly stated by OGBS:[4]

- A clear commitment is made to the Basel Committee on Banking Supervision's Core Principles.
- A clear commitment is made to the 40 Recommendations of the Financial Action Task Force on money laundering, and the 9 Special Recommendations of the Task Force on terrorist financing.

- The necessary legislation and administration to put these commitments into effect is in place or in early prospect.
- There is evidence of either a satisfactory track record of translating the commitments into effect or a detailed plan for doing so within a reasonable time frame.
- The commitments are entered into with the knowledge and support of the relevant political authority.

So, what exactly is wrong with being a member pirate? Beware the language of offshore bankers and financiers; they are cunning, and they are clever. It would seem that offshore banking centers fight terrorism and money laundering, while behind the scenes, they are maintaining banking secrecy. After all, the first rule of a Pirate of Heartless Capitalism is to pretend you are no pirate. So where is their wrongdoing, if any? How can we blame pirates that do no harm? The answer involves banking secrecy and the restriction of the definition of money laundering to a handful of activities including terrorism and drug trafficking, but excluding many other activities.

40 Recommendations (Counter-Measures) on Money Laundering   The Financial Action Task Force (FATF) is an inter-governmental body of 34 members (the world's richest countries) in charge of setting international standards to combat money laundering and terrorist financing. In 2003 the FATF drafted the 40 recommendations on money laundering. According to FATF:[5]

> *The revised 40 Recommendations now apply not only to money laundering but also to terrorist financing, and when combined with the 9 Special Recommendations on Terrorist Financing provide an enhanced, comprehensive and consistent framework of measures for combating money laundering and terrorist financing.*

The 40 recommendations were originally drafted in 1990 and since then have been updated. The 40 recommendations are long, comprehensive, and involve exhaustive monitoring and supervision on behalf of banks and financial institutions.

9 Special Recommendations on Terrorist Financing   The 9 Special Recommendations on Terrorist Financing complement the 40 recommendations on money laundering. They were proposed subsequent to the approval in 1999 of the United Nations International Convention for the Suppression of the Financing of Terrorism.

FATF's Weaknesses   According to Global Witness, FATF's 40 + 9 Recommendations have four significant weaknesses that ought to be tackled if they are to be effective (Global Witness 2009):

1. FATF has no legal enforcement powers of its own, due to its status as an inter-governmental body that consists of its member states.
2. FATF appears to operate in isolation from many of the other actors who are working on anti-corruption efforts.
3. FATF's focus on terrorist financing has not been matched by an equal attention to the fight against corrupt funds, and might even have distracted from it.

4. There are loopholes in the standards that FATF promotes, which means that the anti-money laundering framework that it is promoting is not sufficient to curtail the flows of corrupt money.

The Stop Tax Haven Abuse Act

On March 2, 2009, the Democratic Senator for Michigan Carl Levin introduced the *Stop Tax Haven Abuse Act*. The next day the Democratic Representative from Texas Lloyd Doggett introduced a similar bill in the House of Representatives. The new piece of legislation has two new provisions: (1) any offshore fund with over $50 million of assets that is managed from the United States would be subject to federal corporate income tax; (2) payments made on swaps that reference U.S. equities would be subject to a 30 percent dividend tax.

On March 6, 2009, the Law Firm Cadwalader, Wickersham & Taft LLP, based in New York City, sent a seven-page memo to their Clients & Friends. In the memo the law firm notes that if the law were enacted, "many U.S. managers would either be forced to withdraw from the management of foreign funds or conduct that management activity from London or another offshore location" (Cadwalader 2009).

In March 2009, the Law Firm Hunton & Williams LLP issued a Client Alert to inform its clients about the new bill. In the alert the law firm points out that "the Senate Bill contains provisions that would codify the economic substance doctrine, impose certain rebuttable presumptions regarding control of foreign entities, apply anti-money laundering rules to hedge funds and private equity funds, and extend Patriot Act measures to entities that impede U.S. tax enforcement" (Hunton 2009).

Law Firms warned the Pirates of Heartless Capitalism about the new regulation in place only a handful of days after it was passed. Welcome to the World of the Bretton Woods Elites, where Law Schools issue graduates that become friends with the Pirates of Heartless Capitalism and work to perpetuate a status quo that undermines our ability, as a global community, to move forward in the development agenda, to build a fairer world, and to start writing the History of Tomorrow.

Under the Umbrella of the British Financial Authority

Michael Foot is Chairman of the Promontory Financial Group and is based in London. The Promontory Financial Group is one of the leading financial firms and operates out of eight global offices. According to his biography on Promontory's web site,[6] Foot joined Promontory from the Central Bank of the Bahamas, where he worked as Inspector of Banks & Trust Companies from 2004 to 2007. Prior to his tenure in the Bahamas, Foot was a managing director of the Financial Services Authority (FSA). Foot is certainly an insider.

Peter Neville is the director general of the Guernsey Financial Services Commission. According to Neville, the U.K. government had appointed Foot to undertake a review of the British offshore financial services. I hope a future revision encommended to Foot by the U.K. government will incorporate some of Raymond and John's arguments. What's more, I hope the next U.K. government of Gordon Brown or David Cameron hires Raymond Baker and John Christensen to conduct the review, who could then work with Michael Foot and Promontory. John is introduced hereafter.

The Chief Pirate

The archipelago of the three Cayman Islands is the Chief Pirate of Heartless Capitalism. This archipelago of three islands is the fifth largest banking center in the world, home to 279 banks with a total of $1.5 trillion of banking liabilities (Fessenden-Joseph 2008). Average per-capita income in the three Cayman Islands amounts to $42,000, the twelfth highest in the world. The Cayman Islands are home to some 65,000 inhabitants. As of June 2008, the archipelago is also home to 10,037 funds according to the Cayman Island Monetary Authority, up 11 percent from 8,972 a year before.

45 out of the world's top 50 banks have opened a branch in the Cayman Islands. An IMF report conducted on the Cayman Islands Monetary Authority in 2005 concluded that "an extensive program of legislative, rule and guideline development has introduced an increasingly effective system of regulation both formalizing earlier practices and introducing enhanced procedures" (Fessenden-Joseph 2008).

Switzerland, the Land of Pirates

According to a report by the Boston Consulting Group (BCG), "traditional offshore centers—Switzerland in particular—are not on the verge of surrendering their leadership positions" (Aerni, Juniac, et al., 2008). Figure 10.1 summarizes the Assets under Management (AuM) that sit in offshore financial centers, a majority of which sits in Switzerland. Offshore AuM are assets held in a country that is not the client's residence (Aerni, Juniac, et al., 2008).

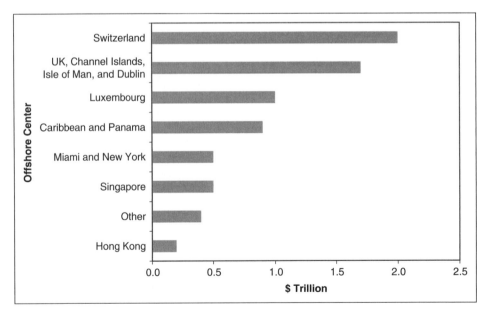

FIGURE 10.1 Assets under Management in Offshore Centers, 2007
Source: Global Wealth 2008: A Wealth of Opportunities in Turbulent Times © 2008, The Boston Consulting Group. Reprinted with permission.

Switzerland earned a reputation of neutrality that has saved the Helvetic Republic from fighting the major armed conflicts of our time. This neutrality has contributed to raising Switzerland's admiration and respect internationally. But when money is concerned, Switzerland is no longer neutral. When it is all about the money, Switzerland takes advantage of its neutrality and independence to serve the interest of the better off, of the wealthy.

The European Union should put phenomenal pressure on Switzerland to interrupt its fiscal incentives to EU-citizens. EU-citizens should choose between being European or Swiss, but not both. Switzerland must end its fiscal malpractices that aim at attracting the wealthy, lowering their level of taxation. I was in Geneva in July 2008. I was not able to see in what specific ways the average Swiss citizen is benefiting from the additional revenue the Swiss tax authority should be earning because of its fiscal malpractices. Public transportation in Switzerland is not better than in the surrounding countries. Public infrastructure in Switzerland is not better either. Fiscal incentives only benefit the better off in Switzerland and harm the European middle class.

MONEY LAUNDERING

Money laundering is equivalent to the flight of illicit financial flows across borders. How did the current financial architecture incorporate so many loopholes that enable the laundering of money across borders? Raymond Baker and Eva Joly provide the following explanation (2008a):

> *Beginning in the 1960s (coincident with the quantification of economics based on modeling of collectable data) a multifaceted structure has been created to handle the movement of illicit money. Minor parts of this structure were available earlier, but the 1960s marked the takeoff point for two reasons. First, it was the decade of independence. From the late 1950s through the end of the 1960s, 48 countries gained their independence from colonial powers. Many of the political and economic elites in these countries, sometimes influenced by risks attendant to the Cold War, wanted to take money out by any means possible, and the West serviced this desire with creative arrangements for capital flight. Second, the sixties marked the spread of multinational corporations. Prior to then an international oil or trading company might have operations in 12 or 15 foreign locales. But from the 1960s forward, multinational corporations widened their presence to hundreds of locations across the globe, frequently utilizing aggressive tax evading techniques in head offices, subsidiaries, and branches. Thus, decolonization and the worldwide reach of corporations propelled the expansion of the global financial structure catering to shifts of illegally generated money.*

What are the main techniques to launder money across borders? Raymond and Eva revise the legal structures that enable the laundering of money internationally (Baker and Joly 2008a). According to the authors of "The Issue of Illicit Financial Flows," the following structures are among the most used instruments to launder money across borders: tax havens, secrecy jurisdictions, disguised corporations, redomiciliation provisions, anonymous trust accounts, fake foundations, falsified pricing, money laundering techniques, and holes left in laws.

A majority of average citizens with average wealth have never heard from these techniques. However, wealthy individuals who can access private bankers, along with corporations, are among the most common users of these legal structures and arrangements whose names are intimidating.

What is the amount and geographic distribution of money laundering? The total capital flight from developing countries amounted to $850 billion to $1 trillion per year in the period 2002 to 2006. What is more concerning is that illicit money flows out of developing countries have increased at a compound rate of 18.2 percent between 2002 and 2006. The good news for Africa is that illicit financial flows from Africa slightly declined between 2002 and 2006 because of incomplete data. As a percentage of the global capital flight the allocation is as follows: Asia (50 percent), Middle East and North Africa (15 percent), Europe (17 percent), Western Hemisphere (15 percent), and Africa (3 percent). The top ten countries with the highest average of illicit capital flows are China, Saudi Arabia, Mexico, Russia, Kuwait, Malaysia, Venezuela, Poland, and Hungary (Kar and Cartwright-Smith 2009).

Greenpeace reports an example of money laundering in the case of the multinational Danzer Group in the Democratic Republic of the Congo (Greenpeace 2008). According to Greenpeace, Danzer would have reported under-invoicing of the sales value of timber. The timber was exported from the Democratic Republic of the Congo (DRC). The technique used by Danzer is denominated false accounting and typically goes unreported. Greenpeace explains its findings as follows (2008):

> *Internal Danzer Group documents show in great detail the price fixing arrangements between the Group's Swiss-based trading arm Interholco AG and the parent firm's subsidiaries in the DRC and the Republic of the Congo. The DRC-based Siforco sells its wood to Interholco at an official price below the true market value of the wood. The shortfall is made up through unofficial payments into offshore bank accounts in Europe, enabling the Danzer Group to evade the payment of a variety of taxes to which it is liable in the DRC.*

Robert Nimmo (FIN) is the former chief risk officer at Barclays Bank. I met Rob at the LSE Garrick in London on October 31, 2006.[7] How can we improve the global banking system so that the current loopholes are eliminated? For Robert, improving the global banking system requires two steps: "firstly establishing a detailed set of principles and practices and secondly establishing regulatory enforcement." Who is more likely to start a global crackdown on tax havens? Robert points out that the United States, the European Union, and Japan need to lead these efforts "because they have collectively the most at stake." For the former banker, "vulnerabilities from Madoff-like Ponzi schemes to over leveraged financial engineering schemes and weak counterparties threaten everyone and are not acceptable."

Private Banking

Two cases emerged in 2008 that recalled taxpayers regarding the importance of cracking down tax havens.

The first case erupted in the summer of 2008. In May 2008 a leading private banker from the Swiss bank UBS was detained in the United States. The UBS private banker was a material witness in the case of German tax evasion into Liechenstein (Simonian 2008). UBS is the world's top private banker. According to the German magazine *Der Spiegel*, as many as 900 German citizens would have laundered as much as 4 billion into the bank accounts of Liechenstein. German Chancellor Angela Merkel recalled, "Responsible behavior from companies is an elementary prerequisite for a functioning socially-responsible market economy." The German Finance Minister at the time Peter Steinbruck pointed out that "it is the elites who are threatening to cause the system to collapse" (Spiegel 2008). The elites are presented in Chapter 12.

The second case was reported by the *Financial Times* on May 14, 2008. According to the London-based newspaper, two bankers had been charged by U.S. authorities on tax evasion. The two bankers would have helped a U.S. billionaire evade income taxes on up to $200 million. One of the two bankers (Bradley Birkenfeld) was a resident of Geneva, whereas the second (Mario Staggl) was a resident of Liechtenstein. According to the *Financial Times*, "UBS has told members of its former private banking team responsible for rich U.S. clients not to travel to the country." Birkenfeld was a subordinate of Martin Liechti, who headed the international private banking business for UBS in the Americas. Liechti remained in the United States as a "material witness" in the ongoing investigation (Chung 2008).

In the aftermath of the disclosure of both tax evasion scandals, the European Commission announced in November 2008 that it would attempt to close the loopholes that exist today in tax evasion legislation (Houlder and Tait 2008). The loopholes exist in the savings tax directive, the European Union's legal code against tax evasion. According to the *Financial Times*, the European Commission "admitted that the directive had dealt only with interest payments made for the immediate profit of individuals resident in the European Union, giving people an opportunity to circumvent the rules by interposing another legal person or arrangement situated in a non-EU country" (Houlder and Tait 2008). Non-EU countries include Andorra, Monaco, Liechtenstein, or Switzerland, all considered tax havens by the OECD. EU countries that are tax havens according to the OECD include Cyprus and Malta.

TAX EVASION

The capital flight from sub-Saharan Africa has amounted to over $600 billion since 1975, which is equivalent to three times the region's external debt. About $1.5 trillion sit today in private accounts offshore (Christensen 2008). What is the reason for this economic loophole? How can trillions remain untaxed? The reason for this twenty-first century absurdity is the current reality of the world's financial architecture.

The Tax Justice Network (TJN) is the world's leading think-tank on tax havens and tax evasion. TJN is an independent organization doing analysis in the field of tax and regulation. The London-based organization's goal is to encourage reform at the national and global levels. TJN's main argument is that tax havens cause poverty. TJN is an advocate of transparency and finds secrecy detrimental.

JOHN CHRISTENSEN (FIN) is one of the world's authorities on tax evasion and money laundering. The British economist is the International Director and co-founder of TJN. I met John in the London suburb of Chiltern on December 19, 2008. According to John, "Tax avoidance presents company directors with a massive headache because those that wish to act with integrity prefer to not engage in aggressive tax avoidance." For John, "The world's super-rich have set themselves apart from the rest of society and have created a vast offshore economy from where they, and powerful corporations, can disengage from regulation and taxes, leaving the rest of us to pay the bills" (Christensen 2008).

Let's embargo tax havens. Let's put phenomenal pressure on their bankers and financiers, on their regulators and policy-makers. They cause incalculable harm and yet are allowed to continue their harmful activity. Coincidentally Germany demanded in October 2008 that its southern neighbor, Switzerland, be reported on a tax blacklist. This is only the beginning of a financial embargo. The then German finance minister Peter Steinbrueck said, "Switzerland offers conditions that invite the German taxpayer to evade taxes. Therefore, in my view, Switzerland belongs on such a list" (Benoit and Hall 2008). The fact of the matter is that the only hope for Western governments resides in the OECD's ability to crackdown uncooperative tax havens.

TAX COMPETITION

Tax competition has been a natural consequence of the principle of competition embraced by the version of capitalism that passed away in 2008. Competition is fundamentally good in certain segments of the private sector. Competition is not part of the equation when we look at the provision of certain public goods such as universal education, health care, the postal service, or the armed forces.

Countries that compete on the basis of reducing taxes are undermining the ability of other countries to sustain their welfare states. Tax competition is similar to environmental degradation. A country could lower its environmental standards in order to host a coal plant that does not fulfill environmental standards. The country would be contributing to global pollution that is harming its neighbors.

Why are tax competition and tax evasion similar concepts? Ireland's low corporate tax has made certain multinationals in the technology and banking sectors move their headquarters to Dublin. Switzerland's low wealth taxes have made the wealthy move their residence to Geneva or Zurich. The Cayman Islands have become the natural setting for hedge funds because they do not tax profits.

Why is tax evasion detrimental to maintaining the welfare state? Ireland has been competing for years with other countries in the European Union, offering a 12.5 percent corporate tax to corporations, many of which have decided to move their headquarters to the world's twentieth largest island to lessen the burden of their tax bill. As a result, the Irish Tax Authority has been able to raise additional corporate taxes, but the overall impact is an aggregate net loss of corporate taxes within the European Union. Macedonia, a republic north of Greece that was part of the former Yugoslavia, is now offering a corporate tax of only 10 percent to corporations that incorporate in its territory. Tax competition undermines the ability of the welfare state to sustain the provision of public goods such as health care and education. There are countries and territories with zero or very low income taxes, which provide no universal health care or education. It is up to the individual to decide which kind of society he or she would like to inhabit. I know very well the kind of society in which I would like to live. It is a society that grants everyone, independent from the level of wealth or income, a basic welfare state that guarantees a minimum level of human dignity.

Corporations that would like to establish their headquarters in Ireland or Macedonia should not be allowed to operate in the European Union. Individuals who decide to move their residence to Switzerland should not be granted entry back in the European Union. The free-riding attitude of individuals and corporations must end once and for all. John Christensen is clear about the impact of tax competition. He asserts the following four conclusions (Christensen 2007b):

1. No empirical evidence to support assertion that tax competition improves public spending efficiency.
2. No evidence that tax competition stimulates growth or job creation.
3. Lower tax on capital shifts tax burden to labor and consumption.
4. Tax competition is fundamentally anti-democratic.

We have to start competing on the basis of our language skills, on the quality of our university graduates, and on the productivity of our workforce. It must be an enhancing competition that makes us improve as a society and reach further goals. We have to stop competing on the basis of undermining our own welfare state, and on the basis of reaching the bottom instead of the ceiling. I know very well what kind of society I dream of for the world. Escalating and exporting the welfare state to the developing world and the extreme poor is only a matter of political will.

Artwork by Claudio Muñoz.

CHAPTER 11

Brain Drain

I dream of the day when these, the African mathematicians and computer specialists in Washington and New York, the African physicists, engineers, doctors, business managers and economists, will return from London and Manchester and Paris and Brussels to add to the African pool of brain power, to enquire into and find solutions to Africa's problems and challenges, to open the African door to the world of knowledge, to elevate Africa's place within the universe of research the information of new knowledge, education and information.

—Thabo Mbeki, *Speech on African Renaissance*

Brain drain is a phenomenon that has increased with the internationalization of migratory flows, and involves that part of the immigrant population considered qualified labor. Brain drain can have a severe impact in the societies of the developing world that see how their best prepared professionals, educated with public money, leave for other countries, hoping for a better future. Brain drain is related to high-skilled migration, which is defined as migration of those who have earned a university or post-secondary education (Lowell, Findlay, et al., 2004).

A PSEUDO POSITIVE DRAIN

Brain drain is typically considered positive from the perspective of the recipient countries hosting qualified labor from the developing world. This qualified labor normally consists of professionals who decide to leave behind their countries of origin to take roots in North America and Europe in order to improve their quality of life. North America and Europe suffer from population aging and a shortage of talent in certain sectors such as technology or health care. Naturally, developed countries welcome and salute these golden eggs of the developing world purchased at a bargain price.

We say in the West that development aid has not been effective in the fight against poverty in many countries that are still trapped in per-capita income levels of half a century ago. We say in the industrialized world that corruption and dictatorial political regimes across the world are detrimental for a country's normal economic development. We like to analyze the reasons behind the failure of the economies of Africa and Latin America from an ex-post macroeconomic dimension. However, we do not realize that some policies of the Western world, such as the attraction of talent from poor countries, act as a catalyst that accelerates their impoverishment, undermining their ability to make further progress. An economy incapable of retaining the self-generated talent is an economy that invests and loses the investment as well as the return on the investment.

We deceive ourselves thinking that, in the end, we are only opening the doors to those individuals willing to escape the nightmare of extreme poverty in the developing world in search for a better life. The truth is that we only open our doors to qualified individuals that in any case would have an opportunity of working in their countries of origin. We forget that a majority of people living in absolute misery lack education because they cannot pay for it. These individuals are born condemned to live without hope.

We deceive ourselves thinking that the individuals we host make a positive impact in their countries of origin, for we believe that remittances benefit those who stayed home. We should at this point distinguish between those unskilled or low-skilled immigrants who send remittances, from those skilled immigrants who send remittances. However, studies have shown that remittances from the latter group impact their countries of origin more than the former.

According to Riccardo Faini, a former professor of political economy at the University of Rome Tor Vergata (2006), there is no empirical evidence that skilled immigrants send more remittances than unskilled or low-skilled immigrants. On the contrary, skilled immigrants spend more time abroad than unskilled or low-skilled immigrants, and take in roots more easily in the destination countries. Faini concludes that skilled labor coming from the better off in the developing world has a smaller incentive to send back remittances, spends a longer time abroad and has the ability to attract family members to the destination country. In conclusion, the brain drain cannot be related to a higher flow of remittances, demystifying the popular belief that the import of skilled labor is more positive for the developing world than the import of unskilled labor.

Richard Black reviews social justice considerations on immigration in his paper "Immigration and Social Justice: Towards a Progressive European Immigration Policy?" Is immigration morally justified? The answer depends on what theory of justice is embraced. For instance, John Rawls believes that social and economic inequalities should be allowed as long as they serve the advantage of the least well off (Black 1996). If brain drain increases the inequality in the sending countries and leaves them worse off, John Rawls may think the outcome is not socially just. Black concludes along these lines, "If the level of immigration were of a significant magnitude and promoted change in the host society of a kind that threatened to undermine principles of social justice themselves, the overall impact of such immigration could not be considered as promoting the cause of social justice" (Black 1996).

FIGURES BEHIND THE PHENOMENON

Professor Richard Devon at Penn State University estimates that the United States invests $200,000 in each student that finishes an undergraduate degree. This indicates the amount of money the industrialized world saves when importing skilled professionals from other countries (Wadhwa 2007).

A survey conducted by the Organization for Economic Cooperation and Development (OECD) shows that among the Indians and Chinese receiving a doctorate in 1990 to 1991, 79 percent of Indians and 88 percent of Chinese continued to work in the United States in 1995 (Cervantes and Guellec 2002). These percentages contrast with 11 percent of Koreans and 15 percent of Japanese who upon earning a doctorate in the United States in 1990 to 91, still worked in the country in 1995.

Figure 11.1 shows the nightmare that some African countries undergo in the health-care sector. The average percentage of African physicians who decide to go abroad is as high as 29 percent in sub-Saharan Africa, reaching peaks above 50 percent in countries like Liberia, Angola, or Mozambique. As a result, we can easily determine why many of these African countries are stuck in poverty traps, for many of them have been hit by epidemics such as malaria or HIV/AIDS and yet are incapable of treating their own population because of this lack of qualified human resources. The case of nurses is less dire than that of physicians, but it is still not promising.

Alan Hudson presents a case study on the crisis of health professionals in developing countries. Hudson remarks, "Africa has the highest disease burden of any continent, but the lowest number of health workers." Hudson remarks that Africa has 0.8 health workers per one-thousand inhabitants, compared with 10.3 in Europe. In these circumstances what can or should the European Union do? Hudson calls for policy coherence between development and other policies. In particular, he recommends to strengthen and enhance the communications between migration and development within the European Commission (Hudson 2006).

Has the European Union improved the dialogue between its migration and its development policies? **Klaus Rudischhauser** (CON) is the director for development and relations with African and Pacific States of the European Commission. I met Klaus on June 23, 2008, at the European Commission Directorate for General Development in Brussels (Belgium). Klaus points out, "In the context of the discussion on policy coherence for development, I agree that this is one of the areas where the European Commission through its Global Approach to Migration has achieved a good dialogue and coherent policy." The European Commission could and should learn from the Commonwealth, as highlighted hereafter.

Geographic Location

What is the nature of migratory flow and its geographical location? William J. Carrington and Enrica Detragiache of the International Monetary Fund raise the question "How Big Is the Brain Drain?" The authors present "estimates of emigration rates from 61 developing countries to OECD countries for three educational categories" (Carrington and Detragiache 1998). The IMF economists divide their results in two sections. The first section covers migration flows to the United States. The second covers migration flows to OECD countries. The results are updated with 1990 data.

The biggest migratory flows from Africa to the United States originated in Egypt, Ghana, and South Africa. These flows are characterized by a majority of individuals with a tertiary education (60 percent of the total). The proportion of low-educated

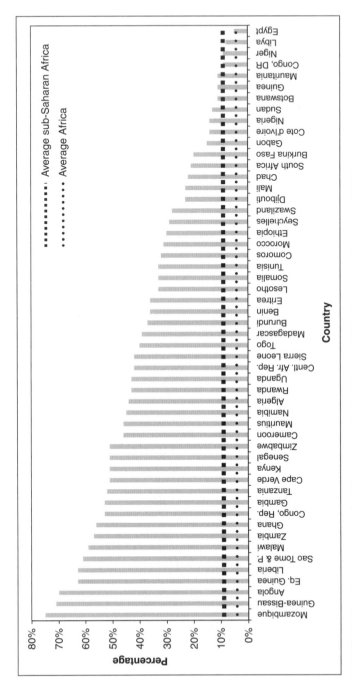

FIGURE 11.1 Physicians Born in Africa Appearing in Census of Nine Receiving Countries, 2000

Source: Clemens et al. (2006). Reprinted with permission of the Center for Global Development, www.cgdev.org.

Africans who migrated to the United States is negligible. As of 1990, five countries contributed 93 percent of the migrants from the developing world to the OECD: the United States, France, Germany, Canada, and Australia (Carrington and Detragiache 1998).

What specific sectors of a developing country's labor market are more likely to be harmed by skilled migration? Education and health care are at the core of many extreme poor countries' loss of talent, in particular in the sub-Saharan African region. Stuart Tannock of Cardiff University points out, "Over half of the doctors trained in Ghana have emigrated, of 200 nurses trained in Swaziland over the past two years, 150 have emigrated, since Zimbabwe gained its independence in 1980, 80 percent of the doctors, nurses and therapists trained at its primary university are thought to have emigrated" (Tannock 2007).

What can the developed world do to help developing countries retain their talent or compensate for the loss of talent? The Ministers of Health of Commonwealth countries met in Geneva on May 18, 2003. They issued a *Commonwealth Code of Practice for International Recruitment of Health Workers*, in which they state, "A consensus approach to dealing with the problem of international recruitment of health workers should be adopted." The code's main purpose is to "discourage the targeted recruitment of health workers from countries which are themselves experiencing shortages" (Commonwealth 2003).

According to Ann Keeling, Director of the Social Transformation Programmes Division at the Commonwealth Secretariat, the Commonwealth Code of Practice "marked the first time that a large group of countries with very different stakes in the matter had sought to codify a set of ethical principles to govern health worker migration" (Keeling 2007). The Commonwealth Code of Practice is a positive development that should be expanded to other developed and developing nations.

A New Architecture needs a leading immigration reformer. **NDIORO NDIAYE** (IMM) is the former deputy director general of the International Organization for Migration (IOM). I spoke with Ndioro on September 30, 2008. Established in 1951, IOM is the leading inter-governmental organization working in the field of migration and counts as many as 125 member states. IOM's four areas of operation are: migration and development, facilitating migration, regulating migration, and forced migration. What is the associated cost of brain drain for Africa? According to Ndioro, in order to compensate for the loss and scarcity of skilled labor due to brain drain, African countries have to allocate four billion dollars to employ 100,000 non-African expatriates that substitute for the vacant positions left behind by the migrant skilled labor, which helps diminish the devastating effects caused by brain drain (Mutume 2003).

Brain Strain

For Georgetown Professor **SUSAN F. MARTIN** (IMM), the concept of brain drain has been replaced by that of brain strain. Susan is the executive director of the Institute of International Migration (IIM) at Georgetown University. The renowned American scholar is also the president of the International Association for the Study of Forced Migration. I met Susan on November 17, 2008, at Georgetown University in Washington, DC. For the Georgetown scholar, "The impact of high skilled and professional emigration will depend on who leaves, what they would have done if they remained, what they are able to do in the destination country, and what type of ties they maintain with their country of origin."

What is brain strain and how does it compare to brain drain? The concept of brain strain was first introduced by the researchers B. Lindsay Lowell, Allan Findlay, and Emma Stewart, all of whom are affiliated with the Institute for Public-Policy Research in the United Kingdom. For the authors, brain strain describes the positive as well as negative impacts that highly skilled out-migration can have on the sending countries (Lowell, Findlay, et al., 2004). The authors suggest that this term is preferable to 'brain drain' because it suggests that two-way flows are often involved and highlights the potential for both positive and adverse consequences inherent in the mobility of highly skilled migrants.

What are the positive and negative factors identified by the authors? For Findlay, Lowell, and Stewart, developing and developed nations can benefit from brain drain in the short, medium, and long runs. In the short and medium run, "temporary labour migration programs linked to strong measures to encourage migrant return hold many advantages." In the long run, the migration "policies that capitalise on expatriate diasporas, support human rights, and harmonise international migration policies of sending and receiving states provide the best policy approaches." According to the authors, it is clear that "the developed world can no longer simply plunder the human resources of the developing world." They add, "It is also clear it neither can nor should close the door to migrants." (Lowell, Findlay, et al., 2004). Is there a balance between too much and too little?

A Brain Drain Tax

Jagdish Bhagwati is a professor of international economics at Columbia University. Bhagwati was introduced in Chapter 7. In 1972 the Indian economist wrote a paper entitled "The United States in the Nixon Era," in which he proposed "extending income tax jurisdiction to expatriate citizens, arguing that citizenship created tax obligations" (Subramanian 2005). Bhagwati's proposal is known as the Bhagwati Tax.

For John Douglas Wilson, a professor of economics at Michigan State University, Bhagwati's proposal "remains remarkably valid after more than thirty years." Bhagwati's proposal suggests to levy a tax on the professional expatriate's income for the first ten years of working activity abroad (Wilson 2006).

How can the collateral damage of brain drain be determined in monetary terms? In 2002 Mihir Desai, Devesh Kapur, and John McHale of Harvard University (determined that in 2001, India lost between 0.24 and 0.58 percent of its GDP because of brain drain to the United States. Although Indian-born residents in the United States represent only 0.1 percent of the Indian population, their income amounts to 10 percent of the country's national income (Ramesh 2002). If a global taxation regime similar to that of the United States was extended by India to India-born residents abroad, the Harvard scholars estimate that India could raise an additional $500 million in tax revenue.

We live in a world needy of new ideas to raise funding for development, a world that has been unable to implement forward-looking ideas such as the Tobin Tax or the Bhagwati Tax. Perhaps it is time to start thinking big again and resuscitate these two great ideas of two great economists. The Tobin Tax is explored in Chapter 22.

SHRINKING POPULATIONS

The thirst to attract skilled migration in the European Union (EU) stems from low fertility rates that are leading to shrinking populations, particularly in Western and Eastern Europe. As Paul Demeny points out (Demeny 2003):

> *Oswald Spengler's prophecy may turn out to be correct after all: depopulation may be slow, rather than precipitous; it could indeed last for centuries. If Europe would prefer a different future for its descendants, corrective action cannot be delayed.*

Much has to be done in the EU in the first half of the twenty-first century if it is to cope with the expectations established in the summit of Lisbon of March 2000 and in view of the failed referenda in France and the Netherlands to approve the cheered Constitution that became a Treaty. The European Union faces increasingly poor demographics that put it on the verge of economic stagnation, compounded by a proven record of inability to sustain its own welfare state.

The EU Lisbon summit of 2000 established an ambitious goal of economic growth beyond the 3 percent mark. Average growth in the EU has been on average lower than three percent ever since. Economists agree that only a higher immigration rate can help the EU grow faster in terms of GDP, and the Lisbon target could only be reached if immigration inflows reach an unlikely three million individuals per year.

Guillermo de la Dehesa summarizes the main economic and demographic challenges faced by the EU in his book *Europe at the Crossroads* (De la Dehesa 2006). De la Dehesa heads the European think-tank Centre for Economic Policy Research. I met De la Dehesa on May 23, 2009, at the Goldman Sachs branch office in Madrid (Spain). For De la Dehesa, the following underlying motives represent concerning evidence of a worsening economic environment (De la Dehesa 2006):

- Age dependency ratio will more than double between 2000 and 2050, spiking up from 24 percent to 49 percent.
- A majority of the new member states coming from Eastern Europe are bringing lower than average fertility rates, contrary to what has historically happened with previous expansions (Greece, Portugal, and Spain). De la Dehesa states, "The likelihood of a big population increase in the fully enlarged EU is much lower than in the United States unless the EU sees a massive influx of African immigrants."
- Life expectancies in the EU have been increasing and are only likely to improve, pushing up dependency ratios even further and putting pressure on the welfare state, which relies on pay-as-you-go pension schemes in a majority of member states, except perhaps for the United Kingdom.

A solution for the EU would be to become more immigrant-friendly and aspire to replicate the successful model of Canada, Australia, or the United States, all of which have and are expected to have lower dependency ratios. If it does, the *Commonwealth Code of Practice* presented earlier in this chapter could be a departing point.

European Trends in Population Growth

Between 1950 and 1975, the average annual rate of population growth was 8.4 per 1,000 inhabitants, a rate that has decreased to 2.9 per 1,000 inhabitants in the subsequent quarter-century. Statistics issued by the Council of Europe show a concerning population decrease in 17 European countries in 2000. In this trajectory, by 2050 half of the European population will be older than 50 years, and the share of the population aged 65 and older will spike up from 14 percent in 2000 to 30 percent (Demeny 2003). In the absence of considerable immigration flows, the populations of the EU-27 and the United States are likely to converge beyond 2050.

The population of the EU increased by an annual average of 2.7 million between 1950 and 1975, by 1.3 million between 1975 and 2000, and is expected to shrink by one million per annum in the first half of the twenty-first century (Demeny 2003). This phenomenon is exacerbated by the fact that out of the eight central European countries that joined the EU in 2004, five showed negative population growth, with the exceptions of Slovakia, Slovenia, and Estonia (Monnier and Rogers 2004).

In a report published by the United Nations in 2000, it becomes clear that the EU has to tackle the issue of demographics and define a medium-term strategy for the admission of third country nationals (Laczko 2002). The report, entitled "Replacement Migration: Is It a Solution to Declining and Ageing Population?", states that a significant increase of immigration flows becomes a necessity if EU member-states wish to maintain the constant size of the working population.

The obvious next step for the technocrats of the European Union based in Brussels is to seriously consider the incorporation of Turkey. The conservatism of European baby boomers coupled with the unfounded fear of accepting a new member-state with a Muslim majority are two drivers that condition a positive out-come for Turkey. In the absence of incentives for EU-citizens to increase the fertility rates, and if the current reluctance on a future Turkish incorporation continues, the European Union's immigration policies could target skilled workers from developing countries.

World Population Trends

With the economic expansion of China and India the world evolves towards a multilateral environment in which the current weight in the international institutions (United Nations Security Council, World Bank, International Monetary Fund) is no longer representative of their demographics. Representative power must overcome the phenomenal asymmetry that overweighs the United States and a handful of European countries.

Europe was a continent of migration in the first part of the twentieth century prior to the eruption of World War I. Between 1790 and 1920, the population of the United States increased from four to 107 million, including 33 million immigrant arrivals (Haines 1994). Between 1900 and 1914, 900,000 new immigrants arrived on U.S. soil every year. Raymond Cohn writes, "This period saw the immigration of a large number of single males who planned to work for a period of months or years and return to their homeland, a development made possible by the steamship shortening the voyage and reducing its cost" (Cohn 2001).

The new world became a magnet for those who looked for a better life and economic prosperity. The United States became a country of migrants and has been better able to cope with minorities. With no further incorporation, the EU-27 will suffer negative demographic growth between 2010 and 2050 close to –0.4 percent per annum, which will severely undermine its ability to remain competitive and maintain its welfare state, as we know it today. The incorporation of Turkey would add two million more citizens each year between 2010 and 2050. De la Dehesa (2006) notes that the three additional million immigrants per year mark would be necessary to maintain EU GDP growth at 3 percent, as decided in the Lisbon summit of 2000.

ILLEGAL IMMIGRATION

Illegal immigration is a highly debated topic and one of the main concerns in the industrialized world. The current income gap and the increasing inequality between developed and developing nations allows for the intensification of human flows between adjacent, yet dissimilar regions in the United States and Europe. Yet while there is a regime of regular migration in North America, the European Union fosters the accumulation and residence of foreigners in an irregular situation (Entorf 2000). Accordingly, the debate in the developed nations has shifted gears and now focuses on illegal immigration, illegal workers, and their impact and consequences.

Leading representatives acknowledge the need to focus a greater deal of effort on immigration. Britain's home secretary John Reid said that managing immigration is now "the greatest challenge facing all European governments" (*Economist* 2006b). Former French President Jacques Chirac said to listeners of the 2006 Bastille Day address, "Africans will flood the world and we have an immense problem, which is that of development" (EurActiv 2006).

Illegal immigration is viewed from an angle of concern from Europe towards North Africa and beyond. The poor integration of some immigrant communities and the turmoil caused by the terrorist attacks of September 11, 2001, in New York, March 11, 2004, in Madrid, and July 7, 2005, in London, have exacerbated the problem of illegal immigration (Lubbers 2004). This should not, however, undermine Europe's commitment to human rights and refugee protection.

In this lack of bipartisan consensus on the issue, policies within countries vary significantly depending on what party—either right or left—rules the government. The absence of a continental regulation leads to the absurd scenario of different approaches undertaken by any two nations in the European Union. Populist messages are thus turning popular among an aging European population that needs migration (whether legal or illegal) to sustain an economic growth able to feed its retirees.

Populist messages are increasingly frequent in Europe. As a matter of fact, 2007 polls showed how a quarter of Denmark's voters support the anti-immigration Danish People's Party; the Swiss gave 29 percent of their votes to the xenophobic Swiss People's Party; Norway's second political force is anti-foreigner; and a fifth of Belgium's Flemish population now votes for the far-right Vlaams Belang (*Economist* 2007d).

It's the Demographics, Stupid

The public opinion in many European countries drifts to undecided on the debate of how to approach illegal immigration. Different countries suggest different policies. The package adopted on July 19, 2006, by the European Commission helps identify the EU's priorities on how to approach and cope with illegal immigration. Tackling illegal employment represents the punch line of a joint effort that should target and help eliminate situations of exploitation of illegal immigrants who work in poor and unsafe conditions in industries such as construction, catering, or the textile sector (EurActiv 2006).

Spain's massive legalization process of some 547,000 undocumented working adults in 2005 triggered a sentiment of discontent in France. Former French Interior Minister Nicolas Sarkozy blamed the Spanish Administration for its lax policies on immigration. Spaniards show most tolerant vis-à-vis immigration among European peers, with 55 percent of respondents believing that immigrants are good for the economy, whereas only 42 percent of Britons share the same view (*Economist* 2007d).

Jesús Caldera (IMM) was Spain's minister of labour and immigration at the time. I met Jesús on July 2, 2008, at the headquarters of Spain's Socialist Party in Madrid (Spain). How can a country like Spain sustain the millions of migrants who were losing their jobs in 2009 and provide them with the same welfare state Spaniards can access in times of economic crisis? For Jesús, the immigration model he embraced attracts foreign labor when there is demand and closes the borders to foreign migration when the demand for labor shrinks, as was the case in 2009. Jesús notes that immigrants should have the same rights and obligations as Spaniards. In times of economic bonanza immigrants helped strengthen Social Security. In times of economic turmoil, immigrants are entitled to the same rights they earned while they contributed to the maintenance of the welfare state. It is an approach that dignifies the country.

On practical grounds, it's all about demographics or in other words: *It's the demographics, stupid.* Europe's native-born workforce is forecast to shrink by 44 million by 2050 (*Economist* 2007d). As a result, skilled workers will be in short supply. The continent will therefore become increasingly dependent on foreign labor. Closed borders are a threat for Europe's own aging population. A common European policy based on the restriction of unskilled workers could prove detrimental for certain countries. Denmark is in strong need of unskilled labor due to the shrinkage of its population participating in the labor force. Germany has kept its economy closed to workers from new EU countries until 2011, but now promotes it due to a skills shortage (*Economist* 2007d).

After all, Demetrios Papademetriou, president of the Washington-based Migration Policy Institute, explains, "Illegal immigration is part of the vital lubricant of our societies. It wouldn't be happening if so many people's interests were not served by the status quo" (Rachman 2006).

Looking Ahead

Forward-looking approaches like the Canadian point system, which favors immigration from high-skilled workers, could be incorporated into the European agenda as an example of a model that could serve as inspiration (Rachman 2006). The fact of the matter is that EU members have a hunger for low-skilled workers in industries where EU citizens no longer want to work.

It makes little sense for a country to get tough on illegal immigrants whereas others are granting amnesty to thousands of them. It only makes it harder to manage illegal immigration. In the meantime policy-makers are in nobody's land and lack the ability to decide whether scarce public resources should be spent fighting against illegal immigration, or whether they should be allocated to other more urgent uses such as public healthcare or education (Entorf 2000).

Italian immigration figures corresponding to 2004 show that only 4 percent of migrants who arrived in Italy in 2004 came by sea (*Economist* 2006a). Frontex, the EU border guard launched by Franco Frattini, Italy's European commissioner, patrols the Mediterranean with military vessels and aircraft with personnel from Spain, Italy, Germany, Portugal, France, and Finland (Caldwell 2006). These efforts are more directly linked to a repressive policy of enforcing the illegal dimension of immigration and forsake the principle of actively working with local administrations in the departing countries to work out common plans of action targeting the elimination of smuggling activity.

Europe has to address the problem of increasing illegal migratory flows by working jointly with the developing nations from which the migrants depart, in order to reduce the lack of opportunity in the departing countries and to foster stability and economic growth leading to self-sustainability. The freeing of people is, after all, like the free movement of goods; "it does not always benefit everybody all the time, but the world is a better place for it, all the same" (Rachman 2006).

POVERTIMMUNE

Povertimmune is one of the three terms that define the New Architecture of capitalism. Povertimmune countries are immune to poverty. In order to hedge against poverty, Decompliant developed and Monfortable developing countries establish a new relationship based on the reform of the six areas that constitute the Axis of Feeble. The three key concepts are explored in subsequent chapters.

Three

Reform

Let's put the house in order, let's clean our own backyard before forcing our poor neighbor to clean his or her own. Let's stop the debate of what is transparency and ethics if we ourselves maintain a double-edged paradigm that does not give the developing world the representative power they not only deserve, but also own. Let's stop the extremely asymmetric negotiation rounds in foreign policy, in trade, in bailout packages that do more harm than good, and give the developing world what belongs to them in a world that is one world, ready or not, in a world that for the first time in history faces global threats that will have global consequences. It is our responsibility to move forward in an agenda that has to put those in need first. It is the responsibility of our time as global citizens to seek and reach transnational agreements that incorporate the worse off and address their vulnerabilities.

Part III explains and justifies what kind of reform is needed in the West and overviews the history of the Bretton Woods institutions. Additional justification is provided about why the World Bank, the International Monetary Fund, and the United Nations (the World Trade Organization is introduced in Chapter 7) are in need of reform. It then reviews what the elites in the developed and developing world think and how they feel about reforming, which is followed by the introduction of the Sleeping Beauty that should wake up to the reality of an unequal world. The Third Sector is then introduced, a sector that truly represents the will of global citizens, to find out what and how they feel about change and reform.

Any time of crisis must bring about reform, for reform moves us forward and reveals new, undiscovered paths where *eutopia* can materialize, and where the desire to move forward conquers the conscience of the human being and removes from us the fear of the unexplored.

Artwork by Andrzej Krauze.

CHAPTER 12

Lobbies and Elites

When we stop trying to feel good about ourselves, or to increase our own power by asserting our innocence, we can begin to look for answers by searching for truth.

—Mitchell Duneier, *Slim's Table*[1]

They live in tax havens such as the Cayman Islands and Switzerland. They work for private banks and hedge funds. They think short-term investing is not speculation. They graduate from the top business schools and law schools and join the best law firms. They are the Pirates of Heartless Capitalism.

They think they maximize economic profit based on the invisible hand of Adam Smith. They minimize the importance of the collateral damage associated with some of their investment decisions. They run multinational corporations and outsource the activities to countries that are unable to enforce minimum labor standards. They are the Pirates of Heartless Capitalism.

They defend the myopic national interest based on a discourse that supports a foreign policy that emphasizes the non-proliferation of nuclear weapons but forgets the damage of the illicit trade of small arms that kill millions, one person at a time. They defend free trade but minimize the importance of fair trade. They defend the elimination of tariffs but justify the maintenance of agricultural subsidies in Europe and North America. They are the Pirates of Heartless Capitalism.

It is time to acknowledge that the Pirates live within our own boundaries. It is time to acknowledge that there is plenty of illicit and unethical behavior within our boundaries. Those who do not acknowledge that there are Pirates within our boundaries are friends of the Pirates of Heartless Capitalism.

I see Pirates all around me who claim they are innocent. I see lobbyists and lawyers and financial engineers and corporate managers who think their work does not carry any collateral damage. We all feel perfectly comfortable based on our own user's manual. We define what is right or wrong based on the same user's manual. We determine the rules of the game with which the developing world simply cannot compete. Those who feel perfectly comfortable with this user's manual are friends of the Pirates of Heartless Capitalism.

The Pirates are too focused on securing their wealth to understand the repercussions of their actions. The Pirates are too focused on maintaining their supremacy using their military and industrial complex. The Pirates do not understand that it is time to change their ways and transition from a heartless to a loving capitalism. The Pirates do not understand that is it time to start the Journey of our Lifetime that will take us to Decemland, the land of 10 percent.

Let's write the History of Tomorrow. Let's defeat the Pirates on the intellectual ring of the idea that defeats by conviction and persuasion and never by imposition. Let's depart from Page One of the rest of our lives. Let's accept that we are all dwellers of the same planet, that we are all inhabitants of the same space, where acute differences and extreme inequality should not take place.

The Pirates shall be defeated in an intellectual war against the Axis of Feeble. It is time to move forward and embrace a new discourse. Let's become men and women of stature; let's become lovers who dream and dreamers who love. The World of Cornucopia and Eutopia is closer than we ever thought possible. We live in the best world we have ever inhabited. We are at a tipping point. Let's get on Tardis and travel in time. Let's believe, dare, and act. I urge those who did not give up their dreams to stand up and shout the urgency of our time. I encourage those who never lost the hope to see the great evils of our time evaporate. It is never too late, dreamers, to stand up and start walking. I stood up and started the walk and decided to never stop because I have found gladiators who fought and continue to fight an intellectual war against the Pirates, who wish to perpetuate a status quo that benefits a minority.

LOBBIES

It is important to understand the role of lobbies in the perpetuation of today's capitalist paradigm, and in the maintenance of the old-fashioned economic principles of free-market economics that prioritize economic profit and forsake human dignity and the environment. Lobbies are groups of power close to the political elite that bias the policy-making process, favoring those they most often represent: the corporations. Lobbies are the trade unions of the better off, although much better organized and funded.

In a sense, Robert B. Reich's book *Supercapitalism* is on Lobbies and Elites (Reich 2007). Reich points out, "Lobbyists swarmed over Washington and other capital cities seeking laws and rules that would give them a competitive advantage (or avoid competitive disadvantage) relative to their rivals, wielding greater and greater influence over decision making" (Reich 2007). Welcome to the World of the Bretton Woods Elites, where lobbies perpetuate the competitive advantages that give corporations the bargaining power to continue the maintenance of the old-fashioned economic principles that are annihilating the little human dignity we have left. Welcome to the world of supercapitalism, the new version of capitalism according to the super rich.

The spending rally on lobbying skyrocketed between 1995 and 2005 from about one billion dollars in 1995 to over two billion dollars in 2005 (Reich 2007). This seems to be a trend that started with the Democrats under President Bill Clinton and skyrocketed with the Republicans under President George W. Bush. Will this trend continue under the presidency of Barack Obama? Figure 12.1 depicts the number of registered lobbyists in Washington, DC, between 1975 and 2005. Figure 12.2 depicts the number of lawyers registered with the DC BAR.[2] In both cases the number of either lobbyists or lawyers increased significantly in the 10 years following 1995.

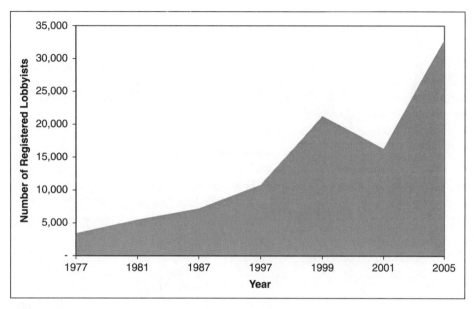

FIGURE 12.1   Number of Registered Lobbyists in Washington, DC
Source: Congressional Budget Office, Reich (2007).

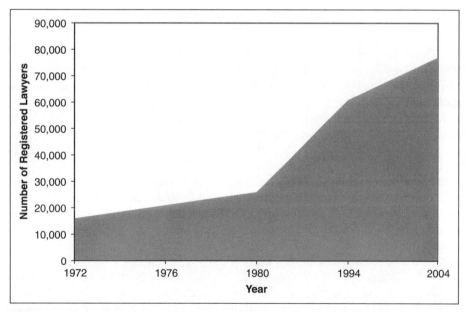

FIGURE 12.2   Number of Lawyers Registered with the DC Bar
Source: District of Columbia BAR Association, Reich (2007).

Economists know well the relation between a nation's number of lawyers and its income growth. It is a negative relation. It is the opposite of the one existing between a country's number of engineers and scientists and its income growth, which is positive. Academia points out that the proliferation of lawyers undermines economic growth. It is time to blow the whistle and acknowledge that lobbies are detrimental to economic development. Hernando de Soto points out in his book *The Mystery of Capital* (2001a):

> *Using economic data from fifty-two countries from 1960 to 1980, Samar K. Datta and Jeffrey B. Nugent have shown that for every percentage point increase in the number of lawyers in the labour force (from say 0.5 to 1.5 percent), economic growth is reduced by 4.76 to 3.68 percent—thus showing that economic growth is inversely related to the prudence of lawyers.*

Charles R. Epp contradicts this finding in his paper "Do Lawyers Impair Economic Growth?" (2006). Epp reexamines the hypothesis that large lawyer populations undermine economic growth. He concludes, "The hypothesis depends on false assumptions about the organization capability and interest of the legal profession; the empirical research in support of the hypothesis depends on flawed lawyer data, unusual combinations of high lawyer populations and low economic growth in one or two countries, and the unjustified use of lawyer population figures from the 1980s in analyses of economic growth prior to that period" (Epp 2006). I would not label Epp's findings inconclusive; after all, I am not an academic referee and do not intend to become one in the foreseeable future. Epp's paper was published by *Law & Social Inquiry*, the Journal of the American Bar Foundation. There could be a latent conflict of interest. The Guild of Pirates of Heartless Capitalism also proves in repetitive pieces of research that their activity is beneficial for capitalism. This is the corruption of knowledge and is presented later in the chapter.

In essence lobbyists are to corporations what private bankers are to wealthy individuals. Small and medium enterprises (SMEs) do not have access to lobbyists because they lack the financial muscle to hire the Washington and Brussels corporate lawyers who can bias the political elite along with their policy-making process. Small and medium wealth owners do not have access to private bankers because they lack the financial muscle to hire the accountants and financial engineers who know the loopholes of the tax code and the imperfections of the financial architecture to take advantage of the tax havens and the tax evasion techniques about which a majority of individuals do not even know.

My favorite lobby of all times is the bipartisan group led by Paul Hoffman in the 1940s. Hoffman was the chief executive officer of the Studebaker Corporation. Hoffman worked alongside Bill Benton of Benton & Bowles Advertising and Marion Folsom of Eastman Kodak. They formed the Committee for Economic Development (Reich 2007). For whom did they lobby? Reich concludes that they lobbied "for the Marshall Plan to rebuild Europe and helped sell the plan to the rest of America" (Reich 2007). As we will see in Chapter 16, Hoffman would subsequently become the first administrator of the Marshall Plan.

Lobbying and Financial Performance

Hui Chen of the University of Colorado at Boulder, David C. Parsley of Vanderbilt University, and Ya-wen Yang of Wake Forest University look at the relation between corporate lobbying and financial performance (Chen, Parsley, et al., 2008). The finance scholars define corporate lobbying activities as "activities designed to influence legislators and thus to further corporate goals by encouraging favorable policies and/or outcomes." The authors explain the purpose of their study and the methodology used (Chen, Parsley, et al., 2008):

> *First, we study the association between a firm's annual lobbying expenditures and its financial performance as reported in the firm's financial statements. We next examine whether a firm's lobbying expenditures are value-relevant to its market price and return.*

The authors compare lobbying with expenditures related to research & development and advertising. Lobbying is an investment activity with an associated return. The authors' conclusions are crystal clear (Chen, Parsley, et al., 2008):

> *First, we find that a firm's lobbying expenses are significantly positively correlated with its accounting based financial performance. We report several robustness and sensitivity analyses, including various measures of financial performance and alternative empirical specifications. Our results appear robust. Secondly, we find that lobbying expenses are also significantly and positively related to firm's market prices and returns, indicating that lobbying expenses are value relevant. Finally, taking a portfolio approach, we compare returns of lobbying firms based on their lobbying intensity, to the returns generated by portfolios of non-lobbying firms. We find that portfolios of firms with the high lobbying intensities outperform their benchmarks of nonlobbying firms.*

The authors also provide insightful data about lobbying activity in the United States among the top lobbying spenders per firm and per sector. Between 1998 and 2005, the number of lobbying firms in the United States increased from 704 to 963 (Chen, Parsley, et al., 2008). Figure 12.3 shows the total lobbying amount per year between 1998 and 2005. The total amount increased by 43.5 percent in the seven-year period. Lastly, Figure 12.4 depicts the percentage change of lobbying dollars between 1998 and 2005 by sector of activity, sorted from highest to lowest. Agriculture, health care, and public administration were the sectors that grew most in relative terms. Manufacturing and Mining & Construction were the sectors whose lobbying dollars shrunk in the seven-year period.

American League of Lobbyists

The American League of Lobbyists (ALL) welcomes its Web visitors with an introduction[3] that stresses the fact that "ALL members adhere to a principled Code of Ethics that focuses on promoting the highest level of ethical lobbying in the country." In the World of the Bretton Woods Elites, there are professional cheaters with

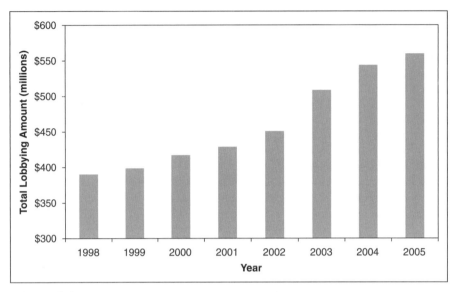

FIGURE 12.3   Total Lobbying Amount in the United States, 1998–2005
Source: Chen, Parsley, et al. (2008). Reprinted with permission.

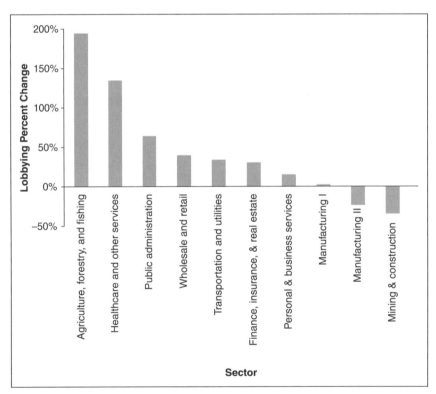

FIGURE 12.4   Lobbying Percentage Change in the United States, 2005 vs. 1998
Source: Chen, Parsley, et al. (2008).

codes of conduct that circumvent the rules by applying the principle that loopholes are there to be taken advantage of. The role of this guild of lobbyists is to defend the interest of lobbyists at large and to promote the profession. ALL is a second-order lobbyist. One of ALL's goals is "to educate people on the lobbying process."

This reminds me of my favorite movie *The Shawshank Redemption*. The movie features Morgan Freeman and Tim Robbins. Tim Robbins' character, Andy Dufresne, is convicted for having killed his wife and her lover. Of course Andy never killed his wife, whom he loved deeply. Andy is imprisoned for life. Andy's best friend in prison is Red, interpreted by Morgan Freeman. Morgan Freeman's performance received a nomination as best actor in the 1994 Academy Awards.

When Andy is finally imprisoned, he realizes every inmate declares innocence. Andy lives in a prison of innocent inmates. That is what this planet has become, a prison of innocent inmates. I am the Andy Dufresne of our prison called market-oriented capitalism. I see around me plenty of Pirates of Heartless Capitalism, including tax haven regulators, private bankers, and lobbyists, all of whom declare innocence, all of whom have a code of ethics, all of whom have established their own bounds of morality and live perfectly comfortable within them.

Andy becomes friends with the prison superintendent. By sending letters to politicians and institutions, he raises funding to set up a library. He is liked by everyone while he prepares for his escape, which he accomplishes 20 years later.

I have become friends with the political elites of our time. I send messages to politicians and institutions. I am prepared to raise funding to set up this venture. I plan to escape from this prison called market-oriented capitalism. I hope to leave the Pirates of Heartless Capitalism declaring innocence behind in 2015, a lifetime after I entered the prison. I hope to take the rest of Humankind with me. The extreme poor come first.

In *The Market as Prison*, Charles E. Lindblom argues against the market, as the market imprisons policy, imprisons thought, and stops the intellectual venture. We live in a market-oriented society (Lindblom 1982).[4] We live in a market-oriented democracy that conditions the policy-making process. A conditioned policy-making process cannot fully work. A conditioned policy-making process cannot fully operate. We live in a society needy of policy changes. The more market-oriented a society becomes, the more incapable it is to adopt changes leading to a new understanding and vision of how the world should function and operate.

The human being is beyond the market. The environment is beyond the market. We need to make sure our policies, whether public or corporate, respect the human being and the environment. We need to make sure our policies guarantee universal access to education, health care, water, and sanitation. These universal rights are beyond market theory and its theorists.

Our will is that of the citizens of the world and is not imprisoned. Our voice is that of the citizens of the world and is not condemned to silence. Market failures and externalities cannot explain the despair of millions. Market failures and externalities are the collateral damage of an economic system that will never work as the theory says or indicates. The system is run by individuals and individuals are human beings who deserve dignity.

I hope to turn as many Pirates of Heartless Capitalism into Reds as possible. Red joined Andy in Mexico's Zihuatanejo. I hope a handful of pirates will one day leave the intellectual prison into which they have confined themselves. If they ever do, they may read this book and decide to join me in Decemland, the land of 10 percent, where they will live happily ever after. *Hope is a good thing. Maybe the best of things and good things never die.*[5]

Lobbying Disclosure Act of 1995

The *Lobbying Disclosure Act* of 1995 is a United States federal law that requires lobbyists to disclose their activity. It was passed in 1995. Under the Act, lobbyists are required to disclose their lobbying activities. A lobbyist is an individual whose lobbying activities represent more than 20 percent of his or her income over a six-month period. Reporting activity is semi-annual.

Lobbying activites are defined as "lobbying contacts and efforts in support of such contacts, including preparation and planning activities, research and other background work that is intended, at the time it is performed, to use in contacts, and coordination with the lobbying activities of others" (United States 1995). Last a lobbying contact is described as any oral or written communication, including electronic communication, to a covered executive branch oficial.

Joan Claybrook reviews the history of the *Lobbying Disclosure Act*. Claybrook summarizes what he understands as the act of lobbying (2005):

> *Lobbying is the process of petitioning government to influence public-policy. This right is one of the most treasured rights in a democracy. Specifically recognized in the Magna Carta of 1215, the right to petition our government was repeatedly affirmed in colonial American treatises, the Declaration of Independence and post-revolutionary federal and state constitutions, including the Bill of Rights. In colonial times, written petitions to local governments were usually simple and brief and almost always answered.*

For Claybrook the first efforts to regulate the lobbying activity go back to 1876, "when the House of Representatives approved a resolution only for that congressional session requiring lobbyists to register for the House Clerk" (Claybrook 2005). The Federal Regulation of Lobbying Act of 1946 targeted domestic lobbyists and provided a framework of registration and financial disclosure for those aiming at influencing the law-making process. According to the author, a 1991 study by the U.S. Government Accountability Office (GAO) revealed that "about 10,000 of the 13,500 individuals and organizations listed as key influence peddlers on Capitol Hill in a book entitled *Directory of Washington Representatives*, were not registered as lobbysts." GAO's findings raised a flag in Capitol Hill. According to Claybrook, as much as 95 percent of registered lobbyists "reported no public relations or advertising expenditures," whereas 90 percent "reported no expenditures for salaries, wages, fees or commissions" (Claybrook 2005). In this context the *Lobbying Disclosure Act* of 1995 was approved under the presidency of Bill Clinton.

ELITES

Elites are groups of power in developed and developing countries that may oppose a change in the current economic paradigm if they sense a change may be contrary to their interests and influence.

Elites in Developing Countries

Inequality in many developing countries tends to be high. This fact was explained in Chapter 5. The Gini coefficient, which measures income inequality, should stay within the range of 0.30 to 0.45 for developing countries. The Gini coefficient is like a human heartbeat: If it stays within the range a person is good to go; if it is too low or too high it is a good idea to go see a doctor.

When it comes to land inequality, developing countries also show a bad allocation of their land resources. As many as a quarter of the world's 1.1 billion poor have no land. An important part of the poor's income comes from agriculture. For the landless poor or those among the poor who have small lots of land, it is difficult to secure sufficient food to remain well fed. For example, in 1994 the top 5 percent of landowners in Bangladesh owned 35 percent of the land. In Bolivia, lots of land larger than 2,500 hectares represent 66.4 percent of the land, while those smaller than 3 hectares represent only 0.8 percent of the land. In Malawi more than 40 percent of small landowners cultivate less than 0.5 hectares, with an average size of only 0.28 hectares.[6] Land reform is important. But those who have control of the resources (large landowners) and the power to introduce land reform (political elite) may be reluctant to move ahead.

Religious Elites

In regard to demographics, many development experts point out that the world's population should not continue growing at the current pace. Major efforts have to be deployed to bring fertility rates down. Basic policies on population growth control focus on the eternal dilemma: education versus contraceptives. The intervention of religious elites is sometimes contrary to the work of policy-makers. Any policy-making that aims at fighting extreme poverty must consider all solutions within range. This is a message of warning for the future policy-maker. Beware the elites and their pressures.

Pope Benedict XVI visited Cameroon and Angola in March 2009. His suggestion that the use of condoms makes the AIDS epidemic worse raised concern among international policy-makers. For *The Economist*, "His statement sounded other-worldly at best, and crass and uncaring at worst" (*Economist* 2009b). The medical journal *The Lancet* responded to Benedict's controversial words with the following statement (*Lancet* 2009):

> *When any influential person, be it a religious or political leader, makes a false scientific statement that could be devastating to the health of millions of people, they should retract or correct the public record. Anything less from Pope Benedict would be an immense disservice to the public and health advocates, including many thousands of Catholics, who work tirelessly to try and prevent the spread of HIV/AIDS worldwide.*

Can a trade off be agreed upon with the religious elites? Is it possible to minimize the extent of their intervention in policies related to birth control and demographics? Policy-making has to be designed based on social science research and not on faith of any kind. This is similar to choosing to build a bridge based on civil engineering or faith.

What bridge would you trust more, a bridge designed based on civil engineering techniques or on religious doctrine? Religion feeds the determination of what is moral and what is not moral. Its ideological fight is a battle of persuasion with the Civil Society, not with the policy-making process. I find that interference of any kind that limits the ability of the policy-maker is an unfortunate event against which policy-makers have to hedge. It does not matter whether population growth control is accomplished through education or birth control techniques. Whatever is most effective in each case should be considered, without the intervening of any faith-based groups.

THINK-TANKS AND FUNDING

As of 2007 there were 5,035 think tanks in the world with the following distribution: South and East Asia (548), Eastern Europe (480), Western Europe (1,187), Africa (265), Latin America (462), Middle East (188), Australia and New Zealand (32), and the United States and Canada (1,873) (McGann 2007). According to James McGann, director of the think-tank Civil Societies Program at Vilanova University. "Think-tanks are organizations that generate policy-oriented research, analysis and advice on domestic and international issues that helps policy-makers and the public make informed decisions about public-policy." For McGann, "The ongoing challenge for think-tanks is to produce timely and accessible policy oriented research that effectively engages policy-makers, the press and the public on the critical issues facing a country" (McGann 2007).

Think-tanks are privately and publicly funded. Corporate funding may bring about the intrusion of the corporate elites in the research outcomes of specific think-tanks. There are numerous examples that uncover this intrusion.

According to the Corporate Europe Observatory (CEO), think-tanks continue to remain reluctant to disclose their sources of finance "despite iniatives such as the European Transparency Initiative" (CEO 2006). CEO approached 22 of the largest multinational corporations that have lobbying offices in Brussels in order to find out more about their funding ties with think-tanks focused on European policy-making. Of the 22 corporations contacted, 13 did not reply, four provided partial information, two gave a basic picture of their financial ties with think-tanks, and three indicated they do not support any think-tanks (CEO 2006). For *The Economist*, "Too many think-tanks accept large chunks of their funding from EU institutions and national governments, others depend on big corporate sponsors, so that the lines between research and lobbying become queasily blurred" (*Economist* 2007c). For CEO's Olivier Hoedeman, "ExxonMobil invests significant amounts in letting think-tanks, seemingly respectable sources, sow doubts about the need for EU governments to take action to reduce greenhouse gas emissions." According to some estimates, ExxonMobil could have spent $19 million since 1998 to fund climate change skeptics (Buncombe and Castle 2006).

According to James Allen Smith, UCLA historian and author of the book *Think Tanks and the Rise of the New Policy Elite*, "corporations have discovered that funding of research, publications, media campaigns and other forms of advocacy on policy issues can serve as an adjunct to traditional corporate lobbying and political contributions." The insurance company AIG is the largest supporter of CATO's study of Social Security privatization (Morgan 2000). In February 2007, *CNN Money* reported that the American Enterprise Institute, a U.S.-based think-tank partly funded by ExxonMobil, had sent letters to scientists providing up to $10,000 "to critique findings in a major global warming study which found that global warming was real and likely caused by burning fossil fuels" (Hargreaves 2007). The Competitive Enterprise Institute (CEI) is another U.S.-based think-tank that received more than two million dollars from ExxonMobil between 1998 and 2005 and has repeatedly cast doubt on the evidence related to climate change. CEI sponsored a TV campaign whose motto was "Carbon dioxide. They call it pollution. We call it life" (Hoedeman 2007).

THE CORRUPTION OF KNOWLEDGE

Who measures the corruption of knowledge, if anyone? Who warns the general public that the message carried by corporate-funded research can be biased and misleading? Where does the funding of our think-tanks come from? What interest do they serve? This section tries to answer some of these questions.

Reich argues, "The corporate takeover of politics also affects how the public understands the issues of the day." He continues and concludes (Reich 2007):

> *Part of the task of lobbying is to provide evidence of the greater wisdom of your point of view, which often requires the work of economists, policy analysts, and other data gatherers and numbers crunchers, as well as word-smiths able to make almost any decision sound reasonable. Legislators need to be able to justify their decision [. . .] Regulators must convince judges they have not acted arbitrarily. Because every side in these contests needs to make the best possible case, large amounts of money are made available to engage experts to provide arguments they may know to be only half-truths or, on occasion, outright deceptions. The result is a broader form of corruption—the corruption of knowledge.*

Does this sound familiar? What about the public campaign sponsored by oil companies to undermine the evidence behind climate change?

Welcome to the World of the Bretton Woods Elites, where the truth is falsified by think-tank research that is funded by partisan groups. Research funding has to be delinked from research outcome. I am not sure many think-tanks would survive if they generated unbiased, independent research that does not necessary fulfill the funder's agenda.

Artwork by Andrzej Krauze.

CHAPTER 13

Institutional Reform

The Soviet delegation to Bretton Woods did sign the Articles and referendum, but Joseph Stalin eventually refused to ratify the agreement, apparently because he feared that Fund policies would be largely controlled by the West. Poland withdrew from membership in 1950. Four years later, Czechoslovakia was forced to withdraw. Shortly after taking power in 1959, Fidel Castro pulled Cuba out.

—J.M. Boughton, *The IMF and the Force of History*

The World Bank and the International Monetary Fund (IMF) are referred to as the Bretton Woods institutions. The World Bank was designed "to facilitate post-war reconstruction in Europe as well as development in other countries." The International Monetary Fund "would ensure a worldwide stable exchange rate regime" (Woods 2000). J.M. Boughton describes it in different words (2004):

Through a combination of national drive, international support— from the U.S. Marshall Plan, the World Bank, and eventually the IMF—, and a homegrown multilateralism in the form of the Common Market and the European Payments Union, much of Europe was growing rapidly and increasingly open to multilateral trade and currency exchange by the late 1950s.

The World Bank and the IMF were designed in the aftermath of World War II, in a world environment that was radically different from today's, under the pressure and the urgency to reconstruct Europe and avoid the threat of Soviet communism. The two World Wars and the resulting lethal destruction accelerated the institution building process of the time. It was the time of our shame as a global community and the visionaries of the twentieth century reacted promptly.

The economic elites of 44 countries met at Bretton Woods in New Hampshire in 1944 and reached a consensus on a new economic and financial architecture. These efforts were led by the British economist John Maynard Keynes and by the American economist Harry Dexter White. Neither of these two lived to see the results of their vision. Keynes died in 1946. Dexter died in 1948. Later visionaries would follow. Will Clayton, George Kennan, Robert Schuman, and Jean Monnet are only four of the names that will come up in subsequent chapters. Where are the visionaries of today?

Many have advocated reform in the Washington-based institutions since the mid 1990s when it became clear that the macroeconomic conditionality and structural reform of the 1980s and early 1990s had not been successful. Many have proposed minor reforms in the aftermath of the mismanagement of successive crises by the IMF: Mexico, Brazil, the Asian Crisis, and Argentina to name only a few of the failed interventions. Minor reforms have not proven to be the right medicine. We need surgery. We need open-heart surgery.

Nobody has flown high enough to have a 30,000-foot view of today's international architecture. Many proposed reform, but did not step back enough to be able to jump further in order to reach the other side, and others did not even attempt to jump. David Dollar minimizes the risk of fall when he states, "There is still room for further improvement because most aid money comes from four big donors who are not particularly selective in either the policy or poverty dimension" (Dollar and Levin 2005).

TWO ISSUES IN CURRENT REFORM

Two issues have driven the Washington elites crazy in the last 15 years. The first is conditionality. The second is representation. Conditionality is a must-have feature in any aid package. There has to be a conditional component when money is given away, otherwise the purpose of helping the poor help themselves is forsaken. It is very difficult to come up with the right amount of conditionality. How much conditionality is too much or too little? Certainly the World Bank and the IMF have leaned towards too much. They have also targeted a definition of conditionality that has been embraced by the Washington Consensus. The Washington Consensus has emphasized privatization and trade liberalization. There is not strong evidence that proves that either privatization or trade liberalization lead to poverty reduction. It depends on whether you see the glass half empty or half full.

I challenge the intellectuals who look at the world from their Ivory Towers and argue that minor reform will lead us to Eutopia. I challenge the political elites who are anchored in twentieth-century capitalism, who miss Reaganonomics and the Washington Consensus and hope a comeback to the 1970s and 1980s is feasible. There is no comeback, I am afraid. There is only one possible way to Eutopia. Today, major reform is not only feasible, but necessary.

Eutopia is Universal Welfare. Eutopia is Global Public Goods. Eutopia is the provision of free health care and education to everyone, starting with the extreme poor. Eutopia is subsidizing water and sanitation to everyone, starting with the extreme poor. I have found a way to Eutopia. The path to Eutopia will take us to Decemland, the land of 10 percent.

Conditionality

Conditionality and structural adjustment have been two of the major policies around which the World Bank has designed and implemented its lending programs to developing countries. In "Can the World Bank Enforce Its Own Conditions," A.M. Thomas points out that the bank increased the percentage of its conditional lending to a high of 64 percent of the total lending in 2002 (Thomas 2004). Thomas concludes, "Aid conditionality is ineffective where reforms lack serious domestic political support and has been counterproductive in some cases" (Thomas 2004). No lending is worse than the one with *imposed* conditionality. Conditionality has to be embraced by the recipient country. There has to be an alignment between the incentive to take the loan and the conditionality that the loan necessarily incorporates. A policy dialogue between donor and recipient is therefore necessary to determine the nature and the degree of the conditionality attached to any lending program.

The European Network on Debt and Development (Eurodad) is a network of 50 nongovernmental organizations from fifteen European countries. Eurodad works on issues related to debt, development finance, and poverty reduction. In June of 2006, Eurodad issued a report entitled "World Bank and IMF Conditionality: a Development Injustice." The report "examines the conditions that the World Bank and the International Monetary Fund attach to their development lending in some of the world's poorest countries" (Eurodad 2006). The results of Eurodad's insightful research are provided in Chapter 20.

Representative Power

The World Bank and the International Monetary Fund are funded by the economic powers of the time of post World War II. The representative power that the economic powers of the time received upon the foundation of the Bretton Woods institutions has not changed ever since and is proportional to the funding provided. Figure 13.1 compares the voting weights of the top 15 countries at the IMF and the World Bank

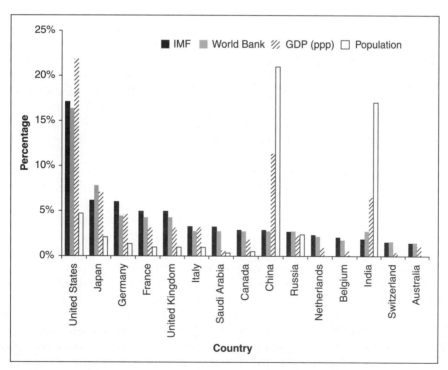

FIGURE 13.1 World Share of Voting Power, GDP, and Population, 2004
Source: Leech and Leech (2005) and Paloni (2006). Reprinted with permission.

with their world share in GDP (purchasing power parity) and population. Countries like the Netherlands, Belgium or Switzerland have a voting weight well above their share of GDP or population. The voting power of China and India should be clearly revised upwards to reflect their economic weight and population.

THE WORLD BANK

Many think that a firm's corporate culture would model any of its employees. The case of the World Bank is different. The Washington-based institution is modeled after its president. It is the president who, over time, has given the institution its personality. The personality has been that of a psychopath. The World Bank has been schizophrenic. The World Bank has been Dr. Jekyll and Mr. Hyde at different times in different decades, depending on whether a Republican or a Democrat was Commander-in-Chief at the White House. Historically, the World Bank president has been an American. The IMF managing director has been a European. So, the presidents of the World Bank have all been American.

Recent Turmoil

Paul Wolfowitz was appointed president of the World Bank on June 1, 2005. Wolfowitz's resignation took place barely two years later in the aftermath of a corruption scandal. Paul Wolfowitz became president with the support of the then President George W. Bush, and became Bush's protégé while at the World Bank. Wolfowitz's presidency was the shortest of any World Bank president in the history of the institution since Eugene Meyer (first president of the World Bank from June to December of 1946). A surprising parallelism can be drawn between Wolfowitz and Robert McNamara.

McNamara was World Bank president from 1968 to 1981. He served as secretary of defense during the Vietnam War. He was appointed president of the World Bank under the presidency of Lyndon B. Johnson. Johnson forced McNamara's election as a compensation for an unfortunate management of the bloody Vietnam War. As deputy secretary of defense, Wolfowitz was the architect of the Iraq War that subsequently became a fatal mistake. George W. Bush forced the election of Wolfowitz as president of a vital institution engaged in the war on poverty. Finally, it was a strategic mistake on behalf of Wolfowitz to allegedly reward his girlfriend, which precipitated his resignation. According to *The Times* Wolfowitz arranged a $50,000 tax-free pay rise for his British girlfriend Shaha Riza (Reid 2007). The resignation was capriciously postponed for months, harming the World Bank's prestige and the extreme poor for whom it is supposed to work day and night.

The collateral damage of Wolfowitz's late resignation has only undermined the patience of European countries that are, along with the United States, the World Bank's major contributors. Wolfwowitz's late resignation catapulted him to the first page of newspapers and tabloids, featuring a history of favoritisms that would have well deserved the application of a preventive policy for his removal from office, which Wolfowitz designed and implemented in the Middle East.

The International Economic institutions are in urgent need of upgrades if they intend to play a role at the beginning of the twenty-first century. Wolfowitz's actions made the World Bank more vulnerable to external critique and exacerbated its diminishing reputation, which Robert McNamara and James Wolfensohn surely improved upon. Wolfensohn was president of the World Bank between 1995 and 2005. Developing countries no longer trust the Washington-based institution. The mistrust is coherent based on the series of pitfalls seen in recent years.

Unfortunately, the presidency of the World Bank is a political position agreed upon between the United States and Europe. There is nothing wrong with the fact that it is a political position. It is wrong, however, that an institution designed for the purpose of helping the developing world cannot be commanded by a president from the developing world.

It is also a bad decision to maintain the World Bank and the International Monetary Fund in Washington, DC, where their policy-making is biased by the intrusion of the U.S. State Department and the White House. That is the unofficial reality. Of course, World Bank and IMF bureaucrats would not admit this publicly.

For years the lending policies of the World Bank have been biased by the West's own interests of spreading democracy and capitalism. There is nothing wrong with spreading democracy and capitalism. It is wrong to use the World Bank as a means to reach this end. It was never designed for this purpose and should never have been used for this purpose. We need institutions that have a *sole* objective: the elimination of hunger and disease and the eradication of extreme poverty. We need to dissociate these goals from the equally admirable but radically different goals of spreading democracy and capitalism that will come naturally once the poor have gotten out of the poverty trap we have helped them build.

Welcome to the World of the Bretton Woods Elites who are afraid of letting the world's institutions move to a developing country, a world in which they are determined to maintain the current status quo, whatever the cost. Let's help the Bretton Woods Elites retire. They have worked hard to maintain the current paradigm. They deserve an early retirement. Subsequent to Wolfowitz's resignation and following the tradition, the American Robert Bruce Zoellick was appointed president of the World Bank in 2007 and became its eleventh president on July 1, 2007. Zoellick is a well-known Republican who worked as deputy secretary of agriculture in the Administration of George Herbert Walker Bush, father of George Walker Bush, whose eight years of presidency came to an end in January 2009. Zoellick was the U.S. representative in the WTO negotiation rounds between 2001 and 2005. Prior to his nomination as president of the World Bank, Zoellick had been deputy secretary of state under Condolezza Rice.

Two Books for Two Presidents

The two most representative presidents of the World Bank in its 60 year history have been Robert McNamara and James Wolfensohn. McNamara was president of the World Bank from 1968 to 1981. Wolfensohn was president of the World Bank from 1995 to 2005. This section reviews the ups and downs of their terms based on the analysis of two authors. Robert L. Ayres wrote *Banking on the Poor* in 1984, focusing on the presidency of Robert McNamara. Sebastian Mallaby wrote *The World's Banker* in 2004, focusing on the presidency of James Wolfensohn.

Banking on the Poor   When McNamara came on board in 1968, the World Bank was not an institution focused on fighting extreme poverty. The World Bank of the time allocated a small share of its budget to extreme poor countries. McNamara changed it all. In his book *Banking on the Poor*, Robert L. Ayres comments, "Only 28 percent of the Bank's agricultural lending in 1972 could be classified as going for projects oriented to the poor." Ayres notes, "By 1977 this had risen to 63 percent. . . . a dramatic shift in a five-year period" (Ayres 1984).

In 1973, 3,000 World Bank delegates met in Nairobi, Kenya, to celebrate the Bank's Annual Meeting. The meeting took place at the Plenary Hall of the Kenyatta Conference Center. The hall was packed. The Nairobi gathering in 1973 represented a major milestone for McNamara, who delivered his best words when he referred to absolute poverty as "a condition of live so degraded by disease, illiteracy, malnutrition and squalor as to deny its victims basic human necessities" (Mallaby 2004). Forty years later the definition of extreme poverty has not changed a bit. What kind of progress has been made?

1973 was a turning point for the McNamara's World Bank. The World Bank would emphasize from that point onward the need to focus on the rural poor in developing countries. Until 1973 the World Bank had only allocated 4 percent of its total lending portfolio of $25 billion to the rural poor. Agriculture lending increased as a result.

In 1980 Ronald Reagan was elected president of the United States. He was inaugurated in 1981, a year in which Ayres reports a fundamental change of approach vis-à-vis the World Bank and its operating policies. Ayres reports that the new administration "questioned the utility of the Bank on many grounds, one of which was the poverty-oriented programs begun under McNamara" (Ayres 1984). With the departure of McNamara, annual agricultural lending dropped from $5.4 billion in the early 1980s to under $4 billion on average in the period 1990 to 1993 (Shaw 2009). McNamara passed away in 2009.

The World's Banker   I phoned Sebastian Mallaby on May 1, 2008. His book *The World's Banker* is a work of art. Mallaby comments, "The shareholders want the Bank to serve their foreign-policy interests; they want it to promote a cleaner environment, human rights, and other values that their voters care about" (Mallaby 2004). Mallaby is right.

During his presidency, Wolfensohn emphasized two main objectives. The first objective was dialogue; the World Bank would have to talk to all the stakeholders, including but not limited to the shareholders. The second objective linked development to noneconomic factors such as corruption. In Wolfensohn's words, "We must learn to have a debate where the mathematics will not dominate humanity." Wolfensohn was right and here is the debate. Mallaby points out that with these words Wolfensohn sounded "remarkably like a structural-adjustment critic from the Fifty Years Is Enough campaign." Mallaby was right again.

James Wolfensohn was the great president of the World Bank in recent times. Mallaby concludes, "The World Bank's next President will need above all to have three qualities: managerial experience, communications flair, and fluency in the issues of development" (Mallaby 2004). Jeffrey Sachs has it all and someone must have told Barack Obama. But there is a better president for a new <u>Bank for the Poor</u>.

Assessing Aid   A critical point in Wolfensohn's presidency was the publication in 1998 of the World Bank report "Assessing Aid." The report criticizes the benefits of (macroeconomic) structural adjustment and donor conditionality (Mallaby 2004).

The report "Assessing Aid" analyzes the role of development aid as well as the World Bank's successes and failures. The report makes explicit that aid can have a positive impact in a good institutional environment (World Bank 1998). According to the report, "countries with public sectors that provide effective, high-quality services are prime candidates for large amounts of financial support." Poor countries with good policies usually attract less aid than countries with mediocre policies. Regarding conditional lending the report concludes, "Conditional lending is worthwhile where reforms have serious domestic support" (World Bank 1998). How can domestic support toward reform be fostered in poor countries? It all depends on what kind of reforms we are talking about and who reforms first. If those who ought to reform first, namely Europe and the United States, move ahead with the reform agenda, those who are worse off may follow suit.

The report also confirms, "A dollar's worth of aid to education may lead to little (or no) additional spending on education" (World Bank 1998). Why do we need to perpetuate the middleman? Chapter 20 recommends avoiding the middleman. Who is the middleman in foreign and development aid? It can be the local government, but also the Bretton Woods institutions and certain NGOs and foundations. Can we get rid of the middleman? Yes, we can.

The report suggests, "Many public services can be provided effectively (often more effectively) by private organizations under contract or holding a concession" (World Bank 1998). This has remained a false premise since 1998. The best run welfare states in the world are those of Western Europe and Canada. Private organizations play little or no role in these countries in the provision of health care and education. Why does the World Bank continue to support a false premise?

Lastly the World Bank proposes, "In difficult environments effective assistance is more about ideas than money or projects." It suggests the following as themes to deliver effective aid under difficult conditions (World Bank 1998): (1) find a champion; (2) have a long-term vision of systemic change; (3) support knowledge creation; and (4) engage Civil Society.

THE INTERNATIONAL MONETARY FUND

The International Monetary Fund (IMF) is much smaller than the World Bank with a workforce of about 2,000 technocrats, compared to over 10,000 at the World Bank. The IMF does help poor countries. At least this is what the institution argues. In 1992 Joshua Aizenman and Robert P. Flood of the International Monetary Fund defined the IMF as follows (Aizenman and Flood 1992):

> *Following World War II the International Monetary Fund was designed and implemented to facilitate aggregate cross-country commercial transactions. The Fund was conceived as an institution responsible for short-term lending primarily for balance of payments purposes and in defense of a system of fixed but adjustable exchange rates. Worldwide capital markets were poorly developed at the time, and the Fund acted as an official version of the yet to be developed international financial structure.*

The IMF identifies the problem of extreme poverty and finds itself a participant in the ambitious target set by the 2015 deadline of the Millennium Development Goals. The IMF's core mission in this context appears to be lending to countries that are experiencing balance of payments problems and exogenous shocks through two programs called Poverty Reduction and Growth Facility (PRGF) and Exogenous Shocks Facility (ESF) (IMF 2007). The interest rate on these loans is only 0.5 percent and the payback period is 10 years.

On top of its lending program, the IMF also assists poor countries with technical assistance and surveillance. PRGF programs target low-income countries that have a reasonable track record of sound policy implementation. ESF programs could help recover from a potential currency depreciation. Countries emerging out of conflict are generally supported through a post-conflict facility. Political factors, and in particular U.S. political factors, play a key role in determining who receives IMF loans (Andersen, Hansen, et al., 2005).

The IMF's workforce was cut by 20 percent in 2008. The projected cut in personnel would save the IMF one hundred million dollars in personnel expenditure. The IMF was in serious need of cutting operating costs in view of its declining lending activity. Dominique Strauss-Kahn, managing director of the IMF at the time said, "I am pleased that this outcome will allow us to achieve our restructuring goals with the least uncertainty for staff and disruption of service to our membership" (Bryant and Guha 2008b).

Domenico Lombardi is the president of Oxonia, the Oxford Institute for Economic Policy. Oxonia is an independent institution devoted to the analysis of economic policy. In *The Role of the IMF in Low-Income Countries*, Lombardi explains that out of the 185 members of the IMF as of year-end 2008, 78 were low-income countries, accounting for more than 40 percent of the organization's membership (Lombardi 2009). The representative power of these 78 countries is roughly 10 percent of the total. By 1990 all 53 African countries had joined the IMF, with a share of the voting power of only 9 percent (Boughton 2004).

According to Lombardi, the IMF lowers the transaction cost of sharing financial information. He comments, "A multilateral institution is in a better position to acquire such data (about the broader investment environment and the quality of policy-making in a given economy) efficiently and to share the informational public goods" (Lombardi 2009). Because of the international credit crunch of the summer of 2008 and the economic recession of 2009, many countries requested financial relief from the IMF, including Iceland and Hungary. If the Fund was on a path to nowhere in 2008, it certainly gained some momentum in 2009.

The latest lending program devised by the IMF in March 2009 is known as Flexible Credit Line (FCL), whereby strong-performing countries hit by the global crisis may use a credit line that "could strengthen further their economic position" (IMF 2009).

THE UNITED NATIONS

The term *United Nations* (UN) was first used by President Franklin D. Roosevelt in 1942 to name the group of allied nations that were fighting against the Axis Powers in World War II.[1] The United Nations was formally constituted at the San Francisco conference of 1945 where 50 countries met. A few scholars object that the sole mission of the United Nations is the maintenance of peace and security. However, a second objective is sometimes included: the protection of human rights.

The UN Charter

The United Nations Charter (UN Charter) is the constitution of the United Nations. The Charter "furnishes the body of rules and norms in accordance with which the powers of the world body and its member states have been exercised" (Joyner 1997). The UN Charter is based on the principle of "sovereign equality of members," members that should be "peace-loving states," which excluded the Axis powers (Germany, Italy, and Japan) and Spain (Karns and Mingst 2007).

The UN Charter determines and makes explicit the context in which collective use of military force can be exerted in cases of aggression by one of the member states. The Charter draws from the previous inability of the League of Nations to stop an act of aggression by one of the member states in violation of the League Covenant.

A lawful use of military force has to comply with the UN Charter's framework for the collective use of force. According to Article 39 of the UN Charter, the Security Council has two roles: (1) the authority to determine if there is a threat to peace; and (2) the power to make recommendations or decide what measures shall be taken to remedy the situation (Arend, Beck, et al., 1996). Upon becoming a member of the United Nations, a member state pledges long in advance of a potential conflict to act unitedly and collectively with all other member states against an actor that has transgressed one of the member's sovereignty.

UN Reform

Jose Antonio Ocampo (FMN) is the former under secretary general for economic and social affairs of the United Nations. I met Jose Antonio on April 16, 2008, at his office at the School of International and Public Affairs of Columbia University in New York City. The overlap of competences between the United Nations and other institutions such as the World Bank is sometimes apparent. Should the United Nations give up its economic capability and focus the purpose for what it was originally designed? Jose Antonio points out, "The United Nations was created to promote peace, human rights and development." The Columbia economist notes that the United Nations started supporting development much earlier than the World Bank. The former Colombian finance minister remarks that Latin America grew more when it was under the influence of the United Nations than when it was under the influence of the World Bank, the IMF, and the Washington Consensus. The Colombia scholar concludes, "The United Nations is much less influenced by Washington and the industrialized world, which grants the United Nations much more independence."

Harvey Morris of the *Financial Times* raised two questions regarding the two runners of the 2008 U.S. election, President Barack Obama and Senator John McCain (Morris 2008):

1. How would a Barack Obama Democratic White House confront the task of reforming the UN?
2. Would John McCain, his Republican opponent, pursue his notion of a League of Democracies?

It is now clear that the United States has probably left behind the idea of a League of Democracies. The League of Democracies would have allowed democratic nations to bypass the veto power of China and Russia and authorize the use of military force when, according to John McCain, the United Nations fails to act (Archibugi 2008).

According to Shashi Tharoor, a former under secretary general for the United Nations, McCain's mini-league would cause only division (Tharoor 2008). Tharoor suggests that not all democracies would eventually join the league. Those that put at risk their relationship with vital trading partners might choose not to participate. For Tharoor, "It is time to renovate and strengthen the UN, not to bypass it" (Tharoor 2008). In the likely scenario that the Obama Administration decides to confront the task of reforming the United Nations, what major changes are likely to occur? Morris adds a third question (2008):

> *Can a postwar system that evolved to safeguard peace in an era of super-power rivalry, decolonization and the nuclear doctrine of mutually assured destruction survive in an age of credit crunch, global warming and the improvised explosive device?*

Chris Joyner (DCA) is the director of the Institute of International Law and Politics at Georgetown University. I met Chris on November 10, 2008, at his office in the government department of Georgetown University in Washington, DC. In a paper entitled "The UN as International Law Giver" (1997), Chris defines the United Nations as a lawgiver who "creates, amends, and implements international law from a variety of sources for its member states." For the Georgetown scholar, the United Nations "surely will maintain its impressive record as a seed bed for developing new rules and norms of international law" (Joyner 1997).

Lucy Law Webster (TNI) is executive director of the Center for War/Peace Studies (CWPC) and the secretary of economists for peace and security. Lucy is also a retired United Nations political affairs officer. CWPC's objective is to replace the law of force with the force of law. The New-York-based nonprofit advocates weighted decision-making and is a supporter of a World Parliamentary Assembly that could broaden the base of UN decisions.

I met Lucy on December 12, 2008, at her fantastic midtown New York apartment. In "A New Deal for the World," Lucy remarks, "The vast inequalities of the present world system are not the only factors contributing to our proclivity to approach our diverse interests in a confrontational way, but reducing these inequalities would reduce mistrust and tension" (Webster 2008). She adds the following:

> *When Jean Monnet and Konrad Adenauer helped create the European Coal and Steel Community, they had a future EU-type institution in mind as well as the efficient use of scarce resources. Thus, one very important how-to principle is to seek structures that make cooperative interaction easy, giving dignity to all participants. Learning by doing is the greatest multiplier; it amplifies, broadcasts, and teaches for an emerging, adaptive interactive global system.*

The former UN political affairs officer does not imply that a world of peace and plenty can be created in a single step. But she believes that a path toward the establishment of a world of peace and plenty can be built. I am in agreement with Lucy. The

Monfort Plan describes a path toward the establishment of Eutopia. The Monfort Plan describes how to start and execute the Journey that will take us to Decemland, the land of 10 percent. It is no longer in my imagination. It is only a matter of feasible priorities. Thank you Lucy for promoting an agenda of peace and plenty. You are an Expert Dreamer upon whose shoulders I stand. I welcome Lucy and the rest of the Expert Dreamers to the new time of optimism that starts on the Decem Date.

The Security Council

The UN Security Council is composed of fifteen seats, five of which are permanent and have veto power. An informal meeting prior to the Security Council's first meeting of January 17, 1946, determined the geographic composition of the six non-permanent members as follows (Kelly 2000): Latin America (2), Middle East (1), Eastern Europe (1), Western Europe (1), and the Commonwealth (1). In 1963 the General Assembly decided to increase the size of the Security Council. As a result, non-permanent seats increased from six to ten with the following geographic allocation: African States (3), Asian States (2), Latin American States (2), Eastern European States (1), and Other States (2). The composition has not changed since 1963. The current 10 non-permanent seats have no veto power and are elected every other year by the General Assembly (Kelly 2000).

Mary Ellen O'Connell of Ohio State University looks at Security Council reform in "Renewing the Council Through Law Reform" (2005). O'Connell raises the question, *What changes can we make that would be real reforms toward the achievement of peace and security in the world?* The three categories of proposals for reforming the Security Council are as follows (O'Connell 2005):

1. Enlarging the Council and reforming the use of the veto power.
2. Reforming the law under which the Council authorizes the use of force.
3. Bypassing the Council in cases where states that want to use force do not get the authorization they seek.

The five members of the Security Council that have veto power are the United States, France, Britain, Russia, and China. The first four are the victors of World War II. According to O'Connell, at the time of design of the Security Council, it was Roosevelt's intent to avoid the pitfalls of the League of Nations. O'Connell concludes, "Roosevelt adhered unswervingly to one central realpolitik derived from his disillusion with the League's enforcement operations, that the four major powers should act as policemen and provide the security for any world organization." O'Connell's own proposal would increase the Security Council from 15 to 21 members, with seven permanent seats. She adds, "The permanent members would be the United States, Russia and China and a representative from Europe, Africa, Asia, and South America, to be decided as those regions wish" (O'Connell 2005).

Michael J. Kelly of Michigan State University proposes a reconfiguration of the veto power. Table 13.1 shows the new allocation according to Kelly's proposal. Three of the five members who currently hold permanent seats with substantive veto power would continue to hold them. France and the United Kingdom along with Germany would rotate for two permanent seats with substantive veto power.

Nine new permanent seats with procedural veto power would be added as indicated by Table 13.1. What is the difference between substantive veto power and

TABLE 13.1 A Reconfiguration of the UN Security Council Veto Power

Term and Veto Power	Member
Permanent Seats with Substantive Veto Power	1.China 2. Russia 3. United States

Permanent Regional Rotating Two-Year Seats with Substantive Veto Power	Europe
	  a. France
	  b. Germany
	  c. United Kingdom

Permanent Regional Rotating Two-Year Seats with Procedural Veto Power	1. Latin America
	  a. Brazil
	  b. Mexico
	  c. Argentina or Chile
	2. Africa
	  a. South Africa
	  b. Egypt
	  c. Nigeria or Kenya
	3. Asia
	  a. India
	  b. Japan
	  c. Indonesia or Pakistan

Source: Kelly (1999).

procedural veto power? With the use of substantial veto power, a matter may be automatically dead. Kelly explains procedural veto power (2000):

> *When the procedural veto is cast, the matter is not automatically dead. Instead it is referred to a special session of the General Assembly for consideration. A majority vote in the Assembly after brief debate, either for or against the matter without possibility of amendment, will then determine the matter's future.*

In "Reforming the Security Council to Achieve Collective Security," Brian J. Foley discusses how the old rules of the UN Charter no longer allow the determination of when it is appropriate to use military force. For Foley, militarism "is alive and well in the world's sole superpower" (Foley 2008) and law cannot by itself eliminate the forces of war. Law can, however, contain them. This is the purpose of his proposal to reform the Security Council.

Foley suggests that a rigorous analysis should be conducted of what he calls alternatives to war. It is his view that a strategy of containment and isolation on Iraq may have worked. Before authorizing the lawfulness of the use of military force, the Security Council would have to assess the harms of war. Foley describes the harms of war as "harm to civilians, soldiers, the environment, cultural artifacts, and economic interests and markets." Once these harms are estimated, the Security Council would be in a position to determine whether the harms outweigh the damages of war (Foley 2008).

Ilyana Kuziemko and Eric Werker of Harvard study "How Much is a Seat on the Security Council Worth" (2006). For the Harvard economists, "A country's U.S. aid increases by 59 percent and its UN aid by 8 percent when it rotates onto the council." Furthermore, "as donor countries use aid strategically, they do not prioritize humanitarian concerns when crafting aid packages" (Kuziemko and Werker 2006).

REFORMING BRETTON WOODS

This section summarizes some of the ideas put forth by academia in recent years to reform the Bretton Woods institutions.

In "The World Bank of the Future," Abhijit V. Banerjee and Ruimin He of MIT examine what the future looks like for the larger of the Bretton Woods institutions (2003). Among their suggestions, the authors note a lack of coordination in default management between the World Bank and the IMF. They suggest "establishing a clear set of rules for dealing with default and enforcing them." The authors also recommend that the Bank "move to a much more scientific process for the selection of projects and ideas" based on "randomized evaluations on convincing quasi-experimental design" (Banerjee and He 2003).

Jeffrey Garten is a professor of international trade and finance at Yale University. Garten argues, "We Need a Bank of the World" (Garten 2008). Garten proposes a Bank of the World instead of a World Bank. According to Garten, a Bank of the World would play the role of a global central bank. A global central bank would regulate and supervise financial institutions.

The main goal of a central bank is typically to control inflation through an appropriate monetary policy. A central bank runs a monetary policy because it controls the interest rates that it can raise or lower at certain times. An interesting example of central banks that no longer run a monetary policy takes place in Europe and the Eurozone. The European Central Bank based in Frankfurt is in charge of setting interest rates for the entire Eurozone. National central banks such as Banca d'Italia or Banque de France no longer control the interest rates that are set from Frankfurt. In this context, what do national central banks in the Eurozone do? They supervise and regulate. They regulate by setting the requirements that financial institutions within their boundaries have to follow. They then supervise to make sure those financial institutions fulfill the regulations dictated in advance.

In the absence of a global currency, a global central bank could not set interest rates for the world. However, a global central bank could play the same role that a national central bank plays in the Eurozone. It could set international standards and then supervise those financial institutions that operate globally to make sure the standards are fulfilled.

In "What Future for the IMF and the World Bank?" Allan H. Meltzer of Carnegie Mellon University summarizes the following three goals that the IMF and the World Bank would need to fulfill going forward (2003):

1. Develop or enhance incentives within client countries for growth.
2. Providing incentives for attainable public goods.
3. Improvements in quality of life and reduction in poverty.

According to Meltzer, the IMF should also focus on two objectives: (1) serving as a quasi lender of last resort; and (2) acting as a provider of financial information that reduces the transaction costs of acquisition. Regarding the first objective Meltzer comments, "Instead of lending to all countries with problems, the IMF should limit its role to preventing the spread of crises from troubled economies to their neighbors, trading partners, and others" (Meltzer 2003).

Regarding the World Bank Meltzer notes, "The Bank can finance global or regional public goods by getting countries to agree on environmental safeguards, disease eradication or reduction, and similar programs with large social benefits and low market returns" (Meltzer 2003). The kind of Global Public Goods the World Bank could finance moving forward is introduced in Chapter 18.

Devesh Kapur and Richard Webb of the Center for Global Development look "Beyond the IMF" (2006). The authors comment, "A consensus has developed that the International Monetary Fund is not fulfilling its role, prompting multiple proposals for reform." They propose five different alternatives for the IMF: crisis resolution, managing the international monetary system, coordination role, surveillance function, and insurance role (Kapur and Webb 2006).

Artwork by Andrzej Krauze.

CHAPTER 14

The Sleeping Beauty

It takes a long time to reach power, but very little to explain to those in power what must be done.

—Jean Monnet

I like <u>Suze Orman</u>.[1] I think she is fresh and inspiring. Her ideas are well explained. She has a good method. She is straightforward. When I tune in to her program, I cannot wait to listen to her say "people first, then money, then things." We all know people come before money, but many often get trapped in the mysterious allure of money regardless.

RICH FIRST, THEN POOR

In the reform agenda the preference is straightforward: Rich first, then Poor. The rich have to lead the reform agenda. We have to reform. We can reform. Many poor countries have to reform as well, but they cannot; they do not have the means, the freedom, the incentive, or simply the funding to accomplish change. We need to acquire inertia. We need to acquire momentum. We need to embrace reform and need to do it at our earliest convenience.

The developing world demands reform. The developing world demands that we reform before imposing our old-fashioned standards to economies that can barely survive and that can barely sustain their own undermined public services. We never thought that the key to a successful development agenda was to start at home, where we never thought reform was necessary.

We do not reform because we are afraid. We are afraid to lose the many privileges we have built over time, sometimes through unjust means. We do not realize that before coming together with the developing world, we have to acknowledge that as Europeans and Americans, we need to do the work that was left incomplete.

I challenge the elites on both sides of the Atlantic to come back with a rhetoric that demonstrates that everything is fine, because it is not. I encourage the elites on both sides of the Atlantic to get in the ring, to fight with their words and persuasion and not through military power or through the abusive power we possess in the international institutions but do not deserve.

Wake up Sleeping Beauty, it is time. Wake up to this unequal world we have built without your consent. You thought the world was the ideal vision in your dreams, but it is not. Wake up, John Maynard Keynes and Jean Monnet. Come back to Earth and see what we have become. Where is our dignity? What did we inherit from the finest men and women of the twentieth century?

Wake up Sleeping Beauty; it is time.

FINALLY WAKING UP

The European Union (EU) is the Sleeping Beauty of the beginning of this twenty-first century. Europe was a devastated continent in the aftermath of World War II. For centuries, European nations fought endless wars. The Marshall Plan for European recovery and the vision of Jean Monnet changed it all.

Europe is now at the forefront of political innovation. It remains, however, a Sleeping Beauty, and at the same time a monster with numerous heads incapable of reaching agreement in foreign policy or common security. The potential on European soil is phenomenal. Today EU members have the unique opportunity and the historic obligation to move ahead and lead the war on poverty and hunger. This section reviews recent challenges and proposes a new environment that may unite younger Europeans and make reform play out in Europe's own advantage as the emerging leading power of the twentieth century.

The Failed European Constitution

On February 20, 2005, Spain became the first EU member country to pass the European Constitution in a nationwide referendum with a low participation rate and a high percentage vote for the Constitution that stood at a strong 77 percent. Spain's enthusiasm with the Constitution was not seconded by France and the Netherlands, which led to a sudden stop and a two-year moratorium that concluded with the emergence of the Treaty in Lisbon in 2007.

Two major lines of argumentation can be linked to the debacle of the ratification of the Constitution of the European Union, both of which played a major role in the failure of the referendum votes in France and Holland. The first topic deals with Turkey's incorporation to the European Union. Turkey would be the second largest country in the EU if it were it to join the Union. With a majority of Muslims and the current confrontation among religious axes, the discussion is likely to perpetuate. The second topic deals with globalization, the role a supranational Europe could play and the loss of sovereignty at the national level. A more cohesive Union necessarily brings about a larger economic market, more labor mobility, and larger cross-border financial flows.

France's vote was used by the Socialists to undermine Chirac's rule of power. Spain's referendum had been supported by both left-wing and right-wing parties. Holland voted in a context of increasing tension between immigrants and natives. It is to a certain extent cumbersome how the controversial Constitution designed by Valerie Giscard d'Estaing, former président de la République in France, and a strong supporter of the European unification process, was rejected in a referendum to be substituted by a Treaty that was subsequently rejected by Ireland.

The Treaty of Lisbon was a lighter version of the Constitution. The European Union is thus farther apart from consolidation. The Treaty of Lisbon owes much of its success to German Chancellor Angela Merkel, the then EU rotatory president, who said at the conclusion of the long negotiation talks, "We are very satisfied with what we have been able to conclude." The Treaty of Lisbon has to be ratified by each member country but is not subject to a referendum vote, except in the case of Ireland, whose citizens had to give the support that no other citizens elsewhere in the European Union would have the opportunity to express, in fear of encountering again the failures of the past that brought down the Constitution. Another failure would have brought to a halt the process of deepening the integration process, once the enlargement process has been ambitiously pursued and accomplished. The failure arrived when Ireland turned down the Treaty in June 2008. Ireland subsequently ratified the Treaty in October 2009. The Treaty was finally a reality after Czech president Vaclav Klaus signed it in November 2009.

According to the EU, the Treaty[2] should provide the EU with "modern institutions and optimized working methods to tackle both efficiency and effectively today's challenges in today's world," an obscure and abstract definition that does not incorporate the European dimension of a continent that seems to be afraid of deepening the bonds that unite its member countries, in a continuous dilemma of regional identity and national independence that is perfectly compatible with a unification process that has to be more explicit about how income redistribution and solidarity schemes are approached, and how the welfare state is maintained.

The Erasmus Program

The EU has consolidated at the vanguard of political advancement in the Western world. The once upon a time six-member European Coal and Steel Community invented in the mind of the French visionary Jean Monnet, has become more than a convenience club and turned into a supranational institution that fosters a climate of understanding among Europeans that once fought in endless wars. The two greatest accomplishments of the EU are the common currency (euro) and the Erasmus Program,[3] a program that fosters exchange studies between European Universities. Whereas the former is well-known in the international arena, the latter is not. However, the Erasmus Program might help the EU consolidate and unify its military capability and foreign policy agenda to have a single voice on the world stage.

The Erasmus Program was started by the then European Economic Community in 1987 as a way to foster understanding among younger Europeans. The Erasmus Program allows a student to complete one academic year abroad in a university of another member state of the European Union. The student abroad receives a stipend and gets credit for his or her academic achievements while abroad.

In terms of the cumulative number of students in the 20 years following the beginning of Erasmus, Germany ranks first with a cumulative number of 263,401 students who have studied a year abroad in other country of the European Union, another followed by France (262,768) and Spain (235,850). In relative terms, Spain leads the ranking in students per-capita who have partaken in the Erasmus Program. The number of Erasmus students was very low in the first year of operation from 1987 to 1988. That year Germany sent a total of 649 students, France sent 895 students, and Spain only 95. On the contrary, in the academic year of 2006 to

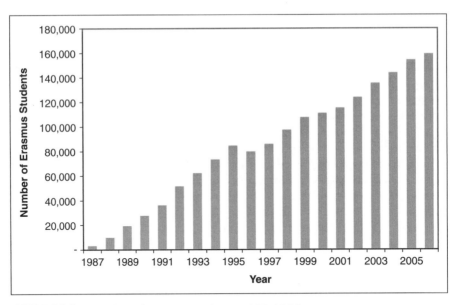

FIGURE 14.1   Number of Erasmus Students, 1987–2006
Data Source: European Commission, Education & Training (2008).

2007, a total of 159,324 college students in Europe studied abroad on the Erasmus Program, of which 23,884 were German; 22,981 French; and 22,322 Spanish. Spain leads the number of incoming Erasmus students per academic year again compared to its peers France, Germany, Italy, and the United Kingdom. The total number of Erasmus students in the first 20 years of the program was 1,683,928. Figure 14.1 shows the number of Erasmus students per year in those initial years:[4]

The Erasmus Program was started in 1987. In its 20 years of operation, it has experienced a significant boom and progressive increase in the number of exchange students sent amongst country members. The program fosters the exchange of college students among member countries, which leverages the students' language skills and widens their base of international friends, with the potential of establishing cross-border relationships that lead to international families whose children will be bilingual or trilingual. The Erasmus Program may actually be the precursor of a new generation of Europeans, born to multinational and multilingual parents, at least one of whom lives abroad.

Economic and Social Issues in the EU

Economic and social issues have been behind the formation of the European Union since the times of the origins of the European Coal and Steel Community. The economic dimension has been enhanced with the Monetary Union, whereas the social dimension has incorporated free-movement across borders (Schengen Agreement) and university-level exchange programs (Erasmus).

The economic integration of 11 countries of the EU-15 has thus far been a success. The later incorporation of Greece, Malta, Slovenia, Cyprus, and Slovakia raises the de-facto Eurozone to a total of 16 countries as of 2009 operating under the same currency, a historical economic achievement that the world is looking upon with the expectation of replicating it in other geographic areas that have previously introduced the idea (ASEAN in Southeast Asia, Mercosur in Latin America, or SADC in Southern Africa).

The social front is enhanced, at last, by the expansion of the Schengen Agreement to a total of 25 countries, 22 member-countries plus Iceland, Liechtenstein, and Norway. In 2009 the United Kingdom, Ireland, Romania, Bulgaria, and Cyprus were still not part of the Schengen Agreement. The Schengen area constitutes a major step toward a single political, economic, and social space where Europeans can freely move, work, travel, and live.

There is no doubt the current state of affairs at the European level has moved forward in the economic agenda that some argue favors the powerful and the multinationals. There is an exciting opportunity ahead of Europeans to consolidate the current process of social cohesion driven by phenomena linked to the Erasmus Program and the Schengen Agreement, from which a generation of Europeans who reckon their belonging to the European Union prior to their country of birth may emerge.

Military Affairs

"The Sleeping Beauty Awakens," according to Wolf von Leipzig (2004). In an article that commemorates the fiftieth anniversary of the Assembly of the Western European Union, Leipzig argues that the European military integration has made major progress. By deploying peacekeeping missions in the Balkans and taking over NATO, the EU started to show some leadership in an area typically dominated by the United States. Leipzig does not hesitate to point out, "The Common Foreign and Security Policy, created by the Maastricht Treaty in 1992, has awakened from its many years of slumber to deal with the challenges and crises in the Balkans, Afghanistan and now also Iraq" (Von Leipzig 2004). It is a mild disruption of the Sleeping Beauty's rest, but it is a beginning.

EU-U.S. Relations

The history of the relations between the United States and the European Union has to be understood in the context of U.S. involvement in World War II, its implementation of the Marshall Plan, and the establishment of the North Atlantic Treaty Organization (NATO). During an official visit to the White House in January 2007, the president of the European Commission José Manuel Durão Barroso reminded those present (White House 2007):

> *This is the most important economic relation in the world, the relation between the United States of America and the European Union. And we believe we can achieve more if we look at it in a comprehensive manner. And I hope that now there will be some concrete work so that in our regular institutional summit between the European Union and the United States we can achieve some more complete results.*

The war in Iraq and the so-called war on terror ruined the joint efforts at a European level to have a homogeneous foreign voice towards the U.S. foreign policy in the Middle East. Britons, Italians, Poles, and Spaniards aligned with the U.S. occupation and its unilateral approach to foreign policy, whereas France and

Germany coupled their efforts with those of Russia to denounce the lack of legitimacy of the U.S.-led invasion.

EU-U.S. relations remain at the forefront of the twenty-first century. Europeans need to strengthen their relations with North America. An Erasmus Program with Canada and the United States is feasible today. The North Atlantic economic cooperation must widen and deepen. The military alliances of the past should be redefined. In what direction should military cooperation be redefined? Chapter 27 delves into a redefinition of military cooperation. The EU and the U.S. must walk together to begin the Journey of our lifetime.

Euro Poll

A successful development plan needs a leading press secretary for the United States. **Mike Mosettig** (PSC) is the senior producer for Foreign Affairs and Defense with the NewsHour of the Public Broadcasting System (PBS) in the United States. Mike thinks the importance of the European Union is underestimated in the United States. I talked to Mark on March 7, 2008. He points out:

> As both a former Brussels and current Washington journalist, I have been following the development and evolution of the European Union for decades. From the perspective of a Washington journalist, what remains surprising all these years is how little effect the process of unification has had on U.S. public opinion, and to a lesser extent, on Washington thinking. This was strikingly clear as the financial crisis spun out of control in the closing months of 2008. For good reason, Washington looked to the major European capitals, not to Brussels, for a European response. But at the same time, Washington can be faulted for not fully appreciating the importance of the euro in preventing things from getting worse, especially competitive devaluations. In some respects, the EU institutionally has seemed to do a less effective job in recent years in explaining itself and the way in which the European idea has become ingrained in much of Europe beyond Britain, and even there. Anecdotally, some of this can be attributed to growing anti-American sentiment, or put another way, the idea that the U.S. is less important to Europe than in the past. In the EU bureaucracies, even its Washington office, a sentiment exacerbated during the Bush years and as well, a historical outgrowth of the post-Cold War years.

A successful development plan needs a respected press secretary for Europe. **Mark Mardell** (PSC) is the BBC's chief political correspondent and has been with the BBC since the end of Margaret Thatcher's era. I phoned Mark on May 2, 2008. Regarding my thoughts on a Marshall Plan for Africa, introduced in Chapter 17, Mark comments:

> You talk of a modern day Marshall Plan. The European Union, while it might be morally inclined to offer the sort of hope you suggest, is politically the worst sort of organization to achieve a visionary coup against the status quo. As I am sure you know every tiny detail is the result of a compromise between 27 nations which all have their own internal strains and debates.

I share Mark's vision. Politically speaking, I think it is unlikely that the 27 countries in the European Union will show any wide consensus in one specific area. The initiative must stem from one country and expand.

The Sleeping Beauty must wake up to the reality of this unequal world into which we have built ourselves. The Sleeping Beauty should lead the effort of redefining capitalism embracing the poor and the environment, and start the journey of poverty eradication and sustainability that will take us to Decemland, the land of 10 percent. It is time, and the second half of this book paves the way for beginning this long journey, a journey of no return, the Journey of our lifetime.

BRIC AND CHINA

BRIC was a term created by the investment bank Goldman Sachs in 2001 to denote the four largest emerging economies: Brazil, Russia, India, and China. The four emerging giants are also waking up. They are growing and catching up with the industrialized nations. They are all members of the G20. China surpassed Germany in GDP terms in January 2009 and became the world's third largest economy behind the United States and Japan. The importance of BRIC is growing. As the world turns multilateral, their voices will be heard more notoriously. Reform must come in Europe and the United States. Reform must also be embraced by the big emerging economies. We have to sit down and finally agree on international standards that save the planet and secure our own survival.

Without international standards that are negotiated and agreed upon under a fair share of representative power, the world becomes a battlefield in which the largest economies fight for the natural resources they need to continue operating on an unsustainable basis. Africa becomes the obvious destination for all, from the Brazilians to the Chinese, including the Americans and the Europeans.

Among the four BRIC countries, China deserves special attention, as it is the emerging economy that has focused its best efforts in conquering Africa with aid and trade. For Goldman Sachs, China's emerging problem is that of population aging. The investment bank confirms, "The growth of the labor force will slow and ultimately decline after 2030." As a result, China "may get old before it gets rich" (Goldman Sachs 2007). Goldman Sachs does not mention in its review of the Asian giant any link between the Chinese increasing investment spree in Africa and its thirst to secure a source of natural resources.

In 2008 Chinese banks continued to pursue their investments in Africa. Trade with Africa was expected to reach $100 billion by 2010, up from $56 billion in 2006 (Green 2008). The annual growth in trade in the four-year period from 2006 to 2010 is equal to 19 percent, nine percentage points above China's average GDP growth of 10 percent. The appetite for resources is increasing at an even faster pace than China's already phenomenal economic growth.

ZhongXiang Zhang is a senior fellow at the East-West Center in Honolulu, Hawaii. In a 2006 paper, he reviews "China's Hunt for Oil in Africa in Perspective" (2006). For the period 2006 to 2010, Zhang predicted that China's domestic energy supply would meet 80 percent of its total consumption. The 20 percent shortfall is to be met through energy imports. How does this appetite for energy translate into China's increasing interest in Africa? For Zhang, Beijing has overpaid its reliance on Africa by "awarding aid and forgiving national debt." He argues (Zhang 2006):

> *Beijing has been building goodwill by strengthening bilateral trade agreements, awarding aid and forgiving national debt. For example, China voluntarily waived $1.2 billion in sovereign African debt in 2000 when the China-Africa Cooperation Forum was formed to promote trade and investment with 44 African countries. To date, Beijing has given more than $5.5 billion in assistance and canceled the debt of 31 African countries. Beijing has helped to build the railroad network in Nigeria, main roads in Rwanda, as well as bridges, stadiums and harbors. In accompanying this, China has forged closer economic relations with Africa. Bilateral trade between China and Africa hit a record of $40 billion in 2005, up 35 percent from 2004. Given that African-Japanese trade totaled US$ 18 billion in 2005, China is outdoing Japan, the world's second largest economy.*

Joshua Eisenman of the American Foreign Policy Council adds, "Under the current Communist Party of China (CPC) Chairman Hu Jintao and the party's fourth generation leadership, China's surging need for energy and minerals to power its impressive economic growth has increased the value of political capital with resource-rich Africa states and, in turn, the importance that the CPC attaches to its political outreach efforts on the continent" (Rotberg 2008).

For Oded Shenkar of Ohio State University, the twenty-first century is *The Chinese Century* (2005). Shenkar remarks that China has become the world's factory and that for over a millennium A.D., China's per capita income was higher than that of Western Europe. One of the keys of China's industrial emergence is its cheap labor compared to other emerging countries. Shenkar notes, "While U.S. manufacturing productivity is five-times higher than productivity in China, the difference is not enough to compensate for a thirty-times higher wage differential" (Shenkar 2005).China's increasing importance as a trade partner and a donor in Africa is noticed by Gernot Pehnelt of the Max Planck Institute of Economics, who writes on "The Political Economy of China's Aid Policy in Africa" (2007). According to Pehnelt, China has already overtaken the World Bank as the major lender in Africa. It is hard to evaluate China's role as a donor in Africa because of China's lack of transparency. China's President Hu Jintao announced at the Beijing Summit of the Forum on China-Africa Cooperation in November 2006 that China would (Penhelt 2006):

- Double the 2006-level of annual assistance to Africa by 2009.
- Provide $3 billion of preferential loans and $2 billion of export buyers' credits.
- Establish a China-Africa development fund with $5 billion in funds to encourage and support Chinese investment in Africa.
- Cancel all interest-free government loans that matured at the end of 2005 owed by nations that have diplomatic ties with China.
- Extend the zero-tariff treatment from currently 190 to 440 exports from African Least Developed Countries and establish three to five trade and economic cooperation zones in Africa over the next three years.

- Train 15,000 African professionals and increase the number of Chinese government scholarships to African students from 2,000 to 4,000 per year.
- Set up 10 special agricultural technology demonstration centers and build 30 hospitals and 100 rural schools.

The China-Africa development fund (CADFund) was set up in 2006 by the Chinese government with the strong support and involvement of the Ministry of Commerce and the Ministry of Foreign Affairs[5] and an initial investment of five billion dollars. The CADFund was designed to foster a strategic partnership between China and Africa. The fund's initial target is to invest between three and four billion dollars in 20 to 30 projects. The goal of the fund is to support African countries with their development of key sectors such as agriculture, infrastructure, and telecommunications. The fund also intends to support the expansion of Chinese corporations (Xinhua 2007). As of November 2009 the CADFund had received one billion dollars from the Chinese government, and had disbursed 500 million dollars (Jopson, 2009a).

For Pehnelt, China's aid engagement in Africa is only a result of China's economic cooperation with the continent. Pehnelt notes that China's economic presence in Africa has risen from four billion dollars in 1995 to $55 billion in 2006 (Pehnelt 2007). China imports energy and raw materials from the African continent. Exports from four sub-Saharan African countries to China have skyrocketed between 1997 and 2006. Gao Jian, the fund's president, points out that the CADFund's goal is not "return on investment but bringing benefit to the two countries" (Lijun 2008).

China's approach to aid and technical cooperation is based on the principle of non-interference. As a result, human rights or quality of governance do not play a role in the allocation of aid to recipients (Penhelt 2007), which could explain why Sudan (lack of human righs) and Nigeria (lack of governance and widespread corruption) are two of China's main trading partners in sub-Saharan Africa. To reinforce its policy of non-interference, China granted a $950 million loan to Mugabe's Zimbabwe in July 2009. In November 2009 the Chinese premier Wen Jiabao announced China would pledge 10 billion dollars in new low-cost loans to Africa at the China-Africa summit in Cairo (Egypt) before an audience that included Sudan's Omar al-Bashir and Zimbabwe's Robert Mugabe. For Wen "There have been allegations for a long time that China has come to Africa to plunder its resources and practice neo-colonialism. This allegation in my view is totally untenable" (Jopson, 2009b).

Hany Besada examines "The Implications of China's Ascendancy for Africa" (2008). For Besada, 1993 represents a turning point in China's approach to Africa and its natural resources. It was in 1993 when China became a net exporter of oil (Besada 2008). Figure 14.2 shows China's outflows of foreign direct investment into Africa in 2006. Table 14.1 shows how China's stock of foreign direct investment in Africa increased between 1990 and 2005.

Jian-Ye Wang looks at "What Drives China's Growing Role in Africa" (2007). For Wang, "because trade and investment have become much more significant in volume than aid flows, economic relations between China and Africa are clearly commercial rather than aid-driven" (Wang 2007). This is a fundamental difference between the relations of China with Africa and those of Europe and North America.

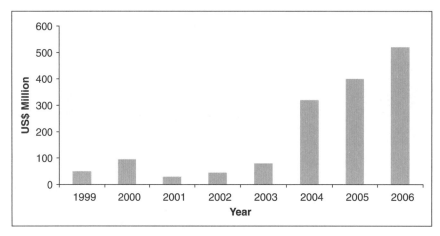

FIGURE 14.2 China's Outflows of FDI to Africa, 1999–2006
Source: Besada (2008). Reprinted with permission of the Centre for International
Governance Innovation.

TABLE 14.1 Chinese FDI Stock in Africa, 1990 and 2005

Region/Country	1990	2005	Region/Country	1990	2005
	(US$ Millions)			*(US$ Millions)*	
Africa	49.2	1595.3	Ghana		7.3
North Africa	3.4	618.4	Guinea		44.2
Algeria	0.4	171.2	Kenya	0.5	58.3
Egypt	1.8	39.8	Liberia		15.9
Libya	1.0	33.1	Madagascar	1.7	49.9
Morocco	0.2	20.6	Mali	0.0	13.3
Sudan		351.5	Mauritania		2.4
Tunisia		2.2	Mauritius	6.3	26.8
Other Africa	45.9	976.9	Mozambique	0.1	14.7
Angola		8.8	Namibia		2.4
Botswana		18.1	Niger	0.1	20.4
Cameroon	0.5	7.9	Nigeria	6.7	94.1
Cape Verde		0.6	Rwanda	2.9	4.7
Central African Republic	1.2	2.0	Senegal	0.2	2.4
Chad	0.1	2.7	Seychelles		4.2
Congo		13.3	Sierra Leone	1.1	18.4
Dem. Rep. of the Congo		25.1	South Africa		112.3
Cote d'Ivoire	0.6	29.1	Togo	0.2	4.8
Equatorial Guinea		16.6	Uganda		5.0
Ethiopia		29.8	Tanzania	1.7	62.0
Gabon	2.9	35.4	Zambia	3.2	160.3
Gambia	0.5	1.2	Zimbabwe	2.5	41.6

Source: Besada (2008). Reprinted with permission of the Centre for International Governance
Innovation.

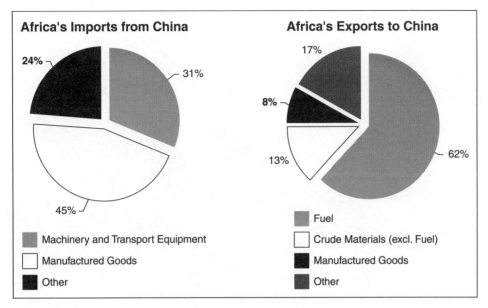

FIGURE 14.3 Composition of Trade Africa-China, 2006
Source: Reprinted with permission of the International Monetary Fund, Wang (2007).

Figure 14.3 shows the nature of the trade between China and Africa. 75 percent of Africa's exports to China are fuel and crude materials. China fundamentally exports machinery and manufactured goods to Africa. The nature of the trade could be described by the phrase *oil for manufactured goods*.

The importance of the ability of African countries to manage the wealth from the exploitation of their natural resources, as described in Chapter 9, is reinforced by the fact that a majority of Africa's exports to its main trade partner consists of fuel and raw materials.

As of 2006, the European Union continued to hold the first spot as the largest donor of development assistance to Africa. Figure 14.3 shows that China was gaining ground, had already surpassed Japan, and was about to catch up to the United States. If trade is added to development assistance, China would surpass the United States to become Africa's second largest aid plus trade partner.

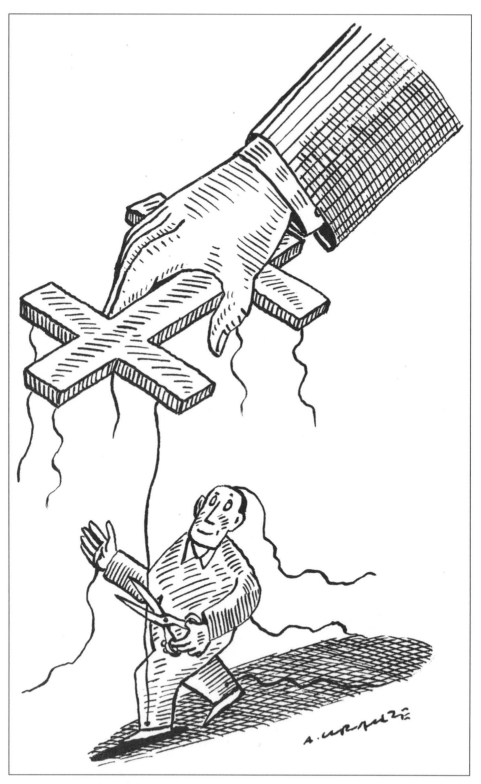

Artwork by Andrzej Krauze.

CHAPTER 15

The Third Sector

A Social Business? Whas is that? It's a business designed to meet a social goal. A Social Business is a business that pays no dividends. It sells products at prices that make it self-sustaining. No profit is paid to investors in the form of dividends. Instead, any profit made stays in the business—to finance expansion, to create new products or services, and to do more good for the world.
—Muhammad Yunus, *Creating a World without Poverty*

The third sector represents many average citizens, who with their time and effort contribute to improving the fabric of society in the developed and developing worlds. Different players in the third sector have different approaches, but they all target an improvement in the welfare of the worse off.

Why is the twenty-first century the time for the third sector? So far the political, economic, and corporate elites have been unable to bring about change in the development arena. We are governed by the same international institutions of the Bretton Woods era; there is no serious alternative to the Washington Consensus and the reform agenda endorsed by the G8 or the G20 does not approach the problems with the necessary largesse the urgency and severity of the moment require. Civil Society, through its associations and its consumers, has the ability to turn the current environment around.

Do the different integrants of the third sector differ in their approach toward poverty eradication? Within the development community there is no clear approach to how poverty should be tackled. Some propose incremental change using tools ranging from microfinance to soft loans. Others suggest that development aid should be increased in order to help the extreme poor fight hunger, conflict, and disease. In the absence of a clear action plan, the multitude of efforts lacks pace and coordination. Thus, synergies cannot be established.

In what areas pertaining to poverty eradication is the third sector most active? The third sector is run through donor support. Donors allocate their funding to those nonprofits they believe are efficient and/or fulfill their own goals.

THE NONPROFIT SECTOR

The twenty-first century nonprofit is a complex reality well defined by SustainAbility, the United Nations Global Compact, and UNEP in the joint report *The 21st Century*

NGO (SustainAbility 2008). The nonprofit sector is worth one trillion dollars a year globally. The report draws two major conclusions. The first is that the market is vital for the very future of non-profits. The marketplace reveals a need and is in a position to provide a solution that satisfies that need. The second conclusion remarks that a nonprofit organization must have a well-designed business model in order to implement its strategy (SustainAbility 2008).

Charities in the United States are much more predominant and active than in Continental Europe. Forbes Magazine ranks the top 200 Charities in the United States. There are over 1.4 million charities in the United States that received $40 billion in private contributions as of 2008. According to Forbes, the top 200 charities had an average revenue equivalent to $515 million, 40 percent of which came from donations (Barrett 2008). The private contributions can either be accumulated in each charity's assets (otherwise called endowment) or spent immediately. The tendency is for a charity to spend a majority of the private contributions it gets in the same fiscal year. A charity's total expenditure is the sum of private support, government support, and other income.

The top 10 recipients of private support in the United States during 2008 were the following: United Way ($4,236 million), Salvation Army ($1,998 million), American Cancer Society ($1,039 million), Food for the Poor ($1,017 million), YMCA ($1,004 million), Feed the Children ($933 million), AmeriCares Foundation ($873 million), Catholic Charities USA ($801 million), Gifts in Kind International ($750 million), and World Vision ($728 million).

Forty-nine out of the top 200 charities work in the area of international needs. The top ten charities in international needs that received most of the private support in 2008 are: Food for the Poor, Catholic Charities USA, Gifts in Kind International, World Vision, MAP International ($393 million), Brother's Brother Foundation ($330 million), Compassion International ($311 million), Operation Blessing International Relief ($278 million), CARE USA ($255 million) and American Jewish Joint Distribution Committee ($242 million).

How much do the top 200 charities spend? What percentage is spent in developing countries? The total volume of private contributions for 2008 amounted to $40.75 billion, up 5 percent from a year before (Barrett 2008). Of this amount, $9.44 billion or 23.16 percent of the total was spent in international needs.

Forbes ranks the top 200 charities according to three categories: charitable commitment, fundraising efficiency, and donor dependency. The categories are defined as follows (Barrett 2008):

1. Charitable commitment: charitable services as percent of total expenses
2. Fundraising efficiency: percent of private support remaining after fundraising expenses
3. Donor dependency: percent of private support remaining after surplus

When the 200 charities are compared against the subset of 49 charities that work in international needs, the latter performs better than the former in all three categories described above. What explains this better performance?

Table 15.1 ranks the best 10 charities in each of the three categories for the sample of top 200 charities and the subsample of 49 charities that work in international needs. Which charities are the leaders in each of the three categories?

TABLE 15.1 Best Ten Performers in Each of the Three Categories

Top 200 Charities

Rank	Fundraising Efficiency	Charitable Commitment	Donor Dependency
1	United Way	PATH	United States Olympic Committee
2	YMCA of the USA	PEF Israel Endowment Fund	Catholic Relief Services
3	Boy Scouts of America	Healthwell Foundation	Direct Relief International
4	Big Brothers Big Sisters of America	Gifts in Kind International	Christian Aid Ministries
5	Cross International Alliance	Smith Center for the Performing Arts	Jewish Federation of Metropolitan Detroit
6	Salvation Army	Rural Economic Development Center	Catholic Medical Mission Board
7	Shriners Hospitals for Children	IMA Worldhealth	Christian Blind Mission International
8	Nature Conservancy	Direct Relief International	Food for the Hungry
9	Mayo Clinic	Christian Aid Ministries	Anti-Defamation League of B'nai B'rith
10	Memorial Sloan-Kettering Cancer Center	American Nicaraguan Foundation	Kingsway Charities

International Needs

Rank	Fundraising Efficiency	Charitable Commitment	Donor Dependency
1	Gifts in Kind International	Gifts in Kind International	Catholic Relief Services
2	Brother's Brother Foundation	Brother's Brother Foundation	Direct Relief International
3	Operation Blessing International Relief	Children's Network International	Christian Aid Ministries
4	PATH	Gleaning for the World	Catholic Medical Mission Board
5	Direct Relief International	Operation Blessing International Relief	Christian Blind Mission International
6	Christian Aid Ministries	Direct Relief International	Food for the Hungry
7	IMA Worldhealth	Christian Aid Ministries	Operation Blessing International Relief
8	American Nicaraguan Foundation	IMA Worldhealth	Kingsway Charities
9	Kingsway Charities	American Nicaraguan Foundation	Brother's Brother Foundation
10	Children's Network International	Kingsway Charities	World Vision

Data Source: Forbes (2008).

What can be learned from the best performers in International needs? Gifts in Kind International and Brother's Brother Foundation are the two top performers in Fundraising Efficiency and Charitable Commitment. Catholic Relief Services is the top performer in Donor Efficiency.

Gifts in Kind International

Gifts in Kind International is one of the top 200 charities in the United States. In 2008 Gifts in Kind International had total expenses of $721 million. The nonprofit spent one million dollars in Management & General expenses and less than one million dollars in Fundraising. Gifts in Kind International got 100 percent of its support from private donors.

Barry Anderson is the former president and chief executive of Gifts in Kind International. I phoned Anderson on January 30, 2009. How has Gifts in Kind International maintained lower operating costs throughout the years? Anderson answers as follows:

> We analyze each program model to ensure that not only does the program breakeven, it also offsets a portion of our operational expense and contributes to our sustainability reserve. We ask donor companies to help fund our operations based on the amount of time and effort required to properly execute their program. For start-up programs we request additional funding for the first year or two. We rely on affiliates where it makes operational sense (particularly internationally). We have ensured that we kept focused on our core business. Low headcount, efficient processes and financial oversight are the key to keeping costs down.

What is the key to a low fundraising efficiency? According to Anderson, "Relying on the networks and contacts of our donors, board members and past grantors has allowed us to keep fundraising down, but it has also limited our ability to secure cash donations."

Catholic Relief Services

Catholic Relief Services (CRS) is the humanitarian agency of the United States Catholic community. Ken Hackett is its president. I phoned Hackett on September 3, 2008. The Catholic nonprofit provides assistance to the needy in more than 100 countries.

CRS is one of the top 200 charities in the United States. In 2008 CRS had total expenses of $597 million. The nonprofit spent $14 million in Management & General expenses and $23 million in Fundraising. CRS got 68 percent of its support through the government. What is Catholic Relief Services' management style like? Hackett states, "One of our guiding principles focuses on the issue of subsidiarity, the idea being that a higher level of government (or organization) should not perform any function or duty that can be handled more effectively at a lower level by people who are closer to the problem and have a better understanding of the issue."

How does Catholic Relief Services approach fundraising? Hackett concludes, "On a fundraising level, CRS seeks to increase our donor base, younger donors in particular, as well as diversify our donor base. We also seek to increase the number of leadership and major donors supporting the agency in addition to focusing on U.S. foundations and corporations which represent philanthropic opportunities for CRS."

What about non-American nonprofits? BRAC is the largest NGO in the world and is presented in Chapter 19.

NONPROFIT MANAGEMENT

What do the following organizations have in common? They are all nonprofit organizations that work in the developing world to lessen the burden of poverty for the worse off. Their leading management provides insight about their worthy activity.

Oxfam America

Oxfam America is the U.S. affiliate of Oxfam International. The organization works in more than 120 countries to fight for social justice. Oxfam America is one of the top 200 charities in the United States. In 2008 Oxfam America had total expenses of $56 million. The nonprofit spent three million dollars in Management & General expenses and $14 million in Fundraising. Oxfam America got 0 percent of its support through the government.

Jeff Ashe is the director of community finance at Oxfam America. I phoned Ashe on March 21, 2008. According to Ashe, "What makes Oxfam America interesting is that we do not take government money because our advocacy work in Washington DC is as important as our development work for the institution."

Pro Mujer

Pro Mujer is an international microfinance network that provides Latin American's poorest women with the financial means to move ahead and leave poverty behind. Pro Mujer's strategy facilitates poor women and their families with microfinance, business training, and health care support. Pro Mujer has subsidiaries in Argentina, Bolivia, Mexico, Nicaragua, and Peru.

VIVIANNE ROMERO (BFP) is Pro Mujer's Director in Bolivia. I met Vivianne at the Pro Mujer headquarters in La Paz (Bolivia) on June 19, 2009. For Vivianne, the financial and health branches of Pro Mujer should be managed separately by individuals who have a proven track record and significant expertise in the area.

Save the Children

Save the Children is one of the top 200 charities in the United States. Save the Children operates internationally. Its focus is the urban children in need in the United States and the developing world. In 2008 Save the Children had total expenses of $350 million. The nonprofit spent $13 million in Management & General expenses and $21 million in Fundraising. Save the Children got 37 percent of its support through the government.

Charles MacCormack is the president of Save the Children. I phoned Mac-Cormack on October 17, 2008. What is Save the Children's management style like? For MacCormack, "Save the Children's management style is results driven, with a premium placed on transparency." How does Save the Children approach fundraising? MacCormack concludes, "Our fundraising approach focuses on low-cost outreach so as to ensure the greatest percentage of our funds go to programs, and that employs the highest of ethical standards."

SOCIAL BUSINESSES

In 2008 Muhammad Yunus published *Creating a World Without Poverty*. Yunus is the founder of Grameen Bank, the world's largest Microfinance Institution. In his book, the Nobel Prize winner raises three questions (Yunus 2007):

1. What is wrong?
2. In a world where the ideology of free enterprise has no real challenger, why have free markets failed so many people?
3. As some nations march toward ever greater prosperity, why has so much of the world been left behind?

For Yunus, a <u>Social Business</u> is a business in which the shareholders are the very own people it serves. In an environment of poverty, the shareholders would be the extreme poor. The incentive to maximize profit is still the same. The only difference is that the earnings are either reinvested to expand or improve the business, or distributed through dividend payments to shareholders, represented by the extreme poor.

Lamiya Morshed (YUN) is the chief executive officer of the Yunus Secretariat. I met Lamiya at the Grameen Tower in Dhaka (Bangladesh) on March 4, 2009. For Lamiya, "Grameen Bank not only provides financial services to its members, but with the rest of the Grameen family of enterprises has been working to meet the diverse economic and social needs of its clients" (Morshed 2006). Every operating business in the Grameen family functions as a Social Business.

Johanna Mair and Oliver Schoen of IESE Business School analyze "Social Entrepreneurial Business Models" (Mair and Schoen 2005). In their paper, the IESE scholars review three different Social Business models, those of Grameen Bank in Bangladesh, Sekem in Egypt, and Mondragón in Spain. The authors argue that the three organizations have created social value and determine the common features of the three business models. In their research the scholars conclude that the three organizations share common features in their approach: the value network, the resource strategy, and the customer interface.

A Social Business changes the nature of the equation of capitalism in developing countries. A good example is the joint venture established by Danone and Grameen in Bangladesh. Yunus points out, "We need a new type of business that pursues goals other than making personal profit—a business that is totally dedicated to solving social and environmental problems" (Yunus 2007).

Yunus is fundamentally right. In today's capitalism it is right to make a profit out of the customer if the customer has a sufficient income. This is, after all, the very essence of capitalism. It is wrong to make a profit out of the extreme poor. We live in a world of limits. We set our own bounds all the time. There are speed limits that cannot be exceeded. There are alcohol limits that cannot be exceeded. Exams are passed above a certain grade and failed below a certain grade. It is a society of limits because it is a society of compromise. We are all part of the same society and mutual respect is essential.

Mutual respect has to be enforced from the bottom up, as well. Mutual respect and compromise have to be global in scope. Before a corporation makes a profit out of the extreme poor, we have to make sure as a global society that the extreme poor leave the poverty trap behind and enter the path to prosperity. Once they reach a sufficient income, corporations may enter and implement a strategy conducive to making a profit.

A Two-Stage Process

In this environment there are clearly two stages in the operation of a corporation that interacts with the extreme poor. In the first stage the corporation functions as a Social Business, in which the corporation's earnings are redistributed to the extreme poor through dividend payments or reinvestment in the improvement and expansion of the business. It is a first stage in which the corporation's earnings help the poor move up the income scale.

A target benchmark is then set. The target benchmark has two conditions. The first condition is to reach a certain average income representative of middle-income countries (set at U.S. $5,000 PPP). The second priority is that the Gini coefficient of the income distribution be below an upper bound, for instance 0.45 as explained in Chapter 5. The corporation shall remain operating as a Social Business until the income and inequality targets are fulfilled. Once targets are fulfilled, the corporation may start operating as a profit-maximizing business and consequently redistributing the earnings to the financial shareholders of the corporation, those who put up the initial capital so that the social venture could take off.

What is the financial incentive for a corporation to enter a market in which it is obliged to function as a Social Business? By entering an underdeveloped market the corporation locks in a future presence. The corporation has to function as a Social Business until the income and inequality targets are fulfilled. Once they are fulfilled it can operate as a regular profit-maximizing business and redistribute the earnings to the shareholders. Only corporations that have started operating as a Social Business during the Window of Opportunity could continue operating in the second stage. Corporations that have not entered the underdeveloped market during the Window of Opportunity would not be allowed to enter the market in the second stage. The Window of Opportunity is described in Chapter 30.

The two-stage scheme rewards long-term investment and sustainability and penalizes greed and short-term speculation. It sends the right signal to the investor community. Only sustainable investors are welcome. Yunus asks, "Why should anybody in his right mind invest his hard-earned money in something that yields no financial return?" (Yunus 2007). The two-stage scheme answers the question. Figure 15.1 depicts the Social Business Life as a function of a country's economic growth and starting per-capita income for Gini coefficients under 0.45 for candidate countries and runners up whose per capita income falls well below the $5,000 mark.

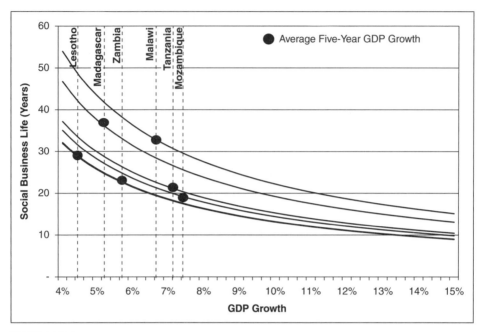

FIGURE 15.1   Economic (GDP) Growth vs. Social Business Life

Danone and Grameen

The French dairy company Danone and the Grameen Group signed a joint venture in 2006 whereby a Social Business was created with an initial capital of one million dollars. The business would manufacture and distribute fortified dairy products in Bangladesh without incurring losses and maximizing the benefits of the clients served. What are these benefits? According to Danone's chairman and chief executive officer Franck Riboud, the benefit is "to bring health through food to the largest number of people in Bangladesh" (Financial Express 2006).

The initial factory was set up in Bogra, 230 kilometers north of Dhaka, the capital of Bangladesh. The business plan targets the construction of 50 plants over the course of a 10-year period. Riboud confirmed on April 29, 2008, that Danone and Grameen would seek to build a second factory in 2009. The new facility would generate 3,000 tons of dairy products every year (France Presse 2008).

I decided to travel to Bogra during my one-week visit to Bangladesh. The Grameen Danone Social Business is a pioneer of what could become a default approach to doing business with the extreme poor in a new capitalist paradigm. Khandoker Mohammad Abu Sohel is the Sales & Distribution Manager at Grameen Danone Foods Ltd. I met Sohel on March 5, 2009, at the Grameen Danone factory in Bogra (Bangladesh). Sohel and his team[1] demonstrated how the way a Social Business is structured helps the extreme poor: from the ladies that deliver the 50 or 100 cups of yogurt in four hour shifts every day to the local farmer and his seven cows that provide the milk to keep the factory operating. I remain convinced the pilot I saw will become mainstream and help the bottom billion get on the ladder of prosperity, once and for all.

What is the next step if the first pilot is successful? Jochen Ebert is general manager with Danone India/South Asia. As of May 2009, Grameen Danone was selling 700,000 cups of yogurt every day, employing 300 women in around 100 locales in Bogra. 150 local farmers provided the necessary milk needed to run the Bogra factory. For Ebert, Grameen Danone is moving ahead slowly, although it is gaining momentum every month. In 2007 Danone proposed a mutual fund that would raise $135 million and pay an interest rate of 3 to 4 percent annually. The investment fund, named danone.communities, enables them to finance the expansion of Danone's Social Business in Bangladesh (Prasso 2007), as well as to start new Social Businesses that fight malnutrition and poverty, mainly in emerging countries.

Asad Kamran Ghalib and Farhad Hossain of the University of Manchester review the case of Grameen Danone Foods Ltd. The authors review the benefits a social enterprise brings (Ghalib and Hossain 2008). For the Manchester scholars the Grameen Danone joint venture brought about a merger of the values of Grameen Bank and Danone Foods. The authors point out, "Social entrepreneurs do not call for the abolition of capitalism altogether; they do not suggest an entirely different business model to run markets; they do not advocate that philanthropy alone can run the world's social markets." Capitalism is, however, understood as a tool to serve the poor, a tool to serve the bottom billion. The authors conclude, "This paper has seen how communities within the proximity of the Bogra facility, a fraction of the bottom billion, have benefited in a number of ways: health, nutrition, employment, and greener environment, all with the possibilties of expanding the operations further afield" (Ghalib and Hossain 2008).

ANTI-GLOBALISTS

Who are the anti-globalists? According to Gijsbert van Liemt of the International Labour Office, anti-globalists "see a world in which the legitimate interests of many people are being crowded out by the power of big corporations, which place the pursuit of short-term profitability above the fulfillment of important needs, such as care for the environment, human rights and poverty reduction" (Van Liemt 2004).

For Jagdish Bhagwati, "anti-capitalism has turned into anti-globalization among left-wing students for reasons that are easy to see" (Bhagwati 2007). For the Columbia professor in a globalized world that lacks global authorities able to enforce standards, an anti-globalist would argue, "Corporations would then be able to seek profits by searching for the most likely locations to exploit workers and nations, thereby putting intolerable pressure on their home states to abandon their gains in social legislation." The Indian scholar concludes, "These anti-corporation arguments are not supported by the facts" (Bhagwati, 2007). If this were true, multinationals would not oppose a paradigm shift that enforces worldwide labor and environmental standards. It remains to be seen whether multinationals join the opposition forces and use the lobbies and the elites as propaganda tools to convey a message that attacks the prioritization of human dignity and the environment. The opposition forces are presented in Chapter 17.

Naomi Klein has become one of the leading thinkers of the anti-globalization movement. Klein's two best-selling books *No Logo* and *The Shock Doctrine* present her thinking. Paul S. Segerstrom of the Stockholm School of Economics analyzes

"Naomi Klein and the Anti-Globalization Movement" (Segerstrom 2003). A Canadian-born journalist, Klein published *No Logo* in 2000, in which she argues against the business practices of multinational corporations and the policies of certain international organizations like the WTO. Segerstrom, a professor of economics at one of the leading economics schools in the world, admits, "My impression is that most economists, including international trade economists, have never read Naomi Klein's book *No Logo*," and adds, "Economists are not responding effectively to the arguments advanced by anti-globalization activists, arguments that resonate with many people, because we do not know what the arguments are" (Segerstrom 2003).

Corporations have shifted their production from the developed world to free-trade zones in countries like Indonesia, China, Mexico, Vietnam, and the Philippines, and have overwhelmingly concentrated their efforts on brand and marketing (Segerstrom 2003). Only ten countries hosted free-trade zones in 1970, compared to 116 countries in 2002 (Kohonen and Mestrum 2009). Labor standards in many of these free-trade zones are questionable according to Klein. Western multinationals have outsourced the manufacturing of their products to developing, sometimes third-world countries with miserable working conditions.

According to Klein, "Wages and standards are being held hostage to the threat of departure in many developing countries" (Segerstrom 2003). Countries compete with each other and downgrade their labor and environmental standards to become the destination of any foreign direct investment with enough bargaining power to discriminate countries that are less restrictive. According to Segerstrom, Klein is "simply wrong about the facts when she states that trade liberalization is not a promising road to economic development." Perhaps we need more fair trade that is also free instead of free trade that is unfair.

Who would you choose to challenge an anti-globalist's opinion? Soederberg uses arguments from research done by strong globalization supporters such as Columbia professors Jagdish Bhagwati and Xavier Sala-i-Martin. Bhagwati's point of view is contrasted with that of Joseph E. Stiglitz in Chapter 7. Sala-i-Martin's methodology to measure income inequality and income distribution is contrasted with that of the World Bank in Chapter 5.

The fact of the matter is that we do not need a violent revolution to embrace a new capitalist paradigm that puts the extreme poor and the environment at the very core of a new consensus. We need a new manifesto for a peaceful revolution, which Wiley's author Laurence J. Brahm provides in his book *The Anti-Globalization Breakfast Club* (Brahm 2009).

Klein joins other representative thinkers of the anti-globalization movement presented in Chapter 3, namely Susan George and Noreena Hertz. If you cannot overtake the mass media, use them to convey your own message. The Weapons of Mass Persuasion are presented in Chapter 30.

Another World is Possible

What kind of other world does an anti-globalist have in mind? According to Van Liempt, there are two main themes in the mind of an anti-globalist. The first theme is a return to the local, involving more emphasis on the local commercial fabric and a more direct link between local producers and consumers. The second theme deals with sustainability and long-term sustainable development (Van Liempt 2004).

The sustainability clause includes: (1) solidarity with the poor that incorporates preferential and fair trade with developing countries; (2) cancellation of foreign debt; (3) closing the wealth, income and inequality gap with the extreme poor; and (4) reform in the financial and global governance architecture (Van Liemt 2004).

The international organization in the global justice movement ATTAC[2] is the best example of what anti-globalists are doing to close the gap between the developed and the developing world, suggesting reform in the international financial architecture. Do not be surprised if the G20 meetings of November 15, 2008, in Washington, DC, and April 2, 2009, in London put on the table a subset of the change suggested by ATTAC in the last decade. In December 1997, Ignacio Ramonet published an article on *Le Monde Diplomatique* entitled "Disarm the Markets" (Ramonet 1997). This is considered to be ATTAC's starting point. ATTAC was subsequently founded in Paris on December 11 to 12, 1998.

On March 5 to 6, 2005, ATTAC Spain presented its political proposal (ATTAC 2005). At the time, ATTAC proposed a change of economic paradigm. ATTAC's proposal included the establishment of the Tobin Tax (presented in Chapter 22), the elimination of tax havens (presented in Chapter 10), the defense of public services (presented in Chapter 5), the cancellation of external debt, and the reduction of financial speculation, otherwise known as short-term investment. Surprisingly AT-TAC's proposals were not seriously considered by the financial and political elites of our time until the previous version of capitalism crashed.

Four

The Building Process

Abeautiful time of change and reform must be started. The international community must get together as it did in times of war, a war that once was and will never be again. We must demand that our elites stop a discourse, which on a daily basis incorporates a military jargon along the lines of nuclear arms and weapons of mass destruction, that belongs in the pockets of our grandparents and should die when they pass away. My grandparents passed away and took with them the old-fashioned views of their generation, a generation who was afraid of yet another World War, a generation who lived through the Cold War—a war that should not and will not happen again.

We have to start building the world of 2050, a world of Global Redistribution and Universal Welfare. We are at a critical time in history, in which a new Bretton Woods summit should take place, triggering a new, creative, and forward-looking building process, a building process that plants today the seeds of tomorrow's institutions and implements a Marshall Plan for Africa that incorporates the poor and transforms their willingness to accept external aid from reactive to proactive.

Part IV looks at the history behind the Marshall Plan and reviews why it worked and what can be learned from it and applied to a Marshall Plan for Africa. Subsequently, it stresses the importance of health care, education, water, and sanitation in the reduction of extreme poverty. Part IV then introduces the core institution of the New Paradigm, an institution that will grant free, basic, and universal access to health care, education, water, and sanitation to the extreme poor without a financial requirement tied to the provision. Finally, the conditionality attached to the provision of Universal Welfare is explained.

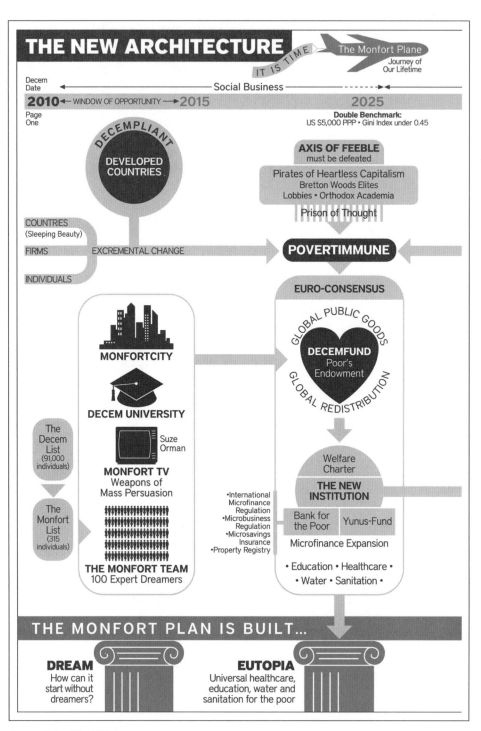

Artwork by Nigel Holmes.

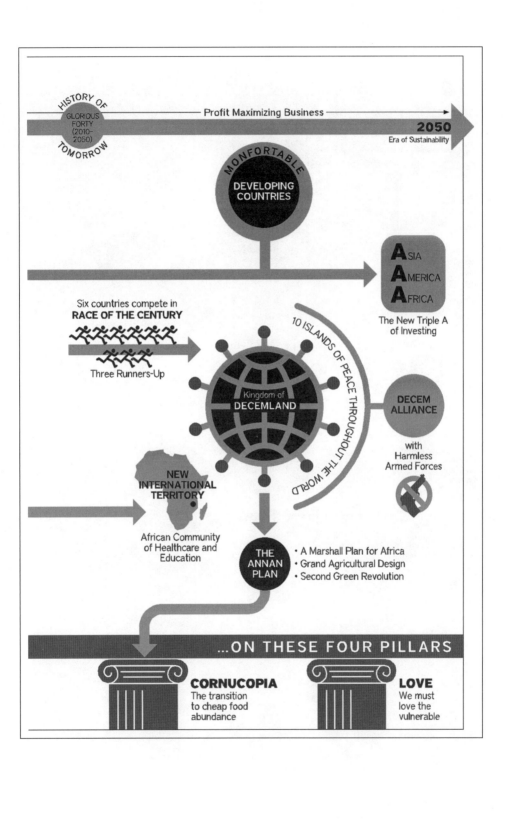

Artwork by Bill Butcher.

CHAPTER 16

Marshall Revisited

*At a press conference around that time, Truman was asked what the United
States "would get" for its aid to Europe. "We are not doing this for credit,"
Truman told the members of the National Conference of Editorial Writers.
"We are doing it because it is right and it's necessary."*
        —Greg Behrman, *The Most Noble Adventure*

A ccording to many political scientists, the Marshall Plan of the twentieth century
was the major accomplishment in foreign policy of the past 100 years. The Marshall Plan's official name was the European Recovery Program. The aid package had
a strong strategic component for the United States. The Marshall Plan proved smart
at a time of desperate need for economic growth and prosperity after three decades
of devastation, which were followed by the Glorious Thirty.[1]

We need to pursue another Forty Glorious Years, The Glorious Forty. We need
to acknowledge the urgency of our time and leave behind the endless debates on
poverty eradication that do not lead us anywhere and only feed the brain power of
our intellectuals. We have to put together ideas that are as big in nature as the plans
described in this chapter. We need to find the visionaries of our time and put them
to work. It is the poor's mandate.

INTRODUCING THE MARSHALL PLAN

The Marshall Plan allocated a total of $13 billion at the time ($120 billion in 2008
purchasing power) to 16 western European countries, namely: Austria, Belgium,
Denmark, France, Germany, Greece, Iceland, Ireland, Italy, Netherlands, Norway,
Portugal, Sweden, Switzerland, Turkey, and the United Kingdom. The largest recipients of Marshall Plan dollars were the United Kingdom ($3.17 billion), France ($2.70
billion), Italy ($1.47 billion), Western Germany ($1.38 billion), and the Netherlands
($1.07 billion) (Price 1955).

Why was the Marshall Plan successful? The plan was successful because the
recipients of the Marshall Plan dollars acknowledged its need in the first place.
Europe was a devastated continent. The winter of 1946 to 1947 was cold and
scarce. Soviet communism was knocking on Europe's doors. Prior to the war, Europe
had been an industrial power. Regaining the industrial fabric was only a matter of

reconstruction for war-torn Europe. Regaining the productivity was only a matter of time for war-torn Europe.

What structural features of the Marshall Plan's design were crucial to its success? The Economic Cooperation Administration (ECA) was the most successful team of public servants that has ever worked in development. ECA was based in Europe and was in charge of administering and supervising the aid. ECA is introduced hereafter.

How did the Marshall Plan deal with the Soviet opposition? The successful North American diplomacy of the time understood well the threat posed by Soviet communism. George F. Kennan, one of the great men of the twentieth century, played a key role in teaching the United States to take careful steps regarding the Soviet involvement in Eastern Europe.

Did the Marshall Plan facilitate the creation of institutions that in the long run have consolidated and proven to be crucial for Europe's stability and peace? At the completion of the Marshall Plan in 1951, French Foreign Affairs Minister Robert Schuman and Jean Monnet continued the legacy of the American visionaries of the time and proposed forward-looking, visionary plans that set the basis of the future European Union.

The Marshall Plan and the Truman Doctrine

The devastation of World War II and the second consecutive surrender of Germany over the course of 25 years, coupled with the Soviet emergence and the rise of communist forces in Western Europe, anticipated the Cold War and set the pace for the foreign policy agendas in the years to come. Europe was torn down. Greg Behrman writes (Behrman 2007):

> *It appeared a medieval work. Millions of people starved in the cities, while farmers and peasants in the country hoarded food for themselves or even their cattle. People had no confidence in the value of their currency or the prospects for their future.*

General George Marshall had been the architect of the war and his military strategies were the basis of the victory in World War II. He was the Supreme Allied Commander in charge of the D-Day invasion. In 1944 Marshall was named Man of the Year by *TIME Magazine*. After the end of the war Marshall was appointed secretary of state and subsequently secretary of defense. Marshall's Harvard speech[2] became the centerpiece of the Marshall Plan.

Marshall was confident about the U.S. motives to undertake the plan. "The consequences to the economy of the United States should be apparent to all. There can be no political stability and no assured peace," he said (Behrman 2007). As a result, the Marshall Plan was motivated by U.S. security and economic interests. The public campaign in the United States was no piece of cake. The Marshall Plan was a major expense that had to be appropriately justified on the grounds of security and economic prosperity. The initiative was driven by the political elite of the United States.

In the days of the fiftieth anniversary of the Marshall Plan the former Chancellor of Germany Helmut Schmidt reminded us, "The United States ought not to forget that the emerging European Union is one of its own greatest achievements: it would have never happened without the Marshall Plan" (Behrman 2007).

France and the United Kingdom were pivotal in the definition of the Marshall Plan and the subsequent allocation of funding. Great Britain was the largest recipient of the Marshall Plan (Diebold 1951). France, on the other hand, was in desperate need for Marshall Plan dollars and accepted the funding conditioned on coordinating its recovery with Germany (Parsons 2002). This set the context for the continuing cooperation between the two core European countries that had been enemies for centuries.

Albrecht Ritschl (ECO) is professor of economic history at the London School of Economics (LSE). I met Albrecht on May 30, 2008, and again on July 6, 2009, at the Economic History department of the LSE. Albrecht notes that the Marshall Plan was not the first development aid plan from the United States to Europe. Albrecht points out, "Already during 1945–1947, the U.S. paid out substantial financial assistance to Europe under various different schemes" (Ritschl 2008).

Harry S. Truman was the thirty-third president of the United States between 1945 and 1953. Truman succeeded Franklin D. Roosevelt and was followed by Dwight Eisenhower. The Truman Doctrine coupled with the Marshall Plan led the U.S. foreign policy in the aftermath of World War II. The Truman Doctrine's core strategy was to aid Greece and Turkey on the political and military fronts so that they would not fall under the communist area of influence. The context of the moment justifies Turkey's early incorporation to NATO in 1952. William C. Cromwell confirms the link between the Marshall Plan and the Truman Doctrine as follows (1979):

> *Most revisioninsts view the Marshall Plan as a fuller elaboration of the Truman Doctrine, designed to erect an economic and political bloc to contain Soviet expansion and to curb the influence of Communist parties in West European countries. Indeed, President Truman gave credence to this view through his later characterization of the Truman Doctrine and the Marshall Plan as "two halves of the same walnut."*

The Truman Doctrine contradicted the Marshall Plan, as the former was targeted to those countries that resisted communism, whereas the Marshall Plan focused on the whole of Europe. In the absence of a clear signal from Washington, there was confusion in Europe regarding the purpose of the Marshall proposal of aid and whether it was simply a substitute for the Truman Doctrine (Cromwell 1979).

The Harvard Address

June 5, 1947, was an important day for U.S. foreign policy. George Marshall had been appointed secretary of state on January 21, 1947, a position he would subsequently hold for two consecutive years. As secretary of state, Marshall was the head of American foreign policy under President Harry S. Truman. His address at Harvard was a critical milestone in the subsequent implementation and completion of the Marshall Plan.

On June 5, Marshall addressed the graduation class at Harvard University in Cambridge, Massachusetts. Marshall's introductory words could not anticipate the historic importance his later message would carry. Marshall started with the following: "I'm profoundly grateful and touched by the great distinction and honor and great compliment accorded me by the authorities of Harvard this morning." Marshall added in subsequent words (1947):

> *I need not tell you, gentlemen, that the world situation is very serious. That must be apparent to all intelligent people. I think one difficulty is that the problem is one of such enormous complexity that the very mass of facts presented to the public by press and radio make it exceedingly difficult for the man in the street to reach a clear appraisement of the situation. Furthermore, the people of this country are distant from the troubled areas of the Earth and it is hard for them to comprehend the plight and consequent reactions of the long-suffering peoples, and the effect of those reactions on their governments in connection with our efforts to promote peace in the world.*

In Marshall's words, there is a strong analogy with today's environment. The world situation is very serious, which seems apparent to many intelligent people I know. The problem is of tremendous complexity. The average man and woman on the street can barely understand the rationale for so much poverty and despair. It is difficult to reach a clear appraisement of the situation. The people in developed countries are distant from the troubled areas of the planet. It is hard for Westerners to understand the urgency of the moment.

Although the world of 1947 was very different from today's world, the urgency of the moment was the same. The challenges of 1947 were very different from today's challenges, but their scope was the same. We need another Marshall address. We need another Marshall Plan. When will it come? Who will give the address and where?

Marshall confirmed that the initiative should come from Europe. Coincidentally, some of Marshall's words are still relevant today. He mentioned, "Our policy is directed not against any country or doctrine but against hunger, poverty, desperation and chaos" (Behrman 2007).

We need men and women with the political stature of George Catlett Marshall, born in Pennsylvania on December 31, 1880, U.S. Army chief of staff from 1939 to 1945, U.S. secretary of state from 1947 to 1949, U.S. secretary of defense from 1950 to 1951, and Nobel Peace Prize winner in 1953. In the Nobel Prize speech given on December 11, 1953, Marshall reminded his listeners (Marshall 1953):

> *We must present democracy as a force holding within itself the seeds of unlimited progress by the human race. By our actions we should make it clear that such a democracy is a means to a better way of life, together with a better understanding among nations. Tyranny inevitably must retire before the tremendous moral strength of the gospel of freedom and self-respect for the individual, but we have to recognize that these democratic principles do not flourish on empty stomachs, and that people turn to false promises of dictators because they are hopeless and anything promises something better than the miserable existence that they endure. However, material assistance alone is not sufficient. The most important thing for the world today in my opinion is a spiritual regeneration which would reestablish a feeling of good faith among men generally. Discouraged people are in sore need of*

the inspiration of great principles. Such leadership can be the rallying point against intolerance, against distrust, against that fatal insecurity that leads to war. It is to be hoped that the democratic nations can provide the necessary leadership.

We learned the lesson of democracy. We now take for granted that we, as Europeans, owe this to the American friend, who sacrified thousands of lives and billions of dollars to pull Europe away from Nazism and out of poverty. Let's become men and women of stature. Let's demand our politicians today to move ahead and to put into practice the lesson we once learned, a lesson that teaches to eradicate once and for all the great evils of our time. The most important thing for the world at this point is to experience a spiritual regeneration. Where are the men and women of political stature? There are only discouraged elites who selfishly defend a myopic interest instead of opening their hearts and minds to the reality of a New Paradigm.

Overall the Harvard address contained two major themes: the first was economics, and the second was security. I cannot think of two better reasons why a second Marshall Plan should today be at the forefront of either the superpower or the Sleeping Beauty. I remain convinced that whoever is the first one to embrace the New Paradigm will have a competitive advantage that will last decades.

Finally, the U.S. Congress passed the Economic Cooperation Act on April 3, 1948. The Marshall Plan dollars for European recovery were approved.

Undermining Marshall

For some academics the Marshall Plan was not the main determinant of the European recovery and its success. *The Marshall Plan: Fifty Years After* is a compendium of papers on the fiftieth anniversary of the Marshall Plan (Schain 2001). The pieces criticize the merits of the Marshall Plan in the European construction process.

As it sometimes happens, the focus of these papers tends to be purely economic and disregards other implications not always fully understood, including the increasing cohesion and mobility of European countries, a social welfare state that grants and guarantees universal health care and education, a social protection network that rewards society as a whole, and a lesser inequality that minimizes social unrest.

As a result of reading and analyzing the book I raised the following three questions that I addressed to Professor Barry Eichengreen at the University of California at Berkeley and to Professor Robert Shapiro at Columbia University. In his piece Eichengreen points out the following remarks (Schain 2001):

- The 1940s were different. There was a belief in the ability of governments to solve problems. Skepticism was reserved for the markets, which had malfunctioned famously in the Great Depression.
- After World War II, a Marshall Plan was necessary because the markets were unable or unwilling to lend. Today a Marshall Plan would be superfluous to all but the very poorest countries, since private capital markets stand ready to do the job.

Shapiro points out, "American public opinion toward the country's involvement in foreign affairs in general, and foreign affairs in particular, would be different today had the Marshall Plan failed" (Schain 2001). I asked the Columbia scholar, "How ready is American society today to spread the wealth with the extreme poor, particularly with an Obama Administration?" Shapiro responds accordingly:

> It has been argued by critics that the U.S., as a percentage of its GDP, has fallen short of other countries in terms of providing foreign aid to the poor. I think President Obama, in succeeding Bush as President, is in a position where he could do more and the American public might support it. Certainly his election showed that the country has moved in a more liberal direction than under Bush. However, the current economic downturn and financial crisis makes it very difficult. If and when the economy improves, there may be an opportunity.

Unfortunately for the Bretton Woods Elites, Eichengreen's first statement no longer holds in today's environment. He points out that the 1940s were different from perhaps 2001. The economic crisis of 2008 and 2009 and the severe malfunction of the financial markets in the aftermath of the credit crunch have brought skepticism back. The 2010s may look an awful lot like the 1940s. Perhaps there will be again a belief in the ability of governments to solve problems. Are we approaching another paradigm?

PRODUCTIVITY AND OUTPUT

Imanuel Wexler, author of *The Marshall Plan Revisited: the European Recovery Program in Economic Perspective*, points out that the main goal of the Marshall Plan was to improve productivity and output of European countries above prewar levels. The Organisation for European Economic Cooperation (OEEC) secretary-general said in an interview in 1952, "The Marshall Plan has raised productivity during four years, but it hasn't created a basis for permanent increase in productivity" (Wexler 1983). This section looks at the accomplishments made in total output increases in industrial and agricultural goods across Europe. Figure 16.1 shows the indices of industrial production in Western Europe for the four Marshall Plan years as a percentage of the level of production in 1938. In 1948 a devastated Europe could only manufacture a fraction of the industrial output of 1938. The Marshall Plan's priority was to increase productivity and output. The increases in output were notorious. The production of certain industrial commodities spiked up as well. Production of steel and cement almost doubled in the four-year period (Price 1955).

The winter of 1946 was cold and scarce. Millions starved in Europe. The scarcity blew a whistle on the other side of the Atlantic. The United States reacted on time. The Marshall Plan also helped increase agricultural output in war-torn Europe. Overall agricultural output increased by 20 percent in the four-year period. Increases by commodity were also significant, which helped Europe feed its population. For instance meat production increased by 40 percent between 1947 and 1952, whereas sugar production increased by 96 percent in the same period (Price 1955), surpassing the 1938 production levels.

A better-fed and healthier population was able to improve productivity and increase industrial output. An increase in agricultural output could also be a

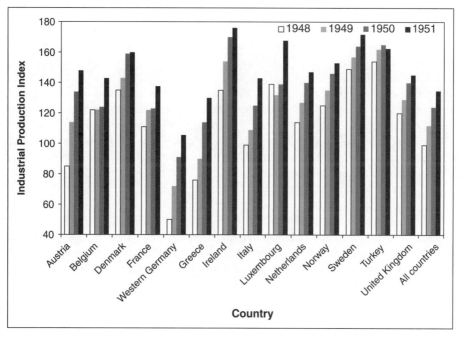

FIGURE 16.1   Indices of Industrial Production in Western Europe, 1948–1951 (1938=100)
Source: Compiled from data from the Organisation for European Economic Co-Operation (OEEC), the Economic Cooperative Administration (ECA), and the Mutual Security Agency (MSA). Wexler (1983).

precondition to pull the extreme poor out of poverty in the 2010s. Overall the gross domestic product of Western Europe increased from $120 billion to almost $160 billion in the four-year period.

WHO WAS WHO IN THE MARSHALL PLAN

The minds behind the Marshall Plan are scrutinized in this section. Behrman points out that "Marshall, Clayton, Lovett and even Kennan never forgot that Europe's confidence, its sense that it could and must assume command of its own destiny, was essential to the success of the Marshall Plan" (Behrman 2007).

MICHAEL INTRILIGATOR (CON) is a professor of economics at the University of California at Los Angeles (UCLA). I phoned Michael on August 28, 2008. In 2008 Michael authored a piece entitled "The Marshall Plan, Foreign Aid, and Overseas Development Assistance," published in the *Encyclopedia of Global Studies* (Intriligator 2008). Michael notes that William L. Clayton was the key figure in the Marshall Plan (Intriligator 2008):

> *The long-forgotten architect of the Marshall Plan was William L. Clayton, a U.S. Assistant Secretary of State, who developed it along with George F. Kennan in 1947. Clayton was also the architect of the General Agreement*

on Tariffs and Trade (GATT) that eventually evolved into the World Trade Organization (WTO). Secretary of State General George C. Marshall unveiled the plan in his Harvard commencement address in June 1947, and it was named for him, but Clayton was the one who designed it.

Behrman notes, "In the spring of 1946, Clayton received Jean Monnet, a French eminence grise in Washington, and negotiated a large loan of several billion dollars in aggregate value for the French" (Behrman 2007). In addition, "On 22 June 1947, barely three weeks after Marshall's speech, William Clayton was dispatched to London, authorized to discuss Marshall's proposal with the heads of the principal governments concerned" (Wexler 1983).

William L. Clayton

William L. Clayton was the architect of the Marshall Plan. In the words of Dean Acheson, Clayton was the catalyst of the Marshall Plan (Fossedal and Mikhail 1997). Clayton was businessman from the South of the United States.

Clayton was born in 1880 and started working in the cotton business in Mississippi. By the end of World War I he had made himself a millionaire. It was Franklin D. Roosevelt who called Clayton up to serve in Washington, DC. His first assignment was to align the Latin American nations against the Axis Powers during World War II (Fossedal and Mikhail 1997).

Clayton became assistant secretary of state in December of 1944. He was later promoted by Truman to under secretary for economic affairs. It was Clayton's intent to help rebuild Europe under the principles of capitalism. Truman asked Clayton to travel to Europe and witness the devastation with his own eyes. Fossedal describes the contents of Clayton's second memorandum to Truman as follows (Fossedal and Mikhail 1997):

> *He crafted this document as a shocking report on the state of Europe rather than a recapitulation of the steps necessary to meet the challenge. He was particularly struck by events in France, where the government faced an inflation crisis and, trying to implement price controls, was unable to persuade farmers to bring their goods to market. People in the cities were literally starving. Something had to be done to restore a modicum of confidence before Europeans could even talk seriously about dropping trade barriers. To encourage free-market reforms, Clayton said, the United States must offer a multi-year grant.*

Marshall drafted his Harvard address using Clayton's two memoranda, a policy planning report from Kennan, and updated information provided by the staffs of Clayton and Acheson (Fossedal and Mikhail 1997).

Paul G. Hoffman

Paul G. Hoffman was appointed head of the Economic Cooperation Administration (ECA). As noted in Chapter 12, Hoffman was the chief executive officer of the Studebaker Corporation. Hoffman worked along with Bill Benton of Benton & Bowles advertising and Marion Folsom of Eastman Kodak. They formed the Committee for Economic Development.

While at ECA Hoffman did not only drive the Marshall Plan to successful completion, he also anticipated that the key to European unification would be a common market (Duignan and Gann 1997). On October 31, 1949, Hoffman, then president of ECA, addressed the Organisation for European Economic Cooperation Council, advocating "a single large market within which quantitative restrictions on the movements of goods, monetary barriers to the flow of payments and eventually all tariff barriers are permanently swept away" (Spagnolo 2003).

The Studebaker Corporation was an automobile manufacturer based in South Bend, Indiana. The company was first incorporated in 1868 under the name of the Studebaker Brothers Manufacturing Company.[3] The company was subsequently purchased by Packard Motor, a car manufacturer based in Arizona. The Packard motor company manufactured luxury cars until it ceased operations in 1958. Roy Gullickson, a mechanical engineer, re-launched the company in 1996.[4]

Hoffman started working for the Studebaker Corporation sales department in 1911 and rose to the presidency at 44 years old. According to Harvard Business School, "In the first nine months of his tenure, sales totaled 30,194 automobiles, which put the company fourth among the independent passenger car producers."[5]

After successfully leading the Marshall Plan efforts, Hoffman became president of the Ford Foundation. Subsequently, he was recruited by the UN to lead the United Nations Development Program (UNDP) for thirteen years. *Fortune* magazine called Hoffman "the father of foreign aid" (Behrman 2007). Alan R. Raucher suggests that Hoffman should be called "the head of the development establishment" (Raucher 1985).

On October 25, 1964, Philip C. Brooks interviewed Paul G. Hoffman in New York City. Hoffman explained during the interview that upon being asked by President Harry S. Truman to head the European Recovery Program, he replied (Truman Library 1964):

> *Mr. President, I am deeply appreciative of your offer, but it would be a mistake for me to accept it because I don't really want to leave Studebaker at this time. I have been working for the last thirteen years trying to help get the Studebaker Corporation to a point where it was making real money. It is there today and I want to be around for the next five years. May I add that it would be a mistake for you to appoint me because I have employed a good many thousand people in my day and I never knew anyone who didn't want the job that was offered to perform satisfactorily.*

To which President Truman replied, "Well, Mr. Hoffman, some of the best people we have in government have to be drafted. We hope you'll prove to be one of them, and I am expecting you to say yes" (Truman Library 1964).

George F. Kennan

George F. Kennan's superb autobiography was awarded the Pulitzer Prize and the National Book Critics Circle Award in 1968, one year after its publication. Kennan is one of the United States' best diplomats and played a key role in the implementation of the Marshall Plan. In the first volume of his autobiography, Kennan comments on his nomination to head the Planning Unit that was in charge of implementing the Marshall Plan throughout Europe (Kennan 1967):

> *I seem to recall that at some time during the first weeks of 1947, while I was still at the War College, Mr. Dean Acheson, then serving as Under Secretary of State, called me to his office and told me that General George Marshall, who had only recently assumed the office of Secretary of State, had in mind the establishment within the department of some sort of a planning unit – something to fill, at least in part, the place of the Divisions of Plans and Operations to which he was accustomed in the War Department. It was likely, Mr. Acheson indicated, that I would be asked to head this new unit when my tour of duty at the War College was completed. I gained no very clear understanding of what was involved.*

The Marshall Plan was first announced by Secretary of State George Marshall in the well-known Harvard speech. Regarding this speech Kennan mentions:

> *We had access to the valuable views and studies of people on the economic side of the department. Will Clayton, then serving as Under Secretary of State for Economic Affairs, did not get back from Europe until mid-May, and the important memorandum he prepared on the subject of European recovery came too late to be of use to us in the preparation of our initial paper; but his views filtered through to us, I am sure in other ways.*

Kennan's deep understanding of the German and Russian foreign policy agendas granted him a key role in the implementation and delivery of the plan. On the last page of the first part of his two-volume autobiography, Kennan wrote a conclusion reminiscent of the political environment in the United States during the second mandate of George W. Bush:

> *"Never before," I wrote on August 14, 1950, "has there been such utter confusion in the public mind with respect to U.S. foreign policy. The President doesn't understand it; Congress doesn't understand it; nor does the public, nor does the press. They all wander around in a labyrinth of ignorance and error and conjecture, in which truth is intermingled with fiction at a hundred points, in which unjustified assumptions have attained the validity of premises, and in which there is no recognized and authoritative theory to hold on to."*

It is time for the United States to shift gears and look beyond what has been the core of its foreign policy agenda in the eight years of George W. Bush; it is time to look beyond a purely anti-terrorist military strategy and address not only the issue of national security, but also the major threats to the environment and the human race.

Overall Kennan's biography fits very well into the storytelling of the Marshall Plan, and his expertise as a diplomat in Germany and Russia conferred him a vision that many lacked at the time. The division of Germany into two parts and the rising popularity of communism throughout Europe at a time of misery were to be fought against with a forward-looking plan that today is seen as one of the major accomplishments in foreign policy of the twentieth century.

In the second volume of his autobiography, Kennan reviews his positions as ambassador in Moscow in the early 1950s and Belgrade in the early 1960s, professes his discrepancies with Secretary of State Dulles, and makes explicit his admiration for President Kennedy (Kennan 1983).

Kennan passed away in 2005 at 101 years old. As one of the key figures in American foreign policy of the twentieth century, Kennan lived under one of the most prominent presidents of the United States in the second half of the previous century, John F. Kennedy. Kennedy wrote to Kennan on October 28, 1963:

> *Dear George: your handwritten note of October 22 is a letter I will keep nearby for reference and reinforcement on hard days. It is a great encouragement to have the support of a diplomat and historian of your quality, and it was uncommonly thoughtful for you to write me in this personal way.*

As a European I am proud of the great contemporary men of Kennan's time who with their great work and passion designed, implemented, and delivered a plan that today is, according to many, the success story of foreign aid of our time. Kennan and his contemporaries understood their moment of truth and urgency and helped build the basis of what is today the European Union, a history of science fiction back in the 1950s.

It is time for the men and women of our time to understand our moment of truth and urgency, to reach new approaches to foreign policy that incorporate the developing world in an international consensus that values the environment and the human being above everything and anything else. "We are not the owners of the planet we inhabit, we are only its custodians," wrote Kennan (Kennan 1983).

THE INCORRIGIBLE OPTIMIST

Jean Monnet is considered the Father of Europe. Otherwise known as Mr. Europe, he is behind the creation of the institutions that accomplished the European Economic Community and subsequently the European Union. The book *Monnet and the Americans* (Hackett 1995) explains in detail the time spent by Monnet in the United States, including with whom he interacted, how influential he was to President Roosevelt to a larger extent and to General Marshall to a lesser extent, and how distant he was from General De Gaulle. Monnet was one of the critical visionaries of his time. The following excerpt reveals some of his insight at a time of change for the world (Hackett 1995):

> *In early summer of 1944, in an interview with a journalist from Fortune magazine, John Davenport, Monnet discussed his thoughts about the future of France and Europe now that the liberation seemed to be at hand. "The countries of Europe," he said, "are too small to give their peoples the prosperity that is now attainable and therefore necessary. The States of Europe must form a federation of 'European entity,' which will make them a single economic unit."*

As a lateral thinker Monnet realized the European Coal and Steel Community would likely trigger an understanding between France and Germany that had been nonexistent in the past. The failure of France and Britain to consensuate agreements and Britain's perennial reluctance to build in the European direction, were key to move forward in the Franco-German axis as the core of the European construction process.

Although Monnet was only slightly involved in the Marshall Plan, he was the main contributor to the Schuman Plan. At the time, Robert Schuman was the French minister of foreign affairs. Monnet was to the Schuman Plan what Clayton was to the Marshall Plan, namely its architect.

The 1940s was a time of challenges on both sides of the Atlantic. Monnet's profound understanding of the British and particularly the American way of conducting politics and foreign policy, proved crucial in his vision for Europe. The Europe we see today is surely a reflection of Monnet's vision. Monnet said, "When our children will look back and consider the period we are going through, I believe they will consider the history of the last 10 years as the charnieres in the course which the world will follow" (Hackett 1995). What about the 10 year period ending in 2020? Will our children look back with pride or in anger?

Monnet was also known as the incorrigible optimist. He was involved in every other plan that had an impact in Europe in the 1940s and the 1950s, including the Monnet Plan, the Pleven Plan, and the Schuman Plan. Douglas Brinkley and Cliffort Hackett point out (Brinkley and Hackett 1991):

> *Monnet was neither politician nor technocrat, nor a charismatic leader of the masses. His unique strength and importance lay in his personal convictions, a network of friendships and influence among the most powerful political figures in France, the United States, Britain, and the other countries of Western Europe, and his extraordinary power to persuade.*

His vision of the future of Europe stems from the failure of the League of Nations to avoid World War II. Monnet was deputy secretary general of the League of Nations at the young age of 30. Brinkley and Hackett point out, "He felt the tragic contrast between inspiring cooperation among allies in wartime, when things were desperate, and its rapid collapse as soon as peace returned, so that the catastrophic cycle started up again." Monnet argued, "Everything I have seen and reflected on here leads me to a conclusion which is now my profound conviction: that to tackle the present situation, to face the dangers that threaten us, and to match the American effort, the countries of Western Europe must turn their national efforts into a truly European effort" (Brinkley and Hackett 1991).

Jean Monnet was a visionary of his time, an optimist of Europe, a European after all. Jean Monnet always looked for the shortcut to tackle problems and was a good friend of some of the leaders of the time. Europeans owe as much to the Marshall Plan as they owe to Mr. Europe, that incorrigible optimist that in his late years had two wishes: win the Nobel Prize and turn 100 years old. Thank you, Jean Monnet.

The Schuman Plan

The Schuman Plan was the most important of the three proposed from France at the time: the Monnet Plan, the Pleven Plan, and the Schuman Plan. The Monnet Plan was a precursor of the Schuman Plan and envisaged shifting the core of Europe's heavy industry from Germany to France (Ritschl 2008). The Pleven Plan was proposed in 1950 by the French Prime Minister Rene Pleven. Pleven suggested building a European army.

The Schuman Plan benefited from the political stability and economic development in Europe fostered by the Marshall Plan dollars. It aimed at European integration by means of a previous unification of the coal and steel industries. Schuman's original declaration included the following words: "If peace is to have a chance there must first of all be a Europe. Europe has not been organized. We have had war" (McKesson 1952). John A. McKesson (1952) summarized the degree of opposition to the Schuman Plan:

> *The Schuman Plan proposes a specific type of economic organization which seeks to combine private initiative with a degree of public supervision. It was inevitable, therefore, that it would be attacked by zealots of every differing shade of opinion. Proponents of extreme liberalism see in it a cartel, and criticize the degree of controls provided. Cartel-minded industrialists attack it as a form of super state control, while doctrinary Socialists attack its failure to provide for nationalization. These criticisms range from the extreme Right to the extreme Left, encompassing those who see too many controls, too few controls, and the wrong kind of controls.*

The Schuman Plan instaurated the European Coal and Steel Community, an institution that was built in times of despair and uncertainty that has proven to be crucial in the future prospects of the European Union as we know it today. In "The Schuman Plan," John A. McKesson points out (1952):

> *The advantages of the scheme are to be twofold. On the political level the "fusion of interests" and the creation of "real solidarity" will eliminate the "age-old enemity* [sic] *between France and Germany," and make any war between the two countries "not only unthinkable, but materially impossible."*

In spite of some opposition, *TIME Magazine* reported December 24, 1951, that the Plan had been approved in the French parliament with an overwhelming majority (*TIME* 1951):

> *Above the squabbles of Europe, and its own internal jealousies, the voice of France sounded bold and clear last week. By a thumping 377-233 majority, the French National Assembly ratified Foreign Minister Robert Schuman's two-year-old plan to pool Europe's coal and steel resources. It was proof—and proof was badly needed—that France can still take the lead in Europe when boldly led herself.*

The European Coal and Steel Community was a major accomplishment of European unification in post-war Europe. *TIME Magazine* reported in 1951, "A supranational High Authority of nine stateless technocrats (no more than two from any one country) will be set up to run the giant combine" (*TIME* 1951). Underneath the High Authority there was a 78-man Assembly elected by the six national parliaments.

LESSONS FROM THE MARSHALL PLAN

What can we learn from the Marshall Plan? This section looks into the lessons that history and historians have suggested were behind the success of the European Recovery Program.

Wood's Memorandum

C. Tyler Wood was an American diplomat who worked as special assistant to the assistant secretary of state for economic affairs. Subsequently, he was deputy to assistant secretary of state in 1947 to1948, assistant to deputy administrator of the Economic Cooperation Administration in 1948 to 1949, assistant Administrator for operations in 1949 to 1950, and deputy U.S. special representative in Europe in 1950 to 1952 (McKinzie and Wilson 1971).

Marshall's Harvard address was a political milestone that sent a first message to the American electorate in preparation for the design and implementation of the Marshall Plan. Wood wrote a policy memorandum on April 7, 1947 that reflected some of the deliberations at the State Department prior to Marshall's speech at Harvard on June 5, 1947. Wood summarized three principles in his memorandum that are presented as follows (Wexler 1983):

1. The initiation of an aid program would have to be preceded by the conclusion of bilateral agreements between the United States and each recipient country, in which the rights of the United States and the obligations of the recipient would be specified.
2. U.S. funds made available under the program could be spent only with the approval, or at least tacit consent, of the United States.
3. The United States would have the right to stop or alter the program at any time, for violation of the agreements or for any other reason.

What lessons can be learned from the basic principles sketched in Wood's memorandum? Chapter 17 looks at the lessons learned from a successful design of a development plan.

The Economic Cooperation Administration

The Economic Cooperation Administration (ECA) was the U.S. Agency in charge of administering the Marshall Plan dollars. Its first director was Paul G. Hoffman, the aforementioned chief executive officer of the Studebaker automobile corporation. President Harry S. Truman appointed Hoffman to head ECA. Congress thought that the European Recovery Program (Marshall Plan) would be best run and managed by people with considerable business and financial experience (Hopkins 1997).

Who would be best positioned to run a second Marshall Plan? What would be the advice for anyone who designed a team of Expert Dreamers with the ability to administer a massive development aid program? ECA offers important lessons regarding the success of the Marshall Plan. First, hire the most talented among the Expert Dreamers. Second, put them to work in the countries where funds are being allocated. These are lessons to take into account. Chapter 29 delves into the recruiting process leading to the formation of the team of Expert Dreamers, inspired by the lessons drawn from ECA.

On November 17, 1947, *TIME Magazine* published an article entitled "The Great Deed" (*TIME* 1947). *TIME* introduced the Economic Cooperation Administration (ECA) as follows:

> *The administering body should have wide and flexible authority to procure goods and facilities, administer and allocate funds. It should work in close cooperation with the State Department. It should make frequent and complete reports to Congress. Appropriations should be on an annual basis.*

Cominform

Cominform represented the Soviet reaction to the Marshall Plan. It was the substitute of the prewar Cominterm.[6] The idea was first discussed by Tito and Stalin in May to June of 1946, a year before Marshall's Harvard address of June 1947. There were three leaders of Cominform: Zhdanov, Malenkov, and Marshal Tito (New International 1947). The first meeting of Cominform took place in September 1947. It exhorted communists worldwide to fight the Marshall Plan, and to fight against American expansionism. The second took place in June 1948 (*TIME* 1949).

On September 22 to 27, 1947, nine Communist parties met at Szlarska Poreba in Poland to debate the formation of a new international Communist organization (Parrish and Narinsky 1994). French and Italian communists attended the conference. The move was the obvious reaction to Marshall's Harvard address and the Marshall Plan. At the conference the representative of the Hungarian communist party pointed out (Parrish and Narinsky 1994):

> *The question of whether Hungary will become a people's democracy or a bourgeois democracy, whether Hungary will join the ranks of the countries of new democracy or become a bastion of Anglo-American imperialism, is not yet decided. Currently in Hungary there exists a mixture of both one and the other types of democracy, and which type of democracy will finally be established depends on the energy, tactics, and talent of the Communist Party.*

Andrei Zhdanov was Stalin's lieutenant at the conference. Stalin ordered him to work with foreign communists in designing a strategy to counter American expansionism. Zhdanov's concluding remarks in the conference were as follows (Parrish and Narinsky 1994):

> *In particular, when discussing mistakes, it is appropriate to note the mistakes of the leadership of the French and Italian parties in response to the new crusade against the working class by world imperialism. The French and Italian leaders have not unmasked in sufficient measure the Truman-Marshall plan, the American plan of enslavement of Europe, and in particular France. The departure of the Communists from the Paul Ramadier government in France was regarded by the French Communist party as an internal French matter, when the real reason for the exclusion of the Communists from the government was American demands. Now it has become completely clear that the removal of the Communists from the government was a prior condition for receipt of American credits.*

The big question for Americans after the Harvard address was whether the Soviet Union would accept to become a recipient of the Marshall Plan dollars. Soviet analysts would admit that America's move was political and aimed at establishing an anti-communist block in Western Europe. They saw the Marshall Plan as a continuation of the Truman Doctrine that would prioritize active pressure against the expansion of communism into Greece and Turkey (Reynolds 1997).

On July 12, 1947, the sixteen recipient countries of the Marshall Plan dollars met in Paris with representatives of the United States. Only a month prior, the United States had issued invitations to the meetings to every European country including the Soviet Union and excluding Franco's Spain (Reynolds 1997). Eastern European countries were pressured by the Soviet Union through Cominform and none of them attended the July 12 meeting in spite of the American invitation.

Why did the Soviet reject the Marshall Plan? Scott D. Parrish of the University of Texas at Austin and Mikhail M. Narinsky of the Institute of Universal History looked at "New Evidence on the Soviet Rejection of the Marshall Plan" (1994). Soviet policy in the aftermath of World War II was increasingly defensive and reactive. The United States feared that the worsening economic environment in 1946 and 1947 could see communists emerge in France and Italy. When Stalin found out about the Marshall Plan he had no other alternative than to provoke a confrontation (Parrish and Narinsky 1994).

The Soviets were concerned about a possible German resurgence after the war. They proposed a $20 billion payment from Germany as reparation costs and suggested a German demilitarization that would yield a prominent role for German communists (Parrish and Narinsky 1994).

When Marshall and Stalin spoke on April 15, 1947, Secretary of State George Marshall pointed out that his desire was to "rebuild the basis of cooperation which had existed during the war and that he had come to Generalissimo Stalin with that hope, feeling that if they cleared away some of suspicion it would be a good beginning for the restoration of that understanding" (Parrish and Narinsky 1994). Soviet doubts on American expansionism in Europe had been reinforced when President Harry S. Truman asked Congress for economic and military support for Greece and Turkey on March 12, 1947, which started the Truman Doctrine.

There is a straightforward analogy between this environment and the environment in the aftermath of September 11, 2001. Some scholars have argued that a second Cold War is about to emerge between Western society and Islamic fundamentalism. The Bush Doctrine would have flooded Iraq and Afghanistan with economic and military support. A Marshall Plan for the area would have then been implemented. A Marshall Plan for Iraq? There is a slight difference. George W. Bush is not Harry S. Truman. There is no such Bush Doctrine. Military and economic support to Iraq and Afghanistan has been unsuccessful, unlike that supplied to Greece and Turkey, and last but not least, there is no such thing as a Marshall Plan for Iraq.

Opposition Forces

There are always a handful of pessimists. It is important to listen to the pessimists because they may be right. But it is also important to move ahead in spite of them. Understanding the opposition forces to any major initiative is important. Identifying them is crucial.

There is a difference between pessimists and opposition forces. Pessimists will undermine a proposal with an objective and constructive critique. They play a role. Because of them a proposal can be refined and eventually improved. Opposition forces will fight by axiom and principle. Opposition forces will divide and conquer, willing to become an alternative. Cominform was an opposition force that divided and conquered Eastern Europe. Eastern Europe then lived in decades of isolationism. The Cold War emerged. What are the opposition forces of our time? Chapter 17 identifies them.

Business Infrastructure

In "The Forgotten Lessons of the Marshall Plan," R. Glenn Hubbard and William Duggan review what many development experts forgot about the European Recovery Program: that to combat poverty in Africa, "government should redirect aid to foster local business" (Hubbard and Duggan 2008).

For the researchers, "Most of the existing proposals represent a great misunderstanding of the intention of the original Marshall Plan and the way it worked." They argue that the Marshall Plan had four key components that led to its success. The fourth component was "a regional coordinating body that handled the distribution of funds among countries," which "ensured that countries would compete for funds." The authors' insightful comments will prove crucial in subsequent chapters. They argue (Hubbard and Duggan 2008):

> *The new plan should require an international commission to provide oversight. And a structure should be put in place, equivalent to the original plan's ECA, to collect and manage the funds on the donor side. Under such a plan, an African country would become eligible by putting policies in place to foster business development; each member government would then have its revolving fund in a special account. In the Marshall Plan, governments spent the repaid loans on economic infrastructure projects approved by the ECA. A Marshall Plan for Africa should establish a similar structure. Given Africa's size and diversity, there might be regional ECAs rather than a single one for the whole continent.*

The authors conclude that the plan should focus on business infrastructure. I make a slight variation of their comment. I think the plan should focus on microbusiness infrastructure. Microbusiness refers to a business run by a microentrepreneur through a microcredit granted by a Microfinance Institution. Microfinance plays a pivotal role in the new version of capitalism. As a result, microfinance empowers the poor by providing basic financial tools that allow the poor to save and borrow in a stable currency. Chapter 22 and Chapter 23 delve more into microfinance. This observation is crucial and has repercussions that reach the new international financial architecture. In the new financial architecture the Bank for the Poor is the alternative to the World Bank.

In "The Marshall Plan: A Strategy that Worked," David W. Ellwood presents the structural features that made the plan a success. For Ellwood the supreme objective of the plan was "to create a healthy economy independent of extraordinary outside assistance" (Ellwood 2008).

Public diplomacy is the term used by Douglas Von Korff to denote how the public opinion in the United States and Europe was persuaded regarding the political convenience of implementing the plan. In Von Korff's words (2007):

> *Proponents of the Plan were able to convince both a traditionally isolationist American public and a Europe desirous for, but debatably dependent upon, foreign aid, that the sacrifices that each needed to make in order to enact the Marshall Plan were well worth their cost.*

How could the domestic public opinion and the international public opinion be persuaded about the convenience of a Marshall Plan for Africa? How can opposition forces be identified and defeated through persuasion? These are questions that will be taken into account in subsequent chapters and will contribute to the design and implementation of a new development plan able to pull extreme poor countries away from poverty once and for all, starting with sub-Saharan Africa.

Artwork by Bill Butcher.

CHAPTER 17

The Annan Plan

I dream things that never were and say, why not?

—Edward F. Kennedy

At 12:35 P.M. on January 20, 1949, Harry S. Truman, then president of the United States, proposed a second Marshall Plan. Truman said that "more than half the people of the world are living in conditions approaching misery." Truman concluded, "For the first time in history, humanity possesses the knowledge and skill to relieve the suffering of these people" (Behrman 2007).

This chapter changes it all. In the preceding chapters, I have analyzed the current status quo with its paradigm, its consensus, its institutions, its lobbies and elites, and its policies. I have explained the current environment and how it is dragging down many developing countries, leaving them worse than they were in pre-independence Africa. Chapter 16 reviewed the most successful development plan in history according to many. There are always a handful of pessimists. It is important to listen to the pessimists because they may be right. But it is crucial to move ahead in spite of them.

Chapter 17 departs from what we know about the elites, the world and its institutions, and the policies implemented in the six areas of the Axis of Feeble, and starts to construct from scratch. Everything is possible in today's environment if a forward-looking action plan is well explained and detailed. Everything is possible in today's status quo if a message of urgency is delivered to Civil Society and the economic and political elites. Change is on the way. Improvement is on the way. It is a long road to Eutopia and Decemland. But the journey of our lifetime must start and continue its course through 2050.

THE HIPC INITIATIVE

Today's environment is in desperate need of another Marshall Plan. The great evils of our time are widespread disease, the variety of armed conflicts throughout the developing world, and the extreme poverty that affects the lives of one billion people. The real problems of today feed second-level problems that control and determine the foreign policy agendas, such as international terrorism, mafias, and immigration. This section reviews the Highly Indebted Poor Countries (HIPC) Initiative.

The HIPC Initiative was triggered by Civil Society and religious organizations during the 1990s in an effort to drastically reduce the external debt burden of the world's poorest countries. The debt burden was linked to the massive lending of the International Financial Institutions (World Bank and International Monetary Fund) and the largest commercial banks during the oil crisis of the 1970s. This crisis drove money flows from the oil importers to the oil exporters and back to the coffers of Wall Street financiers that then flooded many developing countries with dollar-denominated debt.

Much of this dollar-denominated debt exploded because of depreciation episodes linked to inappropriate monetary policies in many developing nations and a rise of the interest rate attached to it. The debt burden as a percentage of GDP reached such high levels that many developing nations had severe difficulties servicing its debt and paying the interest rate on the outstanding debt owed to many creditors. These creditors belong in an institution called the Paris Club.[1]

Macroeconomic conditionality imposed by the World Bank in its lending programs and the International Monetary Fund in its bailout packages encouraged nations to first service its debt burden maintaining a low deficit or running surplus, and to then take care of education and health care. As a result, education and health care in many countries were no longer publicly provided and were therefore discontinued or privatized.

The HIPC Initiative can be considered the first massive development aid plan after the Marshall Plan. Its impact is still ongoing and its results are still uncertain. The following subsection assesses its impact and reviews the adequacy of this sort of scheme in reducing poverty and fostering economic growth.

The World Bank Assessment

As of 2008 the HIPC Initiative had been approved in 33 countries, 27 of which are in Africa. The relief amounted to $49 billion and represents the largest aid package in history after the Marshall Plan, in present value terms (World Bank 2008a). This package was largely motivated by the Millennium Development Goals, in a context that sought their fulfillment by the 2015 deadline. The World Bank concludes in its *2008 Assessment Report* on the HIPC initiative (World Bank 2008a):

> *For the 33 countries for which packages have already been approved, debt service paid on average has declined by about 2 percent of GDP between 1999 and 2006. Yet for debt reduction to have a tangible impact on poverty, the additional resources need to be targeted at the poor. Before the HIPC Initiative, eligible countries were, on average, spending slightly more on debt service than on health and education combined. Now, they have increased markedly their expenditures on health, education and other social services and, on average, such spending is about five times the amount of debt-service payments.*

The fact of the matter is that all low-income countries, whether or not they have benefited from the HIPC Initiative, have improved their policy performance. Among the countries that are part of the Initiative, more is being spent in education, but less on health, agriculture, and transportation (World Bank 2008a).

A second report by the World Bank (2008b) notes, "Net transfers to HIPC countries have doubled from $8.8 billion in 1999 to $17.5 billion in 2004, while transfers to other developing countries have grown by only one-third." Countries that have completed the HIPC process perform better on key policy ratings than other low-income countries. Low-income countries that have not completed the process score the lowest.

The Brady Plan

The Brady Plan was the predecessor of the HIPC Initiative. Nicholas Brady was secretary of the U.S. Treasury during the presidency of George Herbert Bush. Brady said in 1989, "Our objective is to rekindle the hope of the people and leaders of debtor nations that their sacrifices will lead to greater prosperity in the present and the prospect of a future unclouded by the burden of debt" (Hornik and Rudolph 1989).

CAPITALISM AND DEMOCRACY

Capitalism is an economic model with different reincarnations. Capitalism has become a system that fosters income discrepancy beyond bearable limits, discrepancy between those who work to earn an insecure living, and a few who do not need to work to maintain their grotesque wealth (Lewis 2003). Capitalism is "a system dedicated not to providing an equal distribution of wealth to as many people as possible, or ensuring a better quality of life to the majority of people, but rather to create the greatest possible profit for the small minority of the population that own a company" (Sexton 2007). Democracy seems not to be a precondition for capitalism (Bernholz 1998), whereas the opposite remains true. The current capitalism does not lead to Francis Fukuyama's end of civilization (Butcher 1992). The current capitalism is still evolving.

Capitalism is not a steady concept. It does not operate according to predetermined underlying assumptions. There is in actuality a universe of capitalisms, from more liberal to more social, from laissez faire to interventionist, from a purely economic focus to a broader social dimension. Capitalism is, in the end, like many other species in constant evolution, whose strongest specimen will survive. Only when the economic actors that determine capitalism's fate take action, will we become witnesses of a redefined capitalism, able to sustain society over time based on ethics and global justice.

A Troublesome Coexistence

Globalization is not advancing capitalism and democracy at the same time, and corporate interests from the first world are lobbying to secure access to markets where democracy is nothing more than a dream (Street 2000).

Capitalism operates in a race to the bottom environment. In this environment developing nations need to compete against each other. It is ultimately an unfair game where multinational firms use their bargaining power to avoid complying with labor or environmental standards. Capitalism does not guarantee fairness. Capitalism does not guarantee global justice or sustainability. Capitalism is in the end result of greedy first-world individuals who seek a pure economic benefit, and a pure economic return.

Democracy is all about equality, a political regime that fosters equality by adopting redistributive economic policies. Capitalism is all about inequality, an economic regime that welcomes differences in income that will cause individuals to have the incentive to work hard to move up the economic ladder (Kinsley 2003). Political regimes strongly lobbied by the wealthy undermine the poor's ability to influence the social agenda by proposing tax cuts that mostly benefit the better off.

Capitalism is struggling. It is a struggle between two versions of capitalism arising from the Bretton Woods summit in 1944 and the neoliberal manifesto finally named the Washington Consensus, which began when the United States left the fixed exchange rate system in 1971. It is a struggle between two versions of capitalism that have not proven to be adequate. It is a struggle between social capitalism predominant in Europe versus a liberal capitalism widespread in the United Kingdom and its former colonies. A third capitalism seems to have emerged in China, where a centrally ruled and driven capitalism coexists with an authoritarian regime.

Capitalism fosters change whereas democracy promotes stability (Samuelson 2005). Capitalism grants more power and influence to the wealthy, whereas democracy is, in essence, egalitarian. Why don't the worse off simply soak the rich? Surprisingly enough, the size of the middle class would be advantageous to the wealthy, because "a sizeable middle class serves as a buffer against radical demands for redistribution under democracy" (Iversen 2006). A capitalist system unable to account for the loss of physical deterioration or environmental damage (Korten 1998) is a capitalist system with a single concern: that of maximizing economic profit.

Democracy: An Ideal Fit for Capitalism?

In the end, if capitalism is not meant to coexist with democracy, what alternative is left: dictatorship, anarchy? According to Mancur Olson (1993), a two-party democracy is preferable to a stationary-bandit who remains in power. Democracy has historically granted individual rights such as property rights, without which capitalism could not operate (Olson 1993), rights that have systematically been absent in other polities.

In the end capitalism needs democracy for survival. In the end capitalism needs property rights and freedom of expression so that a firm can promote its products and services. And even though capitalism emerged in the world's first democratic regime, it has not stopped state intervention from growing. Corporations may not like regulators, but their cost of complying is inferior to the cost of not doing so, because "by cooperating, the regulations can be made less onerous, there may even be a chance to squeeze out some small competitors, or to keep out potential entrants" (Meltzer and Richard 1978).

The welfare state is not a free lunch but looks like one, with apparent negative consequences on GDP growth (Lindert 2003). This is an interesting discussion because the historical trend seems to have penalized countries with higher levels of redistribution, with a few exceptions such as Scandinavia, in expense of slower rates of growth. However, the excess growth of less redistributive regimes has almost exclusively benefited the rich, with no impact on the worse off (Wolff 1996).

Capitalism may not work in a different polity. Capitalism's ideal companion may be democracy. But in times when capitalism is precipitously introduced in countries that have recently changed political regimes, there should be an introductory time granting the correct establishment of institutions able to regulate the marketplace, a political regime in which "the majority of the population is excluded from participating in political life" (Khakee 2002).

Democracy can learn from capitalism. Capitalism can learn from democracy. Both are necessarily beneficial and desired. Whereas capitalism follows naturally, democracy encounters fierce opposition. It is a fierce opposition from large shareholders, who do not wish to give up their control of public firms. It is a fierce opposition from hedge funds and private equity funds that refuse to be subject to regulation and supervision. It is a fierce opposition from the current international financial architecture that refuses to eliminate unfair jurisdictions such as tax havens (Christensen 2007a). It is a fierce opposition from high net-worth individuals, who flee to low-tax regimes and refuse to be fairly taxed based on the principle of redistribution. It is a fierce opposition from multinational firms that refuse to be transparent and report their environmental and social damage. Lastly, it is a fierce opposition from governments that refuse to eliminate tariffs on agricultural produce in fear of losing the support of the countryside.

Democracy is willing to become more efficient and adopts financing mechanisms from capitalism. Democracy is willing to become more efficient and adopts private-public-partnerships as a way to finance infrastructure-building. Democracy incorporates the economic activity into its own operation. Capitalism is not willing to become more sustainable, ethical, fair, and social. Capitalism is not willing, in the end, to become more democratic.

Here is the crucial difference between democracy and capitalism. The same actors that encourage spreading democracy across the developing world are refusing to make capitalism more intrinsically fair. The same actors that encourage democracy to prevail are refusing to make capitalism more sustainable. Here is the crucial difference between democracy and capitalism.

A NEW SOUL

In *The Soul of Capitalism* best-selling author William Greider reaches the essence of capitalism and from the origin of his discovery, he concludes what should be the core of a new, redefined capitalism (2003). The American author begins his entertaining promenade wondering, "Why must society accept a capitalism that persists in generating greater inequalities, generation after generation, as the required terms for sustaining general abundance?" For Greider, "The future may begin among ordinary people, far distant from established power, who are brave enough to see themselves as pioneers." Greider further notes, "Socialists in Western Europe, while they did not succeed in replacing capitalism with state ownership, created a much gentler version than America's" (Greider 2003).

Who called Barack Obama a Socialist? What if he were a Socialist in the European sense, not in the Soviet sense? Europeans are no Soviet socialists, for Soviet socialists passed away with Stalin and his comrades. Socialist Europeans are mere believers in a welfare state that delivers universal education and health care for all. Some of Greider's ideas are, as he calls them, genuinely new. Greider points out, "In this new moment, when the long ideological conflict with communism has finally ended and general abundance is now secure, some of those old ideas may get a second chance."

In what ways do Greider's ideas fundamentally change today's version of capitalism? Greider anticipates, four years before the credit crunch, some of the greed and avarice that drove Wall Street bankers and the components of the credit risk chain to bankruptcty. Greider notes, "Finance and banking represent the crowning pinnacle of conflict in the collision between society and capitalism, the place where society's values are most visibly and powerfully eclipsed," and adds, "Wall Street finance operates mainly with other people's money, people whose own values and preferences are now effectively excluded in the investing process, people whose own money often is put to uses that do injury to them and to the qualities in life they most value."

Greider sees a conflict of interest between the investors and the shareholders and the bankers and money managers. Do bankers and money managers align their interests with those of their customers and clients? Responsible investing is the answer to the previous questions and is further developed in Chapter 24. Greider concludes (2003):

> *This new concept—understanding pension funds as the universal owner of America's major business corporations—provides an economic rationale, unsentimental and self-interested, for why the funds would enforce social objectives; that is, they should punish corporations for irresponsible behavior by moving their capital elsewhere.*

Two years after Greider published his book, John C. Bogle came out with a follow-up title. In *The Battle for the Soul of Capitalism* (2005), Bogle presents a struggling battle to defend the core of capitalism from the point of view of America's most successful investment manager. Bogle, the founder and retired CEO of the Vanguard Group, is one of the largest money managers in the United States. An economist by training, Bogle created Vanguard in 1974. Bogle points out, "In 1980 the compensation of the average chief executive officer was forty-two times that of the average worker, by the year 2004, the ratio had soared to 280 times that of the average worker" (Bogle 2005). The previous trend looks like the same trend Maddison reported when he compares how the average income in developed and how developing countries increased between 1820 and 1992 (see Chapter 5). Bogle insightfully claims (2005):

> *Only investment America has the power to bend corporate America to its will, and with that power, the ability to reverse the present ethos of managers' capitalism and return to the system of owners' capitalism that has been critical to the building of our nation's economic prosperity and global power.*

The investment genius calls "on the wisdom of some of the sagest minds of present and past, including Henry Kaufman, Felix Rohatyn, Alan Greenspan, Warren Buffett, Adam Smith, Joseph Schumpeter, John Maynard Keynes, Joseph Stiglitz, and Louis Brandeis, all of whom, one way or another, have shared so many of my concerns" (Bogle 2005).

The Three Dimensions of a New Capitalism

We were used to a monodimensional capitalism that only targeted the maximization of economic profit. We were used to monodimensional utility functions that removed from the equation the well-needed sense and sensibility. The new rules of capitalism will change it all.

What are the rules? Who will set them? Will there be a winning version of capitalism? The following years will observe the emergence of one or two new capitalisms. One of them will prevail in the long run. The new rules of a redefined capitalism will incorporate three new dimensions to the old-fashioned economic profit. The three new dimensions are as follows: welfare, human rights and sustainability, and transparency and governance.

1. Welfare: Universal Welfare is the globalization of the welfare state. The welfare state is the first step to building a new capitalism that guarantees the provision of basic education, health care, water, and sanitation before seeking an economic profit.
2. Human Rights and Sustainability: Human rights are related to fair trade and labor standards that seek to guarantee human dignity. Sustainability is about preserving the environment and reversing the effects of climate change.
3. Transparency and Governance: Transparency and governance started to be incorporated to the previous version of capitalism that passed away. Transparency and governance have been defined within the bounds that make Western capitalists comfortable. They have to be redefined and renegotiated in a new consensus that incorporates the point of view of the developing world.

A TALE OF THREE CAPITALISMS

Free-market capitalism passed away. What remains? "It remains for us now to set aside the ancient prejudices and build the Earth" (Pierre Teilhard de Chardin).

Academics typically present dilemmas or trilemmas where only one (dilemma) or two (trilemma) of the variables can be fulfilled simultaneously. There is no trilemma in the tale of three capitalisms. All three dimensions can be fulfilled simultaneously. The three capitalisms are those of China, the United States, and Europe. The three capitalisms differ radically in their approaches and may prevail individually or persist alongside the others for some time going forward.

Chinese Capitalism

China is one of the four emerging economies in the world. The Asian country was reviewed in Chapter 14. China has done a phenomenal job at pulling millions out of poverty. The country's economic growth since 1978 has been able to pull per capita incomes upwards and boost the country's middle class.

Chinese capitalism is centrally driven and market oriented. Chinese capitalism in China is different from Chinese capitalism abroad. China's increasing influence in Africa should be based on a three-dimensional capitalism. The Chinese have so far neglected all three dimensions and have focused on economic profit and economic cooperation. Henry Lee and Shalmon of Harvard University suggest, "Western non-governmental organizations have accused China of using its investments to support some of the more abusive, corrupt, and violent governments in the world" (Rotberg 2008), due to China's refusal to judge the behavior of the countries in which it decides to invest.

American Capitalism

The United States lost two battles during the presidency of George W. Bush. It lost the battle for the soul of capitalism. It also lost the battle of foreign policy. There are always good and bad presidents. There is also reversion to the mean. Because of the latter, President Barack Obama is likely to do a better job than his predecessor. The United States has to accomplish much at home during the first Obama Administration, with historic low levels of international credibility, and a long-lasting trend of unilateralism that has kept the North American giant away from signing the plethora of consensuses and agreements that a majority of developed and developing countries have signed in many of the areas of the Axis of Feeble, described in Part II of this book.

The United States also has the energy and optimism to defy any challenges. It is the land of entrepreneurship and opportunity. There is a generation of Americans who did not fight in World War II or Vietnam, including Barack Obama. This is their time to embrace universal health care and move ahead, leaving unilateralism behind. Many of the Pirates of Heartless Capitalism belong in the generation of baby boomers on both sides of the Atlantic. This is no longer their challenge. We have to fight the war of hunger and disease. It is to this generation that I speak. It is our generation's duty. It is the poor's mandate.

For decades, American capitalism sought to open new markets and foster business-friendly economic environments. American policy-makers emphasized trade and financial flows. In more recent times, American foreign policy has prioritized democracy as a pre-condition for doing business. New schemes of foreign aid such as the Millennium Challenge Corporation (reviewed in Chapter 20) propose aid with accountability based on transparency and governance.

European Capitalism

The Sleeping Beauty remains a beauty with potential. It has not had good or bad presidents because it does not dare to have one. The Sleeping Beauty does not dare to wake up, refuses to open her eyes to the reality of an unequal world. It is easy. It is easy to leave the leading role to the American friend on the other side of the Atlantic. The United States has made mistakes in foreign policy. The United States has made many mistakes in foreign policy during the eight years that President George W. Bush remained in power. Europe simply hides behind the American giant.

There is a Window of Opportunity as capitalism's crisis of identity deepens. It is a Window of Opportunity to redefine capitalism and come together with the developing world. It is a Window of Opportunity to redesign the international institutions and propose new ones. I see changing times in Europe. A generation of Europeans has to wake up and turn the political landscape around. We have to prioritize the extreme poor and their problems in our foreign policy agendas. We have to design a common foreign policy that puts the environment first. Europe can finalize European unification with the accession process of the Balkan republics and Turkey and look beyond its historic fear and lack of leadership.

It is time for the Sleeping Beauty to wake up and conquer the American friend and the developing world. The American friend will fall in love, again, with the Sleeping Beauty that once upon a time was a devastated land full of hatred and pessimism. Together, the American friend and the Sleeping Beauty will unite forces to redefine capitalism's soul and embrace the developing world, once and for all. The momentum could depart from one of the members of the European Union and will continue to spread throughout the continent.

THE BATTLEFIELD

Africa is the battlefield of this century's struggle for the soul of capitalism. The African continent remains underdeveloped and underexploited. It is vast. It is relatively unpopulated and has large stocks of natural resources. There are more inhabitants in India than in the whole of Africa. Africa has to be rescued. It is a battle over what form of capitalism will prevail. It is the battle for the soul of capitalism.

Vast and Unpopulated

Figure 17.1 shows a relative comparison of the population, area and population density for Africa, India, China, the United States, and the European Union. Africa has slightly over 70 percent of China's population, but China only has 30 percent of Africa's area. In terms of population density, Africa and the United States both have about 10 percent of India's population density.

Full of Energy

Figure 17.2 shows the stock of natural gas and oil in Africa. The African continent holds the world's third largest stock of natural gas and oil behind Eurasia (mainly Russia) and the Middle East. Within Africa, Algeria, Libya, and Nigeria have the three major reserves of natural gas and oil.

Mineral-Rich

Africa is a resource-rich continent and has plenty of strategic minerals. It ranks first or second in world reserves of bauxite, cobalt, industrial diamond, phosphate rock, platinum-group metals, verniculite, and zirconium (Yager, Bermudez-Lugo, et al., 2007). Much of the continent remains unexplored, away from mineral exploration and exploitation. Political risk and a lack of enforcement of property rights contribute to the lack of foreign direct investment in many areas. Table 17.1 shows the share of world production for a handful of strategic minerals.

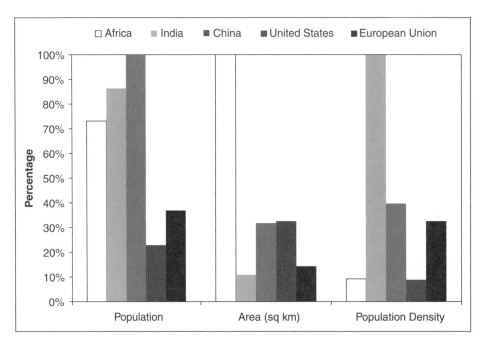

FIGURE 17.1 Population, Area, and Population Density, a Comparative of Countries
Percentages of the maximum population, area and density
Data Source: GeoHive.com (2009).

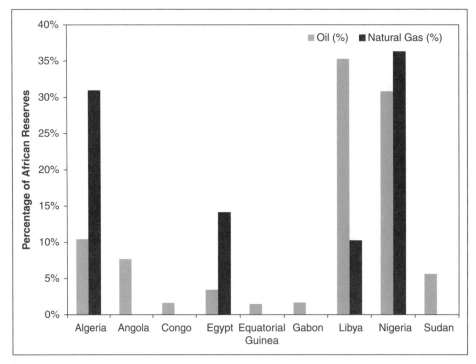

FIGURE 17.2 Africa's Proved Oil and Natural Gas Reserves
Source: United States Department of Energy (2009).

TABLE 17.1 Share of World Production for Minerals, 2005

	Africa	United States	Western Europe	China
Aluminum Bauxite	9%	–	2%	10%
Aluminum Metal	5%	7%	19%	21%
Cement	4%	4%	9%	46%
Chromite	44%	–	3%	1%
Coal	5%	20%	1%	43%
Cobalt	57%	–	–	2%
Copper	5%	8%	1%	9%
Diamond	46%	–	–	–
Gold	21%	11%	1%	9%
Graphite	2%	–	–	71%
Iron ore	4%	4%	2%	27%
Lead	3%	13%	4%	30%
Manganese	39%	–	0%	12%
Petroleum	13%	21%	19%	5%
Phosphate	31%	24%	0%	6%
Steel	2%	8%	15%	31%
Uranium	16%	2%	2%	–
Zinc	2%	8%	7%	26%

Source: United States Geological Survey (2009).

Ongoing projects that started in 2008 include mineral sands in Madagascar, Mozambique, and Kenya; bauxite and alumina in Guinea; nickel in Madagascar; coal in Mozambique; aluminum in South Africa, the Democratic Republic of the Congo and Zambia; crude oil in Nigeria and Sudan; iron ore in Senegal; and natural gas in Nigeria (Yager, Bermudez-Lugo, et al., 2007).

In 2005 Europe received 91 percent of African natural gas and 35 percent of Africa's oil exports. Other countries that imported oil from Africa include the United States (32 percent of total African oil exports), China (10 percent), and Japan (2 percent) (Yager, Bermudez-Lugo, et al., 2007). West Africa exported 45 percent of its oil exports to the United States and 32 percent to China. In the interim, many African countries continue to be highly dependent on mineral and fuel exports. Table 17.2 summarizes the countries that are heavily reliant on mineral and fuel exports.

Strategic minerals are defined as minerals that would be needed to supply the military and industrial needs of a country during an emergency. In particular, cobalt, manganese, chromium, and platinum are vital to American industry and military, without which "it would be virtually impossible to produce many defense products such as jet engine, missile components, electronic components, iron and steel" (Hagerman 1984). Can these four minerals be substituted if supply is disrupted? R.A. Hagerman (1984) provides the answer:

1. Chromium: The extent to which other minerals can be substituted for chromium is quite limited. There is no material that can adequately replace chrome in the steel industry and no substitutes exist for its aerospace industry and nor do they exist for its aerospace applications.

TABLE 17.2   Exports of Fuel and Minerals as a Percentage
of Total Exports, 2005

Above 90%	Above 80%	Above 50%
Algeria	Botswana	Mali
Equatorial Guinea	Congo	Mauritania
Libya	DR Congo	Mozambique
Nigeria	Gabon	Namibia
	Guinea	Zambia
	Sierra Leone	
	Sudan	

Source: United States Geological Survey (2009).

2. Cobalt: 50 to 60 percent of the cobalt consumed is essential in high-temperature alloys for jet engines and steam turbines.
3. Manganese: There is no economical substitute for manganese in steel making. The steel industry could not operate without manganese and would be forced to curtail operations in the event of a loss of supplies.
4. Platinum: Gold, silver, and tungsten are potential substitutes for the platinum group metals in specific electrical uses, but no substitutes exist for the use of the metals as catalysts.

What other major exporters are rich in the four strategic minerals? Republics of the former Soviet Union are among the top producers. Figure 17.3 shows the share of world production of the four strategic minerals chromium, cobalt, manganese, and platinum. African countries produce a majority of the world output.

The World's Breadbasket

Asia was the success story of the last 25 years of the twentieth century. The continent has limited potential for improving its agricultural output because of the limitations to increase food production through increases in arable land. Productivity yields can only increase moderately in Asia, as reviewed in Chapter 6. The increase in demand outpaces the increase in production.

Is there a land that could become the world's breadbasket? If so, where is it and what are the requirements? The next stop for agricultural production is Africa. Productivity increases are feasible in Africa. It is possible to increase the number of hectares available for agriculture. It is also possible to increase yields per hectare if the inputs are improved, as explained in Chapter 6. Figure 17.4 compares population and arable land for Asia, Latin America, and sub-Saharan Africa. Latin America would be the obvious alternative to sub-Saharan Africa. Unlike Latin America, a majority of sub-Saharan Africa falls into the extreme poor category and lacks the necessary infrastructure referred to in Chapter 6. The returns on investment in agriculture and farming remain significant if long-term and sustainable investment can be attracted to some of the poorest regions of the world.

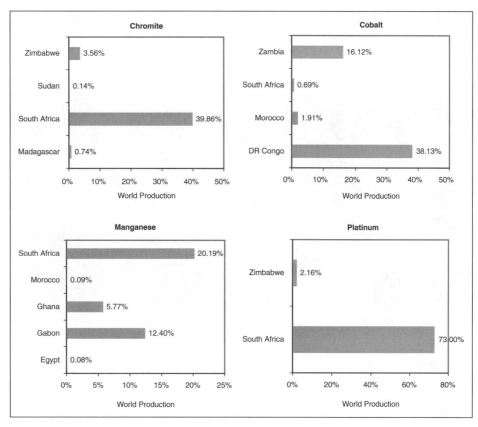

FIGURE 17.3 World Production of Four Strategic Minerals in Africa, 2005
Source: United States Geological Survey (2009).

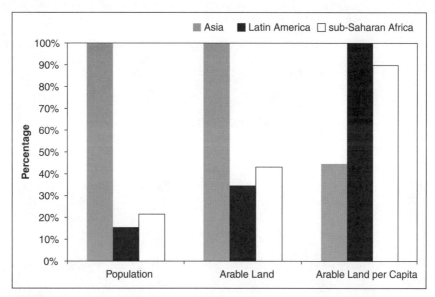

FIGURE 17.4 Population and Arable Land, a Comparative of Continents
Percentages of the maximum population, arable land, and arable land per capita
Data Source: CIA, FAO, and GeoHive.com (2009).

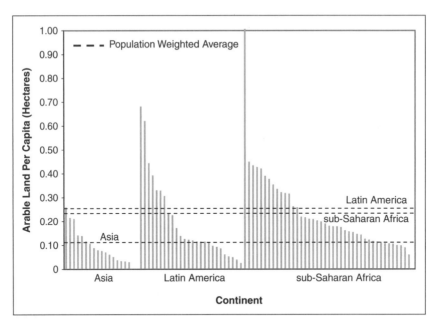

FIGURE 17.5   Arable Land per Capita by Continent
Data Source: CIA, FAO, and GeoHive.com (2009).

What is the arable land in Africa compared to other parts of the world? According to Figure 17.5, average arable land per capita in Latin America and sub-Saharan Africa literally doubles that of Asia.

What is the agricultural output in Africa for the main food staples? Figure 17.6 compares the per capita production for each of the four main food staples in Asia, Latin America, and sub-Saharan Africa.

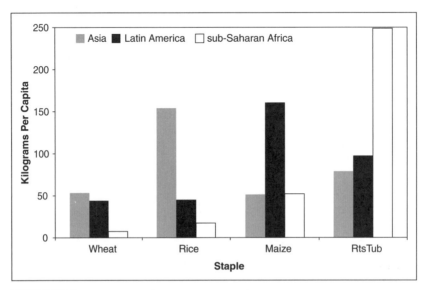

FIGURE 17.6   Average Production per Capita by Continent
Data Source: CIA, FAO, and GeoHive.com (2009).

Land Leases   Sub-Saharan Africa has become the focus of attention for resource-poor countries that are net food importers. Two cases took place at the end of 2008 and at the beginning of 2009. The first case was a deal between South Korean multi-national Daewoo Logistics and the Republic of Madagascar, whereby the former would lease 1.3 million hectares of land from Madagascar for a period of 99 years. 1.3 million hectares is about half the size of Belgium and represent 50 percent of Madagascar's arable land.[2] The second case is the lease of a former Wall Street banker of 400,000 hectares of land in southern Sudan for an undisclosed amount. The two deals were announced in the course of two months between the end of 2008 and the beginning of 2009.

The nature of the deals anticipates what may become the mainstream trend going forward if a global effort is not accomplished to reach international agreements in food production. In the current environment countries, multinationals and investors are likely to continue signing deals of this nature with land-abundant, hopeless developing countries under tremendous pressure of raising income aiming at agricultural production. The bargaining power of developed countries, multinationals, and investors is again a weapon of mass destruction that we deem legitimate. We are using our economic might and not our brain power to fight a race of food scarcity and finite resources.

A MARSHALL PLAN FOR AFRICA

The Annan Plan is a <u>Marshall Plan for Africa</u>. Since he left the United Nations, Kofi Annan has been supporting agricultural investment in the forgotten continent. In 2007 Annan was appointed chairman of the board of the Alliance for a Green Revolution in Africa (AGRA). As chairman, Annan leads the efforts to revitalize agriculture in Africa in order to replace poverty with prosperity.[3]

Chapter 16 reviewed The Marshall Plan and the context in the aftermath of World War II that made possible its political support in the United States. The two priorities in Europe for the United States were: to fight the expansion of Soviet communism, and to increase agricultural and industrial output of war torn Europe to pre-war levels. A Marshall Plan for Africa would have two similar priorities: first, to fight and stop the expansion of heartless capitalism in sub-Saharan Africa; and second, to increase agricultural output beyond pre-independence levels. This section helps clarify the second goal. The remainder of the book explains how to stop the expansion of heartless capitalism and start building a new capitalism that will take us to the World of 2050 and Decemland, the land of 10 percent.

Increasing Agricultural Output per Capita

One of the untold secrets of the successful Chinese growth model in the last 30 years has been China's ability to increase agricultural output. An increase in rice and cereal yields allows the country to better feed its population and utilize less agricultural labor. Consequently, more labor could migrate from rural to urban areas, which helped boost China's manufacturing industry. Table 17.3 compares Africa's and China's agricultural indicators between 1970 and 1992.

TABLE 17.3 Agricultural Indicators for Africa and China, 1970–1992

AFRICA	1970	1975	1980	1985	1990	1992
Share of Agriculture in						
GDP	35	31	30	33	32	33
Labor Force	78	75	73	70	37	66
Trade	63		57	52	49	48
Indices of Output (1979–81 = 100)						
Agriculture		93.9	100.5	111.0	127.9	135.0
Food		93.1	100.4	111.1	129.0	136.7
Crop		97.9	100.6	111.4	129.4	137.2
Food per capita		108.0	100.4	96.1	96.2	93.4
Cereal Output						
Per capita (kg)	169	165	152	151	135	
Per hectare (kg)	837	896	883	1,025	1,049	
Other						
Arable land per capita (hectare)	0.488	0.440	0.393	0.345	0.279	
Fertilizer use per hectare (kg)	6.7	10.0	12.1	13.7	14.7	
CHINA	**1970**	**1975**	**1980**	**1985**	**1990**	**1992**
Share of Agriculture in						
GDP	38	36	35	33	28	27
Labor Force	78	76	74	71	67	66
Trade	35		72	44	33	28
Indices of Output (1979–81 = 100)						
Agriculture		84.7	98.8	130.2	159.2	175.4
Food		84.6	98.8	127.4	157.6	175.8
Crop		85.7	98.4	125.1	144.9	149.8
Food per capita		90.8	98.7	118.6	136.1	145.2
Cereal Output						
Per capita (kg)	251	258	283	321	340	350
Per hectare (kg)	1,875	2,074	2,923	3,837	4,199	4,587
Other						
Arable land per capita (hectare)	0.118	0.106	0.099	0.089	0.081	
Fertilizer use per hectare (kg)	36.1	58.9	134.0	209.1	290.3	

Source: Khan and Khan (1995). Reprinted with kind permission of the Publications Division, Pakistan Institute of Development
Economics, Islamabad, from The Pakistan Development Review, Vol. 34, No. 4 (1995), pp. 429–456. www.pide.org.pk.

Table 17.4 shows the increases and decreases in agricultural output, arable land per capita, and fertilizer per hectare for Africa and China. Africa decreased its food production per capita between 1975 and 1992 by 14 percent, its cereal output per capita between 1970 and 1990 by 20 percent, and its arable land per capita between 1970 and 1990 by 43 percent. The priority for the Annan Plan would be to increase these outputs per capita beyond pre-independence levels, drawing an analogy with post-war Europe and the Marshall Plan. Africa has fought a war that has lasted since the end of colonization. It is time to end this war and help the forgotten continent move out of the poverty trap once and for all.

Figure 17.7 and Figure 17.8 depict agricultural output per capita and cereal production per capita for Africa and China for the period 1970 to 1990. The trend is devastating for the forgotten continent that could and should learn how China accomplished its phenomenal gains in output per capita.

Why has agricultural output per capita fallen so dramatically in sub-Saharan Africa? Africa's share of the world exports have fallen from 8 percent to 2 percent in the last four decades (Haggblade, Hazell, et al., 2004). A shortage of fertilizer has made African soil lose many of its nutrients at a rate of between one billion and three billion dollars per year. HIV/AIDS is cutting the agricultural workforce by half (Haggblade, Hazell, et al., 2004). Certainly population growth explains part of Africa's lost productivity. China's strict and enforced control of its population growth has had a positive impact in productivity gains per capita.

Agricultural output and cereal output in sub-Saharan Africa decreased in relative terms between 1970 and 1992 but increased in absolute terms. There were absolute productivity gains. How are the productivity gains distributed geographically across Africa? Lilyan E. Fulginiti, Richard K. Perrin, and Yu Bingxin of the University

TABLE 17.4 Comparison Africa vs. China in Key Indicators

	Africa	China
Output 1992:1975		
Agriculture	144%	207%
Food	147%	208%
Crop	140%	175%
Food per capita	86%	160%
Cereal Output 1990:1970		
Per capita (kg)	80%	135%
Per hectare (kg)	125%	224%
Other 1990:1970		
Arable land per capita (hectare)	57%	69%
Fertilizer use per hectare (kg)	219%	804%

Source: Khan and Khan (1995). Reprinted with kind permission of the Publications Division, Pakistan Institute of Development Economics, Islamabad, from The Pakistan Development Review, Vol. 34, No. 4 (1995), pp. 429–456. www.pide.org.pk.

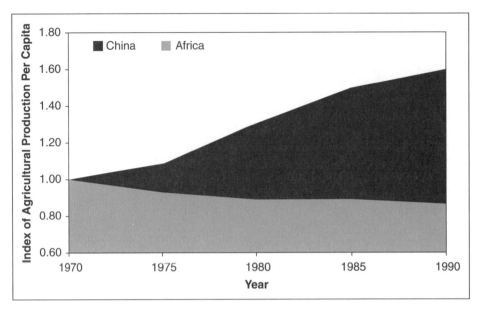

FIGURE 17.7 Agricultural Production per Capita, 1970 = 1.00
Source: Khan and Khan (1995). Reprinted with kind permission of the Publications
Division, Pakistan Institute of Development Economics, Islamabad, from *The Pakistan
Development Review*, Vol. 34, No. 4 (1995), pp. 429–456. www.pide.org.pk.

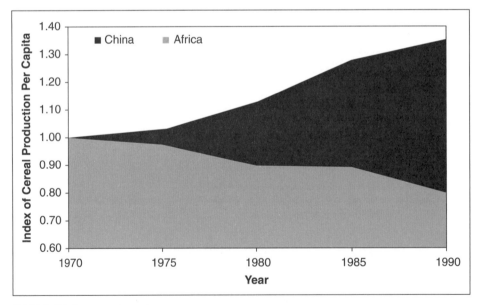

FIGURE 17.8 Cereal Production per Capita, 1970 = 1.00
Source: Khan and Khan (1995). Reprinted with kind permission of the Publications
Division, Pakistan Institute of Development Economics, Islamabad, from *The Pakistan
Development Review*, Vol. 34, No. 4 (1995), pp. 429–456. www.pide.org.pk.

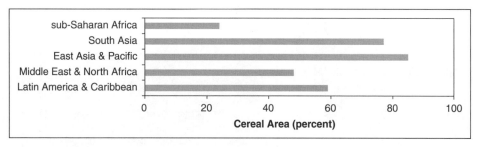

FIGURE 17.9   Use of Improved Varieties of Cereal, 2000
Source: World Bank (2007b).

of Nebraska at Lincoln look at "Agricultural Productivity in sub-Saharan Africa" (Fulginiti, Perrin, et al., 2004). The researchers study agricultural productivity in 41 sub-Saharan African countries between 1960 and 1999.

The Nebraska scholars argue that there is a colonization effect on productivity gains. They report negative productivity gains for the four former Portuguese colonies, averaging −0.26 percent per year. The three former Belgian colonies have a negative productivity gain of −0.17 percent per year. The 14 former French colonies have a positive productivity gain of 0.76 percent. Finally, the 18 former British colonies had the best performance with an average productivity gain of 1.08 percent per year (Fulginiti, Perrin, et al., 2004).

More interesting findings include a correlation between the level of freedom and agricultural productivity. The authors comment, "In a year in which a country was rated partly free, the country is predicted to be 26 percent more technically efficient that when not free." They add, "In a year in which it was rated free, it is predicted to be 39 percent more efficient" (Fulginiti, Perrin, et al., 2004). Why does colonial heritage have an impact on agricultural productivity gains? The authors conclude, "Respect for political and civil rights and absence of conflict are two of the institutional characteristics that contribute to the differences between the colonial groups" (Fulginiti, Perrin, et al., 2004).

Former British and French colonies are, as a result, more likely to trigger a Second Green Revolution. What can be done about agricultural productivity? According to the Rockefeller Foundation, two simple changes could boost productivity. The first is the use of better seeds. The second is the use of more fertilizer (Rockefeller Foundation 2006). Figure 17.9 shows that sub-Saharan Africa ranks last in the use of improved varieties for cereal. Figure 17.10 shows that sub-Saharan Africa ranks last in the use of fertilizer.

REARVIEW MIRROR

There are many similarities between the Marshall Plan and The Annan Plan. The numerous similarities between the two plans raise a question mark. Will the Annan Plan finally take off? If the Annan Plan does not take off, it is because of a lack of political leadership. We need men and women of political stature similar to that of General Marshall or President Truman, similar to that of George Kennan or Will

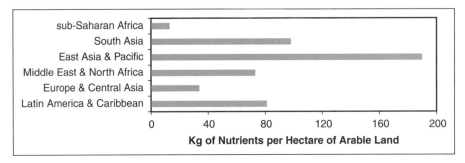

FIGURE 17.10 Fertilizer Use, 2002
Source: World Bank (2007b).

Clayton. We should wonder why the current political leaders perpetuate the defense of national agendas that do not favor the global interest. Table 17.5 summarizes the similarities shared by the Marshall Plan and the Annan Plan.

UNDERMINING THE MONFORT PLAN

This section delves into what can be learned from the pessimists of our time. The ideas of two pessimists in particular, William Easterly and Bruce Bueno de Mesquita, both New York University (NYU) professors, will be discussed. It is important to listen to them. It is more important to move forward in spite of them.

William Easterly's best-selling book *The White Man's Burden* (Easterly 2006) reinforces the notion that to have no plan is the right plan. This is not a good premonition for the success of this book. I should have consulted with Easterly before naming the book *The Monfort Plan*. Easterly adds, "Big plans will always fail to reach the beautiful goal" (Easterly 2006). I guess Easterly is referring to Eutopia and Decemland. What did the NYU professor have in mind when he wrote this line? What is the reader's beautiful goal? The American architect Daniel H. Burnham once said:

> *Make no little plans; they have no magic to stir men's blood and probably will themselves not be realized. Make big plans; aim high in hope and work, remembering that a noble, logical diagram once recorded will not die.*

Many academics comment that the right approach to development is incremental change or incremental improvement. This compares with Jeffrey Sachs' shock therapy. What kind of incremental change are we talking about? Why didn't the United States apply incremental change in Europe in the aftermath of World War II? I am afraid that incremental change works for ordinary times. We are living in extraordinary times. We need Excremental Change. Excremental Change involves cleaning first the loopholes of the system and expelling all the dirt that is inside. Ask the Pirates of Heartless Capitalism where they hide and you will find the dirt. They know where it is. We know where it is. We just do not see it. It is like dirt hiding underneath the carpet.

TABLE 17.5 The Marshall Plan versus The Annan Plan

	The Marshall Plan *Then*	The Annan Plan *Now*
Deathtoll and devastation through war	Millions died in World War I and World War II. The two World Wars were devastating, particularly in Europe. Europe lived at war between 1919 and 1945.	In the post-colonization period when many African countries obtained independence, armed conflict, hunger, and disease have hit the African continent. Millions have died. Africa lived at war between 1961 and 2009.
Restoring industrial and agricultural output	Agricultural and industrial output was well below pre-war levels in war-torn Europe in the late 1940s. Increasing output was a priority for the United States. Europe became the major trade partner of the United States.	Agricultural output is well below pre-independence levels in sub-Sarahan Africa. Increasing agricultural output should be a priority for the world.
Opposition forces	Soviet communism was expanding in Eastern and Western Europe in the aftermath of World War II. Stalin did not give up on his ambition and Greece, Turkey, France, and Italy had strong communist parties willing and able to embrace Soviet propaganda and use it to attack and tear down the Marshall Plan.	Heartless capitalists remain in today's world. They look at short-term profit. They speculate. Heartless capitalism was expanding in sub-Saharan Africa in the 1990s and the 2000s. Heartless capitalists were reluctant to embrace a new version of capitalism. They were reluctant to incorporate a sustainability clause to their modus operandi.
The battlefields	Europe was the obvious battlefield where Americans and Soviets fought to expand their world hegemony and influence.	Africa becomes the obvious battlefield where Americans, Europeans, and Chinese will increasingly fight to expand their world hegemony and influence.
Development planning	A new development plan was implemented with the leadership of the United States.	A new development plan is implemented with the leadership of the European Union.
Recovery programs	The Economic Cooperation Administration (ECA) is set up to administer the Marshall Plan dollars. ECA is the most talented team of corporate managers that have served the public interest.	The Monfort Team (TMT) is set up to administer the Annan Plan dollars. TMT is the most talented team of nonprofit managers that have served the public interest. TMT is presented in Chapter 29.

(Continued)

TABLE 17.5 (*Continued*)

	The Marshall Plan *Then*	The Annan Plan *Now*
New business opportunities	The United States expands its version of capitalism to Western Europe to seek economic profit maximizing opportunities for its business in the long run.	The European Union expands a new version of capitalism to sub-Saharan Africa that seeks social and economic profit maximizing opportunities for its businesses in the long run.
A strategy designed to improve business infrastructure	The American strategy is based upon a model that enhances the multinational corporation in the long run.	The new approach to development seeks to improve microbusiness infrastructure in the long run, empowering the rural and the urban poor and helping them set up business whose dividends and returns can be reinvested in the local community.
Combatting change	Cominform becomes the means through which Soviet communism spreads its propaganda.	Heartless capitalists will persist and fight a new version of capitalism through their instruments: the elites, the lobbies, the think-tanks, and orthodox academia.
A period of devastation followed by glory years	Europe lived the greatest devastation of its history during the first 50 years of the twentieth century. The two World Wars were followed by the Glorious Thirty thanks to the Marshall Plan and the French visionaries Jean Monnet and Robert Schuman who created the European Coal and Steel Community.	Africa lived the most devastating period of its history during the 50 years that followed independence in 1960. This period of devastation will be followed by the Glorious Forty that lead us to the World of 2050 and Decemland, the land of 10 percent.
Cold War	The division of Europe triggered a cold war that lasted forty years.	The division of sub-Saharan Africa among heartless capitalists and loving capitalists could trigger a new cold war that would last another forty years until we reach the World of 2050 and Decemland, the land of 10 percent.
The United States finally joins the international consensus	The United States joined the United Nations. It had previously refused to join the League of Nations.	The United States finally joins the World consensus on small arms trade and the environment.

TABLE 17.5 (*Continued*)

	The Marshall Plan *Then*	The Annan Plan *Now*
New architecture emerging	A New Architecture is born that creates the Bretton Woods Institutions: the World Bank, the International Monetary Fund, the United Nations, and GATT. A majority of the representative power in the Bretton Woods Institutions is given to industrialized nations.	A New Architecture is born that creates The New Institution, the Decemfund, the Yunus-Fund, and the Bank for the Poor. A majority of the representative power in The New Institutions is given to developing nations.
Launching new superpowers	The United States with its military might becomes the only superpower after the end of the cold war.	The European Union becomes the new superpower after the end of an intellectual war between heartless capitalists and loving capitalists.
New headquarters are set	Washington hosts the headquarters of the new financial architecture. New York hosts the United Nations.	Decemland becomes the world's capital and hosts The New Institution, the Bank for the Poor, the Decemfund, and the Yunus-Fund.
New supranational communities	The Marshall Plan facilitates an environment in which the seed of the future European Union can grow with the emergence of the European Community of Coal and Steel.	The Annan Plan facilitates an environment in which the seed of a future united Africa can grow through the establishment of the African Community of Healthcare and Education (presented in Chapter 19).

The next Nostradamus is Professor Bruce Bueno de Mesquita. Bueno de Mesquita recommended looking at his article on foreign aid in the *Journal of Conflict Resolution* of 2007. The paper is called "Foreign Aid and Policy Concessions." Bueno de Mesquita models foreign aid deals under the assumption that political leaders maximize their time in office (Bueno de Mesquita and Smith 2007). In their research, the NYU scholars link the allocation of foreign aid to the survival of the political elite. In Marshall Plan terms, it would be linking the survival in office of President Harry S. Truman during the Marshall Plan years of 1948 to 1951. Truman was president of the United States from 1945 to 1953. He became president on April 12, 1945, taking over for Franklin D. Roosevelt, who died a few weeks after inauguration. When Truman ran for reelection in 1948, the Marshall Plan had already taken off. He beat his opponents and served for a second term.

By modeling the foreign aid transaction process between a donor country and a recipient country that receives aid in exchange for policy concessions, Bueno de Mesquita answers the following questions (Bueno de Mesquita and Smith 2007): "Who gives aid? How much do they give? Who gets aid? How much do they get?"

The political scientist from NYU concludes with two insightful statements. The first statement refers to the recipient countries (Bueno de Mesquita and Smith 2007):

> *Our model offers important policy advice for those who wish to help the needy around the world. Receiving aid is most likely to improve the welfare of citizens in large coalition systems. In such systems, the majority of the additional resources are allocated to public goods, and the leader can retain only limited resources for its own discretionary projects. Aid given to such systems is likely to promote economic growth and enhance social welfare. U.S. reconstruction aid to Western Europe under the Marshall Plan is an example of such a success story. In small coalition systems, aid resources disproportionately end up in the hands of the leader and her cronies in the form of private goods.*

The second statement refers to the donor countries (Bueno de Mesquita and Smith 2007):

> *The survival of leaders in large welfare systems depends on providing for the welfare of their supporters and not on the welfare of people abroad. It is far easier for leaders to buy the public goods that their citizens value from a small coalition state than from a large coalition democratic system. Unless it is the case that the policy goals in the donor state are furthered by enhancing growth in the recipient states (as we might argue was the case under the Marshall Plan) or the citizens in the donor state really care about promoting growth abroad, then leaders in donor states promote their political survival better by buying policy from autocrats than they do by pushing for the institutional reforms necessary for effective development.*

What can we learn from the next Nostradamus? Is Bueno de Mesquita right when he claims a new Marshall Plan is unlikely to take off? In their conclusions, the scholars give the assumptions that have to be fulfilled in order to minimize the probability of failure of any new foreign aid scheme. As a result it is most important to choose a large coalition system. Chapter 19 suggests that the New Architecture start in a large coalition system in Southern Africa.

The second policy advice stresses the importance of implementing a communications strategy that persuades and convinces citizens in donor states about the importance of fostering growth abroad, and that such growth can be accomplished through global redistribution schemes that deliver a Universal Welfare to the extreme poor.

Artwork by Bill Butcher.

CHAPTER 18

A Eutopia of Universal Welfare

*It is easy for anybody with undergraduate training in economics to believe
that taxing some people to pay others who earn little will reduce national
output, and cause deadweight losses of net national well-being. The effects
could be drawn on the blackboard, with two labor market diagrams, one
diagram showing the labor market for those productive persons who pay
taxes and the other showing the labor market of those low-skill persons
who are poor enough to qualify for benefits. The logic is persuasive, but so
far the story is fiction. The deadweight costs are something we imagine, not
something we derived from facts and tests.*
  —Peter Lindert, *Why the Welfare State Looks Like a Free Lunch*

Eutopia is Universal Welfare. Universal Welfare is the provision of free health care
and education to every human being and the provision of subsidized and improved
water supply and sanitation to the extreme poor worldwide, nothing less.

Eutopia is possible today. Universal access reaches further and beyond the Millennium Development Goals. This chapter explains the importance of the provision
of health care and education, a clean water supply and sanitation. This chapter
proposes a first insight regarding how a Universal Welfare could be provided so
that it reaches all of the extreme poor, in urban and rural areas, in low-income and
middle-income countries.

A basic Universal Welfare for those living in extreme poverty should be complemented by disaster response and emergency relief, presented in Chapter 27. The
approach for the provision of a Universal Welfare state for the extreme poor would
include the shift of some of today's military expenditure to emergency relief and
the transformation of part of today's NATO into a worldwide alliance of nations'
armies with the goal of securing emergency assistance in the case of a natural disaster. Chapter 27 delves into a new emergency relief architecture and explores the
concept of Islands of Peace and the Decem Alliance.

WELFARE STATE

International integration and more specifically, European integration, may be releasing competitive forces, "causing a race to the bottom in which social standards and welfare state arrangements are depreciated" (Andersen 2002). As discussed in Chapter 3, globalization is releasing forces that are undermining the ability of developed countries to maintain their welfare states. A market-driven globalization will hurt the welfare infrastructure in developed countries. An institution-based globalization that puts the welfare state above the market will guarantee that the individual is protected independent from his or her level of income or place of birth and residence.

The welfare state can be classified according to three different categories: corporatist, liberal, and social democratic (Esping-Andersen 1990). The Swedish welfare state is an example of a social democratic (Bergh 2004). In the social democratic model, all strata enjoy the same benefits and join the same universal coverage (Esping-Andersen 1990).

How can the welfare state be defined? For Assar Lindbeck of Stockholm University, the welfare state plays the role of providing health and unemployment insurance from a free market economics point of view (Lindbeck 2002). For Lindbeck, the macroeconomic instability of the 1930s coupled with the prosperity of the Glorious Thirty[1] motivated and enabled the implementation and financing of the current welfare state as we know it today. Perhaps the macroeconomic instability of the 2000s coupled with the prosperity of the Glorious Forty will motivate the delivery of a welfare state to the extreme poor. Or perhaps the delivery of a welfare state to the extreme poor will lead to the Glorious Forty.

The difference in social security or social insurance programs between the developed and the developing world remains paramount. According to Peter H. Lindert of the University of California-Davis, "In 1985–1990, such programs absorbed about 16.3 percent of GDP in the rich OECD countries and only 2.7 percent in developing countries, where poverty and inequality are greater" (Lindert 2004).

Hans-Werner Sinn of the University of Munich proposes to move the European welfare state "from a system that pays wage replacement incomes to one that pays wage subsidies" (Sinn 2007). The rationale behind Sinn's proposal is that the welfare state has to be curtailed in an environment of low wage competition from Eastern Europe and China, which is bringing industrial wages down and bringing about a forced migration of industrial labor from Western Europe to Eastern Europe and China. Curtailing the European welfare state would mean "giving up the European dream of an equitable society avoiding crime and social unrest, because it provides useful insurance against the multiple economic risks that the market economy encounters" (Sinn 2007). As a result of all of the above, Sinn proposes that the state should pay wage subsidies to workers instead of paying people benefits while they find a job.

For Lindert, "Since 1980, out of the twenty-one leading OECD countries, only three have cut the share of GDP spent on public health care, only two have cut the share spent on public pensions, only four have cut the share spent on welfare, and only three have cut the share spent on unemployment" (Lindert 2004).

The welfare state can be a free lunch if those who claim benefits are not entitled to receive them. Friedrich Heinemann of the Center for European Economic Research looks at whether the welfare state is self-destructive (Heinemann 2007). Heinemann's insightful research surveys the benefit morale per country over time. The benefit morale is defined as the percentage of a country's individuals who think it is never justifiable to claim government benefits to which they are not entitled. For instance, let's suppose that a Spaniard is not entitled to claim dental insurance, but he claims he should receive it. He would answer negatively to the question, *Do you think it is never justifiable to demand a government benefit when you are not entitled?* Unfortunately 46 percent of Spaniards think it is justifiable to demand a government benefit even when they are not entitled. Best performers are Turkey (89 percent think it is never justifiable to demand a government benefit), Denmark (83 percent), Netherlands (77 percent), Korea (77 percent), and Hungary (75 percent). Worst performers include Greece (24 percent percent), Slovakia (37 percent), France (40 percent), Mexico (44 percent), and Luxembourg (45 percent). The higher the benefit morale score, the easier it is to implement and deliver a welfare state.

The survey spans the time interval of 1981 to 2004. In the long run, the welfare state can be sustained if the benefit morale maintains a high level. Educating citizens about the benefits they are entitled to can play an important role in the maintenance of high benefit morale. The maintenance of high benefit morale is crucial in the successful design and delivery of a Universal Welfare.

Greater flexibility in the work environment, increasing the share of female participation in the labor market, and delaying the retirement age are a few of the policies that could help maintain and enhance the welfare state in Western countries. The welfare state as a concept is static and requires dynamic thinking and innovative policy-making to be maintained. It is possible to maintain and enhance the welfare state in Western countries. It is possible to export the concept and help the developing world build up the infrastructure that once upon a time allowed Europe to become the world's superpower in quality of life.

How can we design Universal Welfare for the developing world if some developed countries do not even provide universal health care to their citizens? Developed countries can provide Universal Welfare, although perhaps they do not because of a lack of political will or popular support. Developing countries need to be helped to build up the infrastructure that would lead to the provision of universal health care and education. This support will pay off in the long run, as is explained throughout this chapter.

In China only 30 percent of the population had access to basic health care in 2009. In April 2009 the Chinese government announced it would extend basic health care to 90 percent of the population by 2012 and to 100 percent of the population by 2020 (Reinoso 2009). In November 2009 the U.S. House of Representatives approved Obama's Health Plan to universalize health care access to all Americans. Access to basic health care and education is becoming universal, and its convenience has proven crucial in times of economic turmoil.

HEALTH CARE

In 2008 Gunilla Backman led a group of researchers who assessed the right to health in 194 countries (Backman 2008). The right to health, along with that of education, was made explicit in the *Universal Declaration of Human Rights* of 1948. Declarations remain statements of good intentions. We need to transition from universal declarations of rights to declarations of universal rights.

The panel of experts led by Backman looked at 72 different indicators classified into the following categories: recognition of the right to the highest attainable standard of health, non-discrimination, health information, national health plan, participation, underlying determinants of health, access to health services, medicines, health promotion, health workers, national financing, international assistance and cooperation, additional safeguards, raising awareness about the right to the highest attainable standard of health, and last but not least, monitoring, assessment, accountability, and redress (Backman 2008). What are the findings of the survey? The researchers try to answer the following two questions (Backman 2008): (1) Do countries' health systems have the relevant right-to-health features?; and (2) Is the relevant data available at the global level?

The quality and quantity of the data is noteworthy. The authors rank 194 countries in order to determine whether the right to health is fulfilled. Whose obligation is it to make sure that the provision of basic health care is fulfilled? I remain convinced it is increasingly a problem of global scope. It remains the responsibility of the local population. But it is the responsibility of the better off to help the extreme poor in a way that avoids the pitfalls of the past. Not surprisingly a majority of countries (192) have ratified treaties that include the right to health (Backman 2008). Many of the 72 indicators require a yes or no answer. Sometimes the data is simply not available. Table 18.1 shows the handful of indicators that had a large proportion of positive or negative answers.

Coincidentally the nonprofit Save the Children, featured in Chapter 15, has been advocating for the free delivery of health care to African children (McGivering 2006). Africa is the region with the highest proportion of child deaths from preventable disease. Many diseases such as measles, pneumonia, or malaria can be cured if prevented in time. Where there is no infrastructure for early prevention and treatment, the outcome is what we see in sub-Saharan Africa today. **Luis Sambo** (HEA) is the regional director for Africa at the World Health Organization[2] (WHO). I phoned Luis on September 30, 2008. Luis is in charge of the WHO regional office of sub-Saharan Africa that includes 46 countries. The Angolan technocrat thinks that poverty reduction has to be approached from a multidisciplinary perspective. WHO's work in Africa does not overlap with that of other institutions. Luis explains

TABLE 18.1   Sample of Healthcare Indicators for 194 countries

Indicator	Description	Yes	No	N/A
7	State law requires registration of births and deaths	188	6	
17	State has comprehensive national health plan	181	13	
21	National health plan recognizes right to health	188	4	2
22	National health plan includes commitment to universal	165	14	15
28	Access to medicines in constitution or other statute	2	188	4
58	State has patients' rights charter	182	12	
59	Patients' rights charter available in official languages	184	1	9

Source: Backman (2008).

that in terms of health WHO has a leading role. Other institutions also contribute to health in terms of funding health services, such as UNICEF or the Global Fund.

The International Finance Corporation (IFC) is one of the five agencies of the World Bank. In 2008 the IFC published a report entitled *The Business of Health in Africa*. In the report, the IFC suggests that the health care sector in Africa may be appealing for investment.[3]

Figure 18.1 shows that approximately 50 percent of all expenditure in health care in Africa in 2005 was private. I think the IFC's approach is biased and fundamentally wrong. It proves once again the interference of free-market advocates in the definition of the strategy of the Washington-based institutions. Public health care is the answer to Africa's problems. It has been proven to work in all OECD countries except the United States. The United States has simply not implemented it and 15 percent of Americans did not have access to health care in 2009, including my friends Armando Cerroblanco from Berkeley and Matt Rossenwasser from New York City.

The United States is the developed country that spends most on health care per capita. It is the only one that leaves one in six citizens outside the health-care radar. If I were to replicate a system of health-care provision I would look at Canada or Germany, I would never look at the United States. I think that the IFC has missed the target with its report. Privatizing health care and education was part of the old paradigm of the Washington Consensus. Foreign direct investment and equity funds will not resolve Africa's health crisis. We need fundamental change that private donors are incapable of providing on their own. We need political will. Where are the men and women of political stature?

Public goods were defined in Chapter 5. Public goods cannot be privately provided, particularly for the worse off. The provision of Global Public Goods cannot

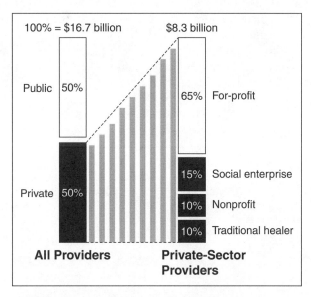

FIGURE 18.1 Healthcare Expenditure in sub-Saharan Africa, Public versus Private, 2005
Source: Adapted from Thatak, Hazlewood, et al. (2008).

be a business in the profit-maximizing sense of the word. It has to be a Social Business in the Yunus sense, as explained in Chapter 15. There are many other sectors that have business appeal, but not health care or education. There are many other income groups that can be a source of economic profit, but not the extreme poor. These axioms have to be the spinal cord of a New Paradigm. Pirates of Heartless Capitalism should be kept away from any perceived business opportunity in health care and education in extreme poor countries, while the extreme poor and the pirates continue to exist.

Testing

Gary Cohen (HEA) is president of BD Medical. I talked to Gary on November 21, 2008. Gary confirms the importance of testing for HIV and tuberculosis. Access to laboratories is often nonexistent in rural areas. Gary adds, "Treatment is commonly administered in the absence of diagnostic testing, potentially accelerating the incidence of drug-related toxicity and the onset of drug resistance if therapy results in incomplete viral suppression." He points out that as policy-makers plan the expansion of health services delivery in developing countries, priority has to be given to the delivery of basic health services that include adequate deployment of laboratory testing (Cohen 2007). Table 18.2 compares the number of diagnostic tests that would be required to provide universal access, along with the associated cost.

HIV/AIDS

A new health delivery requires the incorporation of a leading health expert. **KEVIN FENTON** (HEA) is the director of the National Center for HIV/AIDS, Viral Hepatitis, and Tuberculosis Prevention at the Center for Disease Control and Prevention of the United States. I phoned Kevin on October 31, 2008. According to the National Center for HIV/AIDS, the number of people living with HIV/AIDS increased from 29 million in 2001 to 33 million in 2007. The proportion of people with AIDS globally has remained at 0.8 percent since 2000 (Fenton 2008). New infections peaked in the late 1990s and decreased from 3 million in 2001 to 2.7 million in 2007.

TABLE 18.2 Estimates of Current Testing Rates Compared with Universal Access

Diagnostic Tests	Estimated Current Number of Tests (million)	Estimated Number of Tests at Universal Access (million)	Current Access (percent)	Current Cost per Test (US$)
Rapid HIV test	32	1000	3%	<1
Molecular/PCR HIV test	0.05	1	5%	30–40
CD4 cell count	3	50	6%	3–5
Viral load	0.3	50	<1%	17–35
Tuberculosis culture	18	680	3%	1–4

PCR = Polymerase chain reaction.
Source: Cohen (2007). Reprinted with permission of Becton, Dickinson and Company.

Today, sub-Saharan Africa remains the most infected region in the world. Five percent of sub-Saharan Africans between 15 and 49 years old, or a total of 22 million, were infected in 2007. This represents 67 percent of the total number of infections (Fenton 2008). Table 18.3 shows the number of infections worldwide.

A majority of the infected adults in sub-Saharan Africa are female (over 60 percent). Worldwide there is an equal share of the burden between men and women. UNAIDS is the Joint United Nations Programme on HIV/AIDS. UNAIDS estimates that as of 2007, $10 billion had been allocated to fighting HIV/AIDS, an amount that is running short of the $18 billion necessary (Fenton 2008).

The WHO proposes strategies for an effective response to the HIV pandemic. Among some of the action points for Health Ministries, WHO proposes the following (WHO 2003):

- Generating leadership and stewardship
- Allocating roles and responsibilities
- Achieving a comprehensive governmental response
- Mobilizing non-governmental responses
- Setting achievable goals, objectives and targets
- Obtaining expert, independent advice to inform decision-making
- Assessing the impact of non-health-sector policy on HIV/AIDS
- Priority setting and decision-making that involves major stakeholders
- Accountability, monitoring, and evaluation

The following solutions have been suggested as potential solutions for prevention of HIV transmission: "elimination of concurrent partnerships, circumcision of all men, focusing of prevention efforts on sex workers, universal HIV testing, and provision of antiretroviral therapy" (Piot, Kazatchkine, et al., 2009).

Ninety percent of those living with HIV in 2007 had not been tested and did not know their status (Cohen 2007). In 2005, UNAIDS published "AIDS in Africa:

TABLE 18.3 Number of HIV/AIDS Infections Worldwide, 2007

	Number	Percentage	Newly Infected	Adult Prevalence (15–49)
sub-Saharan Africa	22,000,000	67.0%	1,900,000	5.0%
South/Southeast Asia	4,200,000	13.0%	330,000	0.3%
Latin America	1,700,000	5.0%	140,000	0.5%
Eastern Europe/ Central Asia	1,500,000	5.0%	110,000	0.8%
North America	1,200,000	4.0%	54,000	0.6%
East Asia	749,999	2.0%	52,000	0.1%
West/Central Europe	730,000	2.0%	27,000	0.3%
Middle East/North Africa	380,000	1.0%	40,000	0.3%
Caribbean	230,000	0.7%	20,000	1.1%
Oceania	74,000	0.2%	13,000	0.4%

Source: Fenton (2008).

Three scenarios to 2025." The report identifies the five forces that are driving the future of AIDS in Africa. The five forces are as follows (UNAIDS 2005):

1. The growth or erosion of unity and integration
2. The evolution of beliefs, values, and meanings
3. The leveraging of resources and capabilities
4. The generation and application of knowledge
5. The distribution of power and authority

These five forces operate at every level, from the household level to the international level. Different combinations of the five forces yield the three different scenarios UNAIDS forecasts for 2025.

Tuberculosis

About a third of the world's population is infected with tuberculosis. Most of them are infected "with the latent form that poses little danger to health under normal circumstances, but becomes a major risk for active tuberculosis if the individual acquires HIV" (Cohen 2007).

Gini Williams is the tuberculosis coordinator at the International Council of Nurses. In 2007 Williams authored a piece entitled "Best Practice for the Care of Patients with Tuberculosis." The guide provides "an effective way of implementing and evaluating a series of clinical and organizational interventions aimed at controlling tuberculosis." The five key interventions proposed are the following (Williams 2007):

1. Sustained political commitment to increase human and financial resources and make tuberculosis control a nationwide priority integral to the national health system
2. Access to quality-assured sputum smearmicroscopy for case detection among persons presenting with, or found through screening to have, symptoms of tuberculosis (most importantly, prolonged cough)
3. Standardized short-course chemotherapy for all cases of tuberculosis under proper case management conditions, including direct observation of treatment
4. An uninterrupted supply of quality-assured drugs
5. A recording and reporting system enabling outcome assessment of all patients and assessment of overall program performance

Malaria

Malaria is a lethal disease. It kills one million people every year, a majority of whom are children. A joint report published in 2003 by WHO and UNICEF estimated that malaria costs Africa $12 billion per annum, slowing economic growth by 1.3 percent per year. Since independence, sub-Saharan Africa's GDP is 32 percent lower than what it would have been had malaria been eradicated (Molavi 2003). The Tanzanian malaria researcher Wen Kilama puts it differently: "If seven Boeing 747s full of children crashed into a mountain every day, would the world take measures to prevent it?" (Molavi 2003).

The President's Malaria Initiative (PMI) of the United States was launched in 2005 by former president George W. Bush. On April 9, 2006, Laura Bush signed a letter where she confirmed that the United States had provided the means to reduce the burden of malaria to over 25 million people since PMI was launched. PMI started with an initial allocation of $1.2 billion to spend over a four-year term. PMI proposes four basic preventive methods to reduce the burden of malaria: insecticide-treated bed nets, indoor spraying, new antimalarial drugs, and preventive treatment.

I met **TIMOTHY ZIEMER** (DCA) and **Bernard Nahlen** (HEA) on November 14, 2008, at the USAID Headquarters in Washington, DC. Timothy is the coordinator of the President's Malaria Initiative (PMI) and Bernard is the deputy coordinator. As deputy director of PMI, Bernard provides guidance on malaria technical issues and program coordination. PMI implements at a small level the kind of policies that are necessary globally. Table 18.4 shows the results of PMI in its first two years of operation.

I remain convinced that the pitfalls of George W. Bush in foreign policy in the Middle East overshadow the innovations he pushed in the development aid space with initiatives such as PMI or the Millennium Challenge Coorporation (MCC). Both PMI and MCC have continued to operate under the Obama Administration.

Sexually Transmitted Diseases

Almost a million people acquire a sexually transmitted infection every day. Sexually transmitted diseases include syphilis, chancroid ulcers, and genital herpes. As a result of a sexually transmitted infection, a person greatly increases his or her exposure to

TABLE 18.4   PMI Results in 2006 and 2007

PMI Results	2006	2007	Cumulative Results
Number of people protected by IRS	2,097,056	17,776,105	17,776,105
Number of ITNs procured	1,047,393	5,149,038	6,196,431
Number of mosquito nets re-treated	505,573	677,108	1,182,681
Number of ACT treatments procured	1,229,550	11,536,443	12,766,983
Number of health workers trained in use of ACTs	8,344	20,864	29,208
Number of rapid diagnostic tests procured	1,004,875	2,082,600	3,087,475
Number of IPTp treatments procured	0	1,350,000	1,350,000
Number of health workers trained in IPTp	1,994	3,153	5,147

IRS = Indoor residual spraying; ITN = Insecticide-treated mosquito net; ACT = Artemisinin-based combination therapy; IPTp = Intermittent preventive treatment for pregnant women. *Source:* PMI (2008).

infertility, ectopic pregnancy, and cervical cancer, along with the risk of acquiring and transmitting HIV (WHO 2007). Only in sub-Saharan Africa, 30 percent to 80 percent of women and 10 percent to 50 percent of men are infected with the herpes simplex virus type 2. Human papillomavirus—another sexually transmited infection—causes half a million cases of cervical cancer every year and 240,000 deaths. Preventing sexually transmitted diseases would reduce mortality and prevent infection from HIV.

Francis Ndowa (HEA) is the coordinator of the sexually transmitted infections control team at the World Health Organization. I met Francis on July 17, 2008, at the Headquarters of the World Health Organization in Geneva (Switzerland). What can be done to prevent sexually transmitted diseases? WHO (2007) recommends the following interventions:

1. Promoting healthy sexual behavior
2. Providing condoms and other barrier methods
3. Delivering prevention and care
4. Access to medicines and appropriate technology
5. Scaling up pilot programs

Workforce

McKinsey & Company consultants Michael Conway, Srishti Gupta, and Kamiar Khajavi have studied the shortage of health-care professionals and propose two scenarios for 2030 that would resolve the current shortage of personnel (Conway, Gupta, et al., 2007). Figure 18.2 shows the number of health workers per 1,000 people for different geographical regions.

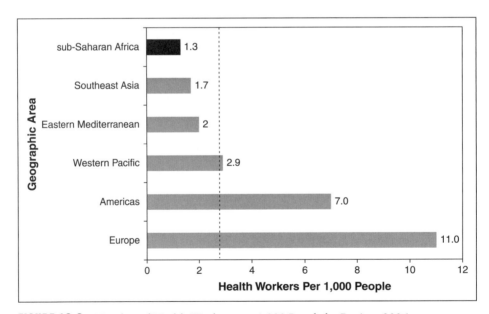

FIGURE 18.2   Number of Health Workers per 1,000 People by Region, 2006
WHO recommends a minimum ratio of 2.5 workers per 1,000 people
Source: WHO (2006).

The authors (2007) review the number of nurses and doctors that would have to be hired to close the gap and reach the 2.5 health workers per 1,000 people recommended by the World Health Organization. In 2007 there were 790,000 nurses and 150,000 doctors working in Africa. In order to cover the gap by 2030, 620,000 additional nurses and 200,000 new doctors would have to be hired. The McKinsey consultants present two scenarios to reach the goal of 1,760,000 health workers by 2030.

In the first scenario, 336,000 new nurses, 132,000 new doctors, and 282,000 paraprofessionals[4] are hired, reaching the magic number. The second scenario does not require hiring more doctors or nurses, and relies on hiring 890,000 paraprofessionals, 150,000 of which would be current nurses who would become paraprofessionals. The basic principle is that it costs less to educate and hire a paraprofessional than it costs to educate and hire a nurse or a doctor. The first scenario has an additional annual cost of $22.4 billion. The second scenario has an additional annual cost of $5.4 billion.

EDUCATION

UNESCO is the United Nations Agency that promotes supranational cooperation in areas that include education, science, and culture. In March 1990 the participants in the World Conference on Education for All, organized by UNESCO, gathered in Thailand to sign a declaration. They did not hesitate to recall that education was a fundamental right and acknowledged that the provision of education was deficient. At the time more than 100 million children had no access to primary education, 60 percent of whom were girls (UNESCO 1990). What has been the progress since then?

A majority of the population in extreme poor countries is under 15 years old. If children in developing nations are not educated they will fall into the many traps present in those countries, including armed guerrilla groups, gangs, smuggling, and prostitution. It is our responsibility to help developing nations reach the target of universal primary and secondary education.

Helen Poulsen explains the impact of HIV/AIDS on education in her paper "The gendered impact of HIV/AIDS on education in South Africa and Swaziland" (Poulsen 2006). In her research she picked two communities in South Africa where the AIDS prevalence rate was 21.5 percent at the time, and two communities in Swaziland where the AIDS prevalence rate was 38.8 percent. Orphan rates are extremely high in these communities. Poulsen reports, "At Naka primary school in South Africa, thirteen percent of students are orphans, while two percent are double orphans" (Poulsen 2006). A majority of the orphans in the second grade happen to be boys. She concludes that girls who are orphans are less likely to attend school. Poulsen's work represents only the tip of the iceberg. It is a good introduction because it connects health care to education and makes the case for a global approach to poverty eradication that incorporates the provision of the four dimensions of a basic welfare state: health care, education, water, and sanitation.

SARAH MOTEN (EDU) is the chief of the Africa Bureau Office of Sustainable Development, Education Division at USAID. I phoned Sarah on November 21, 2008. Sarah manages and coordinates a team that monitors 21 African bilateral education programs that provide $175 million per year. She was also the manager of

President George W. Bush's Africa Education Initiative (AEI). AEI provided a total of $600 million to improve teacher training in Africa. Melvin Foote, president and CEO of Constituency for Africa says that Sarah believes in the African people. "Sarah is very much an Africanist," he asserts (Wickham 2005).

The Dakar Goals

On April 26 to 28, 2000, the World Education Forum met in Senegal, bringing together 1,100 participants, including two heads of state (Nigeria and Senegal) and 100 ministers of education. The participants adopted a text which they called *Education for All: Meeting Our Collective Commitments*. The participants reaffirmed the vision of the *World Declaration on Education for All* of 1990 that departs from the *Universal Declaration of Human Rights*. They acknowledged "the commitments made by the international community to basic education throughout the 1990s," and expanded the definition of education as a fundamental right that goes beyond that of the Millennium Development Goals (UNESCO 2000).[5] The deadline for the fullfilment of the goals was set at 2015.

In 2002 a total of 83 nations were on track to achieve the so-called Dakar goals by the 2015 deadline, whereas according to UNESCO, 70 countries would not reach the target. Christopher Colclough, director of *Global Monitoring Report: Is the World on Track?* argued at the time that "almost one-third of the world's population live in countries where achieving the Dakar goals remains a dream" (UN Foundation 2002).

A new development approach to education needs a leading education authority. **FEDERICO MAYOR ZARAGOZA** (EDU) was deputy director general of UNESCO from 1978 to 1987 and director general of UNESCO from 1987 to 1999. I met Federico on June 5, 2008, at the Fundación Areces in Madrid (Spain). Federico is a strong advocate of Global Redistribution. Do we need new institutions able to deliver education to the extreme poor? Federico's insightful views refer to Nicolas Sarkozy's *refoundation* of capitalism and Angela Merkel's global economic charter as proposal that fall short. Federico noted this book's subtitle should be The New Architecture *After* Capitalism. We need more ambition and enthusiasm, more cooperation and dialogue if we are, as a global society, to defeat the great evils of our time. Thanks to Federico for being a giant on whose shoulders I can envision a fairer capitalism. Thanks for reminding me that "tomorrow is always late." There is a better tomorrow. There is a History of Tomorrow ahead of us. We must act today because if it is never too late if we believe, dream, and love.

The *Education for All Global Monitoring Report 2009* summarizes the progress made in the year 2008. The six goals UNESCO tracks are: early childhood care and education, universal primary education, meeting the lifelong learning needs of youth and adults, adult literacy, gender, and equality (UNESCO 2008). A majority of countries have increased their spending on education since the World Education Forum met in Senegal in 2000. However, the share of national income spent on education decreased in 40 out of 105 countries surveyed between 1999 and 2006. North America and Europe accounted for 55 percent of the global spending on education (UNESCO 2008). The expenditure disparity is manifest: North America and Western Europe (55 percent), East Asia and the Pacific (18 percent), Latin

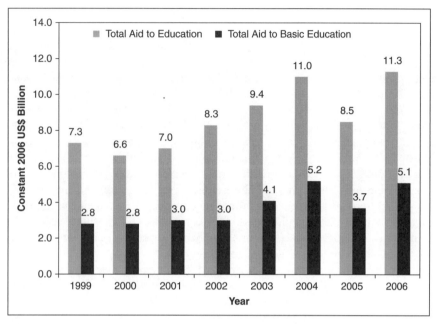

FIGURE 18.3 Total Aid Commitments to Education and Basic Education, 1999–2006
Source: Based on data from OECD.Stat http://stats.oecd.org.

America and the Caribbean (8 percent), Central and Eastern Europe (7 percent), Arab States (3 percent), sub-Saharan Africa (2 percent), and Central Asia (0.3 percent).

Financing Basic Education

A total of $11 billion is estimated to be necessary to fund the three EFA goals in low-income countries. Global aid to education reached $9 billion, up from $5.5 billion in 2002 (UNESCO 2008). Figure 18.3 shows the total aid allocated to education between 1999 and 2006. The general trend is that less than half of the yearly aid to education is allocated to basic education. Aid to education almost doubled between 2000 and 2004 and stagnated thereafter.

WATER AND SANITATION

Water and sanitation are basic needs to which every human being should have access. Between 1990 and 2004 alone, 1.2 billion people worldwide gained access to improved sanitation. As of 2008, 41 percent of the world population, including almost one billion children, lacked access to appropriate sanitation facilities (Black and Fawcett 2008).[6]

A total of 341 million Africans did not have access to drinking water in 2006, up by 61 million from 280 million in 1990. In nine African countries, less than half the population has access to improved drinking water sources (UN Water 2008a).

Better water and sanitation are vital in the fight against HIV/AIDS. The impact of water and sanitation on education is crucial. Overall the number of annual deaths associated with dirt is two million, a majority of which are due to diarrheal disease. Every year diarrheal disease kills 390,000 children under five in West and Central Africa, 262,000 in East and Southern Africa and 536,000 in South Asia (Black and Fawcett 2008). Diarrheal disease could be virtually eliminated with the provision of clean water and sanitation.

Abbas Bhuiya (HEA) is the head social and behavioral sciences at the International Centre for Diarrheal Disease Research in Dhaka, Bangladesh. I had breakfast with Abbas at the BRAC Centre Inn in Dhaka (Bangladesh) on March 6, 2009. Is diarrheal disease a starting point for more severe diseases? According to Abbas, "Diarrhea especially among young children adversely impacts their nutritional status. Repeated diarrheal episodes in the absence of proper management can result in severe malnutrition among children which in turn make children more susceptible to infection and fatal consequences. Thus, diarrhea is a starting point for severe health consequences."

In fact, the direct mortality rates caused by diarrheal disease associated with poor sanitation and hygiene conditions amounted to 5,808 in Cambodia, 20,592 in Indonesia, 10,471 in the Philippines, and 4,136 in Vietnam for 2005 (World Bank 2008c). A universal implementation of improved sanitation and hygiene would mitigate a combined negative economic impact in the four countries that amounts to $8.9 billion per annum (World Bank 2008c).

2008 was the international year of sanitation. As a contribution, a partnership of four institutions including the African Development Bank and the World Bank published a review of the sanitation and hygiene status in 32 African countries. The report raises the question of whether African countries would miss the Millennium Development Goal on water supply and sanitation. According to the report (AMCOW, AfDB, et al., 2008):

> *For Africa to meet its Millennium Development Goals for water supply and sanitation, the number of persons served must more than double from 350 million in 2006 to 760 million by 2015. That still leaves almost 400 million unserved.*

The fact of the matter is that as of 2008 the only countries in Africa that were on track to fulfill the MDGs on water supply and sanitation were in North Africa. The whole of sub-Saharan Africa was off track. Only minor improvements in sanitation took place between 1990 and 2006 in a majority of countries in sub-Saharan Africa (UNICEF, AfDB, et al., 2008): Eritrea (3 percent of the population had access to sanitation facilities in 1990 versus only 5 percent in 2006), Niger (3 percent versus 7 percent), Chad (5 percent versus 7 percent), Ghana (6 percent versus 10 percent), Ethiopia (4 percent versus 11 percent), Madagascar (8 percent versus 12 percent), Togo (13 percent versus 12 percent), Burkina Faso (5 percent versus 13 percent), Guinea (13 percent versus 19 percent), Rwanda (29 percent versus 23 percent), Cote d'Ivoire (20 percent versus 24 percent), Mauritania (20 percent versus 24 percent), Senegal (26 percent versus 28 percent), Nigeria (26 percent versus 30 percent), Central African Republic (11 percent versus 31 percent), Democratic

Republic of the Congo (15 percent versus 31 percent), Liberia (40 percent versus 32 percent), Uganda (29 percent versus 33 percent) and Tanzania (35 percent versus 33 percent).

As a result of the minor improvements in sanitation, the practice of open defecation continues to be widespread in countries like Madagascar (37 percent of the population), Ethiopia (64 percent), Botswana (14 percent), Malawi (11 percent), Mozambique (48 percent), Sao Tome and Principe (59 percent), and Senegal (24 percent). Globally, 1.2 billion people practiced open defecation in 2006, of which 665 million were in India, 66 million in Indonesia, 52 million in Ethiopia, and 50 million in Pakistan (UNICEF, AfDB, et al., 2008).

Provision Disparities

The provision of water and sanitation in many developing countries is linked to income and urban or rural dwelling. Individuals in higher income levels are more likely to have access to water and sanitation. The delivery of water and sanitation is better in urban areas. Generally speaking, for the same level of wealth there will be a greater access to water than to sanitation. Access to both water and sanitation tend to increase with income level.

Providing households with toilets gives only mixed results. It is a better strategy to incentivize households to demand a toilet and help them build it and support it. Consequently, the likelihood that the household uses the toilet increases dramatically. The quality of the toilet during the building process should be monitored, as faulty design of toilets leads to water contamination, particularly bacteriological.

The lack of sanitation is a severe problem in areas where open defecation is widespread. In spite of relative progress, 74 percent of the rural poor in India continue to practice open defecation. This compares with only 18 percent of the urban poor (UNICEF 2008). Rural coverage is generally poorer than urban coverage.

A Worthy Investment

A new development strategy for water and sanitation requires an accomplished chief. **CLARISSA BROCKLEHURST** (WTS) is the chief of water and environmental sanitation at UNICEF, a UN Agency. I met Clarissa on September 8, 2008, at the UNICEF Headquarters in New York City. In "The Case for Water and Sanitation," Clarissa justifies how better water and sanitation makes sense from an economic perspective (Brocklehurst 2004).

Investment in water supply and sanitation is a worthy investment. Table 18.5 shows how for every dollar of investment in water and sanitation an eleven-fold return is obtained.

HANS SPRUIJT (WTS) is the chief of water and environmental sanitation at UNICEF Bangladesh, UNICEF's largest mission. I met Hans on March 2, 2009, at the UNICEF Headquarters in Dhaka (Bangladesh). A successful delivery strategy has allowed UNICEF Bangladesh to reach as many as 30 million individuals in the areas of water and sanitation.

The WHO estimates that improved water and sanitation could help reduce the global disease burden by nine percentage points (Pruss-Ustun, Bos, et al., 2008). The

TABLE 18.5   Benefits and Costs of Improved Access to Water and Sanitation in Africa

Impact of Improved Access to Water Supply and Sanitation	Meeting MDGs	Providing Access to Basic Water and Sanitation for All
Cases of diarrhea avoided annually	173 million cases	245 million cases
Productive days gained annually	456 million days	647 million days
Value of productive days gained annually	US$ 116 million	US$ 168 million
Health sector treatment costs averted annually	US$ 1,695 million	US$ 2,410 million
Value of time saved	US$ 15,877 million	US$ 33,972 million
Schooldays gained annually	99 million schooldays	140 million schooldays
Economic Benefit Cost Analysis		
Cost of investments in improved access per year	US$ 2,020 million	US$ 4,040 million
Total economic benefits per year	US$ 22,910 million	US$ 44,040 million
Benefit cost ratio	11	11

Source: Hutton and Haller (2004). Data reprinted with permission of the Water and Sanitation Program (www.wsp.org).

diseases that are related to a lack of appropriate water supply and sanitation are diarrheal diseases (39 percent of the total), malnutrition (21 percent), and malaria (14 percent). The WHO estimates that it would cost $13 billion per year to meet the drinking water and sanitation target of the MDGs (Pruss-Ustun, Bos, et al., 2008). The benefit cost ratio ranges from a ratio of four to a ratio of 12, as shown in Table 18.6.

The Sanitary Revolution

The sanitary revolution couples the provision of universal sanitation with the necessary education that would foster its widespread use. Providing a toilet for everyone would cost about $10 billion a year, which is less than one percent of global military spending (UN Water 2008b). What is the requirement? The most important aspect is a plan of action that raises awareness and secures sufficient funding. Creating and meeting demand for sanitation are the necessary next steps (UN Water, 2008b). According to Jon Lane, executive director of Water Supply & Sanitation Collaborative Council, the biggest part of the $10 billion "should come from households themselves, which is one of the reasons why aid flows in the sanitation sector must prioritize demand-creation" (Lane 2008).

Creating demand for sanitation is not easy. Many individuals that have never used appropriate sanitation facilities do not know what it is like and do not demand its provision. However, providing appropriate sanitation facilities would have a phenomenal impact on the individual's quality of life, including health and the ability to work. UN Water says, "Building community consensus that open defecation is a serious and shameful problem that can be solved by toilets has proved successful

TABLE 18.6 Benefit-Cost Ratio by Intervention in Developing Regions and Eurasia

Intervention	Annual Benefits in US$ Millions	Benefit-Cost Ratio by Intervention
Halving the proportion of people without access to improved water sources by 2015	18,143	9
Halving the proportion of people without access to improved water sources and improved sanitation by 2015	84,400	8
Universal access to improved water and sanitation services by 2015	262,879	10
Universal access to improved water and improved sanitation and water disinfected at the point of use by 2015	344,879	12
Universal access to a regulated piped water supply and sewage connection by 2015	555,901	4

Source: Hutton and Haller (2004). Data reprinted with permission of the World Health Organization.

in a number of countries" (UN Water 2008b). This is where education plays an important role.

Meeting demand for sanitation, once demand is created through awareness and education, requires supporting and training small local operators, who would be in charge of installing and maintaining the sanitation facilities.

We are closer to Eutopia than we ever thought possible. The Expert Dreamers introduced in this chapter will contribute to reaching the beautiful goal.

Artwork by Bill Butcher.

CHAPTER 19

The New Institution

There is one other approach I would like to see tried in failing states, and that is what is known as independent service authorities. The idea is that in countries where basic public services such as primary education and health clinics are utterly failing, the government, civil society, and donors combined could try to build an alternative system for spending public money.
—Paul Collier, *The Bottom Billion*

This chapter presents a new international legal rule and explains a path toward its establishment. The new legal rule would provide Universal Welfare consisting of free education and health care, and subsidized water and sanitation to the extreme poor. The new international legal rule becomes the charter of The New Institution, responsible for the delivery of the Universal Welfare to the extreme poor worldwide The new <u>Welfare Charter</u> would mimic the United Nations Charter[1] described in Chapter 13. The Welfare Charter would become the constitution of The New Institution.

The purpose of the establishment of the Welfare Charter as a new international rule is first to acknowledge the urgency and raise awareness about the need to fight extreme poverty as an ongoing global concern, and subsequently to describe a scenario in which the provision of a Universal Welfare as a Global Public Good could be accomplished. The establishment of such a rule would universalize the access to a minimum welfare state that would fulfill a person's basic needs. A healthier, better educated population is then more able to make economic progress and leave behind the poverty trap many poor cannot exit today.

UNIVERSAL WELFARE AS AN INTERNATIONAL LEGAL RULE

The Welfare Charter (name given hereafter to the future international legal rule) focuses on the subset of the *Universal Declaration of Human Rights*, which deals with the provision of health care and education. It then expands to the provision of water and sanitation.

On December 10, 1948, member countries of the United Nations signed the *Universal Declaration of Human Rights*. The declaration called upon all member countries "to cause it to be disseminated, displayed, read and expounded principally in schools and other education institutions, without distinction based on the political status of countries or territories." Its dissemination was, however, not a binding requirement to enforce it, not even in the long run.

Articles 25 and 26 of the *Universal Declaration of Human Rights* focus on health care and education. In particular, Article 25(1) states, "Everyone has the right to a standard of living adequate for the health and well-being of himself and of his family, including food, clothing, housing and medical care and necessary social services, and the right to security in the event of unemployment, sickness, disability, widowhood, old age or other lack of livelihood in circumstances beyond his control." Article 26(1) determines that "everyone has the right to education, which shall be free, at least in the elementary and fundamental stages." There is no mention of water and sanitation in the *Universal Declaration of Human Rights*. As described in Chapter 18, water and sanitation are intrinsically connected to hygiene and health. It is important that they be included as part of a basic Universal Welfare. The New Institution will be responsible for the delivery of the Universal Welfare.

International Legal Rules

Dimitry Kochenov (TNI) is a lecturer in European law at Groningen University in the Netherlands and author of the book *EU Enlargement and the Failure of Conditionality* (Kochenov 2008). I talked to Dimitry on November 21, 2008. Dimitry notes "any international legal document certainly contains international legal rules, even if those are merely declarations and have no effect on real world." Not every rule is binding. We are as a result concerned with *binding* international legal rules that oblige state as well as other actors to act.

Anthony Clark Arend is a professor of international law at Georgetown University. I met Arend on January 17, 2008, at the International Center of Georgetown University in Washington, DC. According to Arend, the Welfare Charter would be considered an international legal rule if it shows a certain degree of authority and control. Authority is related to how the decision-making elites perceive the rule to be law. Control indicates whether the rule is reflected in state practice. In Arend's own words, "For a rule of customary international law to exist, two elements must be present: (1) states must engage in an activity; there must be a practice; (2) states must believe that the practice is required by law; they must believe that the practice is obligatory" (Arend 1999).

The *Universal Declaration of Human Rights* never became an international legal rule because it did not reach a sufficient level of control. It became a declaration that a majority of countries have not been able to fulfill after 60 years of existence. There are a total of four different combinations. A rule could have a high degree of authority and a low degree of control and vice versa. But only when a rule has a high degree of both authority and control, it can be considered to be an international legal rule.

The best-known example of a rule that could have become an international legal rule but failed to do so is the United Nations Charter (UN Charter), presented in Chapter 12.[2] More precisely, Article 2(4) of the UN C says, "All Members shall refrain in their international relations from the threat or use of force against the territorial integrity or political independence of any state, or in any other manner inconsistent with the purposes of the United Nations."[3] The UN Charter was signed by 50 of the 51 original member countries at the United Nations Conference on International Organization in San Francisco (California) on June 26, 1945.

Article 2(4) has had a high degree of authority since it was enunciated in 1945 because of the high number of member states that signed the United Nations Charter in 1945 and thereafter. However, it lacks control because there have been many exceptions to its application, many instances in which Article 2(4) has been trespassed. It many instances, states have decided to trespass the law, and therefore have not complied with it. As a result, the level of control is low.

Ideally a declaration that intends to become an international legal rule should fulfill the two requirements put forth by Arend. If a rule has a high level of authority but lacks control, it would be systematically trespassed. On the contrary, if the rule has a high level of control but lacks authority, its application will not be spread out internationally. The provision of Universal Welfare, as a proposed rule, should transition from low to high degrees of authority and control. It is only under that circumstance that the Welfare Charter would become an international legal rule.

If the Welfare Charter became an international legal rule, Universal Welfare would materialize. Consequently health care, education, water and sanitation would reach all the extreme poor. Otherwise we would continue to live in a world where declarations of good intentions that are enunciated but not implemented.

THEORY OF INTERNATIONAL RELATIONS

International law is defined as "a set of binding rules that seek to regulate the behavior of international actors by conferring rights and duties" (Arend, Beck, et al., 1996). The theory of international relations studies how individuals understand the role of states in accepting and implementing international legal rules. There are three main approaches: realism, institutionalism, and constructivism.

In what circumstances would the Welfare Charter become an international legal rule? In this section, the context in which the Welfare Charter could transition into an international legal rule is exposed under the point of view of a realist, an institutionalist, and a constructivist nation-state.

Realism

Realism emerged in the aftermath of World War II and the widespread devastation and horror seen during the two World Wars. In this context, realists believe that human beings are characterized by ambition that often leads to aggressive behavior. Realism substitutes idealism with a Realpolitik approach (Arend, Beck, et al., 1996). According to realists, international affairs are driven by power relations instead of legal institutions, and the world is ruled by anarchy without cooperation, which drives nations to unilateralism instead of multilateralism and does not fully recognize the political legitimacy and law-making authority of a supranational body such as the United Nations. In his article "The False Promise of International Institutions," John Mearsheimer, a professor of political science at the University of Chicago, summarized the essence of realism in five sentences as follows (Mearsheimer 1994):

1. The international system is anarchic.
2. States inherently possess some offensive military capability to hurt and possibly destroy each other.

3. States can never be certain about the intentions of other states.
4. The most basic motive driving states is survival.
5. States think strategically about how to survive.

Why would there be any international cooperation in an anarchic world? The world is an environment in which every country acts individually looking to maximize the benefit of its own citizens, and in which states aspire to power in permanent rivalry. States refuse, therefore, to abide by a common law. According to realism, human beings are evil creatures driven by sin. States, ruled by human beings, can be more evil, and the world—as an aggregation of states—is a dangerous place where each state looks to defend its own interests (Aron 1966). In this environment, distrust among nations is widespread.

Universal Welfare under a Realist Perspective   If realism is driven by power politics and political ambition that stems from economic and military power, what kind of realism, if any, emerges in states with insignificant military and economic might? Many states in the developing world do not have the arsenal of weaponry and military personnel of the great powers.

How is national interest defined? If states are unitary actors that do not believe in international cooperation and defend their own interests, how would this national interest shape a state's foreign policy? In the case of the United States, national interest is based on the maintenance and expansion of democracy and capitalism throughout the world. National interest is undergoing a transition towards a continental interest in the transformation of the European Union.

How would a sub-Saharan African country that suffers from extreme poverty, hunger, disease, and lack of access to education and health care understand the defense of its national interest? A state devastated by extreme poverty is likely to identify its own survival with that of its citizens, if its ruling elite represent the will of its people. This was not the case when a myriad of dictators ruled the developing world, dictators who sought a perpetuation in power to enrich their own pockets, in expense of that of their own citizens. As a result, a poor country that conducts a realist foreign policy will not trust a new supranational institution that delivers a basic welfare state, namely The New Institution. However, such a state will match its policy-making with the defense of its national interest. This national interest could be represented by the provision of Global Public Goods, which include health care and education, and water and sanitation.

The shortest path to the establishment of the Welfare Charter as an international legal rule in a realist world would be, as an independent agent, to persuade poor states to accept additional foreign aid that could help them improve and enhance the well-being of their citizens, thereby strengthening their own national interests. In a world that lacks cooperation and is driven by power politics of self-interest, why would anyone increase foreign aid to benefit a potential enemy? What would be the final purpose of this increase in aid?

The fact of the matter is that unless driven by a merciless dictator whose priority is to enhance its military might (North Korea) or its own economic enrichment (Equatorial Guinea), a poor country that has transitioned into a democracy is more likely to be driven by institutionalism or constructivism, because the principle of noncooperation does not favor the needy. Those in need, in the end, are helpless if they do not accept someone else's help. This is independent from the ultimate reasons that drive individuals, whether or not these reasons are grounded in selfishness and self-interest.

Institutionalism

Institutionalists approach the relations between states as anarchy where cooperation can be beneficial. Institutionalists leave pure unilateralism behind and embrace an approach to international affairs that incorporates some degree of multilateralism.

The concept of regime is important for institutionalists. There are a variety of definitions in the academic literature. John Ruggie, a professor of international affairs at Harvard University, describes regime as "a set of mutual expectations, rules and regulations, plans, organizational energies and financial commitments, which have been accepted by a group of states." Stephen Krasner, a professor of political science at Stanford University, defines regime as "a set of implicit or explicit principles, norms, rules, and decision-making procedures around which actors' expectations converge in a given area of international relations." Lastly, Andrew Hurrell, a professor of international relations at Oxford University, approaches the definition of regime as "an explicit, persistent, and connected sets of rules" (Arend 1999).

Institutionalists believe that the interest of states remains prioritary, but they consider that institutions, by facilitating information sharing and resource pooling, can help reduce transaction costs (Arend 1999). In this context, institutions can facilitate the pursuit of a state's ultimate goals. A regime puts together institutions that define a set of common rules to fulfill by member states, and the relations between the institution and the member states. Contrary to realists that believe in zero cooperation, institutionalists see the advantages they can earn from participating in a regime as defined above

Universal Welfare under an Institutionalist Perspective The concept of regime is important for institutionalist states. In this context, the Welfare Charter as an international legal rule could be presented as a regime driven by a common set of norms that identify common problems among poor states. The common set of norms would establish a mandatory, universal provision of education and health care. The institution exemplified by the regime and the set of norms could facilitate the provision of such a welfare state.

With this perspective in mind, a new supranational institution that delivers a Universal Welfare to adherent countries (The New Institution) could be seen as a supranational Ministry of Health Care and Education, in which resource-pooling and economies of scale help reduce transaction costs. By giving up its own management in two key areas such as health care and education for the extreme poor, which would be subsequently managed by the supranational institution, a state is acknowledging the benefits of cooperation. Yet states are still unitary actors that see the defense of their own interests as paramount. This last statement is compatible with the delivery of a basic welfare state to a nation's extreme poor who are not being reached. And so remains an empty space to fill, which that nation may not be able to cover. Cooperation, in this case, enhances a poor country's own national interest and decreases the exposure to extreme poverty by lessening the burden of lack of education and health care.

An analogy can be drawn with the Eurozone, in which member countries give up the management of its own monetary policy to a supranational institution (the European Central Bank), which yields benefits of cooperation: economic stability and the elimination of exchange rate risk. In both the case of Universal Welfare and the Eurozone, the benefits of the regime match those of the individual member states, and the agency problem is mitigated, which fosters an environment of increased cooperation.

Constructivism

Constructivism emerged in the 1980s, inspired by the British international society approach. According to John Ruggie, the British approach holds that "the system of states is embedded in a society of states, which includes sets of values, rules, and institutions that are commonly accepted by states and which make it possible for the system of states to function" (Ruggie 1998).

For constructivists, states and global norms are interacting. They argue that institutions can teach states to value certain goals. Institutions thus become policymakers with the ability to propose international rules and shape state behavior accordingly. Constructivists add social relationships to the structure of international relations. Constructivists are criticized by realists and institutionalists because of their lack of empirical data to justify their decisions (Arend 1999).

Martha Finnemore, a professor of political science at George Washington University, is a leading constructivist who has written on how institutions and international organizations can help states shape their policies in important areas. For Finnemore, an international organization such as UNESCO can become a teacher of norms (Finnemore 1996). She argues that through membership and involvement in UNESCO, states can shape science policy and create science bureaucracy drawing from international norms set beforehand.

Universal Welfare under a Constructivist Perspective A constructivist would argue that through membership in an institution whose priority is to provide Universal Welfare, countries can learn the benefits and advantages that an unconditional provision of a basic welfare state can have to society, thereby reducing inequality, and decreasing the likelihood and incidence of conflict. Following on Ruggie's view, the society of states that includes a set of values and rules could expand to include the provision of Universal Welfare. Following on Finnemore's view, the creation of a new supranational institution that delivers a Universal Welfare to the extreme poor could help developing countries shape health care and education policy.

The Extractive Industries Transparency Initiative (EITI) is a coalition that includes governments, corporations, and Civil Society organizations and advises resource-rich developing countries on what is the appropriate roadmap to success in the management of their natural resource wealth. EITI is an interesting example of a body that has the ability to shape developing countries' savoir-faire in the field of natural resource management. EITI draws from the expertise and proven success of Norway's oil fund. EITI was described in more detail in Chapter 9.

The previous example has been used to draw the design of the supranational institution able to deliver Universal Welfare, as a constructivist would see it. This supranational institution could draw from the expertise of social democracies in delivering a welfare state, in order to shape developing countries' aspirations to include education and health care as part of the public goods they provide. Developing countries have been driven to the privatization of health care and education in the context of the macroeconomic conditionality imposed by the loans of the World Bank and the bailout packages of the International Monetary Fund. This privatization never occurred in social democracies of Western Europe.

From a constructivist perspective, a world driven by constructivist states could become, in the long run, a global community of states with common norms of Universal Welfare. In this *eutopic* world, the aggregation of states providing Universal Welfare could converge into the creation of a global welfare state, in which a maximum degree of control would be reached and none or few violations of small seriousness and insignificant universality would remain according to Arend's methodology.

ESTABLISHMENT OF THE WELFARE CHARTER

Sub-Saharan Africa is seriously off track in the fulfillment of the three Millennium Development Goals (MDGs) that are directly related to education and health care. The establishment of a Universal Welfare consisting of health care and education would be desirable, because it would contribute to the materialization of the MDGs that a majority of countries embraced in 2000. But leaving behind desirability, this section looks at the most straightforward and likely path towards the establishment of the Welfare Charter, defines a strategy, and suggests a beginning in six countries of sub-Saharan Africa.[4]

In 2000, 189 Heads of State backed the Millennium Development Goals. In 2009 three of the goals were unlikely to be fulfilled in sub-Saharan Africa. sub-Saharan Africa is, as a result, the geographical region in most desperate need of an increase in foreign aid that can contribute to the fulfillment of the MDGs.

The debate is not whether more or less is needed. The debate is how to make additional foreign aid smarter and more effective. Donors, whether they are countries or foundations, are increasingly demanding accountability and transparency in the allocation, delivery, and use of foreign aid. Accountability is a desirable component of the design of any foreign aid allocation, because it engages both the donor and the recipient, aligns their common interests, and maximizes the social return of the aid delivery. In order to increase accountability, donor and recipients should agree on the goals to be fulfilled. This agreement should take the form of a set of conditions that could be used as a benchmark against which a country's performance would be measured. Conditionality is a feature that is more and more present in the policy-making of foreign aid packages. Conditionality can be donor-imposed or negotiated. Conditionality is reviewed in Chapter 20.

Strategy

The strategy of implementation of the Universal Welfare would identify an area within sub-Saharan Africa that has a record of both being cooperative and being willing to subscribe to a program of conditional foreign aid. This strategy would minimize the probability of failure.

The effective provision of Universal Welfare could contribute to the fulfillment of the Millennium Development Goals in the countries of sub-Saharan Africa where it operates. The proposed area would become a pilot that, if successful, could expand to other candidate countries and become an inspiration for similar schemes in Central America and the Caribbean and South Asia.

Supranational Cooperation

How do we measure cooperation? Cooperation has to be understood from the point of view of an institutionalist or a realist as defined in the previous section. Sub-Saharan Africa and, in particular, the southern cone have a recent history of cooperation between countries that has resulted in the formation of a handful of supranational organizations. This cooperative effort is shared through membership in three supranational organizations that promote trade and economic integration, including COMESA, ECOWAS, and SADC. In addition, all African countries are members of the African Union. A brief summary of each follows.

- COMESA is the *Common Market for Eastern and Southern Africa*, an organization of 19 countries with a total GDP of $360 billion and a population of 400 million. COMESA's predecessor is the Preferential Trade Area for Eastern and Southern Africa, adopted in 1978. COMESA seeks economic integration through trade.
- ECOWAS is the *Economic Community of West African States*, a regional group formed in 1975 whose mission is to promote economic integration. ECOWAS consists of four institutions: the Commission, the Community Parliament, the Community Court of Justice, and the Bank for Investment and Development. A total of fifteen West African countries constitute[5] ECOWAS. ECOWAS was the initiative of former Nigerian President Yakubu Gowon (Nugent 2004). Ivory Coast and Senegal were reluctant to join ECOWAS at the time of its formation, fearing that it may be dominated by Nigeria.
- The *Southern African Development Coordination Conference* (SADCC) emerged in 1980 as an alliance of nine Southern African countries, including Angola, Botswana, Lesotho, Malawi, Mozambique, Swaziland, Tanzania, Zambia, and Zimbabwe. SADCC coordinated economic policy to lessen the burden of Apartheid's South Africa. According to Janice Love, author of *Southern Africa in World Politics* (2005), SADCC's goals were "to promote black majority rule and resistance to apartheid destabilization campaigns, to reduce dependence on South Africa and the global economy, and to achieve balanced and sustained development as a region." SADCC later became the *Southern African Development Community* (SADC). In 2009 a total of 15 member states[6] were SADC members.

Supranational cooperation has, as a result, been in the agenda of a subset of sub-Saharan African nations since 1975. Certain sub-Saharan African nations could be seen, through their membership to different organizations, as a collection of countries with a desire to cooperate. As a result nations with a desire to cooperate at a supranational level would be considered institutionalist or constructivist, where the Welfare Charter as an international legal rule is more likely to materialize.

Aid with Accountability

The most representative example of foreign aid subject to accountability that includes conditionality clauses is the United States Millennium Challenge Corporation

(MCC). The MCC is introduced in Chapter 20. Whether or not we agree on the proposed conditionality of the MCC or on the economic rationale behind the selection of the conditions against which conditionality is measured, the voluntary basis on which countries decide to apply for MCC grants denotes an incentive to fulfill the performance required by the MCC. The MCC "assesses the degree to which the political, social and economic conditions in a country promote broad-based sustainable economic growth" (MCC 2008a). Three factors are considered by the MCC's board of directors when considering a new prospect: performance on policy criteria, the opportunity to reduce poverty and generate economic growth in the country, and the funds available to MCC (MCC 2008a).

Countries that are not MCC-compliant either do not fulfill the requirements or have not applied for membership. Therefore, it can be concluded that in sub-Saharan Africa, only MCC-compliant countries[7] have explicitly and openly expressed their willingness to accept the terms of the conditional foreign aid, or as the MCC defines it, aid with accountability.

Yekutiel Gershoni (TNI) is an emeritus professor of African history at the department of Middle Eastern and African history of Tel Aviv University. From 2002 to 2004, Yekutiel was the head of Middle Eastern and African history at Tel Aviv University. I phoned Yekutiel on February 18, 2009. For Yekutiel, "In some cases, African countries accept the conditions not out of free will but out of necessity, due to a disastrous economic situation, when it is obvious that they will not be able to fulfill the conditions."

ACHE

ACHE is the new *African Community of Healthcare and Education*. It is crucial that sub-Saharan Africans from ACHE's Founding Members acknowledge the role played by The New Institution in the areas of education, health care, water, and sanitation. It is also crucial to help sub-Saharan Africa build health care and education infrastructure conducive to the delivery of a basic welfare state. Otherwise, Peter H. Lindert's premonition may become a perpetual reality (Lindert 2004):

> *Most of sub-Saharan Africa, afflicted with rising AIDS mortality and rulers like Mugabe and Arap Moi, is the region where social transfers will remain meager. In social transfers, as in other respects, the main global divergence may be the widening gap between an expanding world and a stagnant Africa. The great divergence in social transfers and in education will probably be a widening of the gap between Africa and the rest of the world.*

Founding Members

ACHE's Founding Members should have shown a high degree of supranational cooperation and the willingness to become part of an ex-ante conditionality scheme similar to the MCC. If ACHE were to start operating in these countries, a moderate degree of authority and control (according to Arend's methodology) could be reached that would bring about some legitimacy and operational recognition that the Welfare Charter may work.

Out of the 10 sub-Saharan African countries that were MCC-compliant in 2009 (the eleventh African country was Morocco), five are members of ECOWAS (Benin, Burkina-Faso, Cape Verde, Ghana, and Mali) and five are members of SADC (Lesotho, Madagascar, Mozambique, Namibia, and Tanzania). Separately, both groups of five countries can be considered to have shown their willingness to cooperate on the economic and trade fronts. Both groups of five countries have also shown their willingness to be subject to ex-ante conditionality in foreign aid schemes.

What group of five countries should be considered as ACHE's Founding Members? Figure 19.1 shows the average political risk and peace index for both groups. The five SADC countries outperform the five ECOWAS countries in both political risk and peace index.[8]

SADC is ahead of the game with an already signed free trade agreement (2008) and expected customs union (2010), common market (2015), monetary union (2016), and a regional central bank with a common currency (2018) (*Lusaka Times* 2008). In addition, SADC includes the region's economic superpower South Africa, the only African member of the G20.

The African Community of Healthcare and Education needs a new executive secretary. **TOMAZ SALOMAO** (TNI) was appointed executive secretary of SADC in 2005. I met Tomaz on April 23, 2009, at the conference center of the Walmont Hotel in Gaborone (Botswana). I met Tomaz a second time on April 24, 2009, at Gaborone's International Airport. For Tomaz, the failed Washington Consensus imposed a set of policies that proved detrimental and did not help poor countries leave poverty behind. The poor continue to be poor.

Botswana is a member of SADC but is not MCC-compliant. Botswana would perfectly qualify to receive MCC grants, but it would not become eligible because its

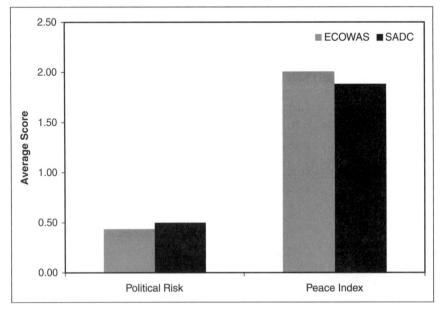

FIGURE 19.1 Average Political Risk and Peace Index
Data Source: Control Risks, Euromoney, and the Peace Index (2009).

per-capita income is the third highest in sub-Saharan Africa. In fact, adding Botswana as a sixth founding member to the five countries suggested beforehand would make sense because: (1) as a champion of governance and transparency Botswana could inspire change in the other five Founding Members; and (2) Botswana only has two million inhabitants, which would not be burdensome for ACHE's finances.

Coincidentally, the Founding Members of the European Coal and Steel Community were also six, had a small country (Luxembourg versus Lesotho) and a large separate country (Italy versus Madagascar). For Yekutiel, "The main difference is that ACHE will be trying to start its work from bottom up while organizations such as ECOWAS were trying to operate from the top down."

Political Alignment   Countries that are politically aligned are more likely to cooperate than countries that are not. Examples would be the United States and Western Europe, or left-wing and right-wing governments on both sides of the Atlantic.

Mozambique and Namibia fought wars against apartheid-backed movements, aligned their struggle, and secured support from outside parties in Angola and Tanzania. This political alignment has brought about a current political elite in the three countries that fought the apartheid regime on the same side. There is mutual understanding among the ruling political parties that not too long ago, armed Marxist guerrillas were supported by Cuba and Scandinavia. For the African Historian Paul Nugent, "The liberation movements envisaged a different kind of freedom, which would not merely substitute black faces for white ones, but transform the very nature of power itself" (Nugent 2004).

The political alignment is yet more holistic if South Africa's African National Congress (ANC) is added to the analysis. Mozambique's FRELIMO or Namibia's SWAPO have close ties with ANC that emerged from their common struggle against South Africa's apartheid. FRELIMO and SWAPO are consequently considered former liberation movements. Other liberation movements include Angola's MPLA, Tanzania's Chama Cha Mapinduzi, and Zimbabwe's Zanu-PF. All liberation movements have dominated their respective national politics since independence. A politics of supranational cooperation is more likely to take off among aligned political forces.

A politics of consensus and cooperation must emerge in today's world, where unfortunately we have become accustomed to a politics of noncooperation and the lack of enforcement of international standards. It is perhaps time to align our forces and best efforts to fight and defeat the great evils of our time. It is our responsibility to deliver a forward-looking vision that unites, one more time, former liberation movements in the quest to start The Glorious Forty that will lead us to Decemland, the land of 10 percent. Figure 19.2 presents a detailed map of Southern Africa.

Conditionality

Conditionality is defined in Chapters 20. The Founding Members should accept that the Universal Welfare state be delivered through the microfinance network by The New Institution. The delivery through microfinance is explained in the next section. Building up the microfinance network includes accepting that local Microfinance Institutions be supervised by the Bank for the Poor, developing new

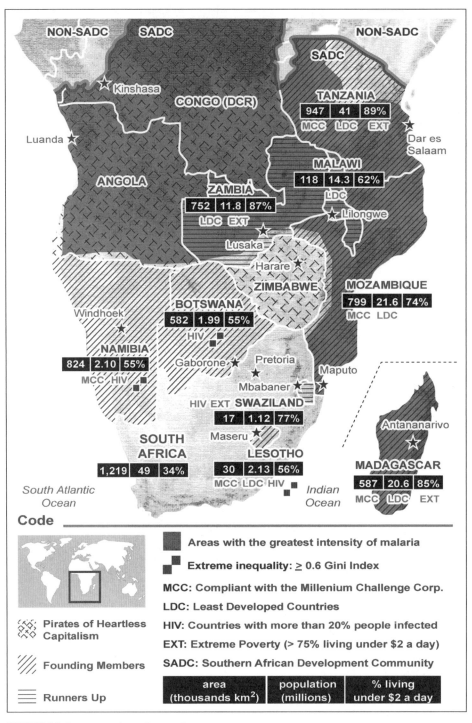

FIGURE 19.2 Map of Southern Africa
Source: Peral (2009).

Microbusiness Regulation, and facilitating the work of a Property Registry. The New Economic Architecture is introduced in Chapters 21, 22, 23, and 24.

Sandra Alzate Cifuentes (TNI) is the director of Colombia's Agency for Social Action and International Cooperation. The Agency administers national and international development aid flows, and channels them in order to reach the vulnerable. I phoned Sandra on August 21, 2008. How can the extreme poor be persuaded to improve their health and education to fulfill the conditionality clause? Sandra stresses that the extreme poor, and in particular mothers living in extreme poverty, hope for a better future for their children. Sandra points out, "There are a series of obstacles that have undermined the delivery of basic health care and education to the extreme poor, even when the delivery is available." Sandra mentions the cost of transportation or school materials such as a uniform or books, along with the additional income brought in by some members of the family who should be in school.

WELFARE DELIVERY THROUGH MICROFINANCE

Microfinance has deserved much attention since Muhammad Yunus won the Nobel Peace Prize in 2006 for his contribution to a growing niche market in the financial services to the poor. Microfinance can be defined as "the supply of small scale financial services such as credit, savings accounts and insurance to poor and low-income people" (Bystrom 2006)

The concept of microfinance defies the widely held belief that the poor lack the ability to move up the ladder, or do not have entrepreneurial skills. Microfinance lends in small quantities—as little as a few hundred dollars—to entrepreneurs in developing countries aiming to establish local businesses, including agricultural, farming, and grocery activities. Microfinance Institutions (MFIs) incorporate group lending to their lending activity. Group lending overcomes the extreme poor's lack of collateral, and enables group members to monitor each other on a regular basis, reinforcing mutual pressure to help ensure repayment (Caouette, Altman, et al., 2008).

Demand for financial services by the poor has been increasing substantially over the last few years. The Microfinance Information Exchange (MIX) is the prominent provider of microfinance information. MIX reports that the numbers of borrowers in 2007 was 71 million. **Adrian Gonzalez** (BFP) is the lead researcher at MIX. I met Adrian at the MIX headquarters in Washington, DC, on May 21, 2009. Adrian works in microfinance because he believes "that expanding access to financial services is good for developing societies, especially when the quality of the services improves and the cost goes down."

The credit crunch that has hit the financial markets since the fall of Bear Stearns has not only castigated shareholders and investors in the developed and emerging markets. The subprime fiasco has also undermined the effort of many MFIs that are unable to fulfill portfolio growth to increase microcredit penetration among the world's poorest, typically rural women in low-income countries, living on under one dollar a day.

Since 2006 the more consolidated MFIs have issued bonds (Grameen), collateralized microcredits (BRAC), or gone public (Compartamos). Grameen and BRAC operate in Bangladesh, the world's most saturated microcredit market along with Bolivia. Compartamos operates in Mexico charging interest rates in the 90 percent range, in a rather uncompetitive market.

In spite of the increasing innovation in the field, many experts advocate a self-financing strategy for MFIs to increase microcredit penetration. This strategy would involve fostering savings among the poor that can then be used to lend to micro-entrepreneurs, thereby increasing the size of microcredit portfolios and microfinance penetration. In order to foster savings, the poor need a stable currency and a deposit insurance scheme that brings trust into the system. National regulations stop many MFIs from raising savings through current accounts for the poor. Developing countries run monetary policies oftentimes unable to maintain the stability of exchange rates away from depreciation. An international deposit insurance scheme for microsavings would bring the necessary credibility into the system, since many developing countries where microcredit operates lack deposit insurance schemes for their mainstream banking sector. A new currency for the poor is presented in Chapter 22. Microsavings Insurance is reviewed in Chapter 23.

José Luis Machinea (FMN) was minister of finance of Argentina from 1999 to 2001. In addition, José Luis was the United Nations executive secretary of the Economic Commission for Latin America and the Caribbean from 2003 to 2008. I met José Luis on January 29, 2009, in Madrid (Spain). For the Argentine, the delivery of education and health care through the microfinance network could be the key feature leading to the success of a new approach to economic development.

Microfinance in Bangladesh

Between March 1 and 7 of 2009, I spent a week in Bangladesh, the pioneer country in microfinance. I had the privilege of meeting with the executive management of BRAC and Grameen. BRAC is the world's largest NGO and the second Microfinance Institution in Bangladesh. Grameen is the world's largest Microfinance Institution. I had the opportunity to see first-hand the challenges microentrepreneurs face in their daily activity. It is time to propose new financial instruments allowing the extreme poor to have access to basic financial services, including microinsurance and Microsavings Insurance.

BRAC was founded by F.H. Abed in 1972. It is the largest nonprofit organization in the world. With a yearly budget of $480 million, it delivers basic education and health care to 110 million people in Bangladesh, roughly 80 percent of the country's population at an annual cost of under five dollars per capita. Grameen was founded in 1976 by Muhammad Yunus and Nurjahan Begum. Grameen and Muhammad Yunus received the Nobel Peace Prize in 2006 for their fight against poverty through microfinance.

Bangladesh has been a laboratory of ideas in the development space during the last 30 years. The reality of the country would be very different without entrepreneurs like F.H. Abed and Muhammad Yunus. Abed and Yunus have brought about a transparent and efficient management of their institutions in a highly populated country where a majority of the land is devoted to agriculture. Abed and Yunus' management contrast with their government, one of Asia's most corrupt.

The portfolio of microloans of the three largest Microfinance Institutions in Bangladesh (Grameen, BRAC, and ASA) amounts to an average of seven million microcredits per institution, for an aggregate total of 21 million microcredits. 96 percent of Grameen's microborrowers are female and the average size of a microloan is $300. A microloan is typically spent to buy cattle and fertilizer for subsistence agriculture.

Microfinance has allowed many women in rural areas of Bangladesh to become microentrepreneurs and earn an additional income for their families. Women no longer play a secondary role and oftentimes the independence they earn through microfinance grants them self-confidence and the conviction that they can make progress without the supervision or custody of their husbands. In conservative societies, microfinance enables the growth of an environment in which women can tear down pre-established cultural barriers that have granted them a secondary role in society.

Subsidies play a role in microfinance but should only help a Microfinance Institution (MFI) take off in its preliminary stage. Maria Otero is the former chief executive officer of Accion International, a private, nonprofit organization operating in 23 countries, where it works with 30 MFIs. Otero comments, "We want to see a strong financial return from our MFIs but also a high social return" (Tully 2007). James Wolfensohn, a former president of the World Bank notes, "Helping 100 million households means that as many as 500–600 million poor people could benefit" (Morduch 1999).

Increasingly, MFIs are coupling the delivery of basic education and health care to microfinance. The American nonprofit Freedom from Hunger and BRAC propose two different models that could be replicated by The New Institution presented in this chapter.

Freedom from Hunger

Freedom from Hunger offers poor women worldwide microfinance solutions combined with basic education and health care. The American nonprofit was established in 1946 under the name Meals for Millions, an organization focused on the eradication of malnutrition through the provision of high-protein powdered food supplements. Freedom from Hunger's Credit with Education reaches 400,000 families living in extreme poverty. Chris Dunford has been the president of Freedom from Hunger since 1991. Dunford and I had a conversation on February 8, 2008. Dunford notes, "When I visit the field to sit among the women at a self-help group meeting, I know I have made a difference. I can feel the impact of my work on their lives. Their spiritual energy renews my own."[9]

Freedom from Hunger fights hunger using the provision of microfinance, education, and health protection. How does the provision of education help mitigate the burden of hunger? The Credit with Education program at Freedom from Hunger "combines microfinance services and health, nutrition, and business education into a single service for women in poor rural areas of the developing world."[10] Coupling two services at the same time reduces the cost of delivery but requires skilled staff able to provide different services. Among the curriculum taught by microfinance experts, there is a malaria component that emphasizes key features needed to prevent the disease, including the importance of sleeping in net-protected beds.

BRAC

BRAC's successful model delivers basic health care and education to 80 percent of the Bangladeshi population at a cost of about five dollars per capita per annum. BRAC's operating model is different from that of Freedom from Hunger. Freedom from Hunger couples education and health protection with microfinance and delivers to poor women in rural areas. BRAC's microfinance branch is separate from its health care and education units. BRAC partly finances the delivery of health care and education to all strata of the population through the profits from its successful microfinance subsidiary. BRAC delivers health care and education to everyone, not only women.

TANIA ZAMAN (TNI) is the chief of staff of BRAC's Chairman F.H. Abed. I met Tania on March 5, 2009, at her office on the twentieth floor of the BRAC Tower in Dhaka (Bangladesh). Can the provision of health care and education increase microcredit repayment rates? For Tania, it would mean "better health resulting in greater ability to work and thus ability to pay back. For education, similar reasoning would apply. Educational skills can increase earnings or literacy may enable them to better manage the credit and therefore earn more and also pay back." Tania's insight is corroborated by Peter H. Lindert, professor of economics at the University of California-Davis, who concludes, "Numerous studies have found that basic public health facilities not only lengthen life, but actually raise people's productivity within each year of their adult lives" (Lindert 2004).

Chapters 22 and 23 explain how microfinance can be scaled up to increase penetration rates substantially. If microfinance is scaled up appropriately, the inclusion of basic health care and education is feasible based on the past success stories of Freedom from Hunger and BRAC, among others.

Institution Design

Building a new institution to address a social problem requires a thorough analysis of the problem, an understanding of the potential solution, and commitment (Fleishman 2007). In addition, if the pilot is successful it could bring about strategic change if others replicate it (Fleishman 2007). ACHE's institutional design must take advantage of economies of scale and avoid the middleman. The design must be able to track down each dollar spent and be able to monitor its direct impact in terms of improvement of health and education indicators.

How would a new institution responsible for the delivery of Universal Welfare be designed? For Dimitry, "The New Institution will need to be responsive to the interests of the states under its jurisdiction and, at the same time, be independent enough to be able to remain faithful to the main tasks ascribed to it. While numerous institutional designs can be envisaged, all of them are likely to include a principle of absolute independence of the Institution from the states under its authority within clearly delimited sphere of competences of the new structure." Dimitry's thoughtful analysis includes the following premises about a successful institution design:

> *Crucial to the success of The New Institution is likely to be the binding nature of the legal-administrative documents generated by it and their direct legal effect within the whole territorial scope of its jurisdiction. It means, first*

of all, that the states will not be able to refuse to follow its decisions or act against it in the broadest possible sense: national law will never acquire an ability to overrule or alter the decisions of The New Institution. Secondly, no intervention of the national law of states should be required for the legal rules of The New Institution to be applicable in practice. Moreover, individual actors in the states concerned should acquire a possibility to rely on the rules generated by The New Institution directly, if necessary, also against their states. Without these basic elements, the functioning of The New Institution is bound to be corrupted by the short-term political interests of the elites of the states under its partial jurisdiction, making the goals set for The New Institution unreachable. The New Institution is bound to be dysfunctional without a strong independent legal panel enjoying unconditional power under the sui generis supranational law of The New Institution to rule against the states under the partial jurisdiction of the Institution in the cases brought by individual legal actors, other states and The New Institution itself. The same panel will also hear the cases of states against The New Institution should conflicts arise, which will empower the states and is to guarantee that The New Institution does not abuse its powers or commit fraud.

Avoid the Middleman   The middleman in the allocation of foreign aid and the lending of structural loans has been the bureaucracy of developing countries. The disbursement of development aid has oftentimes been granted to inefficient structures and only a fraction of the total reaches the extreme poor. Avoiding the middleman implies designing an organization able to hire local nurses and teachers and pay them directly from a central administration. Avoiding the middleman implies avoiding the pitfalls of public systems that rely on public servants who lack the incentive to perform in their jobs. Performance must be measured and enhanced. Underperforming nurses and teachers should be given advice on how to improve their performance. The Universal Welfare must be publicly provided but replicate the incentive structures of privately run organizations.

Measure the Impact of the Welfare Delivery   A leading academic who measures the impact of social policies on poverty eradication should be brought on board in order to measure the impact of the welfare delivery and tweak the inputs to maximize the social return. This talented academic should be a pioneer in the measurement of the impact of policy-making in the mitigation and eradication of poverty.

   Jonathan Morduch (INI) is a professor of public policy and economics at New York University. I talked to Jonathan on March 21, 2008. The talented American is a leading and prominent researcher in the fields of microfinance and microinsurance, and his recent books *Portfolios of the Poor* and *The Economics of Microfinance* are inspirational reads.

Build Up Nursing and Teaching Schools   Rossing Uranium Limited (Rossing) is Rio Tinto's subsidiary in Namibia. Rossing has a foundation, the Rossing Foundation, to which it devotes 2.5 percent of its after-tax profits. On April 15, 2009, I visited the Namibian Institute of Technology, a state-of-the-art vocational school partly funded by the Rossing Foundation. Mike Leech is the managing director of Rossing Uranium Limited. Leech walked me around the fantastic facilities.

The Indian Institutes of Technology were founded in the 1960s and have become elite institutions that produce the world's best engineers. Vijay Mahajan, an Indian-born professor of marketing at the University of Texas at Austin, raises the questions: "Couldn't a similar initiative be created in Africa? Where is the African version of the Indian Institute of Technology or the Indian Institute of Management?" (Mahajan 2008).

The Tanzania National College of Tourism (NCT) is a vocational tourism school based in Dar es Salaam (Tanzania). According to Peter J. Mwenguo, managing director of the Tanzania Tourist Board, NCT is setting the standard in tourism education in Tanzania and is helping build up the skills necessary to boost tourism in the country. NCT was launched as an Agency of the Ministry of Tourism in 2003. According to NCT's chief executive,[11] "The Tanzania hospitality and tourism industry is labor intensive and much of its future success depends significantly on the quality of its employees. Therefore improving skills and knowledge of the employees may assist destination competitiveness and help to establish and maintain a viable industry."

There are two interesting pilots in the area of agriculture that could represent the seed of future academic institutions of the caliber of the Indian Institutes of Technology. The first is the planned Nelson Mandela African Institute of Science and Technology (Mahajan 2008). The second is the Global Open Food and Agricultural University (GO-FAU) (Shaw 2009). The Nelson Mandela African Institutes of Science and Technology were born with the goal of becoming world-class institutions. The initiative was launched in Abuja (Nigeria) in 2005 at a meeting of Heads of State. The four proposed campuses[12] would be based in Arusha (Tanzania), Abuja (Nigeria), Waogadugu (Burkina faso), and Cape Town (South Africa).[13]

The shortage of health care professionals from which sub-Saharan African countries has suffered, stressed by the brain drain of these professionals to Europe and North America explained in Chapter 11, has put the African continent on the verge of a health care catastrophe. We need to help African countries build up state-of-the-art nursing and teaching schools to produce top-notch nurses and teachers, who can then help the African continent revive itself. The Namibian Institute of Technology and Tanzania's NCT are inspiring examples of well-run vocational schools that may set the benchmark for future pilots in the areas of health care and education.

Water and Sanitation   The delivery of clean water and sanitation should rely on organizations that have been working on their provisions such as UNICEF or the African Ministers' Council on Water (AMCOW).

Artwork by Bill Butcher.

CHAPTER 20

Conditionality

After forty-plus years of largely unsatisfactory development aid, we've had
an opportunity to learn at least one thing: you can't just hand over funds
to a government and hope for the best. I'm all for national sovereignty, but
I'm against stupidity, corruption and waste.
                    —Susan George, *Another World is Possible If . . .*

For as long as the human being is human being there has been a debate regarding the stick and the carrot. Is it better to first give and then hit with the stick if the conditions are not fulfilled (ex-post conditionality)? Or is it better to first show the carrot and only give it away if the conditions are fulfilled (ex-ante conditionality)?

Conditionality is a word not very well liked in the development establishment. It recalls the macroeconomic conditionality and the structural reform attached to World Bank loans and the bailout packages of the International Monetary Fund during the 1980s and 1990s. Critics of foreign aid have called for a smarter allocation of aid subject to incentives. This is the approach of the Millennium Challenge Corporation (MCC). The MCC allocates aid subject to a number of conditions.

There have been two generations of conditionality (Stokke 1995). The first generation includes the structural reform and adjustment programs of the 1980s and early 1990s. They were implemented mainly by the World Bank and the IMF and focused on economic reform including privatization and trade liberalization. The second generation of conditionality incorporates policy and governance reform in the areas of human rights, civil rights, and political rights. This second generation is frequent in bilateral aid agreements of the mid and late 1990s.

Conditionality can be ex-ante or ex-post. Paul Collier points out, "Somewhat surprisingly, no agency is doing ex-ante governance conditionality" (Collier 2007). The Millennium Challenge Corporation (MCC) is doing ex-ante governance conditionality. The MCC was founded in 2005 by President George W. Bush and was headed until January 2009 by Ambassador John Danilovich, a former U.S. Ambassador of the United States to Brazil and Costa Rica. In the three-year period starting in 2006, the MCC had allocated a total of $6.1 billion, 74 percent of which was allocated to 11 countries in Africa (10 of which were in sub-Saharan Africa). The *Financial Times* defines the MCC as more of a company than a federal agency, giving out "money in quarterly installments over five years, expecting business plans from its client countries" (Bounds 2006).

The MCC approves compliant countries based on performance across a number of indicators that include a respect for human rights, the fight against corruption, and the adoption of a pro-business environment. Countries join the scheme on a voluntary basis, and the MCC does not proactively search for new compliant countries, called Millennium Challenge Compacts in MCC jargon. As of year-end 2008, the MCC had approved 18 projects in 18 compliant countries that become MCC-compliant.

MCC provides compliant countries with aid with accountability. The accountability is linked to ex-ante conditionality. A country becomes compliant before accessing the pool of funds. In order to become compliant it has to perform across a number of indicators. If it does not perform it does not become compliant and cannot access the pool of funds. Once a country becomes compliant it can lose its status and the aid. Ex-ante conditionality is a very interesting concept that has only been recently tested through the MCC. The concept deserves attention because much of the foreign aid that has failed in the past was granted subject to ex-post conditionality. MCC's ex-ante conditionality is further reviewed in a subsequent section.

Oxford economist Paul Collier summarizes the two problems of old-style conditionality. The first problem has to do with a psychological problem called reactance. He defines reactance as follows (Koeberle, Bedoya, et al., 2005):

> *The point of reactance is that if we tell a person what he's got to do, he does not like being told what to do, and to reestablish his liberty and independence and convince himself that he is free he will try to do the opposite. So if the condition was pretty sensible, his incentives now become to do something that is actually rather foolish.*

Collier's second problem has to do with the credibility of ex-ante conditionality. He remarks that typically the donor's priority is to disburse money very quickly. In this context ex-ante conditionality loses its credibility. Collier concludes, "If ex-ante conditionality works as an incentive, then selectivity is bound to work as an incentive because it has all the incentive effects of ex-ante plus no credibility problems" (Koeberle, Bedoya, et al., 2005).

The debate on conditionality was very much present during the implementation of the Marshall Plan. Richard Bissell was a senior ECA official who wrote a memorandum to Paul Hoffman and William Foster in January 1950. In the memorandum, Bissell notes that that criterion of aid "should progressively move in the direction of performance rather than need" (Wexler 1983). He adds, "Some 20–25 percent of next year's appropriations" should be withheld and be used "frankly and with great toughness as an incentive fund to which the participating countries will have access if, but only if, they perform on a program of national and supranational action which the ECA will work out with their participation in advance" (Wexler 1983). Hoffman was so impressed by the idea that he later implemented it. On February 21, 1950, the ECA asked Congress to earmark a $600 million package of the 1951 Marshall Plan grants "to encourage the aggressive pursuit of a program of liberalized trade and payments" (Wexler 1983).

How can we measure governance? Shantayanan Devarajan reviews the allocation of aid by the Millennium Challenge Corporation and others. He remarks that, among others, the MCC allocates aid based on the productivity of aid in reducing poverty in a particular country, a factor, he argues, "that is a function of the quality of governance." The measure of governance should be done by a mix of country expert reports and surveys. Devarajan proposes to measure governance at a more local level, differentiating between cities and sectors (Devajaran, 2008).

STRUCTURAL REFORM

Structural reform is considered the first generation of conditionality. Kermal Davis is the former finance minister of Turkey. He thinks that a lot of the policy advice around conditionality "especially in the 1980s was driven by the influence of the Reagan/Thatcher conservative revolution where certain ideological buzzwords were more important than the actual substance of the policy" (Koeberle, Bedoya, et al., 2005). For the African historian Paul Nugent, "African governments often had to slash their health budgets in order to conform to conditionality, which has made it very difficult for them to adequately finance the health care which is evidently needed" (Nugent 2004).

Stefan Koeberle, Harold Bedoya, Peter Silarszky, and Gero Verheyen of the World Bank study what kind of policy-based conditionality in lending programs is more likely to be strongly associated with GDP per-capita growth a couple of years after the approval of the loan. They find that only social sector conditionality is associated with economic growth, and no conclusive evidence that conditionality in the areas of economic management, public sector management, or structural policies is associated with economic growth (Koeberle, Bedoya, et al., 2005).

World Bank Conditionality

Between 1980 and 2003, Africa received 34 percent of the total World Bank adjustment lending by number of operations. The share drops to 16 percent by total volume (Koeberle, Bedoya, et al., 2005). The number of associated conditions in any World Bank loan granted to a poor country can reach 100.

Conditions are of two kinds. There are conditions to be fulfilled prior to the extension of the loan. There are also conditions to be fulfilled during the duration of the loan. According to Eurodad,[1] "even if these conditions do not automatically stop development finance flows if they are not met, they do place a massive administrative burden on developing countries which have to monitor and report on their progress a part of a World Bank assessment" (Eurodad 2006).

Eurodad assessed loans granted by the World Bank and the International Monetary to twenty impoverished countries between 2002 and 2005. According to Eurodad, 20 percent of all World Bank conditions for poor countries are related to economic policy, 42 percent are related to public sector reform policies, and 37 percent are related to social and environmental conditions. Eurodad also notes that there is no relation between the number of conditions imposed and a country's performance. In Eurodad's view the better a country's performance, the smaller should be the number of conditions imposed (Eurodad 2006).

IMF Conditionality

According to Eurodad, 43 percent of all IMF conditions for poor countries regarding PRGF[2] programs are related to structural economic policy reforms, whereas

57 percent are related to public sector reform. About half of the conditions in PRGF programs are binding (Eurodad, 2006).

Emmanuel Tumusiime-Mutebile of the Bank of Uganda criticizes IMF conditionality in Africa. He mentions that the failure of conditionality "is not due to the fact that the supported structural reforms are not necessary, but rather because structural performance criteria suffer from several defects." (He also points out that the targets are not easy to monitor and verify. He adds that implementation is much difficult than quantitative targets (Koeberle, Bedoya, et al., 2005).

THE MILLENNIUM CHALLENGE

Ambassador John Danilovich was the chief executive officer of the Millennium Challenge Corporation from when he was confirmed by the U.S. Senate on October 7, 2005, until January 2009. I first met Ambassador John Danilovich at his corner office on Fifteenth Street in Washington, DC, on September 18, 2008. During our second conversation on December 3, 2008, Ambassador John Danilovich spoke persuasively about the innovative aspects of the MCC model and stated, "Foreign aid with accountability was long overdue." He added, "Surely it is not too much to ask of countries who receive hundreds of millions of dollars in aid from the American taxpayer that they adhere to commonly accepted standards of good government and good governance, that they create an institutional infrastructure and build their own capacity to effectively receive our aid and to obtain the sustainable results intended from that aid."

The MCC has replicated some of the structural features of the Marshall Plan reviewed in Chapter 16. Figure 20.1 below shows the allocation of MCC grants by category as of September 2008. There is a strong emphasis on transportation and agriculture and only a slight allocation to health and education.

Figure 20.2 shows how the amount of MCC grants that was allocated to the components of the basic welfare state (health care, education, water supply, and sanitation) compared to the rest of categories. Only 15.3 percent of the total was allocated to the components of the Universal Welfare.

The MCC allocates grants subject to how a compliant country performs across sixteen indicators.[3] The indicators are classified into three different categories: ruling justly (civil liberties, political rights, voice and accountability, government effectiveness, rule of law, and control of corruption), encouraging economic freedom (cost of starting a business, inflation, fiscal policy, trade policy, regulatory quality, and days to start a business), and investing in people (public expenditure on health, public expenditure on primary education, immunization rates, and girls' primary education completion).

Aid Suspension

On December 11, 2008, the MCC Board suspended assistance to Nicaragua. (The MCC was concerned with Nicaragua's commitment to democratic principles). Ambassador John Danilovich commented on the Nicaragua decision that "the MCC model is based on aid with accountability and good governance," concluding,

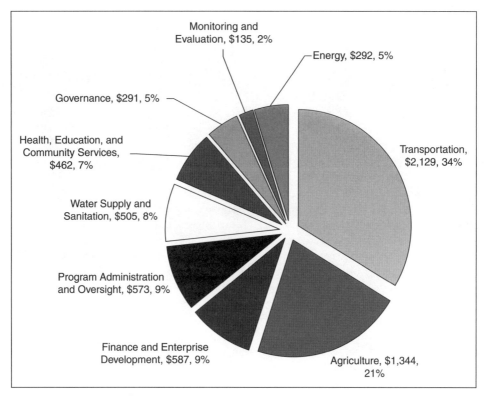

FIGURE 20.1 Allocation of MCC Funds by September 2008, US$ millions
Data Source: MCC (2008).

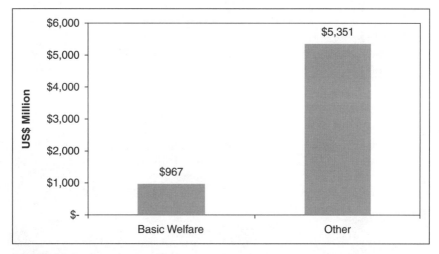

FIGURE 20.2 Allocation of MCC Funds by September 2008, Universal Welfare vs. Other
Data Source: MCC (2008).

"the Board determined that recent actions by the Nicaraguan government were inconsistent with MCC's core principles and therefore had to make this difficult decision" (MCC 2008b).

An Academic Critique

What has been the success of MCC in the first four years of operation? Harvard economists Doug Johnson and Tristan Zajonc look at whether foreign aid can create an incentive for good governance (Johnson and Zajonc 2006). They study the short history of the Millennium Challenge Account and find positive results.

The Harvard scholars point out that the MCC represents "the most significant shift in U.S. foreign aid policy since President Kennedy signed the Foreign Assistance Act of 1961 that separated military and non-military aid and established the U.S. Agency for International Development" (Johnson and Zajonc 2006).

According to the Harvard economists, the MCC's approach to foreign aid is expected to be more effective if it is allocated to countries with good governance. The second expected outcome is that recipient countries will react to the conditional aid by pursuing good policies. Johnson and Zajonc review whether the second expected outcome applies to the case of the MCC. The authors draw two interesting conclusions (Johnson and Zajonc 2006):

1. While our results suggest countries are improving their indicators because of the MCC, we make no claim as to what impact, if any, this has on long-run growth or poverty rates.
2. The statistical and anecotal evidence suggests that when foreign aid is given contingent on past performance, countries respond.

Stephen Kosack of the Brookings Institution looks at how foreign aid is targeted to basic education in countries that show political willingness to improve policy (Kosack 2008). Kosack reviews the cases of the World Bank and the MCC's ex-ante conditional aid to countries that have previously shown good performance in the number of indicators considered. Kosack argues that aid given to education has not followed the pattern of the MCC of past success stories. He mentions the cases of autocratic China, Cuba, Korea, and Taiwan (Kosack 2008). Any of the previous four countries would not have secured aid for basic education from the MCC today.

Kosack's assumption is that MCC-type foreign aid would not be effective if allocated to basic education. This contradicts the results of Johnson and Zajonc reviewed above. What does Kosack understand as efficient in the context of basic education? Kosack mentions the case of Ghana. Ghana was ruled by J.J. Rawlings, who came to power in 1981 through a coup d'etat. The World Bank lent Ghana $260 million in the 15 years following 1986. Other donors followed suit. Ghana improved its primary education, increasing the number of primary students by 60 percent between 1987 and 2000 (Kosack 2008).

For Kosack, "Many democratic governments do depend on the poor and many autocratic governments do not; but there are also many autocratic governments that do depend on the poor—and that invest in primary education—and many democratic goverments that do not" (Kosack 2008). By selecting ex-ante democratic governments as recipients of MCC grants, the MCC is bypassing many autocratic governments that could be investing in primary education.[4] In any case, the MCC's priority does not seem to be health or education, but improving civil and political rights and the investment climate, the type of Western conditionality also incorporated by other European nations to their foreign aid schemes.

Morocco is an interesting example because it received the largest MCC assistance package, worth $697.5 million in 2007. The package is linked, as usual, to improvement in areas pertaining political rights, corruption and economic reforms. Morocco held parliamentary elections in January 2007, but King Mohammed VI continued to hold the real power that the Parliament lacks. Ambassador John Danilovich said at the time regarding Morocco's performance (England 2007):

> *It's about poverty reduction and long-term economic growth, it's about good policies. And as long as whatever government is in power pursues good policies, the personnel in that government, as far as the Millennium Challenge Corporation is concerned, is of no great importance.*

Lex Riefel of the Brookings Institution and James W. Fox of USAID look at how the MCC may be an opportunity for President Barack Obama. Among their recommendations, they include seven steps to strengthen the MCC (Riefel and Fox 2008): more bipartisan support and protection, more flexibility, scaling up, dropping or transferring threshold programs, getting a broader mandate, leveraging foreign investment, and keeping the best that already exists.

Riefel and Fox raise two critical issues in the emergence and success of MCC: (1) the relationship with USAID; and (2) the partnership with NGOs. MCC became a better friend of USAID after the departure of MCC's first CEO Paul Applegarth. The authors comment that the tension between MCC and USAID takes place at the country level. They point out, "Some USAID missions have seen cuts in funding allocations for their country as a direct result of an MCC compact being signed" (Riefel and Fox 2008). For the authors, it is unfortunate that USAID has so few macroeconomits if U.S.-led foreign aid targets economic growth as its main objective. For the authors, the MCC under Ambassador John Danilovich maintained a healthy dialogue with the international NGOs. Ken Hackett, president of Catholic Relief Services, sits in MCC's board of directors. Hackett was featured in Chapter 15.

For James M. Roberts of the Heritage Foundation, "Congress Should Shift USAID Funds to the Millennium Challenge Account." In spite of a proven track record during its short life, Roberts asserts, "The Obama Administration and Congress have primarily embraced the USAID approach and have made significant cuts to MCC funding." Roberts adds, "Congress appropriated $52 billion to USAID funds that do expire, usually within two years, leading to sometimes rash, reckless, and hurried spending" (Roberts 2009).

According to Roberts, the Obama Administration has cut its MCC allocation for Fiscal Year 2009 by 40 percent, whereas it has increased its USAID allocation for the same period by 7 percent. Roberts concludes that allocation for Fiscal Year 2009 should be increased to at least $2.5 billion "by transferring the difference from planned and existing USAID programs (Roberts 2009).

MONFORTABLE

The Monfort Plan's conditionality should make a recipient <u>developing country</u> comfortable, very comfortable, to the extent of being <u>Monfortable</u>.

The conditionality attached to The Monfort Plan is ex-post, subject to an ex-ante agreement on how to deliver the aid. The aid is delivered according to the design of ACHE, as explained in Chapter 19. The Monfort Plan proposes the design of The New Institution that would deliver a basic, free, and Universal Welfare consisting of education and health care. The Monfort Plan would also deliver a subsidized clean water supply and sanitation through existing providers on the ground.

I am the president of Madagascar and I am reading this book. What do I do to become Monfortable? It is very easy, President Marc Ravalomanana.[5] Madagascar would have to agree to the basic principle that for the agreed period of time, education and health care will be provided to the extreme poor in Madagascar by The New Institution (explained in Chapter 19).

BRIAN DONALDSON (DCL) was the former and last U.K. ambassador to Madagascar between 2002 and 2005, and British High Commissioner to Namibia between 1999 and 2002. I met Brian on March 7, 2009, at the Holborn tube station in London (United Kingdom). Ambassador Donaldson knows Madagascar and Namibia extensively. The British diplomat has run a charity since he left the diplomatic mission. Ambassador Donaldson is well aware of the impact of discontinuing foreign aid in the aftermath of a coup d'etat. Madagascar's environment only worsened after major donors such as the European Union or the United States froze or discontinued the inflow of foreign aid in the aftermath of the coup d'etat of March 2009, in a country that has strongly relied on outside contributions.

I am the president of Lesotho and I am reading this book. Is this a free lunch? No, it is not, President Pakalitha Mosisili. As has been explained in Chapter 18, providing health care, education, water supply, and education is an investment. We are investing so that the next generation of sub-Saharan Africans is healthy and educated. We are investing to avoid the death of millions of sub-Saharan African children who will help an aging world continue to move ahead. We are, after all, not doing it for the money. We are doing it because it is right and necessary.

The Agreed Period of Time

I am the president of Mozambique and I am reading this book. For how long will The New Institution provide the basic, free, and Universal Welfare to the extreme poor of Mozambique? It is straightforward, President Armando Guebuza. The provision has a deadline of 2050. The next forty years will be the Glorious Forty. The goal is to reach the World of 2050, the World of Cornucopia and Eutopia with the smallest proportion of extreme poor, and eventually eradicate extreme poverty. We are just opening another stage in the evolution of our race. Those that follow will have to continue the legacy.

The expectation is that a majority, if not all, the extreme poor will leave extreme poverty before 2050. At that time, The New Institution will delegate the delivery in your hands and continue to focus on those who are in extreme need in other countries.

Ex-Ante Conditionality

I am the president of Tanzania and I am reading this book. What does the ex-ante agreement require us to do? It is a piece of cake, President Jakaya Kikwete. The ex-ante agreement acknowledges the urgency of the time. By agreeing to be part of the provision of health care and education, you are delegating the design and implementation of your health care and education for the extreme poor to a supranational institution called The New Institution.

In the Marshall Plan, it was important that Europe acknowledge the urgency of the time and demand the Marshall Plan dollars under the American rules. There will be funds. There will be Monfort Plan dollars and Monfort Plan euros. They will have to be allocated the best possible way in order to maximize the social return. As explained in Chapter 19, the delivery of the basic Global Public Goods by a supranational institution gets rid of the middleman and profits from economies of scale, hiring locally and bypassing inefficient bureaucracies. Each dollar or euro of expenditure can be tracked down and monitored and the social return on the allocated funding can be easily determined.

Only a handful of candidates will be considered Monfortable at the time of the launch of The New Institution. The six candidate countries considered will be Botswana, Lesotho, Madagascar, Mozambique, Namibia, and Tanzania for reasons explained in Chapter 19. The African Community of Healthcare and Education (ACHE) will be later expanded to potential candidate countries on a basis of ex-ante conditionality very similar to that of the European Union. The opportunity will be too good to be true for many developing nations. The extreme poor will have a strong incentive to displace the political elites who do not embrace the necessary requirements to join The New Institution.

Turkey faces a similar challenge with the opportunity of enlargement in the European Union. Piotr Zalewski of the Center for International Relations reviews Turkey's path toward membership of the European Union and the ex-ante human rights conditionality attached. Zalewski concludes (Zalewski 2004):

> *In order to legitimate ex-ante conditionality relationship to have taken root between itself and the Union, the Turkish government must have realized, at one point or another, that the benefits of EU membership significantly outweigh the political and economic costs of EU compliance and convergence. What remains to be addressed is the weight attached by the Turkish government to the benefits of prospective accession: it is this, after all, which is fundamental to our understanding of the strength of the Union's ex-ante conditionality.*

The European Union is a very interesting example of ex-ante conditionality that, in addition, has a strong track record of success. Every nation in Europe has demonstrated, since the emergence of the European Coal and Steel Community, a strong incentive to join the European Union. Countries are willing to undergo reform because "the benefits of EU membership significantly outweigh the political and economic costs of EU compliance" (Zalewski 2004).

Unfortunately there is no similar success story in the development space. But there could be one. This is one of the objectives of The Monfort Plan. If ACHE becomes a success story, many developing nations may be willing to become subject to ex-ante conditionality because the benefits of ACHE membership significantly outweigh the political and economic costs of Monfort-compliance. The Caribbean Community of Healthcare and Education (CCHE) and the South Asian Community of Healthcare and Education (SACHE) could follow.

Can the success story of the European Union and its ex-ante conditionality be replicated in the development space? Gerhard Schumann-Hitzler is the Resource Director in the Directory General of Enlargement at the European Commission in Brussels. I met Schumann-Hitzler in the morning of August 1, 2008, at his office of the European Commission's headquarters in Brussels (Belgium). Schumann-Hitzler remarks, "I do not believe that the success story of the European Union (meaning a far reaching integration of different countries, nations, and cultures) can be reproduced in developing countries of Africa."

Integration would not have happened in Europe without the Marshall Plan and the creation of the European Coal and Steel Commmunity. We should perhaps consider the implementation of the Annan Plan and ACHE before concluding that integration is not feasible in Southern Africa.

Ex-Post Conditionality

I am the minister of health of Botswana and I am reading this book. Have I lost my job? You have not, Minister **SHEILA TLOU** (HEA). As minister of health, you are an accomplished technocrat. The New Institution will hire you. You will be based in Decemland, the land of 10 percent. You will help The New Institution monitor improvement in health and education indicators. It is against this performance that Monfortable countries will be tested. A universal delivery of health care and education must bring about improvements in health and education. Otherwise, the pilot will not be successful and The Monfort Plan will have to be discontinued, at least in your country. Every opportunity has a risk, I am afraid. This is a risk worth taking.

Sheila and I met on April 24, 2009, at Gaborone's International Airport in Botswana. In our conversation, Sheila remarked that The New Institution as presented in Chapter 19 would be welcome in her country. She added that Africans have to contribute improving their governance. Botswana is the best-governed country in sub-Saharan Africa. Sub-Saharan Africans have much to learn from Botswana.

I am the President of Namibia and I am reading this book. Will Namibians with HIV/AIDS be covered by the Universal Welfare? There will have to be a compromise between the available funding and the coverage provided, President Hifikepunye Pohamba. We will work with you toward a feasible solution for the severity of the HIV/AIDS pandemic in Namibia.

Five

Financing Eutopia

Financing Eutopia requires the allocation of new funding throughout the world and a strong commitment on behalf of Civil Society to put pressure on those individuals, governments, and corporations who do not embrace the New Paradigm. Chapters 21 explains how to raise new funding using innovative financing mechanisms that would not require additional taxation. Chapter 22 and 23 propose two new instruments that will contribute to the expansion of microfinance. Chapter 22 proposes a new currency for the poor, called the yunus, inspired by the vision of Bernard Lietaer. Chapter 23 introduces the concept of microsavings insurance that could boost the savings rate among the extreme poor.

The Decem Series, featured in Chapter 24, suggest international taxation mechanisms in the direction of the failed Tobin Tax and explain what could be done to avoid past failures in order to accomplish success. The Decem Series will transform today's capitalism, the sole priority of which has been profit maximization. The invisible hand is no longer individually driven, but orchestrated from above, from our elites who want to perpetuate a set of guidelines that make them richer at the expense of the poor and the planet. The Decem Series suggest the construction of a development fund that will analyze the activities of each and every one of the corporations operating on a global scale. The Decemfund becomes the big brother of twenty-first century capitalism, and provides the free markets with a heart that is well needed, thereby going after the financial speculators of our time, the Pirates of Heartless Capitalism. The Decemfund becomes the Poor's Endowment, able to finance the delivery of health care and education to the extreme poor through 2050.

New investment opportunities arise in the new golden era of capitalism for savvy, sustainable, and long-term investors. The New Triple-A of Investing is composed of Africa-America-Asia. Chapter 25 presents new investment opportunities that will arise in real estate, transportation, distribution, tourism, and beyond.

Artwork by David Bromley.

CHAPTER 21

Collateral

The former communist nations and the Third World are exactly where Europe, Japan and the United States were a couple of hundred years ago. Like the West, they must identify and gather up the existing property representations scattered throughout and bring them into one integrated system to give the assets of all their citizens the fungibility, bureucratic machinery and network required to produce capital.

—Hernando De Soto, *The Mystery of Capital*

The lack of financial services to the poor is sometimes seen as a market failure. The unavailability of credit, insurance, land, and human capital result in underinvestment by the poor, overinvestment by the rich, and a less efficient economy (*Economist* 2005). Credit markets play a fundamental role in a modern economy. Credit markets allow individuals to borrow and lend from financial institutions, which enables the financing of projects and the smoothing of income when income is scarce.

MIND THE COLLATERAL

Collateral is defined as "property that is pledged as security against a debt" (Dyal-Chand 2006). Rashmi Dyal-Chand of Northeastern University explains that there are six requirements an asset pledged as collateral has to fulfill: quantifiable, capable of liquidation, capable of appreciation, meaningul to the borrower, easy to monitor, and transferable (Dyal-Chand 2006).

Microfinance Institutions (MFIs) are the banks of the poor. They serve urban and rural areas in which many people living under the poverty line lack access to almost every sort of basic infrastructure, including health care and education. MFIs lend to the poor in the form of microcredits.[1] MFIs typically borrow from third parties and then lend to the extreme poor. In a risk-averse world the ability of MFIs to sustain portfolio growth is constrained once they reach a certain size, because third-party funding becomes scarce.

Loans can be secured or unsecured. Secured loans pledge collateral as a guarantee that the bank can then sell and cash in the event that the borrower defaults on his or her loan. Unsecured loans do not have such a guarantee and would not recover anything in case the borrower defaulted. It is easier to borrow money from a bank whenever there is a guarantee that the bank can retain in case of default. Increasing the dollar value of any guarantees would make things easier. Commercial banks would lend money to MFIs if these posted collateral in exchange.[2]

Mobilize Assets

There are many assets in today's world that are not being mobilized by either governments or individuals. Governments own buildings and art against which a third party could borrow. Individuals own jewelry against which a third party could borrow.

Why are governments' assets not being appropriately utilized? Governments do not undergo the pressure public corporations receive from their shareholders. Citizens are not fully aware that the government's assets could be mobilized. So far we have not explored the mobilization of government-owned real estate assets in the extremely urgent environment we find ourselves in today. We must consider all possible ways to raise additional funding for development.

How can collateral be used to raise funding for development? A new Bank for the Poor can be created. The role of the Bank for the Poor would be to lend to MFIs to cover the gap that commercial banks and other financial institutions have left empty today. The Bank for the Poor would function as a Central Bank that lends money to MFIs worldwide at a low interest rate. The concept is elaborated in more detail in Chapter 23. For the time being, it is only important to understand that in order to lend substantial funds, the Bank for the Poor would require collateral to hedge against the risk of default. Because the poor lack this collateral, an alternative source of collateral has to be found.

In this section, I propose that governments and individuals in developed countries could exploit idle assets to be used as collateral. What would happen if the collateral had to be used to repay a loan? In the unlikely event of default and in order to minimize losses and maximize recovery rates, the Bank for the Poor would have to foreclose the collateral owned by governments and individuals in order to recover some of the principal value initially lent and pay back the outstanding debt owed to third parties.

Collateral Matters

Collateral lending or secured lending is superior to unsecured lending. In the developed world, unsecured lending carries a higher interest rate because the loss on default of the counterparty is higher. Unsecured lending is typically associated with credit card debt and student loans. In the developing world, the best example of unsecured lending is microcredit. Microcredit has built a track-record of high repayment rates in many countries. The reasons behind this success story are the selection of low-risk individuals that are also highly entrepreneurial and the pressure from peers in a borrower's group. Microcredit is only a first step out of poverty. It confers the poor the ability to borrow small amounts of money to become microentrepeneurs and run small businesses.

In a scenario of asymmetric information,[3] collateral lending is superior to unsecured lending because it reduces moral hazard[4] and adverse selection[5] (Menkhoff,

Neuberger, et al., 2006). Collateral lending also allows borrowing bigger dollar amounts than the typical microcredit. Collateral lending also carries a lower interest rate, lessening the burden on the borrower.

From Dead to Live Capital

Governments and individuals in developed countries can and should mobilize their capital. The poor also should but cannot mobilize their capital. The Peruvian economist Hernando De Soto calls this capital dead capital. Contrary to what many think, the poor do own their houses and lots of land. Unfortunately, oftentimes they have no way to prove ownership, as there is no public registry that confers the title of the land or the real estate to a certain individual. Worst of all, many poor cannot leave their property for fear that someone else will take it. Without legal title, there is no way to prove, after all, that something belongs to someone.

If only the poor could mobilize their assets, they would have collateral against which they could borrow, as is possible in developed countries. Mobilizing capital is only a question of political will. Hernando De Soto's work is covered in this chapter.

MOBILIZING ASSETS

Every nation-state has delegations abroad that represent their citizens and defend the rights of their nationals. The European Union is today a supranational institution with 27 members, each of which maintains individual embassies throughout the world. I am fascinated each time I walk around Embassy Row in Washington, DC, to see so much redundancy, to think of the phenomenal savings Europeans could realize if only we had single representations abroad. Each ministry of foreign affairs has a portfolio of dozens of embassies that are no longer necessary in a united Europe. The European Union is the Sleeping Beauty who has yet to wake.

Once upon a time, the United States was a myriad of states that decided to give up sovereignty and individual foreign policy agendas to become a super state. The vision of Americans is an inspirational example that today could and should be replicated in the European Union, perhaps the most innovative political achievement of our time.

I decided to conduct an intellectual exercise to estimate the value of the real estate portfolios of the ministries of foreign affairs in the European Union. Europeans could use the real estate portfolios of their ministries as collateral to borrow funds to finance some of the ideas put forth in this book.

The section first determines the aggregate value of the real estate portfolio of European Union members. It then explains how the embassies and consulates could be used as collateral to borrow money from financial institutions. The money would then be used by the Bank for the Poor to lend to MFIs worldwide, which they would subsequently lend to microentrepreneurs in the least developed countries.

Real Estate Valuation

The European Union needs a unique foreign policy once and for all. Diplomats may lose their privileges and distinguished positions. Our own pride is an impediment to the pursuit of a fairer world. In today's world we have one single ambassador per country. In tomorrow's world we will no longer need an ambassador for every country. Tomorrow's world starts on the Decem Date.

The Initial Inquiry   On May 7, 2008, I issued an inquiry to the 27 ministers of foreign affairs of the members of the European Union. On May 9, 2008, I sent the same request to 27 senior officials of each of the 27 ministries. The request read as follows:

> *I currently do research on real estate of embassies of EU-member countries, trying to determine how much the set of buildings your Ministry operates abroad is worth (embassies and consulates), and whether you own or rent each of the buildings. I would like to interact with you or one of your advisors about the question I am raising. I am working with each member country (for a total of 27) on this fascinating question.*

Estonia, Ireland, and Sweden   Estonia's Heigo Einblau replied on June 6, 2008. He provided a detailed portfolio of Estonia's sixteen embassies and one consulate abroad. The book value was $34 million.

Ireland's Lavina Collins provided a detailed answer on May 20, 2008. As of 2008, Ireland owned thirty-six properties abroad, twenty-three Residences, nine Chanceries and four combined Chancery/Residences. The value of the properties as of January 1, 2008, was in the region of $179 million. Ireland also rents 98 properties abroad.

Sweden's Annette Walz provided a detailed answer on May 23, 2008. In the two-page letter that Annette attached to her message entitled Real Estate Portfolio, the Swedish diplomat points out that Sweden had 104 missions in 100 cities abroad, a majority of which were embassies (85), with consulates (13) and delegations (6). Annette also facilitated the proportion of rented versus owned properties. Sweden rents 58 percent of its Embassies and 41 percent of its Residences. As of year-end 2007, the Swedish National Property Board published that the book value of Sweden's properties abroad was $400 million.

Valuation Model

The valuation model considers three variables. The first variable is a country's gross domestic product. The higher a country's gross domestic product the more foreign representations it is likely to own. The second variable is the number of foreign representations a country owns abroad. Estonia's 17 owned foreign representations compare with Ireland's 36, or Sweden's 100. The third variable is the average value per property. The model is simple but demonstrates how financial innovation can be used today to raise funding for development. We can create a gold mine with a little creativity and some political will. The only requirement is a good explanation.

Input Data   I used the input data from Estonia, Ireland, and Sweden to create a linear model that will allow us to forecast the number of owned properties for each of the 27 member countries of the European Union. Once we have decided that we will use a country's gross domestic product to predict the number of properties a country owns, we can build a linear regression.

Model Results   The model estimates the total number of properties abroad owned by the 27 countries of the European Union. It then uses the average values for owned property abroad for the three initial countries. Overall, the model departs from a combined GDP for the entire European Union of $15.29 trillion for year-end 2008. The linear model forecasts a total number of 2,667 foreign-owned representations for the aggregate GDP of the 27 member countries of the European Union. Using the lower value ($2 million) and the upper value ($4.98 million) for the average price of a property shown, we can determine lower and upper bounds for the aggregate value of the real estate portfolio of the European Union's 27 ministries of foreign affairs. The lower bound is $5.32 billion and the upper bound is $13.29 billion. According to the Microfinance Information Exchange, the total microfinance portfolio amounted to $49 billion at year-end 2007, of which only $4.5 billion corresponded to Africa Mobilizing European governments' real estate assets abroad would double or triple Africa's microfinance portfolio.

Art in Museums   A similar analysis can be conducted for art held in museums. Art held in museums could be used as collateral that the Bank for the Poor could use to borrow funds from commercial banks. The additional funds borrowed from commercial banks could subsequently be used by the Bank for the Poor to lend to Microfinance Institutions.

Knock, Knock, Knocking on Europe's Door

The Bank for the Poor would use the embassies as collateral against which it could borrow money from commercial banks. The Bank for the Poor would then allocate this pool of new funds competitively among the Microfinance Institutions it supervises. In the worst-case scenario, the extreme poor would default on their microcredits and the commercial banks that have lent to the Bank for the Poor would have to foreclose the foreign representations of the 27 countries of the European Union to maximize their recovery rates from the defaulted loans. This is unlikely to happen due to the high repayment rates associated with microcredit of about 98 percent.

Even so, an event of default could actually benefit the European Union. It is a win-win situation. If default does not occur, EU members keep their foreign representations abroad. If default does occur, EU members would lose their foreign representations abroad, which could trigger a consolidation of all foreign representations into one single EU embassy per capital, with a single EU ambassador per country. The economies of scale would be phenomenal. The European Union would finally have a single voice in foreign policy. The Sleeping Beauty would begin to wake up.

Sometimes countries will not answer specific questions that are delicate because doing so carries a political cost. A French politician may not like to be asked the question, *Do you think agricultural subsidies are fair to the developing world?* The French politician probably knows well they are not, but acknowledging this would be very unpopular in France and would carry a political cost. A German politician may not like to be asked the question, *Should Turkey join the European Union?* The German politician probably knows it is in everybody's advantage to have Turkey join the European Union, although the move may be unpopular in Germany, whose largest minority is of Turkish origin.

By the same token, many politicians across the European Union know it is time to have a single foreign policy with single foreign embassies abroad. Dismantling foreign representations abroad is similar to dismantling agricultural subsidies in France and other EU members. We know we will have to do it sooner or later. We are just lazy Europeans, postponing our work. It is like knowing the Sleeping Beauty must wake up. We are only ignoring the clanging of an alarm clock. We are ignoring the poor knocking on our door. But the alarm clock will not cease. The poor will not go away. We are in a world of ringing and knocking. When will you awake Sleeping Beauty? Ask European politicians whether we should mobilize our real estate assets. They might think it is a good idea. This is similar to acknowledging that we should unite our foreign missions abroad. It is a proxy question that does not entail any political cost. It reveals a preference without being explicit.

HERNANDO'S MYSTERY

Hernando's mystery is the poor's misery. Hernando De Soto is one of the leading economists in the developing world. In his book *The Mystery of Capital*, the Peruvian economist reviews how real estate owned by the extreme poor could be mobilized to raise phenomenal amounts of capital that could trigger sustained episodes of economic growth and prosperity throughout the developing world.

In his masterpiece, the Lima-based economist intends "to demonstrate that the major stumbling block that keeps the rest of the world from benefiting from capitalism is its inability to produce capital." De Soto concludes, "These extralegal systems constitute the most important rebellion against the status quo in the history of developing countries since their independence and in the countries of the former Soviet bloc since the collapse of communism" (De Soto 2001a).

De Soto is right. In many developing countries, a major part of the economic activity remains on the informal side of the economy. Individuals do not have access to bank accounts and basic financial services. Individuals own property but cannot officially attest that it is theirs because there is no official registry where what belongs to whom is recorded.

In his research, De Soto confirms that staying away from the legal system compensates for paying taxes. On the other hand, staying away from the legal system limits the ability of the extreme poor to mobilize their assets and capitalize the value of their real estate collateral. It is no longer a debate of left versus right. De Soto points out (De Soto 2001a):

> Government programs to give property to the poor have failed over the last 150 years whether they followed the bias of the right (private property rights through mandatory law) or of the left (protecting poor people's land in government-run collectives). The crippling political agendas of the 'left vs. right' are largely irrelevant to the needs of most people in developing countries.

Roy Cullen underscores De Soto's insight in commenting, "When informal resources are examined, such as potential land value, the domestic assets that can be tapped are much larger than cumulative FDI or private portfolio flows" (Cullen

2008). Ambassador John Danilovich expresses a similar view (Danilovich and Reckford 2008):

> *Women and children across the globe face many laws and customary practices that don't protect women's tenure rights. Yet, a woman's ability to inherit and hold onto rights to her land is a crucial social safety net that protects her and her children. The lack of tenure rights worsens the plight of HIV/AIDS widows, for example. It threatens children with homelessness, hunger, and loss of education. Children sometimes forgo school to guard their homes and farms for fear of being evicted while their mothers work. This is unacceptable in today's world.*

De Soto concludes, "Economic reformers have left the issue of property for the poor in the hands of conservative legal establishments uninterested in changing the status quo" (De Soto 2001a). As in western countries, the Pirates of Heartless Capitalism of the developing world represented by the conservative legal establishments are stopping today's world from moving ahead. It is time to fight the Pirates of Heartless Capitalism. We know where they are. We have simply been ignoring their presence.

Only in De Soto's native Peru, the poor's assets are worth $90 billion, which is forty times the sum of foreign assistance Peru has received since World War II (De Soto 2001b). The figure is even more impressive for Egypt. The assets of the Egyptian poor are worth a total of $240 billion, or 55 times the value of all foreign direct investment in the past 200 years (De Soto 2001b).

From June 20 to 24, 2009, I was in Lima (Peru). I decided to travel to De Soto's headquarters to determine the validity of his approach. De Soto is based in Lima and heads one of Latin America's leading think-tanks, the Institute of Liberty and Democracy (ILD).

Victor Endo (BFP) is the vice president of international operations at ILD. I met Victor on June 22, 2009, at ILD in Lima (Peru). ILD is active in promoting an agenda of land reform, the priority of which is to bring informal property to the formal economy, so that the extreme poor can mobilize their assets. What incentives should be available so that the extreme poor are willing to legalize their properties and bring them to the informal side of the economy? For Victor, informality carries important associated costs. Victor mentions that if properties are not properly formalized, they are not legally protected against use or occupation by a third party that may claim its ownership. Victor adds that public investment in infrastructure such as electricity or water and sanitation requires that the served communities be legally registered. The Peruvian lawyer concludes that in the absence of legal arrangements, a public authority will not undertake the investments needed to bring public utilities to informal neighborhoods and communities.

I also met Gianfranco Castagnola on June 22, 2009, in Lima (Peru). Castagnola is the executive president of Apoyo Consultoria, Peru's leading economic and financial consultancy. For Castagnola, De Soto's approach to formalize the informal property is only the beginning of legal reform that may enable the mobilization of assets. A more neutral and effective judiciary system is only the next obvious step. An independent and effective judiciary system would enable the foreclosure of a borrower's collateral in case of default.

The next day, I met Raúl Salazar, the managing partner of Macroconsult, Peru's prominent macroeconomic consultancy. For Salazar, De Soto's approach emphasizes the importance of utilizing the poor's collateral to demand credit, but undermines the importance of the poor's paying capability, linked not to the collateral per se, but to their economic activity and income-generating ability. An individual's paying capability may prove as crucial as the value of collateral when requesting credit to a financial institution.

Those of us unwilling to reform are the poor's misery. By fearing to move ahead, we are embracing a new era of protectionism that may revert to radicalism and nationalism. Radicalism and nationalism may exacerbate local riots and escalate into global conflict. We can change the course of history. We can challenge Nostradamus and Bueno de Mesquita's forecasts. We can start a fantastic journey that will lead us to the World of Cornucopia and Decemland where Eutopia is feasible. It is our duty to start building the History of Tomorrow. It is the poor's mandate.

From Dead to Live Capital

De Soto's superb work shows ways of transforming dead capital into live capital, which the poor could use to borrow against. Collateral matters. A revolution lies ahead of us, a silent revolution that will mobilize trillions of dollars. According to De Soto, "citizens inside and outside the bell jar need government to make a strong case that a redesigned, integrated property system is less costly, more efficient and better for the nation than the existing anarchical arrangements" (De Soto 2001a).

Aggregate dead capital amounts to $9.34 trillion. This phenomenal sum is only the beginning. If only dead capital were released from the cage the political elites built in the developing world, perhaps I would not be writing about poverty eradication. If only dead capital were released from the Prison of Thought the economic elites built in the developing world, foreign aid would not play such a significant role. We have been afraid of the extreme poor climbing the ladder of development and gaining representative power in the international institutions. We have been afraid of the extreme poor starting to leave the infamy of poverty behind once and for all.

Dead capital is categorized into urban and rural. A majority of the dead capital is urban. Only in Africa does the amount of rural dead capital rival urban. Hernando De Soto estimates the amount of dead capital as follows (1997 data): Asia ($1.75 trillion urban and $0.59 trillion rural), Africa ($0.58 trillion and $0.39 trillion), Middle East and North Africa ($0.74 trillion and $0.25 trillion), South America ($0.89 trillion and $0.24 trillion), Mexico/Central America and the Caribbean ($0.36 trillion and $0.09 trillion), and China/former Soviet republics and Eastern Europe ($2.16 trillion and $0.8 trillion). As of 1997, the percentage of urban dead capital by country was as high as 57 percent for the Philippines, 53 percent for Peru, 68 percent for Haiti, and 92 percent for Egypt. Rural dead capital amounted to 67 percent in the Philippines, 81 percent in Peru, 97 percent in Haiti, and 83 percent in Egypt (De Soto 2001a).

In urban and rural areas of the developing world, a majority of the capital is locked in, waiting for someone to free it. Let's free the dead capital of the world. Let's hear De Soto's words, which shout the urgency of our time and point in the direction of the journey we as a society must initiate, the Journey of our Lifetime.

I am no longer afraid. I embrace the poor and welcome them to the new era of optimism. Europeans and Americans have to leave their fears behind. Poverty can be eradicated. Read De Soto's work. You will start to believe that change in development is possible and that it can take off sooner than we ever thought possible.

THE INFORMAL ECONOMY

The informal economy is defined as the sector of the economy that remains beyond the legal boundaries of a nation-state. The International Labor Office regards the informal sector as a group of enterprises owned by a household that includes[6] informal own-account enterprises which may employ contributing family workers on an occasional basis, and enterprises of informal employers, which employ one or more employees on a continuous basis (ILO 2002).

The informal economy has two straightforward negative consequences. The first is that it stops the poor from mobilizing their assets. The second is that it undermines the ability of tax authorities to raise revenue to finance the delivery of public goods such as health care or education.

Diana Farrell is director of the McKinsey Global Institute. In her article "Tackling the Informal Economy," Farrell points out what governments should do to reduce the share of the informal economy in the economic activity of a country. For Farrell, there are two myths regarding the informal economy (Farrell 2006):

1. Unlicensed activities by unregistered businesses paying little or no tax do not threaten the growth of the formal, modern economy.
2. For a country experiencing mass rural-urban migration, a growing informal sector is a godsend because it will create jobs much faster than can the formal economy.

Some of the blame for the persistence of the informal economy must be placed on local governments. In particular, in many developing countries it takes ages to register a business. The next subsection reviews the cost of doing business in the developing world.

Another dimension of the costliness of functioning in the formal economy is due to the own competitive nature of business. If it is costly to operate in the formal economy and a firm has competitors that operate more cheaply in the informal economy, there is a strong incentive to shift the business activity to the informal economy (Farrell 2006).

Governments have an incentive to formalize all the informal economy. Government's taxation ability is proportional to the percentage of the economic activity that lies on the formal side. In countries like Venezuela or Nigeria whose public revenues are linked to oil revenues, being able to tax the informal economy would become an alternative source of revenue in times when the price of oil sinks. Figure 21.1 shows the percentage of non-agricultural employment that remains in the informal economy for four geographic areas. As much as a 72 percent of the non-agricultural employment in sub-Saharan Africa remains informal.

Figure 21.2 shows the percentage of a continent's gross domestic product that remains outside the reach of the taxation authorities. As much as 41 percent of the gross domestic product in sub-Saharan Africa remains outside the formal economy. The ability of many nations to raise public revenue from taxation is severely undermined by the high degree of economic activity that remains informal. Many

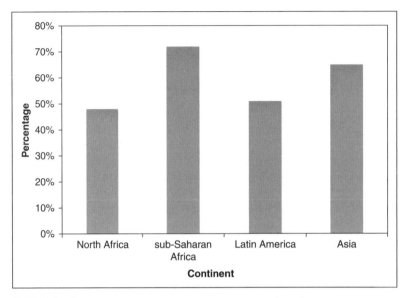

FIGURE 21.1   Informal Employment in Non-Agricultural Sectors (2000)
Source: © International Labour Organization 2002.

developing countries' source of public revenue comes from the taxation of imports and exports at the border through tariffs. Developing countries have been under tremendous pressure to eliminate tariffs in the successive negotiation rounds of the World Trade Organization, as reviewed in Chapter 7.

According to Ehsan Ahmed, J. Barkley Rosser, and Marina V. Rosser of James Madison University, the degree of informal economy is positively correlated with the

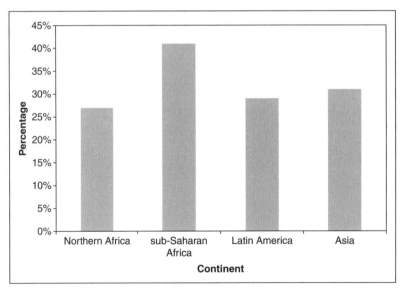

FIGURE 21.2   Contribution of Informal Sector to GDP in Selected Developing Countries, 2000
Source: © International Labour Organization 2002.

incidence of income inequality and the level of corruption (Ahmed, Rosser, et al., 2004). As a result, decreasing the level of the informal economy could bring about a reduction in income inequality and the level of corruption.

The WTO, the World Bank, and the IMF have pursued an agenda of trade liberalization that virtually eliminated tariffs on goods and services, undermining and severely reducing the ability of developing countries to raise public revenue through the taxation of imports and exports. For decades, we in Europe and North America were permissive. We allowed the imposition of a trade liberalization agenda that lowered the ability of governments in the developing world to finance the provision of public services such as health care and education. I carry the blame as my inaction contributed to the sinking of our African neighbors. I understand the urgency of our time. I move ahead because I have raised my level of awareness.

A new world of optimism and enthusiasm must start. We must embrace Eutopia and the belief that there are solutions to the great evils of our time. I found a way out of the hole we helped the extreme poor dig. It may not be the only way out but it can work. I challenge the orthodox thinkers to come up with forward-looking ideas to eradicate extreme hunger and poverty, to deliver basic health care, and education to the one billion extreme poor, who today are born to live in eternal poverty.

Starting a Business

Welcome to the world of the elites whose bureaucracy condemns the poor to live in artificial poverty traps. Why would it take 100 days to set up a business in Peru whereas it only takes four in Denmark? Why would someone need 421 percent of a country's annual per capita income to open a business in Ethiopia when it only costs 1 percent in Sweden? We need to simplify and reduce bureaucracy. We need more and better Microbusiness Regulation that allows the poor to set up a business in order to join the daylight of the formal side of the economy. Table 21.1 shows the number of procedures, time, cost per capita, and total cost that it takes to open a business in a variety of developed and developing countries.

In what ways would more ease and less bureaucracy when it comes to opening a business help the extreme poor move out of the poverty trap we helped to construct?

TABLE 21.1 Indicators for Starting a Business, 2004

Country	Number of Procedures	Time (days)	Cost (US$)	Cost (% of income per capita)
Bolivia	18	67	1,499	166%
Denmark	4	4	0	0%
Ethiopia	8	44	422	421%
Kenya	11	61	194	54%
Nicaragua	12	71	1,335	337%
Peru	9	100	510	24%
Sweden	3	16	190	1%
Tanzania	13	35	557	199%
Uganda	17	36	338	135%

Source: Becker (2004). Reprinted with permission of the Swedish International Development Agency (Sida).

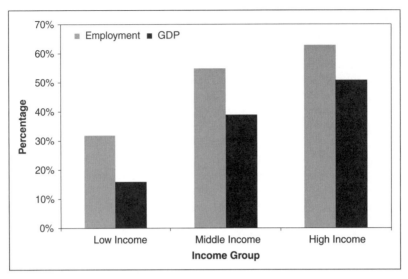

FIGURE 21.3 SME Sector's Contribution to Employment and GDP
(Median Values)
Source: Ayyagari, Beck, et al. (2003).

In a majority of developed economies, small and medium enterprises[7] (SMEs) represent a majority of the economic activity in the developed world. If the barriers to open a business in the developed world were as high as they are in many developing countries a majority of the economic activity would remain informal.

Figure 21.3 shows how SMEs in the formal economy represent a majority of the economic activity and the employment of middle-income and high-income countries. The shares over the total economic activity and total employment rise with income level. Furthermore, the trend as a country develops is that increasingly more of the economic activity and the employment will be related to SMEs. More SMEs will also build up if the number of microenterprises is boosted through microcredit.

Why would I pay three times the annual income in Nicaragua to open a business if I can run it informally instead? The answer is obvious: I would remain informal. Developing countries need to move ahead and approve new regulations and laws that unlock capital, reducing the burden put on microentrepreneurs. In this way, a majority of the informal activity could transition into formal, legal enterprises, from which governments would be able to raise sufficient revenue in order to provide public goods to their citizens. It could take years before the previous scenario takes off unless governments in the developing world are given a phenomenal incentive to reform. Universal Welfare provided by The New Institution could be such a phenomenal incentive. The Race of the Century could contribute to increasing the appeal of the incentive. As explained in Chapter 19, Universal Welfare could start as a pilot of six countries. The Race of the Century is presented in Chapter 28.

The Unbanked

More than 80 percent of households in developed countries have bank accounts compared to less than 20 percent in developing countries (Helms, Littlefield, et al.,

2006). In an exhaustive study, (T. Beck, A. Demirgüç-Kunt, and M.S. Martinez Peria 2005) present indicators of banking sector penetration across 99 countries, finding that greater outreach is correlated with financial development and economic activity.

Increasing the availability of basic financial services would allow the extreme poor to better cope with their financing needs. Better access to microcredit, microsavings, and microinsurance would increase the degree of financial development in many developing countries. There is a way to help the poor leave the informal economy behind by mobilizing their assets. The Monfort Plan provides incentives for governments to introduce new regulation to help the worse off move forward in the quest for a better life, and in the quest for prosperity.

THE MONFORT PLAN'S WAY OUT OF POVERTY

The Monfort Plan's way out of poverty is based on a chain of incentives that the readers will understand entirely once they reach the last chapter of this book. Human beings move ahead because we have incentives. Every person has different incentives or motivations. Many students work harder as the date of an exam approaches. Consultants work harder when the deadline looms. We, as a global society, are faced with a deadline of 2015. We must act now.

We can mobilize assets. The poor can mobilize their dead capital. We can also mobilize a myriad of incentives, some of them of such caliber that they could trigger times of phenomenal change if enough creativity is brought on board.

Why would a group of six sub-Saharan countries embrace an action plan as pilots of a new economic paradigm? It is easy. Propose that they host Decemland, the land of 10 percent. Propose that they host The New Institution, the Bank for the Poor, the Yunus-Fund, and the Decemfund. The process, described in Chapter 28, is called The Race of the Century. Propose that they accept the free delivery of basic health care and education to their extreme poor through 2050 by a new supranational institution called The New Institution. What are the conditions? The conditions are the skeleton of The Monfort Plan's way out of poverty, an easy to follow user's manual that explains step-by-step how to leave poverty behind. Whoever wins The Race of the Century will host Decemland, the land of 10 percent. It is all about the future.

Au Revoir Extreme Poverty

The chain of incentives departs from two components. The first component is the provision of universal health care and education by The New Institution designed to bypass local, inefficient bureaucracies and to profit from economies of scale. The New Institution was introduced in Chapter 19 and will deliver the provision of basic health care and education through the microfinance network, and subsidize clean water supply and sanitation through 2050. The second component is a race to host Decemland, in a five-year contest where six sub-Saharan African countries compete to become the future headquarters of the new institutions that constitute the new economic architecture of a redefined capitalism.

The 40 years of universal provision of basic health care and education become the Glorious Forty, drawing an analogy with the Glorious Thirty that followed in

Europe after the devastation of World War II. The Glorious Forty can bring economic prosperity and welfare to the extreme poor starting in sub-Saharan Africa. We do not need the devastation of another World War, as Nostradamus and Bueno de Mesquita would predict. We have already suffered from the devastation wrought by the myriad of wars stoked by the Cold War. We have already suffered from the devastation of the HIV/AIDS pandemic and the unwillingness of the shareholders of our pharmaceutical corporations to negotiate fair deals with developing countries. We have already suffered from the devastation of episodic famines in sub-Saharan Africa. We have already suffered from the deaths of millions of children from malaria, the disease of our shame. We have only ignored the devastation.

Accession countries must agree to only one condition regarding the universal provision of health care, which is that health care and education has to be provided through the microfinance network. If there is no microfinance infrastructure, we will build it. Chapter 20 explained how to deliver education and health care through the microfinance network. Chapters 22 and 23 explain how to expand the current microfinance fabric to reach further—for example, to reach poor rural women. We shall make microfinance universal. We shall provide basic health care and education

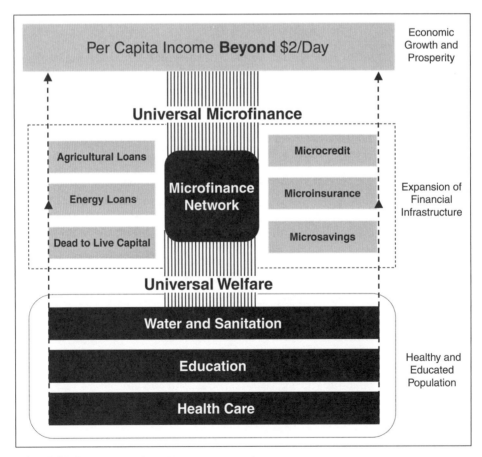

FIGURE 21.4 The Monfort Plan's Way Out of Poverty

to those inhabitants of our same world who were born on the other side of the border. It is a global effort that departs from the most talented group of public servants the world has ever seen. The team of Expert Dreamers is presented in Chapter 29.

Pythagoras would have exclaimed, "Eureka!" The core of the provision of universal health care is the microfinance network. A potential recipient of the Universal Welfare must register within the local microfinance branch. The potential recipient must open a savings account in order to receive coverage. It is here where the financial development of the extreme poor lays its foundation. It is here where the basic financial infrastructure begins to build upward.

Figure 21.4 depicts the three easy steps to exit the poverty trap and leave poverty behind. The first step is to construct the basic financial infrastructure so that the poor can save and borrow, and transmute dead capital into live capital. The second step is to develop a healthy and educated workforce. The third step, economic growth, follows from the first two. A healthy and educated workforce with access to credit and the ability to save in a stable currency should be in a position to tackle the challenge of growing the economy and closing the income gap with the better off.

New Microfinance Architecture

The New Microfinance Architecture is anticipated in Figure 21.5 and further developed in Chapters 22 and 23. Chapter 22 introduces a new currency for the extreme

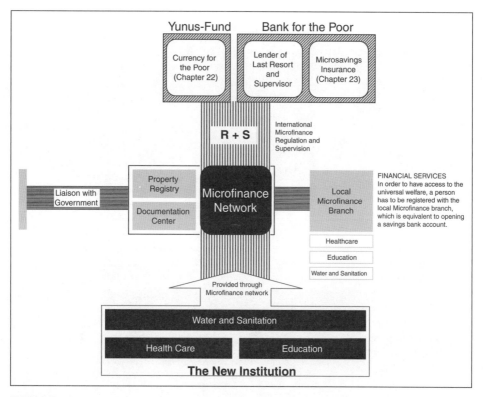

FIGURE 21.5 New Microfinance Architecture

poor's savings. Chapter 23 presents a new Microsavings Insurance to help protect those savings.

In the New Microfinance Architecture, the role of the government is minimized and its involvement is subject to progress in the health and education of the extreme poor. The basic principle is that the provision of the basic welfare state is done exclusively through the microfinance network. The microfinance network offers basic financial services that include savings, credit, insurance, and two additional governmental duties that require a minimal governmental involvement: an official Property Registry that allows the extreme poor to register their land and real estate, and a Documentation Center that assigns each customer an identification card they can then use to access free, basic, and universal health care and education for them and their children, and a subsidized clean water supply and sanitation.

What is the incentive for the extreme poor? Only if the extreme poor open a savings account will they be entitled to receive basic health care and education. The provision of health care and education improves as customers improve their health condition and that of their children. A myriad of arrangements are possible once the basic microfinance infrastructure is built up. The extreme poor can then receive health care and education at a central location. They can also save in a stable currency. In addition the monitoring of their health and education and that of their children can be easily conducted from a central location in rural areas.

Artwork by David Bromley.

CHAPTER 22

The Yunus: A New Currency for the Poor

At this moment, we accept the idea that we will always have poor people among us, that poverty is part of human destiny. The fact that we accept this notion is precisely why we continue to have the poor. If we firmly believe that poverty is unacceptable – that it should have no place in a civilized human society – then we will build appropriate institutions and policies to create a poverty-free world.

—Muhammad Yunus, *Creating a World without Poverty*

In 1944 the economic elite of the allied forces of World War II decided that the exchange rate between any two currencies would be fixed and determined by the amount of gold reserves each country would have deposited in its Central Bank. The price of a dollar was fixed at $35 per troy ounce and other currencies were then pegged to the dollar.

In 1971 when the United States of America decided to abandon unilaterally the gold standard, in a time of economic turmoil brought about by the unexpected rise in the price of oil. As the largest economy in the world, the decision of the United States triggered a chain reaction that meant the definitive good-bye to the gold standard and the adoption of floating exchange rates. In a floating exchange regime, the value of a currency varies with respect to another as a function of a number of macroeconomic variables that determine the economic stability of a country. From the perspective of a developing country that lacks a strong Central Bank with the ability to control and defend the stability of its currency against other stronger currencies such as the dollar, the pound, or the euro, floating exchange rates represent an important risk for which anyone should carefully watch out.

GLOBAL CURRENCY

In 2004 Martin Wolf of the *Financial Times* argued, "A Global Market Economy Needs a Global Currency." Wolf noted that the floating rate exchange system was not a better substitute than the gold standard that had collapsed in 1971. Wolf referred to Ricardo Haussman's coined term *original sin*, by which Haussman addresses developing countries' inability to borrow in their own currencies. Wolf notes that 97 percent of all debt placed in international markets between 1999 and 2001 was issued in a handful of five currencies: U.S. dollar, euro, yen, pound, and Swiss franc (Wolf 2004a). A global currency would allow emerging economies to borrow in their own currency and avoid currency mismatches.

In "A Single Currency for Africa," Paul Masson and Catherine Pattillo of the International Monetary Fund look at the effects that a selective expansion of existing monetary unions would have in Africa (Masson and Pattillo 2004). The IMF economists remind that the goal of a single African currency had been proposed at the creation of the Organization for African Unity in 1963. The authors compare the synergies seen in the Eurozone with those that could be seen in Africa if a monetary union were to emerge. They point out that synergies in Europe are associated with a much better communication and transportation links than in Africa. Masson and Pattillo conclude that a single currency for Africa would only benefit two of the five existing communities, namely ECOWAS[1] and COMESA[2] (Masson and Pattillo 2004), which are the regions with the greatest financing needs.

Jeffrey Frankel of Harvard University notes, "No Single Currency Regime is Right for All Countries or at All Times" (Frankel 1999). The author's own position is that "it is indeed appropriate that some countries, including the crisis currencies, float for the time being; and it is also appropriate for some other countries, such as small countries in Central America, and perhaps also Argentina, to dollarize." Most decisions regarding what currency regime to choose involve tradeoffs. Frankel identifies nine different currency regimes: free floating, managed float, target zone, basket peg, crawling peg, adjustable peg, truly fixed, currency board, and monetary union. For Frankel "emerging market countries have found that an independent monetary policy has not in practice been a useful instrument" (Frankel 1999).

In "Why Not a Global Currency," Kenneth Rogoff of Harvard University asks whether there should be a single currency, as Richard Cooper envisioned in 1984 (Rogoff 2001). A single currency would be equivalent to a system of fixed exchange rates. Rogoff argues that most experts would conclude a fixed exchange rate regime would not allow countries to pursue an independent monetary policy. The associated cost depends, according to Rogoff, on the macroeconomic conditions across regions. Rogoff suggests that his objections to a global currency could be bypassed "by adopting a world currency pegged to a commodity basket" (Rogoff 2001). This idea is elaborated later in this chapter.

Richard N. Cooper of Harvard University presents his "Proposal for a Common Currency Among Rich Democracies" (Cooper 2006). For the Harvard scholar a common currency for the United States, the European Union and Japan "would credibly eliminate exchange rate uncertainty and exchange rate movements among major currencies, both of which are significant sources of disturbance to important economies." For Cooper one currency would require a single monetary policy that could be implemented by a board of governors of national Central Banks (Cooper, 2006).

Benn Steil of the Council of Foreign Relations (CFR) predicted "The End of National Currency" in 2007. In his *Foreign Affairs* article, Steil points out, "The world needs to abandon unwanted currencies, replacing them with dollars, euros, and multinational currencies as yet unborn." Steil comments that because foreigners are unwilling to hold the currencies of developing countries, the financial systems of developing countries end up isolated from the global system (Steil 2007). Are there too many currencies in the world? Brad Setser of the Council on Foreign Relations points out that there may be too many pegs to the dollar (Setser 2006). Ecuador's dollarization in 1999 is credited for the country's strong 2004 performance. Setser argues that the stellar performance was actually related to the price of oil, from which Ecuador benefited. Dollarization has an intrinsic problem, which is the inability to run a tailored monetary policy.

Morrison Bonpasse (YUN) is the president of the Single Global Currency Association.[3] I spoke with Morrison on October 17, 2008. In *The Single Global Currency*, Morrison introduces us into the fascinating world of a single global currency, which he predicts will occur by 2024. The world's financial system is divided into a variety of interrelated currencies that maintain a fixed or floating relation. Morrison presents a well-documented history of the world's currencies, and elaborates on Robert Mundell's optimum currency areas. He sets the European Monetary Union as the reference to follow to inspire other similar monetary unions throughout the world (Bonpasse 2006). A world's single currency is now closer than ever before. The trend started by the European Union sets an inspiring example that other geographic areas of the world could follow. There are many advantages to a common currency, which include stability, low inflation and depreciation, and the ability to save without losing purchasing power.

Global currencies have been proposed by dreamers of past and more recent times. John Maynard Keynes' *bancor* and Bernard Lietaer's *terra* are only two examples of forward-looking concepts that did not materialize but may help a similar idea become a reality in the years to come.

The Bancor

John Maynard Keynes suggested the creation of an international currency that he called bancor. Keynes projected that each national currency be tied to the bancor through a system of fixed exchange rates. The bancor would be fixed in value relative to gold. An International Clearing Union (ICU) would be in charge of exchanging bancors for gold, but gold could not be exchanged for bancors. This assured that there would be no run on bancors (Sardoni and Wray 2007).

Pietro Alessandrini of Universita Politecnica delle Marche and Michele Fratianni of MoFiR do not hesitate to "Resurrect Keynes to Stabilize the International Monetary System." The Italian scholars point out, "A progressive reduction of the dual role of the dollar as a national and international currency can be obtained by introducing a supranational money, albeit gradually." For Alessandrini and Fratianni, the bancor lost to the dollar at Bretton Woods because the United States was the dominant power and the predominant international creditor (Alessandrini and Fratianni 2008).

The Italian economists propose a New International Clearing Unit (NICU) similar to Keynes' ICU. NICU's objective would be "to limit exchange rate risk by issuing supranational money, backed by assets denominated in the national currencies of the participating central bank" (Alessandrini and Fratianni 2008).

The bancor and more recent proposals, such as that of Alessandrini and Fratianni, aim at stabilizing the exchange rate between the major currencies, co-ordinating monetary policies in order to smooth exchange rate fluctuations. They do not serve the purpose of developing economies unless their regimes are pegged to the dollar or the euro.

The Terra

Bernard Lietaer's terra is a suggested new global currency that would use a gold-standard-like system. The terra is crucial in understanding how the yunus could be implemented. In "The Terra TRC White Paper," Bernard proposes the creation of a new currency backed by a basket of the twelve most important commodities in the market. Bernard introduces the currency as follows (Lietaer 2004):

> *The Terra initiative will introduce a reference currency that is fully backed by a dozen or so of the most important commodities and services in the global market, thereby providing for the first time since the gold-standard days, an international standard of value that is inflation-resistant.*

Why twelve commodities and not ten or fifteen? How are the commodities selected and can they vary over time? Bernard suggests that the twelve-commodity proposal would be more stable as a reference than the gold standard (Lietaer 2004). The new twelve-commodity standard would be less volatile than the gold standard and better able to keep its value over time if the commodities are well chosen.

CURRENCY THEORY

The father of currency theory is the Columbia University economist Robert Mundell, who in 1999 was awarded the Nobel Prize in Economics. Mundell's optimum currency areas are at the core of the formation of the Eurozone and explain what geographic areas are most likely to embrace a common currency.

Optimum Currency Areas

Robert Mundell's seminal paper "A Theory of Optimum Currency Areas" set the basis for the modern theory of monetary unions. In his article the Nobel Prize winning economist argues that in a world with fixed and floating exchange rate regimes, an ideal monetary system lies in between (Aizenman and Flood 1992). Mundell sets the conditions that an optimum currency area ought to fulfill. He points out that the currency area should match the region of labor mobility (Aizenman and Flood 1992).

Mundell won the Nobel Prize in Economics in 1999[4] "for his analysis of monetary and fiscal policy under different exchange rate regimes and his analysis of optimum currency areas." Mundell wrote his seminal paper when he was only 29, the same year that he joined the International Monetary Fund. The Columbia economist asks in his 1961 seminal paper, "What is the appropriate domain of a currency area?" He gives three answers (Mundell 1961):

1. Certain parts of the world are undergoing processes of economic integration and disintegration, new experiments are being made, and a conception of what constitutes an optimum currency area can clarify the meaning of these experiments.

2. Those countries, like Canada, that have experimented with flexible exchange rates are likely to face particular problems which the theory of optimum currency areas can elucidate if the national currency area does not coincide with the optimum currency area.
3. The idea can be used to illustrate certain functions of currencies that have been inadequately treated in the economic literature and that are sometimes neglected in the consideration of problems of economic policy.

Floating vs. Fixed

Generally speaking a nation's economic policy-makers have to choose between three alternatives: (1) run a floating currency whose exchange rate is variable; (2) run a fixed currency whose exchange rate is pegged to a major currency like the dollar or the euro; (3) choose an alternative in between the first two. Mundell's theory can help determine whether a country should adopt a floating or a fixed currency.

ALTERNATIVE CURRENCY THEORY

This section presents the theories and views of two leading authorities in the proposal of new currencies. Bernard Lietaer and Margrit Kennedy have been working in the space of alternative currency theory since the 1980s.

A complementary currency operates parallel to the mainstream currency regime. As of 2000, there were 2,500 local currency systems operating in over a dozen countries, including 400 in Britain (Lietaer 2002). A new currency for the poor requires a leading currency expert. **BERNARD LIETAER** (YUN) is a renowned expert on exchange rates and international currencies and author of *The Future of Money*. I phoned Bernard on November 28, 2008. Bernard points out, "The shift in paradigm is not about abandoning the previous system, but complementing it with new money systems that support different sets of values." Bernard concludes, "There are now arguments proving that central banks have in fact an interest in tolerating—and in some circumstances even supporting—well-designed complementary currencies." Bernard suggests that in the case of Switzerland, a complementary currency (WIR system) has proven to have a spontaneous countercyclical effect on the Swiss economy, and as a result has helped the Central Bank (Lietaer 2002).

In *Of Human Wealth*, Bernard introduces the monetary innovations that would contribute to achieving a significant reduction in poverty. Bernard suggests using a combination of three different currencies that he presents as follows (Lietaer 2009):

1. Financial capital could be increased by making available a microsavings tool called "Natural Savings," specifically designed to resist inflation and monetary instabilities.
2. Human capital can be significantly increased through the use of a learning currency called the "Saber."
3. Social capital is improved through the use of interest-free local currencies that encourage cooperative behavior patterns.

Regarding this first proposal, Bernard points out that although microcredit has been repeatedly emphasized, microsavings have not. Bernard suggests issuing a given number of shares and backing them up with growing collateral like trees harvested in a lot of land. The trees would grow and yield timber after a 20-year period. The three requirements to implement this savings tool are the following: "first, legal protection for the property; second, a space where a commercially valuable tree crop can be grown over a period of years, like a plot of land donated, leased, or owned by the community; and third, a modest initial capital investment to get the project started" (Lietaer 2009).

Margrit Kennedy is the author of *Interest and Inflation-Free Money, Creating an Exchange Medium that Works for Everybody and Protects the Earth*. Kennedy suggests the creation of interest and inflation-free money. She deems the solution appropriate but unlikely to be accomplished in a world of Central Bankers. Kennedy proposes two alternative solutions: sectoral currencies and regional currencies that would operate away from the radar of Central Banks. Sectoral complementary currencies are defined as "a means of payment with a built-in target, which are not meant to replace the existing national or international currencies but to complement them" (Kennedy and Kennedy 2007).

Sectoral currencies serve a specific purpose within a specific geographic area. Kennedy provides two examples. The first example takes place in Japan, where in 1995 a retired minister of justice proposed that the younger Japanese accumulated credits in the form of hours for taking care of the elderly. These credits could at a later point in time be spent somewhere else. For instance, the younger Japanese could take care of an older person in their area of residence and later use the earned credit (hours) to pay someone else to take care of their parents who live far away. The second example takes place in Brazil, where an educational currency called saber was proposed. The concept was first introduced by Bernard in 2004. Kennedy explains how the saber operates (Kennedy and Kennedy 2007):

> *When the mobile telephone industry was privatized, the government put a 1 percent surcharge for education on mobile phone bills. This resulted in a fund of $1 billion or 3 billion reais for education in 2004. What could be done with this money? In 2004, Bernard Lietaer proposed to introduce a voucher system called Saber in order to multiply the number of students that can afford to obtain a college level education. In this proposal, the value of the Saber will be nominally the same as the Real. However it will only be redeemable for tuition payments for higher education and lose 20 percent per year to give an incentive to pass it on. The vouchers will be given to schools for their youngest—e.g. the 7 year-old pupils, on the condition that they would chose a mentor from an older class to strengthen a weaker subject. The Saber is then transferred to the older schoolchild, and so on, until at last a senior of 17 years who wants to go to university can use the Sabers to pay a part of the tuition.*

The concept of regional currencies is very interesting because they can only be used in a certain geographic area of the world where they operate. Regional currencies foster local trade because they cannot be used anywhere else. According to Kennedy, regional currencies help to keep the provision of public utilities in the hands of the inhabitants of the region, strengthening the local markets and reducing transport and energy needs (Kennedy and Kennedy 2007). A regional currency has a fixed peg to the national currency (for instance, the euro or the dollar). A regional currency can only be used locally to buy goods and services manufactured in the area. It has an associated circulation fee which typically amounts to 8 percent of its value. This circulation incentive is the substitute of interest rate and motivates an early use of the regional currency. If the regional currency is not used, it will depreciate at an annual rate of 8 percent.

In the case of the Chiemgauer, a regional currency that circulates in Southern Germany, local vendors and tenders get a 3 percent bonus for purchasing vouchers of the regional currency (Kennedy and Kennedy 2007). The Chiemgauer carries a 5 percent transaction fee if exchanged back to euros, which is a Tobin-tax like fee.

THE YUNUS

The yunus is the new currency for the poor. Why do the poor need their own currency? A new currency becomes a savings instrument for many poor who live in small or medium countries. These countries are not able to maintain an appropriate control of their currencies and are subject to the attacks of speculators (Pirates of Heartless Capitalism). Many poor cannot or refuse to save in their local currencies because they do not have access to basic financial services (microfinance); if they do, microcredit is emphasized over savings; their savings would not be guaranteed if they were put in a savings account; and their savings may lose their value (purchasing power) if the local currency is subject to depreciation and hyperinflation.[5]

Many poor have the ability to save even if they do not have access to savings infrastructure. Dambisa Moyo notes, "In Ghana and Tanzania, for example, only about 5–6 percent of the population has access to the banking sector, although some 80 percent of households in Tanzania would be prepared to save if they had access to appropriate products and saving mechanisms" (Moyo 2009). Jonathan Morduch reinforces Moyo's conclusion in his co-authored book *Portfolios of the Poor* (Collins, Morduch, et al., 2009):

> *Perhaps because saving is something that an individual or a household can do without involving others, virtually every diary household saved. In Bangladesh, for example, not a single one of the 42 households [of the survey conducted], even the very poorest, was without some form of do-it-yourself saving.*

What advantages does a new currency bring about? With a new currency the extreme poor can trade with each other without being exposed to currency risk. A Malagasy rice producer can export rice to Bangladesh in exchange for clothing. Because there is no exchange rate risk, the transaction is subject to far less impediments than has traditionally been the case.

A new currency for the poor would profit from economies of scale. The yunus would be used for small transactions. It is an alternative currency, so the national currencies in Madagascar and Bangladesh are always used. The yunus would be the currency of Microfinance Institutions (MFIs) that would lend in yunus. The poor who open a bank account at an MFI would also save in yunus. MFIs from Madagascar and Bangladesh can lend to each other in yunus, provided they are subject to the international regulation and supervision of the Bank for the Poor presented later in the chapter. As a result, currency and exchange rate risk is eliminated. A new currency for the poor would increase the trade between low-income countries. The nature of world trade would change from North-South to South-South.

A new currency for the poor would become a savings instrument that would not lose purchasing power. The most notorious case of a currency that lost all its purchasing power took place in Zimbabwe in 2008. Zimbabwe's inflation rate in 2008 was 516 quintillion percent (516 followed by 18 zeros), a rate that surpasses that of Yugoslavia in 1994 or Hungary in 1946. Consequently, prices in Zimbabwe were doubling every 1.3 days (Berger, 2008). In January 2009, inflation rates in Zimbabwe seemed to halt, with consumer prices falling 2.3 percent (Hawkins, 2009). Had Zimbabweans saved in a stable currency, they would not have lost their savings throughout the hyperinflation episode. A stable currency could have been the euro, the dollar, or the yunus.

Lastly, a new currency for the poor would enable the implementation of a Tobin-like tax. Like the Chiemgauer explained in the previous section, the yunus could charge a transaction fee when exchanged against euros or dollars. The exchange fee would contribute to financing the Universal Welfare provided to the extreme poor through the microfinance network as explained in Chapter 19.

An Investment Fund for the Poor

A global currency for the extreme poor would allow the extreme poor to save without being exposed to speculative attacks disguised as financial trades coming from the financial hubs, a currency with the ability to bring the poor tranquility and peace of mind, and allow them to transform their effort into money they can store, transfer, or spend.

The comeback to the fixed exchange rates gold-standard is not a utopian dream. A proposal that contemplates the creation of the yunus is economically feasible and technically implementable. The creation of the yunus as an exchange currency, would allow the poor to operate a current account in a context of stability similar to saving in a strong currency such as the dollar or the euro, without being exposed to the felonies of speculators or Pirates of Heartless Capitalism. In the operative, an investment fund is set up in each country where the yunus is to be available. The investment fund raises funds from those individuals willing to save, issuing participations denominated yunus in exchange.

The yunus is an alternative currency. The entity operating the yunus would own the monopoly of the currency and be free to restrain access to individuals and institutions from the industrialized world. Contrary to other investment funds, the Yunus-Fund does not borrow any funds or undertake any leverage, investing the extreme poor's savings in a basket of commodities. In exchange for the initial investment, the individual in the developing world receives a number of participations in the fund, each of which would have an intrinsic value linked to the market value of the assets in which the Yunus-Fund invests.

The Yunus-Fund operates through the microfinance network in those countries that allow their poor to invest in the fund. The Yunus-Fund is an investment fund that puts the poor's microsavings into a basket of 12 different commodities, as explained by Bernard. It then issues participations that are considered the new currency of the poor: the yunus. The new financial architecture is part of the New Architecture of Capitalism presented in Chapter 30.

The independence of the Yunus-Fund is guaranteed by the fact that it is not a public institution, but a privately run investment fund owned by its shareholders, the extreme poor. The extreme poor have to be financially savvy and able to choose the managing director of the Yunus-Fund based on performance.

Currency Design

What can we learn from the lessons of Mundell, Bernard, and Kennedy? Mundell's optimum currency areas generally apply for national currencies. Bernard and Kennedy's complementary currencies are operated parallel to the existing monetary order. The two views of the world are complementary and can perfectly coexist.

There are indeed many investment funds that operate today in the world. They buy and sell assets and appreciate or depreciate in value. These funds issue participations to their investors and operate in a world of Central Banks and monetary policies. In the same way, the Yunus-Fund is a fund that operates in a world of Central Banks and monetary policies. It invests in assets and appreciates or depreciates. It issues participations that are then bought and sold by the poor. The poor, in the end, are investing their own savings in a fund that is designed to be stable and maintain its value over time.

Why should a new currency be created instead of using an existing currency such as the euro or the dollar? The goal of the yunus is not to become a substitute but an alternative. It is not a currency per se, but an investment fund that is managed to maintain the value of the savings of the poor. Furthermore, a Tobin tax can be implemented by appropriately designing the investment fund. The investment incentive is to help the poor save and increase the value of their hard-earned money over time.

How much would it cost to set up a Bank for the Poor? Where would it be based? The Bank for the Poor is presented in the next section. It would be based in Decemland, the land of 10 percent. Decemland is the land of the New International Territory presented in Chapter 26 and the Islands of Peace presented in Chapter 27. It is far away from the financial and political centers of our time, far from New York City and Washington, DC, far from Brussels and Geneva, in the antipodes of where the World Bank and the International Monetary Fund stand today.

The Yunus-Fund requires the incorporation of a chief economist. **CHARLES GOODHART** (YUN) is professor emeritus of banking and finance at the London School of Economics. I met Charles on February 2, 2004, at Fundación Cajamadrid in Madrid (Spain). For Charles, the yunus would face two constraints:

1. First, there are transactions costs. The yunus would float against every other currency. Consequently goods and services priced in national currency would constantly vary in value against the yunus. Given network economies of scale, the yunus would never be generally acceptable as a means of payment.
2. Second, there is a problem of control over the scale and nature of the investment policies of the yunus. The governance structure is not well enough controlled.

What are the mitigants to Charles' comments? First, the yunus would be an alternative currency. As such, it would not substitute the national currency but complement it. The yunus would be a stable currency that the extreme poor could use as a savings instrument. If designed appropriately, the exchange rate between the yunus and the euro or the dollar would not vary significantly over time. The governance issue would be mitigated if the incentives between the extreme poor and the Yunus-Fund's management were aligned, avoiding the usual agency problem.

TOBIN TAX REVISITED

James Tobin was a popular economist, internationally known for his simple proposal of taxing international financial transactions dealing with exchange rates. The Tobin tax has been for ages a matter of frustration and discussion among antipoverty groups, who seek to penalize the negative impact of the Pirates of Heartless Capitalism in poor nations, who speculate and destabilize currencies, countries, and societies.

The creation of the yunus would enable the implementation of the Tobin tax in a surprisingly easy way without having to ask the larger commercial banks what they think in this regard. As the new international currency for the poor, the yunus inverts the asymmetry of the economic power, in the hands of the West, and grants relevance to the inhabitants of the developing world.

If the yunus were massively adopted by the poor, a coffee exporter in Brazil could demand that the importer based in Europe or the United States pays in yunus in exchange for the merchandise. If this were the case, the importer, which could be Nestlé or Starbucks, should deposit in the coffee exporter's current account the negotiated amount in yunus. At the time of the exchange rate from euros or dollars to yunus, the entity operating in yunus would establish the payment corresponding to a tax that would amount to a small percentage of the total wire. Nestlé or Starbucks could only exchange euros or dollars into yunus because the coffee exporter would only accept payment in yunus.

The cash-in of the Tobin tax would be asymmetrical. The exchange from yunus to a local currency in a developing country would not incorporate the Tobin tax, in such a way as to let the coffee exporter exchange the yunus into Brazilian reais without being charged a commission at the time of undertaking the conversion mechanism.

A NEW ARCHITECTURE

A new currency needs a new Central Bank. Traditional Central Banks run a national currency's monetary policy. Accordingly, they set the level of interest rates and fight inflation.

The Bank for the Poor is a Central Bank. As a Central Bank its role is to regulate and supervise the use of the yunus throughout the world. Because of this, regulation and supervision are to be defined and implemented. The Yunus-Fund is an Investment Fund. As an Investment Fund, its goal is to carefully select the basket of commodities and determine the composition of the portfolio to maintain and increase its market value.

The Bank for the Poor and the Yunus-Fund represent the new international financial architecture. Contrary to the obsolete Bretton Woods architecture composed by the World Bank and the International Monetary Fund, the New Architecture is designed to work for the poor. How should a Bank for the Poor be designed?

Central Banks

The literature on Central Banks has typically focused on the role of independence and the intrusion of democracy. Central Banks are designed to fight inflation and run an appropriate monetary policy. They are not democratic institutions. Their purpose is not to set the level of interest rates according to popular demand, or according to *vox populi*. Their purpose is to follow the user's manual and implement an independent monetary policy that is not always supported by the median voter. One of the key reasons for an independent Central Bank is the avoidance of partisan/electoral manipulation of monetary policy.

Bernd Hayo of Georgetown University and Carsten Hefeker of the University of Bonn reconsider Central Bank Independence (CBI). The German scholars point out that central bank independence is "neither necessary nor sufficient for monetary stability." For Hayo and Hefeker, CBI is one more way to control inflation. They suggest alternative methods equally effective that would not require CBI: fixed exchange rate and currency board agreements, inflation targets, and central bank contracts. Lastly, they argue that the correlation between CBI and low interest rates found in a number of empirical studies does not mean CBI will bring price stability. In other words, the correlation does not imply causality (Hayo and Hefeker 2001).

Central Banks are not democratic institutions. The democracy versus independence dilemma was well described by David A. Levy of the Levy Economics Institute (Levy 1995):

> *Allowing an independent group of men and women to weigh tradeoffs and make choices that deeply affect the lives of the citizenry is antithetical to democracy when some of them are appointed by boards of directors that are largely elected by bankers, not citizens.*

Forest Capie of the World Bank teaches the lessons learned from Central Banks. According to Capie, CBI was particularly embraced after World War I. At a conference that took place in Brussels in 1920, the participants passed a resolution stating, "Banks should be free from political pressure and should be run solely on the basis of prudent finance." The World Bank economist also emphasizes that the years leading to the Great Depression were characterized by CBI (Capie 1995).

Steven Buigut and Neven T. Valev of Georgia State University study "the consequences of forming a monetary union among a group of countries where the central banks lack independence and are pressured frequently to accommodate government objectives" (Buigut and Valev 2006). The authors confirm that this is usual in developing countries that decide to embrace a common currency.

As an application to their theory, Buigut and Valev determine whether a monetary union would be feasible in the East African Community (Kenya, Tanzania, and Uganda, plus Rwanda and Burundi). In their simulation, Uganda and Tanzania gain from joining the monetary union since they would face less inflation uncertainty than if they were to remain outside the monetary union. The Georgia State scholars conclude, "The benefit of implementing more stable policies in a monetary union may outweigh the costs of losing independent monetary policy" (Buigut and Valev 2006). This may have also been the case for the members of the Eurozone.

For Pierre L. Siklos of Universita Commerciale Luigi Bocconi, "No Single Definition of Central Bank Independence is Right for All Countries" (Siklos 2008). For Siklos, "An institution that is typically wholly owned by government can, at best, be autonomous but not entirely independent of government." An interesting measure that can be used as an explicit sign of CBI is governor turnover, or how long the governor of a central bank actually lasts. For the Bocconi economist, "It would be useful to include a measure of central bank governor turnover in the estimated specification (of CBI)" (Siklos 2008).

The Bank for the Poor

Regulation and supervision of the microfinance network is the role of the new Bank for the Poor. What is meant by regulation and supervision in the context of a Bank for the Poor? The role of the Bank for the Poor is to elaborate international codes of regulation in microfinance that can be implemented to make the Microfinance Expansion a reality. The Bank for the Poor lends to Microfinance Institutions (MFIs) that comply with a strict International Microfinance Regulation and facilitates the provision of Microsavings Insurance, presented in Chapter 23. The Bank for the Poor supports the expansion of microfinance by establishing a legal framework that fosters an environment of governance and risk management that minimizes the probability of default on behalf of microborrowers.

If microfinance is universally provided, the yunus will be a reality as the new international currency for the extreme poor. If microfinance is universally provided, health care and education can be provided through the microfinance network as Global Public Goods delivered to the extreme poor at no cost. The next subsection introduces the concept of International Microfinance Regulation.

Enrique Iglesias (FMN) is the former president of the Inter American Development Bank. I met Enrique on June 10, 2008, and again on February 9, 2009, at the Ibero-American General Secretariat in Madrid (Spain). The Uruguayan was president of the Central Bank of Uruguay from 1966 to 1968 and minister of foreign relations of Uruguay from 1985 to 1988. For Enrique, new vehicles ought to be devised to expand access to microfinancial services among the extreme poor.

INTERNATIONAL MICROFINANCE REGULATION

For Bob Christen of CGAP, the role of regulation in microfinance will not lead its development, as it can repress its development if it is introduced early (Christen 2002). Microfinance regulation has thus far been suggested at a national level. There has not been an attempt to introduce regulation at the international level with which MFIs would have to comply, in the same direction as the Basel I and Basel II framework on Banking Supervision with which financial institutions have to comply. Figure 22.1 shows the number of MFIs that operate under supervision versus the number of MFIs that are not supervised. Supervision is understood at the national level.

In the five-year period ending in 2006, microfinance NGOs had entered a state of consolidation (Attali 2006). In a survey conducted by Elizabeth Rhyne of Accion International (2007), a majority of respondents suggested that the microfinance field will move toward regulated financial institutions and that NGOs will transition into regulated MFIs and continue to grow over the next decade.

The World Savings Bank Institute (WBSI) represents savings banks, credit cooperatives, and Microfinance Institutions worldwide. Jose Antonio Olavarrieta is WBSI's president. I met Olavarrieta in his office at the Spanish Confederation of Savings Banks (CECA) in Madrid on June 4, 2008. For WSBI, international regulation should involve activities and not institutions. WBSI points out, "It would be crucial that regulation focuses on microfinance activities, regardless of the type of Microfinance Institutions that carry them out." WSBI also maintains that regulation should be proportional to the benefits that may arise. WSBI concludes, "Any regulatory and supervisory measures applicable to microfinance activities should have, as a triple objective, to support the enlargement of access to finance, to guarantee a level playing field between all microfinance providers and to equally protect all consumers" (WSBI 2008).

For Beatriz Armendariz de Aghion and Jonathan Morduch of New York University, deposit-taking institutions should be subject to stricter regulation. According

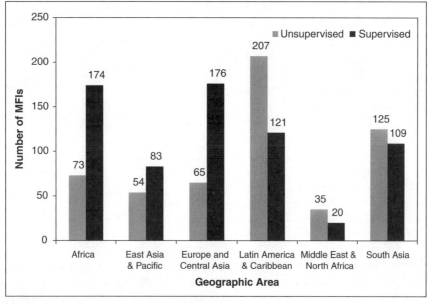

FIGURE 22.1 Supervised MFIs, 2007
Source: MIX Market, Microfinance Information Exchange (2007).

to the NYU scholars, Bangladesh is an example of middle ground in microfinance regulation (Armendariz de Aghion and Morduch 2004):

> *One middle ground reached in Bangladesh is to impose strict regulations on those programs that seek to create truly flexible savings accounts—but for organizations that form as cooperatives, the government tolerates light regulation as long as the institution has a greater volume of loans outstanding than the amount of deposits taken in. If the institution collapses, the winners (borrowers) will at least outnumber the losers (depositors).*

The United Nations' Panel Discussion on Regulation of Microfinance points out the following five directives regarding any future policy-making in the direction of building a regulatory framework for microfinance (United Nations 2007):

1. Whether different agents should be subject to the same type of regulation or whether tiered regulation should be implemented, such as regulation tailored to different institutions.
2. Whether regulation should target agents or activities.
3. Who regulates: state regulation, industry regulation, internal regulation, market discipline.
4. Supervision is very challenging in developing countries due to the multitude of small institutions and limited supervisory capacity. Effectively regulating small institutions without stifling them may entail creating national federations or promoting collaboration between different institutional types. Regulation without supervision would cause costs without benefits.
5. The need for coherence between regulation of microfinance and other national policies.

Bolivia's Superintendencia de Bancos y Entidades Financieras (Superintendencia) was in charge of regulating the microfinance industry in the Andean country until May 2009. In their origins in the 1980s, the microcredit-granting NGOs were not regulated in Bolivia (Superintendencia 2007). As a result of remaining unregulated, they could not take deposits, which stopped their expansion. In this context, Superintendencia moved forward and approved the regulatory framework for the so-called Private Financial Funds (PFFs). This regulatory framework incorporated a specific norm for the provision of services through mobile telephones, and authorization for a money transfer scheme between regulated and unregulated institutions. Finally, specific regulation dealing with credit-scoring bureaus was also put in place. The regulation included aspects regarding corporate governance and customer service. Since the PFF Regulation was passed, there are six intermediaries operating as PFFs in Bolivia, on top of Banco Solidario and Banco Los Andes Procredit, which although they are regulated as banks, also operate in the microfinance sector. According to Superintendencia (2007), during the political turmoil of the years 2002 to 2006, the only institutions that did not suffer from massive deposit retrieval were precisely the PFFs, which stresses the importance of the approved regulation.

Superintendencia became Bolivia's Financial System Supervisory Authority (ASFI) in May 2009. **Ernesto Rivero** (MSI) is the executive director of Bolivia's Financial System Supervisory Authority, the organization in charge of drafting and enforcing the microfinance regulation in Latin America's most crowded microfinance market. I met Ernesto in the morning of June 17, 2009, at the ASFI headquarters in La Paz (Bolivia). Ernesto was appointed executive director on May 8, 2009. Ernesto noted that there had been a shift in strategy under the presidency of Evo Morales to allocate a larger share of the microcredit portfolio to productive activities rather than commercial activities. Productive activities include agriculture and farming.I met **Fernando Romero Moreno** (FMN) in the afternoon of June 17, 2009, in the district of San Jorge of La Paz (Bolivia). Fernando was president of Bolivia's most successful MFI Bancosol, and Bolivia's minister of planning and coordination. For Fernando, the business model of successful commercial microfinance banks such as Bancosol or Compartamos is focusing on a profitable customer and has not managed to reach the rural extreme poor.

Many questions remain open regarding future microfinance regulation. How would an International Microfinance Regulation help boost the delivery of microfinance to the extreme poor? What specific features of microcredit and microsavings should be emphasized by an International Microfinance Regulation? How can the International Microfinance Regulation enforce that microcredit is granted for productive activities? How can the International Microfinance Regulation supervise that the microcredit is not channeled through consumption? Ernesto and Fernando will contribute to drafting a new regulation able to foster the universalization of microfinancial services.

Artwork by David Bromley.

CHAPTER 23

Microsavings Insurance

Poor people are bonsai people. There is nothing wrong with their seeds. Only society never gave them a base to grow on. All that is required to get poor people out of poverty is for us to create an enabling environment for them. Once the poor are allowed to unleash their energy and creativity, poverty will disappear very quickly.

—Muhammad Yunus, *Creating a World without Poverty*

Microfinance was introduced in Chapter 19. The provision of basic financial services to the poor only reaches a tenth of the extreme poor. In most cases Microfinance Institutions (MFIs) provide microcredit, but fail to incorporate microsavings and microinsurance. In countries where penetration rates are significant, such as Bangladesh and Bolivia, the lack of additional financial services such as microsavings accounts or microinsurance is noteworthy. Both microsavings accounts and microinsurance would allow family units to save and protect their precious cattle against theft or disease. It is necessary to expand access to microcredit, microsavings, and microinsurance as a first step conducive to the eradication of extreme poverty.

BANKING FOR THE POOR

The concept of Microsavings Insurance is similar to the Deposit Insurance that operates in the United States and other developed countries. Nowadays, many Microfinance Institutions that can only grant microcredits are unable to offer microsavings accounts because of the local microfinance regulation. The reason for this is to avoid a scenario in which a Microfinance Institution defaults and is not able to reimburse deposits to its microsavers. Microsavings Insurance would help to solve this dilemma.

Compliant Microfinance Institutions would be subject to an International Microfinance Regulation determined by the Bank for the Poor. The Bank for the Poor would lend to Microfinance Institutions and would provide Microsavings Insurance, so that if the Microfinance Institution defaulted, the extreme poor could recover their deposits.

An Emerging Asset Class

An asset class in the financial markets is defined as a unique sort of collateral with structural attributes that differentiate it in terms of risk, return, and correlation with the market. In this sense microfinance is presented as a "new form of decentralized development tool aiming at serving excluded from the formal banking system" (Hudon 2006). The market of microfinance is an aggregation of a variety of regional markets, typically with the prevalence of a specific MFI per region (Portocarrero and Byrne 2003).

In markets where microfinance has consolidated, an increasing competition leads to a reduction of interest rates and the cease of activity of the less efficient MFIs. An optimal scenario is then reached, with a limited number of MFIs offering a homogeneous product at a price that matches marginal revenue with marginal cost (Portocarrero and Byrne 2003). In other countries where microfinance is considered to be competitive, interest rates have remained high, as is the case of Bangladesh, where rates on loans have averaged 15 percent, in spite of fierce competition among the major MFIs. Uganda resembles Bangladesh, whereas Bolivia represents the opposite case, in which a variety of lending modes (group and individual) were available from early on (Porteous 2006) in a more competitive environment, leading to a significant reduction in interest rates.

As nonprofit organizations (NGOs) become MFIs and MFIs mature into more established financial institutions, the poor wonder whether they will ever have access to basic financial services spanning well beyond the simple concept of microloans. The microfinance rating agencies play a key role in this process as independent third-parties with the ability of rating the credit risk of MFIs. These specialized rating agencies provide, according to Standard and Poor's (2007), "useful and insightful ratings and evaluations, but in many cases their products have been designed for different users and purposes, such as providing the owners and management of MFIs with an evaluation of the MFI's ability to meet its social and financial objectives."

The major microfinance rating agencies in terms of number of ratings conducted as of 2007 were (Ada 2008): M-CRIL (15.5 percent market share), Microfinanza Rating (15.1 percent), PlanetRating (11.6 percent), PRIME (11.4 percent), Fitch Ratings (10.4 percent), Class y Asociados (10 percent), MicroRate (8.6 percent), and Crisil (7.6 percent).

As of year-end 2006, the mainstream credit rating agency Fitch Ratings rated a total of 3,078 banks, whereas the microfinance rating agencies had rated a total of 674 MFIs in the period of 1994 to 2005, a third of which were performance evaluations by specialized rating agencies (Rating Fund 2005). The microfinance sector has a long way to go to catch up, but the growth rates in rating actions performed showed in Figure 23.1 denote the progress made to date.

According to Damian Von Stauffenberg of MicroRate, microcredits do not imply the provision of financial services to the poor, but the lending to productive activities. This feature differentiates the microcredit from the consumer loan, which is common in the industrialized world. Before underwriting a loan, an MFI should make sure the borrower has a business able to generate sufficient revenue and cash flow to repay the debt (Martin-Cavanna 2007).

MFIs have to be analyzed differently from traditional banking corporations, since making numerous small loans with much shorter maturities is more expensive than the more traditional commercial bank lending with longer horizons. As a result, ratios such as operating efficiency will be higher for an MFI than for a commercial bank (Standard and Poor's 2007). In the business of lending money to the poor, lenders need to overcome the difficulties of the informal sector, where borrowers typically have no formal records, and need to use alternative ways to assess the risk of default.

Bolivia is one of the success stories in microfinance. The key to success in the Bolivian microfinance is a lesser number of MFIs of bigger size,[1] generating more competition that is translated into lower interest rates, with a portfolio return of 27.1 percent as of 2002 compared with 45.8 percent of Peru (Portocarrero and Byrne 2003). In addition, most Bolivian MFIs provide the borrower with additional services, such as basic health care and social assistance, which strengthens the bond between the borrower and the lender (Castro Valdes, Gil, et al., 2007).

Vivianne Romero is Pro Mujer's director in Bolivia. Pro Mujer Bolivia couples the delivery of preventive health care with the provision of microcredit to all of its 100,000 microfinance customers. Out of its 650 employees, Pro Mujer Bolivia employs 100 medical doctors and nurses. Vivianne finds that for a cost of under $0.60 per month each microborrower, a majority of whom are female, receives a preventive maternal and sexual reproductive care that has a direct impact in the improvement of the lives of the extreme poor Pro Mujer Bolivia serves.

From Microfinance to Banking for the Poor

The market for microfinance is expanding. According to Jacques Attali (2006), as of 2006 there were 2.8 billion people worldwide living on less than two dollars a day, 10,000 MFIs, and 93 million microfinance beneficiaries. The potential market is huge, with an upside of $100 billion and a sector growth of 20 percent per annum. "I think it is quite important to get more of our traditional banking institutions involved in bringing microfinance to the necessary level of density to have an impact on the individual lives of those who receive the loans" says former president Bill Clinton (Baue 2005). According to Deutsche Bank, institutional investment in microfinance is expected to rise ten-fold from $2.4 billion in 2006 to $25 billion in 2015. As of 2007, the untapped demand for microfinance was estimated at $250 billion. Microfinance penetration rates among the poor were above 20 percent only in three countries: Bangladesh (35 percent), Sri Lanka (29 percent) and Vietnam (25 percent) (Dieckmann 2007), the remainder of the developing world being underserved

The Austrian economist Joseph Schumpeter already made clear that banks are the key to economic development because they channel society's savings to entrepreneurs. We need less investment banks and less commercial banks managed by greedy bankers. We need more Microfinance Institutions and more responsible investors. Microfinance can thus play an important role in financial development, strengthening the link between economic growth and poverty alleviation (Barr 2005). MFIs need to go beyond the traditional approach of granting microcredits to the poor with no collateral, to span an array of services beginning with a core package: savings, credit, insurance, and payment products such as money transfers (Rhyne 2007). A greater number of poor people have increasingly demanded savings, insurance, leasing, and other financial services (Meyer 2001).

The world's poor are a majority of the Humankind. As such they have no access to basic financial services that have allowed the West to develop credit markets that are crucial for the development and operation of the entrepreneur and the private enterprise that would find their equivalent in the microentrepreneur and the microbusiness among the extreme poor. Most individuals with a daily per-capita income under two dollars are underserved or totally neglected by the more traditional banking industry mostly active in mature and emerging markets. The poor have no collateral and often live in nation-states that lack basic regulation and property rights, where conducting business and investment is risky and unsafe. The poor live in nation-states unable to enforce regulation and conduct banking supervision.

Regulatory Framework

As MFIs grow and start taking retail deposits, questions arise as to whether or not to regulate them (Barr 2005). The ability of regulation goes along that of supervision. In addition smaller, rural-based MFIs, which often serve the worse off, are more costly to regulate than their urban counterparties. It is not certain that a developing economy has the capability of doing both.

Economies of scale could justify the creation of an International Regulator in charge of enforcing the International Microfinance Regulation presented in Chapter 22, and supervising financial institutions in developing economies that would voluntarily decide to join in. The reality is that microfinance will make progress only if the enabling environment is supportive (Rhyne 2007). In certain countries like Uganda, Indonesia, Peru, and Bolivia, specific microfinance regulatory frameworks have been very helpful.

In particular, Michael Mithika at the School of Applied Microfinance in Nairobi (Kenya) notes, "In spite of the Microfinance Deposit Taking Institutions Act passed in Uganda, there have not been many MFIs that have applied to become deposit taking, and contrary to governmental belief, only a handful of those that applied have experienced significant growth." Mithika points out that savings are not automatic, because individuals choose to whom they lend, contrary to the way financial institutions lend. Even if an institution becomes deposit taking, in a competitive environment it is necessary to learn how to brand, develop, and sell innovative, competitive banking products, which is what many financial institutions have not done appropriately.

Another area that is experiencing tremendous growth is cell-phone banking. Cell-phone banking is emerging but its potential and risks are noteworthy. The issue is complex because it involves the banking regulator on top of the telecommunications regulator. The former should verify whether cell-phone banking meets minimum standards of security, working hands-on with providers and the latter to make sure their systems are up and running at acceptable levels (Rhyne 2007).

Elizabeth Littlefield is chief executive of the Consultative Group to Assist the Poor (CGAP) at the World Bank. I met Littlefield at the CGAP headquarters in Washington, DC, on June 8, 2009. Littlefield is worried that "foreign money, public and private, is not necessarily catalyzing the creation of a sustainable, savings-based financial system in poor countries" (*Economist* 2007b). For Maria Otero, a former president and chief executive officer of Accion International, "To obtain scale, microfinance must be considered a serious asset class and that more companies, banks and non-profits should form alliances to maximize their potential impact" (Tully 2007).

There has been a decrease in newcomers, as donors are not encouraging the creation of nonprofit MFIs that are accordingly heavily subsidized, except for countries where microfinance is still in an initial stage of development. The more successful NGO-type MFIs have become for-profit institutions. Furthermore, fierce competition is decreasing the number of microfinance NGOs in a handful of countries.

New Instruments

Philanthropists and socially responsible investors demand new financial instruments that allow for the maximization of the social return. In 2005, Pierre Omidyar donated $100 million to Tufts University to invest in MFIs (*Economist* 2006c). Omidyar is the founder of eBay. His intent was to attract private capital and turn it profitable. Omidyar established the Omidyar Network in 2004, which he considers a philanthropic investment firm that makes both investments and grants. The Omidyar Network believes that people are the owners of their actions, and that with the right environment and tools, the poor can move ahead on their own.

Jacques Grivel is a Swiss financier founder of the Geneva-based Symbiotics. Grivel would like to see some private funding enter a product that has been heavily reliant on subsidies (Giussani 2006). Private funding coming from institutional investors and pension funds might bolster an already maturing sector.

Microfinance Investment Vehicles (MIVs) are financial instruments that invest in microfinance. In 2005 alone, a total of 54 MIVs nearly doubled their investment in microfinance, reaching one billion dollars by year-end (Von Stauffenberg 2006). This new type of investors will expect the same amount and quality of information that they expect from other more traditional investment opportunities. Prior to the financial crisis of 2007 and 2008, MIVs were undergoing phenomenal growth.

More and more MFIs are turning to the capital markets seeking funding, some of them in pioneering deals like that of BRAC in Bangladesh. With 100,000 employees, BRAC is the largest NGO in the world and second largest MFI in Bangladesh after Grameen. In 2006, BRAC became the first MFI to use microcredit securitization. As a result of the deal, BRAC would receive $180 million in financing over a six-year interval. The collateral was made up of microcredits granted to low-income individuals from rural areas not reached by the country's commercial banks. "This transaction underlines BRAC's commitment to be the leading provider of innovative financing solutions to microentrepreneurs. As one of the largest financing efforts ever dedicated to advancing poverty focused microcredit, this is a landmark for the microfinance industry," pointed out Fazle Hasan Abed, chairperson at BRAC (Citigroup 2006).

SHABBIR A. CHOWDHURY (BFP) is the director of microfinance at BRAC. I met Shabbir on March 1, 2009, at his office in the BRAC Tower in Dhaka (Bangladesh). What is the most likely way to expand financing opportunities in the aftermath of the financial crisis? For Shabbir, "Because of the failure of the present banking system of the West investors will be interested to invest in the microfinance then on the other sector."

DEPOSIT INSURANCE

According to the International Association of Deposit Insurers (IADI), as of September 2008, there were a total of 119 countries in the world with a deposit insurance system in operation, pending, planned, or under serious study (IADI 2008). The problem with deposit insurance schemes in many developing countries is that they only reach the small percentage of the population who has access to a savings account at a commercial bank.

Throughout the world, deposit insurance coverage varies. For instance, Mexico, Turkey, and Japan cover 100 percent of deposits. On the other hand, Chile, Switzerland, and Britain only cover an amount of deposits that is less than their GDP per capita (Demirgüç-Kunt and Kane 2001). Deposit insurance can be explicit or implicit. If a country has elaborated a law that specifies the main features of deposit insurance such as coverage limits, deposit insurance is considered to be explicit. Otherwise, deposit insurance is assumed to be implicit (Demirgüç-Kunt, Karacaovali, et al., 2005), which is equivalent to saying it is nonexistent. A majority of high-income countries have explicit deposit insurance schemes.

For middle-income and low-income countries, Figure 23.1 depicts the distribution of countries with explicit and implicit deposit insurance schemes by geographic area. Sub-Saharan Africa is the worst covered area. It is important to note that even though a country may have an explicit deposit insurance scheme whereby depositors would be covered in case their bank went bankrupt, only the small share of the population in developing countries who can open a bank account at a commercial bank typically benefits from the comfort of a deposit insurance scheme.

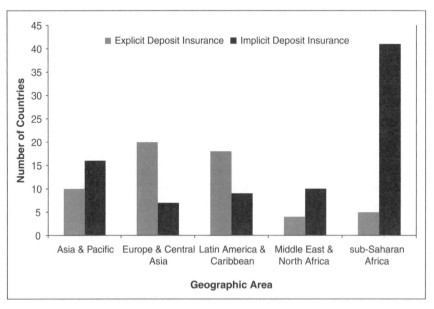

FIGURE 23.1   Countries with Deposit Insurance, Explicit vs. Implicit (Excluding High Income Countries), 2003
Source: Demirgüç-Kunt, Karacaovali, et al. (2005).

Anthony M. Santomero of the Wharton School of the University of Pennsylvania asks whether we need deposit insurance and why. For the Wharton scholar, deposit insurance exists as part of the financial safety net, "an elaborate set of institutional mechanisms for protecting the financial system, which has largely succeeded in preventing contagious runs in the financial sector." According to Santomero, proponents of deposit insurance argue that uninformed depositors are unable to know the true nature of a bank's balance sheet and as a result what sort of risks they may be incurring by depositing their savings at a certain bank (Santomero 1997).

When should deposit insurance be considered? The introduction of deposit insurance schemes in countries lacking an appropriate banking regulation and supervision may, in the end, be an obstacle for financial development and stability (Cull, Senbet, et al., 2003). An adequate and strong banking regulation and supervision system is thus a precondition for a deposit insurance scheme to work properly. Many countries, however, lack the ability to set up an independent bank able to play the regulatory and supervisory role for which it was created. What is needed to guarantee Central Bank independence? The design of an independent Central Bank was presented in Chapter 22.

For Alan D. Morrison of Oxford and Lucy White of Harvard University, deposit insurance should not be financed by banks or depositors, but by taxpayers. The authors conclude that taxpayers who are neither bankers nor depositors should fund deposit insurance because of the following two reasons (Morrison and White 2006):

1. Taxing bankers and then paying this back to depositors in the case of ex-post failure—as has traditionally been advocated—is at best a welfare-neutral policy because it has the adverse effect of reducing the banks' capital base, making moral hazard more likely.
2. A tax upon depositors acts to reduce their investable funds and to deter them from investing.

Luc Laeven of the World Bank looks at the "Pricing of Deposit Insurance" (2002). In order to determine a bank's probability of default, the World Bank economist looks at a bank's credit rating. If a bank goes bankrupt, the deposit insurance scheme would have to rescue depositors and reimburse their deposits. Laeven comments (Laeven 2002):

We use both country and bank credit ratings from Moody's to estimate expected loss rates. The country credit rating acts as a ceiling of the rating for (most) banks in the country. In several countries, country risk is so dominant that bank ratings equal the country rating.

This is a common practice in finance. The international rating agencies Moody's, Standard and Poor's, and Fitch Ratings typically rank countries and public corporations. Countries receive the so-called sovereign rating that determines their ability to pay back their outstanding debt. Corporations receive corporate ratings. Both sovereign and corporate ratings are credit ratings. Therefore, a credit rating determines the ability of the creditor to pay back its debt.

A country's sovereign rating will undermine its ability to set up an appropriate and well-functioning deposit insurance scheme. Because the pricing of deposit insurance is a direct function of a country's sovereign rating, a bank that operates in a country with a low sovereign rating will be less likely to provide a sound deposit insurance scheme. The same bank would be more likely to provide a sound deposit insurance scheme if it operated in a country with a high sovereign rating. From a policy-making point of view, it makes sense to delink a Microsavings Insurance scheme from a country's sovereign rating. Laeven gives more insight about how to design a deposit insurance scheme. He mentions the following structural features (Laeven 2002):

> *To avoid adverse selection, membership of the deposit insurance scheme should be compulsory. To avoid moral hazard, deposit insurance premiums should be risk-adjusted, the insurance coverage should be low, prompt corrective actions should be taken against banks, and early intervention should take place in weak banks. The insurance coverage should aim at insuring the deposits of small depositors, and should exclude part of large deposits, inter-bank deposits, government deposits, and possibly foreign-currency deposits. Low coverage may be complemented with coinsurance for deposits larger than the smallest tranche of deposits.*

What is the typical coverage provided by a deposit insurance corporation? How is the coverage measured? There are two ways to measure the coverage. The first ratio compares the maximum amount a depositor would get reimbursed compared to the country's GDP per capita. The ratio typically ranges between one and three for a majority of countries. The second ratio compares the maximum amount a depositor would get reimbursed compared to the average deposit amount per capita. This second ratio is slightly larger than the first ratio and ranges between one and five for a majority of countries.

MICROSAVINGS INSURANCE

Bhagwan Chowdhry of the University of California at Los Angeles thinks that the savings of the poor could be protected "by allowing, and in fact requiring, financial institutions that offer savings products to buy deposit insurance from the government" (Chowdhry 2005). According to Figure 23.2, a fraction of the extreme poor are able to access a microsavings account, which typically lacks the protection that deposit insurance schemes grant to savings in commercial savings accounts.

There are two types of regulatory frameworks that a country's Central Bank can enforce for its financial institutions: preventive and protective (Chaves and Gonzalez-Vega 1994):

1. Preventive regulation introduces appropriate incentives to reduce moral hazard.
2. Protective regulation serves as an emergency safeguard for depositors when financial institutions get into trouble despite preventive regulation.

The more usual preventive regulation limits the ability of raising deposits to formal banks that comply with a sound regulation including: defined financial services, minimum equity requirements, accounting standards, and mandatory reporting and audits (Fiebig, Hannig, et al., 1999). Typically, only commercial banks in developing

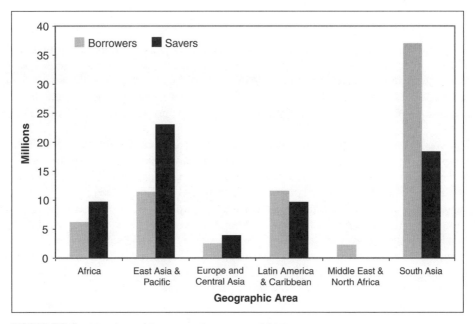

FIGURE 23.2 Number of Savers vs. Borrowers, 2007
Data Source: Microfinance Information Exchange (2007).

countries that serve a small percentage of the population are able to comply with a sound regulation that allows them to raise deposits to continue financing the growth of their loan portfolios.

The Asian Development Bank met in Manila on March 16, 2005, to discuss the building of inclusive financial sectors for development. One of the conclusions of the summit has to do with deposit insurance for microsavings (ADB 2005): "A third issue where there was no resolution in the group was the question of deposit insurance for microsavings. Countries are only beginning to address the questions of offering deposit insurance for MFIs."

Alex Counts is president and chief executive officer of the Grameen Foundation. I phoned Counts on October 12, 2008, and again on October 29, 2008. The Grameen Foundation combines microfinance, technology, and innovative solutions to defeat global poverty, and to create a world without poverty. Counts reviews the potential of deposit insurance for microsavings in his piece "New Frontiers in Microsavings" (Counts and Meriweather 2008). For Counts, most regulatory authorities do not allow MFIs to mobilize deposits because "it puts poor micro-depositors at risk of losing their savings if the MFI collapses or loses the savings of its depositors for any other reason." Counts adds, "Many countries do not have deposit insurance and for those that do, extending it to MFIs that are not already covered could be difficult or even inappropriate, as the insured amount and the cost to the financial institution, if any, were likely designed with traditional financial institutions and their clients in mind" (Counts and Meriweather 2008).

Why is Microsavings Insurance needed? First of all because a Microfinance Institution that offers savings accounts but also lends money could go bankrupt if many of the microcredit borrowers default on their loans. In this case, it is fundamental that the savings accounts of the defaulted Microfinance Institution be protected and therefore insured. Secondly, by insuring savings we build a more inclusive and stable microfinancial infrastructure.

How do we make sure a Microfinance Institution does not default on its loans? The Bank for the Poor would make sure that any MFI signatory of the Microsavings Insurance complies with a strict International Microfinance Regulation, as described in Chapter 22. It is the role of the Bank for the Poor to design and implement the regulation, and then to supervise financial institutions proactively so that the risk of default is minimized.

What would be the impact of a significant increase in the savings capacity of the poor? The savings rate is one of the determinant drivers of economic growth, according to growth economics. If the poor are able to save in a stable currency (the yunus) and open bank accounts that are insured, the incentive to save is fundamentally boosted. If savings increase, the lending capacity of an MFI also increases, and there is more money available for those microentrepreneurs who are willing to start up a business. Savings from one country can be used to lend in another country if microsavers save in a common currency, for instance the yunus, without being exposed to currency risk.

What would be the cost of running a deposit insurance scheme for the bottom billion of the world's population? Alvin James is a senior financial analyst at the Division of Insurance and Research of the U.S. Federal Deposit Insurance Corporation (FDIC). I met James on December 12, 2008, at Dupont Circle in Washington, DC. James suggests looking at the amount of insured deposits in the United States as a proxy. We can then determine the cost of running the deposit insurance scheme for the bottom billion as a fraction of running the FDIC.

As of June 30, 2008, total deposits in the United States amounted to $8.57 trillion, of which the FDIC insured deposit accounts of $100,000 or less with an aggregate balance of $4.46 trillion.[2] The average balance of a microsavings account would be much smaller than the upper bound of $100,000 in the United States. A person in the bottom billion earns under one dollar a day or under $365 a year. If the insured limit was set at $365 or 100 percent of the extreme poor's annual per capita income (compared to the $100,000 of the United States), a new Microsavings Insurance scheme would need to insure a principal amount of $365 billion, which is only a fraction of the principal amount insured by FDIC in the United States.

The upper bound limit of $365 billion assumes that all the extreme poor have access to basic financial services and have indeed opened a bank account. This could be true in the long run. On the short and medium terms, this is far from being accurate and the principal to be insured would be well below this amount.

Expertise in Deposit Insurance

A new Microsavings Insurance scheme requires a new microsavings deposit corporation along with its chief executive officer. **ANTONIO CARLOS DE CAMARGO SILVA** (MSI) is the chief executive officer of Brazil's Fundo Garantidor de Creditos. I spoke with Antonio Carlos on December 5, 2008. For the Brazilian, "Microsavings Insurance is necessary to increase the social inclusion of the poor into society."

Why is Microsavings Insurance needed? Antonio Carlos points out, "As a rule, every insurance system has a positive result, provided it is conceived observing the aspects of costs and moral hazards. The possibility of the creation of an international entity to supervise microsaving insurance ought to take into consideration all socioeconomic characteristics prevailing in each country."

How do we make sure a Microfinance Institution does not default on its loans? In the context of the elaboration of International Microfinance Regulation, Antonio Carlos remarks, "The institution should make use of existing mechanisms of analysis for granting credit limits, or develop its own mechanisms of credit analysis, as it is the practice of ordinary loan systems."

What would be the impact of a significant increase in the savings capacity of the poor? Antonio Carlos concludes, "Microsavings Insurance, if put into practice, should somehow benefit from the participation of government which should contribute with a portion of the costs for the sake of social interest."

VILMA ROSA LEON-YORK (MSI) is the chief executive officer of Nicaragua's Fondo de Garantia de Depositos. I spoke with Vilma Rosa on December 5, 2008. For Vilma Rosa, Nicaragua is an interesting example of what microsavings insurance could do for the extreme poor. Only 15 percent of Nigaraguans have access to a bank account. For the rest, basic financial services are still science fiction.

There should be no overlap between the already operating commercial banks and the current and future Microfinance Institutions. Commercial banks serve the middle and high income earners of developing countries. Microfinance Institutions serve the low-income and the extreme poor who are not profitable for the larger commercial banks.

Artwork by David Bromley.

CHAPTER 24

The Decem Series

*The Decem Tax and the investment fund devoted to projects in develop-
ing countries could in principle help solve a coordination failure. It pools
together the financial effort of many large firms, and therefore provides a
coordinated solution to development problems. In other words, it may make
possible what otherwise would have been impossible. It probably illustrates
well the spirit of Decem.*

—Marcelo Olarreaga

The *Decem Series on Funding for Development* is a series of 10 economic policies
that could significantly increase the amount of funding available for development
in the twenty-first century. The Decem Series propose alternative financial instruments that would feed the <u>Decemfund</u>[1], an investment fund that becomes the poor's
de facto endowment. The Decemfund is introduced in the last section of this chapter, which includes the first three policies in the Decem series. A description of the
complete series can be downloaded at http://Decem.info.

A PUBLIC TREASURE

The first policy of the Decem Series applies to nation-states' Decem-compliance or
Decempliance, a concept introduced later in this chapter.

The national or public debt is a tool that allows governments to finance, in times
of economic crisis and through public spending, infrastructure as well as public
services. These services enable the maintenance of the welfare state and help sustain
employment levels. National economics run deficits and surpluses that alternate
in the ups and downs of the economic cycle. An austere economic policy will set a
maximum ceiling to the deficit, so that a national economy does not borrow in excess.

It is in some respect the way the Republican administration in the United States
financed the war in Iraq or the rescue-packages in post-Katrina New Orleans. A
concern, that of a high leverage, which will have repercussions in our children and
grandchildren, some argue. For what reasons it is worth to increase a nation's debt
level is a matter to which some of our political leaders should respond.

The size of public debt relative to the gross domestic product (GDP) varies
according to the country considered. There are countries that are slightly indebted

such as Luxembourg, whereas others such as Italy or Greece are highly indebted. Among the requirements of the Maastricht Treaty to join the European Economic and Monetary Union, there are two related to the level of debt: (1) the fiscal deficit cannot increase beyond the equivalent of 3 percent of the GDP; and (2) the public debt cannot surpass the level of 60 percent of GDP. In numerous occasions these limits have not been respected, such as in the cases of France and Germany regarding the former, or Greece and Italy regarding the latter. If we observe the current level of debt in several economies of the Eurozone, we can conclude that it would be feasible to increase the debt-to-GDP ratio a number of percentage points, in order to devote the funds raised this way to a great fund for development aid, which I will refer to as the Decemfund hereafter.

Impact of a High Level of Debt

The role played by a rating agency (Moody's, Standard and Poor's, and Fitch are the three main rating agencies) is to determine an institution's credit risk by means of a credit rating. A credit rating is a letter-code denoting how likely a company is to service its outstanding debt and to avoid bankruptcy. In the same way, a rating agency can assign a credit rating to a corporation as well as to a national economy. National ratings are called sovereign.

In 1975, only four national economies were rated by the rating agencies. By 2006, this number has increased notably, counting as many as a hundred. The credit rating is fundamental for an economy, because it is as a function of a credit rating that an economy will have a higher or lower cost of funding when it borrows from the international markets. The level of indebtedness or leverage has a major impact on the probability of default of a national economy. The higher the leverage, the higher the associated probability of default will be.

The current level of a national economy's debt-to-GDP ratio determines whether or not it can undertake an additional increase of leverage of 10 percent. Ten percent of a developed nation's GDP would then be invested in a new development fund, called Decemfund, which is more fully introduced later in this chapter.

Moody's Investors Service analyzes "How Far Can Aaa Governments Stretch Their Balance Sheets." For Moody's, Aaa countries show an exceptional shock absorption capacity and unconstrained access to finance (Moody's 2009). How much additional leverage can an Aaa country undertake to maintain the rating? For Moody's, "Delineating the demarcation between Aaa and Aa governments is to a large extent a normative exercise," because "contrary to lower-rated governments, there is no relevant empirical way to characterize the intrinsic differences between a Aaa government and a Aa government" (Moody's 2007).

Aaa countries are also classified as a function of the percentage of total government revenue they devote to public debt interest payments: Italy, Japan, Ireland, the United States, and the United Kingdom devote more than 10 percent; Germany, Spain, France, Austria, Netherlands, Switzerland, and New Zealand devote between 5 and 10 percent; and finally, Finland, Sweden, Canada, Denmark, Singapore, Norway, Australia, and Luxembourg devote less than 5 percent (Moody's 2009). From more to less leverage, Moody's ranks Aaa countries depending on how much leverage they could undertake while maintaining their Aaa rating (Moody's 2007): United States, Germany, Sweden, France, Switzerland, United Kingdom,

Australia, Canada, Finland, Denmark, Singapore, Austria, Netherlands, New Zealand, Norway, Luxembourg, Ireland, and Spain. Ireland and Spain were subsequently downgraded to Aa in the first half of 2009.

To incur additional leverage carries the obligation of servicing future payments to those investors who decide to purchase the debt. A sustainable level of debt guarantees the future payments, whereas a prudent increase of leverage will not lead to an immediate worsening of the sovereign credit rating. Figure 24.1 summarizes the limitations expressed above.

THE DECEM TAX

The second policy of the Decem Series applies to a firm's Decempliance. Contemporary Western society is sustained on an economic and financial basis formed over recent decades and throughout successive crises that hit countries and societies through forced devaluations, stock market collapses, and government debt defaults that made capitalism mature. It is a society rooted from the very bottom in the principles of a free market, of the law of supply and demand, in which the entrepreneur is rewarded when a project succeeds and goes public through an Initial Public Offering (IPO).

The most advanced societies operate under the rules of the free market, but are sustained thanks to the tax collection ability of public administrations. The inability to collect taxes of economies like those of Russia or Argentina fed the economic crisis that hit their financial structures in 1998 and 2002 respectively.

Corporate profit is an entrepreneur's reward to a job well done, and is normally taxed to a certain degree. Corporate tax represents the basis to determine the market value of a public firm.

The stock market is a key element to understanding the economic stability of a sovereign state. It allows for the financing of large projects, at the same time that it reduces their cost of capital. It makes access to capital more horizontal and democratic and enables the small investor to share the earnings, if any.

The success of multinational firms is not only a result of their good management in the present tense. It is a success linked to the favoritism of the old times, to the abuse of a dominant position, to the malpractices of the negotiation of power with fragile states and states controlled by despotic dictators, and to the exploitation of natural and human resources. Western society provides opportunities, through its multinational firms, to societies in developing economies. But it is to be blamed, nonetheless, for its past policies that had detrimental consequences in the present reality of the poor world.

Let the entrepreneur continue to have the motivation to take risks on a personal project, and to wake up every morning with the passion to see his or her business prosper. Let the entrepreneur be rewarded through the retention of corporate profits. But let societies be compensated, societies that suffered from the abuse of the colonization process throughout centuries of history; let them be compensated with the benefit of sharing part of those earnings, earnings that today represent a key *raison d'etre* of the capitalist system in the so-called industrialized nations of the world.

One of the key principles of financial economics deals with the computation of a firm's equity or market value. The technical definition would say that a firm's market value is determined as the summation of the present value of future cash flows. Such

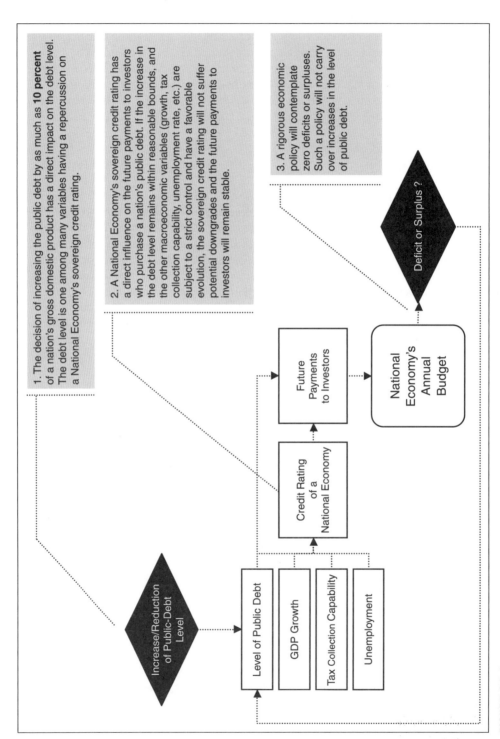

1. The decision of increasing the public debt by as much as **10 percent** of a nation's gross domestic product has a direct impact on the debt level. The debt level is one among many variables having a repercussion on a National Economy's sovereign credit rating.

2. A National Economy's sovereign credit rating has a direct influence on the future payments to investors who purchase a nation's public debt. If the increase in the debt level remains within reasonable bounds, and the other macroeconomic variables (growth, tax collection capability, unemployment rate, etc.) are subject to a strict control and have a favorable evolution, the sovereign credit rating will not suffer potential downgrades and the future payments to investors will remain stable.

3. A rigorous economic policy will contemplate zero deficits or surpluses. Such a policy will not carry over increases in the level of public debt.

Deficit or Surplus ?

National Economy's Annual Budget

Future Payments to Investors

Credit Rating of a National Economy

Increase/Reduction of Public-Debt Level

Level of Public Debt

GDP Growth

Tax Collection Capability

Unemployment

FIGURE 24.1   Impact on a Nation's Sovereign Rating of an Increase in Public Debt

an expression is just the sum of future profits, present-valued to today's value of money. It is not the same to earn one million dollars today, as it is to earn the same million in a year's time, or in 10 years' time. Prices increase because of inflation, an economic force that explains the loss of purchasing power as time passes.

Future profits are subject to uncertainty, to macroeconomic uncertainty, and to risks of various sorts (operational risk, market risk, credit risk, currency risk). As a result, future profits computed to determine a firm's present value are indeed expected profits. It is a game of expectations. If expectations are beaten, the firm's market value will increase; otherwise, the market value will decrease. Based on the previous reasoning, the evolution of a firm's market value as a function of the established corporate tax can be derived. The greater the corporate tax is, the smaller the corporate earnings. Therefore, a firm's market value should diminish as corporate tax increases.

The after-corporate-tax earnings result from subtracting the corporate-tax to before-tax earnings. Of each 100 dollars, the Treasury will retain, for instance, 30 dollars, if the corporate tax is set at 30 percent. To these after-corporate-tax earnings a second tax would be applied, called the Decem Tax[2], which consists of investing 10 percent of the after-corporate-tax earnings in a large investment fund. In the previous example, the firm should devote 7 out of each 100 dollars to this large investment fund.

The reader may think that the After-Decem-Tax earnings decrease from 70 to 63 dollars for each 100 dollars of before-tax earnings. As a result, a firm's market value will automatically drop by 10 percent. The apparent conclusion is that the adoption of such a measure would automatically make the stock market lose 10 percent of its total value when adopted.

The educated reader in financial economics should think in terms of a firm's financial statements: the income statement and the balance sheet. The latter consists of assets and liabilities. The Decem Tax would suggest that 10 percent of the remaining after-corporate-tax earnings be invested in an investment fund (the Decemfund), to be managed according to a set of responsible and sustainable criteria. The profits of this investment fund will be used as funding for development aid in developing economies: health care, education, water, and sanitation. This firm's contribution of 10 percent of its after-corporate-tax earnings will still be an asset to the company that will not be able to manage it directly. This contribution will be freed in case the firm goes bankrupt, a situation in which the firm's senior debt holders will be able to access the firm's contribution to the Decemfund in order to minimize losses and increase the recovery rate accordingly.

The Decem Tax, consisting of retaining a 10 percent of after-corporate-tax earnings, will contribute to increasing the principal of the Decemfund, the profits of which, from the investment strategies, will be devoted to funding for development. In words of Marcelo Olarreaga, a professor of economics at the University of Geneva, "The Decem Tax and the investment fund devoted to projects in developing countries could in principle help solve a coordination failure, as it pools together the financial effort of many large firms, and therefore provides a coordinated solution to development problems."

Would a public firm's market value decrease as a result of applying the Decem Tax? The impact of the Decem Tax on a company's balance sheet is summarized in Figure 24.2.

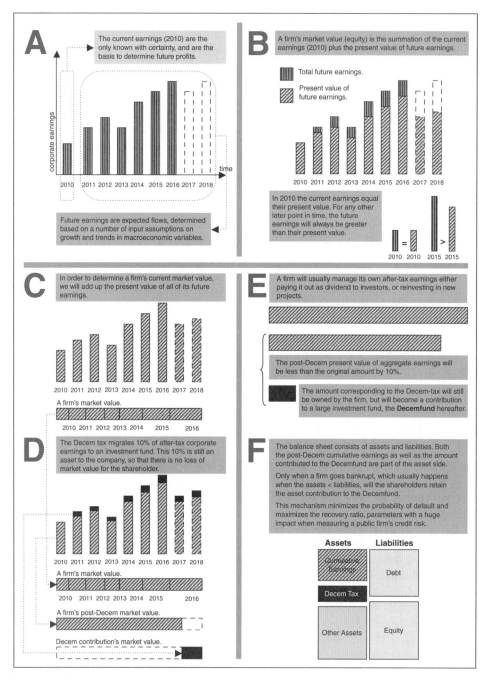

FIGURE 24.2 Impact of the Decem Tax on a Company's Balance Sheet

TAXATION OF PERSONAL WEALTH

The third policy of the Decem Series applies to individuals' Decompliance. The taxation of personal wealth is a concept of global justice. The economies of the industrialized nations that integrate the steam engine of the capitalist system, in which the developing economies belong in the last wagon, have robust taxation systems that enable the public administrations to raise taxes efficiently. This is done through the progressive taxation of the economic activity of individuals with different income levels, who enjoy the stability provided by the well-known welfare state.

Origins of the Redistributive System

The origins of the progressive taxation system, which forms the basis of the principle of redistribution, date back to the times of the economist Adam Smith, who in his masterpiece *The Wealth of Nations* notes, "The indolence and vanity of the rich is made to contribute in a very easy manner to the relief of the poor, by rendering cheaper the transportation of heavy goods to all the different parts of the country," (Smith 1776) making explicit reference to the higher fees affecting the rich class' carriages, which were fundamentally heavier than the poor class' carriages.

Thomas Jefferson argued toward the beginning of the nineteenth century that the tariffs on imports were a way to tax the rich, since the poor would only purchase goods within the country's own borders, and as a result, would not pay tariffs related to imports.

Nowadays, there are taxation systems that are more or less progressive. Generally speaking, societies with an advanced welfare state share a higher taxation of high incomes, higher than the taxation of other societies that have worse social services, otherwise considered universal or of indiscriminate access.

A Tax on Wealth

A recent trend in the taxation arena has benefited the wealthy with the progressive elimination of the wealth tax. This is a logical argument, if it is taken into account that the wealthy individual usually generates abundant yearly income that is correspondingly taxed through the income tax. The wealth tax would incorporate, in this line of argumentation, a second level of disproportionate taxation and would have a negative impact on the wealthy, leading to the massive shift of wealthy individuals to other less punitive and hence more permissive fiscal regimes, like Switzerland, the land of pirates.

However, the precedent line of argumentation is not the only one, nor is it the most reasonable. The majority of wealthy individuals become wealthy by working hard, by having great ideas, and by having market and product insight. Wealth is also generated from inheritance, from luck, from the profits of funds invested in investment vehicles that destabilize and speculate by short-term investing in developing economies, and from the profits of funds invested in multinational firms' equity—the multinationals which exploit the human and natural resources of nations that welcome them as if they were Mr. Marshall. It is a double-edge sword. It is a thin line that separates the income earned fairly from the one that has been obtained by luck or in a rather random way. It is a difficult task to differentiate which is which. Welcome to the world of double standards—the world of the Bretton Woods Elites who allow the Pirates of Heartless Capitalism, who hide from the world on islands and behind mountains, to operate with no mercy. Raymond Baker notes that the third policy of the Decem Series raises a useful question: *Is there a level of wealth that merits taxing in order to achieve redistributions to the poor?* For the American financial authority:

> *The most effective step that can be taken in correcting current imbalances is to engender transparency into the global capitalist system. This means curtailing bank secrecy and canceling the legitimacy of disguised corporations, anonymous trust accounts, and fake foundations, together constituting an illicit financial structure that hides so much wealth today, much of it generated illegally. This has to be accomplished first, before any scheme for taxing high net worth can be effected. Transparency in the global capitalist system is the closest thing to a magic bullet for addressing today's staggering levels of disparity. Then redistribution can begin its long road toward realization.*

A world in which those who earn most do not contribute notably and become a reference with their behavior is not a fair world. A fair world is not a utopia if we do not believe utopia is feasible. A fair world is Eutopia. If the basis of the system that has enabled the generation of phenomenal wealth is not redefined, each and every one of the wealthy will disappear along the rest of society in a world that faces increasingly more difficult challenges.

Milton Pedraza (DCF) is the founder and chief executive officer of The Luxury Institute. I met Milton at the Princeton Club in New York City on January 29, 2008. For Milton, it is time to go beyond net worth and find self-worth by contributing to society.

In the above line of reasoning, it is proposed that 10 percent of an individual's personal wealth above one million dollars be invested in the Decemfund. This contribution is still owned by the wealthy individual and only the profits from the investment strategies are devoted to development aid. Figure 24.3 shows how the wealth tax feeds the Decemfund.

Only with ideas simple to implement and powerful in their conception and scope will we change the current trend, a vital turn in a world on the verge of destruction.

DECEMFUND: THE POOR'S ENDOWMENT

The Decemfund is the new conscience of capitalism. The Decemfund is the new heart of capitalism, used to thinking only with the brain, and only in terms of profit maximization. We forsake the sentiment. It is time to evolve to the principle of sustainability.

For as long as there is extreme poverty, there will be a Poor's Endowment. The Decemfund is the Poor's Endowment. The sections in this chapter have proposed alternative taxation schemes that would feed the Decemfund and contribute to increasing its principal. The Decemfund thereby becomes an endowment invested according to ethical and responsible criteria. The Decemfund will be managed by an

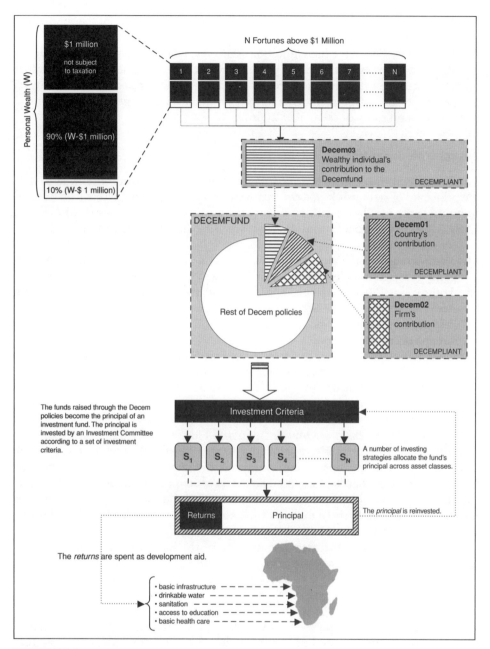

FIGURE 24.3 The Wealth Tax and the Decemfund

experienced investment manager. **KNUT NORHEIM KJAER** (DCF) was executive director of Norges Bank Investment Management, Norway's sovereign oil fund, from 1998 until 2007. I spoke with Knut on May 26, 2008. The Norwegian oil fund is the world's largest sovereign wealth fund of its kind and a well-known example of an investment manager led by the principles of sustainable and responsible investment.

The fund holds equity in more than 3,000 companies. Only in 2006, the fund voted on 23,363 issues in 2,189 companies.

Knut notes, "We have high ambitions with regard to playing a leading role internationally in fostering corporate governance and we are subject to a demanding requirement from the Ministry of Finance to take particular account of an investment horizon that spans many generations ahead, which implies imposing ethical requirements on companies" (Kjoer 2006).

Responsible Investing

The Decemfund will be managed according to responsible investing criteria. What are the principles of responsible investment? Responsible investment necessarily leads to responsible finance. In the words of Harvard Business School professor **MICHAEL CHU** (DCF), there are five principles of responsible finance (Chu 2008):

1. Transparency to the end customers: the terms and conditions under which a good or service is delivered are clearly known by the end-user.
2. Transparency of the financial institutions delivering those goods and services with regards to the public, which includes all the stakeholders, including investors, regulators, and policy makers.
3. Compliance with the law.
4. Compliance with the best practices regarding customer service, being faithful to the spirit rather than to the text of codes of conduct.
5. A regulatory framework to ensure all the above, as well as the solvency of the financial institutions.

I spoke with Michael on March 21, 2008. Have the principles of responsible investing matured with the economic and financial crisis of 2008 and 2009? For Michael, the financial crisis of 2008 confirms the importance of the principles of responsible finance that he outlines. The Harvard scholar concludes that the application of the principles of responsible investing "would have gone a long way to limiting the buildup of the bubble and the subsequent meltdown in U.S. subprime mortgages."

Matt Christensen is the executive director of the European Sustainable Investment Forum (Eurosif). I met Christensen on June 17, 2008, in Paris. Eurosif is Europe's leading sustainable investment forum. It was created in 2001 and it serves as an umbrella association that covers both social and responsible investment at the European level. What are the prospects of sustainable and responsible investments going forward? Among its many initiatives, Eurosif is currently pushing for a mandatory reporting scheme across the EU that would oblige large companies and investors to report on how they are integrating environmental, social, and governance issues with their financial objectives.

DECEMPLIANCE

Decempliance stands for Decem-*com*pliance. There are two levels of compliance in the New Architecture of Capitalism. A developing country should be Monfortable in order to benefit from the New Architecture of Capitalism. Decempliance affects countries, corporations, and individuals in developed countries as explained in the first three Decem Policies presented in this chapter.

A <u>developed country</u> will be <u>Decempliant</u> if it implements the first of the Decem Policies. A corporation will be Decempliant if it implements the second of the Decem Policies. Lastly, an individual will be Decempliant if it implements the third of the Decem Policies. What are the benefits of being Decempliant? The benefits are described in Chapter 30.

Artwork by David Bromley.

CHAPTER 25

Innovative Financing

With the intellectual capacity that exists in the private sector, and similar capacity alleged to exist in the Multilateral Development Banks, it should be possible to design project-specific, as well as generic, schemes for risk-sharing that pave the way for private capital to enter countries where it otherwise might not be prepared to take full exposure risk on its own.
　　　　　　　　　—Percy Mistry, *Financing for Development*

For years the development community has emphasized new approaches to development finance. The number of proposals on the table is considerable. However, a large majority does not move forward because they fail to obtain the consensus of a majority of donors. The usual approach does not increase the size of the pie. Instead, it increases the share of the pie that is then spent as development aid. An alternative approach would increase the size of the pie and devote a share of the increase to development aid. Both approaches are actually necessary. But the second approach has largely remained unexplored.

This chapter proposes how to make the pie larger and use a majority of the new funds for development. We never thought that being in agreement about a specific proposal had a value attached to it. It certainly does. The only requirement is a certain degree of imagination and creativity, a large degree of Civil Society pressure and some political will. The former will indeed lead to the latter. This strategy is called the value of consensus.

Many of the proposals we have seen in recent years incorporate some of the instruments behind the financial crisis and credit crunch of 2007 and 2008. Financial sophistication has proven detrimental and misleading. Many small and institutional investors put their money in instruments they did not understand, but which those who were supposed to understand (the rating agencies) rated as very safe investments (triple-A). The models of the rating agencies failed and with them, a majority of investors fell off a cliff. Any new proposals that aim at raising the investor community's interest and appeal have to be well structured and should be easy to understand. This is the purpose of this chapter.

If only the world community agreed on a handful of decisions, which they viewed as fundamentally positive for the future of humankind and the environment. Human dignity and environmental sustainability can be attained if we prioritize them.

Bubbles appreciate the value of an asset by increasing its demand over its supply in an environment of irrational exuberance.[1] Irrational exuberance is driven by speculative factors. Bubbles burst, sometimes with fatal consequences. This was the case of the real estate bubble in Japan in the late 1980s and early 1990s.

Real estate appreciation can, however, be linked to fundamental factors. The price of real estate in New York City is subject to speculative forces, but it is primarily driven by a variety of fundamental factors, including the fact that the city is home to the financial industry, the United Nations, Columbia University, and New York University. If these integral institutions were to be moved out of Manhattan, it is certain that the price of real estate would drop.

It would, however, not suffice to have New York's financial industry, the United Nations, and two great universities make the price of real estate in any developing country undergo a significant increase. The United States also offers a stable environment, democracy, enforcement of the rule of law and property rights, and very low political risk in a highly predictable environment.

A combination of the factors presented in the last two paragraphs largely drives the price of real estate of any large city. Within the city, there are at the same time large fluctuations in value. A condominium near the UN Headquarters in Manhattan will differ in cost from a condominium on the opposite side of the island near Penn Station. This chapter suggests an innovative investment proposal that could emerge in subsequent years.

A FIRST LOOK AT REAL ESTATE

The origins of the European Union go back to the post-war years of the 1940s, the Marshall Plan, Monnet, Schuman and a plan to pull Europe out of years of destruction and economic stagnation. The devised European Coal and Steel Community tried to unite French and Germans in the production of the raw materials necessary to build up their railroad infrastructure, industry, and weaponry. The wise men of the time constructed a forward-looking plan that aimed at establishing a robust, long-lasting Franco-German cooperation, which later expanded beyond the imagination of many and the borders of the six founding countries.

We look at the issue of borders in the European Union (EU) as if the EU had always existed. A similar comparison would involve looking back at the United States and its current borders today, without realizing that Texas[2] or Southern California[3] could be part of Mexico, and without realizing that Alaska[4] could be part of Russia. A portion of New Mexico and Arizona was purchased by the United States from Mexico in the nineteenth century.[5] Borders are never static; they are always dynamic, part of an on-going process that involves facing the challenges of the times.

Spain is another example of how a former empire lost its last colonies in 1898, when Cuba and the Philippines[6] declared independence in a war that could have otherwise been won by Spain, in which case, Cuba and the Philippines might be part of Spain today, and as a result, be a part of the European Union. The case of Spain recalls the colonies the French and British empires lost in the twentieth century. A number of overseas territories that were not lost by the former empires are today part of the EU, in spite of not being geographically part of Europe, such as the

Azores, the Canary Islands, the French Guiana, Guadeloupe, Madeira, Martinique, Reunion, Saint Barthelemy, and Saint Martin, each of which is an integral part of the EU, and in each of which the euro circulates as the de facto currency.

The rationale behind the generation of a gold mine is simple. In an environment of high country and political risk, foreign direct investment simply does not enter many African countries. Massive foreign invesment inflows will enter sub-Saharan Africa if a part of it falls under the umbrella of the New International Territory, presented in Chapter 26.

No island of its size has the value of Manhattan in the United States. Manhattan is worth as much because of its infrastructure, its role as a global financial center, its access to top universities, and its potential to attract the most talented individuals in the United States and the world. The value of real estate assets is determined by many artificial, man-driven factors that can be easily incorporated to a new territory in sub-Saharan Africa. The appreciation of real estate assets can be carefully monitored to capture the upside financial returns and devote part of the gain to building infrastructure in continental Africa.

If we look at other processes, Hong Kong and Macao went back to China in 1997, after having belonged to the British Empire for over a hundred years. Singapore became independent in 1965. Nothing lasts forever; borders can and should be defined and redefined, when it is our duty to do so. The law, the statutes, and the constitutions of the world ought to be changed by consensus, if consensus is reached, and if technocrats are able to deliver the message of necessity and urgency.

A Goldmine

We need to rescue the poor. We need to raise funding to finance basic health care and education for the next 40 years, to reach Decemland in the World of 2050, a World of Cornucopia and Eutopia. We need to discover a goldmine. So far, developed countries are barely capable of reaching the 0.7 percent target. If a goldmine were discovered we could use the proceeds from the sale of gold to finance basic health care and education.

Gold is a scarce mineral with many uses. Therefore, it is an expensive mineral. If only I could use a wand and transform all the stones in my backyard into gold. If only I could rub Aladdin's lamp and make a wish to transform all the sand in the world into gold. Unfortunately if that were the case, gold would be abundant and cheap.

There is, however, a commodity that is abundant, the price of which is determined by intangible factors: land. Land is abundant. Land is everywhere. Yet the price of an acre or a hectare of land varies significantly from one location to another. An acre in Manhattan is not worth the same as an acre in Madagascar. An acre in the island of Mauritius is not worth the same as an acre in the Comoros.

I have found the wand that may solve the financing problem until the World of 2050 is reached. If only we could control at our will the intangible factors that drive the value of land. If only we could control the price drivers of real estate. The reader should understand that it is possible today to control at our will the price drivers of real estate. We need only a little political will, and a great deal of creativity and enthusiasm.

This chapter explains how to turn cheap land into a goldmine, into real estate that is wanted by real estate developers and investors throughout the world. I booked my piece of land in Decemland, the land of 10 percent. It is a beautiful lot in a land of harmony and understanding. Welcome to the new era of understanding where everything is possible. It is time to start the most creative undertaking of our lifetime. It is time to leave hatred and pessimism behind and look ahead with hope and inspiration. It is time to enter the Glorious Forty, which will lead us to the world of 2050. It is time to start writing the History of Tomorrow. I dare, therefore I am.

FOREIGN DIRECT INVESTMENT

The previous section explained how the drivers that set the price of real estate in the developing world can be influenced to trigger a sudden appreciation of the value of land. This section looks more closely at the rationale behind real estate appreciation.

Drivers of Foreign Direct Investment

Foreign direct investment (FDI) typically originates in developed markets and seeks to enter an emerging country for two purposes: looking for higher returns and diversifying an investment portfolio.

FDI is of two natures: short-term/speculative or long-term/sustainable. The former is detrimental for development and can do more harm than good. The latter should be emphasized over the former in the new capitalist paradigm. We need to find ways to discriminate between short-term and long-term investors. Long-term, sustainable investment should be the only survivor of the financial crisis of 2007 and 2008. Gone are the times of speculation in emerging markets. Whoever wants to speculate should do it where he or she belongs and harm those around him or her. This should and will change the nature of investing.

Figure 25.1 shows the flow of investments into developing countries between 1990 and 2006 in absolute numbers (left scale) and as a percentage of the total capital flows (right scale). Flows are further categorized into private/official. Net capital private flows peaked in 2007 at $929 billion and dropped to $466 billion in 2008, a drop of almost 50 percent (*Economist* 2009d).

What determines the destination of an investment? How does a portfolio manager decide where to invest? The portfolio manager looks at the binome risk and return. Risk and return are typically correlated. A higher return is associated with a higher risk of loss. Hedge funds were speculative investment vehicles with a higher expected return but also a higher expected loss.

Country Risk

How is the risk determined? When assessing whether or not to invest in a country, investment managers look at the three components of country risk: political risk, sovereign risk, and economic risk. All three are explained in detail hereafter.

Political Risk   Control Risks is a U.S.-based risk consultancy that specializes in the estimation of operational risk. The consultancy issues an annual ranking that ranks

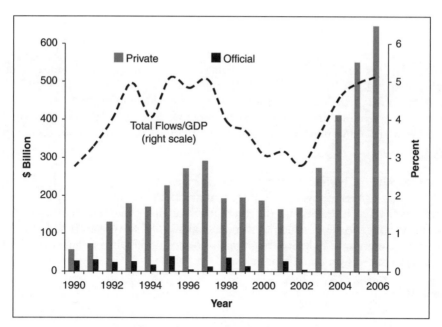

FIGURE 25.1 Net Capital Flows to Developing Countries, 1990–2006
Source: World Bank (2007a).

countries across four categories (political, security, terrorism, and travel) and assigns values of Insignificant, Low, Medium, High, or Extreme to each of them. Control Risks assesses all of the countries and territories in the world in their analysis.

Euromoney is a European consultancy that conducts a variety of analyses in economics and finance, including assessing the political risk of nation-states. The political risk categorization is part of the country risk rankings that Euromoney publishes in its magazine. The country risk ratings have four components: political risk, economic performance, debt indicators, and debt in default or rescheduled, each of which scores in a scale between 0 and 25. The maximum score for country risk is 100 (no risk) and the minimum score is 0 (total risk). As of March 2008, the top five performers were Luxembourg (99.88), Norway (97.47), Switzerland (96.21), Denmark (93.39), and Sweden (92.36). The bottom five performers were Afghanistan (5.45), North Korea (6.01), Iraq (6.11), Somalia (13.32), and the Marshall Islands (13.61).

Control Risks and Euromoney issue independent assessments of political risk that should be related if their estimations are reflective of political risk. As a result, both political risk methodologies are strongly correlated with an R-squared coefficient of 0.31.

When assessing political risk as part of their sovereign risk methodology, the rating agency Standard & Poor's looks at the following components (Standard & Poor's 2006): stability and legitimacy of political institutions, popular participation in political processes, orderliness of leadership succession, transparency in economic policy decisions and objectives, public security, and geopolitical risk.

Political Risk Services is a consultancy that has published the International Country Risk Guide (ICRG) for over 25 years. Political Risk Services determines a country's risk by looking into three different components: political risk, financial risk, and economic risk. In their assessment of political risk, they look at the following variables (Caouette, Altman, et al., 2008): government stability, socioeconomic conditions, investment profile, external conflict, corruption, military in politics, religious tensions, law and order, ethnic tensions, democratic accountability, and bureaucratic quality.

Political risk is the major component of country risk. In the absence of political risk an investment in a developing country can move forward. If political risk is considerable, it may undermine the investment or otherwise demand a return sufficiently high to discard it.

Sovereign Risk   The international rating agencies Moody's, Standard & Poor's, and Fitch Ratings issue sovereign ratings that are indicative of a country's sovereign risk. Sovereign risk is defined as "the risk that a sovereign entity repudiates, delays, or amends its obligations" (Caouette, Altman, et al., 2008). Sovereign risk is second in importance to political risk. Sovereign risk is looked upon when an investor decides to buy debt issued by a country's Central Bank.

Economic Risk   Economic risk is subject to the ups and downs of the local and global economies. As such, it is the risk component that cannot be diversified away. An investment manager can choose to invest in an emerging market with a lower political risk. When it comes to economic risk, the global economy oftentimes drives the recession or expansion of local economies and the investment manager will have a harder time choosing an emerging market that is less exposed to the ups and downs of the economy.

Global Investment Flows

Figure 25.1 showed the share of total capital flows that enter developing countries, a share typically capped at 5 percent. Where does the remaining 95 percent of international capital flows enter? The learned reader should know that international capital flows generally end up in stable environments with legal regimes that enforce property rights.

The consultancy KPMG studies the destination of global corporate capital flows in the five year period 2009 to 2014. The study, published in June 2008, reviews the "investment intentions of companies in 15 countries around the world" (KPMG 2008). The survey reviews where corporations of 15 developed countries intend to invest in the five-year period ending in 2014. Figure 25.2 shows the list of 30 countries that are expected to receive a share of the corporate capital flows in the five-year period ending in 2014.

Not surprisingly, a majority of the countries are either developed or emerging. The countries that are expected to receive a majority of the investment flows are the so-called BRIC countries (Brazil, Russia, India, and China). The only country in Africa that is in the list of 30 countries presented in Figure 25.3 is South Africa.

Figure 25.3 presents the most influential factors that a corporation considers from the point of view of the investment. Factors are rated in a scale of one (least important) to five (most important). Three of the five most important factors are directly related to political risk.

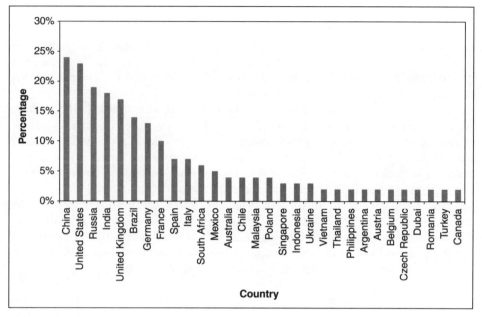

FIGURE 25.2 Percentage of Companies Expecting to Make a Significant Investment in these Countries in the Next Five Years
Source: KPMG (2008).

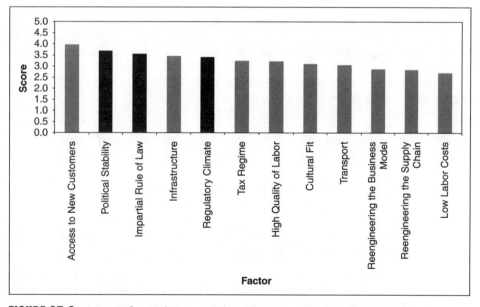

FIGURE 25.3 Most Influential Factors When Choosing a Country for Investment
Political Risk Factors are shaded in black
Source: KPMG (2008).

EXTREME MAKEOVER

How do I attract foreign direct investment if I am the president of Mozambique? Going democratic is an important aspect. Improving governance and transparency is even more important. Diminishing country risk and its three components may be, after all, the most important determinant of foreign direct investment.

Mozambique is a huge country about twice the size of California with half the population. Reducing country risk on all the territory over a short horizon is virtually impossible. If, as the president of Mozambique, I am unable to eliminate country risk throughout Mozambique, I could eventually improve the three components of country risk radically in a smaller part of the territory and then improve the three components gradually throughout the rest of the country.

How is radical improvement over a short horizon accomplished in a small part of a developing country's territory? There must be political will. There must be a phenomenal incentive for a developing country to embrace property rights and a stable legal environment, and guarantee peace and security in a selected area. These can be established in a small part of the territory to start with. Radical improvement may bring about significant economic growth to a small part of the country, which through spillovers would spread out to the rest of the country and beyond.

I hereby propose that one developing country in sub-Saharan Africa leases a small part of its territory to a newly created sovereign state, administered by a pre-agreed board of directors and a city administrator. This new sovereign state is the New International Territory (NIT), part of Decemland. Decemland and NIT are presented in Chapter 26.

NIT becomes the host of the institutions of the New Architecture of capitalism and welcomes the reformed Bretton Woods institutions. NIT is leased territory that reverts to the host country in a fifty-year period.

Positive Shock Therapy

For years, certain economists advocated shock therapy as a way to reform the economics of developing countries. It was a negative shock therapy because it reduced the per-capita income of the poor before improving it. Shock therapy can also be positive.

Positive shock therapy implies shortening the time frame it takes a country like Madagascar to become as prosperous as Mauritius from 40 to only 5 years. Improvement is not holistic or immediate, but localized and gradual. It focuses on radically improving a small part of a developing country to then spread out the improvement to the rest over a 40-year period.

The Example of Madagascar and Mauritius The small island-state of Mauritius has managed to transition from a mono-crop sugar economy to a modern and diversified economy that relies on the financial services and the tourism industry as its two prominent economic sectors. There is no doubt Mauritius benefited from the Preferential Trade Agreement with the European Union in the 1960s and the 1970s, as well as from the opportunities it exploits as an offshore financial center, also called a tax haven. This book proposes a comeback to the former and the elimination of the latter.

Mauritius now sells properties for foreign investors at four million dollars. The phenomenal transformation of land valuation in the country's recent history after its 1960 independence from the United Kingdom is an inspiration for the fundamental drivers behind real estate appreciation.

Abu Twalib Kasenally (DCL) is the minister of housing and lands of Mauritius. I talked to Abu on August 18, 2009 and again on November 13, 2009. Abu's vision is to have a "planned development of the territory of Mauritius where it will be pleasant to live and work, where business can thrive and prosper and where the natural beauty of the country will be preserved for the enjoyment of generations to come."[7] Abu's vision is an inspiration for the design and implementation of Decemland, the land of 10 percent, as presented in Chapter 26 and Chapter 27.

Generally speaking, Mauritius has become a stable democracy with Africa's best governance, strong institutions, and a rule of law that enforces property rights, among other things. On top of all of the above, Mauritius is located in one of the most beautiful enclaves in the world with coral reefs, clear water, and a buoyant luxury tourism industry with an educated workforce fluent in English and able to fulfill the needs of demanding customers.

Mauritius grants residence to foreigners who spend at least a half million dollars in real estate on the Indian Ocean island. Of each single unit investment, the government gets between $150,000 and $200,000 right away, including land transfer and registration costs (Devi 2008). Mauritius uses its appeal as an offshore financial center or tax haven and its privileged location to attract wealthy individuals from across the world, a majority of who come from Europe. The island-state boosts public revenue from the sale of real estate to foreign investors who then obtain residency.

Mauritius has gone from zero to one hundred kilometers an hour in slightly over 40 years. It has been able to minimize political risk and has enforced good governance and the rule of law. Do we need 40-plus years to render an isolated area in a developing country investment worthy? What would happen if we were able to shrink a 40-year process into a 5-year process?

The international rating agencies rate countries based on their ability to repay their domestic and foreign debts. Domestic debt is owed to national investors. Foreign debt is owed to foreign investors. Generally speaking, a country will issue debt to finance its deficit, the building of infrastructure or schools, or the purchase of weaponry, to name a few.

Fitch Ratings studies the correlation between a country's political stability and its sovereign rating (Fox and Kalema 2008). The correlation is strong and has an R-squared coefficient of 0.43, which means that a country's political stability and its rating are strongly related. Typically, a country with a low degree of political stability will have a low sovereign rating and vice versa. According to Fitch Ratings, the following factors would increase investment flows to Africa (Fox and Kalema 2008):

- Debt relief.
- Improved economic management (macro reforms, micro reforms to the business environment, thereby increasing public investment).
- High commodity prices.
- Improved political stability (fewer wars, more democratic transitions/elections).

TABLE 25.1   Average One-Year Rating Migration Rates, 1985–2002

Rating from	Rating to							
	Aaa	Aa	A	Baa	Ba	B	Caa-C	Default
Aaa	93.9%	6.1%	0.0%	0.0%	0.0%	0.0%	0.0%	0.0%
Aa	5.1%	92.5%	1.1%	0.0%	0.0%	0.0%	0.0%	0.0%
A	0.0%	2.7%	90.3%	6.2%	0.9%	0.0%	0.0%	0.0%
Baa	0.0%	0.0%	4.8%	79.6%	8.3%	0.3%	0.0%	0.0%
Ba	0.0%	0.0%	0.0%	3.7%	85.2%	10.0%	0.0%	0.7%
B	0.0%	0.0%	0.0%	0.0%	2.2%	87.7%	2.2%	4.0%
Caa-C	0.0%	0.0%	0.0%	0.0%	0.0%	100.0%	0.0%	0.0%

Source: Varma, Cantor, et al. (2003). © Moody's Investor Services, Inc. and/or its affiliates. Reprinted with permission. All Rights Reserved.

A country like Mauritius is rated Baa by Moody's (triple-B equivalent in the Standard & Poor's ratings scale). A country like Madagascar is rated single-B by Standard & Poor's. A triple-B rating denotes an adequate payment capacity, whereas a single-B rating is considered very speculative with significant credit risk (Caouette, Altman, et al., 2008).

How can we determine how long it would take Madagascar to become as investment-worthy as Mauritius? The two countries share the same geographic location and tourism potential, but Madagascar is much more unstable and poor. Madagascar should secure the same political stability, which is linked to governance, as that of Mauritius. Because political stability and sovereign ratings are strongly related, in order for Madagascar to be as politically stable as Mauritius, the world's fourth largest island would have to improve its rating from single-B to triple-B. Rating transition tables will give us the answer to the previous question. Table 25.1 shows the one-year transition probabilities by rating according to Moody's.

In order to transition from B to Baa, Madagascar would first have to transition from B to Ba and then from Ba to Baa. According to Table 25.1, the probability that a country will transition from B to Ba in one year is 2.2 percent. The probability that a country transitions from Ba to Baa in one year is 3.7 percent. A simple calculation would determine the probability of transition from B to Baa in a two-year period as the product of the two previous, or 0.0814 percent. This means that only one in 1,228 countries that are rated B would transition into Baa in a two-year period.

Figure 25.4 shows 10-year rating transitions for a handful of emerging economies, between the Asian crisis of 1997 and April 2007. Countries that lie along the diagonal line maintained the same sovereign rating. Countries above the diagonal line improved their rating. Countries below the diagonal line worsened their rating. A majority of the underperformers are Asian countries that were impacted by the Asian crisis. We can observe that no country improved its standings from a single-B to a triple-B sovereign rating, as was speculated in the previous paragraph.

There is only one entity that could transform inhabited land in an extreme poor country into land that is investment-worthy in a period as short as five years. The

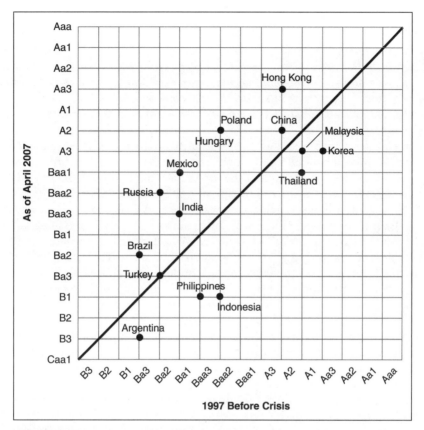

FIGURE 25.4 10-Year Rating Transitions
Source: © Moody's Investor Services, Inc. and/or its affiliates. Reprinted with permission. All Rights Reserved.

radical transformation would be part of the creation process of a New International Territory along with the 10 Islands of Peace presented in Chapter 26 and Chapter 27.

INVESTORS IN DECEMLAND

Decemland is the New International Territory (NIT) and its 10 overseas territories are called Islands of Peace. NIT is a 1,000 square kilometer territory divided into lots the size of one hectare (10,000 square meters). Each lot could be sold separately to individual investors. The target amount to be raised could finance The Monfort Plan. Who could invest? Why? This section describes a wealth of opportunities ahead for savvy investors who are looking to invest in the longer horizon.

Individuals

The Boston Consulting Group (BCG) analyzes "A Wealth of Opportunities in Turbulent Times" (Aerni, Juniac, et al., 2008). In the report, the American consulting firm looks at the world's wealth distribution and its geographic allocation and growth over time. Wealth is measured according to the total Assets under Management (AuM), defined by BCG as follows (Aerni, Juniac, et al., 2008):

> *AuM includes cash deposits, money market funds, listed securities held directly or indirectly through managed investments, and onshore and offshore assets. It excludes wealth attributed to investors' own businesses, residences, or luxury goods. Global wealth reflects total AuM across all households.*

Total wealth in the world as of year-end 2007 stood at $109.5 trillion.[8] The Monfort Plan would be looking at mobilizing a tenth of one percent of the world's global wealth to invest in the land of the future New International Territory. Global wealth had skyrocketed from $66.0 trillion in 2002 to $109.5 trillion in 2007. In 2007, global wealth by geographic area was allocated as follows (Aerni, Juniac, et al., 2008): United States ($39.2 trillion), Latin America ($3.1 trillion), Europe ($38.3 trillion), Middle East and Africa ($3.4 trillion), Asia-Pacific ($13.1 trillion) and Japan ($12.5 trillion). Wealth annual growth in 2006-2007 was led by Latin America and Asia-Pacific (13.1 percent), followed by the Middle East and Africa (8.6 percent), Europe (3.9 percent), North America (3.8 percent), and Japan (0.1 percent).

How is total wealth invested across asset classes? According to BCG, the percentage of total wealth invested in equities doubled between 2002 and 2007 (Aerni, Juniac, et al., 2008). The United States continued to be the region that invested the highest percentage in equities as of year-end 2007.

How has the financial crisis impacted the allocation of wealth? Money has fled from equities and the stock market into more conservative assets. Money has also left hedge funds and private equity funds and has invested in fixed income securities and commodities such as gold.

What opportunities lie ahead for real estate? Real estate has undergone times of bubbles in the United States, Ireland, the United Kingdom, and Spain, among other countries. Real estate used to be appealing in these countries, as it was in Japan in the 1980s. Real estate investors are now looking away from developed countries into the emerging world. Where is the next great investment opportunity? The reader may have discovered it in this chapter.

From an allocation perspective, financial theory recommends to diversify across a number of asset classes. An investor should always invest in real estate, equities, and fixed income securities, and then decide what percentage of his/her total wealth is allocated to each investment class. Thus, real estate will also be part of an investor's portfolio. Contrary to equities, real estate is a tangible asset, the value of which can be recovered if sold. Equities have more volatility and consequently, more uncertainty.

BCG defines the established wealthy as those having more than five million dollars in AuM. The number of established wealthy increased from 660,000 in 2002 to 1,330,000 in 2007, with an annual growth of 15.1 percent. As of year-end 2007, the number of established wealthy individuals by country of origin was the following (Aerni, Juniac, et al., 2008): United States (674,000), Japan (71,000), China (64,000), United Kingdom (54,000), Germany (45,000), Italy (44,000), France (34,000), Australia (26,000), Taiwan (26,000), and Saudi Arabia (24,000). If just one out of every thirteen established wealthy invested in NIT, The Monfort Plan could raise €100 billion[9] to finance the five-year venture that would help fulfill the Millennium Development Goals in sub-Saharan Africa by 2015. It is a matter of political will that can only be accomplished by means of the Weapons of Mass Persuasion.

Capgemini and Merrill Lynch issue a yearly *World Wealth Report* (Capgemini and Lynch, 2009). The 2009 report notes, "At the end of 2008, the world's population of high net worth individuals (HNWI) was down 14.9 percent from the year before, while their wealth had dropped 19.5 percent." The dramatic loss of wealth impacted to a larger extent the ultra high net worth individuals (Ultra-HNWI). HNWI have investable assets of one million dollars or more, excluding primary residence. Ultra-HNWI have more than $30 million. For the French consultancy, "The sharp decline in the number of Ultra-HNWI globally largely resulted from that group's partiality for more aggressive products, which tend to deliver greater-than average returns in good times, but delivered hefty losses in 2008." The United States and the United Kingdom lost a larger share of their HNWI in the list of 12 countries having more HNWI (Capgemini and Lynch 2009). The yearly loss of HNWI was topped by the United Kingdom (–26.2 percent), followed by Canada (–24.2 percent), Australia (–23.6 percent), Spain (–21.1 percent), Italy (–20.7 percent), United States (-18.5 percent), Switzerland (–12.7 percent), France (–12.6 percent), China (–11.8 percent), Japan (–9.9 percent), Brazil (–8.3 percent), and Germany (–2.7 percent).

The more aggressive products often refer to hedge funds and private equity funds such as the ones managed by Bernard Madoff or Allen Stanford, which defaulted, accused of having conducted Ponzi schemes in the first half of 2009. More aggressive products were also structured products that invested in subprime collateral, several of which have gone bankrupt since Bear Stearns announced the default of two of its hedge funds that had heavily invested in subprime collateral in July 2007. The lessons learned stress the need to shift the focus to more solid, long-term investments. A plethora of investment opportunities lie ahead for savvy, sustainable, and long-term investors who are also Decompliant (as was explained in Chapter 24).

Sovereign Wealth Funds

According to Lee Hundson Teslik of the Council on Foreign Relations, Sovereign Wealth Funds (SWFs) controlled as much as $3 trillion as of 2008 (Teslik 2008), an amount that could spike up to $12 trillion in 2012. Sovereign wealth funds would control more money than hedge funds ($1.5 trillion), but still fall well below pension funds and endowments ($53 trillion).

SWFs are likely to invest in the long term. Many SWFs in resource-rich countries increased their principal invested in the commodities boom of 2007 and 2008 and reinvested the proceeds of oil and other commodities, taking stakes in private equity firms (Blackstone) or the financial sector on the verge of the financial crisis of 2008.

Robert Zoellick, who succeeded Paul Wolwofitz as president of the World Bank in 2007, suggested that sovereign wealth funds invest 1 percent of their principal in Africa. A simple calculation determines that 1 percent of the three trillion dollars outstanding is 30 billion dollars. Zoellick's advice is not a requirement, however. Sovereign wealth funds have no predetermined investment constraints and invest as they wish when opportunity arises. Why should they be forced to invest in a world where private equity funds and hedge funds have invested as they've seen fit, thereby contributing to the collapse of the financial markets in 2007 and 2008? I believe in global rules, but global rules need to apply to all investment vehicles and not only sovereign wealth funds.

Zoellick commented in April 2008, "If we can create investment platforms for equity investments in Africa, everybody benefits" (Weisman 2008). I fully agree with Zoellick. We now have to create great investment opportunities and Africa will attract significant foreign investment.

In January 2008 alone, SWFs of the developing world bought a $6.6 billion stake in Merrill Lynch and a $14.5 billion stake in Citigroup. Overall financial institutions of the United States and Europe received a total of $69 billion from sovereign wealth funds in the last 10 months of 2007 (*Economist* 2008).

The top 10 sovereign wealth funds as of year-end 2007 were as follows (*Economist* 2008): Abu Dhabi Investment Authority (United Arab Emirates, $875 billion), Government Pension Fund (Norway, $380 billion), GIC (Singapore, $330 billion), Reserve Fund for Future Generations (Kuwait, $250 billion), China Investment Corporation (China, $200 billion), Temasek Holdings (Singapore, $159 billion), Oil Reserve Fund (Libya, $50 billion), Qatar Investment Authority (Qatar, $50 billion), Fond de Regulation des Recettes (Algeria, $42 billion), and Alaska Permanent Fund Corporation (United States, $38 billion).

Pension Funds

Pension funds are the most common savings instrument for a majority of middle-class Americans and Europeans. Pension funds are conservative instruments of considerable size that diversify their investments wisely between equities and fixed income and between mature and emerging markets. **Stephen Blank** (DCL) is senior fellow in finance at the Urban Land Institute (ULI). I met Stephen for an early breakfast on May 15, 2009, at Michael's in New York City. What percentage of pension fund investments is allocated to real estate? Stephen points out[10] that for those large funds that invest in real estate, the average allocation as of year-end 2008 was 10.71 percent, up from 9.8 percent the prior year. The vast majority of pension funds have no real estate, however. More than 95 percent of all real estate held by pension, foundation, and endowment funds is controlled by fewer than 1,500 funds. The top 600 control more than 90 percent, the top 300, more than 80 percent. New allocations to real estate are expected to be $28 billion in 2009, the lowest in more than 10 years, which does not include uncalled commitments.

What percentage of pension fund real estate investments is allocated to emerging markets? According to Stephen, most do not set specific targets for emerging markets. About 12 percent of current real estate investments are offshore, which includes large emerging markets like India and China. Very little has been allocated to smaller emerging markets. Forty-three percent of ULI's annual plan sponsor survey respondents have made investments in China, 33 percent in India, 24 percent in the emerging markets of Eastern Europe, 27 percent in Central Europe, and 6 percent in Russia. An additional 32 percent have made investments in Mexico, 16 percent in Brazil, and 6 percent in Central America. Three percent have made investments in Africa, and an additional 3 percent have made investments in the Middle East.

What percentage of pension fund real estate investments is allocated to opportunistic real estate strategies? Stephen points out that 17 percent of existing portfolios were characterized as opportunistic, versus a target of 21 percent.

PART

Six

Decemland

Decemland is the land of 10 percent. Decemland consists of the New International Territory along with 10 Islands of Peace throughout the world, that would be considered Decemland's 10 overseas territories.

The New Institutions of the New Architecture of capitalism must be based in the developing world. The New International Territory (NIT) will host the New Institutions of a redefined capitalism, and will welcome the reformed Bretton Woods institutions. NIT is a 1,000-square-kilometer new sovereign nation that a developing country will host in leased territory, slated to revert to the developing nation after a period of 50 years.

The 10 Islands of Peace are Decemland's overseas territories. The 10 Islands of Peace will be leased from developing countries. The valuation methodology to determine how much an island is worth is presented. The determination of the value of an island is based on the fair valuation of the 50-year lease between Decemland and the developing countries that are willing to lease one or several of their islands.

The Race of the Century will determine which of ACHE's six Founding Members hosts NIT during a 50-year period. (ACHE was presented in Chapter 19.) The Race of the Century finds inspiration in similar competitive processes that lead to the selection of a candidate country (the World Cup) or a candidate city (the Olympic Games), among a pool of preselected countries.

The Monfort List is a pool of talent from which the future team of Expert Dreamers will be hired. The Monfort Team becomes the best team of Expert Dreamers that has ever served the public interest, moving the world on a new path to sustainability.

Finally, the new international architecture for a new economic paradigm that embraces the poor and the environment is introduced. The New Architecture starts the Era of Sustainability and the Glorious Forty that will lead to the World of 2050.

Artwork by Mike Luckovich.

CHAPTER 26

The New International Territory

So come with me, where dreams are born, and time is never planned. Just think of happy things, and your heart will fly on wings, forever, in Never Never Land!

—Peter Pan

Decemland is a land where dreams come true. We will build the world's Neverland. It is the land of Eutopia and Cornucopia, where people love and dream. We all build our Neverlands in life. We take care of our friends and families and build a world of trust and love that becomes our own social fabric. It is time to become men and women of stature; it is time to start building the world's Neverland, a land of opportunity that becomes the headquarters of the institutions that make up the New Architecture of Capitalism.

The orthodox thinkers who defend the old paradigms and are reluctant to believe that a paradigm shift is around the corner will continue to live in the Prison of Thought they have built around themselves. The Pirates of Heartless Capitalism who deny the existence of a new world of Eutopia and Cornucopia will perpetuate a life in a monodimensional world that emphasizes the maximization of economic profit and forsakes human dignity and environmental sustainability.

There is a Decemland that belongs to us all. It is the Neverland of Global Redistribution and Global Public Goods. It is the Neverland of which we have all dreamt. It is the aggregation of each of our Neverlands. It is a collective effort that will unite North and South, West and East. It is the new land of opportunity and home of the future World Government.

We must start the Journey of our Lifetime. We must start to build the world of 2050, a world of no borders and no diplomacy. I discovered the world's Neverland. Decemland will not die but remain alive; it will persist, and eventually, it will host the future generations who will inhabit this planet that does not belong to us, of which we are only temporary dwellers.

Six countries in sub-Saharan Africa will participate in The Race of the Century. The winner of the race will host the New International Territory. Decemland consists of the New International Territory and 10 Islands of Peace, presented in Chapter 27. I have discovered the Expert Dreamers that will help build the world's Neverland, those who fought and will continue to fight the great evils of our time, and whose combined strength will defeat the Pirates of Heartless Capitalism. The

Expert Dreamers will show the orthodox thinkers another world is possible if we believe that we are the owners of our fate, and the drivers of our own destiny; we build our own future.

It is time to start building the world's Neverland. I hear the call of the society of the future who inhabits the World of 2050. They shout that a final destination awaits us. We will depart on the Journey of our Lifetime and look ahead. I promise to always look ahead and never stop. I promise to always look ahead and never give up.

I miss the world's Neverland. I miss Decemland, the land of 10 percent, of which I once was an inhabitant. Let's all become children who dream of growing up in a new world of optimism that is not anchored in the fears of the pitfalls of times that were before but will never be again. Let's all become children who dream of growing up in a new world of optimism that is not based in times of devastation and atrocities, or of world wars that left us with an architecture that is no longer able to withstand the challenges of our time.

I woke up and decided to dream. I woke up and decided to imagine the world's Neverland. I found the new land of opportunity. I found Decemland and made a promise, and I shall never stop this journey of no return.

THE LAND OF TEN PERCENT

The United Nations (UN) is headquartered on the east side of Manhattan in New York City. The building emerged in 1952 on land donated by John D. Rockefeller Junior. The Rockefeller family donated six blocks (eighteen acres) of land on Manhattan's east side that at the time were worth $8.5 million. The site is considered international territory. What is exactly international territory in the context of the United Nations? The UN territory would be similar to that of Antarctica or international waters and would not be under the jurisdiction of any nation-state.

The art of building up and administering international territories is called International Territorial Administration (ITA). ITA has been common in war-torn countries in post-war environments. It was the case of Iraq under the administration of Paul Bremer or Kosovo under the administration of the European Union. ITA has never been challenged to take place in a pre-determined, pre-agreed manner. How would a New International Territory be managed? Who would be responsible for its administration? Discover the new land of opportunity at http://Decemland.com.

The Kingdom of Decemland is the land of 10 percent. Decemland consists of the New International Territory (NIT) along with the 10 Islands of Peace. NIT is a 1,000 square kilometer new sovereign nation situated within the borders of one of ACHE's six Founding Members. The process that determines where NIT will be finally based is described in Chapter 28 and is called The Race of the Century. The 10 Islands of Peace are islands that belong to developing nations that are willing to lease them to Decemland voluntarily over a 50-year period.

There can only be one King of Decemland, the land of 10 percent. Nelson Mandela will be appointed the first King of Decemland, the land of 10 percent. Subsequent kings and queens of Decemland will have to be accomplished individuals from the developing world with a strong track record in the fight against the great evils of our time.

NIT becomes the headquarters of the New Institutions of a redefined capitalism. The New Institutions have been presented throughout this book and include The New Institution, the Decemfund, the Bank for the Poor and the Yunus-Fund. NIT also welcomes the reformed Bretton Woods Institutions if political consensus to move them out of Geneva, New York City, and Washington, DC is achieved.

The 10 Islands of Peace are spread throughout the world and are the settlement of the new Harmless Armed Forces that will devote their best efforts to tackle emergency relief and natural catastrophes, mitigating the devastation of natural disasters exacerbated by climate change.

THE LANDSCAPE OF THE NEW INTERNATIONAL TERRITORY

The New International Territory (NIT) was presented in Chapter 25 as an investment opportunity. NIT has an area of 1,000 square kilometers that could be sold to investors in lots of one hectare. Table 26.1 compares Singapore and Hong Kong and gives an idea of the size of successful territories in Asia that obtained independence (Singapore) or reverted back to China (Hong Kong) after the colonial era.

In 1898, Britain signed the 99-year lease of an island by the name of Lantau and the adjacent territories. The ensemble became known as the New Territories. Whereas Hong Kong was transferred to the British, the Lantau Island was leased.

Colin Lewis (ECO) is a professor of economic history at the London School of Economics. I meet Colin every time I am in London. According to Colin, "Technically the United Kingdom was not obliged to return Hong Kong to China at the end of the Patten governorship, only the New Territories and the islands."

Where should NIT be based? The answer has to incorporate a variety of factors. NIT should be based in a poor area so that its economic impact lifts as many poor out of poverty as possible. NIT also has to be based in an area with low political risk so that it becomes a magnet for foreign direct investment.

A Risk Assessment

Sub-Saharan Africa remains the most desolated region in the world in terms of the indicators that measure extreme poverty. It is in sub-Saharan Africa that the HIV/AIDS pandemic has hit hard. It is in sub-Saharan Africa that armed conflicts

TABLE 26.1 Territory Comparison

Territory Comparison	Singapore	Hong Kong
Area (km²)	683	1,042
Population (million)	4.61	7.02
Population density	6,749	6,735
GDP (billion)	$244	$318
Per capita income	$52,900	$45,300
Labor Force (million)	3.67	2.81

Data Source: CIA Factbook (2009).

cause widespread devastation. It is in sub-Saharan Africa that the Millennium Development Goals are unlikely to be accomplished.

It is natural to look at sub-Saharan Africa when the goal is the eradication of extreme poverty. It is the natural place to start. If success is accomplished in sub-Saharan Africa, the same antidote against poverty could then be delivered to other extreme poor countries in the Caribbean (Haiti, Nicaragua, Honduras, Salvador . . .) and South Asia (Laos, Bangladesh, Cambodia . . .).

What would be the best location to host the New International Territory? There are three factors that drive NIT's location: its strategic position, how appealing it would be for investors, and what kind of impact it would have on the eradication of extreme poverty in the surrounding areas.

Choosing sub-Saharan Africa is only the first step. The first decision aims at establishing the new World Headquarters in an extreme poor country where the economic impact could be phenomenal. The world, in particular the extreme poor, needs a positive shock therapy that helps them to once and for all leave extreme poverty behind. The extreme poor need incentives to move ahead and escape the poverty trap. These incentives ought to be driven by creativity and enthusiasm.

Chapter 19 presented the rationale behind choosing six countries in the southern cone of Africa that will become ACHE's Founding Members. The presence of South Africa as a driver of economic growth could be an additional reason for the surrounding countries to move ahead faster than expected if a first stimulus is introduced.

The handful of countries proposed were five countries that have previously shown their willingness to participate in an ex-ante conditional aid scheme through their involvement in the Millennium Challenge Corporation, headed by Ambassador John Danilovich between 2005 and 2009, namely: Lesotho, Madagascar, Mozambique, Namibia, and Tanzania. These five countries are in the same geographic area. The addition of Botswana could only benefit the initial six-country union because of Botswana's good governance and high per-capita income. In the five-plus-one countries involved in the first pilot of The Monfort Plan, Chinese investment remains relatively low. China has entered Africa with the sort of heartless capitalism presented in Chapter 17. In particular, it is heavily present in Angola, Nigeria, Sudan, and Zimbabwe.

Three additional countries, which are in the same geography as the five-plus-one initial countries, could become the Runners Up in a second expansion of the first pilot: Malawi, Swaziland, and Zambia. The analysis throughout this chapter focuses on these nine countries divided into ACHE's six Founding Members and the three Runners Up. All nine countries could participate in The Race of the Century. In order to qualify, the three Runners Up would have to demonstrate their willingness and commitment to work toward becoming Monfortable, as explained in Chapter 20.

How well do the six Founding Members plus three Runners Up rank in terms of political risk vis-à-vis other sub-Saharan African nations? Figure 26.1 shows a ranking of political risk for countries in sub-Saharan Africa, where 100 percent represents zero risk and 0 percent represents maximum risk. Each country's score is the simple average of the political risk scores of Control Risks and Euromoney respectively, as described in Chapter 25. Five of the six Founding Members are among the top nine least risky countries in sub-Saharan Africa. Madagascar and the three Runners Up lag behind.

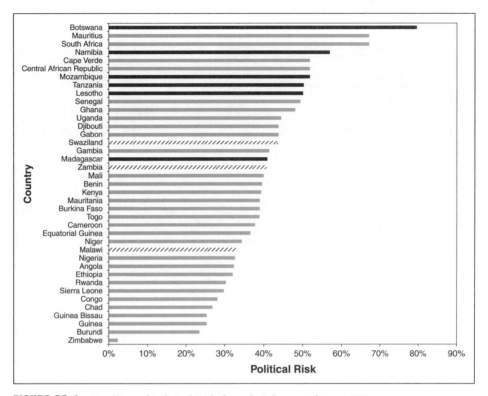

FIGURE 26.1   Ranking of Political Risk for sub-Saharan Africa, 2008
Note: Founding members shaded in black. Runners-up shaded in diagonal stripes.
Source: Control Risks and Euromoney (2008).

From the perspective of country risk and political risk, an investor would decide to invest in five out of six of the Founding Members before investing in many other sub-Saharan African countries. Why is it important to assess countries from a political risk point of view? Only a country with a low political risk will be in a position to attract foreign direct investment of the nature needed to finance The Monfort Plan. Chapter 25 explained why investing in the New International Territory could be an appealing investment opportunity from a real-estate perspective.

What other criteria can be assessed to determine NIT's ideal location? Peace, poverty, and youth are three additional indicators that could help assess the winner of The Race of the Century, which will host Decemland.

Peace Index

Figure 26.2 shows countries in sub-Saharan Africa sorted by their Peace Index score. Four of the six Founding Members rank among the top six of sub-Saharan Africa's most peaceful countries. The United States ranks right below Cameroon, which means that all Founding Members are more peaceful than the United States.[1] The southern cone of Africa, with the exception of South Africa and Zimbabwe, is the most peaceful geographic area in the world outside Western Europe and the southern cone of Latin America (Chile, Argentina, and Uruguay).

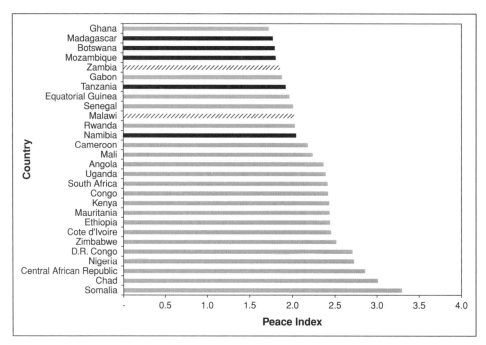

FIGURE 26.2   Peace Index for sub-Saharan Africa, 2007
Note: Founding members shaded in black. Runners-up shaded in diagonal stripes.
Source: Economist Intelligence Unit (2008).

Poverty and Youth

The poverty dimension is crucial. How is poverty assessed? There are many variables that measure poverty. Figure 26.3 looks at the percentage of a country's population who live under the poverty line (less than one dollar a day) and the percentage of a country's population under 15 years old, for the world and sub-Saharan Africa. Both variables are positively correlated. The higher the percentage of people who live under the poverty line, the higher the percentage of young over the total population would be, and vice versa.

Why is it important to focus the efforts of The Monfort Plan in countries where a majority of the population lives under the poverty line but also where a majority of the population is young? African youth are the future of the continent and the future of the planet. They should be able to grow healthy and educated to contribute to Africa's renaissance and reverse the pattern of migration flows from outgoing to incoming. Moreover, 80 percent of the civil conflicts that broke out after the 1960s "took place in countries where at least 60 percent of the population was under 30" (Mahajan 2008). Investing in sub-Saharan Africa will also reduce the likelihood of armed conflict.

According to the top part of Figure 26.3, a majority of the world's poor countries are in this region of Africa. The bottom part of Figure 26.3 shows where the Founding Members and the Runners Up stand compared to their sub-Saharan African

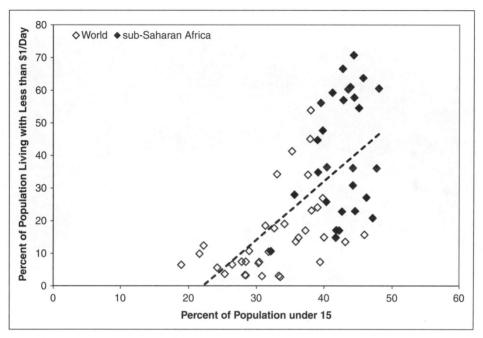

FIGURE 26.3   Poverty and Youth in the World and sub-Saharan Africa, 2005
Data Source: UNDP (2009).

counterparties. Three of the countries (Madagascar, Mozambique, and Tanzania) are among the poorest and most populated countries in sub-Saharan Africa. Botswana and Namibia are better off but face two fundamental constraints: (1) extreme inequality and (2) two of the highest HIV/AIDS infection rates in the world, which are decimating the population. Furthermore, Botswana and Namibia contribute with a small share of the population to the overall population of the six Founding Members.

Artwork by Mike Luckovich.

CHAPTER 27

Islands of Peace

What may in fact be a utopian dream is that the development of cosmopolitan tolerance and mutual respect among sovereign and independent nations, subject to no higher political authority than themselves, will forever spare human civilization from a nuclear war for which the weapons are ready and waiting.

—James A. Yunker, *On the Practicality and Advisability of Federal World Government*

There are thousands of islands in the world, many of them empty or relatively unpopulated. They can be mobilized. They must be mobilized. Decemland consists of the New International Territory along with the 10 Islands of Peace. The Monfort Plan proposes that willing developing countries lease 10 islands on a voluntary basis for a 50-year lease. How is the valuation of an island conducted? What are the requirements to qualify as an island of peace? This chapter provides answers to the questions above.

Indonesia has 17,508 islands, of which only 6,000 are inhabited. The Philippines has 7,107 islands. Vanuatu has 80 islands, of which 65 are inhabited. The list goes on. Whereas it is easy to control the political risk and stability of a small island surrounded by water, it is not easy to control these forces on a mainland territory of many developing countries.

The New International Territory could expand and become a de facto country with overseas territories over the course of the following 50 years. Based in sub-Saharan Africa, NIT could have satellite territories throughout the world based on islands leased from developing nations. A handful of the larger unpopulated islands of the Philippines, Indonesia, Papua New Guinea, Vanuatu, or the Solomon Islands, to name a few, could become international territory under the jurisdiction of a new sovereign nation. They would fall under the umbrella of a stable entity able to guarantee security and stability, and to enforce property rights and a legal environment. The islands would become islands of peace and stability, as presented in the next subsection. Any revenues raised through the commercial exploitation of the islands (real estate development, taxation revenue from property taxes, logistics, harbors and ports, distribution centers, etc.) would help finance health care and education in the countries that accept to lease them. Welcome to the new havens of a loving capitalism where pirates are not welcome.

WHAT ARE ISLANDS OF PEACE?

The Islands of Peace are islands of peace and stability, guaranteed by the Harmless Armed Forces presented in the next section. The Islands of Peace would be home to the world's largest Harmless Armed Forces exclusively devoted to emergency relief. The Harmless Armed Forces would be based closer to where they are needed—in the Caribbean, in the Pacific, and in the Indian Ocean.

A new military alliance would sign a cooperation agreement between the Harmless Armed Forces and the developing countries that decide to lease one of their islands. The Harmless Armed Forces would not only intervene in case of natural and human emergencies. They would also secure peace and stability in the area, minimizing political risk and hence attracting foreign direct investment. Extreme makeover is thus accomplished, which could spread to other parts of the area where the Islands of Peace are located, creating a spillover effect, with which economists are very familiar. This is positive shock therapy.

NATO was the resulting military alliance in the aftermath of World War II. NATO fought the expansion of Soviet communism. We are in desperate need of new military alliances designed to fight the great evils of our time. It is time to use the military muscle appropriately. It is time to help those in desperate need.

ISLAND VALUATION

Island valuation is important because it determines a price tag for an island. Knowing how much an island is worth is an input that has to be used to structure a fair leasing agreement with a developing country.

There are two techniques to determine the potential value of the real estate in a developing country, provided the real estate transitions into a developed economy for a period of 50 to 100 years. The first is to look at former or current overseas territories of Britain, such as Hong Kong or Macao. The valuation of these territories is only a proxy for how much a New Territory in a developing country could be worth if leased temporarily. The second is to look at current transactions of real estate. Welcome to the World of Private Islands.

On February 28, 2008, I contacted four private island brokers:

1. Doug Ingersoll of Caribbean Island Brokers introduced me to the second broker who appraised Marlon Brando's island.
2. Brett Reynolds of FMV helped appraise Marlon Brando's island when it was sold.
3. John Christie of H.G. Christie, a broker of islands in the Bahamas, provided useful information.
4. Farhad Vladi of Vladi Private Islands GmbH participated in the appraisal of the famous Skorpios Island.

How can we determine the value of an island of peace? The value is fundamental to signing a leasing contract with the host country for a 50-year period. According to

Ingersoll, "The value of an island is based on many different factors," including size, location, elevation, vegetation, distance to mainland and other islands, surrounding water quality, and coral/sea life. Ingersoll adds, "When you get to value a very large island, you will need to break it down to its parts." There are three fundamental questions to determine the value of a larger island: (1) does the property have improvements? (2) does the property produce income? and (3) what is the ownership structure?

I asked Ingersoll an obvious question: *What do academic papers have to say on island valuation?* According to Ingersoll, there may not be any. The academic methodology for valuing island properties has not been developed because it has not been needed. Financial innovation could play a fundamental role in this scenario and positively impact the worse off, contrary to the subprime financial crisis. Ingersoll reckons, "The business is way too small of a niche to have many experts in the field." Things may change going forward.

Brett Reynolds is a senior associate at FMV Opinions Inc., a firm based in Irvine (California) that does valuation and financial advisory. For Reynolds, the value of the island can be determined through a discounted cash-flow analysis, where a projection of the potential revenue stream and expenses is undertaken.

I call all developing countries with unpopulated or scarcely populated islands. I call on all developing countries to lease one of their islands to Decemland for a period of 50 to 100 years. The islands will revert to the host country after the leasing period has expired.

John Christie is the vice president of H.G. Christie, The Bahamas' Largest Property Showcase. I sent Christie the following inquiry on May 25, 2008:

The island of Skorpios was valued at $350 million. This might be the largest island ever valued. The other big island would be Marlon Brando's. The island I am looking to value is much larger, but I wonder if the fundamentals used to value Skorpios would also apply to the island I am looking at.

For Christie, "The fundamentals would be the same although different areas have different prices for the islands," concluding that the fundamentals to value a small island like Skorpios or Marlon Brando's island should also apply to the valuation of a large island.

Farhad Vladi (DCL) greets his email messages with a *Welcome to the World of Private Islands*. I spoke with Farhad on November 24, 2009. Vladi Private Islands GmbH is based in Frankfurt. For Farhad, evaluating and appraising islands is similar to appraising paintings. There are three methods for appraising the value of an island according to Farhad:

1. Use comparables from the area or from other countries with the same political and climate conditions.
2. Compare island prices with prices of the real estate opposite the island and interpolate from there.
3. Start from the cost base of the present owner and add interest or the appreciation of real estate in that same wider area.

LEASE AN ISLAND

Decemland consists of NIT along with 10 overseas territories: the 10 Islands of Peace.[1] In order to qualify as an Island of Peace, an island must fulfill the following four requirements:

1. Be relatively large.
2. Be in a developing country.
3. Have a low population density.
4. Must not be ranked as one of the 111 most touristic islands according to National Geographic.

World Islands Info (WII) is the preeminent source for island information. WII ranks an island according to its area and provides additional data. National Geographic ranked the 111 most touristic islands in the world in 2007. Out of the 100 largest islands in the world, only thirteen are featured in National Geographic's ranking of most touristic islands: Puerto Rico, Jamaica, Sicily, Hawaii, Cyprus, Palawan, Crete, Sardinia, Viti Levu, Corsica, Cape Breton Island, Tasmania, and Iceland. Six of the 10 potential Islands of Peace are among the 100 largest in the world, belong to a developing country, and have areas in the range of 10,000 to 15,000 square kilometers and population densities of between 5 and 15 inhabitants per square kilometer. Three of these six potential Islands of Peace are in Indonesia and three are in Papua New Guinea. Four additional islands that could be considered are Boa Vista (Cape Verde), Espiritu Santo (Vanuatu), Juventud (Cuba), and Socotra (Yemen). Figure 27.1 summarizes the population density and area of the 10 potential Islands of Peace.

The Local Population

Leasing foreign territory and switching its sovereignty during a 50-year period raises one question mark immediately. What would happen with the local population? The answer is provided by the Diego Garcia lease agreement between the United Kingdom and the United States.

Diego Garcia is a British territory in the Indian Ocean about 1,000 miles south of the Indian coast. Discovered by the Portuguese in the sixteenth century, the island is part of the Chagos Archipelago and a strategic location in the very center of the Indian Ocean. Diego Garcia is today part of the British Indian Ocean Territory, constituted in 1965 from territory that formerly belonged to Mauritius and the Seychelles.

The United Kingdom and the United States signed a lease agreement that expires in 2016, whereby the United States would use Diego Garcia exclusively for military purposes. The negotiations to lease the island concluded in 1968 with a treaty ratified by Britain called the Exchange of Notes (Global Security 2005). The United Kingdom moved the 2,500 indigenous populations (the Chagossians) out of Diego Garcia during the 1960s and the 1970s to Mauritius and the Seychelles. This move was illicit under the UN Charter and international law.

Olivier Bancoult is the chairman of the Chagos Refugees Group. I phoned Bancoult on July 3, 2009. Bancoult points out that Diego Garcia belongs to an

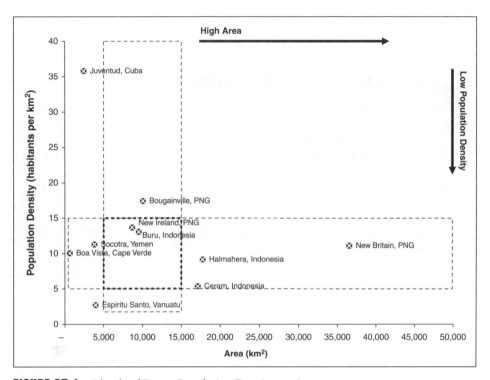

FIGURE 27.1   Islands of Peace, Population Density vs. Area
PNG = Papua New Guinea.
Data Source: World Islands Info and National Geographic (2009).

archipelago that counts as many as 65 islands, of which Diego Garcia is the largest. Peros Banhos and Boddam Salomon were two other islands of the archipelago from which the Chagossians were removed.

In 1998, a British court ruled in favor of the Chagossians and acknowledged their right to return to Diego Garcia, which would not happen until 2016 and unless the United States does not renew the lease agreement, an unlikely move given the strategic position of Diego Garcia in the global war on terror. What did the Chagossians get in exchange? Each Chagossian received a compensation payment, the right to claim British nationality, and the right, at least on paper, to return home.

Ted Morris is a member of the U.S. Air Force as a distinguished graduate of the Reserve Officer Training Corps, who flew as an aircraft commander and instructor pilot in various transport aircraft, and served in various command and staff positions, including one on Diego Garcia. Morris notes, "In 2003, British courts ruled that the Chagossians had received adequate compensation and were entitled to no further compensation," and concludes, "In 2008, the House of Lords of Great Britain[2] ruled that the Chagossians have no right to return to the islands."

According to Peter H. Sand of the Institute of International Law, "The U.S. and U.K. governments have evaded accountability by way of a persistent 'black hole' strategy, contending that some national laws and international treaties for the protection of human rights and the environment do not apply to the island—a position confirmed by a controversial appellate judgment of the House of Lords in October 2008, essentially relying on prerogative colonial law" (Sand 2009).

The Purchase of Property on an Island of Peace

A New International Territory needs a New Governor. **ANDREW SEATON** (DCL) is and has been the British consul general of Hong Kong since 2003. I talked to Andrew on May 28, 2009. Andrew took over for Lord Chris Patten, who was the U.K. governor of Hong Kong from 1992 until the former colony reverted back to China in 1997. Andrew was deputy consul general and trade counselor from 1995 to 2000.

During our conversation Andrew referred to the paradigm one country two systems that has allowed Hong Kong to keep its appeal after reverting back to China. This particular feature would need to be replicated in each of the 10 Islands of Peace and the New International Territory.

Immigration of Foreigners to an Island of Peace

A New International Territory needs an accomplished Immigration Minister. **Martin Brewer** (DCL) is the former chief immigration officer of Bermuda. I phoned Martin on October 21, 2008. About a third of Bermuda's 60,000 inhabitants are foreign. Bermuda constitutes an interesting model that combines a high per-capita foreign population with a lower per-capita local population.

Martin points out that Bermuda's work-permit policies are crucial to understanding the island's successful immigration model. The purpose of the work-permit policies is described by the Bermudian Government[3] as follows:

> *This Government has worked hard to strike the right balance between the understandable desire of business to operate with a minimum of regulatory control and the legitimate and proper aspirations of Bermudians to participate fully in the economy of their island home.*

HARMLESS ARMED FORCES

SOFAs in the United States

The United States armed forces are subject to the U.S. legislation and to a legal code known as Status of Forces Agreement (SOFA). The United States signs individual SOFAs with each of the countries where its troops are present. According to Global Security,[4] a SOFA "sets forth rights and responsibilities between the United States and the host government on such matters as criminal and civil jurisdiction, the wearing of the uniform, the carrying of arms, tax and customs relief, entry and exit of personnel and property, and resolving damage claims."

On December 9, 2008, I met Ambassador **JACKSON McDONALD** (DCA) at the U.S. Department of State in Washington, DC. At the time, Ambassador McDonald was the senior advisor for security negotiations at the Bureau of Political-Military Affairs, and he worked for the U.S. Department of State. In other words, he was in charge of signing SOFAs with the authorities of the countries in which the United States armed forces are based. I appreciated Jackson's advice regarding the countries of which he was ambassador prior to returning to DC, including his insightful views on West Africa.

SOFAs in the European Union

Aurel Sari is a lecturer in law at the University of Exeter. Sari authored a paper called "The EU Status of Forces Agreement: Change and Continuity in the Law of Visiting Forces." When I asked Sari for an electronic version of the paper, he asked about the connection of The Monfort Plan with the EU Status of Forces Agreement. On April 10, 2009, I replied as follows:

> *I propose a concept called "Islands of Peace" in which developing countries would "lease" islands to a newly established international territory that I call Decemland. Armed forces would be established on the islands with two purposes: emergency and disaster relief.*

According to Sari, the scope of application of an EU-SOFA is determined by the Petersberg tasks, namely "humanitarian and rescue tasks, peace-keeping tasks and tasks of combat forces in crisis management, including peacemaking." More precisely, humanitarian tasks are defined as "operations responding to humanitarian emergencies caused by international crises or natural catastrophes, and may include the protection of humanitarian convoys by military escorts or landmine clearance operations" (Sari 2007).

Military Spending

World governments allocate a percentage of their budgets to military spending. The allocation is legitimate if governments represent their citizens. In the world of noncooperation, military might is important to defend nations' strategic interests and integrity. Some of the poorer nations of the world, which are ruled by dictators or have not elected their ruling elite democratically, spend overwhelmingly large amounts in arms and military and forsake other more productive and important sectors such as health care and education.

The Stockholm International Peace Research Institute (SIPRI) reports total military spending for 2007 of $1,339 billion, up 45 percent from a decade before. Total military expenditure amounts to 2.5 percent of the world's GDP. The spending is heavily concentrated in high-income countries, which spend $1,039 billion altogether. Europe is the continent that has experienced the smallest 10-year growth in military expenditure at +16 percent, whereas the Americas have increased their military expenditure by +63 percent compared to a decade earlier (SIPRI 2008).

As of year-end 2006, arms sales by the 100 largest arms manufacturers (excluding China) amounted to $315 billion, 63 percent of which corresponds to 41 U.S. companies, and 29 percent of which corresponds to 34 Western European companies. The top 10 companies include Boeing (U.S.), Lockheed Martin (U.S.), BAE Systems (U.K.), Northrop Grumman (U.S.), Raytheon (U.S.), General

Dynamics (U.S.), EADS (EU), L-3 Communications (U.S.), Finmeccanica (Italy), and Thales (France) (SIPRI 2008).

Total military spending for the top 15 countries amounted to one trillion dollars in 2007 (SIPRI 2008). For decades, peace advocates have been arguing in favor of reducing military spending and increasing development aid. Unfortunately, military spending has only increased. Between 1997 and 2007, military spending increased by 45 percent. Shifting military spending to peace-keeping operations and emergency relief could be a first step to solving the dilemma of reducing military spending. A world that spends more money in peace-keeping and emergency relief is a world that embraces a New Paradigm of cooperation.

New military alliances could then emerge between developing countries and developed countries, whereby developed countries agree to spend up to 10 percent of their military expenditure in peace-keeping operations and emergency relief. The idea could shift up to $100 billion to helping developing countries become more stable, enforce bans on the trade of illicit arms, pursue the fight against malaria, and recover in the case of natural catastrophes. This proposal would literally double the funding for development.

The International Peace Bureau (IPB) is one of the long-standing institutions advocating world peace along a necessary reduction in military spending. IPB was founded in 1891. IPB received the Nobel Peace Prize in 1910 for its efforts to spread out a culture of peace and non-militarization. **Colin Archer** (DCA) is IPB's secretary general. I met Colin on July 16, 2008, at the IPB headquarters in Geneva (Switzerland).

IPB has been a strong supporter of developing creative campaigns on spending priorities. Campaigning is important because it educates the average citizen on what priorities should be given preference over military spending and the impact shifting military spending into sustainable development would have in the lives of millions (Archer 2007). Sustainable development is not a substitute for military spending. Both are necessary. But the latter has been given overwhelming attention since the conclusion of the Cold War.

Daniel Nord (DCA) is the deputy director at the Stockholm International Peace Research Institute (SIPRI). I phoned Daniel on August 14, 2009. For Daniel, certain countries may embrace the idea of shifting a significant part of their military expenditure to emergency relief. SIPRI does not track the share of the military expenditure devoted to humanitarian activities. Daniel acknowledges that all governments may not embrace shifting 10 percent of a country's military expenditure, but it may prove a way to increase humanitarian relief in the short term. In the absence of new horizons where the increase of military expenditure can be reduced or shifted to emergency relief, we will continue to live in a world where priority is given to defense of national interests in lieu of human dignity and environmental sustainability.

THE DECEM ALLIANCE

The Decem Alliance is the new military alliance that all armies in the world are welcome to join. A signatory member of the Decem Alliance is entitled to devote 10 percent of its military resources to emergency relief and to integrate 10 percent of its armed forces into the Harmless Armed Forces based on the 10 Islands of Peace.

Contrary to NATO, all countries are welcome to join. Peacekeeping operations would continue to be the sole responsibility of the United Nations.

A new military alliance requires an accomplished director with significant experience in emergency relief. Timothy Zeimer was introduced in Chapter 18. Prior to becoming coordinator of the president's Malaria Initiative in the United States, Timothy served as executive director of World Relief, which provides disaster response in over 30 countries.

Artwork by Mike Luckovich.

CHAPTER 28

The Race of the Century

We want, on behalf of our continent, to stage an event that will send ripples of confidence from the Cape to Cairo – an event that will create social and economic opportunities throughout Africa. We want to ensure that one day, historians will reflect upon the 2010 World Cup as a moment when Africa stood tall and resolutely turned the tide on centuries of poverty and conflict. We want to show that Africa's time has come.
—Thabo Mbeki, *Celebrate Africa's Humanity*

The six Founding Members were introduced in Chapter 19 and are as follows: Botswana, Lesotho, Madagascar, Mozambique, Namibia, and Tanzania. Three of the six countries obtained their independence from Britain in the 1960s. Mozambique was formerly a Portuguese colony. Madagascar was formerly a French colony. Finally, Namibia split from South Africa in 1990.

THE PARTICIPANTS

The six countries that participate in The Race of the Century have to be Monfortable, the degree of compliance that applies to developing countries in the New Architecture of Capitalism. As such they receive the benefit of participating and become the recipients of Eutopia or Universal Welfare conditioned on the delivery through the microfinance network. In addition, all six countries are SADC members and five have been MCC compliant. Four of the six participants in the Race of the Century are among the group of Least Developed Countries. Botswana and Namibia have a large share of their population living under the poverty line because of extreme inequality.

Former colonies of the British Empire are generally better off than their French and Portuguese counterparties in Africa. Many reasons explain the better performance. Some of them point out to Britain's heritage of property rights enforcement and common law compared to the civil law inherited by former French and Portuguese colonies. A brief description of the six Founding Members is provided in what follows. English is spoken as a second language in Botswana, Lesotho, Namibia, and Tanzania. French is spoken in Madagascar. Finally Portuguese is spoken in Mozambique. Figure 28.1 summarizes the key indicators for each of the six Founding Members and the three Runners Up.

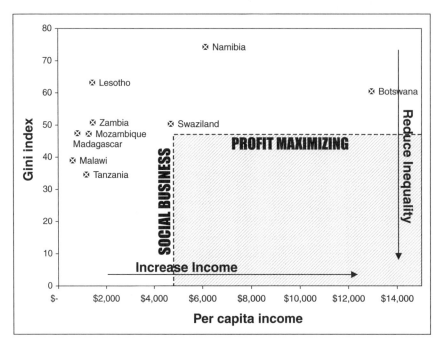

FIGURE 28.1 Key Indicators of Founding Members and Runners Up
Data Source: African Economic Outlook and World Bank (2009).

Botswana

Botswana has proven to be the most successful African nation since independence. The country consistently ranks in the top three in Africa across a number of categories including economic freedom, governance, and transparency. With a population of nearly two million, Botswana is relatively unpopulated compared to other surrounding nations. It is also landlocked, which has historically made development tougher. A British protectorate until 1966, the country changed its name from Bechuanaland to Botswana once it secured independence from Britain.

Botswana is an example of how to wisely administer a natural resource endowment. The country's current challenges include one of the highest HIV/AIDS contagion rates in the continent, surpassing the 20 percent mark, an incidence that is dragging economic development and severely undermining the country's future economic prospects. Botswana should remove obstacles to trade and investment, prioritizing industrial development and improving labor productivity (Chipeta and Schade 2007). Average growth in Botswana has remained above the 7 percent mark since independence, a phenomenal accomplishment that only finds equals among the emerging Asian tigers. Botswana is the only A-rated country in Africa according to Standard and Poor's. Two languages are spoken in the country (Setswana and English), which some academics associate with a lower likelihood of armed conflict and civil war—so frequent in the African continent and so detrimental for a country's stability and prosperity.

Nonofo Molefhi (FMB) is minister of lands and housing of Botswana. I met Nonofo at the Ministry of Lands and Housing in Gaborone (Botswana) on April 21, 2009 and again on July 24, 2009. Nonofo is well aware that nothing lasts forever, not even diamonds. The diamond industry has allowed Botswana to concatenate four decades of strong economic growth. During the 2008 economic crisis, the price of diamonds sunk, severely undermining the ability of the Botswanan Government to finance its public expenditure through diamond revenue. In the first half of 2009, Botswana borrowed $1.5 billion from the African Development to cover a 14 percent deficit in its annual budget. Diversifying the revenue mix to other sectors such as tourism away from the diamond industry is a strategy that could work for sub-Saharan Africa's best managed nation.

Thato Yaone Raphaka (FMB) is the permanent secretary at the Ministry of Local Government of Botswana. I met Thato on July 24, 2009, at the Ministry of Local Government in Gaborone (Botswana). The Ministry of Local Government of Botswana oversees and coordinates the delivery of public goods such as health care, education, water supply, and sanitation in urban and rural areas of Botswana. As one of the least densely populated countries in the world, Botswana faces a difficult challenge when approaching the delivery of public goods to the rural population, who often live in remote areas far away from the Gaborone-Francistown corridor, where a majority of the population is located. Thato acknowledges the right of the rural poor to receive public goods.

Lesotho

The Kingdom of Lesotho is the smallest of the six participants in the Race of the Century. Lesotho is landlocked and has a population of about two million. The country has a per-capita income of $2,000 and a high incidence of HIV/AIDS. In spite of its ties with South Africa, the country has been unable to profit from the spillover effects of the South African economy.

Lesotho boosts a diversified economy that in recent years has grown at a significant rate. All sectors except for agriculture registered positive growth rates in 2007, including mining and quarrying (33.9 percent increase compared with one year earlier), and other manufacturing (37.7 percent). Lesotho is a member of the Common Monetary Area along with Namibia, Swaziland, and South Africa. As a result, the local currency is pegged to the South African Rand, which fosters monetary stability in the African Kingdom. Lesotho remains poor and extremely unequal.

David Mohlomi Rantekoa (FMB) is Lesotho's ambassador to the United States. Mabasia Mohobane is first counsellor at the Lesotho Embassy to the United States. I met Ambassador Rantekoa and Counsellor Mohobane on June 12, 2009, at the Lesotho Embassy in Washington, DC. What would be the economic impact of the Race of the Century for Lesotho? For Ambassador Rantekoa and Counselor Mohobane Lesotho's low per-capita income could be boosted if tourism becomes an engine of economic growth.

Timothy Thahane (FMB) is the minister of finance of the Kingdom of Lesotho. I spoke with Timothy on August 18, 2009. For Timothy, a myriad of universities and experts have proposed new architectures and redefined capitalisms, and it remains to be seen whether the ideas put forth in this book will materialize in the years to come.

Madagascar

Madagascar is the fourth largest island in the world and lies southeast of the African continent between Mozambique and Mauritius.[1] Home to circa 20 million inhabitants, the island has remained poorly developed in spite of its tourism potential and substantial mineral resources, both largely unexploited. A former French colony from 1896, Madagascar obtained independence in 1960. After a decade of peace and steady economic progress, the economy went into steep decline, due to periodic political turmoil, changes in the terms of trade, and economic mismanagement, especially during the 23-year presidency of the "revolutionary socialist" Didier Ratsiraka. The island's already weak infrastructure suffered from lack of maintenance and the level of education—well above the average in sub-Saharan Africa at the time of independence—also declined owing to lack of funds.

The island's political landscape changed after 2002, when a disputed presidential election leading to a minor civil unrest brought president Marc Ravalomanana to power. A wealthy businessman and leading Protestant Christian, president Ravalomanana promised closer relations with the outside world, economic reform, political transparency, and a war on poverty and corruption. In transparency and economic freedom rankings, Madagascar has significantly improved its world's standings, outperforming the average benchmark in economic freedom and approaching the average in transparency. The government's liberalizing economic policies received the approval of the IMF and the donor countries, and the core economic indicators have significantly improved. However economic growth has been impeded by external shocks such as the steep rise in oil prices in 2007 and the impact of periodic devastating cyclones, and improved indicators have not had any significant impact on the desperately poor living standards of the bulk of the population.

President Ravalomanana was re-elected in 2007. But his increasingly autocratic behavior and the failure of his government to alleviate mass poverty led to growing opposition, fostered by disaffected politicians exploiting long-standing regional divisions. The beginning of 2009 saw violent unrest in several towns and popular demonstrations in the capital calling for his resignation. In March 2009, president Ravalomanana was removed from power through a *coup d'etat* conducted by the former mayor of Antananarivo Andry Rajoelina. In August 2009 president Ravalomanana and Rajoelina reached a resolution called the Maputo Agreement whereby they agreed to hold elections within a 15-month period. The Maputo Agreement was facilitated by former Mozambican president Joachim Chissano, who at that time represented SADC, the Southern African Development Community.

Madagascar remains a desperately poor country with inadequate infrastructure and serious economic weaknesses. The infrastructure has been much improved by massive aid inflows. The country has considerable potential for development based on tourism, major mineral resources that are just beginning to be developed and, for the long term, what are thought to be substantial reserves of oil. If the political elite can resolve the problems underlying the present unrest, and the generally sensible, existing economic policies are continued, the gem of the Indian Ocean could well become the Botswana of the first half of the twenty-first century. There is no other country in sub-Saharan Africa as poor as Madagascar and as promising from nearly every angle.

Jocelyn B. Radifera (FMB) is Madagascar's ambassador to the United States. I met Ambassador Radifera on November 17, 2008, and again on June 8, 2009, at the Malagasy Embassy in Washington, DC. How prepared is Madagascar to host a large international event? What would be the economic impact? For Ambassador Radifera, "The spectacular growth of tourists in Madagascar in between 2002 and

2008, a six-fold increase, is proof of the exceptional dynamism of Madagascar's tourism sector. This important growth of demand needs to be supported by the construction of additional accommodation facilities as well as air transport links with major American and European cities."

Zaza Ramandimbiarison (FMB) was deputy prime minister of Madagascar from 2002 to 2004 and was elected chief of staff of Andry Rajoelina in the aftermath of the *coup d'etat* that removed former president Ravalomanana from power in March 2009. I met Zaza on December 15, 2008, at the World Bank in Washington, DC. During our conversation, Zaza acknowledged the necessity to look beyond the current development establishment and embraced the vision to implement new ideas in the development space.

Mozambique

A former Portuguese colony and a vast country of roughly eight times the size of Portugal, Mozambique fought and secured independence from the Portuguese in as late as 1975. The country has a 2,400 kilometer coastline and is home of some 21 million people. Mozambique came out of years of civil war between apartheid-backed RENAMO, and the ruling party's FRELIMO was settled in 1992. RENAMO was taken over by the South Africans after Zimbabwe's independence, providing a home and logistical support. For African Historian Paul Nugent, "RENAMO acquired a well-deserved reputation for being short on ideology and long on terror" (Nugent 2004).

The first multiparty elections were held in 1994. Economic renaissance is occuring in the former Portuguese colony after years of armed conflict settled in the delicate transition through which the country went. In December of 2004, former president Joaquim Chissano voluntarily decided not to run in the presidential election despite the fact that he was entitled to one more five-year term. Armando Guebuza was thus elected president in 2004 and reelected in October 2009. According to *The Economist*, "Armando Guebuza draws support from more radical factions of the ruling party which appear keen to re-establish a firmer grip on power" (*Economist* 2007a).

The country is in the very bottom of the distribution, standing in position 172 out of 177 in the United Nations' Human Development Index. The country is an average performer in transparency compared to its sub-Saharan African peers, and ranks 36 out of 48 countries in sub-Saharan Africa in good governance according to the Ibrahim Index of African Governance, just below Madagascar. Mozambique should develop its financial sector and reduce the high interest rates associated to credit (Chipeta and Schade 2007).

According to Harvard professor Robert I. Rotberg, the RENAMO-FRELIMO war devastated Mozambique, which had to start building the country from scratch after 1997 (Rotberg 2007). Rotberg talks about Mozambique's unquestioned success on the economic, political, social, and developmental fronts. After 2005, president Guebuza has resurrected the fight against corruption. Mozambique's bans on private land ownership stops its farmers from using their property as collateral in a loan that would allow them to finance basic inputs. Mozambique's natural resources are allowing the country to experience significant growth. Rotberg notes that the former Portuguese colony has "signed major exploration agreements with foreign companies seeking oil and gas in the Rovuma River basin between the Tanzanian border and the port city of Nacala." Finally, Rotbert concludes that the country's aluminum mines, offshore natural gas, and hydroelectric power, representing up to 70 percent of exports, are "the big earner and the major driver of Mozambique's economic renaissance" (Rotberg 2007).

Armando Alexandre Panguene (FMB) is Mozambique's former ambassador to the United States. I met Ambassador Panguene on November 13, 2008, and again on May 26, 2009, at the Mozambican Embassy in Washington, DC. How prepared is Mozambique to host a large international event? For Ambassador Panguene:

> *Mozambique is well prepared to host large international events. Maputo, the capital city, has in fact hosted several important events in the past including the African Union Head of States Summit, the African, Caribbean and Pacific (ACP) Summit of Heads of States and Governments, and High Level Meeting of the Smart Partnership that involved high level delegation from more than 25 countries. As far as the logistic arrangements in hosting international events, the hotel and hospitality industry in the country has recently benefited from investments in refurbishment and construction of new hotels and other types of accommodation facilities. In addition, Mozambique has a large Convention Center, the Joaquim Chissano Center located at the Water Front in Maputo.*

What would be the economic impact? The charming ambassador concludes, "The economic impact of large international events would be enormous as this will result in large spending that turns into revenue and employment opportunities in the hotel and hospitality industry."

Fernando Sumbana (FMB) is minister of tourism of Mozambique. I met Fernando on July 14, 2009, at the Pestana Rovuma Hotel in Maputo (Mozambique). Fernando acknowledged Mozambique's potential in tourism if appropriate investment is undertaken in key areas such as education and infrastructure. The country's phenomenal tourism potential could become a driver of economic growth and future prosperity.

Aiuba Cuereneia (FMN) is minister of planning and development of Mozambique. I met Aiuba on July 9, 2009, at the Ministry of Planning and Development in Maputo (Mozambique). For Aiuba, tourism is one of the five development sectors of Mozambique that also include agriculture, fisheries, mining, and energy.

Salvador Namburete is minister of energy of Mozambique. I met Namburete on July 13, 2009, at the Ministry of Energy in Maputo (Mozambique). Namburete points out that Mozambique is making progress expanding access to electricity, which is expected to increase from 14 percent in 2009 to 25 percent in 2014.

Namibia

Namibia is one of the least densely populated countries in Africa, with an area of over 800,000 square kilometers and a population of just over two million. Prior to its independence, Namibia was known as South West Africa (SWA). In the aftermath of World War I, the League of Nations decided that the former German colony should be administered by South Africa. After World War II, South Africa expanded its apartheid to SWA.

Namibia ranks right underneath Botswana in the Human Development Index, at position 125 out of 177 countries. It is, however, one of the richest countries in sub-Saharan Africa in terms of per-capita income. Only Equatorial Guinea, South Africa, Botswana, and Mauritius have a higher per-capita income in sub-Saharan Africa. The country faces the same challenges as Botswana, with a relatively small population of two million and an HIV/AIDS contagion rate that surpasses the 20 percent mark. Namibia ranks underneath Madagascar on economic freedom at sixth out of 40 countries. Namibia is the fifth best performer in transparency, right below Botswana, South Africa, Cape Verde, and Mauritius. In terms of governance, it ranks 12 out of 48 countries in the 2005 Ibrahim Index of African Governance.

The South West Africa People's Organisation (SWAPO) emerged in 1960 as a liberation movement against South Africa's apartheid. SWAPO fought apartheid's South Africa in an ongoing war, which was settled through a United Nations resolution in 1988. Independence came in 1990. SWAPO became the leading political force and has maintained its supremacy ever since. Tommy Nambahu is a member of Parliament with SWAPO. I met Nambahu on April 17, 2009, at the Safari Hotel in Windhoek (Namibia). From 1979 to 1981 Nambahu fought the liberation war against South Africa and subsequently spent ten years in Cuba.

In 2004, SWAPO accomplished a major shift when former president Sam Nujoma stepped down and was substituted by Hifikepunye Pohamba, a former minister of lands. Nujoma however maintained SWAPO's leadership role.

Ben Ulenga (FMB) is Namibia's opposition leader, president of the Congress of Democrats, Namibia's second political force, and former Namibian Ambassador to the United Kingdom. I met Ben on April 17, 2009, at the Safari Hotel in Windhoek (Namibia). During our conversation Ben mentioned that in 1977, he was tried and sentenced to 15 years in prison, a time he spent on Robben Island along with Nelson Mandela. Ben was released in 1985.

Fanuel Tjingaete (FMB) was appointed director of the Namibia Economic Policy Research Unit (NEPRU) in May 2009. NEPRU is an independent think-tank. In addition, Fanuel was Namibia's first auditor general between 1993 and 2003. I met Fanuel on July 21, 2009, at NEPRU in Windhoek (Namibia). Fanuel is disillusioned because the incremental progress to which we have grown accustomed will only change the face of extreme poverty and inequality in the long run.

Tanzania

In spite of its agricultural and tourism potential, Tanzania remains today one of the world's poorest countries. Tanzania has approximately the area of Mozambique and twice as many inhabitants. Tanganyika and Zanzibar obtained independence from Britain in the early 1960s, and subsequently formed Tanzania in 1964. With independence secured, Tanzania hoped to improve poverty, ignorance, and disease In spite of being "endowed with a rich natural resource base, easy geographical access to international markets, peace and tranquillity and political stability," Tanzania remains one of the world's poorest countries 50 years after independence

(Mashindano, Rweyemamu, et al., 2007). In 1967, former Tanzanian president Julius Nyerere pointed out (Nugent 2004):

> *We are making a mistake to think that we shall get money from other countries; first, because in fact we shall not be able to get sufficient money for our economic development; and secondly, because even if we could get all that we need, such dependence upon others would endanger our independence and our ability to choose our own political policies.*

Tanzania ranks in the world's 48 percentile in transparency, and towards the middle of sub-Saharan Africa in the governance distribution at position 22 out of 48. Just under 60 percent of Tanzania's population live under the extreme poverty line, the eighth poorest record in sub-Saharan Africa. Tanzania should allocate more resources to local government administrations responsible for implementing poverty reduction strategies (Chipeta and Schade 2007). Former president Nyerere's view above is reinforced by the fact that in 1967, Tanzanian exports could cover imports, meeting only 62.6 percent of imports by 1976 and 28.6 percent of imports by 1985 (Nugent 2004).

The Tanzania Development Vision 2025 represents the governmental contribution to Tanzania's development in the twenty-first century. According to the American consultancy PricewaterhouseCoopers (1998), "The objective of Tanzania Development Vision 2025 is to awaken, coordinate and direct the people's efforts, minds and national resources towards those core sectors that will enable them to attain development goals and withstand the expected intensive economic competition ahead."

Ernest T. Mallya of the United Nations reviews "A Critical Look at Tanzania's Development Vision 2025." For Mallya, according to Tanzania's Vision the country should accomplish the following goals by 2025: attain a high quality of life, become a peaceful and united country, reach high levels of public governance, expand and enhance education levels and reach, and have a competitive economy (Mallya 2004). The reality is that in 2007, Tanzania only generated 40,000 new jobs annually, barely enough to meet the demand of 700,000 new job seekers that enter the labor market every year in the United Republic (Chipeta and Schade 2007). Tanzania dependency on foreign aid is also noteworthy as almost 20 percent of the recurrent and 90 percent of the development expenditure is provided by foreign aid (Mashindano, Rweyemamu, et al., 2007).

Peter J. Mwenguo (FMB) is the managing director of the Tanzania Tourist Board. I met Peter on July 17, 2009, at the Tanzania Tourist Board in Dar es Salaam (Tanzania). The tourism industry in Tanzania was restructured and privatized in 1992, creating three government agencies that became the liaison between the public and the private sector. According to Peter, the Tanzania Tourist Board is the agency responsible for the promotion of Tanzania abroad and represents the marketing arm of the Tanzanian Government. Tanzania receives under one million tourists a year, with a predominance of European and American visitors. 70 percent of tourism is Safari based. Peter suggests that increases in the number of visitors have to be reasonable to maintain sustainable development. For the Tanzanian tourism expert, investments are necessary in infrastructure and education to trigger an increase in the number of visitors that enter the sub-Saharan country every year.

THE PURPOSE OF THE RACE

What is the purpose of The Race of the Century? The six Founding Members become candidate countries to host the New International Territory, home of the new institutions that will emerge at the conclusion of the Window of Opportunity. As it was explained in Chapter 19 and Chapter 20, these six Founding Members wil receive Universal Welfare for their extreme poor, which will be provided by The New Institution, a supranational Ministry of Health and Education. This is only one of the incentives for the six Founding Members to become part of the New Architecture. The second incentive is equally appealing: to participate in The Race of the Century in order to become the host of the New International Territory, an international event that will receive worldwide attention and become an engine of growth.

The Race of the Century would resemble the competition between candidate countries to host the Football World Cup or between candidate cities to host the Olympic Games. Countries would have to improve across a series of indicators (including health and education indicators) throughout a predetermined time horizon. They would then present their projects to host the New International Territory. A pool of judges would then determine where the NIT would be based at the end of the Window of Opportunity. The Window of Opportunity is presented more fully in Chapter 30. A country may decide to host a global sporting event because of the following (HM Treasury 2007):

- The positive economic impact of visitors during the event and potential for new tourism markets.
- As a catalyst for the economic regeneration of a city or region.
- The intangible benefits often associated with sporting events including increases in national pride and strengthened identity.
- The opportunity to showcase an emerging nation or city.

For Matthew Hensley and Carreen Behrens, "Critics of large-scale events like the World Cup or the Olympics argue that the cost of preparing for and hosting the events negates the projected economic benefits." The authors raise the questions *Can countries in emerging markets identify the benefits and undertake public and private financing approaches to attract major sporting and entertainment market share? Can emerging markets attract and finance major events and business tourism infrastructure?* The case of South Africa is exemplary as the country "has successfully mobilized billions of dollars of private finance into public purpose infrastructure and has created employment and improved service delivery at the national and local levels in a variety of sectors such as health, education or transport" (Hensley and Behrens 2006).

An Engine of Economic Growth

Tourism is a major growth engine in many developed countries. In the European Union, the sector is "dominated by small or medium-sized enterprises (SMEs), with more than 99% of firms employing fewer than 250 people." Only in the European Union, tourism represents the main service industry that generates 13 percent of GDP and 6 percent of employment (EEA 2001). The sector also could be dominated by small and medium microbusinesses that run as social businesses in the participants of the Race of the Century.

Africa's tourism potential remains unexplored. A misperception about political risk and widespread conflict should not include all geographic areas of a vast continent three times the size of the United States. Southern Africa's low political risk and high peace index reinforce the prospects for a medium-term development of its tourism sector. According to the World Tourism Organization, a total of 922 million tourist arrivals took place in 2008 with the following allocation: Europe (53 percent), Asia and the Pacific (20 percent), Americas (16 percent), Middle East (6 percent), and Africa (5 percent) (UNWTO 2009).

Bichaka Fayissa, Christian Nsiah, and Badassa Tadassa review "The Impact of Tourism on Economic Growth and Development in Africa." For the authors, "The contribution of tourism to economic growth and development is reflected in the form of exports since it represents 40 percent of all exports of services." Through a conventional neoclassical growth model that incorporates tourism as one of the sources of growth, the authors conclude, "A 10 percent increase in the spending of international tourists leads to a 0.4 percent increase in the GDP per capita" (Fayissa, Nsiah, et al., 2007).

In July 2009, the World Bank approved a $35 million loan to boost the Ethiopian tourism sector, the first loan of its kind granted to a sub-Saharan African country According to the World Bank, "The Ethiopian tourism sector, which accounts for about 15 percent of foreign currency earnings, represents the third largest export earner and has significant growth potential." The loan would target investments in infrastructure and tourism facilities, skills enhancements, institutional development, and community engagement (Xinhua 2009).

South Africa could become the benchmark and inspiration for the participants in the Race of the Century. What can countries do to increase the tourism share of GDP? Increasing tourism-related infrastructure is a first step, and the Race of the Century could represent a phenomenal incentive to build up tourism infrastructure. Figure 28.2 depicts the share of tourism in a country's GDP and the number of incoming tourists for the Founding Members and the Runners Up.

The 2010 Football World Cup is a major sports event that should impact the surrounding countries through spillover effects. According to FIFA, "Angola, Botswana, Lesotho, Mozambique, Namibia, South Africa, Swaziland, Zambia and Zimbabwe are collectively using the World Cup to develop the seven transfrontier conservation areas (TFCAs) in the region. This TFCA route will offer tourists the unforgettable experience of two oceans, vast landscapes, major rivers, deserts, canyons, mountains and diverse cultures across the nine countries in one trail" (FIFA 2009).

Economic Impact of Major Sports Events

The economic impact of major sports events has been well documented by a myriad of reports. Olympic Games and Football World Cups bring about major improvements in infrastructure coupled with increases in the inflow of tourists. It is likely that the Race of the Century would trigger similar improvements if designed appropriately. In the absence of other fundamental growth sectors such as energy or mining, agriculture and tourism become the two major engines of economic growth for poor countries that remain unindustrialized.

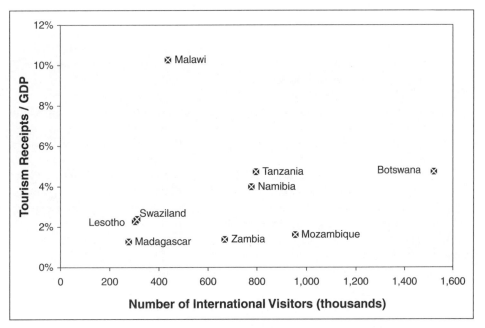

FIGURE 28.2 Share of Tourism Receipts over GDP and Number of Tourists
Data Source: African Economic Outlook and World Tourism Organization (2009).

Olympic Games For PricewaterhouseCoopers (PwC), "While the financial outcome from hosting the Olympic Games can be identified reasonably clearly after the event, it is much more difficult to generalize about the overall economic impact of the Olympic Games" (PwC 2004). The London 2012 Olympic Games may bring about a major positive macroeconomic shock for the malfunctioning British economy. According to PwC, the macroeconomic impact of the London 2012 Olympic Games for the period of 2005 to 2016 would be £1.93 billion for the U.K., £5.90 billion for London, and £525 million for North East London (PwC 2005).

Christian D. Dick and Qingwei Wang of the Centre for European Economic Research study "The Economic Impact of Olympic Games." The authors report, "The stock market reactions to the announcement of the Olympic Games host cities during the last three decades" and find "a significant and positive announcement effect of hosting the Summer Games." As a result the authors conclude, "The Olympic Summer games are considered to have a positive impact on the economy of the host countries" (Dick and Wang 2008).

For Pere Duran, general director of the Turisme de Barcelona Consortium, it is clear that the Barcelona 1992 Olympic Games have contributed to bolster Barcelona as a highly popular tourist destination (Duran 2002). The intangible effects of becoming a participant of the Race of the Century could be phenomenal for the six Founding Members.

Football World Cup In "Hosting the FIFA World Cup," Brian Sturgess and Chris Brady ask *Why should a country bid to host the FIFA World Cup?* For the authors,

"The reputation of economic as the dismal science is well deserved in the case of the pessimistic assessments of the impact of sporting events made by a number of studies." The authors conclude, "There is strong evidence that, in many cases, selecting a country with an underdeveloped football infrastructure provides the incentive to take positive steps to improve the structure of the game in that country" (Sturgess and Brady 2006). This may have been the case in South Africa, particularly if it is compared with the two previous World Cups in Germany (2006) and Japan/South Korea (2002). A straightforward conclusion is that the area that hosts the New International Territory should be underdeveloped, so that the buildup of NIT brings about a strong incentive to improve infrastructure in the area and its whereabouts.

Ramos Mabugu and Ahmed Mohamed review "The Economic Impacts of Government Financing of the 2010 FIFA World Cup." For the scholars, "Those who stand to gain the most via this international soccer event are high income households, while low income households are expected to gain the lowest increase in income" (Mabugu and Mohamed 2008). As a result the gains are regressive, an outcome that should be avoided in The Race of the Century.

Artwork by Mike Luckovich.

CHAPTER 29

The Monfort Team

We know the road to prosperity is a long one. We will travel it with the help of a new school of development thinkers and entrepreneurs, with those who demonstrate they have not just a heart, but also a mind for the poor.
— Paul Kagame, *Africa Has to Find its Own Road to Prosperity*

On June 7, 2009, I had dinner in Washington, DC with World Bank economist Branko Milanovic, one of the leading experts in income inequality and author of *Worlds Apart* (Milanovic 2005). It is after Branko's inspiring book that the introductory section to Chapter 29 is entitled. Branko's book describes the immense income gap between hemispheres. This introductory section describes the immense opinion gap when it comes to approaching the eradication of extreme poverty.

WORDS APART

During the preparation of this book throughout 2008 I approached the microfinance industry in the same manner that I have approached other areas such as agriculture, trade and labor rights, financial architecture, immigration, small arms trade and military spending, or the mining industries. I sampled the industry and tried to reach out to the most relevant experts. I have seen *words apart*. A majority of the experts on the microfinance industry are not even on the same page.

Is there a same page? The wide spectrum of opinions is manifest. There is an intellectual debate, which could be healthy, but this often results in intellectual wars that forsake the ultimate goal: the alleviation of extreme poverty. If poverty is not eradicated, it is not simply because of a lack of political will or interest among developed nations and the elites of the developing world; it is because there is a lack of consensus as to how to mitigate it. The intellectual wars of left-wing and right-wing economists and practitioners do not help. The debate between what approach is most appropriate (for instance, between USAID and the Millennium Challenge Corporation) perpetuates the problem. It is difficult to get everyone on the same page. What is that same page? There are many possibilities, but only one will materialize if a global effort is to be undertaken to create a New Architecture for the extreme poor that sets the basis for the eradication of extreme poverty once and for all.

We have been born in a world that adores criticism in an area where the lack of innovation is second to none. We are all sports journalists broadcasting a football game that has been going on for decades. There is an abundance of commentators and a scarcity of implementors.

For decades, social scientists have been ellaborating theories that had no direct application. The first architecture was built in the aftermath of World War II. It is called the Bretton Woods architecture. For decades, we as a society were reluctant to build a second architecture. We have not looked at the best ideas in the development arena from intellectual giants. The de facto approach has been to channel funds through the existing schemes.

What is the next big idea in the development space? Sampling the universe of opinions in the microfinance industry can only be helpful. The experts may or may not agree on how to tackle extreme poverty through microcredit, microsavings, and microinsurance. But there is one fact. Only when the experts become Expert Dreamers will we be eyewitnesses to the birth of a new consensus, a New Architecture that is designed to work for the extreme poor. It is perhaps time to propose a Page One to start the Glorious Forty that will lead us to the World of Cornucopia and Eutopia. It is perhaps time to start a journey where only dreamers are welcome. It is perhaps time to start asking *why not* instead of *why*. We must dare, and therefore exist.

A WORLDWIDE RECRUITING PROCESS

As reviewed in Chapter 16, the Economic Cooperation Administration (ECA) was the U.S. agency in charge of administering the Marshall Plan dollars. The pool of talent put together at ECA was one of the key structural features why the Marshall Plan was successful. ECA was arguably the best team of people that has ever been put together to serve the (European) public interest. As explained in Chapter 16, ECA offers important lessons about the success of the Marshall Plan: first, hire the most talented among the Expert Dreamers; and second, put them to work in the countries where funds are being allocated. It is a lesson to take into account. The purpose of this chapter is to explain how I came up with a process to identify talent and build the best team of experts that has ever been put together to serve the (global) public interest.

When I studied Telecommunications Engineering at Universidad Politécnica de Madrid (Spain) between 1994 and 1999, I learned to sample an analogue signal. Signal theory shows it is possible to replicate a continuous signal by sampling a series of discrete points and later interpolate. I applied what I learned in signal theory to the world's economic, corporate, and political elites, as well as the Civil Society. The purpose of such an exercise was to reach a representative sample of the world's expert community.

Subsequent sections present The Decem List and The Monfort Team. The Decem List is a list made up of more than 90,497 experts and 17,123 investors. The Decem List contains 819 categories of experts including 10,253 academics organized into 12 academic disciplines, and 13,627 senators and members of Parliament from 33 developed and 47 developing nations. The Monfort List is a subset of the Decem List that identifies the Expert Dreamers, the golden experts of the twenty-first century. Finally, The Monfort Team (TMT) presents One Hundred Expert Dreamers carefully selected from The Monfort List, with whom I have either spoken or met. The Expert Dreamers of the Monfort Team have been introduced throughout this book in different sections and chapters (indicated by boldface type). Accepting Expert Dreamers are featured on http://ExpertDreamers.com. The Expert Dreamers are the seeds of progress and prosperity.

THE DECEM LIST

We have never had a plan of action that put together the best ideas of the best minds of our time. This is one of the purposes of The Monfort Plan, a plan that constructs a credible success story by incorporating the work of some of the most talented and innovative pioneers. Ideas need creativity and enthusiasm to move forward. Ideas need to be commercially appealing, realistic, and viable to move ahead in today's market economies. Ideas need to be original and entertaining to deserve the attention of the consumer in North America and Europe.

The Decem List consists of more than 90,497 experts from around the world in a variety of disciplines and fields. In addition, I put together a list of 17,123 investors who should carefully read Chapter 25. The purpose of building The Decem List was to communicate, to spread an action plan to redefine capitalism, and to eradicate extreme poverty. The objective of spreading the action plan was to find the Expert Dreamers of today to build up the best team of Expert Dreamers the world has seen since the ECA emerged in the late 1940s. I took advantage of the fact that I was an unkown individual among the expert community, with no prestige or reputation, and consequently no fear of moving forward. Many experts in The Decem List were reluctant to establish contact. They most likely would not have turned me down if I had an established reputation.

Members in the Decem List typically receive one message per month. Everybody on The Decem List can request to be removed from the list. I soon realized academics were overwhelmingly requesting to be removed from The Decem List. The trend was so notorious that I decided to create this subsection to express a concern. There is a subset of academia who may be reluctant to embrace a new economic paradigm, as it relies on new ideas not supported by the orthodox theories that for decades have been feeding the intellect of university professors from the world's best universities. The number of scholars in each of the academic categories I included in The Decem List is as follows: Agricultural Economics (722 scholars), Agricultural Engineering (577), Anthropology (227), Economics (1,148), Finance (646), History (1,483), International Affairs (1,595), Materials & Petroleum Engineering (386), Political Science (1,276), Psychology (1,193), Religion (254), and Sociology (746). I chose these 12 categories in the social sciences with the intention of finding talent who could contribute to the design and subsequent implementation of a new economic paradigm.

Only 11.33 percent in the list of 90,497 experts included in The Decem List are academics. However, 54.20 percent of those who requested to be removed from the list are academics. The removal request rate among academics (4.42 percent) is four-fold the average removal request rate (1.11 percent).

I decided to go one step further. I wondered which academic disciplines of the 12 outstanding would show a higher removal request rate. All members in The Decem List are experts. Among the experts, there are Expert Dreamers who will become part of the best team that has been built to serve the public interest. Among the experts there are also expert non-dreamers, those who decided to be removed from The Decem List. Figure 29.1 depicts the percentage of non-dreamers by academic discipline. Anthropology (1.32 percent), Agricultural Engineering (1.73 percent), and Materials & Petroleum Engineering (2.85 percent) are the three academic disciplines with a lower number of expert non-dreamers.

Welcome to the World of the Bretton Woods Elites who perpetuate knowledge created by the baby boomers and their parents and are reluctant to embrace any new ideas that stand beyond their territory of thought and their bounds of rationality. Everything is possible. The only requirement is a good explanation.

The Expert Dreamers found in the following lines the explanation needed to move ahead. The expert non-dreamers, apparently, would prefer to close their minds to the ideas put forth in this book and continue to assume that the axioms, hypotheses, and input conditions that feed their models could eventually be tweaked.

We will eradicate extreme poverty. I will devote my best efforts to contribute to the world I imagine in my dreams. I am confident the team of Expert Dreamers I have presented throughout this book will join me to start this long journey. We shall defeat the Pirates of Heartless Capitalism who undermine our efforts to move ahead. I met the Pirates in New York City and London. I know they hide in Switzerland and the Cayman Islands. It is time to fight them. It is time to say to the pirates once and for all that enough is enough. I hear the winds of change. I feel the aura of that society of 2050 awaiting our final departure.

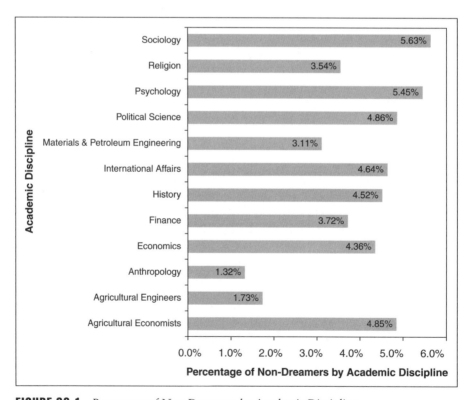

FIGURE 29.1   Percentage of Non-Dreamers by Academic Discipline

It is our generation's duty to contribute to the eradication of extreme poverty. We owe it to the visionaries of the past who contributed to the well-being of Europeans, who no longer fight in eternal wars. We constructed a united Europe out of the devastation of Word War II, thanks to the help of our American friends. Do not dare to think that eradicating poverty is impossible today. It is a matter of feasible priorities. It is a matter of political will. Let's get to work.

During a presentation at the London School of Economics in 2009, Nobel Prize winning economist and Princeton University professor Paul Krugman pointed out, "Most work in macroeconomics in the past 30 years has been useless at best and harmful at worst." The road out of the crisis is uncertain. Economists are used to criticize what policy-makers do. A handful of them including NYU's Nouriel Roubini may have anticipated the crash. Where do we go from here?

I think William Easterly, Jeffrey Sachs and Paul Collier are outstanding scholars with impressive analytical skills and the ability to fight perpetual debates that keep their brains active. Academics are to the policy-making process what phycisists or mathematicians are to civil engineering. Social scientists are well needed; they are a necessary condition, but they do not suffice on their own. They are part of the value chain of the idea. Universities have produced a myriad of theoreticians and a scarcity of implementors. A similar statement could well apply to business schools that produce entrepreneurs with a user's manual based on the previous capitalist paradigm, which is based on the maximization of short-term profit and prioritized to fulfill the shareholders' promise of shareholder value and financial return.

Except for John Maynard Keynes and Harry Dexter White, none of the key figures in the construction of the Bretton Woods architecture were academics. The great men of the 1940s and 1950s were Roosevelt, Truman, Marshall, Kennan, Hoffman, Clayton, Monnet, and Schuman, among others.

Where are the men and women of political stature, the visionaries of today, and the disciples of Marshall and Truman? We may soon find out. A new era takes off on the Decem Date. The train is departing and I do not want to miss it. The next stop is sub-Saharan Africa. The giants of today belong on The Monfort Team.

THE EXPERT DREAMERS

In the process of writing this book, I conducted 225 phone interviews and 325 face-to-face interviews. I visited 25 countries during an 18-month period. I felt that among the categories of experts with whom I interacted during the 18-month interval, academics were the most reluctant to speak to someone with no reputation—no reputation to lose, that is, when it comes to proposing a new economic architecture.

We lived in financial times.[1] We no longer do. We lived the white man's burden. In addition, we now live the academic man's burden. A part of academia is reluctant to embrace change. A part of academia lives in an orthodox world and is imprisoned in the Prison of Thought. Thinking out of the box is not rewarded in today's academic environment. Orthodox academics have become friends with the Pirates of Heartless Capitalism. We ought to evolve as a society according to their models. Let's turn the modus operandi around. Let's turn the status quo around. Let's adapt our models to the reality of an unequal world, to the reality of a world on the wrong path that will not reach sustainability, and to the era of Global Public Goods.

All in all, One-Hundred Expert Dreamers will join the Chief Dreamer to constitute The Monfort Team, the best team of experts that has ever served the global public interest. It is to be a reincarnation of the Economic Cooperation Administration that implemented the Marshall Plan, the success story in development of the twenty-first century.

Over the course of the five-year period ending in 2009, I interacted with the One-Hundred Expert Dreamers. I met 60 of them and talked on the phone with 40. They represent 41 different countries: Angola (1), Argentina (1), Australia (1), Austria (3), Bangladesh (4), Belgium (1), Bermuda (1), Bolivia (3), Botswana (3), Brazil (2), Canada (3), Chile (1), Colombia (3), Costa Rica (1), Cote d'Ivoire (1), Finland (1), Germany (3), Holland (2), Hungary (1), India (3), Israel (1), Jamaica (1), Lesotho (2), Madagascar (2), Mali (2), Mauritus (1), Mozambique (4), Namibia (2), Nicaragua (1), Nigeria (1), Norway (2), Peru (2), Senegal (1), Serbia (1), Spain (5), Sweden (1), Tanzania (1), United Kingdom (7), United States (24), Uruguay (1), and Zimbabwe (1).

The One-Hundred Expert Dreamers have been introduced throughout this book. Forty of them will hold senior positions in 20 different operational areas: Agriculture (AGR), Bank for the Poor (BFP), Chief Executive and Diplomacy (CEO), Conditionality (CON), Decem Alliance (DCA), Decemfund (DCF), Decemland (DCL), Education (EDU), Financial Reform (FIN), Future (FUT), Health (HEA), Immigration (IMM), Income and Inequality (INI), Microsavings Insurance (MSI), Mining (MIN), Small Arms Trade (SAT), The New Institution (TNI), Trade and Labor Rights (TLR), Water and Sanitation (WTS) and the Yunus-Fund (YUN). In addition there are five transversal areas: Chief of Staff (CST), Press Secretary (PSC), Economic Historian (ECO), Founding Member (FMB), and Finance Minister (FMN).

I propose that the 20 operational areas be headed by the following Expert Dreamers: Joachim Von Braun, Shabbir A. Chowdhury, John Danilovich and Cheick Diarra, Michael Intriligator, Timothy Ziemer, Knut Norheim Kjaer, Brian Donaldson, Federico Mayor Zaragoza, Raymond Baker, Hazel Henderson, Kevin Fenton, Ndioro Ndiaye, Branko Milanovic, Antonio Carlos Bueno de Camargo Silva, Preston Chiaro, Christiane Agboton-Johnson, Tomaz Salomao, Robert Wade, Clarissa Brocklehurst, and Bernard Lietaer. Figure 29.2 summarizes Who is Who in The Monfort Plan. A complete diagram of the One-Hundred Expert Dreamers is provided on http://TheMonfortNews.net.

There are many initiatives set to launch for The Monfort Plan, including a Headquarters[2] and University,[3] as well as travel and communication channels.[4]

THE CHIEF DREAMER

The Monfort Team should be led by the Chief Dreamer. In today's environment a paradigm shift is feasible if we raise the awareness of the citizens of Europe and North America, whose leaders have driven capitalism to a point of no-return, where the myriad of bailouts and stimuli have only postponed a well-needed and deserved reform of other non-financial components of the reform agenda.

We have constrained the reform agenda to one of the six components of the Axis of Feeble, the financial sphere, a good and necessary beginning that is not sufficient to drive the world to the path of sustainable growth and prosperity.

A paradigm shift is feasible if we dream and lead a change. We are in desperate need of a Chief Dreamer able to transmit a forward-looking vision that enables North and South, developed and developing countries to get on the same page and start writing the History of Tomorrow. What are the requirements to become the Chief Dreamer? Jonathan Swift wrote *A Modest Proposal* in 1729 and divided readers into three classes:

> *Readers may be divided into three classes—the superficial, the ignorant and the learned, and I have with much felicity fitted my pen to the genius and advantage of each. The superficial reader will be strangely provoked to laughter, which clears the breast and the lungs, is sovereign against the spleen, and the most innocent of all diuretics. The ignorant reader (between whom and the former the distinction is extremely nice) will find himself disposed to stare, which is an admirable remedy for ill eyes, serves to raise and enliven the spirits, and wonderfully helps perspiration. But the reader truly learned, chiefly for whose benefit I wake when others sleep, and sleep when others wake, will here find sufficient matter to employ his speculations for the rest of his life.*

The Chief Dreamer must remain awake while others sleep, must work in the interest of the developing world and propose forward-looking ideas that are realistic so that the reader finds sufficient matter to employ his or her speculations for the rest of her life. The Chief Dreamer must be a twenty-first century Jules Verne who conquers through persuasion and not imposition. The Chief Dreamer must combine the qualities of George Kennan and Jean Monnet and be determined to defend the priorities of the vulnerable. The Chief Dreamer must be multilingual to address a variety of audiences in different geographies and must be multidisciplinary to understand the complex roots that drive today's increasing inequality gap and inequality.

The Chief Dreamer must surround him or herself by the most talented team of Expert Dreamers to have served the global public interest. The Chief Dreamer must be able to identify the Expert Dreamers from the expert non-dreamers. The Chief Dreamer must be energetic and enthusiastic, must ask *why not* instead of *why*, and must never give up to defeat the opposition forces who defend the non-reform agenda, the opposition forces who replicate the Soviet Union's Cominterm, and who oppose the expansion of loving capitalism. The Chief Dreamer must identify who belongs in the opposition forces, and who is reluctant to embrace a paradigm shift, in order to persuade and conquer the hearts and minds of the orthodox, and be ready to defeat the Pirates of Heartless Capitalism who are not ready to acknowledge the urgency of our time.

The Chief Dreamer must be loving and understanding, must prioritize human dignity and environmental sustainability and be able to persuade the political and economic elites to embrace a paradigm shift that puts developed and developing countries on the same page, Page One of the History of Tomorrow.

It is time to move ahead once and for all. It is time to start a wonderful creative process that accelerates trends in order to become a catalyst of global accomplishments. Let's get to work and accomplish in 40 years what many thought would happen in two centuries. Let's drive today's society to the World of 2050, a world of Global Public Goods and a global currency, a world without diplomacy or

1. John Danilovich 2. Cheick Diarra 3. Branko Milanovic 4. Tomaz Salomao
5. Federico Mayor Zaragoza 6. Raymond Baker 7. Brian Donaldson 8. Knut Norheim Kjaer
9. Michael Intriligator 10. Kevin Fenton 11. Clarissa Brocklehurst

FIGURE 29.2 Who is Who in The Monfort Plan
Artwork by Joe Cummings.

12. Preston Chiaro 13. Shabbir Ahmed Chowdhury 14. Bernard Lietaer 15. Hazel Henderson
16. Joachim Von Braun 17. Robert Wade 18. Christiane Agboton-Johnson
19. Ndioro Ndiaye 20. Timothy Ziemer 21. Antonio Carlos Bueno de Camargo Silva

borders, where every human being can access health care and education, where every newborn can start living the World Dream.

The Chief Dreamer needs a chief of staff. **Enrique Mora** (CST) is the chief of staff of the former EU High Representative of Foreign Affairs and Common Security Javier Solana. I met Enrique on June 24, 2008, at the Justus Lipsius Building of the Council of Europe in Brussels (Belgium).

The Chief Dreamer will inhabit La Monfortcloa along with the five Spaniards and The Africans.[5] Fore more information see http://www.la-Monfortcloa.es.

I am an aspiring candidate for the role of Chief Dreamer.[6]

THE BEGINNING OF HISTORY AND THE FIRST MAN

Do we need a New Architecture? Should the current architecture be reformed? Have the Bretton Woods institutions served the purpose for which they were created? What are the roots of poverty? Poverty is originated and perpetuated because we are reluctant to reform in six key areas that represent the Axis of Feeble of today's capitalism. We, as a global society, are driving a vintage car that was designed and built in the 1940s and 1950s. There are two possibilities if we wish to travel faster and more comfortably. Either take the car to a garage or get a new one. We are in desperate need of a New Architecture. I have decided to dream of a new world of no poverty, a World of Cornucopia and Global Public Goods, where we live the World dream, where education and health care are globally provided. The new world begins on January 1, 2050, when the beginning of history takes off, when the first man is born in a world of no war and infinite possibilities.

I decided to look at the future and propose ideas that will allow us to write the History of Tomorrow. The theory of international relations is based on times that once were and will never be again, as well as on World Wars and Cold Wars, and on foreign policy agendas where unilateralism is predominant. This is not our world. Our world is a world full of optimism, where we can dream and love.

The 1940s and 1950s were times of phenomenal change because of the devastation brought about by World War II. The architecture designed in the 1940s and 1950s sought the economic reconstruction of war-torn Europe and the building of a system of collective security where peace-loving states would be able to avoid the pitfalls of another World War. We need a New Architecture whereby the priority is to look ahead and dare as we never dared before. It is time to think big again, it is time to feel the urgency and fight the great evils of our time with creativity and passion.

There will be a beginning of history where the first man will be born once we reach a society of global justice and global opportunity. There will be a beginning of history once we align the incentives of the poor with those of the rich, once we incorporate the long-term vision to the investment strategies of our money managers, and once we incorporate the long-term horizon to the corporate strategies of our corporations.

It is up to us as a global society to set the pace at which we would like to drive the car that drives us along the path of sustainability. It is up to us as a global society to drive a vintage care or to design a new car that will become a catalyst able to accelerate trends. The Bretton Woods institutions are instruments of foreign policy of our parents and grandparents; they represent the ideals of the baby boomers. The Bretton Woods institutions are politicized instruments of foreign policy of the United States and Europe. They forsake their ultimate goal because they prioritize the interest of the rich and the powerful above all else.

The shortest way to Eutopia is the proposition and implementation of an alternative architecture that is designed to work for the poor, where the developing world has a majority of the representative power. The shortest way to Eutopia is the creation of Global Public Goods through Global Redistribution.

There are two strategies when it comes to influencing the powerful. One can play the role of George Kennan or Jean Monnet and become an intermediary between the citizenry and the elites. Kennan and Monnet influenced the political elites of their time and brought about shifts in policy-making that helped secure peace and economic stability in war-torn Europe. One can also become powerful and lead the change through excremental change and reform.

This is a warning to the elites who rule today's capitalism. Hear the winds of change that come from our generation. Hear the winds of change that come from the Southern Hemisphere. It is time to become men and women of political stature. It is time to embrace the urgency of our time. It is time to wake up to the reality of an unequal world that perpetuates the great evils of our time. It is time to identify the Axis of Feeble and defeat it in an intellectual war that uses the Weapons of Mass Persuasion. We owe the current state of affairs to the great men and women of the 1940s and 1950s. It is time to follow their steps and learn the lessons of time and history.

Artwork by Mike Luckovich.

CHAPTER 30

The New Economic Architecture

*We of this generation did not create the civilization of which we are part
and, only too obviously, it is not we who are destined to complete it. We
are not the owners of the planet we inhabit; we are only its custodians.*
—George F. Kennan, *Memoirs 1950–1963*

The first two G20 summits that took place in Washington, DC, in November
2008, and in London in April 2009, set the pace of the financial reform that
should change the structure of the economic and financial architecture that has been
operating since the Bretton Woods summit of 1944. The big winner of the first two
summits was the International Monetary Fund (IMF). The IMF tripled its reserves.
The big losers were the fiscal and tax havens. This is a victory and a loss for the
alter-globalist movement that would have expected and hoped for a more radical
transformation of the Bretton Woods Institution. It is, however, not a bad beginning
in the difficult financial times we are currently experiencing, times where the lack of
creativity and leadership among our political elite is manifest.

A financial reform agreed upon by 20 countries is better than a reform agreed
upon by seven or eight countries. It seems that the the global community matures,
albeit at a slow pace. It seems that the West incorporates the representative power of
certain emerging countries to the decision-making process that rules today's capitalism. We should not forget other pending issues that today remain far away from the
radar of the leaders who met in Washington and London. Trade reform, investment
in agriculture, demographic control, agreements to limit the small arms trade, or an
increase and better allocation of development aid to deliver health care and education to the extreme poor, are all fundamental issues that will determine the future of
humankind.

Considering only financial reform is similar to adopting a myopic modus
operandi. The aim of those of us who expect to live through 2050 is to be demanding
of our political elite. We live in times that will determine whether we transition from
today's heartless capitalism to a loving capitalism, which will allow us to enter the
new Era of Sustainability, leaving the Pirates of Heartless Capitalism behind. The
perpetuation of short-term investment and the lack of responsible investors along
with ethical standards in our corporate policies will aggravate the already concerning
environment of poverty, pollution, and inequality we face as a society.

We are constantly looking at the performance of our stock markets to determine how well the economy is functioning. However, we forget to observe other trends in education and health care in many sub-Saharan African countries which the future of the planet inhabits. In a majority of countries of sub-Saharan Africa, almost half the population is under 18 years old. They are the future. It is important that they grow up healthy and educated, strong and prepared to face a challenging state of our evolution where capitalism must embrace the extreme poor. The Washington and London summits were summits that maintained the pattern of capitalism. There was no evolution. There was no world evolution. There are solutions to today's problems that do not seek the destruction of the current world order. There are solutions that propose an alternative architecture, one that is able to build a robust basis for a new capitalism.

We should not forget that the current ongoing crisis is not only economic or financial, but also geo-political. With the lack of consensus in the European Union, the U.S.-China relationship has deserved much focus and attention. The world has a long road ahead to transition from a superpower environment to a multilateral one. As long as the European Union is not ready to move ahead with a common foreign policy, Europeans will continue to lack the well-needed leadership when the United States' foreign policy is faulty, a United States that rules the world in a manner that is a far cry from the political stature of past times when Roosevelt or Truman inhabited the White House.

WORLD EVOLUTION

Thomas Friedman wrote his best-selling book *The World is Flat* in 2006. The *New York Times* columnist observed the part of globalization fundamentally positive, particularly to the West, but neglected to underline the collateral damage of globalization, the lack of labor standards in many countries, and the assymetric bargaining power of multinational companies that seek to minimize the labor and environmental standards of the locations in which they establish their headquarters. Friedman's vision stresses the positives and minimizes the negatives, transmitting a reality that does not hold.

In his book *Africa Rising*, the former dean of the Indian School of Business and professor of business at the University of Texas at Austin Vijay Mahajan, reminds us of the importance of Africa as a market (Mahajan 2008). Africa, in the eyes of Mahajan, is a market of 900 million consumers who, in per-capita income terms, earn more than the Indians. If Africa was a unique economy, it would be the world's tenth largest. Mahajan is an optimist who emphasizes the business appeal of areas that include health care and education. The market will not fill the gap left behind by nation-states that fail to deliver basic health care and education to their extreme poor. The market is not the solution to market failures or externalities that condemn the poor to live in a poverty trap that perpetuates over time. Market-advocates learned the lesson during the current economic crisis.

We need strong institutions able to deliver Global Public Goods. We need new institutions that sign a manifesto with developing countries that accept the direct delivery and provision of a basic welfare state to their extreme poor. We need long-term investors who are ethical, sustainable, and responsible. We need a compromise between the business sector and developing countries. It is easy to understand the appeal of Africa, according to Mahajan. The conflict of interest and hard-fought debate is whether or not profit-maximizing enterprises should exploit the extreme poor, commercially speaking.

For Benard Lietaer, "Duane Elgin claimed that humanity has always been at its best when its capacities are challenged to the maximum" (Lieater 2002). **DUANE ELGIN** (FUT) is the author of *Awakening Earth*. I spoke with Duane on December 5, 2008. For Duane, "To be sustainable, a civilization must maintain the integrity of the physical, social, and spiritual foundations upon which it is established." Duane concludes, "We have reached a pivotal time in our species evolution when we must make a momentous turn to reconnect with the natural world from which we struggled so mightily to escape and to heal the separations that divide us as a human family" (Elgin 1993).

HAZEL HENDERSON (FUT) is the founder and president of Ethical Markets LLC and a renowned futurist who celebrates cultural and biodiversity and a new *earth ethics* beyond *economism*. I talked to Hazel on June 12, 2009. In her book *Ethical Markets*, Hazel presents the core of her vision when she introduces the unpaid love economy, fair trade, renewable energy, shareholder activism, health and wellness, and the future of socially responsible investing. For Hazel, it is time to clarify the difference between money and wealth, GDP-growth, and quality of life. Hazel concludes, "We have learned that narrow, fragmented, short-term thinking is now too costly and is unsustainable" (Henderson 2006).

A WINDOW OF OPPORTUNITY

There is a Window of Opportunity that is opening up and will not remain open forever. The Social Business paradigm proposed by Nobel Peace Prize winner Muhammad Yunus should dominate the profit-maximizing model so long as the poor remain poor. It is time to align the incentives of corporations, and their shareholders and corporate managers, with those of the poor. Corporations should be required to embrace a modus operandi that fulfills the Social Business paradigm in the Yunus sense. Corporations would only transition to a <u>Profit-Maximizing</u> modus operandi when two triggers are hit: (1) a minimum per-capita income of $5,000 in purchasing power parity; and (2) a maximum Gini coefficient of 0.45, as explained in Chapter 5.

We cannot continue to operate under the previous economic paradigm, a unidimensional capitalism that prioritizes the interest of shareholders and emphasizes the shorter horizon over the longer horizon. We need ways to discriminate between short-term and long-term investors. We need to be aware of the pros and cons of globalization. Better times lie ahead of us if we put global priorities on the agendas of Europe and North America. If we do not dare, we risk losing a unique opportunity. History will judge the ability of our men and women of political stature to defeat the great evils of our time.

John F. Kennedy shouted twice in 1963, "*Ich bin ein Berliner.*" It is time for President Barack Obama and his counterparties in Europe to shout the urgency of our time, to fight the Pirates of Heartless Capitalism who wish to perpetuate an economic model that prioritizes the interests of a few. The global agency problem stems from the fact that the political and economic elites on both sides of the Atlantic do not propose reform in a direction that benefits both Hemispheres. The United States emphasizes the war on terror and continues to maintain a foreign policy that is too focused on Israel and the Middle East. The European Union is a monster with 27 heads unable to become a credible superpower. Europeans continue to hide behind the American friend, who rescues and bails out according to its user's manual, which is not representative of the interests of the global population.

The opportunity cost of not undertaking reform during this Window of Opportunity could be huge. The Window of Opportunity should not become the Widow of Opportunity. We cannot afford spoiling this opportunity. The elites, lobbies, think tanks, and orthodox academia are what Cominform was during the late 1940s, an instrument of propaganda of the Pirates of Heartless Capitalism, one that seeks to perpetuate an evil economic system responsible for creating wealth in the North at the expense of those in the South, and has allocated the wealth with tremendously unequal patterns. The U.S. middle class is not richer today in purchasing power parity than it was 30 years ago. We need more middle class, more sustainable and better allocated economic growth, and less inequality.

Where are the men and women of political stature? Let's displace the elites who are not ready to undertake reform. It is time to move one step forward, acknowledge the blame, and dare. The Window of Opportunity begins on the <u>Decem Date</u>. The first developed country that becomes Decempliant on or after the Decem Date will host Monfortcity, the headquarters of The Monfort Team, from where The Monfort Plan will be implemented.

THE FOUR PILLARS

The New Architecture of capitalism is based upon <u>Four Pillars</u>. Every new vision, every new doctrine, and every New Paradigm ought to be based upon Four Pillars. Three would make the structure fall on its knees. Five would be redundant. The Four Pillars are <u>Dream</u>, <u>Love</u>, <u>Cornucopia</u>, and <u>Eutopia</u>. We must dream and love to reach the world of Cornucopia and Eutopia. Those who do not dream, and those who do not love will lag behind and become dwellers of the Prison of Thought and the cage of the orthodox.

We must dream. If we do not dream awake, a better world will never materialize. Only if we dream will we be able to defeat the Pirates of Heartless Capitalism, who argue strongly in favor of returning to the old Washington Consensus, and who prioritize the market above human dignity, global justice, and environmental sustainability.

We must love. If we do not love, we will continue to ignore those among us who live in extreme poverty. If we do not love, we will perpetuate an income and inequality gap, we will continue to allocate wealth disproportionately, and we will not share the rewards of globalization in a fairer way.

Dream and Love will channel our best efforts and thinking to a proposal of solutions to the great evils of our time. Dream and Love will prepare an environment in which a New Paradigm can take off. Dream and Love will conquer the hearts and minds of the dwellers of this world, a majority of whom believe that poverty will be eternal. Dream and Love will set the path to start the Journey of our Lifetime that will take us to the world of Cornucopia and Eutopia.

The World of 2050 is a world of Cornucopia and Eutopia. Cornucopia is global food abundance. Eutopia is the delivery of Global Public Goods, the delivery of a Universal Welfare state that reaches the extreme poor. We have to invest today to realize the returns of our investment in the next 40 years. We must start the Glorious Forty that will take us to the World of 2050. We will make progress in 40 years equivalent to what many thinkers thought would happen in two centuries. The world of 2050 is the world of World Government and terra, the world's new currency.

The Four Pillars of the New Architecture will help global society write the History of Tomorrow. The journey that starts on the Decem Date will take us to Decemland, the land of 10 percent, where the New Institutions emerging in the New Paradigm will be based.

Only if we invest in the developing world will we obtain long-term, sustainable returns. We must start the Journey of our Lifetime. We will create the Decemfund, which becomes the Poor's Endowment, able to finance the Universal Welfare state from the Decem Date to 2050. Welcome to the new era of Global Public Goods, welcome to the era of Global Redistribution in which we ask *why not* instead of *why*.

I embrace the Four Pillars of the New Architecture. I dream and love, therefore I am. I found the Expert Dreamers who dream and love. Only a world of Cornucopia and Eutopia will prevail. Only a world of Cornucopia and Eutopia will guarantee that our children and grandchildren have the opportunities we inherited in the West from our parents and grandparents. It is time to leave the fears of the baby boomers behind. It is time to look ahead and imagine a better future. It is time to get to work.

The United States' President Barack Obama's four pillars were enumerated in *The American Spectator* as follows (Shattan 2009): cosmopolitanism, soft power, appeasement, and global meliorism. What does each of the four pillars mean and how do they interact with the Four Pillars of the New Architecture of capitalism?

Obama is the United States' first cosmopolitan president, as is "already evident from his trips abroad." Obama's soft power "doesn't just mean giving the U.N. a larger say" but also "pursuing greater economic justice and redistributing wealth." Obama's appeasement has much to do with his willingness to sit down, sans preconditions, with the leaders of countries that his predecessor included in the Axis of evil. Lastly, Obama's global meliorism was first embraced by President Truman and his Point Four program launched in 1949, which Truman described as "a bold new program for making the benefits of our scientific advances and industrial progress available for the improvement and growth of underdeveloped areas" (Shattan 2009).

Obama's hope and change message that catapulted him to the presidency of the most powerful nation on Earth has much to do with the Dream component of the New Architecture. Obama's soft power could be associated with the Love component of the New Architecture. His cosmopolitanism and likely global meliorism could contribute to reaching Cornucopia and Eutopia through Global Redistribution and the delivery of Global Public Goods.

DECEMPLIANT, MONFORTABLE, AND POVERTIMMUNE

There are three words that define the New Architecture of capitalism: Decempliant, Monfortable, and Povertimmune. Developed countries can become Decempliant.

Developing countries can become Monfortable. Decompliant developed countries and Monfortable developing countries can then establish a Povertimmune relationship that becomes the antidote against poverty in a new capitalist paradigm.

What does it mean to become Decompliant and Monfortable? Developed countries can become Decem-compliant or Decompliant. Firms and wealthy individiduals in developed countries can also become Decompliant. Decompliant describes the ability to become Decem-compliant. Decem-compliance is fulfilled if the Decem Policies are fulfilled, as explained in Chapter 24. In order to fulfill its respective Decem policy a country should raise 10 percent of its GDP in debt and contribute to the Poor's Endowment, otherwise called the Decemfund. A company should also contribute to the Decemfund with an allocation equivalent to 10 percent of its after-tax corporate earnings, a contribution called the Decem Tax. Finally, an individual should invest 10 percent of his or her wealth in excess of one million dollars in the Decemfund.

A developing country will be Monfortable if it agrees to receive the provision of Global Public Goods through a new institution called The New Institution. The New Institution delivers health care, education, water, and sanitation through an expanded microfinance network, getting rid of the middleman (the local administrations) and taking advantage of economies of scale. Developing countries that accept to become recipients of the delivery of such Global Public Goods agree to participate in an ex-ante conditionality scheme.

The new relationship between Decompliant countries and Monfortable countries enables the construction of a new geographic space that is Povertimmune. The Povertimmune environment hedges developing countries against the threat of the Pirates of Heartless Capitalism and the pitfalls of the six components of the Axis of Feeble. Developing countries can start to sustain economic growth and prosperity away from the externalities that many experts have attributed with the origination and perpetuation of poverty.

Decompliant and Monfortable countries are signatory of new rules in the areas of agriculture, trade and labor rights, small arms trade, extractive and mining industries, financial architecture, and brain drain. The new rules guarantee that Monfortable developing countries are Povertimmune and can grow away from the areas that originate and perpetuate the poverty trap.

Only Decompliant countries will take advantage of a new economic space that offers a healthy and educated workforce able to reach a middle-income status on the mid run. Companies will be able to operate in Monfortable countries if they decide to become Decompliant during the Window of Opportunity that opens up on the Decem Date. In the 40 year span that begins on the Decem Date and ends in 2050, Decompliant companies will operate according to a Social Business corporate model until the Monfortable countries reach two benchmarks: a per-capita income of $5,000 and a Gini coefficient under 0.45. From that point onwards and until 2050, Decompliant companies will be able to operate with a profit-maximizing corporate model to extract a profit out of those who once were extreme poor.

In the New Architecture of capitalism, incentives of developed and developing countries are aligned, and corporations that invest on the long run will become the victors of a new, redefined, and loving capitalism. This is the New Architecture where short-term investors are discriminated from long-term investors. This is the New Architecture that penalizes the Pirates of Heartless Capitalism.

THE HISTORY OF TOMORROW

The History of Tomorrow starts on the Decem Date. The History of Tomorrow triggers the Glorious Forty, able to push the globe forward toward the world of 2050, a world of Cornucopia and Eutopia, the world of Decemland, the land of 10 percent. I call all dreamers to start envisioning the world of which they dreamt. I call all dreamers to imagine the design of their utopia. I call the Expert Dreamers of our time. I call the wise men and women of our time. I call the disciples of Marshall and Truman. It is your time, a time when we must dare, and therefore exist.

I call all those who decided to never give up, who thought a better world was around the corner. There will be a Window of Opportunity that we cannot forsake. There will be a Window of Opportunity that we cannot afford missing. Those that do not get on the train of optimism will live in the Prison of Thought for the rest of their lives.

I call the orthodox thinkers and academics to convert, to become believers in a New Paradigm, to leave their user's manuals behind and embrace new horizons that lie ahead of us for which there are no quantitative models to predict future outcomes.

I call the right and the left, the progressive and the conservative. Let's get on the same page. Let's prioritize the interests of the developing world. Let's build toward a World of Cornucopia and Eutopia. Let's dream and love.

I call the Pirates of Heartless Capitalism to get ready to fight the battle of their lifetime. I call the Pirates of Heartless Capitalism to fight against the best team of Expert Dreamers that has ever served the global public interest. I found them hidden in the United Nations, the International Monetary Fund and the World Bank. I found them in Africa, Latin America, and Asia, in Europe and North America. I identified them in my numerous trips. Let's fight the battle of our lifetime. Let's defeat the Pirates of Heartless Capitalism once and for all. I call all human beings to believe that a paradigm shift is around the corner. I call all human beings to get ready for the Journey of our Lifetime. We will write Page One of the History of Tomorrow. A better world lies ahead of us if we are determined to improve and move ahead, leaving the fears of the baby boomers and the two World Wars behind.

Bretton Woods does not represent our generation. Our problems are those of the extreme poor. There are solutions to the great evils of our time that our current elites forgot or abandoned, that our current elites thought belonged in the imagination of our children, and that our current elites decided to leave for Hollywood movies or science-fiction books.

There is a Decemland waiting around the corner. There are Harmless Armed Forces to be deployed on 10 Islands of Peace. There are Decempliant countries and Monfortable countries. There are Povertimmune countries. There is a Race of the Century leading to the establishment of the New International Territory. As far as I know, I am not a character from a Hollywood movie or a science-fiction book. As far as I know, the Expert Dreamers who I identified are not figments of my imagination.

The potential to build a better world is only feasible if we believe change is around the corner. Let's export the welfare state to those who were born to live in eternal poverty. Let's eradicate disease and hunger once and for all. Let's start building a new world, the world of no diplomacy, the world without borders.

The New Architecture of Capitalism is the beginning of The History of Tomorrow. We will determine our own fate. We do not need Nostradamus or the Next Nostradamus to dictate that the models predict a World War III. There will be no World War III if we defeat the Axis of Feeble. There will be no World War III if we embrace the extreme poor and the environment.

It is time to shout the urgency of our time. It is time to become men and women of political stature. Where are the disciples of Marshall and Truman? Where are the disciples of Monnet and Schuman? Will you wake up Sleeping Beauty? Will you conquer the American friend?

Let's move ahead, let's start the Journey of our Lifetime, and let's ask *why not* instead of *why*. There is a new world ahead of us, there is a society waiting for us in 2050, expecting that we will undertake change and reform, expecting that we will prioritize the interest of the most vulnerable.

We extradited the excitement from the policy-making process. We adopted a modus operandi dictated by the rules and formulae that economists of the second half of the twentieth century invented. We have accepted the reality of armed conflict and food shortage with no reaction capacity. They are, after all, problems that shake remote societies, away from our daily routines, removed from our daily concerns.

The History of Tomorrow is not uncertain. The History of Tomorrow is not a reality beyond our own control, subjected to the ups and downs of the market and the randomness of fate. Today we can start building the History of Tomorrow. It is a history that brings both hemispheres closer together in issues related to income, welfare, health, human rights, and opportunity.

Progressive economists argue in favor of redistribution. Conservative economists defend that it is fundamental to increase the size of the pie by promoting economic growth. If we reform in the West and incorporate the emerging and poor countries, we will succeed at increasing the size of the pie and will more effectively redistribute it. Poor countries are a world to be explored, a world that will take off if we are determined to construct our own destiny, if we understand that today's capitalism is heading in the wrong direction. We determine the course of capitalism with our actions, decisions, behavior, and attitude.

We live a time of change on both sides of the Atlantic. The emerging world holds increasing influence. Asia has earned the relevance and importance that once upon a time belonged only to Europe and the United States. The world has gone through times of redefinition, when humankind has climbed the stairs of human evolution. We have banned the intellectual advancement and have substituted it with the monodimensional maximization of economic profit. We have ignored the collateral damage of economic principles that disregard human dignity and do not respect the environment.

We believed we had explored each corner of the globe. We announced the end of history. We were mistaken by our forecast. We forgot that the global society of the twenty-first century still has much to learn. It is a process of vertical growth, a growth in maturity and wisdom that draws us nearer to the society of tomorrow, to the society of 2050. Looking forward, I anticipate more understanding among countries, more cooperation and less competition, a more moderate consumption, the penalization of excess, and the adoption of dialogue and diplomacy instead of preventive war and silent struggles that should have expired with the fall of the Berlin wall. The time of Global Redistribution has arrived, a time of Global Public Goods, of economic and social returns, of functions of emotional utility. My satisfacion increases when I become fully aware that the worse off enter the path of self-reliance and economic sustainability, thereby leaving behind the poverty trap.

I believe in class mobility, in the reduction of inequality, in the abolition of extreme poverty, and in North-South cooperation. I anticipate changing times that take into account a horizontal world making vertical progress in the maturity of ideas, one which discovers new dimensions of understanding and change based on persuasion and the transmission of excitement—an excitement that sees a world moving ahead on the path of sustainable economic growth. Sustainable growth will grant each citizen of the blue planet access to a basic welfare state and the opportunity to build up wealth and assets, thanks to hard work and dedication.

It is time. It is our time. Let's move ahead.

Artwork by Mike Luckovich.

Notes

CHAPTER 1 Bretton Woods and the Washington Consensus

1. Richard Woodward is a Lecturer in political economy at the University of Hull. For Woodward, "Adam Smith was very sensitive to the non-economic effects of economic activity, and had a much more complicated perspective on human nature than many modern economists and economic models."
2. I would like to thank the directors of the master's programs that I have attended for having supported my applications: Linda Kreitzman of the *University of California at Berkeley*, Andrés Rodríguez Pose of the *London School of Economics and Political Science*, Guillermo Calvo of *Columbia University in the City of New York*, Anthony Clark Arend of *Georgetown University*, and Ros Plowman of the *London School of Hygiene and Tropical Medicine*.

   I would also like to thank Jesús Galvache Pina of Barclays Bank, which facilitated a credit line to finance the master's program at Berkeley, and to Adolfo Aznar Gil of the Spanish savings bank CajaDuero which provided a student loan to finance the master's program at Georgetown.

CHAPTER 2 Redefining Capitalism

1. This section is the translation of an article published on *El Mundo Mercados* on August 3, 2008 entitled "El Cambio de Paradigma."
   See http://www.elmundo.es/2008/08/03/mercados.

CHAPTER 3 Globalization and Poverty

1. Héctor Pérez Saiz contributed to improving this section. Héctor was part of the *5spaniards* team, which also included Silvia Montero-Ramos and Pablo Swedberg-González. For more information about 5spaniards see http://5spaniards.org
2. European Commission Employment, Social Affairs and Equal Opportunities.
   See http://ec.europa.eu/social.
3. Sometimes also known as speculator.
4. In order to qualify as a *Least Developed Country*, a country needs to have a three-year average of the gross national income under $750; severe problems in the areas of nutrition, health, education, and adult literacy; and be considered economically vulnerable in agriculture and exports.
5. Tunisia's National Solidarity Fund.
   See http://www.26-26.org.
6. Tunisia's National Solidarity Fund.
   See http://www.26-26.org.

CHAPTER 4   The Reality of Aid

1. The United States GDP for 2007 GDP was $13.80 trillion, according to the Bureau of Economic Analysis at the U.S. Department of Commerce.
2. Foundacion Center.
   See http://foundationcenter.org.

CHAPTER 5   The World's Income Distribution

1. Extreme poverty was subsequently redefined by the World Bank as having a disposable income of under $1.25 a day (U.S.) in 2005 purchasing power terms.
2. The history of AFS is worth mentioning. In 1947, a group of thirteen American volunteers who had driven ambulance units in war-torn Europe during World War II decided to create a nonprofit organization that would foster international understanding by exchanging students between any pair of countries. I owe much of who I am to the wonderful American volunteers who decided to give up their time and open their hearts and homes to a handful of European teenagers who arrived from overseas, willing to discover their particular American dream.
   The visionaries of AFS challenged their time with a forward-looking approach that helped secure European peace in the long run. In particular, I owe much of who I have become to AFS volunteers John and Ellen Evans and John and Barbara Thabet, and to AFSers Elisabeth Linhart from Austria, Francesco Cilloni from Italy, and Özgür Akdemir from Turkey.
3. Structural Funds.
   See http://ec.europa.eu/regional_policy.
4. Nobel Prize Simon Kutznets.
   See http://nobelprize.org/nobel_prizes/economics/laureates/1971.
5. The Gini coefficient measures income inequality and ranges between a value of 0 and 1. A Gini coefficient of 0 indicates perfect equality (everybody earns the same income), whereas a Gini coefficient of 1 indicates perfect inequality (one person holds all the wealth and the rest earn nothing). Denmark's Gini coefficient is the lowest in the world at 0.23. Namibia's Gini coefficient is the highest in the world at 0.74.

CHAPTER 6   Agriculture

1. Thomas Malthus (1766-1834).
   See http://www.ucmp.berkeley.edu.
2. Thomas Robert Malthus, 1766-1834.
   See http://cepa.newschool.edu.
3. IRRI is located in Los Baños, a town two hours south of Manila. IRRI's welcoming staff including the charming Bita Avendaño, Ria Anna Dimapilis and Duncan Macintosh.
4. The WFP's chief librarian, the charming Andreas Psoroulas, arranged the one-day visit to the headquarters of the Rome-based institution.
5. The great Pozuelo-Monfort family is a treasure that resides in Southeastern Spain, in the land of Francisco Salzillo and Juan de la Cierva. The family includes parents Antonio and Rita, siblings Ana, Jaime, Antonio, Maita, Carmela, Emilio, Miguel, Amalia, cousin Rodrigo Hernández Pozuelo and brother-in-law Ricardo Navarro Ropero.
6. The welcoming IRRI team in Dar es Salaam (Tanzania) included the welcoming Anna Nyacho and Ezekiel Shilili.

CHAPTER 7   Trade Liberalization and Labor Rights

1. David Ricardo, 1772-1823.
   See http://cepa.newschool.edu.
2. As of July 23, 2008. The last two members to join were Ukraine on May 16, 2008, and Cape Verde on July 23, 2008.
3. Idea proposed by Muhammad Yunus, who intends to open a poverty museum in Bangladesh once extreme poverty is eradicated from the Asian country.
4. Technical Comments on the WTO's "GATS – Fact and Fiction" Paper.
   See http://www.gatswatch.org.
5. What are intellectual property rights?
   See http://www.wto.org.
6. Standards concerning the availability, scope and use of Intellectual Property Rights.
   See http://www.wto.org.
7. Stolper-Samuelson for the real world.
   See http://rodrik.typepad.com.
8. Everything-But-Arms (EBA).
   See http://stats.oecd.org/glossary.
9. Decent work for all.
   See http://www.ilo.org.

CHAPTER 8   Small Arms Trade

1. The Illicit Arms Trade.
   See http://www.fas.org.
2. Land-mines: A deadly inheritance.
   See http://www.unicef.org.
3. Data for 1990 to 1993 includes the mandatory arms embargo on South Africa. The Figure only shows mandatory UN embargoes. Voluntary embargoes were established by UN Security Council resolutions on Afghanistan in October 1996 and on Eritrea and Ethiopia in 1999.

CHAPTER 9   The Extractive Industries

1. An agency problem arises when the goals of two different stakeholders with overlapping interests differ.
2. This has been the case between two Peruvian regions that have been fighting to claim the right to the revenues paid by the company Southern Copper (IB Times 2008). Southern Copper exploits two mining sites in the Peruvian regions of Moquegua and Tacna. The residents of Moquegua are requesting that the revenues be allocated on the amount of metal produced, instead of on the amount of earth removed from the mining site. This scheme would benefit them over the neighboring region of Tacna.

CHAPTER 10   Financial Architecture

1. Between May 2005 and May 2008, I worked for CIFG, a family of financial guaranty companies, in the offices of New York City and London. I would like to thank CIFG's chief executive officer Jacques Rolfo and recruiter Pamela Brown for their unconditional support that allowed me to study at the *London School of Economics* and at *Columbia*

University while working part-time. It was a pleasure to work for my two supervisors, Victor Mahoney and Joe Keepers.

2. OCDE 35 Jurisdictions Committed to Improving Transparency and Establishing Effective Exchange of Information in Tax Matters.
   See http://www.oecd.org.

3. Offshore Group of Banking Supervisors Conclude 25th Annual Meeting in the Cayman Islands.
   See http://www.ogbs.net.

4. Conditions of Membership.
   See http://www.ogbs.net.

5. The 40 Recommendations.
   See http://www.fatf-gafi.org.

6. Our People.
   See http://www.promontory.com.

7. Robert is one of the four co-authors of *Managing Credit Risk* (Wiley), along with John B. Caouette, Edward I. Altman, and Paul Narayanan. I worked as research assistant for the four co-authors from July 2006 to December 2007. The part-time work helped finance graduate studies at the London School of Economics.

CHAPTER 12   Lobbies and Elites

1. Bill Falloon, executive editor at Wiley, purchased a copy of *Slim's Table* for me at a University of Chicago bookstore on October 3, 2008. Without Bill's openmindedness and dreamer attitude, this book would have never been published. I thank Bill for being a dreamer who asks *why not* instead of *why*. Meg Freeborn, development editor with Wiley, gave fantastic feedback that helped improve the final manuscript and showed tremendous patience necessary to bear the persistence and infatigable attitude of this energetic Spaniard. Melissa Lopez, production editor with Wiley, completed the revision of The Monfort Plan.

2. The BAR examination is a qualification that enables law graduates to work in a particular jurisdiction.

3. American League of Lobbyists.
   See http://www.alldc.org.

4. These comments were originally posted on http://corporateresponsibility.blogs.ie.edu.

5. These are the final words in Andy Dufresne's letter to Red in *The Shawshank Redemption*.

6. Land statistics.
   See http://www.ruralpovertyportal.org.

CHAPTER 13   Institutional Reform

1. About the United Nations.
   See http://www.un.org.

CHAPTER 14   The Sleeping Beauty

1. Ambassador Jorge Pinto Mazal will be the Spanish-speaking anchor of Monfort Television.

2. Also known as the Treaty of Lisbon or Reform Treaty.

3. I have been *Erasmus student* twice at Télécom Paris in the academic year 1997-1998 and at Universität Stuttgart in the academic year 1999-2000.

4. European Commission Education & Training.
   See http://ec.europa.eu/education.
5. Chairman's Message.
   See http://www.cadfund.com.

CHAPTER 15 The Third Sector

1. Members of the Grameen Danone team in Bogra included the dynamic Brice Lewillie and Rémi Carpentier.
2. Association for the Taxation of Financial Transactions fo the Aid of Citizens.

CHAPTER 16 Marshall Revisited

1. The Glorious Thirty were the thirty years that followed World War II. The term was originally French (*Les Trente Glorieuses*) and related to France's resurgence after World War II.
2. Formally known as Marshall's Harvard address.
3. History.
   See http://www.studebakermotorcompany.com.
4. Packard Motors.
   See http://www.packardmotors.com.
5. Paul G. Hoffman.
   See http://www.hbs.edu/leadership/database/leaders.
6. Cominterm was the international communist organization in charge of spreading communist propaganda. Cominterm was officially dismantled by the Soviet Union in 1943.

CHAPTER 17 The Annan Plan

1. Members of the Paris Club include: Australia, Austria, Belgium, Canada, Denmark, Finland, France, Germany, Ireland, Italy, Japan, Netherlands, Norway, Russian Federation, Spain, Sweden, Switzerland, the United Kingdom, and the United States.
2. The lease precipitated the fall of former president Marc Ravalomanana in March in a *coup d'etat* that raised former mayor of Antananarivo Andry Rajoelina into power.
3. Board & Staff.
   See http://www.agra-alliance.org.

CHAPTER 18 A Eutopia of Universal Welfare

1. Years of economic growth in Europe in the aftermath of World War II.
2. The World Health Organization (WHO) is the health policy-making unit of the United Nations. It works with governments and Health Ministries to establish national strategies to prevent and treat diseases.
3. Between 1997 and 2007, IFC approved 54 investment projects in the health sector amounting to $580 million, a majority of which was invested in middle-income countries (IEG 2009).
4. A paraprofessional is an aide physician who has the knowledge but not the license to perform medical duties.
5. In particular, the text specifies two additional requirements, namely: (1) achieving a fifty percent improvement in levels of adult literacy by 2015, especially for women, and

equitable access to basic and continuing education; and (2) improving all aspects of the quality of education and ensuring excellence of all so that recognized and measurable learning outcomes are achieved by all, especially in literacy, numeracy, and essential life skills.

6. Sanitation is related to excreta management and liquid and solid waste management.

CHAPTER 19 The New Institution

1. The United Nations Charter is the constitution of the United Nations.
2. One goal of this chapter is to explain in what circumstances the Welfare Charter could be enforced, contrary to the United Nations Charter.
3. Charter of the United Nations Chapter I.
   See http://www.un.org.
4. (1) Goal 2: achieve universal primary education;
   (2) Goal 4: reduce child mortality; and
   (3) Goal 6: combat HIV/AIDS, malaria and other diseases.
5. Benin, Burkina Faso, Cape Verde, Cote d'Ivoire, Gambia, Ghana, Guinee, Guinee Bissau, Liberia, Mali, Niger, Nigeria, Senegal, Sierra Leone, and Togo.
6. Angola, Botswana, Democratic Republic of the Congo, Lesotho, Madagascar, Malawi, Mauritius, Mozambique, Namibia, Seychelles, South Africa, Swaziland, Tanzania, Zambia, and Zimbabwe.
7. Benin, Burkina Faso, Cape Verde, Ghana, Lesotho, Madagascar, Mali, Morocco, Mozambique, Namibia, and Tanzania.
8. Botswana has the lowest political risk in sub-Saharan Africa and a political risk score of 0.79 whereas Zimbabwe has the highest political risk and a political risk score of 0.02. Ghana is the most peaceful country in sub-Saharan Africa and has a peace index of 1.72, whereas Somalia is the most violent country in sub-Saharan Africa and has a peace index of 3.82. The peace index was not available for Benin, Cape Verde, and Lesotho.
9. At the BRAC Centre Inn in Dhaka (Bangladesh) I felt at home thanks to the welcoming Sales Manager Abul Hossain and his team of energetic gentlemen.
10. Christopher Dunford.
    See http://www.freedomfromhunger.org.
11. Integration of Microfinance and Other Services.
    See http://www.freedomfromhunger.org.
12. Chief Executive's Message.
    See http://nctcollege.ac.tz.
13. Institutions under the Ministry.
    See http://www.mst.go.tz.

CHAPTER 20 Conditionality

1. Eurodad is a network of 55 non-governmental organizations from eighteen European countries working in three areas: debt, development finance, and poverty reduction.
2. Poverty Reduction and Growth Facility, described in Chapter 13.
3. As of year-end 2008.
4. The combination of health, education, and community services received only 7 percent of all the MCC grants between 2005 and 2007.
5. Marc Ravalomanana was the democratically elected president of the Republic of Madagascar until former mayor of Antananarivo Andry Rajoelina took over through a *coup d'etat* in March 2009.

CHAPTER 21   Collateral

1. A microcredit is a small loan granted to a low income, entrepreneurial individual; it has no collateral attached and is typically used to set up a small business activity, otherwise called microbusiness.
2. The availability of collateral reduces the losses of a bank if the borrower goes bankrupt.
3. In this scenario, a borrower knows more than the financial institution about his or her repayment ability and does not disclose all the facts.
4. Moral hazard takes place when an individual takes greater risks because he or she is insured.
5. Adverse selection occurs when the individual to be insured knows more about the risk to be covered than the insurance company. The individual, by not facilitating some of the information, may lower the cost of the insurance coverage.
6. According to the ILO, a majority of countries exclude agriculture from their measurement of the informal sector and sometimes only the urban informal sector is considered.
7. Small and medium enterprises are defined as enterprises having less than 250 employees.

CHAPTER 22   The Yunus: A New Currency for the Poor

1. ECOWAS (Economic Community of West African States) is a group of 15 countries in West Africa whose mission is the promotion of economic integration.
2. COMESA (Common Market for Eastern and Southern Africa) is a supranational institution in Southeast Africa that includes the following countries: Burundi, Comoros, Democratic Republic of the Congo, Djibouti, Egypt, Eritrea, Ethiopia, Kenya, Libya, Madagascar, Malawi, Mauritius, Rwanda, Seychelles, Sudan, Swaziland, Uganda, Zambia, and Zimbabwe. The area has a population of over 400 million and a GDP of over $360 billion.
3. Single Global Currency Association.
   See http://www.singleglobalcurrency.org.
4. Nobel Prize Robert A. Mundell.
   See http://nobelprize.org/nobel_prizes/economics/laureates/1999.
5. As has been the case in Zimbabwe.

CHAPTER 23   Microsavings Insurance

1. Coincidentally, the same analysis would apply to microfinance in Bangladesh, another success story.
2. FDIC Statistics.
   See http://www.fdic.gov/sdi.

CHAPTER 24   Decemland

1. The Decemfund's principal will be invested according to a set of sustainable and responsible criteria. The return on the investment will be spent as development funds and will typically amount to 0.7% of a country's GDP if the return on the invested principal is on average 7% and the fund's principal is equivalent to a country's 10% of GDP. The Decemfund shifts today's 0.7% pay-as-you-go contribution to a more predictable return on an endowment that becomes the Poor's endowment.
2. The *Alcabala* is a precursor of the Decem Tax and was a ten-percent-tax on sales adopted in 1342 under Alfonso XI in the Crown of Castile.

CHAPTER 25   Innovative Financing

1. Book written by Yale economist Robert Shiller.
2. In 1836, Texas became independent from Mexico, and in 1945, it joined the United States.
3. Southern California was arguably part of Mexico between 1821 and 1846.
4. Alaska was purchased by the United States from the Russian Empire in 1867.
5. The Gadsden Purchase took place in 1853 to 1854 between the United States and Mexico.
6. Cuba and the Philippines were lost by Spain to the United States in the Spanish-American war of 1898, better known as *Desastre* in Spanish contemporary history.
7. See http://www.gov.mu/portal/site/housing.
8. Total wealth shrank during the financial crisis of 2008.
9. Provided that each lot of one hectare in NIT is sold for €1 million.
    See http://Decemland.com.
10. According to a survey conducted by Institutional Real Estate, Inc. and Kingsley Associates.

CHAPTER 26   The New International Territory

1. With the exception of Lesotho, which is not ranked by the *Economist Intelligence Unit.*

CHAPTER 27   Islands of Peace

1. The 10 Islands of Peace will receive the following names in the order in which they are leased from developing countries: Unos, Duo, Tres, Quattuor, Quinque, Sex, Septep, Octo, Novem, and Decem.
2. The equivalent of the Supreme Court of the United States.
3. Government of Bermuda.
    See http://www.gov.bm.
4. Status-of-Forces Agreement.
    See http://www.globalsecurity.org.

CHAPTER 28   The Race of the Century

1. Mervyn Brown, former U.K. Ambassador to Madagascar and author of *The History of Madagascar* (Brown 1993) contributed to improving the section on the world's fourth largest island.

CHAPTER 29   The Monfort Team

1. "We live in financial times" is the logo of the *Financial Times*, a leading international newspaper.
2. Monfortcity is the headquarters where The Monfort Team will be established during the Window of Opportunity presented in Chapter 30. Monfortcity will also be home of Decem University and Monfort Television (Monfort.TV).
3. Decem University will become the leading university of a Redefined Capitalism. The Expert Dreamers will teach the variety of disciplines involved in the implementation of The Monfort Plan and will educate the loving capitalists in the art of sustainable development.
4. Monfort Television will broadcast the work of The Monfort Team throughout the world. Monfort Television will entertain and educate viewers. Using the Weapons of Mass Persuasion, the Expert Dreamers, with their vision and work will raise the level of

awareness that will facilitate a necessary reform in Western countries in order to defeat the Axis of Feeble and start the Journey of our Lifetime on the Decem Date. Jenny Alonzo will be the chief executive officer of Monfort Television.

More can be found at http://Monfort.TV.

The Monfort Team will travel the world in The Monfort Plane that will become the world's most popular plane. Pablo Estrada will be the pilot of The Monfort Plane. *The Monfort News* is a blog aggregator that will feature the thoughts about a New Economic Paradigm of the Expert Dreamers. *The Monfort News* can become the equivalent of *The Huffington Post* in the development space. *The Monfort News* could subsequently be published as a newspaper in North America and Europe. Only native citizens from Povertimmune countries would be eligible to sell *The Monfort News* and the business would work as a Social Business, as explained in Chapter 15; that is, any profits would be reinvested in extreme poor countries through the delivery of global public goods.

More can be found at http://TheMonfortNews.net

5. The Africans are the Chief Dreamer's six African advisors. I met these fine ladies and gentlemen in 2009 during my trips to the Southern African cone. They are Micus Chimbombi (Botswana), Mabasia Mohobane (Lesotho), Fidele Rabenamanjara (Madagascar), Mohamed Harun (Mozambique), Charlotte Keyter (Namibia) and Richard Kasesela (Tanzania).

Fore more information about The Africans see http://TheAfricans.org.

6. Marketing strategist Daniel Pérez-Vidal and technology strategist Fernando Fernandes De Aquino will help the aspiring candidate to Chief Dreamer campaign to reach a thin consensus leading to the beginning of The Glorious Forty. I am proud of the men and women of my generation that will contribute to a changing world.

CHAPTER 30   The New Economic Architecture

1. There is a Next Generation that will be waiting our arrival in 2050 if we begin the Journey of our lifetime during the Window of Opportunity. Otherwise we risk missing a golden opportunity to explore new venues of understanding that will catalyze an acceleration of trends capable of bringing about peace and harmony to the society of 2050. It is a travel in time that will spare Humankind two hundred years of turmoil and uncertainty.

Bibliography

Aaronson, Susan. "Obama, the Optimist on Trade." *Financial Times*. July 22, 2008.

Acemoglu, Daron, and James A. Robinson, "The Political Economy of the Kuznets Curve," *Review of Development Economics* 6 (2002): 183–203.

Ada. *The Microfinance Rating Outlook Report 2008*. Ada (2008).

ADB. "Building Inclusive Financial Sectors for Development." Asian Development Bank. March 16, 2005.

AECI. "Microcredit Fund." Agencia Española de Cooperación Internacional, 2006.

Aerni, Victor, Christian de Juniac, Bruce Holley, and Tjun Tang. "A Wealth of Opportunities in Turbulent Times." Boston Consulting Group, September 2008.

Africa Recovery. "New African Initiative Stirs Cautious Hope." *Africa Recovery* 15. no. 3 (October 2001).

AFRIK. "Arms Convention for ECOWAS to Be Ready by the End of the Year." AFRIK, October 7, 2008.

Ahmed, Ehsan, J. Barkley Rosser, and Marina V. Rosser. "Income Inequality, Corruption, and the Non-Observed Economy: a Global Perspective," December 2004.

Aizenman, Joshua, and Robert P. Flood. "A Theory of Optimum Currency Areas." Working Paper 92/39 (Washington, DC: International Monetary Fund, 1992).

Alessandrini, Pietro, and Michele Fratianni. "Resurrecting Keynes to Stabilize the International Monetary System." December 4, 2008.

AMCOW, AfDB, the World Bank, and WSP. "Can Africa Afford to Miss the Sanitation MDG Target? A Review of the Sanitation and Hygiene Status in 32 Countries," 2008.

Andersen, T.B., H. Hansen, and T. Markussen. "US Politics and World Bank IDA-Lending." Institute of Economics, University of Copenhagen, May 2005.

Andersen, Torben M. "International Integration and the Welfare State." Working Paper No. 2002–2. (2002).

Anderson, Kym, Lee Ann Jackson, and Chantal Pohl Nielsen. "Genetically Modified Rice Adoption: Implications for Welfare and Poverty Alleviation." *Journal of Economic Integration* 20, no. 4 (December 2005): 771–88.

Anderson, Kenneth. "The Ottawa Convention Banning Landmines, the Role of International Non-governmental Organizations and the Idea of International Civil Society." *European Journal of International Law* 11 (2000): 91–120.

Africa Progress Panel. *An Agenda for Progress at a Time of Global Crisis*. Annual Report of the Africa Progress Panel, 2009.

Archer, Colin, *Whose Priorities? A Guide for Campaigners on Military and Social Spending*, by Colin Archer. Geneva: International Peace Bureau, 2007.

Archibugi, Daniele. "A League of Democracies or a Democratic United Nations." *Harvard International Review*, 2008.

Arend, A.C., R.J. Beck, and R.D. Vander Lugt. *International Rules*. London: Oxford University Press, 1996.

Arend, Anthony Clark. *Legal Rules and International Society*. London: Oxford University Press, 1999.

Armendariz de Aghion, Beatriz, and Jonathan Morduch. "Microfinance: Where Do We Stand?" (2004).

Aron, Raymond. *Peace and War: A Theory of International Relations.* Garden City, NY: Doubleday & Company, 1966, 591–600.

Asia-Pacific News. "Leaders seek to boost Africa's agriculture output." May 29, 2008.

Attac. Contributions to Attac's Political Project. 2005.

Attali, J. "Microfinance And Banks." *Planet Finance,* March 17, 2006.

Ayres, R.L. *Banking on the Poor.* Boston: The MIT Press, 1984.

Ayyagari, Meghana, Thorsten Beck, and Asli Demirguc-Kunt. "Small and Medium Enterprises Across the Globe." *Small Business Economics* 29, no. 4 (December 2007): 415–34.

Backman, Gunilla. "Health Systems and the Right to Health: An Assessment of 194 Countries." *The Lancet,* December 10, 2008.

Baker, Raymond, and Eva Joly. "The Issue of Illicit Financial Flows." *Commentaire Hiver 2008–2009,* 31, no. 124 (2008a).

Baker, Raymond, John Christensen, and Nicholas Shaxson. "Catching Up with Corruption." *The American Interest* (September–October 2008b).

Baker, Raymond. *Capitalism's Achilles Heel.* Hoboken, NJ: John Wiley & Sons, 2005.

Balasubramanian, V., M. Sie, R.J. Hijmans, and K. Otsuka. "Increasing Rice Production in Subsaharan Africa: Challenges and Opportunities." *Advances in Agronomy* 94 (2007).

Baldwin, Richard, and Simon Evenett. *What World Leaders Must Do to Halt the Spread of Protectionism.* London: Centre for Economic Policy Research, 2008.

Banerjee, Abhijit V., and Ruimin He. "The World Bank of the Future." Working Paper 03-06, Massachusetts Institute of Technology Department of Economics Working Paper Series, January 2003.

Bardhan, Ashok, Jackie Begley, Cynthia A. Kroll, and Nathan George. "Global Tourism and Real Estate." Fisher Center for Real Estate and Urban Economics, Haas School of Business. Paper prepared for the Sloan Industry Studies Conference, Boston, Massachusetts, May 2, 2008.

Barr, M.S. "Microfinance and Financial Development." *Michigan Journal of International Law* (2005).

Barrett, William P. "America's 200 Largest Charities." *Forbes Magazine,* November 19, 2008.

Barry, Christian, and Sanjay G. Reddy. *International Trade and Labor Standards: A Proposal for Linkage.* New York: Columbia University Press, 2008.

Bates, Robert H. Prosperidad y Violencia. Edited by Antoni Bosch, 2004.

Baue, W. "Consortium Advances Microfinance as an Emerging New Asset Class." *Social Funds,* November 9, 2005.

Becchetti, Leonardo, and Fabrizio Adriani. "Fair Trade: a Third Generation Welfare Mechanism to Make Globalisation Sustainable." Tor Vergata, Centre of Economic and International Studies Research Paper Series, Rome, Italy, November 15, 2004.

Becchetti, Leonardo, and Furio Rosati. "Global Social Preferences and the Demand for Socially Responsible Products: Empirical Evidence from a Pilot Study on Fair Trade Consumers." Working Paper No. 91 (Rome, Italy: Tor Vergata, Centre of Economic and International Studies Research Paper Series, February 2007).

Beck, T., A. Demirguc-Kunt, and M.S. Martinez Peria. "Reaching Out: Access to and Use of Banking Services across Countries." Working Paper 3754 (Washington, Dc: World Bank Policy Research Working Paper Series, April 2005.

Becker, Kristina Flodman. *The Informal Economy.* Swedish International Development Agency, March 2004.

Behrman, G. *The Most Noble Adventure: The Marshall Plan and the Time When America Helped Save Europe.* New York: Free Press, August 2007.

Beintema, Nienke M., and Gert-Jan Stads. "Measuring Agricultural Research Investments." *Asti Background Note,* October 2008.

Bellemare, Marc F. "Hunger in Africa: A Structural Problem." Office of News & Communications, Duke University (April 18, 2008).

Benoit, Bertrand, and Ben Hall, "Berlin calls for Swiss to be on tax blacklist," *Financial Times*, October 22, 2008

Berger, Sebastian. "Zimbabwe Hyperinflation Will Set World Record within Six Weeks." *Telegraph*, November 13, 2008.

Bergh, Andreas, "The Universal Welfare State: Theory and the Case of Sweden." *Political Studies* 52 (2004): 745–766.

Berkol, Ilhan. *Analysis of the ECOWAS Convention on Small Arms and Light Weapons and Recommendations for the Development of the Action Plan.* Group for Research and Information on Peace and Security, April 2007.

Bernholz, P. "Democracy and Capitalism: Are They Compatible in the Long-Run?" Paper presented at the meeting of the International Schumpeter Society, Vienna, Austria 1998.

Besada, Hany. "The Implications of China's Ascendancy for Africa." Working Paper 40 (Waterloo, Ontario: The Centre for International Governance Innovation, October 2008).

Bhagwati, Jagdish. *In Defense of Globalization.* New York: Oxford University Press, 2004.

———. *Termites in the Trading System: How Preferential Agreements Undermine Free Trade.* New York: Oxford University Press USA, 2008.

Bhagwati, Jagdish. "Obama and Trade: An Alarm Sounds." *Financial Times*, January 8, 2009.

Birdsall, Nancy, and Devesh Kapur. "The Hardest Job in the World." Center for Global Development, June 1, 2005.

Birdsall, Nancy. "World Bank Revisions in PPP GDP Show China and India 40 percent Poorer." Center for Global Development, 2008.

Black, Maggie, and Ben Fawcett. *The Last Taboo: Opening the Door on the Global Sanitation Crisis.* London: Earthscan Publications, 2008.

Black, Richard. "Immigration and Social Justice: Towards a Progressive European Immigration Policy?" *Transactions of the Institute of British Geographers, New Series* 21, no. 1 (1996): 64–75.

Bogle, J.C. *The Battle for the Soul of Capitalism.* New Haven: Yale University Press, 2005.

Bonpasse, Morrison. *The Single Global Currency: Common Cents for the World.* The Single Global Currency Association, 2006.

Borger, Julian. "US Biofuel Subsidies Under Attack at Food Summit." *The Guardian*, June 3, 2008.

Boswell, C. "The External Dimension of EU Immigration and Asylum Policy." *International Affairs* 79, No. 3 (2003): 619-38.

Bouet, Antoine. *The Expected Benefits of Trade Liberalization for World Income and Development.* International Food Policy Research Institute, 2008.

Boughton, J.M. "The IMF and the Force of History: Ten Events and Ten Ideas That Have Shaped the Institution." Working Paper WP/04/75 (Washington, DC: International Monetary Fund, May 2004).

Bounds, Andrew. "US Aid Chief Faces Challenge of Tight Funds." *Financial Times*, April 7, 2006.

Bourguignon, François, Victoria Levin, and David Rosenblatt. "Global Redistribution of Income." Working Paper 3961 (Washington, DC: World Bank Policy Research Working Paper Series, July 2006).

Bourguignon, François, Agnes Benassy-Quere, Stefan Dercon, Antonio Estache, Jan Willem Gunning, Ravi Kanbur, Stephan Klasen, Simon Maxwell, Jean-Philippe Platteau, and Amedeo Spadaro. "Millennium Development Goals at Midpoint: Where do we stand and where do we need to go?" (2008).

Brahm, Laurence J. *The Anti-Globalization Breakfast Club.* Hoboken, NJ: John Wiley & Sons, 2009.

Brinkley, Douglas, and Clifford Hackett. *Jean Monnet: The Path to European Unity.* New York: St. Martin's Press, 1991.

Brocklehurst, Clarissa. "The Case for Water and Sanitation." *Water and Sanitation Program,* November 2004.

Brown, Mervyn. *The History of Madagascar.* Markus Wiener Publishers, 2002

Brown, Lawrence D., and Lawrence R. Jacobs. *The Private Abuse of the Public Interest.* Chicago: University of Chicago Press, 2008.

Bruntrup, Michael. "Everything but Arms and the EU-Sugar Market Reform—Development Gift or Trojan Horse?" Discussion Paper for the German Development Institute, October 2006.

Bryant, Chris, and Javier Blas. "Food Inflation Threatens Progress on Poverty." *Financial Times,* April 9, 2008a.

Bryant, Chris, and Krishna Guha. "IMF Cost Cuts Spur Almost 500 Redundancies." *Financial Times,* April 30, 2008b.

Bueno de Mesquita, Bruce, and Alastair Smith. *Foreign Aid and Policy Concessions, Journal of Conflict Resolution,* Vol. 51, No. 2, 251–284, 2007.

Buigut, Steven, and Neven Valev. "Monetary Union and Central Bank Independence." Working Paper 06–54, Andrew Young School of Policy Studies Research Paper Series, May 2006.

Buncombe, Andrew, and Stephen Castle. "Exxon Spends Millions to Cast Doubt on Warming." *The Independent,* December 7, 2006.

Butcher, A. Allen. "Democracy and capitalism: are they critical elements of a climax human culture?," Progressive Living, 1992. http://www.progressiveliving.org/DEMCAP.htm

Byström, Hans. "The Microfinance Collateralized Debt Obligation: a Modern Robin Hood?", *World Development,* Vol. 36, pages 2109–2126, 2006.

Cadwalader. "Clients & Friends Memo." Cadwalader Wickersham & Taft LLP, March 6, 2009.

Calderisi, Robert. *The Trouble with Africa: Why Foreign Aid Isn't Working.* New York: Palgrave Macmillan, 2006.

Caldwell, C. "Utopia with border control." *Financial Times,* August 12, 2006.

Caouette, Jack, Edward I. Altman, Paul Narayanan, and Robert Nimmo. *Managing Credit Risk: The Great Challenge for Global Financial Markets.* Hoboken, NJ: John Wiley & Sons, 2008.

Capgemini, and Merrill Lynch. *World Wealth Report 2009,* June 24, 2009.

Capie, Forest. "The Evolution of General Banking." Working Paper 1534 (Washington, DC: World Bank Policy Research Working Paper Series, November 1995).

Carrington, W.J., and Detragiache E. "How Big is the Brain Drain?" Working Paper 98 (Washington, DC: International Monetary Fund, 1998).

Castro Valdes, J., J.P. Gil, G. Kabance, S. Fox. "Rating Methodology For Bolivian Microfinance Credits." *Fitch Ratings,* 2007.

CCM. *Convention on Cluster Munitions.* Diplomatic Conference for the adoption of a convention on cluster munitions, May 30, 2008.

CECP. Giving in Numbers. Committee Encouraging Corporate Philanthropy, 2008. http://www.corporatephilanthropy.org/benchmarking.html

CEO. *Brussels Think Tanks Survey 2006.* Corporate Europe Observatory, December 2006.

Cervantes, Mario, and Dominique Guellec. "The Brain Drain: Old Myths, New Realities." *OECD Observer* No. 230, January 2002.

Chaves, R.A., and Claudio Gonzalez-Vega. "Principles of Regulation and Prudential Supervision and their Relevance for Microenterprise Finance Organizations." In *The New World of Microenterprise Finance.* Edited by M. Otero, and E. Rhyne. West Hartford: Kumarian, 1994: 55–75.

Chen, Hui, David Parsley, and Ya-Wen Yang. *Corporate Lobbying and Financial Performance,* June 2008. http://papers.ssrn.com/sol3/papers.cfm?abstract_id=1014264

Chipeta, Chinyamata, and Klaus Schade. "A Comparative Analysis of 10 Country Studies and Surveys of Business and Non-State Actors." *Regional Integration in Southern Africa* 12 (May 2007).

Chowdhry, Bhagwan. "Regulators Need to be Open to Innovation." *The Financial Express*, 2005.

Christen, Robert. "Regulation and Supervision of Microfinance." CGAP, October 2002.

Christensen, John. "Tax Avoidance, Tax Havens and the Genesis of the Tax Justice Network." Tax Justice Network, January 2005.

———. "Closing the Floodgates." Tax Justice Network, 2007a.

———. "Towards Tax Justice for Europe." Sbilanciamoci Forum, Marghera L'impresa di un'economia diversa, September 6–9, 2007b.

———. "Can Pay... Won't Pay!" *New Internationalist* 416 (October 2008).

Christiaensen, Luc, and Lionel Demery. *Down to Earth: Agriculture and Poverty Reduction in Africa*. Washington, DC: The World Bank, 2007.

Chu, Michael. "Why Do We Care About Responsible Finance?" Frankfurt Forum 2008: Responsible Finance, Kfw & Frankfurt School of Finance and Management, February 21, 2008.

Chung, Joanna, and Haig Simonian. "Bankers Charged in US Tax Evasion Case." *Financial Times*, May 14, 2008.

Chung, Joanna. "Former UBS Banker Expected to Plead Guilty in Tax Evasion Case." *Financial Times*, May 30, 2008.

Citigroup. "Bangladesh: Citigroup Supports World's First AAA-Rated Microcredit Securitization." *Citigroup Press Release*, July 6, 2006.

Clark, Renata, Lee-Ann Jaykus, Marion Woolridge, J. Michael Frank, Marina Miraglia, Abigail McQuatters-Gollop, Cristina Tirado, and Mary Friel. "Climate Change: Implications for Food Safety." FAO, 2008.

Clark, Gregory. *A Farewell to Alms*. Princeton, NJ: Princeton University Press, 2007.

Claybrook, Joan. "History of the Lobbying Disclosure Act." *Public Citizen*, July 23, 2005.

Clemens, Michael A., and Moss, Todd J. "Ghost of 0.7 Percent: Origins and Relevance of the International Aid." *International Journal of Development Issues* Vol. 6 No. 1, pp. 3–25, 2007.

Clemens, Michael A., and Gunilla Peterson. "A New Database of Health Professional Emigration from Africa." Working Paper Number 95 (Center for Global Development, August 2006). http://www.cgdev.org/content/publications/detail/9267.

Clift, Jeremy. "Beyond the Washington Consensus." *Finance & Development*, September 2003.

Cohen, Gary M. "Access to Diagnostics in Support of HIV/AIDS and Tuberculosis Treatment in Developing Countries." *AIDS* 21, suppl 4 (2007): S81–S87.

Cohn, Raymond. "Immigration to the United States." EH.Net Encyclopedia. Edited by Robert Whaples. (August 14, 2001), http://eh.net/encyclopedia/article/cohn.immigration.us.

Collier, Paul. "On the Economic Consequences of Civil War." *Oxford Economic Papers* 51 (1999): 168–83.

Collier, Paul. *The Bottom Billion: Why the Poorest Countries are Failing and What Can be Done About it*. London: Oxford University Press, 2007.

Collier, Paul. "A Chance to Crack Down on Africa's Loot-Seeking Elites." *The Guardian*, October 7, 2008.

Collins, Daryl, Jonathan Morduch, Stuart Rutherford, and Orlanda Ruthven. *Portfolios of the Poor*. Princeton: Princeton University Press, 2009.

Commonwealth. "Commonwealth Code of Practice for the International Recruitment of Health Workers." Adopted at the Pre-Wha Meeting of Commonwealth Health Ministers, 2003.

Conway, Michael D., Srishti Gupta, and Kamiar Khajavi. "Addressing Africa's Health Workforce Crisis." *The McKinsey Quarterly*, November 2007.

Cooper, Richard N. "Proposal for a Common Currency of Rich Democracies." Paper Presented at Harvard University, 2006.

Counts, Alex, and Patrick Meriweather. "New Frontiers In Microsavings." Grameen Foundation, March 2008.

Cromwell, William C. "The Marshall Non-Plan, Congress and the Soviet Union." *The Western Political Quarterly* 32, no. 4 (December 1979) 422–443.

Crook, Clive. "Obama Has to Lead the Way on Trade." *Financial Times*, December 22, 2008.

Crowther, Greg. "Counting the Cost: the Economic Impact of Cluster Ammunition Contamination in Lebanon." *Landmine Action*, 2008.

Cull, Robert, Lemma W. Senbet, and Marco Sorge. "Deposit Insurance and Financial Development." World Bank Policy Research Working Paper No. 2682. March 2003.

Cullen, Roy. *The Poverty of Corrupt Nations*. Toronto: Blue Butterfly, 2008.

Daly, H.E., and J.B. Cobb Jr. *For The Common Good*. Boston: Beacon Press, 1989.

Dammasch, S. "The System of Bretton Woods: A Lesson from History." 2000. http://www.unimagdeburg.de/fwwdeka/student/arbeiten/006.pdf

Danilovich, John J., and Jonathan T.M. Reckford. "An End to Global Poverty Starts with Property Rights." *The Atlanta Journal-Constitution*, November 25, 2008.

Davis, Graham A., and John E. Tilton. "Why the Resource Curse Is a Concern." Colorado School of Mines, 2007.

De la Dehesa, G. *Europe at the Crossroads*. New York: McGraw-Hill, 2006.

De Soto, Hernando. *The Mystery of Capital: Why Capitalism Triumphs in the West and Fails Everywhere Else*. Black Swan, 2001a.

———. "The Secret of Non-Success." *TIME Magazine*, April 16, 2001b.

Deardorff, Alan V. "What Might Globalization's Critics Believe?" Discussion Paper No. 492, University of Michigan, December 2002.

Deen, Thalif. "Binding Treaty Eludes Small Arms Trade." *IPS News*, August 8, 2008.

Demeny, P. "Population Policy in Europe at the Dawn of the Twenty-First Century." *Population and Development Review* 29, no. 1 March (2003): 1–28.

Demirgüç-Kunt, Asli, and Edward J. Kane. "Deposit Insurance Around the Globe: Where Does it Work?" World Bank Policy Research Working Paper No. 2679. September 2001.

Demirgüç-Kunt, Asli, Baybars Karacaovali, and Luc Laeven. "Deposit Insurance Around the World: A Comprehensive Database." Working Paper 3628 (Washington, DC: World Bank Policy Research Working Paper Series, June 2005).

Devarajan, Shantayanan, William R. Easterly, and Howard Pack. "Low Investment Is Not the Constraint on African Development." Center for Global Development Working Paper No. 13. October 2002.

Devarajan, Shantayanan. Two Comments on "Governance Indicators: Where Are We, Where Should We Be Going?," Daniel Kaufmann and Aart Kraay, The World Bank Observer, February 19, 2008.

Devi, Sharmila. "Real Estate: Fancy a Pad in Paradise?" *Financial Times*, March 11, 2008.

Dick, Christian D., and Qingwei Wang. "The Economic Impact of the Olympic Games: Evidence from Stock Markets." Discussion Paper No. 08-060 (Centre for European Economic Research, 2008).

Diebold, William, Jr. "American Mobilization and European Recovery." *Proceedings of the Academy of Political Science* 24, no. 3, Mobilizing American Power for Defense (May 1951: 3–18).

Dieckmann, Raimar. "*Microfinance: an Emerging Investment Opportunity*." Deutsche Bank Research, December 19, 2007.

Dollar, David, and V. Levin. "The Increasing Selectivity of Foreign Aid 1984–2002." Working Paper 3299 (Washington, DC: World Bank Policy Research Working Paper Series, March 2004).

Dowden, Richard. Africa's Leadership Crisis." *TIME Magazine*, June 11, 2008.

Dreyfus, Pablo, Luis Eduardo Guedes, Ben Lessing, Antonio Rangel Bandeira, Marcelo de Sousa Nascimento, and Patricia Silveira Rivero. "Small Arms in Rio de Janeiro." *Small Arms Survey*, 2008.

Duignan, Peter J., and Lewis H. Gann. "The Marshall Plan." *Hoover Digest* 4, 1997.

Duneier, Mitchell. *Slim's Table*. Chicago: University of Chicago Press, 1992.

Duran, Pere. "the Impact of the Olympic Games on Tourism." Centre D'estudis Olimpics, 2002.

Dyal-Chand, Rashmi. "Human Worth as Collateral." Working Paper Series No. 09-2006, Northeastern Public Law and Theory Faculty, October 2006.

Easterly, William, and Ross Levine. "Africa's Growth Tragedy: Policies and Ethnic Divisions." *Quarterly Journal of Economics* 112, no. 4 (1997): 1203–1250.

Easterly, William. *The Elusive Quest for Growth*. Cambridge, MA: The MIT Press, 2001.

———. "The Cartel of Good Intentions: The Problem of Bureaucracy in Foreign Aid." *Foreign Policy* 131 (July/August 2002: 40–49).

———. "Can Foreign Aid Buy Growth?" *Journal of Economic Perspectives* 17, no. 3 (Summer 2003): 23–48.

———. *The White Man's Burden: Why the West's Efforts to Aid the Rest Have Done So Much Ill and So Little Good*. New York, Penguin Books, 2006.

Economist, The. "Copenhagen Consensus: Putting the World to Rights," June 3, 2004a.

———. "More or Less Equal?" March 11, 2004b.

———. "The Hidden Wealth of the Poor," November 3, 2005.

———. "Illegal immigration to Italy," August 24, 2006a.

———. "Migration Migraine," September 14, 2006b.

———. "The Birth of Philanthrocapitalism," February 23, 2006c.

———. "Not Quite as Stellar as It Looks," November 29, 2007a.

———. "Small Loans and Big Ambitions," March 15, 2007b.

———. "The Think-Tanks That Miss the Target," June 7, 2007c.

———. "The Trouble with Migrants," November 22, 2007d.

———. "Sovereign-Wealth Funds: Asset-Backed Insecurity," January 17, 2008.

———. "Give and Count the Cost," May 7, 2009a.

———. "Sex and Sensibility," March 19, 2009b.

———. "Sin Aqua Non," April 8, 2009c.

———. "Swing Low Swing Right," June 11, 2009d.

EEA, *Indicator Fact Sheet Signals 2001*. European Environment Agency, 2001.

Efrat, Asif. "Regulating Rifles: International Control of the Small Arms Trade." 3rd Annual Conference on Empirical Legal Studies Papers July 22, 2008.

Ehui, Simeon, and Marinos E Tsigas. "Identifying Agricultural Research and Development Investment Opportunities in Subsaharan Africa." *Afjare* 1.1 (December 2006).

Eichenwald, Kurt. "Will Capitalists End Capitalism?" *El País*, July 7, 2002.

El Mundo. "Spain Is the World's Main Ammunition Exporter to Subsaharan Africa," June 16, 2006.

Elgin, Duane. *Awakening Earth: Exploring the Evolution of Human Culture and Consciousness*. New York: William Morrow & Co., 1993.

Ellwood, David W. "The Marshall Plan: A Strategy that Worked." *Peace & Security*, May 8, 2008.

England, Andrew. "Us Gives Morocco Assistance Package." *Financial Times*, August 31, 2007.

ENS. "WWF: Stopping Climate Cange Is Possible." *Environment News Service*, May 2, 2007.

Entorf, H. "Rational Migration Policy Should Tolerate Non-Zero Illegal Migration Flows: Lessons from Modelling the Market for Illegal Migration." *Iza Dp* 199 (September 2000).

Epp, Charles R. "Do Lawyers Impair Economic Growth?" *Law & Social Inquiry, Journal of the American Bar Foundation* 17, No. 4 (July 28, 2006): 585–622.

Epstein, Richard A. "Aids Drugs: Are Property Rights and Human Rights in Conflict?" *Financial Times*, May 7, 2007.

Esping-Andersen, G. *The Three Worlds of Welfare Capitalism.* Princeton, NJ: Princeton Univesity Press, 1990.

Euractiv. "Commission Tries to Get to Grips with Recent Immigration Crises," July 20, 2006.

Eurodad. "World Bank and Imf Conditionality: a Development Injustice," June 2006.

Faini, Riccardo. "Remittances and the Brain Drain." IZA Discussion Paper No. 2155. May 2006.

Fairtrade. "Doha: Fairtrade Response," July 31, 2008.

FAO. Crop Prospects and Food Situation No. 2 (April 2008). http://www.fao.org/docrep/010/ai465e/ai465e00.htm

Fayissa, Bichaka, Christian Nsiah, and Badassa Tadasse. "The Impact of Tourism on Economic Growth and Development in Africa." Department of Economics and Finance Working Paper Series, Middle Tennessee State University, August 2007.

Farrell, Diana. "Tackling the Informal Economy." *BusinessWeek*, May 8, 2006.

Fenton, Kevin. "Global HIV Trends." The National Center for HIV/AIDS, 2008.

Fessenden-Joseph, Lea Ann. "Three Offshore Islands Fifth Biggest Banking Centre." *Caribbean Property Magazine* 23, December 2008.

Fiebig, Michael, Alfred Hannig, and Sylvia Wisniwski. "Savings in the Context of Microfinance." Cgap, 1999.

FIFA. "KE NANO Celebrate Africa's Humanity." 2010 FIFA World Cup Organising Committee South Africa, 2009.

Financial Express. "Grameen Group, Group Danone Teamup to Set up Social Business Enterprise," April 10, 2006.

Financial Times. "Lessons Learnt for Capitalism's Future," May 12, 2009.

Finnemore, M. *National Interests in International Society.* Ithaca: Cornell University Press, 1996.

Fleishman, Joel L. *The Foundation.* New York: PublicAffairs, 2007.

Foley, Brian J. "Reforming the Security Council to Achieve Collective Security." Edited by Miller & Bratspies. *Progress in International Law* (2008): 573–592.

Fossedal, Gregory, and Bill Mikhail. "A Modest Magician: Will Clayton and the Rebuilding of Europe." *Foreign Affairs*, May/June 1997.

Fox, Richard, and Veronica Kalema. "Africa: Politics to the Fore." *Fitch Ratings*, February 5, 2008.

France Presse. "Danone to Open a Second Yogurt Plant in Bangladesh." April 30, 2008. http://www.industryweek.com/articles/danone_to_open_second_yogurt_plant_in_banglad esh_16227.aspx

Franck, Thomas M. "European Communities in Africa." *The Journal of Negro Education* 30, no. 3, African Education South of the Sahara (Summer 1961): 223–231.

Frankel, Jeffrey A. "No Single Currency Regime Is Right for All Countries." New Century Chair, the Brookings Institution. May 21, 1999.

Fruchart, Damien, Paul Holtom, Siemon T. Wezeman, Daniel Strandow, and Peter Wallensteen. *United Nations Arms Embargoes: Their Impact on Arms Flows and Target Behaviour.* Stockholm International Peace Research Institute and Uppsala University, Department of Peace and Conflict Research, November 2007.

Fulginiti, Lilyan E., Richard K. Perrin, and Yu Bingxin. *Institutions and Agricultural Productivity in Subsaharan Africa.* Agricultural Economics, 31, 2–3, December 2004.

Global Security, "Diego Garcia Camp Justice." Global Security, 2005.

Garten, Jeffrey E. "We Need a Bank of the World." *Newsweek Magazine*, November 3, 2008.

Geneva Declaration. Global Burden of Armed Violence, 2008. http://www.genevadeclaration.org/pdfs/Global-Burden-of-Armed-Violence.pdf

George, Susan. *Another World is Possible If*. London and Brooklyn: Verso Books, 2004.

———. "The World Trade Organization Could Have Had Alternative Finances." *Le Monde Diplomatique*, July 2007.

Ghalib, Asam Kamran, and Farhad Hossain. "Social Business Enterprises—Maximizing Social Benefits or Maximising Profits? The Case of Grameen-Danone Foods Limited." Working Paper 51, Brooks World Poverty Institute (BWPI), University of Manchester, July 2008.

Ghana Business News. "Nigeria Suspends Global Bond Issue," March 4, 2009.

Ghosh, Bimal. "Economic Effects of International Migration: A Synoptic Overview," *World Migration*, Chapter 8, 2005.

Gibb, R. "Post-Lome: The European Union and the South." *Third World Quarterly* 21, no. 3 (June 2000): 457–481.

Giussani, B. "Macro Microfinance." *The Wall Street Journal*, November 15, 2006.

Global Witness. "Undue Diligence: How Banks Do Business with Corrupt Regimes," March 2009.

Gluckman, Ron. "The Fort Knox of Rice," *Asia Inc.*, 1992.

Goldman Sachs. "BRICs and Beyond." Goldman Sachs Global Economics Group, November 2007.

Goussikindey, Eugene. "Worse than AIDS: The Arms Trade in Africa." *Woodstock Report* 85, June 2006.

Green, Matthew. "China Trade with Africa Hit by Deal Rethink." *Financial Times*, December 17, 2008.

Greenpeace. "Conning the Congo." Greenpeace International, July 2008.

Greider, William. *The Soul of Capitalism*. New York: Simon & Schuster, 2003.

GRIPS, *Report Review of Our Common Interest: Report of the Commission for Africa*, GRIPS, March 2005

Hackett, Clifford P. *Monnet and the Americans: The Father of a United Europe and His U.S. Supporters*. Washington, DC: Jean Monnet Council, 1995.

Hagerman, R.A. "U.S. Reliance on Africa for Strategic Minerals." United States Marine Corps, April 1984.

Haggblade, Steven, Peter Hazell, Ingrid Kirsten, and Richard Mkandawire. "Building on Successes in African Agriculture" International Food Policy Research Institute, Focus 12, Brief 1 of 10, April 2004.

Haines, Michael R. "The Population of the United States 1790–1920." Working Paper No. H0056 (National Bureau of Economic Research, NBER Working Papers, June 1994).

Hanson, Stephanie. "African Agriculture." Council on Foreign Relations, May 28, 2008.

Hargreaves, Steve. "Exxon Linked to Climate Change Pay Out." *CNN Money*, February 5, 2007.

Haug, Maria, Martin Langvandslien, Lora Lumpe, and Nicholas Marsh. "Shining a Light on Small Arms Exports: The Record of State Transparency." Norwegian Initiative on Small Arms Transfers, January 2002.

Hawkins, Tony. "Zimbabwe Reins in Hyperinflation." *Financial Times*, March 24, 2009.

Hayek, F.A. *The Road to Serfdom*. Chicago: University of Chicago Press, 2007.

Hayo, Bernd, and Carsten Hefeker. "Reconsidering Central Bank Independence." *European Journal of Political Economy* 18 (2002): 653–674.

Heinemann, Friedrich. "Is the Welfare State Self-destructive?" Discussion Paper No. 07-029 (Center for European Economic Research, May 2007).

Held, David. *Global Covenant*. Cambridge, Oxford, and Boston: Polity, 2004.

———. *Debating Globalization*. Cambridge, Oxford, and Boston: Polity, 2005.

Helms, B., E. Littlefield, and D. Porteous. "Financial Inclusion 2015: Four Scenarios for the Future of Microfinance." CGAP FocusNote, October 2006.

Henderson, Hazel. *Ethical Markets*. White River Jct., VT: Chelsea Green Publishing Company, 2006.

Hensley, Matthew, and Carreen Behrens. "PPP and the World Cup: Strategies to Help Emerging Markets Attract Major Events and Finance New Infrastructure." Institute for Public-Private Partnerships, 2006.

Hertz, Noreena. *The Silent Takeover*. London: Arrow Books, 2002.

HM Treasury. "Hosting the World Cup: A Feasibility Study." February 2007.

Hoda, Anwarul, and Ashok Gulati. "WTO Negotiations on Agriculture and Developing Countries." International Food Policy Research Institute, IFPRI Issue Brief 48, June 2008.

Hoedeman, Olivier. "Exxonmobil Funds Global Warming Spectics—Will Brussels Clear the Air?" *EU Observer*, March 13, 2007.

Hopkins, Martha. "For European Recovery." Library of Congress Information Bulletin, Vol. 56, No. 11, June 23, 1997

Hornik, Richard, and Barbara Rudolph. "Enter the Brady Plan." *TIME Magazine*, March 20, 1989.

Houlder, Vanessa, and Nikki Tait. "Brussels to Close Loopholes in Tax Evasion Legislation." *Financial Times*, November 13, 2008.

Hubbard, R. Glenn, and William Duggan. "The Forgotten Lessons of the Marshall Plan." *Policy Innovations*, June 20, 2008.

Huber, Juergen. "The Past, Present and Future ACP-EC Trade Regime and WTO." *European Journal of International Law (EJIL)* 11, no. 2 (2000): 247–438.

Hudon, M. "Subsidies and Financial Performances of the Microfinance Institutions: Does Management Matter?" Solvay Business School Working Paper, January 2006.

Hudson, Alan. "Case Study on EU Strategy for Action on the Crisis in Human Resources for Health in Developing Countries." Policy Coherence for Development in the EU Council, 2006, 147–151.

Humphreys, Macartan, Jeffrey D. Sachs, and Joseph E. Stiglitz, eds. *Escaping the Resource Curse*. New York: Columbia University Press, 2007.

Hunton. *"Client Alert."* Hunton & Williams LLP, March 2009.

Hutton, Guy, and Laurence Haller. "Evaluation of the Costs and Benefits of Water and Sanitation Improvements at the Global Level." World Health Organization (WHO), 2004.

IAC. *Realizing the Promise and Potential of African Agriculture*. Interacademy Council (IAC), 2004.

IADI. "List of Countries with Deposit Insurance." International Association of Deposit Insurers, September 30, 2008.

IANSA. *Gun Violence: The Global Crisis*. International Action Network on Small Arms (IANSA), 2008.

IB Times. "Peruvian Regional Battle over Mining Tax Revenue Disribution Erupts Again." *International Business Times*, October 31, 2008.

ICRC. *Humanitarian, Military, Technical and Legal Challenges of Cluster Munitions*. International Committee of the Red Cross (Icrc), April 2007.

IEG. *Improving Effectiveness and Outcomes for the Poor in Health, Nutrition, and Population*. Independent Evaluation Group (IEG), World Bank, IFC, and MIGA, 2009.

IHT. "Brazil's Petrobras Creates Subsidiary for Biofuels, Plans to Raise Oil Output." *International Herald Tribune*, March 4, 2008.

ILO. *Women and Men in the Informal Economy: A Statistical Picture*. International Labour Office (Ilo), 2002.

IMF. "Financing for Development: Implementing the Monterrey Consensus." Paper prepared by the International Monetary Fund (IMF) and World Bank for the Spring 2002 Development Committee Meeting, April 11, 2002.

IMF. "How the Imf Helps Poor Countries." International Monetary Fund, Factsheet, October 2007.

IMF. "IMF Overhauls Lending Framework." International Monetary Fund Press Release 09/85, March 24, 2009.

Independent, The. "Marshall Plan for Africa Approved by the Eu," by Alex Duval Smith, October 11, 2001.

Independent, The. "Global Arms Trade: Africa and the Curse of the Ak-47," April 6, 2006.

Intriligator, Michael. "The Marshall Plan, Foreign Aid, and Overseas Development Assistance." In *The Encyclopedia of Global Studies*. Thousand Oaks, CA: Sage Publications, 2009.

IRRI. "The Rice Crisis: What Needs to be Done?" International Rice Research Institute (IRRI), 2008.

Iversen, T. "Capitalism and Democracy." in The Oxford Handbook of Political Science, Oxford Handbooks in Political Science, Oxford University Press, 2006.

Jackson, Thomas, Nicholas Marsh, Taylor Owen, and Anne Thurin. *Who Takes the Bullet? the Impact of Small Arms Violence*. Norwegian Church Aid, Understanding the Issues, March 2005.

Jeucken, M. *Sustainability in Finance*. The Netherlands: Eburon Academic Publishers, 2004.

Johnson, Thomas H., Robert O. Slater, Pat McGowan. "Explaining African Military Coups d'Etat 1960–1982." *The American Political Science Review* 78, no. 3 (September 1984: 622–640.

Johnson, Doug, and Tristan Zajonc. "Can Foreign Aid Create an Incentive for Good Governance? Evidence from the Millenium Challenge Corporation." Working Paper 11, Center for International Development (Cid) at Harvard University, Cid Graduate Student and Postdoctoral Fellow Working Paper Series, April 2006.

Johnston, Daniel. *International Exploration, Economics, Risk, and Contract Analysis*. Tulsa, OK: PennWell Books, 2003.

Jopson, Barney. "China Seeks African Joint Ventures", *Financial Times*, November 9, 2009.

———. "China Pledges $10bn in Loans to Africa", *Financial Times*, November 9, 2009.

Jowit, Juliette. "UN Says Eat Less Meat to Curb Global Warming." *The Observer*, September 7, 2008.

Joyner, Christopher C., ed. *The United Nations As International Law Giver*. Chapter Sixteen, Part III: Internal Law. New York: Press Syndicate of the University of Cambridge, 1997.

Kajisa, Kei. "The Revolution Keeps Rolling." *Rice Today*, April–June 2008.

Kanina, Wangui. "Annan to Lead Green Revolution for African Agriculture." *Reuters*, July 16, 2007.

Kanter, James. "EU Fund to Ease Globalization Pain." *International Herald Tribune*, March 1, 2006.

Kapur, Devesh, and Richard Webb. "Beyond the IMF." Working Paper 99 (Washington, DC: Center for Global Development, August 2006).

Kar, Dev, and Devon Cartwright-Smith. *Illicit Financial Flows from Developing Countries: 2002–2006*. Global Financial Integrity, January 2009.

Karns, Margaret P., and Karen A. Mingst. *The United Nations in the 21st Century*. Boulder, CO: Westview Press, 2007.

Kaul, Inge, Isabelle Grunberg, and Marc A. Stern. *Global Public Goods*. London: Oxford University Press, 1999.

Kaul, Inge. "What Is a Public Good?" *Le Monde Diplomatique*, June 2000.

Keeling, Ann. "The Politics of Health Worker Migration in the Commonwealth," Global Forum for Health Research, October-November 2007.

Kelly, Michael J. "UN Security Council Permanent Membership: A New Proposal for a Twenty-First Century Council." *Seton Hall Law Review* 320 (2000): 319–399.

Kennan, George F. *Memoirs 1925–1950.* New York: Pantheon Books, 1967.

———. *Memoirs 1950–1963.* New York: Pantheon Books, 1983.

Kennedy, Margrit, and Declan Kennedy. "Complementary Currencies and the Chiemgauer Project." Prepared for the Tenth Annual Digital Money Forum, The Tower of London, March 2007.

Kenny, C. "What is Effective Aid? How Would Donors Allocate It?" Working Paper 4005 (Washington, DC: World Bank Policy Research Working Paper Series, September 2006).

Keynes, John Maynard. *The Economic Consequences of the Peace.* Book Jungle, 2007.

Khakee, A. "Democracy and Marketization in Central and Eastern Europe: Case Closed?" *East European Politics and Societies* 16, No. 2 (2002).

Khan, Mahmood H., and Mohsin S. Khan. "Agricultural Growth in China and Sub-Saharan Countries." *The Pakistan Development Review,* Winter 1995.

Killicoat, Phillip. "Weaponomics: The Global Market for Assault Rifles." Post-Conflict Transitions Working Paper 10, Department of Economics, Oxford University, April 2007.

Kinsley, M. "Capitalism's 'Deal' Falls Apart." *Washington Post,* June 8, 2003.

Kjoer, Knut N. "From Oil to Equities." Address at the Norwegian Polytechnic Society, November 2, 2006. Norges Bank Investment Management.

Kochenov, Dimitry. *EU Enlargement and the Failure of Conditionality,* European Monographs, 2006.

Koeberle, Stefan, Harold Bedoya, Peter Silarszky, and Gero Verheyen, eds. *Conditionality Revisited: Concepts, Experiences, and Lessons.* Washington, DC: The World Bank, 2005.

Kohonen, Matti, and Francine Mestrum, *Tax Justice,* Pluto Press, 2009

Korten, D.C. (1998), *Life after capitalism,* FEASTA Review 1.

Kosack, Stephen, *Directing Foreign Aid for Basic Education: Taking Account of Political Will,* the Brookings Institution, Policy Brief 2008–01, May 2008

KPMG, *Global Corporate Capital Flows, 2008/9 to 2013/14,* June 2008

Krugman, Paul, *Development, Geography and Economic Theory,* Antoni Bosch Editor, 1995

Kuziemko, Ilyana, and Eric Werker. "How Much is a Seat on the Security Council Worth? Foreign Aid and Bribery at the United Nations." *Journal of Political Economy* 114, 5: 905–930, 2006.

Laczko, F. "New Directions for Migration Policy in Europe." *Philosophical Transactions: Biological Sciences* 357, no. 1420, Reviews and a Special Collection of Papers on Human Migration (April 29, 2002): 599–608.

Laeven, Luc. "Pricing of Deposit Insurance." Working Paper 2871 (Washington, DC: World Bank Policy Research Working Paper Series, July 2002).

Lancet, *Redemption for the Pope?,* The Lancet, Volume 373, Issue 9669, Page 1054, 28 March 2009

Lane, John. "Aid Effectiveness in the New Age of Demand-Driven Sanitation." *Asian Water,* October 2008.

Lawson, Nigel. "Capitalism Needs a Revived Glass-Steagall Act." *Financial Times,* May 12, 2009.

Lebo, Jerry, and Dieter Schelling. *Design and Appraisal of Rural Transport Infrastructure,* World Bank Technical Paper No. 496. Washington, DC: The World Bank, 2001.

Lederman, Daniel, and William F. Maloney. *Natural Resources, Neither Curse nor Destiny.* Palo Alto, CA: Stanford Universty Press, 2007.

Leech, Dennis, and Robert Leech. "Voting Power in the Bretton Woods Institutions.", *Homo Oeconomicus* 22, no. 4 (2005): 1–23; also in Chapter 1 of *The IMF, World Bank and Policy Reform.* Edited by Alberto Paloni and Maurizio Zanardi. New York: Routledge, 2006, 29–48.

Levy, David A. "Does an Independent Central Bank Violate Democracy?" Working Paper 148, Levy Economics Institue, November 1995.

Lewis, S. "Are Democracy and Capitalism Incompatible?" *Student Economic Review* (2003).

Lietaer, Bernard. *The Future of Money*. Century, 2002.

———. "The Terra TRC White Paper." Self-published. 2004.

———. *Of Human Wealth*. Century, 2009.

Lijun, Mao. "Development Fund Signs First Deal in Africa." *China Daily*, January 16, 2008.

Lindbeck, Assar. "Changing Tides for the Welfare State." Working Paper 645, Cesifo Working Paper Series, January 2002.

Lindblom, Charles E., *The Market As Prison*, 1982.

Lindert, Peter H. "Why the Welfare State looks like a Free Lunch." Working Paper 9869 (Cambridge, MA: National Bureau of Economic Research Working Paper, 2003).

———. *Growing Public*. Cambridge and New York: Cambridge University Press, 2004.

Lombardi, Domenico. "The Role of the IMF in Low-Income Countries: An Institutional Approach." In *Finance, Development, and the IMF*, James Boughton, and Domenico Lombardi, eds. Oxford, U.K.: Oxford University Press, 2009.

Love, Janice. *Southern Africa in World Politics*. Boulder, CO: Westview Press, 2005.

Lowell, B. Lindsay, Allan Findlay, and Emma Stewart. "Brain Strain: Optimising Highly Skilled Emigration from Developing Countries." Working Paper 3 (London: Institute for Public Policy Research, Asylum and Migration, 2004).

Lubbers, R. "Eu Should Share Asylum Responsibilities, Not Shift Them." Unhcr, January 11, 2004.

Lusaka Times. "Zambia to Maintain SADC, COMESA Membership," June 3, 2008.

Lyman, Princeton N., and Patricia Dorff. *Beyond Humanitarianism: What You Need to Know about Africa and Why It Matters*. New York: Council on Foreign Relations, 2007.

Mabugu, Ramos, and Ahmed Mohamed. "The Economic Impacts of Government Financing of the 2010 FIFA World Cup," 2008.

Mahajan, Vijay. *Africa Rising*. Philadelphia, PA: Wharton University Press, 2008.

Mair, Johanna, and Oliver Schoen. "Social Entrepreneurial Business Models: an Exploratory Study." Working Paper No. 610. Iese Business School, October 2005.

Malia, Martin. *Introduction to The Communist Manifesto*. New York: Signet Classics, 1998.

Mallaby, Sebastian. *The World's Banker*. New York: Penguin Books, 2004.

Mallya, Ernest T. "A Critical Look at Tanzania's Development." *Vision 2025*. 2005.

Marshall, George. The Marshall Plan speech at Harvard University, June 5, 1947.

Marshall, George. Nobel Lecture, December 11, 1953.

Martin, Will, and Aaditya Mattoo. "The Doha Development Agenda: What's on the Table?" Working Paper 4672 (Washington, DC: World Bank Policy Research Working Paper Series, July 2008.

Martin-Cavanna, Javier. Interview With Damian von Stauffenberg. *Compromiso Empresarial*, May–June 2007.

Marx, Karl. *The Communist Manifesto*. New York: Signet Classics, 1998.

Mashindano, Oswald, Dennis Rweyemamu, and Daniel Ngowi. "Deepening Integration in SADC: Tanzania—Torn between EAC and SADC." Friedrich Ebert Foundation, *Regional Integration in Southern Africa* 9, February 2007.

Masson, Paul, and Catherine Pattillo. "A Single Currency for Africa?" Imf Finance & Development, December 2004.

Mathiason, Nick. "Mining and Oil Face World Tax Exposure." *the Observer*, September 21, 2008.

———. "Obama Bid to Stamp out Tax Havens." *the Guardian*, March 4, 2009.

MCC. *Guide to the MCC Indicators and the Selection Process Fiscal Year 2008*. Millennium Challenge Corporation, 2008a.

MCC. "MCC Reiterates U.S. Commitment to Fight Poverty." Millennium Challenge Corporation Press Release, December 11, 2008b.

McGann, James G. *2007 Survey of Think Tanks: A Summary Report.* Foreign Policy Research Institute, Vilanova University, August 2007.

Mcgivering, Jill. "Plea for Free Africa Healthcare." *BBC News,* May 30, 2006.

McKesson, John A. "The Schuman Plan." *Political Science Quarterly* 67, no. 1 (March 1952): 18–35.

Mckinnon, Ronald I. "Optimum Currency Areas and Key Currencies: Mundell I Versus Mundell II." *Journal of Common Market Studies* 42, No. 4 (2004): 689–715.

McKinzie, Richard D., and Theodore A. Wilson. *Oral History Interview with C. Tyler Wood.* June 18, 1971.

Mearsheimer, J.J. "The False Promise of International Institutions." *International Security* 19, no. 3 (Winter 1994/1995): 5–49.

Meltzer, Allan H., and Richard, S.F. "Why Government Grows (and Grows) in a Democracy." *Public Interest* 52 (1978).

Meltzer, Allan H. *What Future for the IMF and the World Bank?* Quarterly International Economics Report, July 2003.

Menkhoff, Lukas, Doris Neuberger, and Chodechai Suwanaporn, *Collateral-based lending in emerging markets: evidence from Thailand,* 2004

Meyer, R. "The Demand for Flexible Microfinance Products: Lessons from Bangladesh." Rural Finance Program, The Ohio State University, 2001.

Milanovic, Branko. *Worlds Apart.* Princeton, NJ: Princeton University Press, 2005.

———. "Where in the World are You?" Working Paper 4493 (Washington, DC: World Bank Policy Research Working Paper Series, World Bank Development Research Group, February 2007).

Mitchell, Daniel J. "Why Tax Havens Are a Nlessing." *Foreign Policy,* March 2008.

Molavi, Afshin. "Africa's Malaria Death Toll Still Outrageously High." *National Geographic News,* June 12, 2003.

Monnier, A., and G.I. Rogers. "The European Union at the Time of Enlargement." *Population (English Edition, 2002–)* 59, no. 2 (March/April 2004): 315–336.

Moody's Investors Service. *How Far Can Aaa Governments Stretch Their Balance Sheets?* Moody's Global Sovereign Special Comment, February 2009.

———. *International Policy Perspectives.* New York, 2007.

Morduch, J. "The Microfinance Promise." *Journal of Economic Literature* XXXVII (December 1999): 1569–1614.

Morgan, Dan. "Corporate Funding of Think Tanks Raises Questions of Credibility." *Washington Post,* February 16, 2000.

Morris, Harvey. "UN's Disunited Members Ponder Reform." *Financial Times,* September 23, 2008.

Morrison, Alan D., and Lucy White. "Is Deposit Insurance a Good Thing, and If So, Who Should Pay for It?," Oxford Financial Research Centre Working Paper No. 2004-FE-08. June 2006.

Morshed, Lamiya. "Lessons Learned on Improving Replicability of Successful Microcredit Programs." Paper prepared for the Microcredit Summit Campaign, 2006.

Moyo, Dambisa. *Dead Aid.* New York: Farrar, Straus and Giroux, 2009.

Muggah, Robert. "Emerging from the Shadow of War: A Critical Perspective on DDR and Weapons Reduction in the Post-Conflict Period." *Contemporary Security Policy* 27, no. 1 (April 2006): 190–205.

Mundell, R.A. "A Theory of Optimum Currency Areas." *American Economic Review* 51 (1961): 657–665.

Murphy, Richard. *Country-By-Country Reporting: How to Make Multinational Companies More Transparent.* Tax Justice Network, Tax Justice Briefing, March 2008.

Mutume, Gumisai. "Reversing Africa's Brain Drain." *Africa Recovery*, Vol. 17 #2, page 1, July 2003.

Nairobi Protocol. *the Nairobi Protocol for the Prevention, Control and Reduction of Small Arms and Light Weapons in the Great Lakes Region and the Horn of Africa*, May 21, 2004.

Neary, J. Peter. "The Stolper-Samuelson Theorem." *Encyclopedia of World Trade Since 1450*. J.J. McCusker et al., New York, 2004.

New African Initiative. New Partnership for Africa's Development (NEPAD), July 2001.

New International. *The New International* 13, no. 8 (October 1947): 227–231.

Nolutshungu, Sam C. "Soviet Involvement in Southern Africa." *Annals of the American Academy of Political and Social Science* 481, Soviet Foreign Policy in an Uncertain World (September 1985): 138–146.

Nugent, Paul. *Africa Since Independence*. Basingstroke: Palgrave Macmillan, 2004.

O'Connell, Mary Ellen. "The United Nations Security Council and the Authorization of Force: Renewing the Council Through Law Reform." Working Paper 31, Public Law and Legal Theory Working Paper Series, April 2005.

OECD. "Agricultural Policies in OECD Countries." Organisation for Economic Co-operation and Developent (OECD), Monitoring and Evaluation, 2007.

———. "Debt Relief Is Down: Other Oda Rises Slightly." Organisation for Economic Co-Operation and Developent (OECD), April 4, 2008.

———. "Jurisdictions Committed to Improving Transparency and Establishing Effective Exchange of Information in Tax Matters." Organisation for Economic Co-operation and Developent (OECD), 2009.

Ogodo, Ochieng. "Africa: Low Agricultural Output Blamed on Policies." AllAFrica.com, April 13, 2008.

Olson, M. "Dictatorship, Democracy and Development." *The American Political Science Review* 87, no. 3 (1993).

Owens, Jeffrey, and Pascal Saint-Amans. "Overview of the OECD's Work on Countering International Tax Evasion." Organisation for Economic Co-operation and Developent (OECD), July 16, 2009.

Owuor, Peter. "Plans Underway to Reduce Small Arms Trade in Africa." Inter Press Service, January 18, 2000.

Oxfam. "Everything but Arms and Sugar?" Oxfam Parliamentary Briefing, no. 13, December 2000.

———. "Paying the Price," 2005.

———. "Africa's Missing Billions." 107 Briefing Paper, October 2007.

———. "Irresponsible Transfers," 2008.

Pandey, Sushil, Mark W. Rosegrant, Timothy Sulser, and Humnath Bhandari. "Investing in the Future." *Rice Today*, January–March 2009.

Parrish, Scott D., and Mikhail M. Narinsky. *New Evidence on the Soviet Rejection of the Marshall Plan*. 1947: two reports, Woodrow Wilson International Center for Scholars, Working Paper No. 9, March 1994.

Parsons, Craig. "Showing Ideas as Causes: The Origins of the European Union." *International Organization* 56, no. 1 (Winter 2002: 47–84.

Pehnelt, Gernot. "The Political Economy of China's Aid Policy in Africa." JENA Economic Research Papers 2007-051.

Perkins, Anne. "The Future for Agriculture Is Africa." *The Guardian*, July 9, 2008.

Pinstrup-Andersen, Per, Rajul Pandya-Lorch, and Mark W. Rosegrant. *World Food Prospects: Critical Issues for the Early Twenty-First Century*. Food Policy Report, International Food Policy Research Institute, October 1999.

Piot, Peter, Michael Kazatchkine, Mark Dybul, and Julian Lob-Levyt. "AIDS: Lessons Learnt and Myths Dispelled." *The Lancet*, March 20, 2009.

PMI. *The President's Malaria Intiative Second Annual Report*, President's Malaria Initiative, March 2008.

Pogge, Thomas, and Sanjay Reddy. "How Not to Count the Poor." Version 6.2, 29, October 2005.

Porteous, David. "Competition And Microcredit Interest Rates." CGAP FocusNote, February 2006.

Portocarrero, F., and G. Byrne. "Market Structure and Competition In Microcredit." (original version in Spanish) Consorcio de investigacion economica y social, July 2003.

Poulsen, Helen. "The Gendered Impact of HIV/AIDS on Education in South Africa and Swaziland: Save the Children's Experiences." *Gender & Development* 14, no. 1 (March 2006).

Prasso, Sheridan. "A Yogurt Maker Wants to Change the World." *Fortune*, April 18, 2007.

Price, Harry Bayard. *The Marshall Plan and Its Meaning*. Ithaca, NY: Cornell University Press, 1955.

Pruss-Ustun, Annette, Robert Bos, Fiona Gore, Jamie Bartram. *Safer Water, Better Health*. World Health Organization, 2008.

PwC. *Tanzania Development Vision 2025*, PricewaterhouseCoopers, 1998.

———. *European Economic Outlook*. PricewaterhouseCoopers (PwC), June 2004.

———. *Olympic Games Impact Study Final Report*. PricewaterhouseCoopers, December 2005.

Rachman, G. "Hysteria, Hypocrisy and the World's Immigrant Hordes." *Financial Times*, September 12, 2006.

Ramesh, Jairam. "A Taxing Idea at the Right Time?" *The Times of India*, October 21, 2002.

Ramonet, Ignacio. "Disarm the Markets." *Le Monde Diplomatique*, February 1997.

Ramzy, Austin. "A New Book Reveals Why China Is Unhappy." *TIME Magazine*, March 20, 2009.

Rapoport, Hillel. "Who is Afraid of the Brain Drain?" Policy Brief, Stanford Institute for Economic Policy Research, 2002.

Rating Fund. The Microfinance Rating Market Outlook—The Rating Fund Market Survey 2005.

Raucher, Alan R. *Paul G. Hoffman: Architect of Foreign Aid*. Lexington, KY: University Press of Kentucky, 1985.

Ravallion, Martin, and Dominique van de Walle. "Land and Poverty in Reforming East Asia." *Finance & Development*, September 2008a.

———. *Land in Transition: Reform and Poverty in Rural Vietnam*. Palgrave Macmillan and The World Bank, 2008b.

Raventós, Daniel. *Basic Income: The Material Conditions of Freedom*. London: Pluto Press, 2007.

Reich, Robert B. *Supercapitalism*. New York: Vintage Books, 2007.

Reid, Tim. "Wolfowitz resigns after scandal over girlfriend's pay rise", *The Times*, May 18, 2007.

Reinoso, Jose. "China Demands Its Role as Superpower." *EL PAIS*, April 12, 2009.

Reuters. "Biofuels Take Off in Some Countries," June 9, 2005.

———. "Reuniting Ivory Coast Would Boost GDP," March 16, 2007.

———. "Africa Can Triple Food Output," June 16, 2008a.

———. "IMF to Give Ivory Coast $66 Million in Post-War Aid," April 7, 2008b.

———. "G8 Summit to Pledge $15 Billion to Boost Food Supply." July 9, 2009.

Reynolds, David. "Marshall Plan Commemorative Section: The European Response: Primacy of Politics." *Foreign Affairs*, May/June 1997.

Rhyne, E., and M. Otero. "Microfinance Matures: Opportunities, Risks, and Obstacles for an Emerging Global Industry." *Innovations, MIT Press*, Winter and Spring 2007.

Richardson, Martin, and Frank Stahler. *Fair Trade*, June 2007. http://papers.ssrn.com/sol3/papers.cfm?abstract_id=1001146.

Riefel, Lex, and James W. Fox. "The Millennium Challenge Corporation: An opportunity for the next President." Working Paper 30, Brookings Global Economy and Development, December 2008.

Rifkin, Jeremy. *The European Dream*. New York: Tarcher Penguin, 2004.

———. "Europe and the Future of Capitalism." *EL PAIS*, June 23, 2005.

Ringmar, Erik. *Surviving Capitalism*. London: Anthem Press, 2005.

Ritschl, Albrecht. "The Marshall Plan, 1948–1951." Edited by Robert Whaples. EH.Net Encyclopedia, February 10, 2008.

Roberts, James M. "Foreign Aid: Congress Should Shift USAID Funds to the Millennium Challenge Account." Heritage Foundation WebMemo #2574, August 4, 2009.

Rockefeller Foundation. *Africa's Turn: A New Green Revolution for the 21st Century*, July 2006.

———. *The Rockefeller Foundation 2007* Annual Report, 2007.

Rodriguez-Suanzes, Pablo. "How to Fix the World with $75 Billion." *El Mundo*, June 1, 2008.

Rodrik, Dani. *Has Globalization Gone Too Far?* Washington, DC: Institute for International Economics, 1997.

———. "*Feasible Globalizations*." Harvard University, May 2002.

Rogoff, Kenneth. *On Why Not a Global Currency*, Economics Department, Harvard University, To be presented at the American Economic Association Meeting session on "Exchange Rates and Choice of Monetary Regimes," January 8, 2001.

Rosser, J. Barkley, and Marina Vcherashnaya Rosser. Failure of the Washington Consensus on Inequality and the Underground Economy in the Transition Economies, *Challenge: The Magazine of Economic Affairs*, vol. 44, no. 2, pp. 39–50, March-April 2001.

Rotberg, Robert I. *Africa's Successes: Evaluating Accomplishment*. Belfer/WPF Report Number 43, 2007.

———. *China into Africa: Trade, Aid and Influence*. Washington, DC: Brookings Institution Press, 2008.

Ruggie, John Gerard. "What Makes the World Hang Together? Neoutilitarianism and the Social Constructivist Challenge." *International Organization* 52.4 (Autumn 1998): 855–885.

Sachs, Jeffrey. *The End of Poverty*. New York: Penguin Books, 2006.

Samuelson, R.J. "Capitalism vs. Democracy." *Newsweek*, October 3, 2005.

Sand, Peter H. "Diego Garcia: British-American Legal Black Hole in the Indian Ocean?" *Journal of Environmental Law* (2009).

Santomero, Anthony M. "Deposit Insurance: Do We Need It and Why?" Wharton Financial Institutions Center, August 1997.

Sardoni, C., and L.R. Wray. "Fixed and Flexible Exchange Rate and Currency Sovereignty." Working Paper No. 489, the Levy Economics Institute, January 2007.

Sari, Aurel. "The EU Status of Forces Agreement: Change and continuity in the Law of Visiting Forces." *The Military Law and the Law of War Review* 1–2 (2007).

Schaefer, Brett D., and Daniella Markheim. "The Free Trade Future of AGOA." The Heritage Foundation, June 5, 2006.

Schain, Martin A. *The Marshall Plan: Fifty Years After*. New York: Palgrave Macmillan, 2001.

Schroeder, Matt, and Guy Lamb. "The Illicit Arms Trade in Africa." *African Analyst*, Third Quarter (2006).

Segal, Paul. "The Resource Dividend: Natural Resource Rents and Global Poverty." University of Oxford, February 21, 2009.

Segerstrom, Paul S. "Naomi Klein and the Anti-Globalization Movement," CEPR Discussion Paper No. 4141. December 2003

Setser, Brat. "Too Many Currencies? Or Too Many Dollar Pegs?" Council on Foreign Relations, January 22, 2006.

Sexton, T. "Capitalism and Democratic Ideals: Opposites Attracting or a Match Made in Heaven?" *Associated Press*, 2007.

Shattan, Joseph. "The Four Pillars of Obamaism." *The American Spectator*, May 5, 2009.

Shaw, John D. *Global Food and Agricultural Institutions*. New York: Routledge, 2009.

Shenkar, Oded. *The Chinese Century*. Philadelphia, PA: Wharton School Publishing, 2005.

Shi, Jacylyn. "TRIPS and Development—A Dilemma Facing International Trade Law." Norman Patterson School of International Affairs, Crleton University, December 2004.

Siklos, Pierre L. "No Single Definition of Central Bank Independence Is Right for All Xountries." Research Paper 2008-02, Universita Commerciale Luigi Bocconi, Paolo Baffi Centre Research Paper Series, March 2008.

Simonian, Haig. "Private Banks Face Tax Evasion Clampdown." *Financial Times*, May 8, 2008.

Sinn, Hans-Werner. "The Welfare State and the Forces of Globalization." Working Paper 1925, CESifo Working Paper Series, February 2007.

SIPRI. *United Nations Arms Embargoes: Their Impact on Arms Flows and Target Behaviour*. SIPRI and Uppsala Universitet, 2007.

―――. *Yearbook 2008 Armaments, Disarmaments and International Security*. Stockholm International Peace Research Institute (SIPRI), 2008.

Smaling, Eric, Moctar Toure, Nico de Ridder, Nteranya Sanginga, and Henk Breman. "Fertilizer Use and the Environment." Background paper prepared for the African Fertilizer Summit, Abuja, Nigeria, June 9–13, 2005.

Smaling, Eric. "Harvest for the World." Inaugural Address, November 2, 2005.

Small Arms Survey. Small Arms Survey 2007: Guns and the City.Susanne Soederberg. *The Politics of the New International Financial Architecture*. London: Zed Books, 2004.

Smith, Adam. "The Wealth of Nations", 1776.

Somma, Abigail. "The 10 Percent that Could Change Africa." International Food Policy Research Institute (IFPRI) Forum, October 2008.

Soros, George. *George Soros on Globalization*. New York: PublicAffairs, 2002.

Spagnolo, Carlo. "The Bretton Woods System and the Birth of the European Paments Union." 1st EUI Alumni Conference, Florence, October 3–4, 2003.

Spiegel. "The Liechtenstein Connection." *Der Spiegel*, February 16, 2008.

Standard & Poor's. "Sovereign Credit Ratings: A Primer." New York, October 19, 2006.

Standard and Poor's. *S&P Microfinance*, 2007.

Steil, Benn. "The End of National Currency." *Foreign Affairs*, May/June 2007.

Stiglitz, Joseph E., and Andrew Charlton. *Free Trade for All*. New York: Oxford University Press, 2005.

Stiglitz, Joseph E. *Globalization and its Discontents*. W.W. Norton & Company, 2003.

Stokke, Olav. "Aid and Political Conditionality." Frank Cass & Co., 1996.

Storper, Michael. "The Poverty of Radical Theory Today: from the false promises of Marxism to the mirage of the cultural turn." *International Journal of Urban and Regional Research* 25, no. 1 (2001): 155–179.

Street, P. "Capitalism and Democracy Don't Mix Very Well, Reflections on Globalization." *Z magazine*, February 2000.

Sturgess, Brian, and Chris Brady. "Hosting the FIFA World Cup." *World Economics* 7, no. 4 (October–December 2006).

Subramanian, Arvind. "The Globalization Guru." *Finance & Development* 42, no. 3 (September 2005).

Superintendencia. Regulation and Supervision of Microfinance Institutions in Bolivia (original version in Spanish), Superintendencia de Bancos y Entidades Financieras de Bolivia, 2007.

SustainAbility. *The Global Compact*, UNEP, The 21st Century NGO, In the Market for Change, 2008.

Talbott, John R. *Obamanomics*. New York: Seven Stories Press, 2008.

Tall, Tidjane. *Fixing Africa Once and for All*. Self-published. 2009.

Tannock, Stuart. "Beyond National Borders: Refraining the Global Brain Debate." SKOPE Research Paper No. 73, June 2007.

Teruel-Soria, Ana. "The World Bank Opens Its Own Store of Fair Trade." *Cinco Dias*, March 13, 2006.

Teslik, Lee Hudson. "Sovereign Wealth Funds." Council on Foreign Relations, January 17, 2008.

Tharoor, Shashi. "This Mini-League of Nations Would Cause Only Division." *The Guardian*, May 27, 2008.

Thatak, Arnab, Judith G. Hazlewood, and Tony M. Lee. "How Private Health Care Can Help Africa." *The McKinsey Quarterly*, March 2008.

Thomas, A.M. "Can the World Bank Enforce Its Own Conditions: The World Bank and the Enforcement Critique of Conditionality." *Development and Change* 35, no. 3 (June 2004): 485–497.

TIME. "The Great Deed." *TIME Magazine*, November 17, 1947.

———. "The Last Straw?" *TIME Magazine*, December 12, 1949.

———. "France & the Schuman Plan." *TIME Magazine*, December 24, 1951.

Transparency. *2008 Bribe Payers Index*. Transparency International, 2008.

Truman Library. *Oral History Interview with Paul G. Hoffman*, October 25, 1964.

Tully, K. "Microfinance: From The Ground Up." *Financial Times*, February 16, 2007.

Tupy, Marian L. "The False Promise of Gleneagles." CATO Institute, April 2009.

Ukpe, Aniekan Iboro. *Defining the Character of the Enabling Clause: Towards a More Beneficial GSP Scheme*, 2007. http://papers.ssrn.com/sol3/papers.cfm?abstract_id=1265733

UN Foundation. "Dakar Goals Unlikely In 70 Nations." *UN Wire*, November 14, 2002.

UN Water. *A Snapshot of Drinking Water and Sanitation in Africa*. Unicef and World Health Organization, 2008a.

UN Water. "A Toilet for Everyone: We can do It." Factsheet 5, International Year of Sanitation, 2008b.

UNAIDS. *AIDS in Africa: Three Scenarios to 2025*, January 2005.

UNECA. "Perspectives of African Countries on the Monterrey Consensus.". United Nations Economic Commission for Africa, October 2007.

UNESCO. "World Declaration on Education for All." World Conference on Education For All, 1990.

———. *Education For All: Meeting Our Collective Commitments*, 2000.

———. *EFA Global Monitoring Report 2009*, 2008.

UNICEF. *WASH for Children: Investing in Water, Sanitation and Hygiene in East Asia and the Pacific*. Bangkok, Thailand: Unicef East Asia and Pacific Regional Office, 2008.

———. *WHO/UNICEF Joint Monitoring Programme for Water Supply and Sanitation*, 2008.

UNICEF and WHO. *Progress on Drinking Water and Sanitation: Special Focus on Sanitation*. UNICEF and World Health Organization, 2008.

United Nations. *It Is Time for a Green Revolution in Africa*. World Economic and Social Survey, 1995.

———. *Monterrey Consensus of the International Conference on Financing for Development*. United Nations Department of Economic and Social Affairs, Division for Sustainable Development, 2002.

———. *Panel Discussion Regulation of Microfinance.* April 10, 2007.

———. *Follow-up International Conference on Financing for Development to Review the Implementation of the Monterrey Consensus,* December 9, 2008a.

———. *Making Globalization Work for the Least Developed Countries.* United Nations Office of the High Representative for the Least Developed Countries, March 2008b.

United States. *Lobbying Disclosure Act of 1995* (1995).

UNWTO "World Tourism Barometer." *World Tourism Organization* 7, no. 2 (June 2009).

USTR. *2008 Comprehensive Report on U.S. trade and investment policy toward Subsaharan Africa and implementation of the African Growth and Opportunity Act.* Office of the United Sates Trade Representative, May 2008a.

———. *Report Shows AGOA Continues to Grow and Diversity U.S.-Africa Trade.* Office of the United States Trade Representative, May 16, 2008b.

Van Liemt, Gijsbert. "Towards a Different Kind of Globalization, or How the Anti-Globalists View the World." Working Paper 38 (World Commission on the Social Dimension on Globalization, International Labour Office (ILO), March 2004).

Varma, Praveen, Richard Cantor, David Hamilton, David Levey, Sharon Ou, and Vincent Truglia. *Sovereign Bond Defaults, Rating Transitions, and Recoveries (1985–2002).* Moody's Investors Service Special Comment, February 2003.

Von Braun, Joachim, and Rajul Pandya-Lorch, eds. *Food Policy for the Poor: Expanding the Research Frontiers.* Washington, DC: International Food Policy Research Institute, 2005.

Von Braun, Joachim. *The World Food Situation.* IFPRI Food Policy Report No. 18, December 2007.

Von Korff, Douglas. *The Public Diplomacy of the Marshall Plan,* Self-published, 2007.

Von Leipzig, Wolf. "The Sleeping Beauty Awakens." *Luxemburger Wort,* December 4, 2004.

Von Stauffenberg, Damian. "Microfinance Investment Vehicles, An Emerging Asset Class." *MFInsights,* November 2006.

Wade, Robert. "Why Free Trade Has Costs for Developing Countries." *Financial Times,* August 11, 2005.

———. "Some Forms of Protection Have to Be Deployed." *Financial Times,* December 2, 2008.

Wadhwa, Vivek. "The Reverse Brain Drain." *BusinessWeek,* August 22, 2007.

Wang, Jian-Ye. "What Drives China's Growing Role in Africa?," IMF Working Paper 07/211 (Washington: International Monetary Fund), August 2007.

Webster, Lucy Law. "A New Deal for the World." Center for War/Peace Studies, 2008.

Webster, Philip. "G8 Summit: $15 Billion Aid Pledge for Developing Countries." *the Times,* July 10, 2009.

WEF. *Building on the Monterrey Consensus.* World Economic Forum (WEF), September 2005.

Weisman, Steven R. "World Bank Calls on Sovereign Funds to Invest in Africa." *Washington Post,* April 3, 2008.

Weitzman, Hal. "Boom Fattens Cargill's Balance Sheet." *Financial Times,* April 14, 2008.

Welsh, David. *Ethnicity in Subsaharan Africa, International Affairs.* (Royal Institute of International Affairs 1944–) 72, no. 3, Ethnicity and International Relations (July 1996): 477–491.

Wexler, Imanuel. "The Marshall Plan Revisited: The European Recovery Program in Economic Perspective." Greenwood Press, Contributions in Economics and Economic History, No. 55, 1983.

WFP. *World Hunger Series 2007: Hunger and Health.* World Food Program, 2007.

White House. "George Bush Welcomes European Commission President Jose Barroso to the White House." White House Office of the Press Secretary, January 8, 2007.

WHO. *Global Health-Sector Strategy for HIV/AIDS 2003–2007.* World Health Organization (WHO), Department of HIV/AIDS, Family and Community Health, 2003.

———. *Global Strategy for the Prevention and Control of Sexually Transmitted* 2006–2015. World Health Organization (WHO), 2007.

———. *World Health Report*. World Health Organization, 2006.

Wickham, DeWayne. "Bush's Africa policy Is Being Driven by the Right Wom *Today*, October 10, 2005.

Williams, Gini. "Best Practice for the Care of Patients with Tuberculosis." Internatio Against Tuberculosis and Lung Disease, 2007.

Williamson, John. "Did the Washington Consensus Fail?" Peterson Institute for Inte Economics, November 6, 2002.

Wilton Park. "Reducing Poverty: The Roles of Parliaments, Government and N Actors." Report on Wilton Park Conference 917, June 5–9, 2006.

Wolf, Martin. *A Global Market Economy Needs a Global Currency*. *Financial Times* 4, 2004a.

———. *Why Globalization Works*. New Haven, CT: Yale University Press, 2004b.

———. "Seeds of Its Own Destruction." *Financial Times*, May 12, 2009a.

———. "Why Davos Man Is Waiting for Obama to Save Him?" *Financial Times*, F 4, 2009b.

Wolff, Edward N. "Time for a Wealth Tax?" *Boston Review*, February/March 1996.

Woods, N. "The Challenge of Good Governance for the IMF and the World Bank selves." *World Development* 28, no. 5 (May 2000).

World Bank. *Assessing Aid: What Works, What Doesn't, and Why*. New York: University Press, 1998.

———. *Financial Flows to Developing Countries: Recent Trends and Prospects*. Wash DC: Global Development Finance, 2007a.

———. *World Development Report 2008*. World Bank, 2007b.

———. *World Development Indicators*, 2007c.

———. *Debt relief under the Heavily Indebted Poor countries Initiative*, March 2008.

———. *The Enhanced HIPC Initiative*, 2008b.

———. *Economic Impacts of Sanitation in Southeast Asia*. World Bank Water and Sani Program, February 2008c.

———. *Global Economic Prospects: Commodities at the Crossroads*, World Bank, 20(

Wright, Quincy. "Western Diplomacy since 1945." *Annals of the American Acade* *Political and Social Science* 336, Is International Communism Winning?, (July 1 144–153.

WBSI. "The Regulation of Microfinance Services." World Savings Banks Institute (W June 2008.

WTO. "*GATS Facts and Fiction*." World Trade Organization (WTO), 2001.

Xinhua. "China Approves China-Africa Development Fund," May 14, 2007.

———. "World Bank Okays $35 Million Credit for Ethiopia's Tourism Development," 3, 2009.

Yager, Thomas R., Omayra Bermudez-Lugo, Philip M. Mobbs, Harold R. Newman, David R. Wilburn. "The Mineral Industries of Africa." United States Geological Sur August 2007.

Yunker, J.A. *Rethinking World Government: A New Approach*. Lanham, MD: Univer Press of America, 2005.

Yunus, M. *Creating a World Without Poverty*. New York: PublicAffairs, 2007.

Zalewski, Piotr. *Sticks, Carrots and Great Expectations: Human Rights Conditionality a Turkey's Path Towards Membership of the European Union*. Center for Internatio Relations, December 17, 2004.

Zhang, ZhongXiang. "China's Hunt for Oil in Africa in Perspective." In September 20(http://mpra.ub.uni-muenchen.de/12829/

About the Author

Jaime **Pozuelo-Monfort** graduated from *Universidad Politécnica de Madrid* in 2000 with a master's and a bachelor's in telecommunications engineering, having also studied two years as an exchange student at *Télécom Paris* and *Universität Stuttgart*. Subsequently, he earned master's degrees in business administration from *Collège des Ingénieurs in Paris*, in financial economics from *Universidad Carlos III de Madrid*, in financial engineering from the *University of California at Berkeley*, in economic development from the *London School of Economics*, and in public administration from *Columbia University*. He currently pursues a master's in international law and politics at *Georgetown University* and a master's in public health at the *London School of Hygiene and Tropical Medicine*.

He has worked in the technology sector in Madrid, Stuttgart, and Paris, and in the financial industry in New York City and London. His interests lie in the interaction between financial economics and economic development. In addition, he is a columnist in both written and electronic publications. He speaks English, French, German, and Spanish fluently, and has an intermediate level in Russian and a beginner's level in Italian, and Portuguese. Jaime is the multidisciplinary European and aspiring candidate to Chief Dreamer. For more information, or to contact Jaime, visit http://Monfort.org.

Index